OPERATIONS RESEARCH

OPERATIONS RESEARCH

By

Dr. Qazi Shoeb Ahmad
Professor
Department of Mathematics
Integral University
Lucknow

Dr. Shakeel Javed
Assistant Professor
Department of Statistics & O.R.
AMU, Aligarh

Dr. Mohd Vaseem Ismail
Assistant Professor
Faculty of Pharmacy
Jamia Hamdard
New Delhi

UNIVERSITY SCIENCE PRESS
(An Imprint of Laxmi Publications Pvt. Ltd.)

BANGALORE • CHENNAI • COCHIN • GUWAHATI • HYDERABAD
JALANDHAR • KOLKATA • LUCKNOW • MUMBAI • RANCHI
NEW DELHI • BOSTON, USA

Published by :
UNIVERSITY SCIENCE PRESS
(An Imprint of Laxmi Publications Pvt. Ltd.)
113, Golden House, Daryaganj,
New Delhi-110002

Phone : 011-43 53 25 00
Fax : 011-43 53 25 28

www.laxmipublications.com
info@laxmipublications.com

First Edition : 2013

OFFICES

✆ **Bangalore**	080-26 75 69 30	✆ **Chennai**	044-24 34 47 26
✆ **Cochin**	0484-237 70 04, 405 13 03	✆ **Guwahati**	0361-251 36 69, 251 38 81
✆ **Hyderabad**	040-24 65 23 33	✆ **Jalandhar**	0181-222 12 72
✆ **Kolkata**	033-22 27 43 84	✆ **Lucknow**	0522-220 99 16
✆ **Mumbai**	022-24 91 54 15, 24 92 78 69	✆ **Ranchi**	0651-220 44 64

UOR–9686–350–OPERATION RESEARCH-ISM

C—

Typeset at : ABRO Enterprises, Delhi.

Printed at : Repro Knowledgecast Limited, Thane

Contents

Preface

The authors feel great pleasure in presenting the first edition of the book **"Operations Research".** This book is designed to meet the requirement of B.Tech, M.B.A., B.B.A. students of different Universities.

The subject matter has been discussed in such a way that the students will find no difficulty to understand it. Each chapter of this book contains complete self-explanatory theory and a large number of solved examples, followed by a collection of good exercises.

The language of the book is simple and easy to understand. The authors hope that the students, teachers and other readers will find the book interesting and to the point covering the whole course. We hope that the students will receive the book warmly.

We have taken great care in eliminating the misprints, but if there are still any, we shall be highly obliged to those who will take trouble of pointing them out. Suggestions for the improvement of the book will be gratefully acknowledged.

—Authors

UNIT—I

LINEAR PROGRAMMING

CHAPTER 1

Graphical Solution and Formulation

1.1 LINEAR PROGRAMMING

Linear programming deals with the maximization or minimization (or optimization) of a function of variables known as objective function, subject to a set of linear equalities and/or inequalities known as constraints. Here, the objective function can be cost, profit or production capacity, which is to be obtained in the best possible manner. The constraints may be imposed by different sources such as market demand, storage capacity, raw material availability etc. The word 'linear' here implies that the variables, considered here do not certain any powers greater than one.

Thus, a given change in one variable will always cause a resulting proportional change in another variable.

The word programming refers to modelling and solving a problem mathematically that involves the economic allocation of limited resources by choosing a particular course of action or a strategy among various alternative strategies to achieve the desired objective.

G.B. Dantzig developed the technique primarily for solving military logistics problems. But nowadays, it is being used widely in all the areas of management, education, transportation planning, military operations, healthcare systems, education etc.

1.2 STRUCTURE OF LINEAR PROGRAMMING MODEL

The general structure of LP model consists of mainly three basic components:

(*a*) **Decision variables.** The Operation Researcher needs to evaluate various alternatives (or courses of action) for arriving at the optimal value of the objective function. If there is no alternative to be selection among various alternatives, then there is no need of linear programming. The evaluation of various alternatives can be obtained by the nature of objective function and availability of resources. Once the objective is decided, we pursue certain activities (also called as decision variables) usually denoted x_i's ($i = 1, 2, ..., n$). The value of these activities represents the extent to which each of these is performed. There are certain variables (decision), which are not always under the control of decision maker, and are called as uncontrollable variables. If the values are under the control of decision maker, then these variables are called as controllable variables. These decision variables, usually interrelated in terms of consumption of limited resources, require simultaneous solutions. One thing is to be kept in mind that all the decision variables in linear programming model are controlable, continuous and non-negative.

$$i.e., \ x_j \geq 0, \ (j = 1, 2, ..., n)$$

(*b*) **The objective function.** The main aim (or goal or objective) of each linear programming problem (LPP) is to either maximize the profit or minimize the costs involved. Thus, the objective function of each LPP can be expressed in terms of the decision variables to optimize (maximize or minimize) the criterion of optimality, for example, profit, cost, revenue, distance etc. Thus, the objective function of any LPP, by using the decision variables (discussed above) can be expressed as

Maximize/Minimize $Z = C_1x_1 + C_2x_2 + ... + C_nx_n$

or $\quad$ $$\text{Max/Min } Z = \sum_{j=1}^{n} C_j x_j \quad (j = 1, 2, ..., n)$$

where Z is the value of the objective function and C_j: represents the contribution of a unit of the respective variables x_j ($j = 1, 2, ..., n$), so that the value of z may be maximum or minimum. Now, the optimal value of Z (maximum or minimum) can be obtained graphically or by using the well known method known as simplex method (will be discussed later on).

(*c*) **The constrants.** Constraints are imposed while formulating the linear programming model, as there is always a limitation of using the available resources. For example, man hour, labour, machine, raw-material, money, space etc. can be utilized upto a limit. These limited resources can be used upto some extent to which an objective of the model can be achieved. All the solutions obtained after simplifying the LP model, must satisfy the constraints imposed.

(*d*) **Non-negative restriction.** All the decision variables must assume non-negative values as negative values of physical quantities is an impossible solution.

1.3 ADVANTAGES OF LINEAR PROGRAMMING

There are various advantages in using the linear programming. Some of the advantages are discussed below:

1. It is very much helpful in attaining the optimum use of productive resources. If the resources are limited, then the linear programming model gives the optimum result after using the limited available resources. Linear programming shows how a decision maker can use his available limited resources effectively by selecting and distributing these resources.
2. Linear programming also helps in re-evaluating the basic plan for changing conditions. For example, if a particular plan is started and after sometime, certain conditions are changed that effects the model, then LP can determine other conditions that will adjust the remainder of the plan for best result.
3. With the use of linear programming, the executive builds into his planning a true reflection of the limitations and restrictions under which he must operate and whenever it becomes

necessary to deviate from the best programme he can evaluate the cost or penalty involved.

4. In LPP, high lighting the bottlenecks in the process is the most significant advantage of this technique. For example, whenever bottleneck problem occurs, some of the machines remain idle for sometime while few cannot meet the respective demands.

1.4 GENERAL MATHEMATICAL MODEL OF LINEAR PROGRAMMING PROBLEM

The general linear programming problem with n decision variables and m constraints can be stated in the following form:

Find the values of decision variables $x_1, x_2, ..., x_n$ so as to

Maximize or Minimize $Z = C_1x_1 + C_2x_2 + ... + C_nx_n$

Subject to the linear constraints

$$\begin{array}{ccccccc} a_{11}x_1 & + & a_{12}x_2 & + ... + & a_{1n}x_n & = & b_1 \\ a_{21}x_1 & + & a_{22}x_2 & + ... + & a_{2n}x_n & = & b_2 \\ \vdots & & \vdots & & \vdots & & \vdots \\ \vdots & & \vdots & & \vdots & & \vdots \\ \vdots & & \vdots & & \vdots & & \vdots \\ a_{m1}x_1 & + & a_{m2}x_2 & + ... + & a_{mn}x_n & = & b_m \end{array}$$

The above formulation can also be written as follows:

$$\text{Max or Min } Z = \sum_{j=1}^{n} C_j x_j \qquad ...(1)$$

subject to linear constraints

$$\sum_{j=1}^{n} c_{ij} x_j = b_i \qquad i = 1, 2, ..., m \qquad ...(2)$$

$$j = 1, 2, ..., n$$

and $$x_j \geq 0 \qquad ...(3)$$

The equation represented by (1) is the objective function; equation (2) is the set of constraints and equation (3) is the non-negativity condition.

In the above LPP model, instead of equality sign (=), ≤ or ≥ (less than or equal to or greater than or equal to) sign can be used as per requirement in equation (2) for constraints.

Here: C_j: represents the coefficient of per unit contribution (profit/cost) of decision variables x_j to the value of the objective function; the coefficients a_{ij} (i = 1, 2, ..., m and j = 1, 2, ..., n) are referred to as the substitution or technological coefficients. These represents the amount of resources consumed per unit of variable a_{ij} and b_i (i = 1, 2, ..., m) is the constant representing the requirement or availability of the ith constant.

The above constrained optimization (maximization or minimization) problem may have

(*i*) a unique optimal feasible solution

(*ii*) no feasible solution, in otherwords, there may not exist any x_j; $j = 1, 2, ..., n$ that satisfy every constraint or restriction

(*iii*) more than one optimal feasible solution

(*iv*) unbounded solution, in otherwords, the value of the objective function can be made as large as possible in a maximization problem or as small as possible in a minimization problem.

1.5 AREAS OF APPLICATION OF LINEAR PROGRAMMING

Linear programming is widely used in various fields such as industry, business, military operation etc.

1. **In Industry.** Linear programming is used in the field of industrial problems. Examples of industries, where LP can be used are:
   (*a*) Production scheduling
   (*b*) Product-mix problem
   (*c*) Trim loss
   (*d*) Blending problem
   (*e*) Transportation of goods from factory of customers etc.
2. **In Management**
   (*a*) Assignment of right persons for the right job
   (*b*) Travelling sales man problem.
   (*c*) Manpower planning
   (*d*) Portfolio selection
   (*e*) Profit planning etc.

1.6 BASIC DEFINITIONS

(*a*) **Solution to a LPP.** Any set $x = \{x_1, x_2, ..., x_{m+n}\}$ of variables is called a solution to LP, if it satisfies the set of constraints (2).

(*b*) **Feasible Solution.** Any set $x = \{x_1, x_2, ..., x_{m+n}\}$ of variables is called a feasible solution of LPP, if it satisfies the set of constraints (2) and the non-negativity restrictions.

(*c*) **Basic Solution.** A basic solution is a solution obtained by setting any n variables (among $m + n$ variables) equal to zero and solving for remaining m variables, provided the determinant of the coefficients of these m variables is non-zero. Such m variables are called basic variables and the remaining n zero-valued variables are called non-basic variables.

(*d*) **Basic Feasible Solution.** A basic feasible solution is a basic solution that also satisfies the non-negativity restriction. The following are two types of basic feasible solution:

(*i*) **Non-degenerate basic feasible solution.** A non-degenerate basic feasible solution is the basic feasible solution that has exactly m positive x_i ($i = 1, 2, ..., n$) *i.e.*, all m basic variables are positive and the remaining n variables will be all equal to zero.

(*ii*) **Degenerate basic feasible solution.** A basic feasible solution is called degenerate, if one or more basic variables are zero valued.

(*e*) **Optimum Solution.** A basic feasible solution is said to be optimum, if it also optimizes the objective function (1).

(*f*) **Unbounded Solution.** If the value of the objective function can be increased or decreased in definitely, then such solution are called as unbounded solution.

1.7 GRAPHICAL METHOD OF SOLUTION LPP

The graphical method is used for solving two variable linear programming problem and it involves the following main steps:

1. **Formulation of the Problem.** First of all the problem under consideration is formulated as an LPP containing the objective function and the constraints.
2. **Plotting Each of the Formulated Constraints.** After the problem is formulated as an LPP, the next step is to draw the graph of the constraints of the LPP. For this, we have to follow the following steps:
   (*a*) The inequality of the constraint equations are changed into equality sign.
   (*b*) We then suppose $x_1 = 0$ and calculate the corresponding value of x_2 from first constraint equation.
   (*c*) Then we suppose $x_2 = 0$ and again calculate the corresponding value of x_1 from the same constraint equation.
   (*d*) This process is repeated until all the constraint equations are utilized.
   (*d*) Then the co-ordinates so obtained from each constraints are plotted so that a straight line may be drawn by connecting these points.
   (*f*) Thus, there will be as many straightlines as there are equations, whereas each straight line represents one constraint equation.
3. **Locating the Feasible Region (or Solution Space).** The feasible region is that region which satisfies all the constraints simultaneously.

   For less than sign in constraint equation, the feasible region will be the area which lies below these lines and for greater than sign in constraint the feasible region will be the area which lies, above the constraint lines. But for less than or equal to sign and greater than or equal to sign in constraints, the feasible region includes the points on the constraint lines also.
4. **Selection of the Graphic Solution Technique.** The following two techniques are used for graphical solution.
   (*a*) **Corner Point Method (or Extreme Point Method).**
      (*i*) Identify each of extreme (or corner) points of the feasible region either by inspection or by the method of simultaneous equations.
      (*ii*) Compute the value of profit or cost at each corner point by substituting the coordinates of that point in the given objective function.
      (*iii*) Then locate the extreme points (corner points) at which the value of the objective function is maximum (in case of maximization problem) and minimum (in case of minimization problem).

(*b*) **Iso-Profit or Iso-Cost Method.**

(*i*) Choose any specific profit or cost value and draw an iso-profit (iso-cost) line so that it falls within shaded region.

(*ii*) Then move this iso-profit (iso-cost) line parallel to itself and further (closer) from (to) the origin until further movement would take the iso-profit (iso-cost) line completely outside the feasible region.

(*iii*) Then identify the optimal solution as the coordinates of that point on the feasible region that are touched by either iso-profit (highest possible) or iso-cost (lowest possible) line. The coordinates of the optimal point are chosen.

(*iv*) Compute the optimal profit or the cost.

1.8 SOME SPECIAL CASES IN LPP

Inspite of unique solution, there may exist no solution or an unbounded solution or even multiple solution for a given LPP.

1. In Feasible Solution (or No Solution)

Whenever, there is no solution to an LPP that may satisfy all the constraints of LPP, then it is said that there exists an infeasible solution for that LPP.

In other words, there exists no feasible region in graph plotted.

Example: Max $2x_1 + x_2$

Subject to $2x_1 + 3x_2 \leq 18$

$2x_1 + 2x_2 \geq 20$

$x_1, x_2 \geq 0$

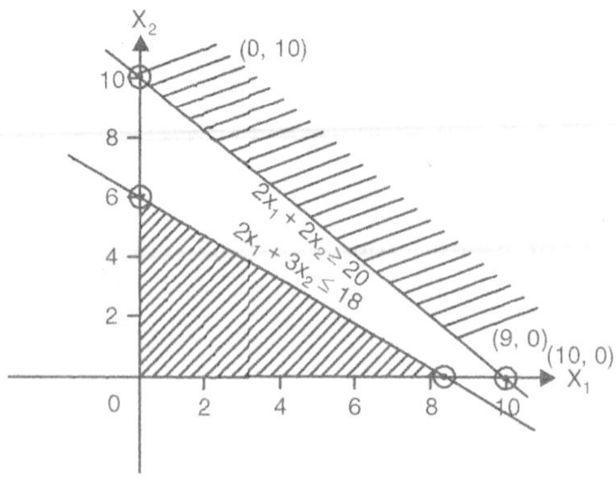

Fig. 1.1

Since in the above graph, there is nocommon shaded region among the constraints. Thus the set of points satisfying one constraint includes none of the points satisfying the other. Thus the given LPP has no feasible solution.

2. Multiple Optimal Solution

If the optimal solution of a LPP occurs at an extreme point of the feasible region, then the optimal solution is unique, which means that no other solution yields the same value of the objective function. But sometimes, the cases arises when more than one optimal solution yields the same value of the objective function, thus, multiple optimal solution can be obtanied, for an alternative optimal solution to exist.

(*i*) The given objective function is parallel to the constraint that forms the boundary of the feasible region.

(*ii*) The constraint line should form a boundary on the feasible region in the direction of the movement of objective function line.

Example: Maximize $Z = 8x_1 + 6x_2$

Subject to
$$6x_1 + 8x_2 \leq 48$$
$$4x_1 + 3x_2 \leq 24$$
$$2x_1 \leq 10$$
$$x_2 \leq 6$$
$$x_1, x_2 \geq 0$$

The points obtained by converting the inequality sign into equality sign are:

(*i*) (0, 6) and (8, 0) from first constraint

(*ii*) (0, 8) and (6, 0) from second constraint

(*iii*) $x_1 = 5$ from third constraint

(*iv*) $x_2 = 6$ from fourth constraint

After simplifying 2nd and 3rd constraint coordinates of point B are $\left(\frac{24}{7}, \frac{24}{7}\right)$ and C are $\left(5, \frac{4}{3}\right)$.

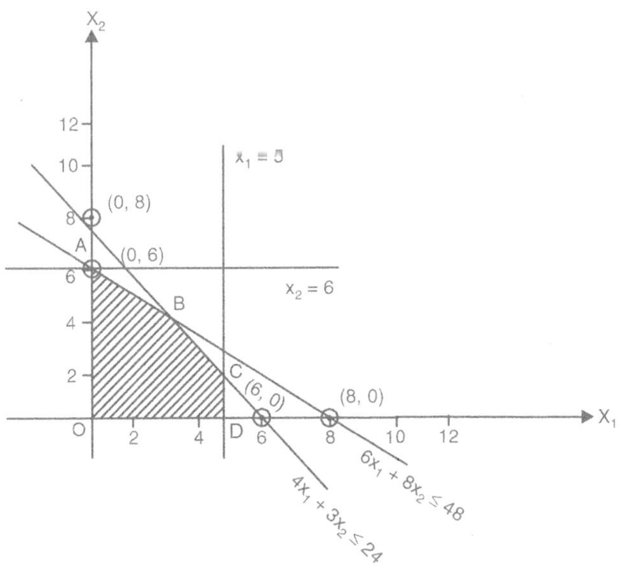

Fig. 1.2

In the above graph, the feasible region is represented by ODCBA.

Thus, the value of the objective function Z is calculated as:

A: (0, 6) $Z(A) = 8(0) + 6(6) = 36$

B: $\left(\frac{24}{7}, \frac{24}{7}\right)$ $Z(B) = 8\left(\frac{24}{7}\right) + 6\left(\frac{24}{7}\right) = \frac{192}{7} + \frac{144}{7} = \frac{336}{7} = 48^*$

C: $\left(5, \frac{4}{3}\right)$ $Z(C) = 8(5) + 6\left(\frac{4}{3}\right) = 40 + \frac{24}{3} = 40 + 8 = 48^*$

D: (6, 0) $Z(D) = 8(6) + 6(0) = 48^*$

Since Z_{max} occurs at points B, C and (marked with *). Thus we have multiple optimal solutions.

3. Unbounded Solution

A LPP may have unbounded solution which means that it has no limits on the constraints. The objective of the LPP can be made infinitely large without violating any of the constraints.

Example: Maximize $Z = 3x_1 + 2x_2$

Subject to

$$3x_1 - 6x_2 \leq 3$$
$$2x_1 + 4x_2 \geq 6$$
$$x_1, x_2 \geq 0$$

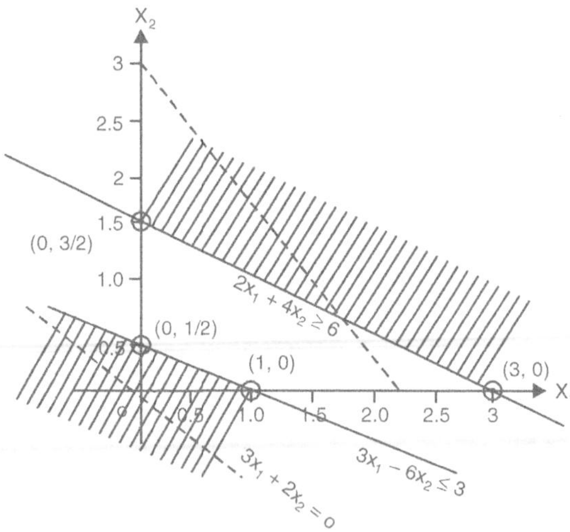

Fig. 1.3

Now the value of the objective function at 0 (0, 0) is $3x_1 + 2x_2 = 0$, and is represented by the dotted line, passing through the origin 0, in the graph above.

We cannot find the maximum value of the objective function, as feasible region cannot be located and the furthest point on the graph cannot be located to get the maximum value of the objective function. The maximum value of the objective function cannot be found as the furthest point occurs at infinity. Thus, the above problem has an unbounded solution.

Example 1. *Use the Graphical method to solve the following LPP*

Maximize $Z = 15x_1 + 10x_2$

Subject to constraints $2x_1 - 3x_2 \leq 180$

$$x_1 \leq 60$$
$$x_2 \geq 40$$
$$x_1, x_2 \geq 0$$

Solution. Now we shall treat x_1 as the horizontal axis while x_2 as the vertical axis in plotting the graph.

Each constraint of the LPP is connected from inequality to equality sign.

(*i*) So $2x_1 + 3x_2 = 180$

Now put $x_1 = 0 \Rightarrow x_2 = 60$ so the point is (0, 60)

and $x_2 = 0 \Rightarrow x_1 = 90$ so the point is (90, 0)

(*ii*) $x_1 = 60$

(*iii*) $x_2 = 40$

Then all these points and lines are drawn as:

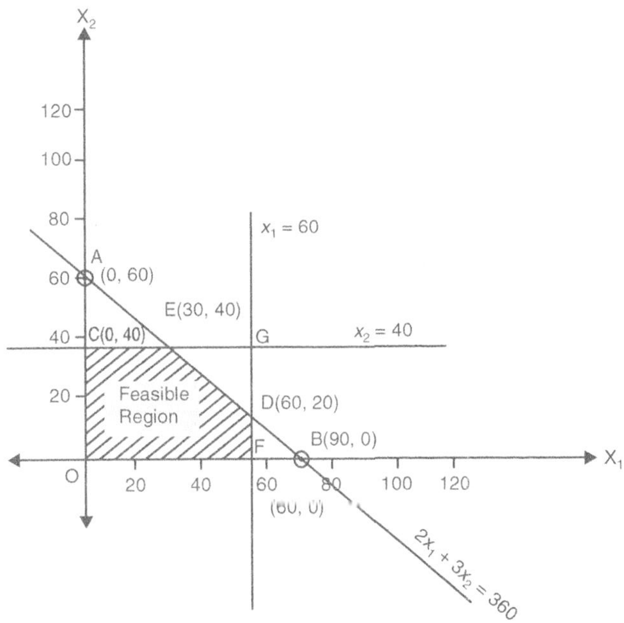

Fig. 1.4

Since all constraints have been graphed, the area that is bounded by all the constraints lines including all the boundary points is called the feasible region. The feasible region is shown above and is represented by OFDEC.

(*i*) $2x_1 + 3x_2 \leq 180$

Any point above the constraint line violates the inequality condition and any point below the constraint line satisfies the constraints.

(*ii*) $x_1 \leq 60$

Any point lying in the left hand side satisfies the constraint while points lying in the right hand side violates the constraints.

(*iii*) $x_1 \leq 40$

Similarly we can say that any point above the constraint violates the inequality condition and the points below the constraint line satisfies the constraints.

Remark: For satisfying the constraint

We proceed as follows:

(*i*) $2x_1 + 3x_2 \leq 180$

If we put $x_1 = 0$ and $x_2 = 0$

then $0 + 0 \leq 180$

$0 \leq 180$ (True)

Since the above statement is true, the shaded region of the feasible region will pass through the origin of the graph, otherwise not

(*ii*) $x_1 \leq 60$

$0 \leq 60$ (True)

(*iii*) $x_2 \leq 40$

$0 \leq 40$ (True)

In both the cases the shaded portion will cover the origin.

The points E and D are obtained by simplifying (*i*) and (*iii*) and constraints (*i*) and (*iv*)

For coordinates of E $\quad 2x_1 + 3x_2 = 180$ and $\quad x_2 = 40$

i.e., $\quad 2x_1 + 3(40) = 180 \Rightarrow 2x_1 = 60 \Rightarrow x_1 = 30$

$\Rightarrow$ coordinate E is (30, 40).

For coordinates of *D* $\quad 2x_1 + 3x_2 = 180$ and $\quad x_1 = 60$

$2(60) + 3x_2 = 180 \Rightarrow 3x_2 = 60 \Rightarrow x_2 = 20$

$\Rightarrow$ coordinate D is (60, 20).

Since we have got the shaded region in terms of feasible region OFBDEC, we want to find the maximum value of the objective function as the problem is of maximization type.

Thus, the points are as follows:

Points (Extreme)	Coordinates	Value of Z_0
O	(0, 0)	$15 \times (0) + 10(0) = 0$
F	(60, 0)	$15 \times (60) + 10(0) = 900$
D	(60, 20)	$15(60) + 10(20) = 1100$*
E	(30, 40)	$15(30) + 10(40) = 850$
C	(0, 40)	$15(0) + 10(40) = 400$

Since the value of Z = 1100 (marked with '*') is the maximum one. Thus, the graphical solution of the given

LPP is Max $\quad Z = 1100$

$x_1 = 60$

$x_2 = 20$

Example 2. *Use the graphical method to solve the following LPP.*

Max $\quad Z = 5x_1 + 10x_2$

Subject to the constraints

$$2x_1 + 4x_2 \leq 20$$
$$2x_1 + 2x_2 \leq 12$$
$$2x_1 + 2x_2 \leq 4$$
$$2x_1 - 4x_2 \leq 2$$
$$x_1, x_2 \geq 0$$

Solution. First of all, we will change all the inequality sign into equality signs and then plot the graph.

(*i*) $2x_1 + 4x_2 = 20$

If $x_1 = 0 \Rightarrow x_2 = 5 \Rightarrow (0, 5)$

If $x_2 = 0 \Rightarrow x_1 = 10 \Rightarrow (10, 0)$

(*ii*) $2x_1 + 2x_2 = 12$

If $x_1 = 0 \Rightarrow x_2 = 6 \Rightarrow (0, 6)$

If $x_2 = 0 \Rightarrow x_1 = 6 \Rightarrow (6, 0)$

(*iii*) $2x_1 + 2x_2 = 4$

(0, 2) and (2, 0)

(*iv*) $2x_1 - 4x_2 = 2$

$\left(0, \frac{1}{1}\right)$ and (1, 0)

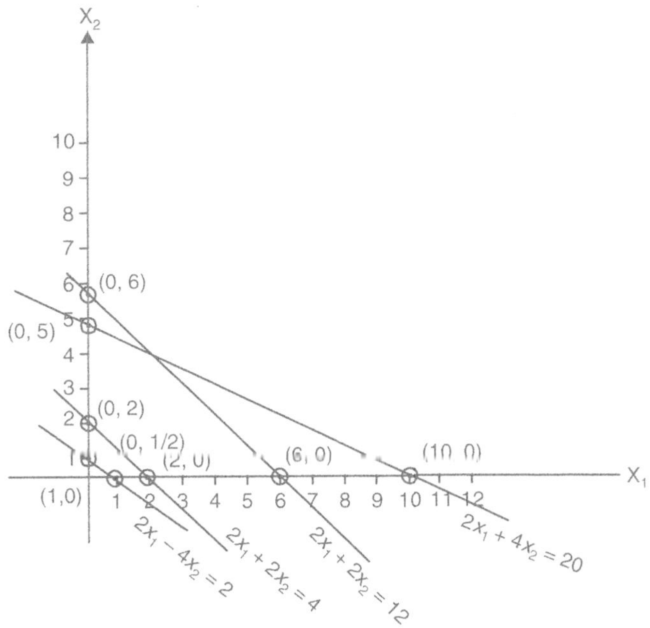

Fig. 1.5

Example 3. *Solve the following LPP using graphical method.*

Max $Z = 20x_1 + 30x_2$

Subject to

$$2x_1 + 4x_2 \le 80$$
$$6x_1 + 3x_2 \le 90$$
$$12x_1 + 8x_2 \le 240$$
$$x_1, x_2 \ge 0$$

Solution. From the given constraints, the coordinates are obtained as:

(i) $2x_1 + 4x_2 = 80 \Rightarrow (0, 20)$ and $(40, 0)$

(ii) $6x_1 + 3x_2 = 90 \Rightarrow (0, 30)$ and $(15, 0)$

(iii) $12x_1 + 8x_2 = 240 \Rightarrow (0, 30)$ and $(20, 0)$

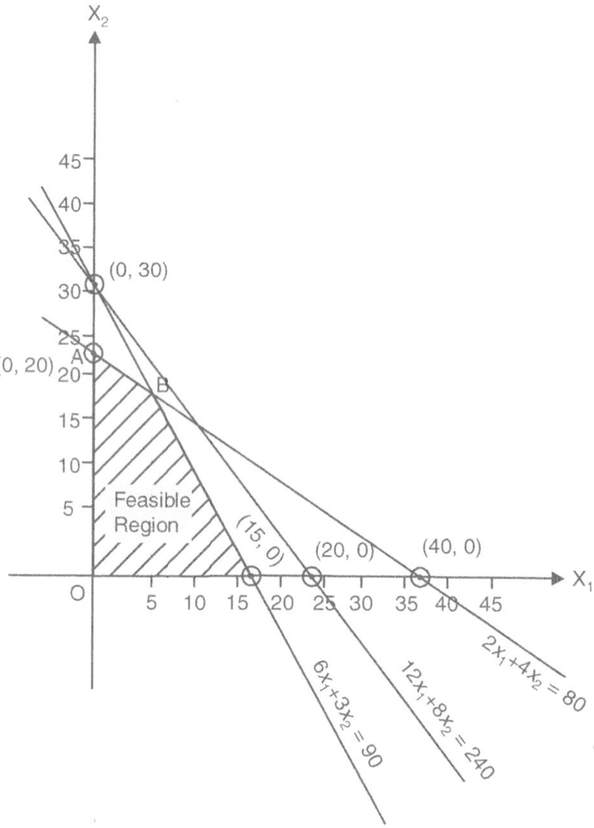

Fig. 1.6

The feasible region is denoted by OABC.

The coordinates of point B are obtained by simplifying the constraints $6x_1 + 3x_2 = 90$ and $2x_1 + 4x_2 = 80$

$$B\left(\frac{20}{3}, \frac{50}{3}\right)$$

The value of the objective function can be calculated as

Now O(0, 0) $\quad Z(O) = 20(0) + 30(0) = 0$

A(0, 20) $\quad Z(A) = 20(0) + 30(20) = 600$

$B\left(\frac{20}{3}, \frac{50}{3}\right) \quad Z(B) = 20\left(\frac{20}{3}\right) + 30\left(\frac{50}{3}\right) = \frac{1900}{3} = 633.33^*$

C (15, 0) $\quad Z(C) = 20(15) + 30(0) = 300$

The value of the objective function is maximum at point $B\left(\frac{20}{3}, \frac{50}{3}\right)$ the optimal solution is

$$Z_{max} = 633.33$$

$$x_1 = \frac{20}{3}$$

$$x_2 = \frac{50}{3}$$

Example 4. *Find the maximum value of* $Z = 15x_1 + 13x_2$

Subject to the constraints

$$2x_1 + 2x_2 \leq 12$$

$$6x_1 + 9x_2 \geq 18$$

$$0 \leq x_1 \leq 4$$

$$0 \leq x_2 \leq 5$$

Solution.

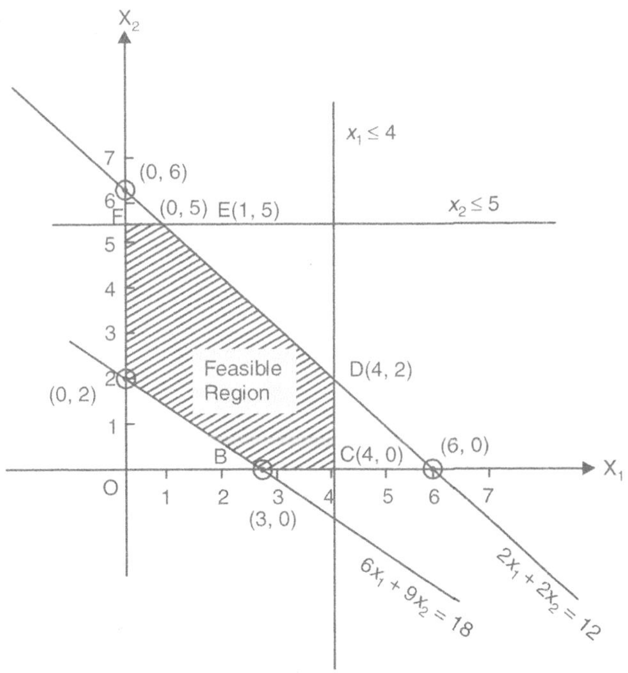

Fig. 1.7

The feasible region is represented by ABCDEF.

Thus the value of the objective function Z at the points

O(0, 0)	15(0) + 13(0)	= 0
A(0, 2)	15(0) + 13(2)	= 26
F(0, 5)	15(0) + 13(5)	= 65
E(1, 5)	15(1) + 13(5)	= 15 + 65 = 80
D(4, 2)	15(4) + 13(2)	= 60 + 26 = 86*
C(4, 0)	15(4) + 13(0)	= 60
B(3, 0)	15(3) + 13(0)	= 45

So the maximum value is 86.

Thus, the optimum solution is $Z_{max} = 86$

$x_1 = 4$

$x_2 = 2$

Example 5. *Solve the following LPP graphically and show that there is an infeasible solution.*

Maximize $Z = 2x_1 + x_2$

Subject to

$$3x_1 + 2x_2 \leq 12$$
$$x_1 \leq 2$$
$$2x_1 + 2x_2 \geq 6$$
$$-2x_1 + 2x_2 \geq 8$$
$$x_1 \geq 0 \text{ and } x_2 \geq 0$$

Solution.

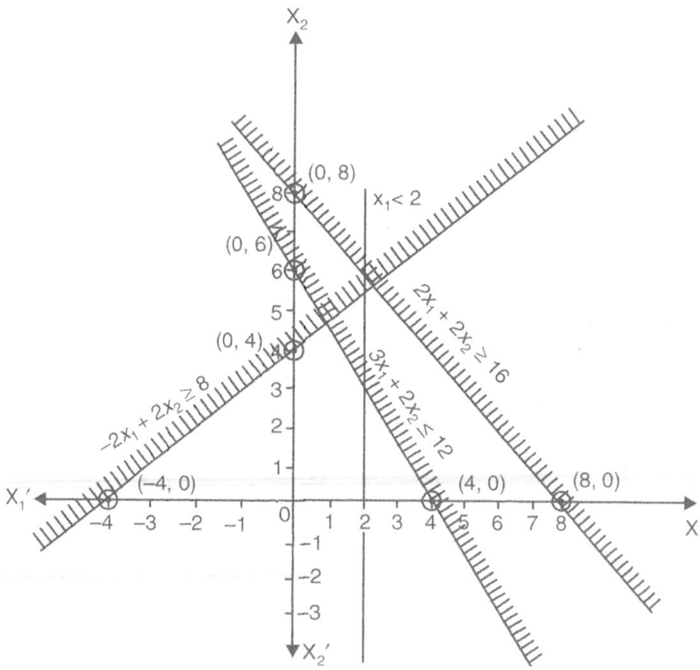

Fig. 1.8

In the above example, feasible region cannot be located as there is no common shaded region.

Thus there is no feasible region for the above problem which satisfies all the three constraints simultaneously.

Hence, there is an infeasible solution.

Example 6. *Solve graphically the following problem.*

Maximize $Z = 7x_1 + 14x_2$

Subject to

$$x_1 + 2x_2 \geq 3$$
$$x_1 + x_2 \leq 4$$
$$0 \leq x_1 \leq 1.5$$
$$0 \leq x_2 \leq 2.5$$

Solution. Coordinates of B are $\left(\frac{3}{2}, \frac{3}{4}\right)$

Coordinates of C are (1.5, 2.5)

Coordinates of D are (0, 2.5)

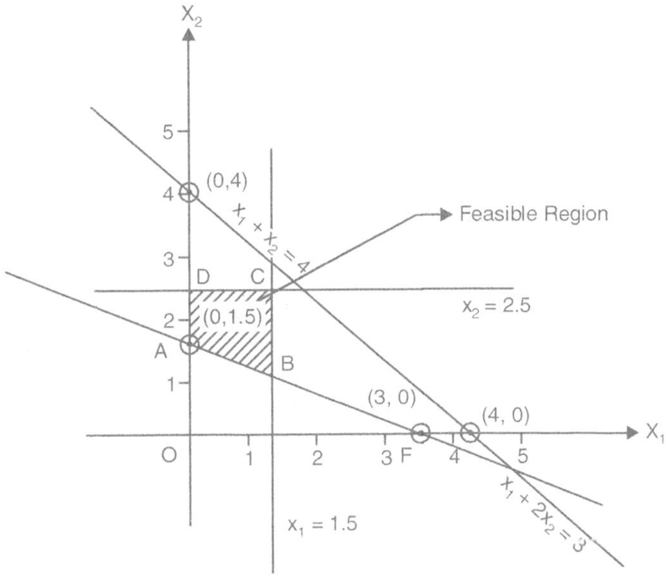

Fig. 1.9

Thus, the feasible region is represented by ABCD.

Now the value of the objective function at points

A(0, 1.5) $Z(A) = 7(0) + 14(1.5) = 21$

$B\left(\frac{3}{2}, \frac{3}{4}\right)$ $Z(B) = 7\left(\frac{3}{2}\right) + 14\left(\frac{3}{4}\right) = 21$

C(1.5, 2.5) $Z(C) = 7(1.5) + 14(2.5) = 45^*$

D(0, 2.5) $Z(D) = 7(0) + 14(2.5) = 35$

Since the value of Z is maximum at point C(1.5, 2.5)

Then $Z_{max} = 45$ and $x_1 = 1.5$, $x_2 = 2.5$

Example 7. *Solve graphically the following problem and show that there is an unbounded solution.*

Max $Z = 10x_1 + 20x_2$

Subject to

$$2x_1 - 2x_2 \leq 2$$
$$x_1 + x_2 \geq 3$$
$$x_1, x_2 \geq 0$$

Coordinates of B are (2, 1)

Solution.

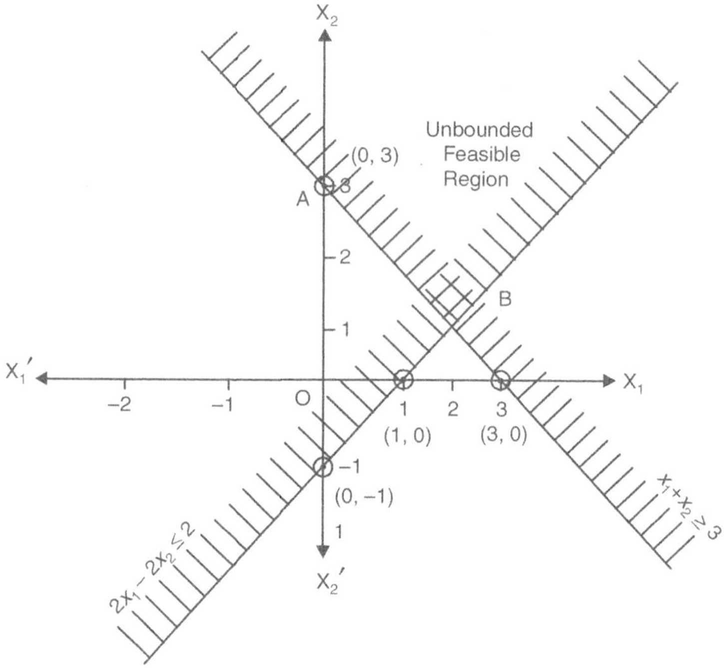

Fig. 1.10

Since the extreme points of the feasible region are only A and B and the value of the objective function at these points are.

A(0, 3) Z(A) = 10(0) + 20(3) = 60

B(2, 1) Z(B) = 10(2) + 20(1) = 40

But there are infinitely many points lying in feasible region for which the value of the objective function is more than 60. Thus for large values of x_1 and x_2 the value of the objective function will be increased. Hence the problem has an unbounded solution.

Example 8. *Solve the following LPP graphically*

Maximize $Z = 10x_1 + 20x_2$

Subject to

$$2x_1 + 3x_2 \leq 30$$
$$3x_1 + 2x_2 \leq 24$$
$$x_1 + x_2 \geq 3$$
$$x_1, x_2 \geq 0$$

Solution. Thus the feasible region is denoted by ABCDE.

The coordinates of point B are $\left(\frac{12}{5}, \frac{42}{5}\right)$.

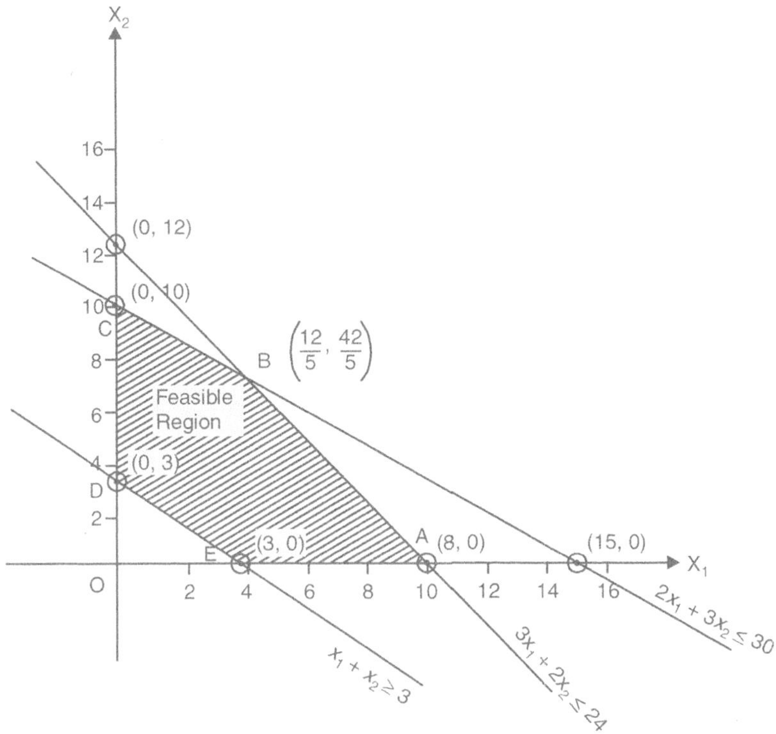

Fig. 1.11

Thus the value of the objective function at various extreme points are:

$A(8, 0) \Rightarrow 10(8) + 20(0) = 80$

$$B\left(\frac{12}{5}, \frac{42}{5}\right) \Rightarrow 10\left(\frac{12}{5}\right) + 20\left(\frac{42}{5}\right) = 24 + 168 = 192$$

$C(0, 10) \Rightarrow 10(0) + 20(10) = 0 + 200 = 200^*$

$D(0, 3) \Rightarrow 10(0) + 20(3) = 0 + 60 = 60$

Thus, the value of the objective function is maximum at (0, 10).

Thus optimal solution is $z_{max} = 200; x_1 = 0, x_2 = 10$

Example 9. *Solve the following LPP graphically*

Max $Z = 30x_1 + 20x_2$

Subject to

$$10x_1 + 8x_2 \leq 800$$
$$x_1 \leq 60$$
$$x_2 \geq 75$$

and $\quad x_1, x_2 \geq 0$

Solution.

Thus, the coordinates of C and B can be calculated by solving the constraints $10x_1 + 8x_2 = 800$ and $x_2 = 75$, $x_1 = 60$ and $10x_1 + 8x_2 = 800$.

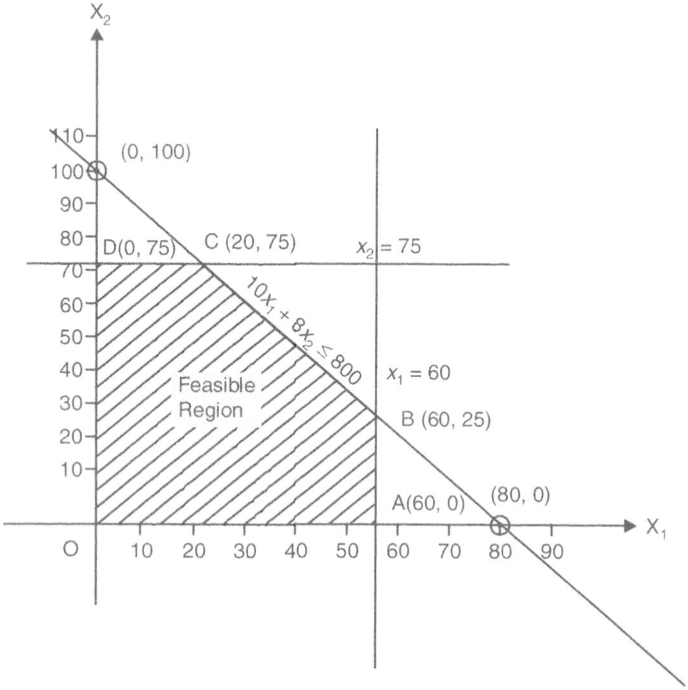

Fig. 1.12

The feasible region is denoted by OABCD. Now we calculate the value of the objective function at various extreme points of the feasible region.

O(0, 0)	$\Rightarrow 30(0) + 20(0)$	$= 0$
A(60, 0)	$\Rightarrow 30(60) + 20(0)$	$= 1800$
B(60, 25)	$\Rightarrow 30(60) + 20(25)$	$= 1800 + 500 = 2300^*$
C(20, 75)	$\Rightarrow 30(20) + 20(75)$	$= 600 + 1500 = 2100$
D(0, 75)	$\Rightarrow 30(0) + 20(75)$	$= 1500$

Thus, the value of the objective function is maximum at B.

Thus, the optimal solution is $Z_{max} = 2300$

$x_1 = 60$

$x_2 = 25$

1.9 FORMULATION OF PROBLEM AS AN LPP

In this section, we give an outline that how the problems are formulated as an LPP. This can only be done easily after gaining some experiences. The following steps should be kept in mind while formulating a problem as an LPP.

Step 1: Before the formulation of the problem as an LPP, it is necessary that the problem should be clear and should have a detailed verbal description so that the constraints, objective function and the restrictions may be used.

Step 2: After going through the problem, the next step is to make the objective of the problem under consideration, very clear, that whether it is a maximization (profit, revenue) or a minimization (cost, time etc), and act accordingly.

Step 3: Then determine all the factors or constraints that are used as an restriction in the problem to obtain the constraint equations.

Step 4: After make a clear picture of the objective function and the constraints, define the decision variables to be used.

Step 5: Then use these decision variables with the cost functions (c_j's) to formulate the objective function, and with the physical rate of substitution coefficients (a_{ij}'s) to formulate the constraints equations and finally with the available resources or requirements (b_i's) to make the right hand side of the constraints so formed.

Step 6: Then the suitable equality or inequality sign is used in the constraints equation so formed above.

1.10 EXAMPLES ON THE APPLICATIONS OF LINEAR PROGRAMMING

In this section we illustrate the applications of linear programming in various fields with the help of examples. In this section, emphasis is given how a given problem can be formulated as a LPP, by analysis of the given problem. The main aim is how the problem is formulated instead of what is the solution of the given problem?

Example 10 (Production Problem). *A company XYZ produces two products P_1 and P_2. These products are processed on the same machine. If one unit of product P_1 and one unit of product P_2 are processed, then the machine takes 20 minutes and 25 minutes respectively. The machine can be operated for a maximum of 50 hours in a week. Product P_1 requires 10 kg and P_2 requires 15 kg of the raw material per unit, if the total supply of the raw material is 500 kg per week. The cost of product P_1 is ₹ 50 per unit and its selling price is ₹ 100, whereas the cost of product P_2 is ₹ 16 per unit and its selling price is ₹ 60. Determine the number of units of product P_1 and P_2 produced per week so that the profit is maximum. It is also given that the market demand of product P_2 is minimum 1000 units per week.*

Solution.

Formulation of Objective Function. For product P_1 and product P_2, let x_1 and x_2 be the number of units produced per week.

Since the cost of product P_1 is ₹ 50 and its selling price is ₹ 100 per unit.

Thus, the profit on one unit of product P_1 is = ₹ 100 – ₹ 50

= ₹ 50

Hence profit on x_1 units of product P_1 is = ₹ $50x_1$

Similarly the profit on x_2 units of product P_2 is = ₹ $(60 - 16)x_2$

= ₹ $44x_2$

Since the objective is to maximize the profit.

Thus maximize $Z = 50x_1 + 44x_2$ ...(1)

Formulation of Constraints. Since one unit of product P_1 and product P_2 takes 20 minutes and 25 minutes respectively.

Thus 1 unit of P_1 takes = 20 minutes

x_1 units of P_1 takes = $20x_1$ minutes

and x_2 units of P_2 takes = $25x_2$ minutes

Since machine can be operated for a maximum of 50 hours (= 50 × 60 = 3000 minutes) in a week.

We have $20x_1 + 25x_2 \leq 3000$ ...(2)

Since one unit of product P_1 uses 10 kg of raw material while one unit of product P_2 uses 15 kg and the total supply of raw material per week is 500 kg.

Thus $10x_1 + 15x_2 \leq 500$.

Also in the market, atleast 1000 units of product p_2 is required.

Thus $x_2 \geq 1000$.

Hence the LPP can now be summarized as

Maximize $Z = 50x_1 + 44x_2$

Subject to constraints

$$20x_1 + 25x_2 \leq 300$$
$$10x_1 + 15x_2 \leq 500$$
$$x_1 \geq 1000$$
$$x_1, x_2 \geq 0$$

Example 11 (Production Allocation Problem). *A company produces three different products A, B and C and these products are to be processed on three different Machines I, II and III. The daily capacity of all the three machines as well as the time required by these machines to produce one unit of each product is given in the following table.*

Machine	*Time in minutes (per unit) Product*			*Machine Capacity (minutes per day)*
	A	*B*	*C*	
I	4	1	2	510
II	3	2	1	635
III	—	5	7	495

It is to determine that how many units of each product are produced daily. If all the products produced are consumed in that market, then formulate the above problem as on LPP, given that the profit per unit of each product A, B and C is obtained as ₹ 10, ₹ 20 and ₹ 50 respectively.

Solution. Formulation of LPP

Let x_1: be the number of units produced daily for product A

x_2: be the number of units produced daily for product B

x_3: be the number of units produced daily for product C

(*a*) **Formulation of objective function.** Since the profit gained in each of the product A, B and C is respectively ₹ 10, ₹ 20 and ₹ 50.

Profit on one unit of product A: ₹ 10

Profit on x_1 unit of product A = ₹ $10x_1$

Profit on one unit of product B = ₹ 20

Profit on x_1 unit of product B $= ₹\ 20x_2$

Profit on one unit of product C $= ₹\ 50$

Profit on x_3 unit of product C $= ₹\ 50x_3$

Hence the objective is to maximize the profit.

Thus maximize $Z = 10x_1 + 20x_2 + 50x_3$ ...(1)

(*b*) Formulation of Constraints

Time required for producing one unit of product A = 4

Time required for producing x_1 unit of product A = $4x_1$

Time required for producing one unit of product B = 1

Time required for producing x_2 unit of product B = x_1

Time required for producing one unit of product C = 2

Time required for producing x_3 unit of product C = $2x_3$

Since the machine capacity for operating is 510 minutes/day. Thus using above data the first constraint can be written as:

$$4x_1 + x_2 + 2x_3 \le 510$$

Similarly $3x_1 + 2x_2 + x_3 \le 635$

and $5x_2 + 7x_3 \le 495$

The LPP formulation is as follows:

$$\text{Max } Z = 10x_1 + 20x_2 + 50x_3$$

$$\text{Subject to } \begin{aligned} 4x_1 + x_2 + 2x_3 &\le 510 \\ 3x_1 + 2x_2 + x_3 &\le 635 \\ 5x_2 + 7x_3 &\le 495 \\ x_1, x_2, x_3 &\ge 0 \end{aligned}$$

Example 12 (Diet Problem). *A doctor advises a patient to ensure certain minimum intake of carbohydrates, fats, proteins and minerals for the patient. The minimum daily needs of these for the patient are 40, 30, 25 and 20 respectively. The doctor told to eat only following two foods continuously, till the disease is cured. The table below gives the details of the foods:*

Food	*Carbohydrates*	*Fats*	*Proteins*	*Minerals*
A	17 units	15 units	13 units	12 units
B	15 units	13 units	14 units	13 units

The food A costs ₹ 50 per unit and the food B costs ₹ 30 per unit. Formulate the above problem as a LPP which results the quantity of food A and food B to buy to fulfill the daily requirements of carbohydrates, fats, proteins and minerals for the patient to keep his bill for purchasing the food as low as possible.

Solution. Let x_1: be the patient purchase x_1 units of food A.

x_2: be the patient purchase x_2 units of food B.

(*a*) **Formulations of Objective Functions**

The cost of 1 unit of food A costs $= ₹\ 50$

The cost of x_1 units of food A costs $= ₹\ 50x_1$

The cost of 1 unit of food B costs $= ₹\ 30$

The cost of x_2 units of food B costs $= ₹\ 30x_2$

Thus, the objective function is of minimization as its involves costs.

Hence Minimize $Z = 50x_1 + 30x_2$.

(*b*) **Formulation of Constraints**

Carbohydrates Constraints $17x_1 + 15x_2 \leq 40$

Fats constraints $15x_1 + 13x_2 \leq 30$

Proteins constraints $13x_1 + 14x_2 \leq 25$

Minerals constraints $12x_1 + 13x_2 \leq 20$

Thus, the formulations is

$$
\begin{aligned}
\text{Minimize } Z &= 50x_1 + 30x_2 \\
\text{Subject to } \quad & 17x_1 + 15x_2 \leq 40 \\
& 15x_1 + 13x_2 \leq 30 \\
& 13x_1 + 14x_2 \leq 25 \\
& 12x_1 + 13x_2 \leq 20 \\
& x_1, x_2 \geq 0
\end{aligned}
$$

Example 13 (Inspection Problem). *In a company there are two Inspectors of calibre I_1 and I_2, who control the quality of goods by inspection. At least 2500 must be inspected in 10 hour per day. Inspector I_1 can check 50 pieces in an hour and 95% accuracy. Inspector I_2 can check 25 pieces in an hour with 90% accuracy.*

The daily amount received by inspectors I_1 and I_2 are ₹ 100 per hour and 150 per hour respectively. If a product with defect is passed by these inspectors, then the company gets a lost of ₹ 30. If there are 20 I_1 inspectors and 25 I_2 inspectors appointed for this purpose, then find the optimal assignment of inspectors so as to minimize the daily inspection cost.

Solution. Formulation of LPP

Let x_1: represents the number of I_1 inspectors and

x_2: represents the number of I_2 inspectors

(*a*) **Formulation of Objective Function.** The company has to incur two types of costs:

(*i*) Wages paid to both the inspectors I_1 and I_2

(*ii*) Cost of their errors while checking the products.

Thus cost of I_1 inspector per hour would be

₹ $(100 + 30 \times 0.10 \times 50)$ = ₹ 250

($\because$ As I_1 inspector has 90% accuracy, *i.e.*, 10% is for error he makes).

Similarly cost of I_2 inspector per hour would be

₹ $(150 + 30 \times 0.05 \times 25)$ = ₹ 187.50

$\therefore$ The objective function becomes

Minimize $Z = 10(250x_1 + 187.50x_2)$ ($\because$ for 10 hours inspection by these inspectors)

$= 2500x_1 + 1875x_2$ ...(1)

(*b*) **Formulation of Constraints**

Total number of I_1 inspectors deputed; $x_1 \leq 20$ ...(2)

Total number of I_2 inspectors deputed; $x_2 \leq 25$ ...(3)

Now the total number of pieces inspected daily in 10 hours.

$$50 \times 10x_1 + 25 \times 10x_2 \geq 2500$$

i.e., $$500x_1 + 250x_2 \geq 2500 \quad ...(4)$$

Thus, the LPP can be formulated as:

Minimize $Z = 2500x_1 + 1875x_2$

Subject to
$$x_1 \leq 20$$
$$x_2 \leq 25$$
$$500x_1 + 250x_2 \geq 2500$$
$$x_1, x_2 \geq 0$$

Example 14 (Production Scheduling Problem). *A company produces its 3 products P_1, P_2 and P_3 which passes through three process I_1, I_2 and I_3. The time available for machine for processing on I_1, I_2 and I_3 are 75 hours, 100 hours and 150 hours respectively. The product are sold at the rate of ₹ 35, ₹ 20 and ₹ 30 per unit respectively, after being made through different alternative routes as shown in the table. The customer also pays ₹ 20, ₹ 15 and ₹ 10 per unit for extra units of products respectively. Formulate the problem as an LPP assuming that the orders of product P_1, P_2 and P_3 are fixed as 200 units, 150 units and 100 units.*

Machines	Product P_1		Product P_2		Product P_3		Machine hours Available
	Route		Route		Route		
	I	II	I	II	I	II	
I_1	2	3	5	6	1	5	75
I_2	3	1	0	2	6	1	100
I_3	2	7	1	3	4	4	150

Solution. Formulation of LPP

Let x_{11}: be the number of units of product P_1 be produced through Route I_1

x_{12}: be the number units of product P_1 be produced through Route I_2

x_{21}: be the number of units of P_2 be produced through I_1

x_{22}: be the number of units of P_2 be produced through I_2

x_{31}: be the number of units of P_3 be produced through I_1

x_{32}: be the number of units of P_3 be produced through I_2

(*a*) **Formulation of Objective Function**

Maximum $Z = 35(x_{11} + x_{12}) + 20(x_{21} + x_{22}) + 30(x_{31} + x_{32})$

(cost of p_1 product passing through route I_1, ₹ selling price is ₹ 35 = $35x_{11}$

cost of p_1 product passing through route I_2, ₹ selling price is = $35x_{12}$

So total of cost of units for both the routes is

$$= 35x_{11} + 35x_{12}$$
$$= 35(x_{11} + x_{12})$$

(*b*) **Formulation of Constraints**

(*i*) The machine hours available for each machine for process through

I_1: $2x_{11} + 3x_{12} + 5x_{21} + 6x_{22} + x_{31} + 5x_{32} \leq 75$

I_2: $3x_{11} + x_{12} + 2x_{22} + 6x_{31} + x_{32} \le 100$

I_3: $2x_{11} + 7x_{12} + x_{21} + 3x_{22} + 4x_{31} + 4x_{32} \le 150$

(*ii*) Since the fixed order is 200 units for product P_1, 150 units for product P_2 and 100 units for product P_3.

Thus the total number of units of product P_1 produced are $(x_{11} + x_{12})$ and in order to satisfy the fixed order it must also satisfy the fixed order of 200 units.

Thus
$$x_{11} + x_{12} \ge 200$$
$$x_{21} + x_{22} \ge 150$$
$$x_{31} + x_{32} \ge 100$$

Thus the new objective function can now be calculated after involving the selling prices and the fixed order of all the three products as.

$$\text{Max } Z = 200 \times 35 + 20(x_{11} + x_{12} - 200) + 150 \times 20 + 15(x_{21} + x_{22} - 150) + 100 \times 30 + 10(x_{31} + x_{32} - 100)$$

or
$$\text{Max } Z = 7000 + 20(x_{11} + x_{12}) - 4000 + 3000 + 15(x_{21} + x_{22}) - 2250 + 3000 + 10(x_{31} + x_{32}) - 1000$$
$$= 20(x_{11} + x_{12}) + 15(x_{21} + x_{22}) + 10(x_{31} + x_{32}) + 5750$$

Thus formulation of above problem as an LPP is written as follows:

Maximize $Z = 20(x_{11} + x_{12}) + 15(x_{21} + x_{22}) + 10(x_{31} + x_{32}) + 5750$

Subject to the constraints

$$2x_{11} + 3x_{12} + 5x_{21} + 6x_{22} + x_{31} + 5x_{32} \le 75$$
$$3x_{11} + x_{12} + 2x_{22} + 6x_{31} + x_{32} \le 100$$
$$2x_{11} + 7x_{12} + x_{21} + 3x_{22} + 4x_{31} + 4x_{32} \le 150$$
$$x_{11} + x_{12} \ge 200$$
$$x_{21} + x_{22} \ge 150$$
$$x_{31} + x_{32} \ge 100$$
$$x_{11}, x_{12}, x_{21}, x_{22}, x_{31}, x_{32} \ge 0$$

Example 15 (Transportation Problem). *A company produces 2 different products at two different factories A and B. These products are to be distributed at three different demand centres I, II and III. The requirement of these products and its availability are given in the following table.*

Demand Centres

		I	*II*	*III*	*Availability*
Factories	*A*	*5*	*7*	*9*	*10*
↓	*B*	*2*	*6*	*12*	*5*
Requirement		*5*	*6*	*4*	

Solution. Formulation of LPP

Let x_1: be the quantity or the number of products transported from factory A to demand centre I.

x_2: be the quantity of products transported from factory A to demand centre II.

Thus, the transportation of products are shown in the table below.

		I	II	III	Availability
Factories	A	x_1	x_2	$10 - (x_1 + x_2)$	10
	B	$5 - x_1$	$6 - x_2$	$5 - \{(5 - x_1) + (6 - x_2)$	5
Requirement		5	6	4	

(*a*) **Formulation of Objective Function:**

Minimize Z $= 5x_1 + 7x_2 + 9(10 - x_1 - x_2) + 2(5 - x_1) + 6(6 - x_2) + 12\{5 - (5 - x_1) - (6 - x_2)\}$

or Minimize Z $= 5x_1 + 7x_2 + 90 - 9x_1 - 9x_2 + 10 - 2x_1 + 36 - 6x_2 + 60 - 60 + 12x_1 - 72 + 12x_2$

or $= 6x_1 + 2x_2 + 64$

(*b*) **Formulation of Constraints:**

$10 - (x_1 + x_2) \geq 0$ or $x_1 + x_2 \leq 0$

$5 - x_1 \geq 0$ or $x_1 \leq 5$

$6 - x_2 \geq 0$ $x_2 \leq 6$

$5 - \{(5 - x_1) + (6 - x_2)\} \geq 0$ $x_1 + x_2 \geq 6$

Thus, the above problem is formulated as an LPP as follows:

Minimize Z $= 6x_1 + 2x_2 + 64$

Subject to constraints

$$x_1 + x_2 \leq 10$$
$$x_1 + x_2 \geq 6$$
$$x_1 \leq 5$$
$$x_2 \leq 6$$
$$x_1, x_2 \geq 0$$

Example 16. *A factory produces two products A and B, and has a total production capacity of 1000 products per day. The factory supplies at least 500 pieces of product A and at least 400 pieces of product B per day to the market. Each piece of product A requires 2 machine hours production time and each piece of product B requires 5 machine hours production time. The daily maximum hours for machine to work is 18 hours.*

The profit on a piece of product A is ₹ 8 while on product B is ₹ 12. Then formulate the above problem as an LPP in order to maximize the profit.

Solution.

Let x_1: be the number of product A be produced.

x_2: be the number of product B be produced.

Thus, the LPP formulation is

Maximize Z $= 8x_1 + 12x_2$

Subject to

$$x_1 + x_2 \leq 1000$$
$$x_1 \geq 500$$
$$x_2 \geq 400$$
$$2x_1 + 5x_2 \leq 18$$
$$x_1, x_2 \geq 0$$

Example 17 (Product Mix Problem). *There are two types of foods F_1 and F_2 available in a college canteen. Food F_1 contains 16 units of vitamin A per gram and 17 unit of vitamin B per gram. The cost of food F_1 is ₹ 2.50 per gram. Food F_2 contains 18 units of vitamin A per gram and 22 units of vitamin B. The costs of food F_2 is ₹ 2.00 per gram. If the daily minimum requirement of vitamin A and vitamin B are 120 units and 140 units respectively, then formulate the above problem as an LPP to minimize the cost of product mix.*

Solution.

Let x_1: be the quantity of Food F_1 be purchased.

x_2: be the quantity of Food F_2 be purchased.

Then LPP formulation is

Minimize $Z = 2.5x_1 + 2x_2$

Subject to $16x_1 + 18x_2 \geq 120$ (Vitamin A constant)

$17x_1 + 22x_2 \geq 140$ (Vitamin B constant)

$x_1, x_2 \geq 0$

Example 18. *An animal feed company must produce 350 kgs of a mixture consisting of ingradients A and B daily. Gradient A costs ₹ 16 per kg and gradient B costs ₹ 20 per kg. No more than 100 kgs of A can be used and at least 120 kgs of B must be used. Formulate the above problem as an LPP so as to minimize the cost.*

Solution.

Let x_1: be the quantity of gradient A

x_2: be the quantity of gradient B

Formulation of the problem as an LPP

Minimize $Z = 16x_1 + 20x_2$

Subjects to constraints

$$x_1 + x_2 \geq 350$$
$$x_1 \leq 100$$
$$x_2 \geq 120$$
$$x_1, x_2 \geq 0$$

Example 19. *A firm has an advertising budget of ₹ 80,000 and wishes to allocate these budgets to televisions and newspapers, so that the total exposure of the firm may be maximized. Each page of the newspaper advertising is estimated for ₹ 35,000 exposures, while each advertisement on television is estimated for ₹ 55,000 exposures. Each spot on television costs ₹ 15,000 whereas each page of newspaper costs ₹ 8000. An additional condition of the firm is imposed that it has specified that at least 3 pages of newspaper advertising and at least 2 spots on televisions be used. Formulate the above problem as an LPP.*

Solution.

Maximize $Z = 35{,}000x_1 + 55{,}000x_2$

Subject to $8{,}000x_1 + 15{,}000x_2 \leq 80{,}000$

$$x_1 \geq 3$$
$$x_2 \geq 2$$
$$x_1, x_2 \geq 0$$

(where x_1: Number of pages and x_2: Number of spots on TV)

Example 20 (Diet Problem). *A doctor advises his patient regarding the diet so that the daily requirements of carbohydrates, fats and proteins be fulfilled at a minimum cost. The choice is to be made from four different types of foods he usually takes. The yields per unit of different types of foods are given as follows.*

Type of Food	*Yield per unit*			*Cost per unit (in ₹)*
	Carbohydrates	*Fats*	*Proteins*	
A	6	5	9	49
B	7	5	7	36
C	11	10	10	90
D	9	8	7	75
Minimum Requirement	1200	450	950	

Formulate the above problem as LPP.

Solution. Formulation of the LPP:

(*a*) **Formulation of the Objective Function:**

Let x_1: be the number of unit of Food A to be used

x_2: be the number of units of Food B to be used.

x_3: be the number of units of Food C to be used.

x_4: be the number of units of Food D to be used.

Since cost of one unit of Food *A* costs = ₹ 49

Thus cost of x_1 unit of Food A costs = ₹ $49x_1$

Since cost of 1 unit of Food B costs = ₹ 36

Thus cost of x_2 units of Food B costs = ₹ $36x_2$

Since cost of 1 unit of Food C costs = ₹ 90

Thus cost of x_3 units of Food C costs = ₹ $90x_3$

Since cost of 1 unit of Food D costs = ₹ 75

Thus cost of 1 unit of Food D costs = ₹ $75x_4$

Since the main is to minimize the cost. Thus the objective function is formulated as:

Minimize $z = 49x_1 + 36x_2 + 90x_3 + 75x_4$ ...(1)

(*b*) Formulation of the Constraints.

Constraints for carbohydrates

$$6x_1 + 7x_2 + 11x_3 + 9x_4 \geq 1200$$

Constraints for fats

$$5x_1 + 5x_2 + 10x_3 + 8x_4 \geq 450$$

Constraints for proteins

$$9x_1 + 7x_2 + 10x_3 + 7x_4 \geq 950$$

Thus the formulation of the above problem as an LPP is

$$\text{Minimum } Z = 49x_1 + 36x_2 + 90x_3 + 75x_4$$

Subject to the constraints

$$6x_1 + 7x_2 + 11x_3 + 9x_4 \geq 1200$$
$$5x_1 + 5x_2 + 10x_3 + 8x_4 \geq 450$$
$$9x_1 + 7x_2 + 10x_3 + 7x_4 \geq 950$$
$$x_1, x_2, x_3, x_4 \geq 0$$

OBJECTIVE TYPE QUESTIONS

1. Which of the following is not a characteristic of LPP.
(*a*) limited amount of resources (*b*) an objective function of maximization type
(*c*) alternative courses of action (*d*) non-negativity restriction.

2. A constraint in LPP model restricts
(*a*) use of the available resources (*b*) value of decision variables
(*c*) value of objective function (*d*) All of the above.

3. Before the formulation of an LPP, it is always better to express
(*a*) the objective function in words (*b*) each constraints in words
(*c*) by writing decision variables used (*d*) All of the above.

4. Linear programming is a
(*a*) mathematical technique (*b*) statistical technique
(*c*) heuristic technique (*d*) physical technique.

5. The constraints involved in LPP represents
(*a*) the requirements or limitations
(*b*) the objective of the problem under consideration
(*c*) non-negativity restriction
(*d*) None of the above.

6. LPP can be used in:
(*a*) Military applications
(*b*) Production, financial and marketing management
(*c*) Agricultural applications
(*d*) All of the above.

7. Linear programming problems treats all the relationships among decision variables as:
(*a*) linear (*b*) curvilinear
(*c*) non-linear (*d*) quadratic.

8. Linear programming problem, the constraints may be defined by using
(*a*) equal of sign (*b*) less than or equal to sign
(*c*) greater than or equal to sign (*d*) All of the above.

9. A feasible solution to the linear programming problem should satisfy.
(*a*) the non-negativity restriction
(*b*) the constraints of the problem

(*c*) the problem constraints and non-negativity constraints
(*d*) None of the above.

10. Linear programming is a
(*a*) constrained decision-making model
(*b*) constrained optimization model
(*c*) constrained mathematical programming
(*d*) All of the above.

11. The graphical method is useful because
(*a*) It gives heuristic solution of the problem
(*b*) It gives analytical solution of the problem
(*c*) It gives geometric insight into the model and the meaning of optimality
(*d*) None of the above.

12. All variables obtained in the solution of a LPP are either zero or positive, but never negative, because of
(*a*) objective function of LPP
(*b*) structural constraints of LPP
(*c*) limited resources involved in LPP
(*d*) None of the above.

13. The non-negativity requirement is included in a LP because it makes the model
(*a*) easier to solve
(*b*) correspond more closely to the real-world problem
(*c*) gives best solution
(*d*) None of the above.

14. Linear Programming is a
(*a*) constrainted optimization problem
(*b*) mathematical programming problem
(*c*) constrained decision-making problem
(*d*) All of the above.

15. Constraints appear as .... when plotted on graph
(*a*) simply a coordinate point
(*b*) always a perpendicular line
(*c*) always a parallel line
(*d*) any straight line.

16. If a point on the boundary of the feasible region is considered, the such a point
(*a*) will be the optimal solution
(*b*) have the maximum objective function value
(*c*) have the minimum objective function value
(*d*) satisfies all the constraints.

17. The non-negativity requirement is included in a LPP because
(*a*) It makes the model easier to solve
(*b*) Its calculation procedure formulation is very tough
(*c*) It makes the model correspond more closely to the real-world problem.
(*d*) It formulation is very easy.

18. The unbounded solution of an LPP means that
(*a*) It cannot be plotted on the graph paper
(*b*) It cannot be solved by any other method except graphical method

(*c*) At least one decision variable can be made arbitrarily

(*d*) the objective contours can be moved as far as desired, in the optimizing directions, and still touch at least one point in the constraint set.

19. All the variables in the solution of a LPP are either positive or zero because of the existence of

(*a*) scarce resources (*b*) limited raw materials

(*c*) some extra constraints (*d*) None of the above.

20. Which of the following statement is incorrect.

(*a*) LP takes into consideration the effect of time, uncertainty and quadrite form.

(*b*) All the variables in the solution of a LPP are either zero or positive.

(*c*) Decision variables in a LPP may be more or less than the number of constraints.

(*d*) None of the above.

EXERCISES

1. What do you understand by the term linear programming?

2. What are the major assumptions and limitations of linear programming?

3. What is meant by a feasible solution to an LPP?

4. What is the role of linear programming in managerial decision making?

5. Give a mathematical and economic structure of linear programming problem. What are the requirements for applying the linear programming?

6. Discuss the advantages and the limitations of linear programming.

7. Discuss various fields where LPP can be applied.

8. Write the General Structure of an LPP.

9. What are the advantages and the limitations of LPP?

10. Discuss in brief, that linear programming is used as a technique for resource utilization.

11. Illustrate graphically the special cases encountered in LPP.

(*a*) Unbounded solution

(*b*) Multiple optimal solution

12. Explain the graphical method of solving an LPP involving two variables.

13. Each linear programming problem with a feasible solution area offers infinite number of solutions. Do you agree with this statement.

Use the graphical method to solve the following LPPS.

14. Max $Z = 3x_1 + 4x_2$

Subject to
$$2x_1 + x_2 \le 40$$
$$2x_1 + 5x_2 \le 180$$
$$x_1, x_2 \ge 0$$

15. Min $Z = 600x_1 + 400x_2$

Subject to
$$3x_1 + 3x_2 \ge 40$$
$$3x_1 + x_2 \ge 40$$

$$2x_1 + 5x_2 \geq 44$$
$$x_1, x_2 \geq 0$$

16. Min $Z = 2x_1 + x_2$

Subject to
$$5x_1 + 10x_2 \leq 50$$
$$x_1 + x_2 \geq 1$$
$$x_1 \leq 4$$
$$x_1, x_2 \geq 0$$

17. Max $Z = 15x_1 + 13x_2$

Subject to
$$3x_1 + 5x_2 \leq 15$$
$$15x_1 + 6x_2 \leq 30$$
$$x_1, x_2 \geq 0$$

18. Min $Z = 17x_1 + 18x_2$

Subject to
$$6x_1 + 2x_2 \geq 16$$
$$2x_1 + 6x_2 \geq 22$$
$$x_1, x_2 \geq 0$$

19. Min $Z = 2x_1 + x_2$

Subject to
$$2x_1 + 2x_2 \leq 80$$
$$6x_1 + 2x_2 \geq 60$$
$$8x_1 + 6x_2 \geq 120$$
$$x_1, x_2 \geq 0$$

20. Max $Z = 3y_1 + 4y_2$

Subject to
$$2y_1 + 2y_2 \leq 200$$
$$8y_1 + 5y_2 \leq 600$$
$$3y_1 + 4y_2 \leq 500$$
$$y_1, y_2 \geq 0$$

21. Max $Z = 20x_1 + 15x_2$

Subject to
$$x_1 - 2x_2 \leq 5$$
$$3x_1 - 6x_2 \geq 18$$
$$x_1, x_2 \geq 0$$

22. Solve the following graphically:

Max $Z = 15x + 10y$

Subject to
$$2x + 2y \leq 70$$
$$3x - 3y \leq 20$$
$$x, y \geq 0$$

23. Solve graphically the following:

Max $Z = 2x_1 + 4x_2$

Subject to
$$x_1 + 2x_2 \leq 10$$
$$3x_1 + 3x_2 \geq 3$$
$$x_2 \leq 4$$
$$x_1, x_2 \geq 0$$

24. Solve graphically:

$$\text{Min } Z = 10x_1 + 9x_2$$

Subject to

$$\begin{aligned} 2x_1 &\leq 16 \\ 3x_2 &\leq 30 \\ 5x_1 + 3x_2 &\geq 45 \\ x_1, x_2 &\geq 0 \end{aligned}$$

25. Solve graphically:

$$\text{Max } Z = 3x_1 + 2x_2$$

Subject to

$$\begin{aligned} -x_1 + 2x_2 &\leq 4 \\ 3x_1 + 2x_2 &\leq 14 \\ 2x_1 - 2x_2 &\leq 6 \\ x_1, x_2 &\geq 0 \end{aligned}$$

EXERCISES

1. A firm manufactures scooters and bikes. The available man hours are 500, available machine hours 500 and availability of raw materials is 2000 tonnes of steel. The production of 1 scooter requires 30 man hours, 21 machine hours and 2 tonnes of steel. Whereas the production of one bike requires 45 man hours, 30 machine hours and 2.5 tonnes of steel. The prices of one scooter is ₹ 40,000 and that of one bike is ₹ 55,000, then determine maximum profit.

2. A factory XYZ manufactures two articles A_1 and A_2. To manufacture articles A_1 and A_2, the machine hours required are 1.5 hours and 2.5 hours respectively, whereas man hours required are 2 hours and 1.5 hours respectively. The total available machine hours and man hours in the factory are 100 hours and 90 hours respectively. The profit on each articles A_1 and A_2 are respectively ₹ 150 and ₹ 140. Formulate the problem as an LPP so as to maximize the profit per week.

   [**Hints:** $\text{Max } P = 150x_1 + 140x_2$

   Subject to
   $$\begin{aligned} 1.5x_1 + 2.5x_2 &\leq 100 \\ 2x_1 + 1.5x_2 &\leq 90 \\ x_1, x_2 &\geq 0 \end{aligned}$$]

3. An animal feed company must produce 500 kg of a mixture consisting of foods A and B. The food A cost ₹ 30 per kg whereas food B cost ₹ 50 per kg. Not more than 120 kg of food A can be used and at least 90 kg of food B must be used. Formulate the problem as an LPP and find the minimum cost of the mixed food.

   [**Hints:** $\text{Min } Z = 30x_1 + 50x_2$

   Subject to
   $$\begin{aligned} x_1 + x_2 &\leq 500 \\ x_1 &\leq 120 \\ x_2 &\geq 90 \\ x_1, x_2 &\geq 0 \end{aligned}$$]

4. A company manufactures automobile spare parts A, B and C. The profits per unit for these spareparts are ₹ 20, ₹ 16 and ₹ 9 respectively. The time required for manufacturing spareparts A are 12 hours machine work, 15 hours in drilling work and 10 hours used while packing.

The time required for B are 8 hours on machine, 7 hours in drilling and 12 hours in packing. The time required for sparepart C are 10, 15, and 16 hours respectively. The total number of hours available for machine hours are 200 hours, for drilling 300 hours and for packing 500 hours respectively. Determine the most profitable mix, assuming that all the spareparts produced, are sold in the marked and formulate the problem.

[**Hints:** Max $P = 20x + 16y + 9z$

Subject to $12x + 8y + 10z \le 200$

$15x + 7y + 15z \le 300$

$10x + 12y + 16z \le 500$

$x, y, z \ge 0$]

5. A company produces two types of products A and B. Each type of product is manufactured by passing these products on two different machines for drilling and finishing of the products. The processing time for each unit of two products on two different machines are as follows:

Product	*Machine for Drilling (hours/unit)*	*Machine of Finishing (hours/unit)*
A	4	6
B	8	4

For a permit of one month, the availability of drilling machine and finishing machine are 260 hours and 240 hour The maximum sale price of products A and B are ₹ 45 per unit and ₹ 55 per unit respectively. Then formulate the problem as an LPP if a maximum profit is to obtain.

[**Hints:** Max $P = 45x_1 + 55x_2$

Subject to $4x_1 + 8x_2 \le 260$

$6x_1 + 4x_2 \le 240$

$x_1 \le 50$

$x_2 \le 35$

$x_1, x_2 \ge 0$]

6. A manufacturer uses 3 raw products A, B and C priced at ₹ 30, 50 and 120 per kg respectively. The raw products can be obtained in limited quantities as 20 kg/day, 15 kg/day and 10 kg/day. The manufacturer can make three products x, y and z, which can be sold at ₹ 90, 100 and 120 per kg respectively. If we mix 2 kg of A, 1 kg of B and 1 kg of C, then 4 kg of x will be produced. Similarly 3 kg of A, 2 kg of B and 2 kg of C will yield 7 kg of y, while 2 kg of A and 2 kg of B and 1 kg of C will yield 3 kg of Z. Formulate the above problem as an LPP.

7. A retailer deals with two times A and B. He has ₹ 30,000 for investment and 1 big godown for storing atmost 100 pieces of these products. Item A costs ₹ 250 and item B costs ₹ 100. The net profit on item A and B are respectively ₹ 300 and ₹ 200 respectively. Formulate the above problem as an LPP, assuming that all the items are sold for maximizing his profit.

[**Hints:** Max $Z = 300x_1 + 200x_2$

Subject to $x_1 + x_2 \le 100$

$250x_1 + 100x_2 \le 30{,}000$

$x_1, x_2 \ge 0$]

8. Two types of paper x and y are produced on a paper machine. Because of the limited raw material, not more than 400 kg of grade x and 300 kg of grade y can be produced in a week. There are 160 production hours in a week. It requires 2 hours and 4 hours to produce one kg of products x and y respectively with corresponding profits of ₹ 2 and ₹ 5 per kg. Find the optimum product mix using graphical solution after its formulations.

9. A small manufacturer employs 15 skilled men and 20 semi-skilled men and makes an article in two qualities, a super model and a simple model. The making of a super model requires 5 hours work by a skilled man and 5 hours work by a semi-skilled man. The simple model requires 2 hours by a skilled man and 4 hours by a semi-skilled man. There is a condition that no worker can work more than 8 hours a day. The manufacturers profit of super model is ₹ 20 and that of simple model is ₹ 15. Formulate the problem as an LPP and solve the problem graphically to maximize its profit.

[Hints: Max $Z = 20x_1 + 15x_2$

Subject to $5x_1 + 2x_1 \leq 15 \times 8$ (hours for skilled)

$5x_1 + 4x_2 \leq 20 \times 8$ (hours for semi-skilled)

$x_1, x_2 \geq 0$]

10. A company XYZ sells its two different products A and B, making a profit of ₹ 50 and ₹ 40 per unit on them. They are processed in a common production process and are sold in 2 different places. The productions process has a total capacity of 5000 man hours. It takes 2 hours to product a single unit of A and 3 hours to produce a single unit of B. After the careful study of the market, the decision maker of the company estimated that the maximum number units of product A and product B can be sold are 500 units and 900 units. Formulate this problem to maximize the profit and find the solution graphically.

[Hints: Max $Z = 50x_1 + 40x_2$

Subject to $2x_1 + 3x_2 \leq 5000$ (man hour constraints)

$x_1 \leq 500$ (marketing constraints)

$x_2 \leq 900$ (marketing constraints)

$x_1, x_2 \geq 0$]

11. A company produces two types of belts. Presently, 500 belts of both types are produced per week. The various cost and machine hours are given in the following table.

Types of Belt	*Total Cost*	*Man Hours Required*	*Machine Hours Required*	*Selling Price per Belt*
I	80	5	2	130
II	75	3	1.5	125

Formulate the above problem as an LPP so as to maximize the profit.

12. A manufacturer produces two types of jeans, one jeans and another cargo jeans. Both these jeans are to be processed on two different machines. Jeans requires 2 hours on machine I and one hour on machine II. Cargo jeans require one hour on machine I and 2 hours on machine II. If machine I and machine II have total available hours as 25 hours and 30 hours respectively. The profit on both the machines are ₹ 60 and ₹ 100 respecively. Then formulate the above problem as an LPP, assuming that all of his products are sold.

[Ans. Max $P = 60x_1 + 100x_2$

Subject to $2x_1 + x_2 \leq 25$

$x_1 + 2x_2 \leq 30$

$x_1, x_2 \geq 0$]

13. Old hens can be bought at ₹ 20 each and their young ones at ₹ 50 each. The old hen lays 3 eggs per week while young one lays 5 eggs per week, each egg being worth ₹ 2. A hen cost ₹ 6 per week to feed. Mr. x has ₹ 200 to spend on hens. If he wants to get a profit of ₹ 25, per week, then formulate the above problem as an LPP if not more than 30 hens can be housed.

14. A housewife is health conscious and she wants to decide the constituents of a diet, that fulfils the daily requirement of carbohydrates, proteins and fats at the minimum cost. The housewife has to make her choice among the three foods she wants to serve. The yields per unit of these foods are given in the table below. Formulate the problem as an LPP.

Food Type	*Carbohydrates*	*Proteins*	*Fats*	*Cost per Unit*
F_1	5	3	2	₹ 49
F_2	4	5	1	₹ 58
F_3	8	7	6	₹ 83
Minimum Requirement	875	1320	600	

[**Ans.** Max $Z = 49x_1 + 58x_2 + 83x_3$

Subject to
$$5x_1 + 4x_2 + 8x_3 \geq 875$$
$$3x_1 + 5x_2 + 7x_3 \geq 1320$$
$$2x_1 + x_2 + 6x_3 \geq 600$$
$$x_1, x_2, x_3 \geq 0]$$

15. Three different products are to be produced on three different machines. All the three machines can operate upto a maximum of 150 hours, 160 hours and 120 hours per week. The profit on these products are respectively ₹ 30, ₹ 20 and ₹ 40 respectively. The time required in hours per unit of each machine is given as follows:

Machine	*Product A*	*Products B*	*Product C*
I	5	6	2
II	3	2	1
III	4	2	5

Formulate the above problem as an LPP.

[**Ans.** Max $P = 30x_1 + 20x_2 + 40\,x_3$

Subject to
$$5x_1 + 6x_2 + 2x_3 \leq 150$$
$$3x_1 + 2x_2 + x_3 \leq 160$$
$$4x_1 + 2x_2 + 5x_3 \leq 120$$
$$x_1, x_2, x_3 \geq 0]$$

16. A parent has been advised to eat the food with some specified nutrients in it. He use to take 2 different types of foods F_1 and F_2, for which the nutrition values and the minimum requirement of the nutrients are given in the following table. Food F_1 and food F_2 costs ₹ 25 and ₹ 15 per plate. Formulate the above problem as an LPP.

Nutrients	*Food F_1*	*Food F_2*	*Minimum Requirement*
	A	*B*	
I	30	20	60
II	11	16	65
III	5	10	90

[**Ans.** Min $C = 25x_1 + 15x_2$

Subject to
$$30x_1 + 20x_2 \geq 60$$
$$11x_1 + 16x_2 \geq 65$$
$$5x_1 + 10x_2 \geq 90$$
$$x_1, x_2 \geq 0]$$

17. A second hand scooter dealer wants to maximize his profit by spending ₹ 80,000 in this business. He can sell the scooters: (Chetak, Kinetic Honda, Activa) at ₹ 15,000, 25,000 and 12,000 respectively whose actual costs after purchase was ₹ 8000, ₹ 17,000 and ₹ 9000 respectively. The probabilities of sale for each type of scooters in one month are given in the following table. Then formulate the problem as an LPP.

Scooter	*Probability*
Chetak	0.5
K. Honda	0.3
Activa	0.7

18. A company ABC produces two products x and y. The products are produced by using the raw materials A and B. By using 3 units of material A and 5 units of material B, one unit of product x is produced and by using 4 units of material A and 3 units of mateiral B, one unit of product y is produced. There is a limitation on the availability of the raw materials A and B. Only 50 units of A and 40 units of B material can be arranged for the production. If the cost of these materials used are ₹ 5 per unit and ₹ 8 per unit for x and y. Formulate the above problem as an LPP.

[**Ans.** Minimize $C = \{(5 \times 3) + (8 \times 5)\}x_1 + \{(5 \times 5) + (8 \times 3)\}x_2$

Subject to
$$3x_1 + 4x_2 \leq 50$$
$$5x_1 + 3x_2 \leq 40$$
$$x_1, x_2 \geq 0]$$

19. A paper will produces two types of paper card sheets and century A4 size. Because of the limited raw materials availability, not more than 800 tonnes of card sheets and 650 tonnes of century. A4 size can be produced in one month. Total production hours in one month are 1000 cardsheets requires 30 minutes and century A4 size neels 50 minutes for the production of one tonne of each produce. The profit on cardsheets is ₹ 500 and on century A4 size is ₹ 300 per tonne. Then formulate as an LPP to maximize the profit for the above product mix problem.

20. Three different grades of coal I, II and III contains ash and phosphorus as impurities. In a particular process in industry, fuels upto a maximum 100 tonnes is required that can contain the impurity as ash not more than 2.5% and phosphorus not more than 0.02%. It is desired to maximize the profit while the above conditions are satisfied. All the three different coals, the percentage of impurities and the profits of coals are given as follows:

Grade of Coal	*Ash*	*Phosphorus*	*Profit in ₹ (per tonne)*
I	2.0%	0.01%	15
II	1.5%	0.03%	20
. III]	4.0%	0.25%	16

Formulate the above problem as an LPP and solve it graphically.

[**Ans.** Max $P = 15x + 20y + 16z$

Subject to $x + y + z \leq 300$

Ash constraint: $2.0x + 1.5y + 4.0z \leq 25(x + y + z)$

Phosphorus constraint $0.01x + 0.03y + 0.25y \leq 0.02(x + y + z)$

$x, y, z \geq 0$]

21. An automobile spareparts manufacturing company received an order for three different types of spareparts for its regular supply. The management of the company is considering to denote the available excess capacity to one or more of the three types of the spareparts x, y and z. The available capacity on the machines, are given in the following table:

Types of Machine	*Machine Hours available/week*	*Production in Machine (hr/unit)*		
		Spare Part (X)	*Spare Part* (Y)	*Spare Part* (Z)
A	125	3	6	3
B	160	8	1	—
C	245	7	2	0

The profit per unit on the spareparts is ₹ 15, ₹ 16 and ₹ 9 respectively for the spareparts x, y and z. Formulate the problem as an LPP.

[**Ans.** Max $Z = 15x + 16y + 9z$

Subject to $3x + 6y + 3z \leq 125$

$8x + y \leq 160$

$7x + 2y \leq 245$

$x, y, z \geq 0$]

22. The readymade garments owner stores two types of T-shirts, viz: V-shape or round-shape T-shirts if he makes ₹ 20 and ₹ 35 per T-shirt on V-shape and round-shape T-shirts. He has two skilled workers x and y, who can devote at the most 10 hours and 12 hours per day respectively. Both the types of T-shirts are to stitched by the skilled workers x and y. If worker x spends 4 hours and 5 hours for stitching the V-shaped and round shaped T-shirts, whereas worker y spends 7 hours and 4 hours for stiching V-shaped and round-shaped T-shirts. In order to maximize the profit, formulate the problem as an LPP.

[**Ans.** Maximize $P = 20x_1 + 35x_2$

Subject to $4x_1 + 5x_2 \leq 10$

$7x_1 + 4x_2 \leq 12$

$x_1, x_2 \geq 0$]

Answers of Objective Type Questions

1. (*b*)	**2.** (*d*)	**3.** (*d*)	**4.** (*a*)	**5.** (*a*)	**6.** (*d*)
7. (*a*)	**8.** (*d*)	**9.** (*c*)	**10.** (*d*)	**11.** (*c*)	**12.** (*d*)
13. (*b*)	**14.** (*d*)	**15.** (*d*)	**16.** (*d*)	**17.** (*a*)	**18.** (*d*)
19. (*d*)	**20.** (*a*)				

❑❑❑

CHAPTER 2

Linear Programming—Simplex Method

2.1 STANDARD FORM OF LINEAR PROGRAMMING PROBLEM

The standard form of LPP with m constraints and n variables is represented as follows:

Optimize (Maximize/Minimize)

$$Z = \sum_{j=1}^{n} C_j x_j$$

Subject to $$\sum_{j=1}^{n} a_{ij} x_j (\leq, =, \geq)\, b_i;\ i = 1, 2, \ldots, m$$

and $$x_j \geq 0;\ j = 1, 2, \ldots, n$$

Remark:

(*i*) All the variables are restricted to be non-negative.

(*ii*) All the constraints are expressed as equations.

(*iii*) The objective function is of the maximization type and can be converted into minimization by multiplying the objective function by (–1).

(*iv*) The right hand side constant (b_i) of each of the constraint is non-negative.

2.2 SOME BASIC DEFINITIONS

(1) Basic Variable

A variable x_1 is said to be a basic variable in a given equation if it appears with a unit coefficient in that equation and zeros in all other equations. Those variables which are not basic are called non-basic variables.

(2) Basic Solution

For a system of m simultaneous linear equations in n variables ($n > m$), a solution obtained by setting ($n - m$) variables equal to zero and solving for the remaining m variables is called a basic solution.

(3) Basic Feasible Solution

A basic feasible solution to a LPP is a basic solution for which the m variables solved, for are all greater than or equal to zero. The basic solution which is feasible is known as basic feasible solution.

(4) Slack Variable

A variable added to the left hand side to the inequality "less than or equal to" to convert the constraint into an equality is called a slack variable. Slack variables represent unused capacity and the contribution (cost or profit coefficients) associated with them is zero.

i.e., Slack = Requirement – Production

(5) Surplus Variable

A variable subtracted from the left hand side to the inequality "greater than or equal to" to convert the constraint into an equality is called a surplus variable. Surplus variables represent excess amount above the required minimum level.

i.e., Surplus = Production – Requirement

(6) Optimal Solution

Any basic feasible solution which optimizes (minimizes or maximizes), the objective function of a general LPP is called an optimal basic feasible solution to the general LPP.

(7) Degenerate Basic Feasible Solution

A basic feasible solution is called degenerate, if one or more basic variables are zero-valued.

(8) Non-degenerate Basic Feasible Solution

A non-degenerate basic feasible solution is the basic feasible solution which has exactly m positive x_i ($i = 1, 2, ..., m$).

(9) Unbounded Solution

If the value of the objective function Z can be increased or decreased infinitely, then such solutions are called unbounded solution.

(10) Simplex Tableaus

Whenever the LPP is solved by using the simplex method, then it is always necessary to represent each iteration in the simplex tableau form.

(11) Pivot Column

The column which has the largest (maximum) value of the net-evaluation ($C_j - Z_j$) in the maximization problem and has the minimum (smallest) value in minimization problem.

(12) Pivot Row

The pivot row is the smallest quantity that is obtained by the ratio of quantity column and pivot column values for each row.

(13) Pivot Number

The element that lies at the intersection of pivot row and pivot column is called pivot number.

2.3 SIMPLEX METHOD

We have till now studied that LPP can be solved graphically. This is only possible when the decision variables considered are only two. Thus it is not possible to obtain the graphical solution to the LPP if the decision variables are more than 2 in numbers and usually this happens in real-life problem.

In 1947, G. Dantzig developed an iterative procedure which is widely used in simplifying the LPP's, where more than two variables are used.

The simplex method is an algorithm (the step-by-step procedure to solve a particular problem), which is based on the fundamental theorem of linear programming. The simplex method provides a systematic algorithm that consists of moving from one basic feasible solution (one vertex) to another in a prescribed manner so that the value of the objective function is always improved. Repeating the process may lead to the optimal vertex in a finite number of steps. The computational procedure is summarized in the following steps.

Step 1: Reformulate the given LPP as a standard maximization LPP.

i.e., $\quad \text{Max } Z = Cx$

Subject to $\quad Ax \le b$

$\quad x \ge 0$

i.e., $\text{Max Z} = C_1x_1 + C_2x_2 + \ldots + C_nx_n$

Subject to

$$\begin{aligned} a_{11}x_1 + \ldots + a_{1n}x_n &\le b_1 \\ a_{21}x_1 + \ldots + a_{2n}x_n &\le b_2 \\ &\vdots \\ a_{m1}x_1 + \ldots + a_{mn}x_n &\le b_m \\ x_1, x_2, \ldots, x_n &\ge 0 \end{aligned}$$

Step 2: Then add slack variables in the left hand side to convert the given inequality constraints into equality constraints. Assign a zero coefficients to these slack variables in the above objective function.

$$\text{Max } Z = C_1x_1 + C_2x_2 + \ldots + C_nx_n + 0_1 \cdot s_1 + 0_1 \cdot s_2 + \ldots + 0 \cdot s_m$$

Subject to

$$\begin{aligned} a_{11}x_1 + a_{12}x_2 + \ldots + a_nx_n + s_1 &= b_1 \\ a_{21}x_1 + \ldots + a_{2n}x_n + s_2 &= b_2 \\ \vdots \qquad\quad \vdots \qquad \vdots \quad &\quad \vdots \\ a_{m1}x_1 + \ldots + a_{mn}x_n + s_m &= b_m \\ x_1, x_2, \ldots, x_n \ \& \ s_1, s_2, \ldots, s_m &\ge 0 \end{aligned}$$

Step 3: Obtain the initial basic feasible solution of the given LPP

i.e., If we put $x_1 = x_2 = \ldots = x_n = 0$

then, we get $s_1 = b_1$

$$s_2 = b_2$$
$$\vdots$$
$$s_m = b_m$$

Step 4: Construct the initial simplex tableaus for computation, the initial basic feasible solution, the constraint and the objective function are displayed in the simplex tableaus as:

Initial Simplex Tableau

C_j (contribution)		per unit	C_1	C_2	C_3	...	C_n	0	0	...	0	
C_B	Basic variable (Y_B)	Value of Basic variables X_B	Coefficient of Matrix x_1	x_2	x_3	...	x_n	Slack variables s_1	s_2	...	s_m	Minimum Ratio ↓
0	s_1	b_1	a_{11}	a_{12}	a_{13}	...	a_{1n}	1	0	...	0	
0	s_2	b_2	a_{21}	a_{22}	a_{23}	...	a_{2n}	0	1	...	0	
⋮	⋮	⋮	⋮	⋮	⋮		⋮	⋮	⋮		⋮	
0	s_m	b_m	a_{m1}	a_{m2}	a_{m3}	...	a_{mn}	0	0	...	1	
Net contribution per unit		$C_j - Z_j$	C_1	C_2	...	...	C_n	0	0	...	0	

Step 5: Then the net evaluation $Z_j - C_j$ is calculated by

$$Z_j - C_j = C_B X_B - C_j$$

and test the basic solution for optimality.

Step 6: For testing of optimality; any of the following condition is checked.

(*i*) If all $Z_j - C_j \geq 0$, the solution under consideration is an optimal one. The alternative solution may exist if any non-basic $Z_j - C_j$ is also zero.

(*ii*) If at least one $Z_j - C_j$ is negative, then the current solution is not optimal then proceed to the next step 6 for the improvement of the solution.

(*iii*) If corresponding to any negative $Z_j - C_j$, all elements of the column x_j are negative, and if so, the solution (current) is unbounded.

Step 7: Whenever, the basic feasible solution is improved, the "outgoing vector" and "incoming vector" are to be located in the simplex tableau, which is done as follows:

Whenever $Z_j - C_j$ (the net evaluation) is calculated, by the above formula, locate the vector x_k that corresponds to the most negative value of $Z_j - C_j$. The most negative value corresponding to column x_k is termed as pivot column. This pivot column is marked with a recantangle ☐ and is called as "incoming vector".

After finding the pivot column, locate the pivot row by dividing the x_B vector with corresponding pivot column vectors *i.e.*, $\frac{x_{Br}}{x_{rk}}$ and then we choose the minimum of this ratio (provided that $x_{ck} > 0$), which is marked as a rectangle ☐ and is called as "outgoing vector". The intersection of pivot column and pivot row is the pivot element. This pivot element is then made unity and then subtract appropriate multiples of this pivot row from the remaining (other) rows, to obtain zeros in the remaining positions of the column x_k.

Step 8: The step 5 and step 6 are repeated until an optimum solution is obtained.

Example 1. *Use the simplex method to solve the following LPP.*

Maximize $Z = 3x_1 + 5x_2 + 4x_3$

Subject to $2x_1 + 3x_2 \leq 8$

$$2x_2 + 5x_3 \leq 10$$

$$3x_1 + 2x_2 + 4x_3 \leq 15$$

$$x_1, x_2, x_3 \geq 0$$

Solution.

Step 1: Since the given LPP is of maximization problem and all the b_i's (RHS of constraints) are positive.

Now introducing the slack variables s_1, s_2 and s_3 to convert the inequality constraints into equality constraints. So the LPP can now be rewritten as

Maximize $Z = 3x_1 + 5x_2 + 4x_3 + 0{\cdot}s_1 + 0{\cdot}s_2 + 0{\cdot}s_3$

Subject to

$$2x_1 + 3x_2 + s_1 = 8$$

$$2x_2 + 5x_3 + s_2 = 10$$

$$3x_1 + 2x_2 + 4x_3 + s_3 = 15$$

$$x_1, x_2, x_3, s_1 \text{ and } s_2 \geq 0.$$

Step 2: The initial basic feasible solution will be

if $x_1 = x_2 = x_3 = 0$

then, $s_1 = 8$, $s_2 = 10$ and $s_3 = 15$ and $Z_{\text{max}} = 0$

Constructing the initial simplex tableau for computation. After writing in matrix form, we can construct the table as follows:

Iteration–0

	C_j		3	5	4	0	0	0
C_B	Y_B	X_B	x_1	x_2	x_3	s_1	s_2	s_3
0	s_1	8	2	3	0	1	0	0
0	s_2	10	0	2	5	0	1	0
0	s_3	15	3	2	4	0	0	1
	$Z_j - C_j$	0	–3	–5	–4	0	0	0

Step 3: To calculate that the initial solution is optimal or not. So we compute $Z_j - C_j = C_B X_B - C_j$

Calculation: For iteration–0

For column I ($j = 1$) $Z_1 - C_1 = (0.2 + 0.0 + 0.3) - 3 = -3$

For column II ($j = 2$) $Z_2 - C_2 = (0.3 + 0.2 + 0.2) - 5 = -5$

For column III ($j = 3$) $Z_3 - C_3 = (0.0 + 0.5 + 0.4) - 4 = -4$

and for column IV, V and VI.

Since all $Z_j - C_j \leq 0$, the current solution is not optimal, and –5 (corresponding to x_2) is the most negative $Z_j - C_j$. So x_2 column will enter the basis and is a pivot column. So we mark the pivot column using a rectangle as:

			3	5	4	0	0	0
C_B	Y_B	X_B	x_1	x_2	x_3	s_1	s_2	s_3
0	s_1	8	2	3	0	1	0	0
0	s_2	10	0	2	5	0	1	0
0	s_3	15	3	2	4	0	0	1
	$Z_j - C_j$		–3	–5	–4	0	0	

↓ pivot column

x_2 enter s the basis with its cost 5 (*i.e.*, $C_B = 0$ must be replaced by 5).

Then we compute the pivot row (or the outgoing vector) by minimum ratio by using

$$\frac{x_{Br}}{x_{rk}} = \min_i \left[\frac{x_{Br}}{x_{ik}}, x_{ik} > 0\right]$$

Thus for $k = 2$ and $r = 1$

$$\frac{x_{B1}}{x_{12}} = \frac{8}{3}$$

for $k = 2$ and $r = 2$ $\quad \frac{x_{B2}}{x_{22}} = \frac{10}{2}$

for $k = 2$ and $r = 3$ $\quad \frac{x_{B3}}{x_{32}} = \frac{15}{2}$

Thus, $\quad \frac{x_{Br}}{x_{rk}} = \min\left[\frac{8}{3}, \frac{10}{2}, \frac{15}{2}\right] = \min[2.67, 5, 7.5] = 2.67 = \frac{8}{3}$

Thus we mark the row, corresponding to 2.67 (as minimum ratio) with a rectangle. So, s_1 will be an outgoing vector and the first row becomes the pivot row as follows:

C_B	Y_B	X_B	x_1	x_2	x_3	s_1	s_2	s_3	Minimum ratio
0	s_1	8	2	3*	0	1	0	0	$\frac{8}{3}$ ← Pivot row
0	s_2	10	0	2*	5	0	1	0	
0	s_3	15	3	2	4	0	0	1	

↓ pivot column

Step 4: Since the intersection of pivot column and pivot row, gives the pivot element. So pivot element is 3 (marked with *).

Since pivot element is not 1, so to make the pivot element as 1, we divide the whole row (*i.e.*, first row) by 3 to obtain the new values of the elements in this row.

The new values of the elements in the remaining rows (2nd and 3rd row) for iteration–1, can be obtained by performing the following elementary row operations on all rows so that all the elements in the pivot column becomes zero except the pivot element (equal to 1).

Iteration–1

			3	5	4	0	0	0
C_B	Y_B	X_B	x_1	x_2	x_3	s_1	s_2	s_3
5	x_2	$\frac{8}{3}$	$\frac{2}{3}$	1	0	$\frac{1}{3}$	0	0
0	s_2	$\frac{14}{3}$	$\frac{-4}{3}$	0	5	$\frac{-2}{3}$	1	0
0	s_3	$\frac{29}{3}$	$\frac{5}{3}$	0	4	$\frac{-2}{3}$	0	0
	$Z_j - C_j$	$\frac{40}{3}$	$\frac{1}{3}$	0	–4	$\frac{5}{3}$	0	0

Calculations:

Elementary Row Operations

For Row 1: $R_1(\text{New}) \rightarrow \dfrac{R_1(\text{Old})}{3}$ (where denominator is the pivot element)

Thus, $R_1(\text{New}) \rightarrow \left(\dfrac{8}{3}, \dfrac{2}{3}, \dfrac{3}{3}, \dfrac{0}{3}, \dfrac{1}{3}, \dfrac{0}{3}, \dfrac{0}{3}\right)$

$R_1(\text{New}) \rightarrow \left(\dfrac{8}{3}, \dfrac{2}{3}, 1, 0, \dfrac{1}{3}, 0, 0\right)$

For Row 2: $R_2(\text{New}) \rightarrow R_2(\text{Old}) - 2R_1(\text{New})$

R_2(Old)	10	0	2	5	0	1	0
$2[R_1$(New)]	$\frac{16}{3}$	$\frac{4}{3}$	2	0	$\frac{2}{3}$	0	0
(Subtract)	–	–	–	–	–	–	–
	$\frac{14}{3}$	$\frac{-4}{3}$	0	5	$\frac{-2}{3}$	1	0

For Row 3: $R_3(\text{New}) \rightarrow R_3(\text{Old}) - 2R_1(\text{New})$

R_3(Old)	15	3	2	4	0	0	1
$2R_3$(New)	$\frac{16}{3}$	$\frac{4}{3}$	2	0	$\frac{2}{3}$	0	0
(Subtract)	–	–	–	–	–	–	–
	$\frac{29}{3}$	$\frac{5}{3}$	0	4	$\frac{-2}{3}$	0	1

Calculations of $Z_j - C_j$ for iteration–2.

For column I ($j = 1$) $\quad Z_1 - C_1 = 5 - \frac{2}{3} + 0\left(\frac{-4}{3}\right) + 0\left(\frac{5}{3}\right) - 3$

$$= \frac{10}{3} - 3 = \frac{1}{3}$$

For column II ($j = 2$) $\quad Z_2 - C_2 = 5.1 + 0.0 + 0.0 - 5 = 0$

For column III ($j = 3$) $\quad Z_3 - C_3 = 5.0 + 0.5 + 0.4 - 4 = -4$

Since all $Z_j - C_j \ngtr 0$, so the current solution is not optimal. So we locate x_3 (most negative) to enter the basis. Column corresponding to III column will enter the basis and becomes the pivot column as:

			3	5	4	0	0	0	Minimum Ratio
C_B	Y_B	X_B	x_1	x_2	x_3	s_1	s_2	s_3	
5	x_2	$\frac{8}{3}$	$\frac{2}{3}$	1	0	$\frac{1}{3}$	0	0	
0	s_2	$\frac{14}{3}$	$\frac{-4}{3}$	0	5	$\frac{-2}{3}$	1	0	
0	s_3	$\frac{29}{3}$	$\frac{5}{3}$	0	4	$\frac{-2}{3}$	0	0	
	$Z_j - C_j$	$\frac{40}{3}$	$\frac{1}{3}$	0	–4	$\frac{5}{3}$	0	0	

↑ Pivot Column

Now we compute the pivot row using the

$$\frac{x_{Br}}{x_{rk}} = \min_i \left[\frac{x_{Br}}{x_{ik}}, x_{ik} > 0\right].$$

for $k = 3$ (III column) and $r = 1$

$$\frac{x_{B1}}{x_{13}} = \frac{8/3}{0}, \; x_3 < 0.$$

So, we will not find the ratio for I row as denominator is 0 and it violates the condition of $x_{ik} > 0$)

for $k = 3$ and $r = 2$

$$\frac{x_{B2}}{x_{23}} = \frac{14/3}{5} = \frac{14}{15} = 0.93$$

for $k = 3$ and $r = 3$

$$\frac{x_{B3}}{x_{33}} = \frac{29/3}{4} = \frac{29}{12} = 2.42$$

Thus, $$\frac{x_{Br}}{x_{rk}} = \min\,[0.93,\ 2.42] = 0.93.$$

So, we mark the row (II) corresponding to 0.93 $\left(\frac{14/3}{5}\right)$ with a rectangle. Thus s_2 will be an outgoing vector and the II row becomes the pivot row.

C_B	Y_B	X_B	x_1	x_2	x_3	s_1	s_2	s_3	
5	x_2	$\frac{8}{3}$	$\frac{2}{3}$	1	0	$\frac{1}{3}$	0	0	
0	s_2	$\frac{14}{3}$	$\frac{-4}{3}$	0	5*	$\frac{-2}{3}$	1	0	← Pivot Row
0	s_3	$\frac{29}{3}$	$\frac{5}{3}$	0	4	$\frac{-2}{3}$	0	0	
					↑ Pivot Column				

In the above table, 5* is the pivot element, and in order to make the pivot element 1 (one), we divide all elements of pivot row by 5 to obtain the new values of the elements in this row. The new values of the elements in the remaining rows for the new iteration–2, are obtained by performing the elementary row operations on all rows so that all the elements except the pivot element 1 in the pivot column are zero.

Iteration–2

			3	5	4	0	0	0
C_B	Y_B	X_B	x_1	x_2	x_3	s_1	s_2	s_3
5	x_2	$\frac{8}{3}$	$\frac{2}{3}$	1	0	$\frac{1}{3}$	0	0
4	x_3	$\frac{14}{15}$	$\frac{-4}{15}$	0	1	$\frac{-2}{15}$	$\frac{1}{5}$	0
0	s_3	$\frac{89}{15}$	$\frac{41}{15}$	0	0	$\frac{-2}{15}$	$\frac{-4}{5}$	0
	$Z_j - C_j$	$\frac{256}{15}$	$\frac{-11}{15}$	0	0	$\frac{17}{15}$	$\frac{4}{5}$	0

Calculations for iteration–2

For II Row: R_2(New) $\rightarrow \frac{R_2(\text{Old})}{5}$

$$\rightarrow \left(\frac{14}{15}, \frac{0}{5}, \frac{5}{5}, \frac{-2}{15}, \frac{1}{5}, 0\right)$$

For III Row: $R_3(\text{New}) \rightarrow R_3(\text{Old}) - 4R_2(\text{New})$

Now	$R_3(\text{Old}) \rightarrow$	$\frac{29}{3}$	$-\frac{5}{3}$	0	4	$\frac{-2}{3}$	0	1
and	$4R_2(\text{New}) \rightarrow$	$\frac{56}{15}$	$\frac{16}{15}$	0	4	$\frac{-8}{15}$	$\frac{4}{5}$	0
	(Subtract) –	–	–	–	–	+	–	–
		$\frac{89}{15}$	$\frac{41}{75}$	0	0	$\frac{-2}{15}$	$\frac{-4}{5}$	1

For I Row: $R_1(\text{New}) \rightarrow R_1(\text{Old}) - 0.R_2(\text{New})$

The row will be same.

$\therefore$ $R_1(\text{New}) \rightarrow R_1(\text{Old})$.

To calculate that the current solution is optimal or not, we compute $Z_j - C_j = C_B X_B - C_j$.

Calculation for iteration–2 of $(Z_j - C_j)$

for column I (j = 1) $Z_1 - C_1 = 5\times\frac{2}{3}+4\left(\frac{-4}{15}\right)+0\cdot\frac{41}{15}-3 = \frac{-11}{15}$

for column II (j = 2) $Z_2 - C_2 = 5 \times 1 + 4.0 + 0.0 - 5 = 0$

for column III (j = 3) $Z_3 - C_3 = 5.0 + 1.4 + 0.0 - 4 = 0$

for column IV (j = 4) $Z_4 - C_4 = 5\frac{1}{3}+4\left(\frac{-2}{15}\right)+0\left(\frac{2}{15}\right)-0=+\frac{17}{15}$

for column V (j = 5) $Z_5 - C_5 = 5\cdot 0+4\cdot\frac{1}{5}+0\left(\frac{-4}{5}\right)-0=+\frac{4}{5}$

for column VI (j = 6) $Z_6 - C_6 = 5.0 + 4.0 + 0.0 - 0 = 0$

Since $Z_1 - C_1 < 0$ $\left(i.e., \frac{-11}{75}<0\right)$, so the current solution is not optimal and $\left(\frac{-11}{15}\right)$ corresponding to column x_1 becomes the pivot column as.

			3	5	4	0	0	0
C_B	Y_B	X_B	x_1	x_2	x_3	s_1	s_2	s_3
5	x_2	$\frac{8}{3}$	$\frac{2}{3}$	1	0	$\frac{1}{3}$	0	0
4	x_3	$\frac{14}{15}$	$\frac{-4}{15}$	0	1	$\frac{-2}{15}$	$\frac{1}{5}$	0
0	s_3	$\frac{89}{15}$	$\frac{41}{15}$	0	0	$\frac{2}{15}$	$\frac{-4}{5}$	1
	$Z_j - C_j$	$\frac{256}{15}$	$\frac{-11}{75}$	0	0	$\frac{17}{15}$	$\frac{4}{5}$	0

↑ Pivot Column

The pivot column is marked with the rectangle as shown above.

So, x_1 enters the basis with cost 3. Then pivot row is computed by using

$$\frac{x_{Br}}{x_{rk}} = \min_i \left[\frac{x_{Br}}{x_{ik}}, x_{ik} > 0\right].$$

Thus for $k = 1$ and $r = 1$

$$\frac{x_{B1}}{x_{11}} = \frac{8/3}{2/3} = 4$$

for $k = 1$ and $r = 2$, the ratio is not calculated as $\frac{-4}{15} \not> 0$. Since it does not satisfies $x_{ik} > 0$.

for $k = 1$ and $r = 3$

$$\frac{x_{B3}}{x_{31}} = \frac{89/15}{41/15} = \frac{89}{41}.$$

Here, $$\frac{x_{Br}}{x_{rk}} = \min\left[\frac{8/3}{2/3}, \frac{89/15}{41/15}\right] = \min\left[4, \frac{89}{41}\right] = \frac{89}{41}.$$

Since the minimum ratio occurs for III row, so row III is the pivot row and is marked with the rectangle and s_3 leaves the basis.

			3	5	4	0	0	0	
C_B	Y_B	X_B	x_1	x_2	x_3	s_1	s_2	s_3	Minimum Ratio
5	x_2	$\frac{8}{3}$	$\frac{2}{3}$	1	0	$\frac{1}{3}$	0	0	
4	x_3	$\frac{14}{15}$	$\frac{-4}{15}$	0	1	$\frac{-2}{15}$	$\frac{1}{5}$	0	
0	s_1	$\frac{89}{15}$	$\frac{41}{15}$*	0	0	$\frac{2}{15}$	$\frac{-4}{5}$	1	$\frac{89}{41}$ ← Pivot Row
			$\frac{-11}{15}$	0	0	$\frac{17}{15}$	$\frac{4}{5}$	0	

So the pivot element now becomes $\frac{41}{15}$ (marked with *). In order to make the pivot element 1, divided it by $\frac{41}{15}$.

Iteration–3

			3	5	4	0	0	0
C_B	Y_B	X_B	x_1	x_2	x_3	s_1	s_2	s_3
5	x_2	$\frac{50}{41}$	0	1	0	$\frac{15}{41}$	$\frac{8}{41}$	$\frac{-10}{41}$
4	x_3	$\frac{62}{41}$	0	0	1	$\frac{-6}{41}$	$\frac{5}{41}$	$\frac{4}{41}$
3	x_1	$\frac{89}{41}$	1	0	0	$\frac{-2}{41}$	$\frac{-12}{41}$	$\frac{15}{41}$
	$Z_j - C_j$	$\frac{756}{41}$	0	0	0	$\frac{45}{41}$	$\frac{24}{41}$	$\frac{11}{41}$

Calculation: To get the improved solution of iteration–3, perform the following elementary row operations.

$$R_3(\text{New}) \Rightarrow \frac{R_3(\text{Old})}{\frac{41}{15}} = R_3(\text{Old}) \times \frac{15}{41}$$

$$= \left(\frac{89}{15}\times\frac{15}{41}, \frac{41}{15}\times\frac{15}{41}, 0\times\frac{15}{41}, 0\times\frac{15}{41}, \frac{-2}{15}\times\frac{15}{41}, \frac{4}{5}\times\frac{15}{41}, 1\times\frac{15}{41}\right)$$

$$= \left(\frac{89}{41}, 1, 0, 0, \frac{-2}{41}, \frac{-12}{41}, \frac{15}{41}\right)$$

$$R_1(\text{New} \Rightarrow R_1(\text{Old}) - \frac{2}{3}R_3(\text{New})$$

$R_1(\text{Old})$	$\Rightarrow$	$\frac{8}{3}$	$\frac{2}{3}$	1	0	$\frac{1}{3}$	0	0
$\frac{2}{3}R_3(\text{New})$	$\Rightarrow$	$\frac{178}{123}$	$\frac{2}{3}$	0	0	$\frac{4}{123}$	$\frac{-24}{23}$	$\frac{30}{123}$
(Subtract)		–	–	–	–	–	+	–
$R_1(\text{Old}) - \frac{2}{3}R_3(\text{New})$	$\Rightarrow$	$\frac{450}{369}$	0	1	0	$\frac{45}{123}$	$\frac{24}{123}$	$\frac{-30}{123}$
or		$\frac{50}{41}$	0	1	0	$\frac{15}{41}$	$\frac{8}{41}$	$-\frac{10}{41}$

Now, $$R_2(\text{New}) \rightarrow R_2(\text{Old}) + \frac{4}{15}R_3(\text{New})$$

$\therefore$	R_2(Old)	$\Rightarrow$	$\frac{14}{15}$	$\frac{-4}{15}$	0	1	$\frac{-2}{15}$	$\frac{1}{5}$	0
	$\frac{4}{15} R_3$(New)	$\Rightarrow$	$\frac{356}{615}$	$\frac{4}{15}$	0	0	$\frac{-8}{615}$	$\frac{-48}{615}$	$\frac{60}{615}$
	(Add)		+	+	+	+	+	+	+
	$R_2(\text{Old}) - \frac{4}{15} R_3(\text{New})$	$\Rightarrow$	$\frac{930}{615}$	0	0	1	$\frac{-90}{615}$	$\frac{75}{615}$	$\frac{60}{615}$
	or		$\frac{62}{41}$	0	0	1	$\frac{-6}{41}$	$\frac{5}{41}$	$\frac{4}{41}$

Calculation of $Z_j - C_j$

for column ($j = 1$) $\quad Z_1 - C_1 = 5.0 + 4.0 + 3.1 - 3 = 0$

for column ($j = 2$) $\quad Z_2 - C_2 = 5.1 + 4.0 + 3.0 - 5 = 0$

for column ($j = 3$) $\quad Z_3 - C_3 = 5.0 + 4.1 + 3.0 - 4 = 0$

for column ($j = 4$) $\quad Z_4 - C_4 = 5 \cdot \frac{15}{41} + 4\left(\frac{-6}{41}\right) + 3\left(\frac{-2}{41}\right) - 0$

$$= \frac{75}{41} - \frac{24}{41} - \frac{6}{41} - 0 = \frac{75 - 24 - 6}{41} = \frac{45}{41}$$

for column ($j = 5$) $\quad Z_5 - C_5 = 5 \cdot \frac{8}{41} + 4 \cdot \left(\frac{5}{41}\right) + 3\left(-\frac{12}{41}\right) - 0$

$$= \frac{40}{41} + \frac{20}{41} - \frac{36}{41} = \frac{40 + 20 - 36}{41} = \frac{24}{41}$$

for column ($j = 6$) $\quad Z_6 - C_6 = 5\left(\frac{-10}{41}\right) + 4\left(\frac{4}{41}\right) + 3\left(\frac{15}{41}\right) - 0$

$$= \frac{-50}{41} + \frac{16}{41} + \frac{45}{41} = \frac{-50 + 16 + 45}{41} = \frac{-50 + 61}{41} = \frac{11}{41}$$

Since in iteration–3, all $Z_j - C_j$ are positive (≥ 0),

Therefore the optimal solution is attained at iteration–3.

Thus, the optimal solution is

$$x_1 = \frac{89}{41}$$

$$x_2 = \frac{50}{41}$$

$$x_3 = \frac{62}{41}$$

and $\quad Z_{\max} = \frac{765}{41}$.

Example 2. *Solve the following LPP using simplex method.*

Maximize $Z = 3x_1 + 2x_2$

Subject to

$$x_1 + x_2 \le 4$$
$$x_1 - x_2 \le 2$$
$$x_1, x_2 \ge 0$$

Solution.

Step 1: Check whether b_i's (RHS) are positive or not, if not, then make it positive by multiplying with –1. Then convert the inequality sign (≤) by introducing non-negative slack variables. The coefficients of slack variables are always considered as zero in the given objective functions.

Here we add two slack variables s_1 and s_2 such that $s_1 \ge 0$ and $s_2 \ge 0$, as there are only two constraints to convert the constraints into equality sign.

Thus, the given problem can now be rewritten as:

Maximize $Z = 3x_1 + 2x_2 + 0 \cdot s_1 + 0 \cdot s_2$

Subject to

$$x_1 + x_2 + s_1 = 4$$
$$x_1 - x_2 + s_2 = 2$$
$$x_1, x_2, s_1, s_2 \ge 0.$$

Then we write the above LPP into matrix form as follows by using the coefficients of A_i and slack variables.

$$\begin{bmatrix} 1 & 1 & 1 & 0 \\ 1 & -1 & 0 & 1 \end{bmatrix} \begin{bmatrix} x_1 \\ x_2 \\ s_1 \\ s_2 \end{bmatrix} = \begin{bmatrix} 4 \\ 2 \end{bmatrix} \qquad [\because Ax = B]$$

Step 2: Now construct in initial simplex tableau. The values of nonbasic variables are always zero

i.e., $x_1 = x_2 = 0$

Thus, $s_1 = 4$ and $s_2 = 2.$

We use the above matrix from of the given problem to write in the simplex tableau.

Iteration–1

	C_j		3	2	0	0
C_B	Y_B	X_B	x_1	x_2	s_1	s_2
0	s_1	4	1	1	1	0
0	s_2	2	1	–1	0	1
	$Z_j - C_j$	0	–3	–2	0	0

In the above table we compute $Z_j - C_j$ as follows:

$$Z_1 - C_1 = C_B X_1 - C_1 \text{ (for } j = 1) \qquad [\because Z_j - C_j = C_B X_B - C_j]$$
$$= 0.1 + 0.1 - 3 = -3$$
$$Z_2 - C_2 = C_B X_2 - C_2 \text{ (for } j = 2)$$
$$= 0 \times 1 + 0 \times (-1) - 2 = -2$$
$$Z_3 - C_3 = C_B X_3 - C_3 \text{ (for } j = 3)$$
$$= 0 \times 1 + 0 \times 0 - 0 = 0$$
$$Z_4 - C_4 = C_B X_4 - C_4 \text{ (for } j = 4)$$
$$= 0 \times 0 + 0 \times 1 - 0 = 0$$

Since all $Z_j - C_j \leq 0$, the optimal solution has not been attained. We proceed to locate the pivot column and the pivot element:

For Pivot Column: Find the most negative $Z_j - C_j$ for $j = 1, 2, 3, 4$.

Here, most negative $Z_j - C_j = -3$

So we mark this column using a rectangle as a pivot column. Thus x_1 (variable corresponding to pivot column) is the entering or incoming variable.

		C_j	3	2	0	0	Minimum Ratio ↓
C_B	Y_B	X_B	x_1	x_2	s_1	s_2	
0	s_1	4	1	1	1	0	
0	s_2	2	1*	–1	0	1	2
	$Z_j - C_j$	0	–3	–2	0	0	

↓ Pivot Column.

Then we compute the minimum ratio to locate the outgoing vector by using

$$\frac{x_{Br}}{x_{rk}} = \min_i \left[\frac{x_{Br}}{x_{ik}}, x_{ik} > 0\right].$$

Thus for $k = 1$ and $r = 1$

$$\frac{x_{B1}}{x_{11}} = \frac{4}{1}$$

and for $k = 1$ and $r = 2$

$$\frac{x_{B2}}{x_{21}} = \frac{2}{1}$$

Thus, $$\frac{x_{Br}}{x_{rk}} = \min\left[\frac{4}{1}, \frac{2}{1}\right] = 2.$$

Thus we mark the row corresponding to value 2 (as minimum ratio) with a rectangle. Thus the slack variable s_2 (corresponding to minimum ratio) will be a outgoing variable. Thus we mark it with a rectangle to make it pivot row.

In iteration–1, the pivot element is already 1 in the above table, so we make elementary row operations on R_1 only.

$R_1(\text{New}) \rightarrow R_1(\text{Old}) - R_2(\text{New})$

$R_1(\text{Old})$	$\Rightarrow$	4	1	1	1	0
$R_2(\text{New})$	$\Rightarrow$	2	1	– 1	0	1
Substract		–	–	+	–	–
Thus, $R_1(\text{Old}) - R_2(\text{New})$	$\Rightarrow$	2	0	2	1	–1

Iteration–2

			3	2	0	0	Minimum Ratio ↓
C_B	Y_B	X_B	x_1	x_2	s_1	s_2	
0	s_1	2	0	2*	1	–1	1
3	x_1	2	1	–1	0	1	
	$Z_j - C_j$	6	0	–5 ↑	0	3	

Calculations for $Z_j - C_j$

for column I (j = 1) $Z_1 - C_1$ = 0.0 + 3.1 – 3 = 0

for column II (j = 2) $Z_2 - C_2$ = 0.2 + 3(–1) – 2 = – 5*

for column III (j = 3) $Z_3 - C_3$ = 0.1 + 3.0 – 0 = 0

for column IV (j = 4) $Z_4 - C_4$ = 0(–1) + 3(1) – 0 = 3

Since $Z_2 - C_2$ is most negative so x_2 enters the basis. Thus 2 (marked with *) becomes the pivot element. Now make the pivot element as 1. And for this divide the row 1 by 2.

Iteration–3

			3	2	0	0
C_B	Y_B	X_B	x_1	x_2	s_1	s_2
2	x_2	1	0	1	$\frac{1}{2}$	$-\frac{1}{2}$
3	x_1	3	1	0	$\frac{1}{2}$	$\frac{1}{2}$
	$Z_j - C_j$	11	0	0	$\frac{5}{2}$	$\frac{1}{2}$

Calculation

$$R_1(\text{New}) \rightarrow \frac{R_1(\text{Old})}{2}$$

$$\Rightarrow \left(\frac{2}{2}\ \frac{0}{2}\ \frac{2}{2}\ \frac{1}{2}\ \frac{-1}{2}\right)$$

$$\Rightarrow \left(1\ 0\ 1\ \frac{1}{2}\ \frac{-1}{2}\right)$$

$R_2(\text{New}) \rightarrow R_2(\text{Old}) + R_1(\text{New})$

$R_2(\text{Old})$	=	2	1	–1	0	1
$R_1(\text{New})$	=	1	0	1	$\frac{1}{2}$	$\frac{-1}{2}$
(Add)		+	+	+	+	+
		3	1	0	$\frac{1}{2}$	$\frac{1}{2}$

Calculations of $Z_j - C_j$

for column I ($j = 1$) $Z_1 - C_1 = C_B X_B - C_1$

$= 2.0 + 3.1 - 3 = 0$

for column II ($j = 2$) $Z_2 - C_2 = 2.1 + 3.0 - 2 = 0$

for column III ($j = 3$) $Z_3 - C_3 = 2\cdot\frac{1}{2} + 3\cdot\frac{1}{2} - 0 = \frac{5}{2}$

for column IV ($j = 4$) $Z_4 - C_4 = 2\cdot\left(-\frac{1}{2}\right) + 3\cdot\frac{1}{2} = \frac{1}{2}$

for objective function $2.1 + 3.3 = 2 + 9 = 11$

Since, all $Z_j - C_j \geq 0$.

Optimal solution has been attained.

$$\therefore \quad Z_{\max} = 11$$
$$x_1 = 3$$
$$x_2 = 1.$$

Example 3. *Maximize* $Z = 4x_1 + 10x_2$

Subject to

$$2x_1 + x_2 \leq 50$$
$$2x_1 + 5x_2 \leq 100$$
$$2x_1 + 3x_2 \leq 90$$
$$x_1, x_2 \geq 0.$$

Solution. Since the problem is of maximization and the right hand side of the inequality (b_i) are already positive. Thus introducing the slack variables s_1, s_2 and $s_3 \geq 0$.

Thus the above problem can be rewritten as

Maximize $Z = 4x_1 + 10x_2 + 0.s_1 + 0.s_2 + 0.s_3$

Subject to

$$2x_1 + x_2 + s_1 = 50$$
$$2x_1 + 5x_2 + s_2 = 100$$
$$2x_1 + 3x_2 + s_3 = 90$$
$$x_1, x_2, s_1, s_2, s_3 \geq 0$$

Iteration–0

	C_j		4	10	0	0	0	
C_B	Y_B	X_B	x_1	x_2	s_1	s_2	s_3	Minimum Ratio
0	s_1	50	2	1	1	0	0	50
0	s_2	100	2	5*	0	1	0	20 ←
0	s_3	90	2	3	0	0	1	30
	$Z_j - C_j$	0	–4	–10	0	0	0	

Calculations for $Z_j - C_j$

for column I ($j = 1$) $Z_1 - C_1 = C_B X_B - C_1$

$= 0.2 + 0.2 + 0.2 - 4 = -4$

for column II ($j = 2$) $Z_2 - C_2 = 0.1 + 0.5 + 0.3 - 10 = -4$

for column III ($j = 3$) $Z_3 - C_3 = 0.1 + 0.0 + 0.0 - 0 = 0$

Similarly for column IV and V, $Z_j - C_j$ can be calculated.

Now, all $Z_j - C_j \ngeq 0$ because $Z_2 - C_2 = -10 < 0$

Thus column 2 (because of –10) will enter the basis and this becomes the pivot column.

To locate the pivot row, we find the minimum ratio by

$$\frac{x_{Br}}{x_{rk}} = \min\left[\frac{x_{Br}}{x_{rk}}, x_{rk} > 0\right] = \min\left[\frac{50}{1}, \frac{100}{5}, \frac{90}{3}\right] = \min[50, 20, 30] = 20$$

So, row II corresponds to the minimum ratio, thus row II becomes the pivot row and 5* (marked with *) becomes the pivot element.

In order to make the pivot element we divide the whole row by 5.

The new values of the elements for other rows are evaluated by performing elementary operations.

Iteration–1

	C_j		4	10	0	0	0
C_B	Y_B	X_B	x_1	x_2	s_1	s_2	s_3
0	s_1	30	$\frac{8}{5}$	0	1	$\frac{-1}{5}$	0
10	x_2	20	$\frac{2}{5}$	1	0	$\frac{1}{5}$	0
0	s_3	30	$\frac{4}{5}$	0	0	$\frac{-3}{5}$	1
	$Z_j - C_j$	200	0	0	0	2	0

Calculations for Row Operations

$$R_2(\text{New}) \rightarrow \frac{R_2(\text{Old})}{5}$$

i.e., $$\left(\frac{100}{5} \quad \frac{2}{5} \quad \frac{5}{5} \quad \frac{0}{5} \quad \frac{1}{5} \quad 0\right)$$

$$R_2(\text{New}) \rightarrow 20 \quad \frac{2}{5} \quad 1 \quad 0 \quad \frac{1}{5} \quad 0$$

$R_1(\text{New}) \rightarrow R_1(\text{Old}) - R_2(\text{New})$

	R_1(Old)	⇒	50	2	1	1	0	0
	R_2(New)	⇒	20	$\frac{2}{5}$	1	0	$\frac{1}{5}$	0
	(Subtract)		–	–	–	–	–	–
Thus,	R_1(New)	⇒	30	$\frac{8}{5}$	0	1	$\frac{-1}{5}$	0

$R_3(\text{New}) \rightarrow R_3(\text{Old}) - 3R_2(\text{New})$

	R_3(Old)	⇒	90	2	3	0	0	1
	R_2(New)	⇒	60	$\frac{6}{5}$	3	0	$\frac{3}{5}$	0
	(Subtract)		–	–	–	–	–	–
Thus,	R_3(New)	⇒	30	$\frac{4}{5}$	0	0	$\frac{-3}{5}$	1

Calculations for $Z_j - C_j$ for iteration–1

for column I ($j = 1$) $\quad Z_1 - C_1 = 0\cdot\frac{8}{5} + 10\cdot\frac{2}{5} + 0\cdot 30 - 4 = 0$

for column II ($j = 2$) $\quad Z_2 - C_2 = 0.0 + 10.1 + 0.0 - 10 = 0$

for column III ($j = 3$) $\quad Z_3 - C_3 = 0.1 + 10.0 + 0.0 - 0 = 0$

for column IV ($j = 4$) $\quad Z_4 - C_4 = 0\cdot\left(\frac{-1}{5}\right) + 10\left(\frac{1}{5}\right) + 0\left(\frac{-3}{5}\right) - 0 = 2$

for column V ($j = 5$) $\quad Z_5 - C_5 = 0.0 + 10.0 + 0.1 - 0 = 0$

Since all $Z_j - C_j$ in iteration–1 are positive

i.e., all $\quad Z_j - C_j \geq 0$

Thus an optimal solution has been attained.

$$\therefore \quad Z_{max} = 200$$
$$x_1 = 0$$
$$x_2 = 20.$$

Remark: Since the net evaluation corresponding to non-basic variable x_1 is zero, which is an indication that an alternative basic solution exists. Thus z can be brought into the basis instead of s_1 and s_5. Then the resulting new basic feasible solution will also be an optimum solution. But in this case too, the optimum value of Z remains the same, *i.e.*, $Z_{max} = 200$.

Example 4. *Solve the following LPP using Simplex method.*

Maximize $Z = 2x_1 + 4x_2$

Subject to

$$-2x_1 + 4x_1 \leq 16$$
$$3x_1 + 6x_2 \leq 36$$
$$4x_1 - 8x_2 \leq 12$$
$$x_1, x_2 \geq 0.$$

Solution. Introducing the slack variables as it is already in standard form (maximization type).

i.e.,

$$-2x_1 + 4x_2 + s_1 = 16$$
$$3x_1 + 6x_2 + s_2 = 36$$
$$4x_1 - 8x_2 + s_3 = 12$$

where $s_1 \geq 0$, $s_2 \geq 0$ and $s_3 \geq 0$ are the slack variables.

Thus the LPP can be rewritten as:

$$\text{Max } Z = 2x_1 + 4x_2 + 0 \cdot s_1 + 0 \cdot s_2 + 0 \cdot s_3$$

Subject to

$$-2x_1 + 4x_2 + s_1 = 16$$
$$3x_1 + 6x_2 + s_2 = 36$$
$$4x_1 - 8x_2 + s_3 = 12$$
$$x_1, x_2, s_1, s_2, s_3 \geq 0$$

Initial basic feasible solution

If $x_1 = x_2 = 0$, then
$$s_1 = 16$$
$$s_2 = 36$$
$$s_3 = 12.$$

Simplex Tableau

	C_j		2	4	0	0	0	Ratio	
C_B	Y_B	X_B	x_1	x_2	s_1	s_2	s_3		
0	s_1	16	–2	4*	1	0	0	$\frac{16}{4} = 4$	Minimum
0	s_2	36	3	6	0	1	0	$\frac{36}{6} = 6$	
0	s_3	12	4	–8	0	0	1		
	$Z_j - C_j$		–2	–4	0	0	0		
				Minimum					

Here, 4 (marked with *) is the pivot element.

In the above table, we compute the net evaluations $Z_j - C_j$ and find that –2 is the most negative. So, x_2 corresponding to –2 enters the basis (in coming vector) and then compute the ratio for outgoing vector.

i.e., $$\min\left\{\frac{x_{Br}}{x_{rk}}, x_{rk} > 0\right\}$$

i.e., $$\min\left\{\frac{16}{4}, \frac{36}{6}\right\} = 4$$

Thus the column corresponding to vector x_2 is the pivot column and the row corresponding to ratio 4 is the pivot row.

Hence, the pivot element now becomes 4. The pivot element is made '1' by dividing the pivot row by the pivot element.

The incoming vector is x_2 and the outgoing vector is s_1.

Now, the new iterated simplex tableaus is obtained by applying the row operations

$$\text{New element} = \text{Old element} - \frac{\left[\begin{array}{c}\text{Associated no. in pivot row} \times \\ \text{Corresponding no. in pivot colum}\end{array}\right]}{\text{Pivot Element}}$$

i.e., wave element $= 36 - \dfrac{6 \times 16}{4} = 12$

Iteration–1

			2	4	0	0	0	
C_B	Y_B	X_B	x_1	x_2	s_1	s_2	s_3	Ratio
4	x_2	4	$\frac{-1}{2}$	1	$\frac{1}{4}$	0	0	
0	s_2	12	6*	0	$\frac{-3}{2}$	1	0	2 ← Pivot Row
0	s_3	44	0	0	2	0	1	
	$Z_j - C_j$	16	–4	0	1	0	0	

Pivot Column

Iteration–2

			2	4	0	0	0
C_B	Y_B	X_B	x_1	x_2	s_1	s_2	s_3
4	x_2	5	0	1	$\frac{1}{8}$	$\frac{1}{12}$	0
2	x_1	2	1	0	$\frac{-1}{4}$	$\frac{1}{6}$	0
0	s_3	44	0	2	0	0	1
	$Z_j - C_j$	24	0	0	0	0	0

Since all $Z_j - C_j \geq 0$

$\therefore$ Optimal solution has been attained.

Thus, $x_1 = 2$

$x_2 = 5$

and $Z_{max} = 24$

Example 5. *Maximize* $Z = 2x_1 + 4x_2 + 3x_3$

Subject to $3x_1 + 2x_2 + x_3 \leq 60$

$4x_1 + x_2 + 3x_3 \leq 40$

$2x_1 + 2x_2 + 2x_3 \leq 80$

$x_1, x_2, x_3 \geq 0.$

Solution. Since the problem is of maximization and again the right hand side (b_i's) of the constraints are positive. So, only introducing the slack variables ($s_1 \geq 0$, $s_2 \geq 0$ and $s_3 \geq 0$), the above LPP can be rewritten as follows.

If $x_1 = x_2 = x_3 = 0$, then $s_1 = 60$, $s_2 = 40$ and $s_3 = 80$, be the initial solution for which the value of the objective function would be $Z = 0$.

Max $Z = 2x_1 + 4x_2 + 3x_3 + 0 \cdot s_1 + 0 \cdot s_2 + 0 \cdot s_3$

Subject to $3x_1 + 2x_2 + x_3 + s_1 = 60$

$4x_1 + x_2 + 3x_2 + s_2 = 40$

$2x_1 + 2x_2 + 2x_3 + s_3 = 80,$

$x_1, x_2, x_3, s_1, s_2, s_3 \geq 0$

Iteration–0

	C_j		2	4	3	0	0	0		
C_B	Y_B	X_B	x_1	x_2	x_3	s_1	s_2	s_3	Min. Ratio	
0	s_1	60	3	2*	1	1	0	0	$\frac{60}{2} = 30$	←
0	s_2	40	4	1	3	0	1	0	$\frac{40}{1} = 40$	
0	s_3	80	2	2	2	0	0	1	$\frac{80}{2} = 40$	
	$Z_j - C_j$	0	–2	–4	–3	0	0	0		

Calculations of $Z_j - C_j = C_B X_B - C_j$

for column I ($j = 1$) $Z_1 - C_1 = 0.3 + 0.4 + 0.2 - 2 = -2$

for column II ($j = 2$) $Z_2 - C_2 = 0.2 + 0.1 + 0.2 - 4 = -4$*

for column III ($j = 3$) $Z_3 - C_3 = 0.1 + 0.3 + 0.2 - 3 = -3$

Similarly $Z_j - C_j$ for column 4 and 5 can be computed.

Here $Z_2 - C_2 < 0$ (most negative value).

Thus column II is the pivot row and x_2 enters the basis.

Now try to locate the pivot row by using the relation

$$\frac{x_{Br}}{x_{rk}} = \min\left[\frac{x_{Br}}{x_{rk}}, x_{rk} > 0\right]$$

$$= \min\left[\frac{60}{2}, \frac{40}{1}, \frac{80}{2}\right]$$

$$= \min [30, 40, 40]$$

$$= 30$$

Since minimum ratio is 30.

Here the minimum ratio occurs for I Row. Thus Row I is the pivot row and element 2 (intersection of pivot column and pivot row) marked with asterisk (*) becomes the pivot element. So s_1 leaves the basis. In order to make the pivot element 1, divide it by 2 to compute the new values of the elements of Row 1, while new values of the elements of other rows are evaluated by performing elementary row operation.

Iteration–1

			2	4	3	0	0	0	
C_B	Y_B	X_B	x_1	x_2	x_3	s_1	s_2	s_3	Min. Ratio
4	x_2	30	$\frac{3}{2}$	1	$\frac{1}{2}$	$\frac{1}{2}$	0	0	60
0	s_2	10	$\frac{5}{2}$	0	$\frac{5}{2}$*	$\frac{-1}{2}$	1	0	4
0	s_3	20	–1	0	1	–1	0	1	20
	$Z_j - C_j$	120	4	0	–1	2	0	0	

Calculations for Row Operations

$$R_1(\text{New}) \rightarrow \frac{R_1(\text{Old})}{2}$$

$$R_2(\text{New}) \rightarrow R_2(\text{Old}) - R_1(\text{New})$$

	R_2(Old)	⇒	40	4	1	3	0	1	0
	R_1(New)	⇒	30	$\frac{3}{2}$	1	$\frac{1}{2}$	$\frac{1}{2}$	0	0
	(Subtract)		–	–	–	–	–	–	–
i.e.,	R_2(New)		10	$\frac{5}{2}$	0	$\frac{5}{2}$	$\frac{-1}{2}$	1	0

R_3(New) → R_3(Old) − $2R_1$(New)

	R_3(Old)	⇒	80	2	2	2	0	0	1
	$2R_1$(New)	⇒	60	3	2	1	1	0	0
	(Subtract)		–	–	–	–	–	–	–
i.e.,	R_3(New)		20	−1	0	1	−1	0	1

Calculations of $Z_j - C_j$ for Iteration–2

for column I (j = 1) $Z_1 - C_1 = 4 \cdot \frac{3}{2} + 0 \cdot \frac{5}{2} + 0\,(-1) - 2 = 4$

for column II (j = 2) $Z_2 - C_2 = 4.1 + 0.0 + 0.0 - 4 = 0$

for column III (j = 3) $Z_3 - C_3 = 4 \cdot \frac{1}{2} + 0 \cdot \frac{5}{2} + 0.1 - 3 = -1^*$

for column IV (j = 4) $Z_4 - C_4 = 4 \cdot \frac{1}{2} + 0\left(\frac{-1}{2}\right) + 0\,(-1) - 0 = 2$

Only $Z_3 - C_3 < 0$ (= −1). Thus, the current solution is not optimum and can be improved.

Here III column becomes the pivot column and so x_3 enters the basis. Locate the variable that leaves the basis by using the relation.

$$\frac{x_{Br}}{x_{rk}} = \min_i \left[\frac{x_{Br}}{x_{ik}}, x_{ik} > 0\right]$$

$$= \min \left[\frac{30}{1/2}, \frac{10}{5/2}, \frac{20}{1}\right]$$

$$= \min\,[60, 4, 20]$$

$$= 4$$

Here pivot row is the second row as minimum ratio is for II row.

Here s_2 leaves the basis and so pivot element becomes $\frac{5}{2}$, and in order to make pivot element as 1 and to compute the new values of the elements of R_1 and R_3, we apply the elementary row operations for proceeding to iteration–2.

Iteration–2

			2	4	3	0	0	0
C_B	Y_B	X_B	x_1	x_2	x_3	s_1	s_2	s_3
4	x_2	28	1	1	0	$\frac{6}{10}$	$\frac{-1}{5}$	0
3	x_3	4	1	0	1	$\frac{-1}{5}$	$\frac{2}{5}$	0
0	s_3	16	− 2	0	0	$\frac{-4}{5}$	$\frac{-2}{5}$	1
	$Z_j - C_j$	124	5	0	0	$\frac{9}{5}$	$\frac{2}{5}$	0

Calculations Performing Row Operations.

$$R_2(\text{New}) \rightarrow \frac{R_2(\text{Old})}{5/2}$$

$$R_2(\text{New}) \rightarrow \frac{2}{5} R_2(\text{Old})$$

$$R_2(\text{New}) \; : \; \left(10\cdot\frac{2}{5} \quad \frac{5}{2}\cdot\frac{2}{5} \quad 0.\frac{2}{5} \quad \frac{5}{2}\cdot\frac{2}{5} \quad \frac{-1}{2}\cdot\frac{2}{5} \quad 1\cdot\frac{2}{5} \quad 0\cdot\frac{2}{5}\right)$$

$$\therefore \quad R_2(\text{New}) \; : \; \left(4 \quad 1 \quad 0 \quad 1 \quad \frac{-1}{5} \quad \frac{2}{5} \quad 0\right)$$

$$R_1(\text{New}) \rightarrow R_1(\text{Old}) - \frac{1}{2} R_2(\text{New})$$

	Now $R_1(\text{Old})$	:	30	$\frac{3}{2}$	1	$\frac{1}{2}$	$\frac{1}{2}$	0	0
	and $\frac{1}{2} R_2(\text{New})$	:	2	$\frac{1}{2}$	0	$\frac{1}{2}$	$\frac{-1}{10}$	$\frac{1}{5}$	0
	(Subtract)		–	–	–	–	+	–	–
∴	$R_1(\text{New})$		28	1	1	0	$\frac{6}{10}$	$\frac{-1}{5}$	0

$R_3(\text{New}) \rightarrow R_3(\text{Old}) - R_2(\text{New})$

Now	$R_3(\text{Old})$	:	20	–1	0	1	–1	0	1
and	$R_2(\text{New})$	:	4	1	0	1	$\frac{-1}{5}$	$\frac{2}{5}$	0
	(Subtract)		–	–	–	–	+	–	–
∴	R_3 (New)	:	16	–2	0	0	$\frac{-4}{5}$	$\frac{-2}{5}$	1

Calculations for $Z_j - C_j$

$$Z_1 - C_1 = 4.1 + 3.1 + 0.(-2) - 2 = 5$$

$$Z_2 - C_2 = 4.1 + 3.0 + 0.0 - 4 = 0$$

$$Z_3 - C_3 = 4.0 + 3.1 + 0.0 - 3 = 0$$

$$Z_4 - C_4 = 4\cdot\frac{6}{10} + 3\left(\frac{-1}{5}\right) + 0\left(\frac{-4}{5}\right) - 0 = \frac{9}{5}$$

$$Z_5 - C_5 = 4\left(\frac{-1}{5}\right) + 3\left(\frac{2}{5}\right) + 0\left(\frac{-2}{5}\right) - 0 = \frac{2}{5}$$

$$Z_6 - C_6 = 4.0 + 3.0 + 0.1 - 0 = 0$$

Since, all $Z_j - C_j \geq 0$

Therefore an optimal solution has been attained.

Now, the value of the objective function Z

$$Z = 4\cdot(28) + 3\cdot(4) + 0\cdot(16)$$
$$= 112 + 12 + 0$$
$$= 124.$$

∴ The optimal solution is

$$Z_{max} = 124$$
$$x_1 = 0$$
$$x_2 = 28$$
$$x_3 = 4.$$

Example 6. *Maximize* $Z = x_1 - x_2 + 3x_3$

Subject to $x_1 + x_2 + x_3 \leq 10$

$$2x_1 + 0x_2 - x_3 \leq 2$$
$$2x_1 - 2x_2 + 3x_3 \leq 0$$
$$x_1, x_2, x_3 \geq 0$$

Solution. Since the given problem is of maximization one and the right hand side (b_i) of the constraints are positive. So only introducing slack variables $s_1 \geq 0$, $s_2 \geq 0$ and $s_3 \geq 0$, the LPP can be rewritten as:

$$\text{Maximize } Z = x_1 - x_2 + 3x_3 + 0\cdot s_1 + 0\cdot s_2 + 0\cdot s_3$$

Subject to $x_1 + x_2 + x_3 + s_1 = 10$

$$2x_1 + 0.x_2 - x_3 + s_2 = 2$$
$$2x_1 - 2x_2 + 3x_3 + s_3 = 0$$
$$x_1, x_2, x_3, s_1, s_2, s_3 \geq 0$$

The initial solution of the problem after

$x_1 = 0 = x_2 = x_3$, is $s_1 = 10$

$s_2 = 2$

and $s_3 = 0$.

Iteration–0

	C_j		1	–1	3	0	0	0	
C_B	Y_B	X_B	x_1	x_2	x_3	s_1	s_2	s_3	Minimum Ratio
0	s_1	10	1	1	1	1	0	0	$\frac{10}{1} = 10$
0	s_2	2	2	0	–1	0	1	0	
0	s_3	0	2	–2	3*	0	0	1	$\frac{0}{3} = 0$
	$Z_j - C_j$	0	–1	1	–3	0	0	0	
					↑				

Calculations for $Z_j - C_j = C_B X_B - C_j$

for column I ($j = 1$), $Z_1 - C_1 = 0.1 + 0.2 + 0.2 - 1 = -1$

for column II ($j = 2$) $Z_2 - C_2 = 0.1 + 0.0 + 0(-2) + 1 = 1$

for column III ($j = 3$) $Z_3 - C_3 = 0.1 + 0(-1) + 0(3) - 3 = -3$

Similarly $Z_4 - C_4$, $Z_5 - C_5$ and $Z_6 - C_6$ can be computed.

Since $Z_3 - C_3 = -3 < 0$, is most negative.

Thus III column becomes the pivot column, and so x_2 enters the basis.

Then find the minimum ratio by using the relation

$$\frac{x_{Br}}{x_{rk}} = \min_i \left[\frac{x_{Bi}}{x_{ik}}, x_{ik} > 0\right]$$

$$i = 1, ..., m$$

So
$$\frac{x_{Br}}{x_{rk}} = \min\left[\frac{10}{1}, -, \frac{0}{3}\right]$$ (as -1 is negative, we can't find the ratio as it violates the condition $x_{ik} > 0$).

$$= \min [10, -, 0]$$

$$= 0$$

Thus the pivotal element becomes 3 (marked with *), as row III is the pivot row because of minimum ratio. Here, s_3 leaves the basis now.

In order to make the pivot element 1, we divide the pivot row by 3 and the new values of the elements are computed by performing elementary row operations, as discussed in calculations of iteration–1.

Iteration–1

	C_j		1	−1	3	0	0	0	
C_B	Y_B	X_B	x_1	x_2	x_3	s_1	s_2	s_3	Min. Ratio
0	s_1	10	$\frac{1}{3}$	$\frac{5}{3}$*	0	1	0	$\frac{-1}{3}$	6
0	s_2	2	$\frac{8}{3}$	$\frac{2}{3}$	0	0	1	$\frac{1}{3}$	3 ←
3	x_3	0	$\frac{2}{3}$	$\frac{-2}{3}$	1	0	0	$\frac{1}{3}$	–
	$Z_j - C_j$	0	1	−1 ↑	0	0	0	1	

Calculations of Row Operations

$$R_3(\text{New}) \rightarrow \frac{R_3(\text{Old})}{3}$$

$$R_3(\text{New}) \Rightarrow \left(\frac{0}{3}\ \frac{2}{3}\ \frac{-2}{3}\ \frac{3}{3}\ \frac{0}{3}\ \frac{0}{3}\ \frac{1}{3}\right)$$

i.e., $R_3(\text{New}) \Rightarrow \begin{pmatrix} 0 & \frac{2}{3} & \frac{-2}{3} & 1 & 0 & 0 & \frac{1}{3} \end{pmatrix}$

$R_1(\text{New}) \to R_1(\text{Old}) - R_3(\text{New})$

	$R_1(\text{Old})$	$\Rightarrow$	10	1	1	1	1	0	0
	$R_3(\text{New})$	$\Rightarrow$	0	$\frac{2}{3}$	$\frac{-2}{3}$	1	0	0	$\frac{1}{3}$
	(Subtract)		–	–	+	–	–	–	–
$\Rightarrow$	$R_1(\text{New})$	$\Rightarrow$	10	$\frac{1}{3}$	$\frac{5}{3}$	0	1	0	$\frac{-1}{3}$

$R_2(\text{New}) \to R_2(\text{Old}) + R_3(\text{New})$

	$R_2(\text{Old})$	$\Rightarrow$	2	2	0	–1	0	1	0
	$R_3(\text{New})$	$\Rightarrow$	0	$\frac{2}{3}$	$\frac{-2}{3}$	1	0	0	$\frac{1}{3}$
	(Add)		+	+	+	+	+	+	+
$\Rightarrow$	$R_2(\text{New})$		2	$\frac{8}{3}$	$+\frac{2}{3}$	0	0	1	$\frac{1}{3}$

Calculations of $Z_j - C_j$

for column I (j = 1), $Z_1 - C_1 = 0\cdot\frac{1}{3} + 0.\frac{8}{3} + 3\cdot\frac{2}{3} - 1 = 1$

for column II (j = 2) $Z_2 - C_2 = 0\cdot\frac{5}{3} + 0\cdot\frac{2}{3} + 3\left(\frac{-2}{3}\right) + 1 = -1$

for column III (j = 3) $Z_3 - C_3 = 0.0 + 0.0 + 3.1 - 3 = 0$

for column IV (j = 4) $Z_4 - C_4 = 0.1 + 0.0 + 3.0 - 0 = 0$

for column V (j = 5) $Z_5 - C_5 = 0.0 + 0.1 + 3.0 - 0 = 0$

for column VI (j = 6) $Z_6 - C_6 = 0\cdot\left(\frac{-1}{3}\right) + 0\cdot\left(\frac{1}{3}\right) + 3\cdot\left(\frac{1}{3}\right) - 0 = 1$

Since $Z_2 - C_2 = -1$ (<0), is the most negative, so the current solution can be further improved. Column 2nd, has x_2 is the pivot column.

Thus IInd column corresponding to x_2 (because of –1) enters the basis and minimum ratio is

$$\frac{x_{Br}}{x_{rk}} = \min_i \left[\frac{10}{5/3}, \frac{2}{2/3}, \ldots\right] \quad \text{because for II row, } x_{ik} < 0.$$

$$= \min\,[2, 3] = 2$$

So $\frac{5}{3}$ (marked with asterisk *) becomes the pivot element and in order to make the pivot element 1, perform the following elementary row operations as done in iteration–2.

Iteration–2

			1	– 1	3	0	0	0
C_B	Y_B	X_B	x_1	x_2	x_3	s_1	s_2	s_3
–1	x_2	6	$\frac{1}{5}$	1	0	$\frac{3}{5}$	0	$\frac{-1}{5}$
0	s_2	–2	$\frac{38}{15}$	0	0	$\frac{-1}{5}$	1	$\frac{7}{5}$
3	x_3	4	$\frac{4}{5}$	0	1	$\frac{1}{5}$	0	$\frac{1}{5}$
	$Z_j - C_j$	6	$\frac{6}{5}$	0	0	0	0	$\frac{4}{5}$

Calculations for Row Operations

$$R_1(\text{New}) \to \frac{R_1(\text{Old})}{5/3}$$

$$\to R_1(\text{Old}) \times \frac{3}{5}$$

i.e., $R_1(\text{Old}) = 10 \quad \frac{1}{3} \quad \frac{5}{3} \quad 0 \quad 1 \quad 0 \quad \frac{-1}{3}$

$$\Rightarrow \frac{3}{5} R_1(\text{Old}) = \left(10 \cdot \frac{3}{5} \quad \frac{1}{3} \cdot \frac{3}{5} \quad \frac{5}{3} \cdot \frac{3}{5} \quad 0 \cdot \frac{3}{5} \quad 1 \cdot \frac{3}{5} \quad 0 \cdot \frac{3}{5} \quad \frac{-1}{3} \cdot \frac{3}{5}\right)$$

$$\Rightarrow R_1(\text{New}) = -6 \quad \frac{1}{5} \quad 1 \quad 0 \quad \frac{3}{5} \quad 0 \quad \frac{-1}{5}$$

$$R_2(\text{New}) \to R_2(\text{Old}) - \frac{2}{3} R_1(\text{New})$$

Now	$R_2(\text{Old})$	= 2	$\frac{8}{3}$	$\frac{2}{3}$	0	0	1	$\frac{1}{3}$
and	$\frac{2}{3} R_1(\text{New})$	= 4	$\frac{2}{15}$	$\frac{2}{3}$	0	$\frac{1}{5}$	0	$\frac{-2}{15}$
(Subtract)		–	–	–	–	–	–	+
$\Rightarrow$	$R_2(\text{New})$	= –2	$\frac{38}{15}$	0	0	$\frac{-1}{5}$	1	$\frac{7}{15}$

$$R_3(\text{New}) \rightarrow R_3(\text{Old}) + \frac{2}{3} R_1(\text{New})$$

Now	$R_3(\text{Old})$ =	0	$\frac{2}{3}$	$\frac{-2}{3}$	1	0	0	$\frac{1}{3}$
and	$\frac{2}{3}R_1(\text{New})$ =	4	$\frac{2}{15}$	$\frac{2}{3}$	0	$\frac{1}{5}$	0	$\frac{-2}{15}$
(Add)		+	+	+	+	+	+	+
⇒	$R_3(\text{New})$	4	$\frac{4}{5}$	0	1	$\frac{1}{5}$	0	$\frac{1}{5}$

Calculations for $Z_j - C_j = C_B X_B - C_j$

for column I ($j = 1$), $Z_1 - C_1 = -1 \cdot \frac{1}{5} + 0 \cdot \frac{38}{15} + 3 \cdot \frac{4}{5} - 1 = \frac{6}{5}$

for column II ($j = 2$) $Z_2 - C_2 = -1.1 + 0.0 + 3.0 + 1 = 0$

for column III ($j = 3$) $Z_3 - C_3 = -1.0 + 0.0 + 3.1 - 3 = 0$

Similarly calculate $Z_j - C_j$ for $j = 4$, 5 and 6 and we find that all $Z_j - C_j \geq 0$.

Therefore, an optimal solution has been attained.

$$Z_{max} = 6$$
$$x_1 = 0$$
$$x_2 = -1$$
$$x_3 = 4$$

Example 7. *Solve the following LPP using Simplex method.*

Maximize $Z = 3x_1 + 5x_2 + 4x_3$

Subject to
$$2x_1 + 3x_2 \leq 8$$
$$3x_1 + 2x_2 + 4x_3 \leq 15$$
$$2x_2 + 5x_3 \leq 10$$
$$x_1, x_2, x_3 \geq 0$$

Solution. Introducing slack variables as $s_1 \geq 0$, $s_2 \geq 0$ and $s_3 \geq 0$, the above LPP can again be rewritten as:

Maximize $Z = 3x_1 + 5x_2 + 4x_3 + 0.s_1 + 0.s_2 + 0.s_3$

Subject to
$$2x_1 + 3x_2 + s_1 = 8$$
$$3x_1 + 2x_2 + 4x_3 + s_2 = 15$$
$$2x_2 + 5x_3 + s_3 = 10$$
$$x_1, x_2, x_3, s_1, s_2, s_3, \geq 0$$

If $x_1 = 0 = x_2 = x_3$ then the values of $s_1 = 8$, $s_2 = 15$, and $s_3 = 10$.

Iteration–0

	$C_j \to$		3	5	4	0	0	0	
C_B	Y_B	X_B	x_1	x_2	x_3	s_1	s_2	s_3	Min. Ratio
0	s_1	8	2	3*	0	1	0	0	$\frac{8}{3}$ ←
0	s_2	15	3	2	4	0	1	0	$\frac{15}{2}$
0	s_3	10	0	2	5	0	0	1	$\frac{10}{2}$
	$Z_j - C_j$	0	–3	–5	–4	0	0	0	

Calculations for $Z_j - C_j$

for column I ($j = 1$), $Z_1 - C_1 = C_B X_B - C_1$

$= 0.2 + 0.3 + 0.0 - 3 = -3$

for column II ($j = 2$) $Z_2 - C_2 = 0.3 + 0.2 + 0.2 - 5 = -5^*$

for column III ($j = 3$) $Z_3 - C_3 = 0.0 + 0.4 + 0.5 - 4 = -4$

Since $Z_2 - C_2 \leq 0$ (most negative)

So it becomes the pivot column. So x_2 enters the basis. Locate the pivot row by computing the minimum ratio by using

$$\min_i \left[\frac{x_{Br}}{x_{rk}},\quad x_{ik} > 0\right] = \min\left[\frac{8}{3}, \frac{15}{2}, \frac{10}{2}\right] = \frac{8}{3}$$

Thus Row I becomes the pivot row and 3 the pivot element, but s_1 leaves the basis here.

To make the pivot element 1, make elementary row operations as discussed later after iteration–1.

Iteration–1

			3	5	4	0	0	0	
C_B	Y_B	X_B	x_1	x_2	x_3	s_1	s_2	s_3	Min. Ratio
5	x_2	$\frac{8}{3}$	$\frac{2}{3}$	1	0	$\frac{1}{3}$	0	0	—
0	s_2	$\frac{29}{3}$	$\frac{5}{3}$	0	4	$\frac{-2}{3}$	1	0	$\frac{29}{3/4}$
0	s_3	$\frac{14}{3}$	$\frac{-4}{3}$	0	5*	$\frac{-2}{3}$	0	1	$\frac{14}{3/5}$
	$Z_j - C_j$	$\frac{40}{3}$	$\frac{1}{3}$	0	–4	$\frac{5}{3}$	0	0	

Calculations for Row Operations

$$R_1(\text{New}) \rightarrow \frac{R_1(\text{Old})}{3}$$

$$R_1(\text{Old}) : \quad (8 \;\; 2 \;\; 3 \;\; 0 \;\; 1 \;\; 0 \;\; 0)$$

$$\frac{R_1}{3}(\text{Old}) : \quad \left(\frac{8}{3} \;\; \frac{2}{3} \;\; \frac{3}{3} \;\; 0 \;\; \frac{1}{3} \;\; 0 \;\; 0\right)$$

$$: \quad \left(\frac{8}{3} \;\; \frac{2}{3} \;\; 1 \;\; 0 \;\; \frac{1}{3} \;\; 0 \;\; 0\right)$$

$R_2(\text{New}) \longrightarrow R_2(\text{Old}) - 2R_1(\text{New})$

Now	$R_2(\text{Old})$	:	15	3	2	4	0	1	0
and	$2R_1(\text{New})$	:	$\frac{16}{3}$	$\frac{4}{3}$	2	0	$\frac{2}{3}$	0	0
	(Subtract)		–	–	–	–	–	–	–
			$\frac{29}{3}$	$\frac{5}{3}$	0	4	$\frac{-2}{3}$	1	0

$R_3(\text{New}) \longrightarrow R_3(\text{Old}) - 2R_1(\text{New})$

Now	$R_3(\text{Old})$:		10	0	2	5	0	0	1
and	$2R_1(\text{New})$	:	$\frac{16}{3}$	$\frac{4}{3}$	2	0	$\frac{2}{3}$	0	0
	(Subtract)		–	–	–	–	–	–	–
			$\frac{14}{3}$	$\frac{-4}{3}$	0	5	$\frac{-2}{3}$	0	1

Calculations for $Z_j - C_j$

$$Z_1 - C_1 = 5 \cdot \frac{2}{3} + 0 \cdot \frac{5}{3} + 0\left(\frac{-4}{5}\right) - 3 = \frac{1}{3}$$

$$Z_2 - C_2 = 5.1 + 0.0 + 0.0 - 5 = 0$$

$$Z_3 - C_3 = 5.0 + 0.4 + 0.5 - 4 = -4$$

$$Z_4 - C_4 = 5 \cdot \frac{1}{3} + 0 \cdot \left(\frac{-2}{3}\right) + 0\left(\frac{-2}{3}\right) - 0 = \frac{5}{3}$$

$$Z_5 - C_5 = 0 + 0 + 0 - 0 = 0$$

$$Z_6 - C_6 = 0 + 0 + 0 - 0 = 0$$

Since $Z_3 - C_3 = -4$ (<0), is most negative, so III column become the pivot column and x_3 enters the basis.

Locate the minimum ratio by

$$\min_i \left[\frac{x_{Br}}{x_{rk}},\quad x_{ik} > 0\right]$$

$$\Rightarrow \qquad \min\left[-, \frac{\frac{29}{3}}{4}, \frac{\frac{14}{3}}{5}\right] \qquad (\because 0 \text{ violates the condition } x_{ik} > 0, \text{ so it is not used})$$

$$\Rightarrow \qquad \min\left[-, \frac{29}{12}, \frac{14}{15}\right] = \frac{14}{15}$$

Since minimum ratio occurs for 3rd row, it becomes the pivot row and so the variable (slack) s_3 leaves the basis. In order to make the pivot element 1, divide it by 5, and for the new values of elements for remaining rows, elementary row operations are performed in iteration–2.

Iteration–2

			3	5	4	0	0	0	
C_B	Y_B	X_B	x_1	x_2	x_3	s_1	s_2	s_3	Min. Ratio
5	x_2	$\frac{8}{3}$	$\frac{2}{3}$	1	0	$\frac{1}{3}$	0	0	$\frac{15}{2}$
0	s_2	$\frac{89}{15}$	$\frac{41}{15}$	0	0	$\frac{-2}{15}$	1	$\frac{-4}{5}$	0 ←
4	x_3	$\frac{14}{15}$	$\frac{-4}{15}$	0	1	$\frac{-2}{15}$	0	$\frac{1}{5}$	–
$Z_j - C_j$		$\frac{256}{15}$	$\frac{-11}{15}$	0	0	$\frac{17}{15}$	0	$\frac{4}{5}$	

Calculations for Row Operations

$$R_2(\text{New}) \longrightarrow \frac{R_1(\text{Old})}{5}$$

$$\left(\frac{14}{3}\cdot\frac{1}{5} \quad \frac{-4}{3}\cdot\frac{1}{5} \quad 0\cdot\frac{1}{5} \quad 5\cdot\frac{1}{5} \quad \frac{-2}{3}\cdot\frac{1}{5} \quad 0\cdot\frac{1}{5} \quad 1\cdot\frac{1}{5}\right)$$

$$\left(\frac{14}{15} \quad \frac{-4}{15} \quad 0 \quad 1 \quad \frac{-2}{15} \quad 0 \quad \frac{1}{5}\right)$$

$R_1(\text{New}) \longrightarrow R_1(\text{Old}) - 0.R_1(\text{New})$

Now	$R_1(\text{Old})$	:	$\frac{8}{3}$	$\frac{2}{3}$	1	0	$\frac{1}{3}$	0	0
and	$0.R_1(\text{New})$ (Subtract)	:	0 –	0 –	0 –	0 –	0 –	0 –	0 –
⇒	$R_1(\text{New})$		$\frac{8}{3}$	$\frac{2}{3}$	1	0	$\frac{1}{3}$	0	0

$R_2(\text{New}) \longrightarrow R_2(\text{Old}) - 4R_1(\text{New})$

Now	R_2(Old)	:	$\frac{29}{3}$	$\frac{5}{3}$	0	4	$\frac{-2}{3}$	1	0
and	$4R_1$(New)	:	$\frac{56}{15}$	$\frac{-16}{15}$	0	4	$\frac{-8}{15}$	0	$\frac{4}{5}$
	(Subtract)		–	+	–	–	+	–	–
⇒	R_2(New)	:	$\frac{89}{15}$	$\frac{41}{15}$	0	0	$\frac{-2}{15}$	1	$\frac{-4}{5}$

Calculations for $Z_j - C_j$

$$Z_1 - C_1 = 5\cdot\frac{2}{3} + 0\cdot\frac{41}{15} + 4\left(\frac{-4}{15}\right) - 3 = \frac{10}{3} - \frac{16}{15} - 3 = \frac{34}{15} - 3 = \frac{-11}{15}$$

$$Z_2 - C_2 = 5\cdot 1 + 0\cdot 0 + 4\cdot 0 - 5 = 0$$

$$Z_3 - C_3 = 5\cdot 0 + 0\cdot 0 + 4\cdot 1 - 4 = 0$$

$$Z_4 - C_4 = 5\cdot\frac{1}{3} + 0\cdot\left(\frac{-2}{15}\right) + 4\left(\frac{-2}{15}\right) - 0 = \frac{5}{3} - \frac{8}{15} = \frac{17}{15}$$

$$Z_5 - C_5 = 5.0 + 0.1 + 4.0 - 0 = 0$$

$$Z_6 - C_6 = 5.0 + 0.\left(\frac{-4}{5}\right) + 4\left(\frac{1}{5}\right) = \frac{4}{5}$$

Since all $Z_j - C_j$ are positive except $Z_1 - C_1$. Thus the current solution can be further improved.

Here first column becomes the pivot column and x_1 enters the basis.

Then by using

$$\min_i \left[\frac{x_{Br}}{x_{rk}}, \quad x_{ik} > 0\right]$$

$$\min\left[\frac{5}{\frac{2}{3}}, \frac{0}{\frac{41}{15}}, -\right] \qquad \left(\because \frac{-4}{15} \text{ violates the condition}\right)$$

$$\min\left[\frac{15}{2}, 0, -\right] = 0$$

Thus, II row becomes the pivot row and so s_2 leaves the basis. $\left(\frac{41}{15}\right)$ is the pivot element.

			3	5	4	0	0	0
C_B	Y_B	X_B	x_1	x_2	x_3	s_1	s_2	s_3
5	x_2	$\frac{50}{41}$	0	1	0	$\frac{15}{41}$	$\frac{-10}{41}$	$\frac{8}{41}$
3	x_1	$\frac{89}{41}$	1	0	0	$\frac{-2}{41}$	$\frac{15}{41}$	$\frac{-12}{41}$
4	x_3	$\frac{62}{41}$	0	0	1	$\frac{-6}{41}$	$\frac{4}{41}$	$\frac{5}{41}$
$Z_j - C_j$			0	0	0	$\frac{45}{41}$	$\frac{11}{41}$	$\frac{24}{41}$

Calculations for Row Operations

$$R_2(\text{New}) \longrightarrow \frac{R_2(\text{Old})}{41/15}$$

$$R_2(\text{Old}) \times \frac{15}{41}$$

$$\left(\frac{89}{15} \div \frac{41}{15} \quad \frac{41}{15}\cdot\frac{15}{41} \quad 0\cdot\frac{15}{41} \quad 0\cdot\frac{15}{41} \quad \frac{-2}{15}\cdot\frac{15}{41} \quad 1\cdot\frac{15}{41} \quad \frac{-4}{5}\cdot\frac{15}{41}\right)$$

Thus, $R_2(\text{New}) \; : \; \left(\frac{89}{41} \quad 1 \quad 0 \quad 0 \quad \frac{-2}{41} \quad \frac{15}{41} \quad \frac{-12}{41}\right)$

$$R_1(\text{New}) \longrightarrow R_1(\text{Old}) - \frac{2}{3}R_2(\text{New})$$

Now	$R_1(\text{Old})$	:	$\frac{8}{3}$	$\frac{2}{3}$	1	0	$\frac{1}{3}$	0	0
and	$\frac{2}{3}R_2(\text{New})$	:	$\frac{178}{123}$	$\frac{2}{3}$	0	0	$\frac{-4}{123}$	$\frac{30}{123}$	$\frac{-24}{123}$
	(Subtract)		–	–	–	–	+	–	+
$\therefore$	$R_1(\text{New})$	:	$\frac{150}{123}$	0	1	0	$\frac{45}{123}$	$-\frac{30}{123}$	$\frac{24}{123}$
		:	$\frac{50}{41}$	0	1	0	$\frac{15}{41}$	$-\frac{10}{41}$	$\frac{8}{41}$

$$R_3(\text{New}) \longrightarrow R_3(\text{Old}) + \frac{4}{15}R_2(\text{New})$$

Now	R_3(old)	:	$\frac{14}{15}$	$\frac{-4}{15}$	0	1	$\frac{-2}{15}$	0	$\frac{1}{5}$
and	$\frac{4}{15}R_2$(New)	:	$\frac{356}{615}$	$\frac{4}{15}$	0	0	$\frac{-8}{615}$	$\frac{4}{41}$	$\frac{-48}{615}$
	(Add)		+	+	+	+	–	+	+
∴	R_3(New)	:	$\frac{930}{615}$	0	0	1	$\frac{-90}{615}$	$\frac{4}{41}$	$\frac{75}{615}$
		:	$\frac{62}{41}$	0	0	1	$\frac{-6}{41}$	$\frac{4}{41}$	$\frac{5}{41}$

Calculation for $Z_j - C_j$

$$Z_1 - C_1 = 5{\cdot}0 + 3{\cdot}1 + 4{\cdot}0 - 3 = 0$$
$$Z_2 - C_2 = 5{\cdot}1 + 3{\cdot}0 + 4{\cdot}0 - 5 = 0$$
$$Z_3 - C_3 = 5{\cdot}0 + 3{\cdot}0 + 4{\cdot}1 - 4 = 0$$
$$Z_4 - C_4 = 5\cdot\frac{15}{41} + 3\left(\frac{-2}{41}\right) + 4\left(\frac{-6}{41}\right) - 0 = \frac{75}{41} - \frac{6}{41} - \frac{24}{41} = \frac{45}{41}$$
$$Z_5 - C_5 = 5\cdot\left(\frac{-10}{41}\right) + 3\left(\frac{15}{41}\right) + 4\cdot\left(\frac{4}{41}\right) - 0 = \frac{-50}{41} + \frac{45}{16} + \frac{16}{41} = \frac{11}{41}$$
$$Z_6 - C_6 = 5\cdot\frac{8}{41} + 3\left(\frac{-12}{41}\right) + 4\cdot\frac{5}{41} - 0 = \frac{40}{41} - \frac{36}{41} + \frac{20}{41} = \frac{24}{41}$$

and objective function $Z = 5\left(\frac{50}{41}\right) + 3\left(\frac{89}{41}\right) + 4\left(\frac{62}{41}\right) = \frac{250}{41} + \frac{267}{41} + \frac{248}{41} = \frac{765}{41}$

Since all $Z_j - C_j \geq 0$.

Thus, the optimal solution has been attained.

$$Z_{\max} = \frac{765}{41}$$
$$x_1 = \frac{89}{41},\ x_2 = \frac{50}{41}$$
$$x_3 = \frac{62}{41}$$

Formulation of LPP and its Solution

Example 8. *A furniture manufacturer produces chairs and tables. He has two different types of wood used, and labours for the construction of chairs and tables. Each table is constructed by using 5 board-feet of teak, 2 board-feet Sheesham and 4 labour-hours, while each chair is constructed by using 2 board-feet of teak, 3 board of sheesham and 2 labour-hour. The manufacturer makes a profit of ₹ 12 per table and ₹ 8 per chair, if all the products produced are sold. There are only 150 board-feet of teak and 100* *board-feet of sheesham and 80 labour-hours are available for their construction. How many tables and chairs can be produced so as to maximize the overall profit.*

Solution. Formulation of LPP

Let x_1 : Number of tables be produced

and x_2 : Number of chairs be produced.

Formulation of Objective Function

Since profit on selling 1 table is ₹ 12

Hence, profit on selling x_1 table is ₹ $12x_1$

Profit on selling 1 chair is ₹ 8

Hence, profit on selling x_2 chair is ₹ $8x_2$

∴ The objective function can be written as

$$12x_1 + 8x_2$$

Formulation of Constraints

Since each table requires 5 board-feet and each chair requires 2 board-feet of teak. However, only 150 board-feet of teak wood is available.

Thus, $5x_1 + 2x_2 \leq 150$

and each table requires 2 board-feet and each chair requires 3 board-feet of sheesham and only 100 board-feet of sheesham is available.

Thus, $2x_1 + 3x_2 \leq 100$.

Similarly the labour hour constraints can be written as:

$$4x_1 + 2x_2 \leq 80$$

(only 80 labour-hours are available)

Since the problem is to maximize the profit, so the problem can be formulated as LPP as follows:

$$\text{Maximize } Z = 12x_1 + 8x_2$$

$$\text{Subject to } 5x_1 + 2x_2 \leq 150$$

$$2x_1 + 3x_2 \leq 100$$

$$4x_1 + 2x_2 \leq 80$$

$$x_1, x_2 \geq 0.$$

Solution of LPP using Simplex Method

Introducing slack variables s_1, s_2 and s_3.

∴ Maximize $Z = 12x_1 + 8x_2 + 0.s_1 + 0.s_2 + 0.s_3$

Subject to

$$5x_1 + 2x_2 + s_1 = 150$$

$$2x_1 + 3x_2 + s_2 = 100$$

$$4x_1 + 2x_2 + s_3 = 80$$

$$x_1, x_2, x_3, s_1, s_2, s_3 \geq 0.$$

Iteration–0 By putting $x_1 = x_2 = x_3 = 0$, we get $s_1 = 150, s_2 = 100, s_3 = 80$

	C_j		12	8	0	0	0	
C_B	Y_B	X_B	x_1	x_2	s_1	s_2	s_3	Min. Ratio
0	s_1	150	5	2	1	0	0	$\frac{150}{5} = 30$
0	s_2	100	2	3	0	1	0	$\frac{100}{2} = 50$
0	s_3	80	4*	2	0	0	1	$\frac{80}{4} = 20$
	$Z_j - C_j$	0	–12	–8	0	0	0	

Calculations for $Z_j - C_j$

$$Z_1 - C_1 = (0.5 + 0.2 + 0.4) - 12 = -12$$
$$Z_2 - C_2 = (0.2 + 0.3 + 0.2) - 8 = -8$$

Since $Z_1 - C_1$ is most negative. Hence I column becomes the pivot column and thus x_1 enters the basis.

Now pivot row is determined by

$$\min_i \left[\frac{x_{Br}}{x_{rk}}, x_{ik} > 0 \right]$$

$$\min \left[\frac{150}{5}, \frac{100}{2}, \frac{80}{4}, \right] = \min [30, \ 50, \ 20] = 20$$

Since III has the minimum ratio, thus III row becomes the pivot row and so 4 becomes the pivot element.

In order to make the pivot element 1 (unity) and to compute the new values of the elements of the remaining rows, elementary operations are performed in iteration–1

Iteration–1

			12	8	0	0	0		
C_B	Y_B	X_B	x_1	x_2	s_1	s_2	s_3	Min. Ratio	
0	s_1	50	0	$\frac{-1}{2}$	1	0	$\frac{-5}{4}$		
0	s_2	60	0	2*	0	1	$\frac{-1}{2}$	$\frac{60}{2}$	←
12	x_1	20	1	$\frac{1}{2}$	0	0	$\frac{1}{4}$	$\frac{20}{1/2}$	
	$Z_j - C_j$	240	0	–2	0	0			
				↑					

Calculations for Row Operations

$$R_3(\text{New}) \longrightarrow \frac{R_3}{4}(\text{Old})$$

i.e., $$\left(\frac{80}{4}\ \frac{4}{4}\ \frac{2}{9}\ \frac{0}{4}\ \frac{0}{4}\ \frac{1}{4}\right)$$

$$R_3(\text{New}) : \left(20\ 1\ \frac{1}{2}\ 0\ 0\ \frac{1}{4}\right)$$

$R_1(\text{New}) \longrightarrow R_1(\text{Old}) - 5R_3(\text{New})$

Now	R_1(old)	:	150	5	2	1	0	0
and	$5R_3$(New)	:	100	5	$\frac{5}{2}$	0	0	$\frac{5}{4}$
	(Subtract)		–	–	–	–	–	–
∴	R_1(New)	:	50	0	$\frac{-1}{2}$	1	0	$\frac{-5}{4}$

$R_2(\text{New}) \longrightarrow R_2(\text{Old}) - 2R_3(\text{New})$

Now	R_2(Old)	:	100	2	3	0	1	0
and	$2R_3$(New)	:	40	2	1	0	0	$\frac{1}{2}$
	(Subtract)		–	–	–	–	–	–
∴	R_2(New)	:	60	0	2	0	1	$\frac{-1}{2}$

Calculations for $Z_j - C_j$

$$Z_1 - C_1 = 0.0 + 0.0 + 12.1 - 12 = 0$$

$$Z_2 - C_2 = 0\cdot\left(\frac{-1}{2}\right) + 0\cdot 2 + 12\cdot\frac{1}{2} - 8 = -2^*$$

$$Z_3 - C_3 = 0.1 + 0.0 + 12.0 - 0 = 0$$

$$Z_4 - C_4 = 0.0 + 0.1 + 12.0 - 0 = 0$$

$$Z_5 - C_5 = 0\cdot\left(\frac{-5}{4}\right) + 0\left(\frac{-1}{2}\right) + 12\left(\frac{1}{4}\right) - 0 = 3$$

Since $Z_2 - C_2$ is most negative.

So II column becomes the pivot column and thus x_2 enters the basis.

And the pivot row is located as

$$\min_i\left[\frac{x_{Br}}{x_{rk}},\ x_{ik} > 0\right]$$

$$\min\left[-, \frac{60}{2}, \frac{20}{1/2}\right] \quad \left(\text{as } \frac{-1}{2} \text{ violates the inequality } x_{ik} > 0, \text{ so it is left unused}\right)$$

$$\min[-, 30, 40]$$
$$= 30$$

Thus 2nd row becomes the pivot row and 2 becomes the pivot element (marked with *).

Iteration–2

			12	8	0	0	0
C_B	Y_B	X_B	x_1	x_2	s_1	s_2	s_3
0	s_1	65	0	0	1	$\frac{1}{4}$	$\frac{-11}{8}$
8	x_2	30	0	1	0	$\frac{1}{2}$	$\frac{-1}{4}$
12	x_1	5	1	0	0	$\frac{-1}{4}$	$\frac{3}{8}$
	$Z_j - C_j$	300	0	0	0	1	$\frac{5}{2}$

Calculations for Row Operations

$$R_2(\text{New}) \longrightarrow \frac{R_2(\text{Old})}{2}$$

i.e.,
$$\left(\frac{60}{2} \quad \frac{0}{2} \quad \frac{2}{2} \quad \frac{0}{2} \quad \frac{1}{2} \quad \frac{\frac{-1}{2}}{2}\right)$$

$$\therefore \quad R_2(\text{New}) : \left(30 \quad 0 \quad 1 \quad 0 \quad \frac{1}{2} \quad \frac{-1}{4}\right)$$

$$R_1(\text{New}) \rightarrow R_1(\text{Old}) + \frac{1}{2} R_2(\text{New})$$

	$R_1(\text{Old})$:	50	0	$-\frac{1}{2}$	1	0	$\frac{-5}{4}$
	$\frac{1}{2} R_2(\text{New})$:	15	0	$\frac{1}{2}$	0	$\frac{1}{4}$	$\frac{-1}{8}$
	(Add)	+	+	+	+	+	+
∴	$R_1(\text{New})$:	65	0	0	1	$\frac{1}{4}$	$\frac{-11}{8}$

$$R_3(\text{New}) \rightarrow R_2(\text{Old}) - \frac{1}{2} R_2(\text{New})$$

$R_3(\text{Old})$:	20	1	$\frac{1}{2}$	0	0	$\frac{1}{4}$

$\frac{1}{2}R_2$(New):	15	0	$\frac{1}{2}$	0	$\frac{1}{4}$	$\frac{-1}{8}$
(Subtract)	–	–	–	–	–	+
∴ R_3(New) :	5	1	0	0	$\frac{-1}{4}$	$\frac{3}{8}$

Calculations for $Z_j - C_j$

$$Z_1 - C_1 = 0.0 + 8.0 + 12.1 - 12 = 0$$
$$Z_2 - C_2 = 0.0 + 8.1 + 12.0 - 8 = 0$$
$$Z_3 - C_3 = 0.1 + 8.0 + 12.0 - 0 = 0$$
$$Z_4 - C_4 = 0 \cdot \frac{1}{4} + 8 \cdot \frac{1}{2} + 12\left(\frac{-1}{4}\right) - 0 = 4 - 3 = 1$$
$$Z_5 - C_5 = 0 \cdot \left(\frac{-11}{8}\right) + 8 \cdot \left(\frac{-1}{4}\right) + 12\left(\frac{3}{8}\right) - 0 = \frac{5}{2}$$

Objective function $Z = 0.65 + 8.30 + 12.5 = 0 + 240 + 60 = 300$

Since all $Z_j - C_j \geq 0$.

Thus an optimum solution has been attained

$$Z_{max} = 300$$
$$x_1 = 5$$
$$x_2 = 30$$

Example 9. *A manufacturer produces three different types of automobile spareparts X, Y and Z, which are to be processed on three different machines M_1, M_2 and M_3. Sparepart X requires M_1 machine for 2 hours, M_3 machine for 3 hours, while sparepart Y requires M_1 machine for 3 hours, M_2 machine for 2 hours and M_3 machine for 2 hours Sparepart Z requires M_2 machine for 5 hours and M_3 machine for 4 hour M_1 machine, M_2 machine and M_3 machine are available for 8 hours, 10 hours and 15 hours respectively per day. The profits from selling these spareparts are respectively ₹ 3.00, ₹ 5.00 and ₹ 4.00 per piece. Find the daily production of each type of sparepart so as to maximize the profit.*

Solution. Formulation of LPP

Let x_1 : Sparepart X is produced.

x_2 : Sparepart Y is produced.

x_3 : Sparepart Z is produced.

Thus the above problem can be formulated as a LPP as

Maximze $Z = 3x_1 + 5x_2 + 4x_3$

Subject to Constraints for

$2x_1 + 3x_2 + 0.x_3 \leq 8$ (Machine M_1)

$0x_1 + 2x_2 + 5x_3 \leq 10$ (Machine M_2)

$3x_1 + 2x_2 + 4x_3 \leq 15$ (Machine M_3)

$x_1, x_2, x_3 \geq 0$

Introducing slack variables $s_1 \geq 0$, $s_2 \geq 0$ and $s_3 \geq 0$

Thus the LPP can be rewritten as:

Maximize $Z = 3x_1 + 5x_2 + 4x_3$

Subject to

$$2x_1 + 3x_2 + 0.x_3 + s_1 = 8$$
$$0.x_1 + 2x_2 + 5x_3 + s_2 = 10$$
$$3x_1 + 2x_2 + 4x_3 + s_3 = 15$$
$$x_1, x_2, x_3, s_1, s_2, s_3 \geq 0$$

If $x_1 = x_2 = x_3$, then $s_1 = 8$, $s_2 = 10$ and $s_3 = 15$

Iteration–0

	$C_j \rightarrow$		3	5	4	0	0	0	
C_B	Y_B	X_B	x_1	x_2	x_3	s_1	s_2	s_3	Minimum Ratio
0	s_1	8	2	3*	0	1	0	0	$\frac{8}{3}$
0	s_2	10	0	2	5	0	1	0	$\frac{10}{2}$
0	s_3	15	3	2	4	0	0	1	$\frac{15}{2}$
	$Z_j - C_j$	0	–3	–5	–4	0	0	0	
				↑					

Calculations for $Z_j - C_j = C_B X_B - C_j$

$$Z_1 - C_1 = 0.2 + 0.0 + 0.3 - 3 = -3$$
$$Z_2 - C_2 = 0.3 + 0.2 + 0.2 - 5 = -5^*$$
$$Z_3 - C_3 = 0.0 + 0.5 + 0.4 - 4 = -4$$

Since $Z_2 - C_2$ is most negative, thus II column is the pivot column and x_2 enters the basis.

Now,
$$= \min_i \left[\frac{x_{Br}}{x_{rk}}, \quad x_{ik} > 0\right]$$
$$= \min\left[\frac{8}{3}, \frac{10}{2}, \frac{15}{2}\right] = \frac{8}{3}$$

Thus I row becomes the pivot row and 3 becomes the pivot element. To make the pivot element (as per algorithm) equal to 1, divide the whole I row by 3 and the new values of the elements of remaining rows are computed by performing elementary row operation as done in iteration–1.

Iteration–1

			3	5	4	0	0	0
C_B	Y_B	X_B	x_1	x_2	x_3	s_1	s_2	s_3
5	x_2	$\frac{8}{3}$	$\frac{2}{3}$	1	0	$\frac{1}{3}$	0	0
0	s_2	$\frac{14}{3}$	$\frac{-4}{3}$	0	5*	$\frac{-2}{3}$	1	0
0	s_3	$\frac{29}{3}$	$\frac{5}{3}$	0	4	$\frac{-2}{3}$	0	1
$Z_j - C_j$		$\frac{40}{3}$	$\frac{1}{3}$	0	–4	$\frac{5}{3}$	0	0

Calculations for Row Operations

$$R_1(\text{New}) \longrightarrow \frac{R_1}{3}(\text{Old})$$

$$i.e., \left(\frac{8}{3} \quad \frac{2}{3} \quad \frac{3}{3} \quad \frac{0}{3} \quad \frac{1}{3} \quad \frac{0}{3} \quad \frac{0}{3}\right)$$

$$\therefore \quad R_1(\text{New}) : \left(\frac{8}{3} \quad \frac{2}{3} \quad 1 \quad 0 \quad \frac{1}{3} \quad 0 \quad 0\right)$$

$R_2(\text{New}) \rightarrow R_2(\text{Old}) - 2R_1(\text{New})$

Now	$R_2(\text{Old})$	:	10	0	2	5	0	1	0
	$2R_1(\text{New})$	:	$\frac{16}{3}$	$\frac{4}{3}$	2	0	$\frac{2}{3}$	0	0
	(Subtract)		–	–	–	–	–	–	–
∴	$R_2(\text{New})$	:	$\frac{14}{3}$	$\frac{-4}{3}$	0	5	$\frac{-2}{3}$	1	0

$R_3(\text{New}) \rightarrow R_3(\text{Old}) - 2R_1(\text{New})$

Now	$R_3(\text{Old})$	:	15	3	2	4	0	0	1
and	$2R_1(\text{New})$	:	$\frac{16}{3}$	$\frac{4}{3}$	2	0	$\frac{2}{3}$	0	0
	(Subtract)		–	–	–	–	–	–	–
∴	$R_3(\text{New})$	:	$\frac{29}{3}$	$\frac{5}{3}$	0	4	$\frac{-2}{3}$	0	1

Calculations of $Z_j - C_j$

$$Z_1 - C_1 = 5 \cdot \frac{2}{3} + 0 \cdot \left(\frac{-4}{3}\right) + 0 \cdot \frac{5}{3} - 3 = \frac{10}{3} - 3 = \frac{1}{3}$$

$$Z_2 - C_2 = 5.1 + 0.0 + 0.0 - 5 = 0$$
$$Z_3 - C_3 = 5.0 + 0.5 + 0.4 - 4 = -4^*$$
$$Z_4 - C_4 = 5 \cdot \frac{1}{3} + 0 \cdot \left(\frac{-2}{3}\right) + 0 \cdot \left(\frac{-2}{3}\right) - 0 = \frac{5}{3}$$

Since $Z_3 - C_3$ is most negative, the current solution can be further improved. Thus III column becomes the pivot column. So x_3 enters the basis.

Now $$\min_i \left[\frac{x_{Br}}{x_{rk}},\ x_{ik} > 0\right]$$

$$\min\left[-,\ \frac{\frac{14}{3}}{5},\ \frac{\frac{29}{3}}{4}\right] \quad \text{(As 0 does not satisfy the condition } r_{ik} > 0)$$

$$\min\left[-,\ \frac{14}{15}\ \frac{29}{12}\right]$$

$$= \frac{14}{15}$$

So s_2 leaves the basis as by minimum ratio II row becomes the pivot row and 5 becomes the pivot element. In order to make the pivot element 1 and to compute the new values of the remaining columns, perform the elementary row operations as done in next iteration.

Iteration–2

		C_j	3	5	4	0	0	0		
C_B	Y_B	X_B	x_1	x_2	x_3	s_1	s_2	s_3	Min Ratio	
5	x_2	$\frac{8}{3}$	$\frac{2}{3}$	1	0	$\frac{1}{3}$	0	0	$\frac{8}{3}\Big/\frac{2}{3}$	
4	x_3	$\frac{14}{15}$	$\frac{-4}{15}$	0	1	$\frac{-2}{15}$	$\frac{1}{5}$	0	–	
0	s_3	$\frac{89}{15}$	$\frac{41}{15}^*$	0	0	$\frac{-2}{15}$	$\frac{-4}{5}$	1	$\frac{89}{15}\Big/\frac{41}{15}$	←
	$Z_j - C_j$	$\frac{256}{15}$	$-\frac{11}{15}$	0	0	$\frac{17}{15}$	$\frac{4}{5}$	0		

Calculations for Row Operations

$$R_2(\text{New}) \rightarrow \frac{R_2(\text{Old})}{5}$$

i.e., $$\left(\frac{\frac{14}{3}}{5}\ \frac{\frac{-4}{3}}{4}\ \frac{0}{5}\ \frac{5}{5}\ \frac{\frac{-2}{3}}{5}\ \frac{1}{5}\ \frac{0}{5}\right)$$

$$i.e., \left(\frac{14}{15} \quad \frac{-4}{15} \quad 0 \quad 1 \quad \frac{-2}{15} \quad \frac{1}{5} \quad 0\right)$$

R_1(New) $\rightarrow$ R_1(Old) $-$ 0. R_2(New)

i.e. R_1(New) $\rightarrow$ R_1(Old)

$$\left(\frac{8}{3} \quad \frac{2}{3} \quad 1 \quad 0 \quad \frac{1}{3} \quad 0 \quad 0\right)$$

R_3(New) $\rightarrow$ R_3(Old) $-$ 4R_2(New)

Now	R_3(old)	:	$\frac{29}{3}$	$\frac{5}{3}$	0	4	$\frac{-2}{3}$	0	1
and	4R_2(New)	:	$\frac{56}{15}$	$\frac{-16}{13}$	0	4	$\frac{-8}{15}$	$\frac{4}{5}$	0
	(Subtract)		$-$	+	$-$	$-$	+	$-$	$-$
$\therefore$	R_3(New)	:	$\frac{89}{15}$	$\frac{41}{15}$	0	0	$\frac{-2}{15}$	$\frac{-4}{5}$	1

Calculations for $Z_j - C_j$

$$Z_1 - C_1 = 5\cdot\frac{2}{3} + 4\left(\frac{-4}{15}\right) + 0\left(\frac{41}{15}\right) - 3$$

$$= \frac{10}{3} - \frac{16}{15} - 3 = \frac{50 - 16 - 45}{15} = \frac{-11}{15}$$

$$Z_2 - C_2 = 5.1 + 4.0 + 0.0 - 5 = 0$$

$$Z_3 - C_3 = 5.0 + 4.1 + 0.0 - 4 = 0$$

$$Z_4 - C_4 = 5\cdot\frac{1}{3} + 4\left(\frac{-2}{15}\right) + 0\left(\frac{-2}{15}\right) - 0 = \frac{5}{3} - \frac{8}{15} = \frac{17}{15}$$

$$Z_5 - C_5 = 5\cdot 0 + 4\cdot\frac{1}{5} + 0\left(\frac{-4}{5}\right) - 0 = \frac{4}{5}$$

$$Z_6 - C_6 = 5.0 + 4.0 + 0.1 - 0 = 0$$

Since $Z_1 - C_1 < 0$, therefore the current solution can be further improved as I column becomes the pivot column and x_1 enters the basis.

Now
$$\min_i \left[\frac{x_{Br}}{x_{rk}}, \quad x_{ik} > 0\right]$$

$$\min\left[\frac{8/3}{2/3}, \quad -, \quad \frac{89/15}{41/15}\right]$$

$$\min\left[4, \quad -, \quad \frac{89}{41}\right] = \frac{89}{41}$$

Since minimum ratio corresponds to row R_3, thus s_3 leaves the basis. The elementary operations are done in next iteration.

Iteration–3

	C_j		3	5	4	0	0	0
C_B	Y_B	X_B	x_1	x_2	x_3	s_1	s_2	s_3
5	x_2	$\frac{50}{41}$	0	1	0	$\frac{15}{41}$	$\frac{8}{41}$	$\frac{-10}{41}$
4	x_3	$\frac{62}{41}$	0	0	1	$\frac{-6}{41}$	$\frac{5}{41}$	$\frac{4}{41}$
3	x_1	$\frac{89}{41}$	1	0	0	$\frac{-2}{41}$	$\frac{-12}{41}$	$\frac{15}{41}$
	$Z_j - C_j$	$\frac{765}{41}$	0	0	0	$\frac{45}{41}$	$\frac{24}{41}$	$\frac{11}{41}$

Since all $Z_j - C_j \geq 0$

$\therefore$ the optimum solution has been attained.

$$Z_{max} = \frac{765}{41}$$

$$x_1 = \frac{89}{41}$$

$$x_2 = \frac{50}{41}$$

$$x_3 = \frac{62}{41}$$

Example 10. *Minimize* $f = 8x_1 - 2x_2$

Subject to $-4x_1 + 2x_2 \leq 1$

$5x_1 - 4x_2 \leq 3$

$x_1, x_2 \geq 0$

Solution. Since the given LPP is of minimization, convert it into maximization problem by

$$\text{Minimum } Z = -\text{Maximum } (-Z)$$

i.e., $$Z = -8x_1 + 2x_2$$

Since all the b_i's are positive in the right hand side. Thus introducing slack variables s_1 and s_2, we can rewrite the LPP as follows:

$$\text{Maximize } Z = -8x_1 + 2x_2 + 0.s_1 + 0.s_2$$

Subject to $-4x_1 + 2x_2 + s_1 = 1$

$5x_1 - 4x_2 + s_2 = 3$

$x_1, x_2, s_1, s_2 \geq 0$

If we put $x_1 = x_2 = 0$, the initial basic feasible solution can be obtained as $s_1 = 1$ and $s_2 = 3$.

Iteration–0

C_B	Y_B	X_B	x_1	x_2	s_1	s_2	Minimum Ratio
$C_j \rightarrow$			–8	2	0	0	
0	s_1	1	–4	2*	1	0	$\frac{1}{2}$ ←
0	s_2	3	5	–4	0	1	–
$Z_j - C_j$		0	8	–2 ↑	0	0	

Iteration–1

C_B	V_B	X_B	x_1	x_2	s_1	s_2
			–8	2	0	0
2	x_2	$\frac{1}{2}$	–2	1	$\frac{1}{2}$	0
0	s_2	5	–3	0	4	1
$Z_j - C_j$		1	4	0	1	0

Since all $Z_j - C_j \geq 0$

$$Z_{max} = 0$$

$$x_1 = 0$$

$$x_2 = \frac{1}{2}$$

Since the given LPP was of minimization.

Thus optimal solution is as:

$$f_{min} = 1$$

$$x_1 = 0 \quad \text{and} \quad x_2 = \frac{1}{2}.$$

Example 11. *Minimize* $f = -x_1 + 2x_2$

Subject to
$$-x_1 + 3x_2 \leq 10$$
$$x_1 + x_2 \leq 6$$
$$x_1 - x_2 \leq 2$$
$$x_1, x_2 \geq 0$$

Solution. Since the given LPP is of minimization, therefore convert into maximization by

Minimum Z = –Maximum (–Z)

i.e., $Z = x_1 - 2x_2$

and since all b_i's in the right hand side are positive.

Thus introducing slack variables are s_1, s_2 and s_3.

The problem can now be re-written as:

$$\text{Maximize } Z = x_1 - 2x_2 + 0.s_1 + 0.s_2 + 0.s_3$$

$$\text{subject to} \quad -x_1 + 3x_2 + s_1 = 10$$
$$x_1 + x_2 + s_2 = 6$$
$$x_1 - x_2 + s_3 = 2$$
$$x_1, x_2, x_3, s_1, s_2, s_3 \geq 0.$$

If $x_1 = x_2 = x_3$, then $s_1 = 10$, $s_2 = 6$, and $s_3 = 2$.

Iteration–0

	$C_j \rightarrow$		1	–2	0	0	0	
C_B	V_B	X_B	x_1	x_2	s_1	s_2	s_3	Minimum Ratio
0	s_1	10	–1	3	1	0	0	
0	s_2	6	1	1	0	1	0	$\frac{6}{1}$
0	s_3	2	1*	–1	0	0	0	$\frac{2}{1}$ ←
	$Z_j - C_j$	0	–1 ↑	2	0	0	0	

Iteration–1

			1	–2	0	0	0
C_B	V_B	X_B	x_1	x_2	s_1	s_2	s_3
0	s_1	12	0	2	1	0	0
0	s_2	4	0	2	0	1	0
1	x_1	2	1	–1	0	0	0
	$Z_j - C_j$	2	0	1	0	0	0

Since all $Z_j - C_j \geq 0$, *i.e.*, Optimum solution has been attained.

Thus, $Z_{\max} = 2$

$x_1 = 1$ and $x_2 = 0$

Hence, $f_{\min} = -2$

$x_1 = 1$

and $x_2 = 0$

2.4 MINIMIZATION PROBLEMS (ALL CONSTRAINTS OF TYPE ≥)

Till now, we have studied the linear programming problems that involved ≤ (inequality) signs. This was the case when the profit was to maximized. Few examples were also solved involving ≤ inequality sign, but of minimization type. So, if the problem is of maximization or minimization, then it is not to worry how to obtain the optimal solution, if the inequality is ≤. But if the inequality is of ≥ sign or = sign, then in such cases, the simplex method is somewhat different.

Consider the following LPP

Maximize or Minimize $Z = C_1x_1 + C_2x_2 + \dots + C_nx_n$

Subject to

$$a_{11}x_1 + a_{12}x_2 + \dots + a_nx_n \geq b_1$$
$$a_{21}x_1 + a_{22}x_2 + \dots + a_{2n}x_n \geq b_2$$
$$\vdots$$
$$a_{m1}x_1 + a_{m2}x_2 + \dots + a_{mn}x_n \geq b_m$$
$$x_1, x_2, x_3, \dots x_n \geq 0.$$

The method is known as **Big *M* method** or **Method of Penalties** as we use surplus (negative slack) variable and artificial variable.

When the constraints are of ≥ type.

i.e., $$\sum_{j=1}^{n} a_{ij}x_j \geq bi \quad x_1 \geq 0$$

Whenever the inequality ≥ are converted into equality sign we add surplus variable.

i.e., $$\sum_{j=1}^{n} a_{ij}x_j - s_j = b_j;\ x_j \geq 0,\ s_j \geq 0$$

If we put $x_j = 0$ $(j = 1, 2, \dots, n)$, then we get an initial solution as

$$-s_i = b_i \text{ or } s_i = -b_i$$

This initial solution is not a feasible solution as it violates the non-negativity condition of surplus variable, *i.e.*, $s_i \geq 0$.

In order to overcome this difficulty, we add artificial variables A_i $(i = 1, 2, \dots, m)$ to get an initial basic feasible solution.

Then the above constraint can be written as.

$$\sum_{j=1}^{n} a_{ij}x_j - s_i + A_i = b_i$$
$$x_j, s_i, A_i \geq 0;\ l = 1, 2, \dots, m$$

The initial basic feasible solution can now be obtained by equating $(n + m)$ variables equal to zero. Thus the new solution to the given LPP will be $A_i = b_i$ $(i = 1, 2, \dots, m)$, which does not constitute a solution to the original system of equations.

To get back to the original problem, artificial variables must be dropped from the optimal solution as these variables are extraneous to the problem. There are the following two methods of solve a linear programming problem that involves artificial variables.

2.5 (A) THE BIG-M METHOD (METHOD OF PENALTY)

This method is used to remove the artificial variables from the basis. In this method, if the objective function Z is to be minimized, then a very large positive or high penalty $(+M)$ is assigned, while $(-M)$ is assigned (a large negative or high negative penalty) for the maximization problem, where $M > 0$.

The following steps are involved for solving the LPP using Big-M method.

Step 1: Express the given LPP in the standard form either by adding slack variables surplus variable or/and artificial variable. If slack and/or surplus variable are added, then assign zero coefficients to both of them, while a very high penalty $+M$ (for minimization) and $-M$ (for maximization) to artificial variables in the objective function of the given LPP.

Step 2: Then the initial basic feasible solution is obtained by assigning zero value to original values.

i.e., $x_j = 0$ for $j = 1, 2, ..., n$.

Step 3: Calculate the net evaluations and check.

(*a*) If all $Z_j - C_j \geq 0$, then the current basic feasible solution is optimal.

(*b*) If for any column K, $Z_k - C_k$ is most negative and all other entries in this column are negative, then the problem has an unbounded solution.

(*c*) If one or more $Z_j - C_j < 0$ (minimization case), then select the variable to enter the basis with the largest negative $Z_j - C_j$ value.

i.e., $Z_k - C_k = \text{Min } (Z_j - C_j, Z_j - C_j < 0)$

Step 4: Determine the pivot row and pivot element as usual (already discussed in simplex algorithm) of the maximization case.

At any iteration of the simplex algorithm any one of the following case may arise.

(*a*) If atleast one artificial variable is present in the basis with positive value and the coefficient of M in each $Z_j - C_j$ ($j = 1, 2, ..., n$) values is negative, then the given LPP has no solution *i.e.*, the current solution is degenerate solution.

(*b*) If atleast one artificial variable is present in the basis with positive value and the coefficient of M in each $Z_j - C_j$ ($j = 1, 2, ..., n$) values is negative, then the given LPP has no optimum basic feasible solution. In this case, the solution is pseudo optimum basic feasible solution.

Example 12. *Solve the following LPP using the Big-M method.*

$$\text{Maximize } Z = 3x_1 + 2x_2$$

Subject to

$$2x_1 + x_2 \leq 2$$
$$3x_1 + 4x_2 \geq 12$$
$$x_1, x_2 \geq 0.$$

Solution. Since first constraint is of $\leq$ type, thus introducing slack variable $s_1 \geq 0$.

But the second constraint involves $\geq$ inequality, so introduce surplus variable $s_2 \geq 0$ and an artificial variable $A_1 \geq 0$. Thus the above LPP can be rewritten after introducing slack variable, surplus variable and artificial variable as:

Maximize $Z = 3x_1 + 2x_2 + 0.s_1 + 0.s_2 - MA_1$

Subject to

$$2x_1 + x_2 + s_1 = 2$$
$$3x_1 + 4x_2 - s_2 + A_1 = 12$$
$$x_1, x_2, s_1, s_2 \geq 0$$
$$A_1 \geq 0.$$

If we put $x_2 = x_1 = 0$,

then, $s_1 = 2$ and $A_1 = 12$

Iteration–0

	$C_j \rightarrow$		3	2	0	0	$-M$	
C_B	Y_B	X_B	x_1	x_2	s_1	s_2	A_1	Minimum Ratio
0	s_1	2	2	1*	1	0	0	$\frac{2}{1}$
$-M$	A_1^*	12	3	4	0	-1	1	$\frac{12}{4}$
	$Z_j - C_j$	$-12M$	$-3M - 3$	$-4M - 2$	0	$+M$	0	

Calculations for $Z_j - C_j$

$$Z_1 - C_1 = 0.2 + (-M) \cdot 3 - 3 = -3M - 3$$
$$Z_2 - C_2 = 0.1 + (-M) \cdot 4 - 2 = -4M - 2$$
$$Z_3 - C_3 = 0.1 + (-M) \cdot 0 - 0 = 0$$
$$Z_4 - C_4 = 0.0 + (-M) \cdot (-1) - 0 = M$$
$$Z_5 - C_5 = 0.0 + (-M) \cdot 1 - M = 0$$

Since $Z_2 - C_2$ is most negative.

Therefore x_2 enters the basis and by minimum ratio $\min\left[\frac{2}{1}, \frac{12}{4}\right] = \min[2, 3] = 2$,

s_1 leaves the basis.

Thus 1 becomes the pivot element.

Iteration–1

			3	2	0	0	$-M$
C_B	Y_B	X_B	x_1	x_2	s_1	s_2	A_1
2	x_2	2	12	1	1	0	0
$-M$	A_1	4	-5	0	-4	-1	1
	$Z_j - C_j$	$-4M + 4$	$5M + 1$	0	$4M + 2$	M	0

Calculations for Row Operations:

$$R_1(\text{New}) = \frac{R_1(\text{Old})}{1}$$

$$R_1(\text{New}) = R_1(\text{Old}) - 4R_1(\text{New})$$

Now	R_2(Old)	:	12	3	4	0	–1	1
and	$4R_1$(New)	:	8	8	4	4	0	0
	(Subtract)		–	–	–	–	–	–
∴	R_2(New)	:	4	–5	0	–4	–1	1

Calculations for $Z_j - C_j$

$$Z_1 - C_1 = 2.2 + (-M) \cdot (-5) - 3 = 5M + 4 - 3 = 5M + 1$$

$$Z_2 - C_2 = 2.1 + (-M) \cdot 0 - 2 = 0$$

$$Z_3 - C_3 = 2.1 + (-M) \cdot (-4) - 0 = 4M + 2$$

$$Z_4 - C_4 = 2.0 + (-M) \cdot (-1) - 0 = M$$

$$Z_5 - C_5 = 2.0 + (-M) \cdot (1) + M = -M + M = 0.$$

Since all the coefficient of M in each $Z_j - C_j$ (in iteration–1) is non-negative and an artificial vector also appears in the basis, but not at zero level.

Thus the given LPP does not have any feasible solution.

Example 13. *Minimize* $F = 12x_1 + 20x_2$

Subject to $6x_1 + 8x_2 \geq 100$

$$7x_1 + 12x_2 \geq 120$$

$$x_1, x_2 \geq 0.$$

Solution. Since the problem is of minimization one, we can convert it into maximization.

Also ≥ sign are there in both the costraints.

Thus introducing surplus variables $s_1 \geq 0$ and $s_2 \geq 0$ and the artificial variables $A_1 \geq 0$ and $A_2 \geq 0$.

Thus the given LPP can now be rewritten as

Maximize $Z = -12x_1 - 20x_2$

Subject to

$$6x_1 + 8x_2 - s_1 + A_1 = 100$$

$$7x_1 + 12x_2 - s_2 + A_2 = 120$$

$$x_1, x_2, s_1, s_2 \geq 0$$

$$A_1, A_2 \geq 0.$$

The initial basic feasible solution is

$$A_1 = 100$$

and $A_2 = 120$

Iteration–0

	$C_j \rightarrow$		-12	-20	0	0	$-M$	$-M$	
C_B	V_B	X_B	x_1	x_2	s_1	s_2	A_1	A_2	Min. Ratio
–M	A_1	100	6	8	–1	0	1	0	$\frac{100}{8}$
–M	A_2	120	7	12*	0	–1	0	1	$\frac{120}{12}$
	$Z_j - C_j$	$-220M$	$-13M + 12$	$-20M + 20$	$+M$	M	0	0	

Calculations of $Z_j - C_j$

$$Z_1 - C_1 = -M.6 + (-M)\cdot 7 + 12 = -1.3M + 12$$
$$Z_2 - C_2 = -M.8 + (-M)\cdot 12 + 20 = -20M + 20^*$$
$$Z_3 - C_3 = -M.(1) + (-M)\cdot(0) - 0 = M$$
$$Z_4 - C_4 = -M\ (0) + (-M)\cdot(-1) - M = M$$
$$Z_5 - C_5 = -M(1) + (-M)\cdot(0) + M = 0$$
$$Z_6 - C_6 = -M(0) + (-M)\cdot(1) + M = 0$$

Since the coefficient of M in $Z_2 - C_2$ is most negative, thus x_2 enters the basis.

$$\min\left[\frac{100}{8}, \frac{120}{12}\right] = \min[125, 12] = 12$$

So artificial variable A_2 leaves the basis.

Iteration–1

			-12	-20	0	0	$-M$	
C_B	Y_B	X_B	x_1	x_2	s_1	s_2	A_1	Min. Ratio
$-M$	A_1	20	$\frac{4}{3}$*	0	–1	$\frac{2}{3}$	1	$\frac{20}{3/4}$ ←
–20	x_2	10	$\frac{7}{12}$	1	0	$\frac{-1}{12}$	0	$\frac{10}{12/7}$
$Z_j - C_j$		$-220M$ –20	$\frac{-4M}{3} + \frac{1}{3}$	0	M	$\frac{-2M}{3} + \frac{5}{3}$	0	

Calculations of Row Operations

$$R_2(\text{New}) \longrightarrow \frac{R_2(\text{Old})}{12}$$

$$R_1(\text{New}) \longrightarrow R_1(\text{Old}) - 8R_2(\text{New})$$

Now	R_1(Old)	:	100	6	8	–1	0	1
and	$8R_2$(New)	:	80	$\frac{14}{3}$	8	0	$\frac{-2}{3}$	0
	(Subtract)		–	–	–	–	+	–
∴	R_1(New)	:	20	$\frac{4}{3}$	0	–1	$\frac{2}{3}$	1

Calculation for $Z_j - C_j$

$$Z_1 - C_1 = -M\cdot\left(\frac{4}{3}\right) + (-20)\cdot\frac{7}{12} + 12 = \frac{-4M}{3} + \frac{1^*}{3}$$

$$Z_2 - C_2 = -M.0 - 20\cdot(1) + 20 = 0$$

$$Z_3 - C_3 = -M\cdot(-1) + (-20).0 - 0 = M$$

$$Z_4 - C_4 = M\cdot\left(\frac{2}{3}\right) - 20\cdot\left(\frac{-1}{12}\right) - 0 = \frac{-2M}{3} + \frac{5}{3}$$

$$Z_5 - C_5 = -M\cdot(1) - 20\cdot(0) + M = 0$$

Since coefficient of M in $Z_1 - C_1$ is most negative. Hence it enters the basis.

Calculations for Minimum Ratio

$$\min_i \left[\frac{20}{\frac{3}{4}}, \frac{10}{\frac{12}{17}}\right] = \min[15, \ 17.14] = 15$$

So, the artificial variable A_1 leaves the basis.

Iteration–2

			–12	–20	0	0
C_B	V_B	X_B	x_1	x_2	s_1	s_2
–12	x_1	15	1	0	$\frac{-3}{4}$	$\frac{-1}{12}$
–20	x_2	$\frac{5}{4}$	0	1	$\frac{7}{48}$	$\frac{-9}{24}$
	$Z_j - C_j$	–205	0	0	$\frac{1}{4}$	$\frac{17}{2}$

Calculations of Row Operations

$$R_1(\text{New}) \to \frac{R_2(\text{Old})}{\frac{4}{3}}$$

or $$\frac{3}{4}R_2(\text{Old})$$

$$i.e., \quad \left(20 \times \frac{3}{4} \quad \frac{4}{3}\cdot\frac{3}{4} \quad 0\cdot\frac{3}{4} \quad -1\cdot\frac{3}{4} \quad \frac{2}{3}\cdot\frac{3}{4}\right)$$

$$R_1(\text{New}) \quad \left(15 \quad 1 \quad 0 \quad \frac{-3}{4} \quad \frac{1}{2}\right)$$

$$R_2(\text{New}) \rightarrow R_2(\text{Old}) - \frac{7}{12} R_1\ (\text{New})$$

Now	R_2(Old)	:	10	$\frac{7}{12}$	1	0	$\frac{-1}{12}$
and	$\frac{7}{12} R_1$(New)	:	$\frac{35}{4}$	$\frac{7}{12}$	0	$\frac{-7}{16}$	$\frac{7}{24}$
	(Subtract)		–	–	–	+	–
∴	R_2 (New)	:	$\frac{5}{4}$	0	1	$\frac{7}{16}$	$\frac{-9}{24}$

Calculations for $Z_j - C_j$

$$Z_1 - C_1 = -12.1 - 20.0 + 12 = 0$$

$$Z_2 - C_2 = -12.0 - 20.1 + 20 = 0$$

$$Z_3 - C_3 = -12\cdot\left(\frac{-3}{4}\right) - 20\cdot\left(\frac{-7}{16}\right) - 0 = 9 - \frac{35}{4} = \frac{1}{4}$$

$$Z_4 - C_4 = -12\cdot\left(\frac{-1}{12}\right) - 20\cdot\left(\frac{-9}{24}\right) - 0 = \frac{7}{12}$$

In iteration–2, all the net evaluations $Z_j - C_j \geq 0$

Thus an optimal solution has been attained

$$\therefore \quad Z_{max} = -205, \quad x_1 = 15, \quad x_2 = \frac{5}{4}$$

But the given LPP was of minimization.

Thus minimum $Z = -(-205) = 205$

$$\therefore \quad Z_{min} = 205, \quad x_1 = 15, \quad x_2 = \frac{5}{4}.$$

Example 14. *A manufacturer produces 200 kg of a mixture consisting of ingredients A and B. The cost of A is ₹ 3 per kg while the cost of B is ₹ 5 per kg. For the mixture to be of little bit good quality, he cannot mix more than 80 kg of A and must mix atleast 60 kg of B. Find the minimum cost of the mixture.*

Solution. Let x_1 : number of kgs of ingredient type A

x_2 : number of kgs of ingriedient type B.

Since the cost of 1 kg of A is ₹ 3

$\therefore$ the cost of x_1 kg of A is ₹ $3x_1$

Since the cost 1 kg of B is ₹ 5

$\therefore$ the cost x_2 kg of B is ₹ $5x_2$

Thus the objective function can be written as

$$C = 3x_1 + 5x_2$$

200 litres of the mixture is produced by A and B ingredients

$$\therefore \quad 200 = x_1 + x_2$$

and not more than 80 kg of ingredient A can be mixed

$$x_1 \leq 80$$

atleast 60 kg of ingredient B must be used.

$$x_2 \geq 60$$

The above problem can be formulated as LPP

Minimize $\quad C = 3x_1 + 5x_2$

subject to

$$x_1 + x_2 = 200$$
$$x_1 \leq 80$$
$$x_2 \geq 60$$
$$x_1, x_2 \geq 0.$$

Change the given LPP into standard form.

$$\therefore \quad \text{Max } Z = -3x_1 - 5x_2$$

Subject to

$$x_1 + x_2 = 200$$
$$x_1 \leq 80$$
$$x_2 \geq 60$$
$$x_1, x_2 \geq 0.$$

Now introducing artificial variable A_1 in constraint one, slack variable s_1 in second constraint and surplus and artificial variable s_2 and A_2 respectively in third constraint.

$$\text{Maximize } Z = -3x_1 - 5x_2 - M.A_1 - M.A_2$$

i.e.,

$$x_1 + x_2 + A_1 = 200$$
$$x_1 + s_1 = 80$$
$$x_2 - s_2 + A_2 = 60$$
$$x_1, x_2, s_1, s_2, A_1, A_2 \geq 0.$$

The initial basic feasible solution is

$$A_1 = 200$$
$$s_1 = 80$$
$$A_2 = 60$$

Iteration–0

	C_j		–3	–5	0	0	–M	–M		
C_B	Y_B	X_B	x_1	x_2	s_1	s_2	A_1	A_2	Minimum Ratio	
–M	A_1	200	1	1	0	0	1	0	200	
0	s_1	80	1	0	1	0	0	0		
–M	A_2	60	0	1*	0	–1	0	1	60	←
	$Z_j - C_j$	–260 M	–M + 3	–2M + 5	0	0	0	0		
				↑						

Iteration–1

			–3	–5	0	0	–M	
C_B	V_B	X_B	x_1	x_2	s_1	s_2	A_1	
–M	A_1	140	1	0	0	1	1	140
0	s_1	80	1*	0	1	0	0	80
–5	x_2	60	0	1	0	–1	0	
	$Z_j - C_j$	+40M – 300	–M – 3	0	0	–M + 5	0	
			↑					

Iteration–2

			–3	–5	0	0	–M
C_B	Y_B	X_B	x_1	x_2	s_1	s_2	A_1
–M	A_1	60	0	0	–1	1*	1
–3	x_1	80	1	0	1	0	0
–5	x_2	60	0	1	0	–1	0
	$Z_j - C_j$	–60M – 540	0	+5	+M + 3	–M + 5	0
						↑	

Iteration–3

			–3	–5	0	0
C_B	Y_B	X_B	x_1	x_2	s_1	s_2
0	S_2	60	0	0	–1	1
– 3	x_1	80	1	0	1	0
– 5	x_2	120	0	1	–1	0
$Z_j - C_j$		–840	0	0	2	0

Since all $Z_j - C_j \geq 0$.

Thus an optimal solution has been attained.

$$\therefore \quad Z_{max} = -840$$
$$x_1 = 80$$
$$x_2 = 120$$

Since the given LPP was of minimization.

Thus Minimum $\quad Z = -(-840) = 840$

Hence Optimum Solution in

$$\therefore \quad Z_{max} = 840$$
$$x_1 = 80$$
$$x_2 = 120.$$

Example 15. *Use penalty (Big M) method to solve the following LPP.*

$$Max\ Z = x_1 + 2x_2 + 3x_3 - x_4$$

Subject to constraints

$$x_1 + 2x_2 + 3x_3 = 15$$
$$2x_1 + x_2 + 5x_3 = 20$$
$$x_1 + 2x_2 + x_3 + x_4 = 10$$
$$x_1, x_2, x_3 \leq 0.$$

Solution. Since the problem is in standard form (maximization) and all the constraints are of equality sign. Thus adding only artificial variables A_1, A_2 and A_3.

Iteration–0

	$C_j \rightarrow$		1	2	3	–1	–M	–M	–M	
C_B	Y_B	X_B	x_1	x_2	x_3	x_4	A_1	A_2	A_3	Minimum Ratio
–M	A_1	15	1	2	3	0	1	0	0	$\frac{15}{3}$
–M	A_2	20	2	1	5*	0	0	1	0	$\frac{20}{5}$ ←
–M	A_3	10	1	2	1	1	0	0	1	$\frac{10}{1}$
	$Z_j - C_j$	–45M	–4M –1	–5M –2	–9M – 3 ↑	–M + 1	0	0	0	

$Z_j - C_j$ are calculated as usual.

Since $Z_3 - C_3 = -3M - 5M - M - 3 = -9M - 3$ is most negative. Hence x_3 enters the basis and the minimum ratio is calculated as.

$$\text{Min.} \left[\frac{15}{3}, \frac{20}{5}, \frac{10}{1}\right] = 4.$$

Here artificial variable leaves the basis and so it is dropped out. Thus 5, becomes the pivot element.

Iteration–1

	C_j		1	2	3	–1	–M	–M	
C_B	Y_B	X_B	x_1	x_2	x_3	x_4	A_1	A_3	Min. Ratio
$-M$	A_1	3	$\frac{-1}{5}$	$\frac{7}{5}$	0	0	1	0	$\frac{3}{7/5}$ ←
3	x_3	4	$\frac{2}{5}$	$\frac{1}{5}$	1	0	0	0	$\frac{4}{1/5}$
$-M$	A_3	6	$\frac{3}{5}$	$\frac{9}{5}$	0	1	0	0	$\frac{6}{9/5}$
$Z_j - C_j$		$-9M + 12$	$-2M/5 + 1/5$	$-2M/5 - 7/5$ ↑	0	$M - 1$	0	M	

Calculations of Row Operations

$$R_2(\text{New}) \longrightarrow \frac{R_2}{5}(\text{Old})$$

i.e.,
$$\left(\frac{20}{5}\ \ \frac{2}{5}\ \ \frac{1}{5}\ \ \frac{5}{5}\ \ \frac{0}{5}\ \ \frac{0}{5}\ \ \frac{1}{5}\right)$$

$$R_2(\text{New}) \quad \left(4\ \ \frac{2}{5}\ \ \frac{1}{5}\ \ 1\ \ 0\ \ 0\ \ \frac{1}{5}\right)$$

$$R_1(\text{New}) \rightarrow R_1(\text{Old}) - 3R_2(\text{New})$$

$$\begin{array}{llcccccccc}
\text{Now} & R_1(\text{Old}) & : & 15 & 1 & 2 & 3 & 0 & 1 & 0 \\
\text{and} & 3R_2(\text{New}) & : & 12 & \frac{6}{5} & \frac{3}{5} & 3 & 0 & 0 & 0 \\
 & (\text{Subtract}) & & - & - & - & - & - & - & - \\
\hline
\therefore & R_2(\text{New}) & : & 3 & \frac{-1}{5} & \frac{7}{5} & 0 & 0 & 1 & 0
\end{array}$$

$$R_3(\text{New}) \longrightarrow R_3(\text{Old}) - R_2(\text{New})$$

$$\begin{array}{llcccccccc}
\text{Now} & R_3(\text{Old}) & : & 10 & 1 & 2 & 1 & 1 & 0 & 0 \\
\text{and} & R_2(\text{New}) & : & 4 & \frac{2}{5} & \frac{1}{5} & 1 & 0 & 0 & 0 \\
 & (\text{Subtract}) & & - & - & - & - & - & - & - \\
\hline
\therefore & R_2(\text{New}) & : & 6 & \frac{3}{5} & \frac{9}{5} & 0 & 1 & 0 & 0
\end{array}$$

Calculations of $Z_j - C_j$

$$Z_1 - C_1 = -M\cdot\left(-\frac{1}{5}\right) + 3\cdot\left(\frac{2}{5}\right) - M\cdot\left(\frac{3}{5}\right) - 1$$

$$= \frac{1}{5}M + \frac{6}{3} - \frac{3}{5}M - 1 = \frac{-2}{3}M + \frac{1}{5}$$

$$Z_2 - C_2 = -M\frac{(-7)}{5} + \frac{3}{5} - M\left(\frac{9}{5}\right) - 2 = \frac{7}{5}M - \frac{9}{5}M - \frac{7}{5} = \frac{-2}{5}M - \frac{7}{5}$$

Similarly we can find the remaining net evaluations.

Since $Z_2 - C_2$ is most negative.

Thus x_2 enters the basis.

$$\therefore \text{ Min.}\left[\frac{3}{7/5}, \frac{4}{1/5}, \frac{6}{9/5}\right] = \text{min.}\left[\frac{3\times5}{7}, 4\times5, \frac{6\times5}{9}\right]$$

$$= \text{min.}\left[\frac{15}{7}, 20, \frac{30}{9}\right] = \frac{15}{7}$$

Now Artificial variable leaves the basis.

Iteration–2

			1	2	3	– 1	– M	
C_B	Y_B	X_B	x_1	x_2	x_3	x_4	A_3	Minimum Ratio
2	x_2	$\frac{15}{7}$	$\frac{-1}{7}$	1	0	0	0	—
3	x_3	$\frac{15}{7}$	$\frac{3}{7}$	0	1	0	0	$\frac{25}{3}$
$-M$	A_3	$\frac{15}{7}$	$\frac{6}{7}$	0	0	0	0	$\frac{15}{6}$ ←
	$Z_j - C_j$	$\frac{-15}{7}M + 15$	$\frac{-6}{7}M$ ↑	0	0	0	0	

Calculations for Row Operations

$$R_1(\text{New}) \longrightarrow \frac{R_1}{7/5}(\text{Old})$$

$$: \frac{5}{7}R_1(\text{Old})$$

$$: \left(3.\frac{5}{7}\ \frac{-1}{5}.\frac{5}{7}\ \frac{7}{5}.\frac{5}{7}\ 0\cdot\frac{5}{7}\ 0\cdot\frac{5}{7}\ 0\cdot\frac{5}{7}\right)$$

$$R_1(\text{New}) : \left(\frac{15}{7}\quad \frac{-1}{7}\quad 1\quad 0\quad 0\quad 0\right)$$

$$R_2(\text{New}) \longrightarrow R_2(\text{Old}) - \frac{1}{5}R_1(\text{New})$$

Now	R_2(Old) :	4	$\frac{2}{5}$	$\frac{1}{5}$	1	0	0
and	$\frac{1}{5}R_1$(New) :	$\frac{3}{7}$	$\frac{-1}{35}$	$\frac{1}{5}$	0	0	0
(Subtract)		–	+	–	–	–	–
∴	R_2(New) :	$\frac{25}{7}$	$\frac{3}{7}$	0	1	0	0

$$R_3(\text{New}) \longrightarrow R_3(\text{Old}) - \frac{9}{5}R_1(\text{New})$$

Now	R_3(Old) :	6	$\frac{3}{5}$	$\frac{2}{5}$	0	1	0
and	$\frac{9}{5}R_1$(New) :	$\frac{27}{7}$	$\frac{-9}{35}$	$\frac{9}{5}$	0	0	0
	(Subtract)	–	+	–	–	–	–
∴	R_3(New) :	$\frac{15}{7}$	$\frac{6}{7}$	0	0	1	0

Calculations of $Z_j - C_j$

$$Z_1 - C_1 = 2\cdot\left(\frac{-1}{7}\right) + 3\cdot\left(\frac{3}{7}\right) + (-M)\cdot\left(\frac{6}{7}\right) - 1 = \frac{-6}{7}M - \frac{2}{7} + \frac{9}{7} - 1 = \frac{-6}{7}M$$

$$Z_2 - C_2 = 2.1 + 3.0 + (-M)\cdot 0 - 2 = 0$$

$$Z_3 - C_3 = 0 + 3 + 0 - 3 = 0$$

$$Z_4 - C_4 = 0 - 0 = 0$$

$$Z_5 - C_5 = 0 - 0 = 0$$

Thus x_1 enters the basis.

$$\text{Now min.} \left[-\frac{25/7}{3/7}, \frac{15/7}{6/7}\right] \quad \text{as } [-1/7 \text{ violates } x_k > 0]$$

$$\text{min.} \left[-, \frac{25}{3}, \frac{15}{6}\right] = \frac{15}{6}$$

So A_3 leaves the basis and is dropped out. Here $\frac{6}{7}$ is the pivot element.

Iteration–3

	$C_j \rightarrow$		1	2	3	–1
C_B	Y_B	X_B	x_1	x_2	x_3	x_4
2	x_2	$\frac{5}{2}$	0	1	0	0
3	x_3	$\frac{5}{2}$	0	0	1	0
1	x_1	$\frac{5}{2}$	1	0	0	0
	$Z_j - C_j$		0	0	0	1

Calculations for Row Operations

$$R_3(\text{New}) \longrightarrow \frac{R_3}{6/7}(\text{Old})$$

i.e., $\left(\frac{15}{7}\cdot\frac{7}{6} \quad \frac{6}{7}\cdot\frac{7}{6} \quad 0.\frac{7}{6} \quad 0.\frac{7}{6} \quad 0.\frac{7}{6}\right)$

$\therefore$ $R_3(\text{New})$ $\left(\frac{5}{2} \quad 1 \quad 0 \quad 0 \quad 0\right)$

$$R_1(\text{New}) \longrightarrow R_1(\text{Old}) + \frac{1}{7} R_1(\text{New})$$

Now	$R_1(\text{Old})$:	$\frac{15}{7}$	$\frac{-1}{7}$	1	0	0
and	$\frac{1}{7} R_1(\text{New})$:	$\frac{5}{14}$	$\frac{1}{7}$	0	0	0
(Add)		+	+	+	+	+
$\therefore$	$R_1(\text{New})$:	$\frac{35}{14}$	0	1	0	0

$$R_2(\text{New}) \longrightarrow R_2(\text{Old}) - \frac{3}{7} R_1(\text{New})$$

Now	$R_2(\text{Old})$:	$\frac{25}{7}$	$\frac{3}{7}$	0	1	0
and	$\frac{3}{7} R_1(\text{New})$: (Subtract)	$\frac{15}{14}$	$\frac{3}{7}$	0	0	0
		–	–	–	–	–
$\therefore$	$R_2(\text{New})$:	$\frac{35}{7}$	0	0	1	0

Calculations for $Z_j - C_j$

$$Z_1 - C_1 = 2.0 + 3.0 + 1.1 - 1 = 0$$
$$Z_2 - C_2 = 2.1 + 3.0 + 1.0 - 2 = 0$$
$$Z_3 - C_3 = 2.0 + 3.1 + 1.0 - 3 = 0$$
$$Z_4 - C_4 = 2.0 + 3.0 + 1.0 + 1 = 1$$

Since all $Z_j - C_j \geq 0$, an optimal solution has been attained.

Now the value of objective function Z is

$$Z = 2\left(\frac{5}{2}\right)+3\left(\frac{5}{2}\right)+1\left(\frac{5}{2}\right)=\frac{10}{2}+\frac{15}{2}+\frac{5}{2}=\frac{30}{2}=15$$

Thus the optimal solution is

$$Z_{max} = 15$$
$$x_1 = \frac{5}{2}$$

$$x_2 = \frac{5}{2}$$

and $$x_3 = \frac{5}{2}.$$

Example 16. *A manufacturer produces two types of torches, A and B. Torch A makes a profit of ₹ 50 per unit and Torch B makes a profit of ₹ 30. These torches are produced by using two types of plastics X and Y. At least 18 kg of Plastic X and 12 kg of plastic Y must be used daily. Torch A uses 2 kg of X and 1 kg of plastic Y, while torch B uses 1 kg of X and 1 kg of Y plastics. For torch A and B, 3 hours and 2 hours are required for manufacturing them and at most 34 hours of labour are to be utilized. How many units of each torches should be produced so as to maximize the profit.*

Solution. Formulation of LPP

Let x_1 : number of units of torch A be manufactured

x_2 : number of units of torch B be manufactured

The profit for 1 torch A is ₹ 50

The profit for x_1 torch A is ₹ $50x_1$

The profit for 1 torch B is ₹ 30

The profit for x_2 torch B is ₹ $30x_2$

Thus the objective function can be written as:

$$\text{Maximize } 50x_1 + 30x_2$$

Since 2 kg of plastic X is used in torch A and 1 kg of plastic is used in torch B. The total availablitity of plastic X is 18 kg.

$$\therefore \quad 2x_1 + x_2 \geq 18$$

1 kg of plastic Y is used in torch A and 1 kg of plastic y is used in Torch B and the total availability of plastic Y is 12 kg.

$$\therefore \quad x_1 + x_2 \geq 12.$$

Total available labour time is 34 hours and for producing torch A and B, the labour hours are 3 hours and 2 hours respectively.

Thus $$3x_1 + 2x_2 \leq 34$$

Hence the above problem can be written as an LPP as

$$\begin{aligned} \text{Maximize } Z &= 50x_1 + 30x_2 \\ \text{Subject to} \quad & 2x_1 + x_2 \geq 18 \\ & x_1 + x_2 \geq 12 \\ & 3x_1 + 2x_2 \leq 34 \\ & x_1, x_2 \geq 0. \end{aligned}$$

Using Simplex Method for its Solution

Since the problem is in maximization form, thus introducing surplus variables s_1 and s_2 and the artificial variables A_1 and A_2 for the first two constraints, while slack variable s_3 in third constraint. Thus after introducing surplus, artificial and slack variables, the given LPP can be written as

$$\text{Maximize } Z = 50x_1 + 30x_2 + 0{\cdot}s_1 + 0{\cdot}s_2 + 0{\cdot}s_3 - MA_1 - MA_2$$

$$\text{Subject to } \quad 2x_1 + x_2 - s_1 + A_1 = 18$$

$$x_1 + x_2 - s_2 + A_2 = 12$$

$$3x_1 + 2x_2 + s_3 = 34$$

$$x_1, x_2, s_1, s_2, s_3, A_1, A_2 \geq 0.$$

The initial basic feasible solution is

$$A_1 = 18$$

$$A_2 = 12$$

$$s_3 = 34.$$

Iteration–0

			50	30	0	0	0	$-M$	$-M$	
C_B	Y_B	X_B	x_1	x_2	s_1	s_2	s_3	A_1	A_2	Min. Ratio
$-M$	A_1	18	2*	1	–1	0	0	1	0	$\frac{18}{2}$ ←
$-M$	A_2	12	1	1	0	–1	0	0	1	$\frac{12}{1}$
0	s_3	34	3	2	0	0	1	0	0	$\frac{34}{3}$
	$Z_j - C_j$	$-30M$	$-3M - 50$ ↑	$-2M - 30$	M	M	0	0	0	

Calculations for $Z_j - C_j$ (for Iteration–0)

$$Z_1 - C_1 = -M.2 + (-M){\cdot}1 + 0.3 - 50 = -3M - 50$$

$$Z_2 - C_2 = -M.1 - M.1 + 0.2 - 30 = -2M - 30$$

$$Z_3 - C_3 = -M{\cdot}(-1) - M.0 + 0.0 - 0 = M$$

Similarly, remaining net evaluations can be computed.

x_1 enters the basis as $Z_1 - C_1$ is most negative.

$$\text{Now min.} \left[\frac{18}{2}, \frac{12}{1}, \frac{34}{3}\right] = \frac{18}{2}$$

Here, artificial variable A_1 leaves the basis and is dropped out. Thus, 2 becomes the pivot element.

Iteration–1

			50	30	0	0	0	$-M$	
C_B	Y_B	X_B	x_1	x_2	s_1	s_2	s_3	A_2	Min. Ratio
50	x_1	9	1	$\frac{1}{2}$	$\frac{-1}{2}$	0	0	0	18
$-M$	A_2	3	0	$\frac{1}{2}$	$\frac{1}{2}$	-1	0	1	6
0	s_3	7	0	$\frac{1}{2}$	$\frac{3}{2}$*	0	1	0	$\frac{14}{3}$ ←
	$Z_j - C_j$	$-3M$ +450	0	$\frac{-1}{2}M-5$	$\frac{-1}{2}M$ −25 ↑	M	0	0	

Calculation of Row Operations for Iteration–1

$R_1(\text{New}) \longrightarrow \frac{R_1}{2}(\text{Old})$

i.e.,
$$\left(\frac{18}{2} \quad \frac{2}{2} \quad \frac{1}{2} \quad \frac{-1}{2} \quad \frac{0}{2} \quad \frac{0}{2} \quad \frac{0}{2}\right)$$

$\therefore$ $R_1(\text{New})$ $\left(9 \quad 1 \quad \frac{1}{2} \quad \frac{-1}{2} \quad 0 \quad 0 \quad 0\right)$

$R_2(\text{New}) \longrightarrow R_2(\text{Old}) - R_1(\text{New})$

Now	R_2(Old)	:	12	1	1	0	-1	0	1
and	R_1(New)	:	9	1	$\frac{1}{2}$	$\frac{-1}{2}$	0	0	0
(Subtract)			–	–	–	+	–	–	–
$\therefore$	R_2(New)	:	3	0	$\frac{1}{2}$	$\frac{1}{2}$	-1	0	1

$R_3(\text{New}) \longrightarrow R_3(\text{Old}) - 3R_1(\text{New})$

Now	R_3(Old)	:	34	3	2	0	0	1	0
and	$3R_1$(New)	:	27	3	$\frac{3}{2}$	$\frac{-3}{2}$	0	0	0
	(Subtract)		–	–	–	+	–	–	–
$\therefore$	R_3(New)	:	7	0	$\frac{1}{2}$	$\frac{3}{2}$	0	1	0

Calculations of $Z_j - C_j$ for Iteration–1

$$Z_1 - C_1 = 50.1 - M.0 + 0.0 - 50 = 0$$

$$Z_2 - C_2 = 50\cdot\frac{1}{2} - M.\frac{1}{2} + 0.\frac{1}{2} - 30 = -\frac{1}{2}M - 5$$

$$Z_3 - C_3 = -\frac{1}{2}50 - M.\frac{1}{2} + 0.\frac{3}{2} - 0 = \frac{-1}{2}M - 25$$

$$Z_4 - C_4 = 50.0 - M(-1) + 0.0 - 0 = M$$

$$Z_5 - C_5 = 50.0 - M.0 + 0.1 - 0 = 0$$

$$Z_6 - C_6 = 50.0 - M.1 + 0.0 + M = 0$$

Since $Z_2 - C_2$ is most negative, therefore x_2 enters the basis.

Now Min. $\left[\frac{9}{1/2}, \frac{3}{1/2}, \frac{7}{1/2}\right] = \frac{6}{3}$

So artificial variable A_2 leaves the basis and is dropped out. Therefore 1/2 becomes pivot element.

Iteration–2

			50	30	0	0	0	$-M$	
C_B	Y_B	X_B	x_1	x_2	s_1	s_2	s_3	A_2	Min. Ratio
50	x_1	$\frac{34}{3}$	1	$\frac{2}{3}$	0	0	$\frac{2}{3}$	0	17
$-M$	A_2	$\frac{2}{3}$	0	$\frac{1}{3}$*	0	-1	$\frac{-1}{3}$	1	2 ←
0	x_3	$\frac{14}{3}$	0	$\frac{1}{3}$	1	0	$\frac{2}{3}$	0	14
$Z_j - C_j$			0	$\frac{-1}{3}M + \frac{20}{6}$	0	M	$\frac{1}{3}M + \frac{50}{3}$	0	

$\therefore$ x_2 enters the basis as $Z_2 - C_2$ is most negative and A_2 leaves the basis and is dropped out.

(All the row operation and net evaluation are to be calculated by the Reader)

Iteration–3

			50	30	0	0	0
C_B	Y_B	X_B	x_1	x_2	s_1	s_2	s_3
50	x_1	10	1	0	0	2	1
30	x_2	2	0	1	0	-3	-1
0	x_3	4	0	0	1	1	-1
	$Z_j - C_j$	560	0	0	0	10	20

Since all $Z_j - C_j \geq 0$

$$\therefore \quad Z_{max} = 560$$
$$x_1 = 10$$
$$x_2 = 2$$
$$x_3 = 4$$

Example 17. *Vitamins A and B are present in foods X and Y. One unit of food X contains three units of vitamin A and four units of vitamin B. One unit of food Y contains six units of vitamin A and three units of vitamin B. One unit of food X and Y costs ₹ 4 and 5 respectively. The minimum daily requirement of vitamins A and B is 80 and 100 units respectively. Formulate this problem as an LP model to find the optimum mixture of food X and Y at the minimum cost that meets the daily requirement of vitamins A and B.*

Solution. Let x_1 : number of vitamins units purchased for food X.

x_2 : number of vitamins units purchased for food Y.

Thus, Minimize $F = 4x_1 + 5x_2$

Subject to $3x_1 + 6x_2 \geq 80$ (Vitamin A constraint)

$4x_1 + 3x_2 \geq 100$ (Vitamin B constraint)

$x_1, x_2 \geq 0.$

Solution of LPP using Charni's Method (or Big-M method). Converting minimization problem into maximization and introducing slack and artificial variables ($s_1 \geq 0$ and $A_1 \geq 0$) in first constraint and ($s_1 \geq 0$ and $A_2 \geq 0$) in second constraint.

Thus, Maximize $Z = -4x_1 - 5x_2 + 0{\cdot}s_1 + 0{\cdot}s_2 - MA_1 - MA_2$

subject to $3x_1 + 6x_2 - s_1 + A_1 = 80$

$4x_1 + 3x_2 - s_2 + A_2 = 100$

$x_1, x_2 \geq 0$

Iteration–0

	$C_j \rightarrow$		–4	–5	0	0	–M	–M	
C_B	Y_B	X_B	x_1	x_2	s_1	s_2	A_1	A_2	Min. Ratio
–M	A_1	80	3	6*	–1	0	1	0	$\frac{80}{6}$ ←
–M	A_2	100	4	3	0	–1	0	1	$\frac{100}{3}$
	$Z_j - C_j$	–180M	–7M + 4	–9M + 5	M	M	0	0	
				↑					

Since $Z_2 - C_2$ is most negative, so x_2 enters the basis and by computing the minimum ratio A_1 leaves the basis and is dropped out.

Iteration–1

			-4	-5	0	0	$-M$	
C_B	Y_B	X_B	x_1	x_2	s_1	s_2	A_2	Min. Ratio
-5	x_2	$\frac{40}{3}$	$\frac{1}{2}$	1	$\frac{-1}{6}$	0	0	
$-M$	A_2	60	$\frac{5}{2}$*	0	$\frac{1}{2}$	$\frac{-1}{2}$	1	24 ←
	$Z_j - C_j$	$-60M + \frac{200}{3}$	$\frac{-5}{2}M + \frac{5}{2}$ ↑	0	$\frac{-1}{2}M + \frac{5}{6}$	$\frac{1}{2}M$	0	

Since $Z_2 - C_2$ is most negative.

Thus x_2 enters the basis.

While by computing the minimum ratio, it is found that A_2 leaves the basis and is dropped out.

Thus $\frac{5}{2}$ becomes the pivot element.

Iteration–2

			-4	-5	0	0
C_B	Y_B	X_B	x_1	x_2	s_1	s_2
-5	x_2	$\frac{4}{3}$	0	1	$\frac{-4}{15}$	$\frac{-1}{5}$
-4	x_1	24	1	0	$\frac{-1}{5}$	$\frac{-1}{5}$
	$Z_j - C_j$	$\frac{-308}{3}$	0	0	$\frac{32}{15}$	$\frac{9}{5}$

Since all $Z_j - C_j \geq 0$.

Thus an optimal solution has been attained.

$$\therefore \qquad Z_{\max} = \frac{-308}{3}$$

$$x_1 = 24$$

$$x_2 = \frac{4}{3}.$$

But the objective function is of minimization.

Therefore, $$Z_{min} = \frac{308}{5} \quad (\text{Min} = -\text{Max})$$

$$x_1 = 24$$

$$x_2 = \frac{4}{3}.$$

2.6 SOLVING LPP WHEN VARIABLES ARE UNRESTRICTED

The non-negativity condition $x_j \geq 0$, ($j = 1, ..., n$) are called *unrestricted variables*. In any LPP, usually it is assumed that all the variables x_j should have non-negative values. For example if a company produces two types of belts A and B, then there number of units produced should be ≥ 0, as the company will produce zero belts either of type A or B or more than zero. It cannot produce negative number of belts. In an LP problem, the values x_j are non-negative. However, in some real life situations, one or more of the variables can have either, negative, zero or positive value.

Simplex algorithm requires that all x_j's must have non-negative value at each iteration, therefore to convert an LP problem involving unrestricted variables into an equivalent problem having only restricted variables, the unrestricted variables must be expressed as the difference of two non-negative variables.

Example 18. *Solve the following LPP using Big-M method, when one of the decision variable is unrestricted.*

Maximize $Z = 3x_1 + 2x_2 + x_3$

subject to $$2x_1 + 5x_2 + x_3 = 12$$
$$3x_1 + 4x_2 = 11$$
$$x_2, x_3 \geq 0$$

and x_1 *unrestricted.*

Solution. Since in the above LPP, x_1 is unrestricted.

Thus expressing x_1 variables as the difference of two non-negative variables as:

$$x_1 = x_1' - x_1''$$

Now, the given LPP is in its standard form (maximization) so introducing artificial variables A_1 and A_2 in the given constraints. Thus the above LPP can be written as:

Maximize $Z = 3(x_1' - x_1'') + 2x_2 + x_3 - MA_1 - MA_2$

Subject to $$2(x_1' - x_1'') + 5x_2 + x_3 + A_1 = 12$$
$$3(x_1' - x_1'') + 4x_2 + A_2 = 11$$
$$x_1', x_1'', x_2, x_3, A_1, A_2 \geq 0$$

∴ The initial basic feasible solution is

$$A_1 = 12$$
$$A_2 = 11.$$

Iteration–0

	$C_j \rightarrow$		3	–3	2	1	–M	–M	
C_B	Y_B	X_B	x_1'	x_1''	x_2	x_3	A_1	A_2	Min. Ratio
–M	A_1	12	2	–2	5*	1	1	0	12/5 ←
–M	A_2	11	3	–3	4	0	0	1	$\frac{11}{4}$
	$Z_j - C_j$	–33M	–5M – 3	–5M + 3	–9M – 2 ↑	–M – 1	0	0	

Computation of $Z_j - C_j$ are same as done previously. So 5 is the pivot element. x_2 enters the basis while A_1 leaves the basis and is dropped out.

Computations for Row Operations for Iteration–1

$R_1(\text{New}) \longrightarrow \frac{R_1}{5}(\text{Old})$

i.e., : $\left(\frac{12}{5} \quad \frac{2}{5} \quad \frac{-2}{5} \quad \frac{5}{5} \quad \frac{1}{5} \quad \frac{0}{5}\right)$

∴ $R_1(\text{New})$: $\frac{12}{5} \quad \frac{2}{5} \quad \frac{-2}{5} \quad 1 \quad \frac{-1}{5} \quad 0$

$R_2(\text{New}) \longrightarrow R(\text{Old}) - 4R_1(\text{New})$

Now R_2(Old) :	11	3	– 3	4	0	1
and $4R_1$(New) :	$\frac{48}{5}$	$\frac{8}{5}$	$\frac{-8}{5}$	4	$\frac{4}{5}$	0
(Subtract)	–	–	+	–	–	–
∴ R_2(New) :	$\frac{7}{5}$	$\frac{7}{5}$	$\frac{-7}{5}$	0	$\frac{-4}{5}$	1

Iteration–1

	$C_j \rightarrow$		3	–3	2	1	–M	
C_B	V_B	X_B	x_1'	x_1''	x_2	x_3	A_2	Min. Ratio
2	x_2	$\frac{12}{5}$	$\frac{2}{5}$	$\frac{-2}{5}$	1	$\frac{1}{5}$	0	$\frac{12/5}{2/5}$
–M	A_2	$\frac{7}{5}$	$\frac{7}{5}$	$\frac{-7}{5}$	0	$\frac{-4}{5}$	1	$\frac{7/5}{7/5}$ ←
	$Z_j - C_j$	$\frac{-7}{5}M + \frac{24}{5}$	$\frac{-7}{5}M + \frac{4}{5}$ ↑	$\frac{7}{5}M + \frac{11}{5}$	0	$\frac{4}{5}M - \frac{3}{5}$	0	

Calculations for $Z_j - C_j$

$$Z_1 - C_1 = 2.\frac{2}{5} - M.\frac{7}{5} - 3 = \frac{4}{5} - \frac{7}{5}M = \frac{-7M}{5} + \frac{4}{5}$$

$$Z_2 - C_2 = 2\cdot\left(\frac{-2}{5}\right) - M\cdot\left(\frac{-7}{5}\right) - 3 = \frac{7}{5}M - \frac{4}{5} + 3 = \frac{7}{5}M + \frac{11}{5}$$

$$Z_3 - C_3 = 2.1 + (-M)\cdot 0 - 2 = 2$$

$$Z_4 - C_4 = 2.\frac{1}{5} + (-M)\cdot\left(\frac{-4}{5}\right) - 1 = \frac{2}{5} + \frac{4}{5}M - 1 = \frac{4}{5}M - \frac{3}{5}$$

$$Z_5 - C_5 = 2.0 + (-M)\cdot 1 + M = 0.$$

Now minimum ratio can be computed as:

$$\text{Minimum}\left[\frac{12/5}{2/5}, \frac{7/5}{7/5}\right] = \text{Minimum } [6, 1] = 1.$$

x_1', enters the basis and A_2 leaves the basis and is dropped out.
Thus the pivot element in iteration –1 is 7/5.

Iteration–2

			3	–3	2	1	
C_B	Y_B	X_B	x_1'	x_1''	x_2	x_3	Min. Ratio
2	x_2	2	0	0	1	$\frac{3}{7}$*	$\frac{2}{3/7}$
3	x_1'	1	1	–1	0	$\frac{-4}{7}$	–
$Z_j - C_j$		7	0	0	0	$\frac{-67}{35}$ ↑	

Calculations for Row Operations

$$R_2(\text{New}) \longrightarrow \frac{R_2}{7/5}(\text{Old})$$

$$i.e., R_2(\text{New}) \quad : \quad \left(\frac{7}{5}\cdot\frac{5}{7} \quad \frac{7}{5}\cdot\frac{5}{7} \quad \frac{-7}{5}\cdot\frac{5}{7} \quad 0.\frac{5}{7} \quad \frac{-4}{5}\cdot\frac{5}{7}\right)$$

$$\left(1 \quad 1 \quad -1 \quad 0 \quad \frac{-4}{7}\right)$$

$$R_1(\text{New}) \longrightarrow R_1(\text{Old}) - \frac{2}{5}R_2(\text{New})$$

Now	R_1(Old)	:	$\frac{12}{5}$	$\frac{2}{5}$	$\frac{-2}{5}$	1	$\frac{1}{5}$
and	$\frac{2}{5}R_2$(New)	:	$\frac{2}{5}$	$\frac{2}{5}$	$\frac{-2}{5}$	0	$\frac{-8}{35}$
(Subtract)			–	–	+	–	+
$\therefore$	R_1(New)	:	2	0	0	1	$\frac{3}{7}$

Calculations for $Z_j - C_j$

$$Z_1 - C_1 = 2.0 + 3.1 - 3 = 0$$
$$Z_2 - C_2 = 2.0 + 3(-1) + 3 = 0$$
$$Z_3 - C_3 = 2.1 + 3.0 - 2 = 0$$
$$Z_4 - C_4 = 2.\frac{2}{5} + 3\left(\frac{-4}{7}\right) - 1 = \frac{4}{5} - \frac{12}{7} - 1$$

Here x_3 enters the basis while x_2 leaves the basis and so $\frac{2}{5}$ is the pivot element.

Iteration–3

			3	–3	2	1
C_B	Y_B	X_B	x_1'	x_1''	x_2	x_3
1	x_3	$\frac{14}{3}$	0	0	$\frac{7}{3}$	1
3	x_1^1	$\frac{11}{3}$	1	–1	$\frac{4}{3}$	0
	$Z_j - C_j$	$\frac{47}{3}$	0	0	$\frac{13}{3}$	0

Calculations of Row Operations

$$R_1(\text{New}) \longrightarrow \frac{R_1}{3/7}(\text{Old})$$

i.e., R_1(Old) : $\left(2 \quad 0 \quad 0 \quad 1 \quad \frac{3}{7}\right)$

$\frac{7}{3}R_1$(Old) : $\left(2.\frac{7}{3} \quad 0.\frac{7}{3} \quad 0.\frac{7}{3} \quad 1.\frac{7}{3} \quad \frac{3}{7}.\frac{7}{3}\right)$

i.e., : $\left(\frac{14}{3} \quad 0 \quad 0 \quad \frac{7}{3} \quad 1\right)$

$$R_2(\text{New}) \longrightarrow R_2\ (\text{Old}) + \frac{4}{7}R_1(\text{New})$$

Now,	R_2(Old) :	1	1	–1	0	$\frac{-4}{7}$
and	$\frac{4}{7}R_1$ (New) :	$\frac{8}{3}$	0	0	$\frac{4}{3}$	$\frac{4}{7}$
(Addition)		+	+	+	+	+
∴	R_2(New) :	$\frac{11}{3}$	1	–1	$\frac{4}{3}$	0

Calculations for $Z_j - C_j$

$$Z_1 - C_1 = 1.0 + 3.1 - 3 = 0$$

$$Z_2 - C_2 = 1.0 + 3(-1) + 3 = 0$$

$$Z_3 - C_3 = 1.\frac{7}{3} + 3.\frac{4}{3} - 2 = \frac{7}{3} + \frac{12}{3} - 2 = \frac{13}{3}$$

$$Z_4 - C_4 = 1.1 + 3.0 - 1 = 0$$

In iteration–3, all the net evaluations $Z_j - C_j \geq 0$, therefore the optimal solution has been attained.

Thus, $x_1' = \frac{11}{3}, x_3 = \frac{14}{3}, x_1'' = 0, x_1 = 0.$

Since, $x_1 = x_1' - x_1'' = \frac{11}{3} - 0 = \frac{11}{3}$

$x_2 = 0$

$x_3 = \frac{14}{3}$

Thus, $Z_{max} = \frac{47}{3}$

$x_1 = \frac{11}{3}$

$x_2 = 0$ and $x_3 = \frac{14}{3}$.

Example 19. *Solve the following* LPP

$$\textit{Maximize } Z = 2x_1 + 3x_2$$

Subject to $-x_1 + 2x_2 \leq 4$

$x_1 + x_2 \leq 6$

$x_1 + 3x_2 \leq 9$

x_1 *and* x_2 *are unrestricted.*

Solution. Since the given LPP is in maximization form and all the constraints are of ≤ inequality sign. Thus, introducing slack variables $s_1 \geq 0$, $s_2 \geq 0$ and $s_3 \geq 0$.

Since x_1 and x_2 are unrestricted. s_2 replacing them with non-negative variables x_1', x_1'', x_2' and x_2'' as follows:

$$x_1 = x_1' - x_1''$$

$$\text{and} \quad x_2 = x_2'' - x_2'$$

After introducing the slack variables and the non-negative variables, the above LPP can be re-written as:

$$\text{Maximize } Z = 2(x_1' - x_1'') + 3(x_1' - x_2'') + 0.s_1 + 0.s_2 + 0.s_3$$

$$\text{subject to} \quad (x_1' - x_1'') + 2(x_2' - x_2'') + s_1 = 4$$

$$(x_1' - x_1'') + (x_2' - x_2'') + s_2 = 6$$

$$(x_1' - x_1'') + 3(x_2' - x_2'') + s_3 = 9$$

$$x_1', x_1'', x_2', x_2'', s_1, s_2, s_3, \geq 0$$

The initial solution of the problem is

$$s_1 = 4$$

$$s_2 = 6$$

$$\text{and } s_3 = 9$$

Iteration–0

	$C_j \rightarrow$		2	–2	3	–3	0	0	0	
C_B	Y_B	X_B	x_1'	x_1''	x_2'	x_2''	s_1	s_2	s_3	Min. Ratio
0	s_1	4	–1	1	2*	–2	1	0	0	$\frac{4}{2}$
0	s_2	6	1	–1	1	–1	0	1	0	$\frac{6}{1}$
0	s_3	9	1	–1	3	–3	0	0	1	$\frac{9}{3}$
	$Z_j - C_j$	0	–2	2	–3	3	0	0	0	

Calculations of $Z_j - C_j$

$$Z_1 - C_1 = 0.(-1) + 0\,(1) + 0.1 - 2 = -2$$

$$Z_2 - C_2 = 0.1 + 0(-1) + (0.1) + 2 = 2$$

$$Z_3 - C_3 = 0.2 + 0.1 + 0.3 - 3 = -3$$

Similarly, remaining net evaluations can be computed.

Here $Z_3 - C_3$ is most negative.

So x_2' enters the basis.

$$\text{Minimum ratio is min} \left[\frac{4}{2}, \frac{6}{1}, \frac{9}{3}\right] = \frac{4}{2} = 2$$

$\therefore$ s_1 leaves the basis and 2 becomes the pivot element.

Iteration–1

			2	−2	3	−3	0	0	0	
C_B	Y_B	X_B	x_1'	x_1''	x_2'	x_2''	s_1	s_2	s_3	Min. Ratio
3	x_1	2	$\frac{-1}{2}$	$\frac{1}{2}$	1	−1	$\frac{1}{2}$	0	0	
0	s_2	4	$\frac{3}{2}$	$\frac{-3}{2}$	0	0	$\frac{-1}{2}$	1	0	$\frac{4}{3/2}$
0	s_3	3	$\frac{5}{2}$	$\frac{-5}{2}$	0	0	$\frac{-3}{2}$	0	1	$\frac{3}{5/2}$ ←
	$Z_j - C_j$	6	$-\frac{7}{2}$	$\frac{7}{2}$	0	0	$\frac{3}{2}$	0	0	

Calculations of Row Operations

$R_1(\text{New}) \longrightarrow \frac{R_1}{2}(\text{Old})$

i.e., : $\left(\frac{4}{2} \quad \frac{-1}{2} \quad \frac{1}{2} \quad \frac{2}{2} \quad \frac{-2}{2} \quad \frac{1}{2} \quad \frac{0}{2} \quad \frac{0}{2}\right)$

$\therefore$ $R_1(\text{New})$: $\left(2 \quad \frac{-1}{2} \quad \frac{1}{2} \quad 1 \quad -1 \quad \frac{1}{2} \quad 0 \quad 0\right)$

$R_2(\text{New}) \longrightarrow R_2(\text{Old}) - R_1(\text{New})$

Now,	$R_2(\text{Old})$:	6	1	−1	1	−1	0	1	0
and	$R_1(\text{New})$:	2	$\frac{-1}{2}$	$\frac{1}{2}$	1	−1	$\frac{1}{2}$	0	0
(Subtract)		−	+	−	−	+	−	−	−
$\therefore$	$R_2(\text{New})$:	4	$\frac{3}{2}$	$\frac{-3}{2}$	0	0	$\frac{-1}{2}$	1	0

$R_3(\text{New}) \longrightarrow R_3(\text{Old}) - 3R_1(\text{New})$

Now,	$R_3(\text{Old})$:	9	1	−1	3	−3	0	0	1
and	$3R_1(\text{New})$:	6	$\frac{-3}{2}$	$\frac{3}{2}$	3	−3	$\frac{3}{2}$	0	0
	(Subtract)	−	+	−	−	+	−	−	−
$\therefore$	$R_3(\text{New})$:	3	$\frac{5}{2}$	$\frac{-5}{2}$	0	0	$\frac{-3}{2}$	0	1

Calculations of $Z_j - C_j$

$$Z_1 - C_1 = 3\left(\frac{-1}{2}\right) + 0\left(\frac{-3}{2}\right) + 0\left(\frac{5}{2}\right) - 2 = \frac{-3}{2} - 2 = \frac{-7}{2}$$

$$Z_2 - C_2 = 3.\frac{1}{2} + 0\left(\frac{-3}{2}\right) + 0\left(\frac{-5}{2}\right) + 2 = \frac{3}{2} + 2 = \frac{7}{2}$$

$$Z_3 - C_3 = 3.1 + 0.0 + 0.0 - 3 = 0$$

$$Z_4 - C_4 = 3(-1) + 0.0 + 0.0 + 3 = 0$$

$$Z_5 - C_5 = 3\left(\frac{1}{2}\right) + 0\left(\frac{-1}{2}\right) + 0\left(\frac{-3}{2}\right) - 0 = \frac{3}{2}$$

$$Z_6 - C_6 = 3(0) + 0.1 + 0.0 - 0 = 0$$

$$Z_7 - C_7 = 3.0 + 0.0 + 0.1 - 0 = 0$$

Since $Z_1 - C_1$ is most negative, so x_1' enters the basis.

Here, Min. $\left[-, \frac{4}{3/2}, \frac{3}{5/2}\right]$ ($\because$ $\frac{-1}{2}$ for I column does not satisfy the condition $x_{1k} > 0$)

$$\text{Min.} \left[-, \frac{8}{3}, \frac{6}{5}\right] = \frac{6}{5}$$

So s_3 leaves the basis and $\left(\frac{5}{2}\right)$ becomes the pivot element.

Iteration–2

			2	−2	3	−3	0	0	0	
C_B	Y_B	X_B	x_1'	x_1''	x_2'	x_2''	s_1	s_2	s_3	Min. Ratio
3	x_2'	$\frac{13}{5}$	0	0	1	−1	$\frac{1}{5}$	0	$\frac{1}{5}$	$\frac{13/5}{1/5}$
0	s_2	$\frac{11}{5}$	0	0	0	0	$\frac{2}{5}$*	1	$\frac{-3}{5}$	$\frac{11/5}{2/5}$
2	x_1'	$\frac{6}{5}$	1	−1	0	0	$\frac{-3}{5}$	0	$\frac{2}{5}$	—
	$Z_j - C_j$	$\frac{51}{5}$	0	0	0	0	$\frac{-3}{5}$	0	$\frac{7}{5}$	

Calculations of Row Operations

$$R_3(\text{New}) \longrightarrow \frac{R_3}{5/2}(\text{Old})$$

$$\text{Or} \qquad \longrightarrow \frac{2}{5} R_3(\text{Old})$$

$$: \left(\frac{5}{2}.\frac{2}{5} \quad \frac{-5}{2}.\frac{2}{5} \quad 0.\frac{2}{5} \quad 0.\frac{2}{5} \quad \frac{-3}{2}.\frac{2}{5} \quad 0.\frac{2}{5} \quad 1.\frac{2}{5}\right)$$

$$\therefore \quad R_3(\text{New}) \quad : \left(1 \quad -1 \quad 0 \; 0 \quad \frac{-3}{5} \quad 0 \quad \frac{2}{5}\right)$$

$$R_1(\text{New}) \longrightarrow R_1(\text{Old}) + \frac{1}{2} R_3(\text{New})$$

Now,	R_1(Old)	:	2	$\frac{-1}{2}$	$\frac{1}{2}$	1	–1	$\frac{1}{2}$	0	0
and	$\frac{1}{2}R_3$(New)	:	$\frac{3}{5}$	$\frac{1}{2}$	$\frac{-1}{2}$	0	0	$\frac{-3}{10}$	0	$\frac{1}{5}$
(Add)		:	+	+	+	+	+	+	+	+
∴	R_1(New)	:	$\frac{13}{5}$	0	0	1	–1	$\frac{1}{5}$	0	$\frac{1}{5}$

$$R_2(\text{New}) \longrightarrow R_2(\text{Old}) - \frac{-3}{2} R_3(\text{New})$$

Now,	R_2(Old)	:	4	$\frac{3}{2}$	$\frac{-3}{2}$	0	0	$\frac{-1}{2}$	1	0
and	$\frac{3}{2}R_3$(New)	:	$\frac{9}{5}$	$\frac{3}{2}$	$\frac{-3}{2}$	0	0	$\frac{-9}{10}$	0	$\frac{3}{5}$
	(Subtract)		–	–	+	–	–	+	–	–
∴	R_2(New)	:	$\frac{11}{5}$	0	0	0	0	$\frac{2}{5}$	1	$\frac{-3}{5}$

Calculations of $Z_j - C_j$

$$Z_1 - C_1 = 3.0 + 0.0 + 2.1 - 2 = 0$$
$$Z_2 - C_2 = 3.0 + 0.0 + 2(-1) + 2 = 0$$
$$Z_3 - C_3 = 3.1 + 0.0 + 2.0 - 3 = 0$$
$$Z_4 - C_4 = 3(-1) + 0.0 + 2.0 + 3 = 0$$
$$Z_5 - C_5 = 3\left(\frac{1}{5}\right) + 0\left(\frac{2}{5}\right) + 2\left(\frac{-3}{5}\right) - 0 = \frac{3}{5} - \frac{6}{5} = \frac{-3}{5}$$
$$Z_6 - C_6 = 3.0 + 0.(1) + 2.0 - 0 = 0$$
$$Z_7 - C_7 = 3\left(\frac{1}{5}\right) + 0\left(\frac{-3}{5}\right) + 2\left(\frac{2}{5}\right) - 0 = \frac{3}{5} + \frac{4}{5} = \frac{7}{5}$$

Since $Z_5 - C_5$ is most negative, thus s_1, enters the basis.

Here, $\min.\left[\frac{13/5}{1/5}, \frac{11/5}{2/5}, -\right] = \min\left[13, \frac{11}{2}, -\right] = \frac{11}{2} = 6.5$

Thus $\frac{2}{5}$ is the pivot element.

Iteration–3

		c_j	2	–2	3	–3	0	0	0
C_B	Y_B	X_B	x_1'	x_1''	x_2'	x_2''	s_1	s_2	s_3
3	x_2'	$\frac{3}{2}$	0	0	1	–1	0	$\frac{-1}{2}$	$\frac{1}{2}$
0	s_1	$\frac{11}{2}$	0	0	0	0	1	$\frac{5}{2}$	$\frac{-3}{2}$
2	x_1'	$\frac{9}{2}$	1	–1	0	0	0	$\frac{3}{2}$	$\frac{-1}{2}$
$Z_j - C_j$		$\frac{27}{2}$	0	0	0	0	0	$\frac{3}{2}$	$\frac{1}{2}$

Calculations of Row Operations

$$R_2 \text{ (New)} \longrightarrow \frac{R_2}{2/5}\text{(Old)}$$

i.e., $\frac{5}{2} R_2\text{(Old)}$: $\left(\frac{11}{5}.\frac{5}{2} \quad 0.\frac{5}{2} \quad 0.\frac{5}{2} \quad 0.\frac{5}{2} \quad 0.\frac{5}{2} \quad \frac{2}{5}.\frac{5}{2} \quad 1.\frac{5}{2} \quad \frac{-3}{5}.\frac{5}{2}\right)$

$\therefore$ $R_2\text{(New)}$: $\left(\frac{11}{2} \quad 0 \quad 0 \quad 0 \quad 0 \quad 1 \quad \frac{5}{2} \quad \frac{-3}{2}\right)$

$$R_1 \text{ (New)} \longrightarrow R_1\text{(Old)} - \frac{1}{5} R_2\text{(New)}$$

Now, R_1(Old)	:	$\frac{13}{5}$	0	0	1	–1	$\frac{1}{5}$	0	$\frac{1}{5}$
and $\frac{1}{5} R_2$(New)	:	$\frac{11}{10}$	0	0	0	0	$\frac{1}{5}$	$\frac{1}{2}$	$\frac{-3}{10}$
(Subtract)	:	–	–	–	–	–	–	–	+
$\therefore$ R_1(New)	:	$\frac{3}{2}$	0	0	1	–1	0	$\frac{-1}{2}$	$\frac{1}{2}$

$$R_3\text{(New)} \longrightarrow R_3\text{(Old)} + \frac{3}{5} R_2\text{(New)}$$

Now, R_3(Old)	:	$\frac{6}{5}$	1	–1	0	0	$\frac{-3}{5}$	0	$\frac{2}{5}$
and $\frac{3}{5} R_2$(New)	:	$\frac{33}{10}$	0	0	0	0	$\frac{3}{5}$	$\frac{3}{2}$	$\frac{-9}{10}$
(Add)	:	+	+	+	+	+	+	+	+
$\therefore$ R_3(New)	:	$\frac{9}{2}$	1	–1	0	0	0	$\frac{3}{2}$	$\frac{-5}{10}$

Calculations of $Z_j - C_j$

$$Z_1 - C_1 = 3.0 + 0.0 + 2.1 - 2 = 0$$
$$Z_2 - C_2 = 3.0 + 0.0 + 2.(-1) + 2 = 0$$
$$Z_3 - C_3 = 3.1 + 0.0 + 0.0 - 3 = 0$$
$$Z_4 - C_4 = 3(-1) + 0.0 + 2.0 + 3 = 0$$
$$Z_5 - C_5 = 3.0 + 0.1 + 2.0 - 0 = 0$$
$$Z_6 - C_6 = 3\left(\frac{1}{2}\right) + 0\left(\frac{-3}{2}\right) + 2\left(\frac{-1}{2}\right) - 0 = \frac{1}{2}$$
$$Z_7 - C_7 = 3\left(\frac{1}{2}\right) + 0\left(\frac{-3}{2}\right) + 2\left(\frac{-1}{2}\right) - 0 = \frac{3}{2} + 0 - \frac{2}{2} = \frac{3}{2} - \frac{2}{2} = \frac{1}{2}$$

and value of objective function $= 3\left(\frac{3}{2}\right) + (0)\left(\frac{11}{2}\right) + 2\left(\frac{9}{2}\right) = \frac{27}{2}$

Since all the net evaluations are positive, the optimum solutions has been attained.

$\therefore \quad x_1' = \frac{9}{2} \quad x_1'' = 0$

$\therefore \quad x_2' = \frac{2}{5} \quad x_2'' = 0$

Since $\quad x_1 = x_1' - x_1'' = \frac{9}{2} - 0 = \frac{9}{2}$

and $\quad x_2 = x_2' - x_2'' = \frac{3}{2} - 0 = \frac{3}{2}$

$\therefore \quad Z_{max} = \frac{27}{2}$

$\therefore \quad x_1 = \frac{9}{2}$

and $\quad x_2 = \frac{3}{2}$

Example 20. *Minimize* $Z = 2x_1 + 2x_2 + 2x_3$

Subject to $\quad 2x_1 - 6x_2 + 8x_3 = 10$

$2x_1 - 4x_2 \leq 6$

$4x_2 - 2x_3 \geq 8$

$x_1, x_2 \geq 0$

and x_3 is unrestricted.

Solution. Convert the given LPP in standard form (maximization)

$\therefore \quad$ Maximize $Z = -2x_1 - 2x_2 - 2x_3$

Subject to $\quad 2x_1 - 6x_2 + 8x_3 = 10$

$2x_1 - 4x_2 \leq 6$

$4x_2 - 2x_3 \geq 8$

$$x_1, x_2 \geq 0$$

and x_3 is unrestricted.

Thus introducing artificial variable in first constraint, $A_1 \geq 0$.

Slack variable in second constraint, $s_1 \geq 0$

Surplus and artificial variable in third constraint $s_2 \geq 0$, $A_2 \geq 0$ and since x_3 is unrestricted

So replace x_3 by $(x_3' - x_3'')$, the above LPP can further be written as:

$$\text{Maximize } Z = -2x_1 - 2x_2 - 2(x_3' - x_3'') = M.A_1 + 0{\cdot}s_1 + 0{\cdot}s_2 - MA_2$$

$$\text{Subject to} \quad 2x_1 - 6x_2 + 8(x_3' - x_3'') + A_1 = 10$$

$$2x_1 - 4x_2 + s_1 = 6$$

$$4x_1 - 2(x_3' - x_3'') - s_2 + A_2 = 8$$

$$x_1, x_2, x_3', x_3'' \geq 0$$

$$s_1, s_2, A_1, A_2 \geq 0.$$

Thus the initial basic feasible solution is

$$A_1 = 10, s_1 = 6 \text{ and } A_2 = 8.$$

Iteration–0

	C_j		–2	–2	–2	2	0	0	–M	–M	
C_B	Y_B	X_B	x_1	x_2	x_3'	x_3''	s_1	s_2	A_1	A_2	Min. Ratio
–M	A_1	10	2	–6	8*	–8	0	0	1	0	$\frac{10}{8}$
0	s_1	6	2	–4	0	0	1	0	0	0	—
–M	A_2	8	0	4	–2	2	0	–1	0	1	—
	$Z_j - C_j$	–18M	–2M + 2	2M + 2	–6M + 2	6M – 2	0	M	0	0	

Calculations for $Z_j - C_j$

$$Z_1 - C_1 = -M(2) + 0.2 - M(0) + 2 = -2M + 2$$

$$Z_2 - C_2 = -M(-6) + 0(-4) - M(4) + 2 = 6M - 4M + 2 = 2M + 2$$

$$Z_3 - C_3 = -M.8 + 0.0 - M(-2) + 2 = -8M + 2M + 2 = -6M + 2^*$$

$$Z_4 - C_4 = -M(-8) + 0.0 - M(2) - 2 = 8M - 2M - 2 = 6M - 2$$

$$Z_5 - C_5 = -M.0 + 0.1 - M.0 - 0 = 0$$

$$Z_6 - C_6 = -M.0 + 0.0 - M(-1) - 0 = M$$

$$Z_7 - C_7 = -M.1 + 0.0 - M.0 + M = -M + M = 0$$

$$Z_8 - C_8 = -M.0 + 0.0 - M.1 + M = 0$$

Since $Z_3 - C_3$ is most negative, therefore x_3' enters the basis.

Here, minimum ratio is min $= \left[\frac{10}{8}, -, -\right] = \frac{10}{8}$

Thus A_1 leaves the basis and is dropped out.

Iteration–1

			x_2 ↓						
	C_j		-2	-2	-2	2	0	0	$-M$	
C_B	Y_B	X_B	x_1	x_2	x_3'	x_3''	s_1	s_2	A_1	Min. Ratio
-2	x_3'	$\frac{5}{4}$	$\frac{1}{4}$	$\frac{-3}{4}$	1	-1	0	0	0	—
0	s_1	6	2	-4	0	0	1	0	0	—
$-M$	A_2	$\frac{21}{2}$	$\frac{1}{2}$	$\frac{5}{2}^*$	0	0	0	-1	1	$\frac{21/2}{5/2}$ ←
	$Z_j - C_j$	$-\frac{21}{2}M - \frac{5}{2}$	$\frac{-M}{2} + \frac{3}{4}$	$\frac{-5M}{2} + \frac{7}{2}$ ↑	0	0	0	M	0	

Calculations of Row Operations

$$R_1(\text{New}) \longrightarrow \frac{R_1}{8}(\text{Old})$$

i.e., : $\left(\frac{10}{8} \quad \frac{2}{8} \quad \frac{-6}{8} \quad \frac{8}{8} \quad \frac{-8}{8} \quad \frac{0}{8} \quad \frac{0}{8} \quad \frac{0}{8}\right)$

$\therefore$ $R_1(\text{New})$: $\left(\frac{5}{4} \quad \frac{1}{4} \quad \frac{-3}{4} \quad 1 \quad -1 \quad 0 \quad 0 \quad 0\right)$

$$R_2(\text{New}) \longrightarrow R_2(\text{Old}) - 0.R_1(\text{New})$$

Now $R_2(\text{Old})$	:	6	2	-4	0	0	1	0	0
and $0.R_1(\text{New})$	:	0	0	0	0	0	0	0	0
(Subtract)	:	–	–	–	–	–	–	–	–
$\therefore$ $R_2(\text{New})$	:	6	2	-4	0	0	1	0	0

$R_3(\text{New}) \longrightarrow R_3(\text{Old}) + 2R_2(\text{New})$

Now $R_3(\text{Old})$	:	8	0	4	-2	2	0	-1	1
and $2R_2(\text{New})$	:	$\frac{5}{2}$	$\frac{1}{2}$	$\frac{-3}{2}$	2	-2	0	0	0
(Add)	:	+	+	+	+	+	+	+	+
$\therefore$ $R_3(\text{New})$	:	$\frac{21}{2}$	$\frac{1}{2}$	$\frac{5}{2}$	0	0	0	-1	1

Calculations for $Z_j - C_j$

$$Z_1 - C_1 = -2.\frac{1}{4} + 0.2 - M.\frac{1}{2} + 2 = \frac{1}{2} - \frac{1}{2}M + 2 = -\frac{1}{2}M + \frac{3}{2}$$

$$Z_2 - C_2 = -2.\left(\frac{-3}{4}\right) + 0.(-4) - M\left(\frac{5}{2}\right) + 2 = \frac{3}{2} - \frac{5}{2}M + 2 = -\frac{5}{2}M + \frac{7}{2}*$$

$$Z_3 - C_3 = -2.1 + 0.0 - M.0 + 2 = 0$$

$$Z_4 - C_4 = -2.(-1) + 0.0 - M(0) - 2 = 2 - 2 = 0$$

$$Z_5 - C_5 = -2.0 + 0.1 - M.0 - 0 = 0$$

$$Z_6 - C_6 = -2.0 + 0.0 - M.(-1) - 0 = M$$

$$Z_7 - C_7 = -2.0 + 0.0 - M(1) + M = 0$$

Thus $Z_2 - C_2$ enters the basis as $Z_2 - C_2$ is most negative.

$$\text{Now } \min\left[-, -\frac{21/2}{5/2}\right] = \frac{21}{5}$$

So, A_2 leaves the basis and is dropped out.

Iteration–2

			−2	−2	−2	2	0	0
C_B	Y_B	X_B	x_1	x_2	x_3'	x_3''	s_1	s_2
−2	x_3'	$\frac{22}{5}$	$\frac{2}{5}$	0	1	−1	0	$\frac{1}{4}$
0	s_1	$\frac{114}{5}$	$\frac{14}{5}$	0	0	0	1	$\frac{-8}{5}$
−2	x_2	$\frac{21}{5}$	$\frac{1}{5}$	1	0	0	0	$\frac{-2}{5}$
	$Z_j - C_j$		$\frac{4}{5}$	0	0	0	0	$\frac{3}{10}$

$$R_3(\text{New}) \longrightarrow \frac{R_3}{5/2}(\text{Old})$$

$$i.e., \quad : \quad \left(\frac{21}{2}.\frac{2}{5} \quad \frac{1}{2}.\frac{2}{5} \quad \frac{5}{2}.\frac{2}{5} \quad 0.\frac{2}{5} \quad 0.\frac{2}{5} \quad 0.\frac{2}{5} \quad -1.\frac{2}{5}\right)$$

$$\therefore \quad R_3(\text{New}) \quad : \quad \left(\frac{21}{5} \quad \frac{1}{5} \quad 1 \quad 0 \quad 0 \quad 0 \quad \frac{-2}{5}\right)$$

$$R_1(\text{New}) \longrightarrow R_1(\text{Old}) + \frac{3}{4}R_3(\text{New})$$

Now	R_1(Old)	:	$\frac{5}{4}$	$\frac{1}{4}$	$\frac{-3}{4}$	1	–1	0	0
and	$\frac{3}{4}R_3$(New)	:	$\frac{63}{20}$	$\frac{3}{20}$	$\frac{3}{4}$	0	0	0	$\frac{-6}{20}$
(Add)	:		+	+	+	+	+	+	+
∴	R_1(New)	:	$\frac{89}{20}$	$\frac{88}{20}$	0	1	–1	0	$\frac{-6}{20}$

R_2(New) ⟶ R_2(Old) + $4R_3$(New)

Now	R_2(Old)	:	6	2	–4	0	0	1	0
and	$4R_3$(New)	:	$\frac{84}{5}$	$\frac{4}{5}$	4	0	0	0	$\frac{-8}{5}$
	(Add)		+	+	+	+	+	+	+
∴	R_2(New)	:	$\frac{114}{5}$	$\frac{14}{5}$	0	0	0	1	$\frac{-8}{5}$

Calculations for $Z_j - C_j$

$$Z_1 - C_1 = -2.\frac{2}{5} + 0.\frac{14}{5} - 2.\frac{1}{5} + 2 = \frac{-4}{5} - \frac{2}{5} + 2 = \frac{-6+10}{5} = \frac{4}{5}$$

$$Z_2 - C_2 = -2.0 + 0.0 - 2.1 + 2 = -2 + 2 = 0$$

$$Z_3 - C_3 = -2.1 + 0.0 - 2.0 + 2 = 0$$

$$Z_4 - C_4 = -2.(-1) + 0.0 - 2.0 - 2 = 0$$

$$Z_5 - C_5 = -2.0 + 0.1 - 2.0 - 0 = 0$$

$$Z_6 - C_6 = -2.\frac{1}{4} + 0.\left(\frac{-8}{5}\right) - 2.\left(\frac{-2}{5}\right) - 0 = -\frac{1}{2} + \frac{4}{5} = \frac{-5+8}{10} = \frac{3}{10}$$

Since all $Z_j - C_j \leq 0$, thus the optimal solution has been attained.

Value of objective functions is

$$Z = -2.\left(\frac{22}{5}\right) + 0\left(\frac{114}{5}\right) - 2\left(\frac{21}{5}\right)$$

$$= \frac{-44}{5} - \frac{42}{5} = \frac{-86}{5}$$

$x_1 = 0,\ x_2 = \frac{21}{5},\ x_3' = \frac{22}{5},\ x_3'' = 0$

$\therefore\ x_3 = x_3' = x_3'' = \frac{22}{5} - 0 = \frac{22}{5}$

∴ Optimum solution is minimum $Z = -\left(\frac{-86}{5}\right) = \frac{86}{5}$

$$\therefore \quad Z_{max} = \frac{86}{5}$$
$$x_1 = 0$$
$$x_2 = \frac{21}{5}$$
$$\text{and } x_3 = \frac{22}{5}.$$

2.7 TWO PHASE METHOD

Two phase is another method for solving a LPP that involves artificial variables. This method involves two phase, as the name indicates; Phase I and Phase II.

Algorithm

Phase I

Step 1. Convert the given LPP into maximization, if it is in minimization form.

Step 2. Assign and add surplus and artificial variables, if necessary to convert the inequality constraints into equality constraints.

Step 3. Then assign zero coefficients to each of the decision variables (x_j) and to the surplus variables. Assign –1 coefficient to each of the artificial variable.

Step 4. Check the optimality criteria as:

(*a*) If $Z^* = 0$, and at least one artificial variable is present in the basis with positive value, then no feasible solution exists for the original LPP.

(*b*) If $Z^* = 0$, and no artificial variable is present in the basis, then the basis consists of only decision variables and hence go to phase II to obtain an optimum basic feasible solution of the original LPP.

(*c*) If $Z^* = 0$ and at least one artificial variable is present in the basis at zero value; then a feasible solution to the above LPP is also a feasible solution to the original LPP. Now in order to arrive at the basic feasible solution, proceed directly to phase II or else eliminate the artificial basic variable and then proceed to next phase II where $Z^* = \sum_{i=1}^{m} (-1)A_i$

An artificial variable is never considered again to enter into the basis.

Phase II

Now assign actual coefficients to the variables in the objective function and zero to the artificial variables that appeared at zero level (value) in the basis at the end of first phase.

In other words, the last simplex table of phase I is used as the initial simplex table for phase II.

Now apply the usual simplex algorithm to obtain the optimal solution to the original problem. Artificial variables that do not appear in the basis can be removed.

Remark:

(1) It is to be noted that in the phase II, the sequence of variables entered into the basis will in general be different from the sequence in Big-M method due to the presence of artificial vectors in the basis.

(2) The LPP defined in the above phases is also called as an auxiliary problem. The value of the objective function in this problem is bounded from below by zero because the objective function represents the sum of artificial variables with negative unit coefficients. Thus, the solution to this problem can be obtained in finite number of steps.

Example 21. *Maximize* $Z = -x_1 - x_2$

Subject to $3x_1 + 2x_2 \geq 30$

$-2x_1 - 3x_2 \leq -30$

$x_1 + x_2 \leq 5$

$x_1, x_2 \leq 0$

Solve the above LPP *using Two phase method.*

Solution.

$\therefore$ Maximize $Z = -x_1 - x_2$

Subject to $3x_1 - 2x_2 \geq 30$

$2x_1 + 3x_2 \geq 30$

$x_1 + x_2 \leq 5$

$x_1', x_2 \geq 0$

Introducing slack, variables $s_3 \geq 0$, surplus variables $s_1 \geq 0$, $s_2 \geq 0$ and artificial variables $A_1 \geq 0$ and $A_2 \geq 0$ in the given constraints as follows.

$$3x_1 + 2x_2 - s_1 + A_1 = 30$$

$$2x_1 + 3x_2 - s_2 + A_2 = 30$$

$$x_1 + x_2 + x_3 = 5$$

$$x_1, x_2, s_1, s_2, s_3, A_1 \text{ and } A_2 \geq 0.$$

Thus the above LPP, after introducing slack, surplus and artificial variables can be written as:

Maximize $Z = -x_1 + x_2 + 0.s_1 + 0.s_2 + 0.s_3 - A_1 - A_2$

Subject to $3x_1 + 2x_2 - s_1 + A_1 = 30$

$2x_1 + 3x_2 - s_2 + A_2 = 30$

$x_1 + x_2 + s_3 = 5$

$x_1, x_2, s_1, s_2, s_3, A_1$ and $A_2 \geq 0$.

Phase I. Now the first phase, Phase I starts by considering the following auxiliary LPP.

Max $Z^* = -A_1 - A_2$

Subject to $3x_1 + 2x_2 - s_1 + A_1 = 30$

$2x_1 + 3x_2 - s_1 + A_2 = 30$

$x_1 + x_2 + s_3 = 5$

$x_1, x_2, s_1, s_2, s_3, A_1, A_2 \geq 0.$

The initial basic feasible solution is

$$A_1 = 30$$
$$A_2 = 30$$
$$s_3 = 5$$

Iteration–0

	$C_j \rightarrow$		0	0	0	0	0	–1	–1	
C_B	Y_B	X_B	x_1	x_2	s_1	s_2	s_3	A_1	A_2	Min. Ratio
–1	A_1	30	3	2	–1	0	0	1	0	$\frac{30}{3}$
–1	A_2	30	2	3	0	–1	0	0	1	$\frac{30}{2}$
0	s_1	5	1*	1	0	0	1	0	0	$\frac{5}{1}$
	$Z_j - C_j$	–60	–5 ↑	–5	1	1	0	0	0	

Calculations for $Z_j - C_j$

$$Z_1 - C_1 = -1.3 + (-1).\ 2 + 0.1 - 0 = -3 - 2 = -5$$
$$Z_2 - C_2 = -1.2 - 1.3 + 0.1 - 0 = -5$$
$$Z_3 - C_3 = -1.(-1) + (-1).0 + 0.0 - 0 = 1$$
$$Z_4 - C_4 = -1.0 - 1.(-1) + 0.0 - 0 = 1$$
$$Z_5 - C_5 = -1.0 + (-1)\ .\ 0 + 0.1 - 0 = 0$$
$$Z_6 - C_6 = -1.1 + (-1)\ .\ 0 + 0.0 + 1 = 0$$
$$Z_7 - C_7 = -1.0 - 1.1 + 0.0 + 1 = 0$$

Since $Z_1 - C_1$ and $Z_2 - C_2$ has same and are most negative, choose $Z_1 - C_1$. x_1 enters the basis (or x_2 enter the basis)

Here $\min \left[\frac{30}{3}, \frac{30}{2}, \frac{5}{1}\right] = 5$

Thus s_1 leaves the basis

1 becomes the pivot element.

Iteration–1

			0	0	0	0	0	–1	–1
C_B	Y_B	X_B	x_1	x_2	s_1	s_2	s_3	A_1	A_2
–1	A_1	15	0	–1	–1	0	–3	1	0
–1	A_2	20	0	1	0	–1	–2	0	1
0	s_1	5	1	1	0	0	1	0	0
	$Z_j - C_j$	–35	0	0	1	1	5	0	0

Calculation of Row Operations

$R_1(\text{New}) \longrightarrow R_1(\text{Old}) - 3R_3(\text{New})$

Now R_1(Old)	:	30	3	2	–1	0	0	1	0
and $3R_3$(New)	:	15	3	3	0	0	3	0	0
(Subtract)	:	–	–	–	–	–	–	–	–
∴ R_3(New)	:	15	0	–1	–1	0	–3	1	0

$R_2(\text{New}) \longrightarrow R_2(\text{Old}) - 2R_3(\text{New})$

Now R_2(Old)	:	30	2	3	0	–1	0	0	1
and $2R_3$(New)	:	10	2	2	0	0	2	0	0
(Subtract)	:	–	–	–	–	–	–	–	–
∴ R_2(New)	:	20	0	1	0	–1	–2	0	1

Calculations of $Z_j - C_j$

$$Z_1 - C_1 = -1.0 + (-1)\ .0 + 0.1 - 0 = 0$$
$$Z_2 - C_2 = -1(-1) + (-1)\ 1 + 0.1 - 0 = 0$$
$$Z_3 - C_3 = -1(-1) + (-1).0 + 0.0 - 0 = 1$$
$$Z_4 - C_4 = -1.0 + (-1).\ (-1) + 0.0 - 0 = +1$$
$$Z_5 - C_5 = -1.(-3) - 1.(-2) + 0.1 - 0 = 5$$
$$Z_6 - C_6 = -1.1 - 1.0 + 0.0 + 1 = 0$$
$$Z_7 - C_7 = -1.0 - 1.1 - 0.0 + 1 = 0$$

Since $Z_j - C_j \geq 0$, and the two artificial variables A_1 and A_2 still appears in the basis at positive level, therefore the original problem has no feasible solution.

Example 22. *Solve the following LPP using two phase simplex method.*

$$\text{Maximize } Z = -x_1 - x_2$$
$$\text{Subject to } \quad 2x_1 + x_2 \geq 4$$
$$x_1 + 7x_2 \geq 7$$
$$x_1, x_2 \geq 0$$

Solution. Now introducing surplus and artificial variables in given constraints.

$$2x_1 + 9x_2 - s_1 + A_1 = 4$$
$$x_1 + 7x_2 - s_2 + A_2 = 7$$
$$x_1, x_2, s_1, s_2, A_1 \text{ and } A_2 \geq 0.$$

Thus the above LPP, after introducing surplus and artificial variables can be written as:

$$\text{Maximize } Z = -x_1 - x_2 + 0{\cdot}s_1 + 0{\cdot}s_2 - A_1 - A_2$$
$$\text{Subject to } \quad 2x_1 + x_2 - s_1 + A_1 = 4$$
$$x_1 + 7x_2 - s_2 + A_2 = 7$$
$$x_1, x_2, s_1, s_2, A_1, \text{ and } A_2 \geq 0.$$

The initial solution is $A_1 = 4$ and $A_2 = 7$.

Iteration–0

	$C_j \rightarrow$		0	0	0	0	−1	−1	
C_B	Y_B	X_B	x_1	x_2	s_1	s_2	A_1	A_2	Min. Ratio
−1	A_1	4	2	1	−1	0	1	0	$\frac{4}{1}$
−1	A_2	7	1	7*	0	−1	0	1	$\frac{7}{7}$
	$Z_j - C_j$	−11	−3	−8	1	1	0	0	

The net evaluation can be computed in the same manner, as done earlier. Here $Z_2 - C_2 = -8 < 0$, is most negative.

Thus x_2 enters the basis.

Since minimum ratio is 1 $\left(=\frac{7}{7}\right)$, thus A_2 leaves the basis and can be dropped out from the simplex table.

So 7, becomes the pivot element.

Iteration–1

	$C_j \rightarrow$		0	0	0	0	−1	
C_B	Y_B	X_B	x_1	x_2	s_1	s_2	A_1	Min. Ratio
−1	A_1	3	$\frac{13}{7}$*	0	−1	$\frac{1}{7}$	1	$\frac{3}{13/-7}$ ←
0	x_2	1	$\frac{1}{7}$	1	0	$\frac{-1}{7}$	0	$\frac{1}{1/7}$
	$Z_j - C_j$	−3	$\frac{-13}{7}$ ↑	0	1	$\frac{-1}{7}$	0	

Calculations for Row Operations

$$R_2(\text{New}) \longrightarrow \frac{R_2}{7}(\text{Old})$$

$$i.e., \quad : \quad \left(\frac{7}{7} \quad \frac{1}{7} \quad \frac{7}{7} \quad \frac{0}{7} \quad \frac{-1}{7} \quad \frac{0}{7} \quad \frac{1}{7}\right)$$

$$\therefore R_2(\text{New}) \quad : \quad \left(1 \quad \frac{1}{7} \quad 1 \quad 0 \quad \frac{-1}{7} \quad 0 \quad \frac{1}{7}\right)$$

$R_1(\text{New}) \longrightarrow R_1(\text{Old}) - 1.R_2(\text{New})$

Now R_1(Old)	:	4	2	1	–1	0	1
and R_2(New)	:	1	$\frac{1}{7}$	1	0	$\frac{-1}{7}$	0
(Subtract)	:	–	–	–	–	+	–
$\therefore$ R_1(New)	:	3	$\frac{13}{7}$	0	–1	$\frac{1}{7}$	1

Calculations for $Z_j - C_j$

$$Z_1 - C_1 = -1.\frac{13}{7} + 0.\frac{1}{7} = \frac{-13}{7}$$

Similarly, calculate the remaining net evaluations.

Since $Z_1 - C_1$ is most negative, therefore, x_1 enters the basis.

Here, Min. Ratio is min $\left[\frac{3}{13/7}, \frac{1}{1/7}\right]$

$$\min\left[\frac{3\times7}{13}, 1\times7\right] = \min\left[\frac{21}{13}, 7\right] = \frac{21}{13}$$

Now x_1 enters the basis and A_1 leaves the basis, thus A_1 is dropped out.

Iteration–2

	$C_j \rightarrow$		0	0	0	0
C_B	Y_B	X_B	x_1	x_2	s_1	s_2
0	x_1	$\frac{21}{13}$	1	0	$\frac{-7}{13}$	$\frac{1}{13}$
0	x_2	$\frac{10}{13}$	0	1	$\frac{1}{13}$	$\frac{-14}{91}$
	$Z_j - C_j$	0	0	0	0	0

Calculations for Row Operations

$$R_1(\text{New}) \longrightarrow \frac{R_1}{13/7}(\text{Old}) \text{ or } \frac{7}{13}R_1(\text{Old})$$

$$\therefore R_1(\text{New}) \quad : \quad \left(3.\frac{7}{13} \quad \frac{13}{7}.\frac{7}{13} \quad 0.\frac{7}{13} \quad -1.\frac{7}{13} \quad \frac{1}{7}.\frac{7}{13}\right)$$

$$i.e., \quad : \quad \left(\frac{21}{13} \quad 1 \quad 0 \quad \frac{-7}{13} \quad \frac{1}{13}\right)$$

$$R_2(\text{New}) \longrightarrow R_2(\text{Old}) - \frac{1}{7} R_1(\text{New})$$

$\therefore R_2(\text{Old})$	:	1	$\frac{1}{7}$	1	0	$-\frac{1}{7}$
$\frac{1}{7} R_1(\text{New})$	:	$\frac{3}{13}$	$\frac{1}{7}$	0	$\frac{-1}{13}$	$\frac{1}{91}$
(Subtract)	:	–	–	–	+	–
$\therefore R_2(\text{New})$	:	$\frac{10}{13}$	0	1	$\frac{1}{13}$	$\frac{-14}{91}$

Calculations for $Z_j - C_j$

$$Z_1 - C_1 = 0.1 + 0.0 - 0 = 0$$
$$Z_2 - C_2 = 0.0 + 0.1 - 0 = 0$$
$$Z_3 - C_3 = 0.\frac{-7}{13} + 0.\frac{-1}{13} - 0 = 0$$
$$Z_4 - C_4 = 0.\frac{1}{13} + 0.\left(\frac{-14}{91}\right) = 0$$

Since all $Z_j - C_j \geq 0$, therefore an infeasible solution is obtained. Instead of entering x_1 variable, now enters s_2 variable, so as to obtain an optimal solution.

Again consider iteration–1.

Iteration–1

			0	0	0	0	–1	
C_B	Y_B	X_B	x_1	x_2	s_1	s_2	A_2	Min. Ratio
–1	A_1	3	$\frac{13}{7}$	0	–1	$\frac{1}{7}$*	1	←
0	x_2	1	$\frac{1}{7}$	1	0	$\frac{-1}{7}$	0	
$Z_j - C_j$		–3	$\frac{-13}{7}$	0	1	$\frac{-1}{7}$	0	

To avoid infeasibility, s_2 is entered into the basis and A_1 leaves the basis and is dropped out.

Iteration–2

			0	0	0	0
C_B	Y_B	X_B	x_1	x_2	s_1	s_2
0	s_2	21	13	0	–7	1
0	x_2	4	2	1	–1	0
$Z_j - C_j$		0	0	0	0	0

Calculations for Row Operations

$$R_1(\text{New}) \longrightarrow \frac{R_1(\text{Old})}{1/7}$$

i.e., $7R_1(\text{Old})$

$$R_1(\text{New}) \quad : \quad \left(3.7 \quad \frac{13}{7}.7 \quad 0.7 \quad -1.7 \quad \frac{1}{7}.7\right)$$

$$\therefore R_1(\text{New}) \quad : \quad (21 \quad 13 \quad 0 \quad -7 \quad 1)$$

$$R_2(\text{New}) \longrightarrow R_2(\text{Old}) + \frac{1}{7} R_1(\text{New})$$

Now $R_2(\text{Old})$	:	1	$\frac{1}{7}$	1	0	$-\frac{1}{7}$
and $\frac{1}{7} R_1(\text{New})$	:	3	$\frac{13}{7}$	0	–1	$\frac{1}{7}$
(Add)	:	+	+	+	+	+
$\therefore R_2(\text{New})$	:	4	2	1	–1	0

Calculations for $Z_j - C_j$

$$Z_1 - C_1 = 13.0 + 2.0 - 0 = 0$$

Similarly all $Z_j - C_j = 0.$

Since all $Z_j - C_j \geq 0$, the optimal solution has been attained.

$$Z_{max} = 0$$
$$x_1 = 0$$
$$x_2 = 4$$

However, the above solution may or may not be the basic feasible solution to the original LPP. Thus, Phase II is considered to obtain an initial basis feasible solution.

Example 23. *Use two phase simplex method to solve the following LPP*

$$\textit{Maximize } Z = -\frac{15}{2} x_1 + 3x_2$$

$$\textit{Subject to} \quad 3x_1 - x_2 - x_3 \geq 3$$
$$x_1 - x_2 + x_3 \geq 2$$
$$x_1, x_2, x_3 \geq 0.$$

Solution. Introducing surplus and artificial variables, s_1, s_2, A_1 and A_2. the above LPP can be written as:

$$\text{Maximize } Z = -\frac{15}{2} x_1 + 3x_2$$

$$\text{Subject to} \quad 3x_1 - x_2 - x_3 - s_1 + A_1 = 3$$
$$x_1 - x_2 + x_3 - s_2 + A_2 = 2$$
$$x_1, x_2, s_1, s_2, A_1 \text{ and } A_2 \geq 0.$$

Then formulating the new objective function Z^*, containing only the artificial variables whose costs are –1.

$$\text{Maximize } Z = -A_1 - A_2$$

$$\text{Subject to} \quad 3x_1 - x_2 - x_3 - s_1 + A_1 = 3$$

$$x_1 - x_2 + x_3 - s_2 + A_2 = 2$$

$$x_1, x_2, s_1, s_2, A_1, \text{ and } A_2 \geq 0.$$

The initial basic feasible solution is

$$A_1 = 3 \text{ and } A_2 = 2.$$

Iteration–0

			0	0	0	0	0	–1	–1	
C_B	Y_B	X_B	x_1	x_2	x_3	s_1	s_2	A_1	A_2	Min. Ratio
–1	A_1	3	3*	–1	–1	–1	0	1	0	$\frac{3}{3}$ ←
–1	A_2	2	1	–1	1	0	–1	0	1	21
$Z_j - C_j$		–5	–4 ↑	2	0	1	1	0	0	

Since $Z_j - C_j$ is most negative, x_1 enters and A_1 leaves the basis.

Iteration–1

			0	0	0	0	0	–1	
C_B	Y_B	X_B	x_1	x_2	x_3	s_1	s_2	A_2	Min. Ratio
0	x_1	1	1	$\frac{-1}{3}$	$\frac{-1}{3}$	$\frac{-1}{3}$	0	0	—
–1	A_2	1	0	$\frac{-2}{3}$	$\frac{4}{3}$*	$\frac{1}{3}$	–1	1	$\frac{3}{4}$ ←
$Z_j - C_j$		–1	0	$\frac{2}{3}$	$\frac{-4}{3}$	$\frac{-1}{3}$	1	0	

Calculations for Row Operations for Iteration–2

$$R_1(\text{New}) \longrightarrow \frac{R_1}{3}(\text{Old})$$

$$i.e., \quad \left(\frac{3}{3} \quad \frac{3}{3} \quad \frac{-1}{3} \quad \frac{-1}{3} \quad \frac{-1}{3} \quad \frac{0}{3} \quad \frac{0}{3}\right)$$

$$\therefore R_1(\text{New}) \quad : \quad \left(1 \quad 1 \quad \frac{-1}{3} \quad \frac{-1}{3} \quad \frac{-1}{3} \quad 0 \quad 0\right)$$

$R_2(\text{New}) \longrightarrow R_2(\text{Old}) + R_1(\text{New})$

Now R_2(Old)	:	2	1	–1	1	0	–1	1
and R_1(New)	:	1	1	$\frac{-1}{3}$	$\frac{-1}{3}$	$\frac{-1}{3}$	0	0
(Subtract)		–	–	+	+	+	–	–
$\therefore$ R_2(New)	:	1	0	$\frac{-2}{3}$	$\frac{4}{3}$	$\frac{1}{3}$	–1	1

Calculations for $Z_j - C_j$

$$Z_1 - C_1 = 0.1 - 1.0 - 0 = 0$$

$$Z_2 - C_2 = 0.\left(-\frac{1}{3}\right) - 1\left(-\frac{2}{3}\right) - 0 = \frac{2}{3}$$

$$Z_3 - C_3 = 0.\left(-\frac{1}{3}\right) - 1\left(\frac{4}{3}\right) - 0 = \frac{4}{3}$$

$$Z_4 - C_4 = 0.\left(-\frac{1}{3}\right) - 1\left(\frac{1}{3}\right) - 0 = \frac{-1}{3}$$

$$Z_5 - C_5 = 0.0 - 1.(-1) - 0 = 1$$

$$Z_6 - C_6 = 0.0 - 1.1 + 1 = 0$$

Since $Z_3 - C_3$ is most negative, thus x_3 enters the basis

and $$\min\left[-, \frac{1}{4/3}\right] = \frac{3}{4}$$

A_2 leaves the basis and is dropped out.

$\left(\frac{4}{3}\right)$ becomes the pivot element.

Iteration–2

	$C_j \rightarrow$		0	0	0	0	
C_B	Y_B	X_B	x_1	x_2	x_3	s_1	s_2
0	x_1	$\frac{5}{4}$	1	$\frac{-1}{2}$	0	$\frac{-1}{4}$	$\frac{-1}{2}$
0	x_3	$\frac{3}{4}$	0	$\frac{-1}{2}$	1	$\frac{1}{4}$	$\frac{-3}{4}$
	$Z_j - C_j$	0	0	$\frac{3}{4}$	0	$\frac{15}{8}$	$\frac{15}{8}$

Since all $Z_j - C_j \geq 0$ we have attained the optimal solution in phase I and this solution does not contain any artificial variable at zero or positive level.

Calculations for Row Operations in Iteration–2

$R_2(\text{New}) \longrightarrow \frac{3}{4} R_1(\text{Old})$

$$R_2(\text{New}) \quad : \quad \left(1.\frac{3}{4} \quad 0.\frac{3}{4} \quad \frac{-2}{3}.\frac{3}{4} \quad \frac{4}{3}.\frac{3}{4} \quad \frac{1}{3}.\frac{3}{4} \quad -1.\frac{3}{4} \right)$$

$$\therefore R_2(\text{New}) \quad : \quad \left(\frac{3}{4} \quad 0 \quad \frac{-1}{2} \quad 1 \quad \frac{1}{4} \quad \frac{-3}{4} \right)$$

$R_1(\text{New}) \longrightarrow R_1(\text{Old}) + \frac{1}{3} R_2(\text{New})$

$\therefore$ Now R_1(Old)	:	1	1	$\frac{-1}{3}$	$\frac{-1}{3}$	$\frac{-1}{3}$	0
and $\frac{1}{3} R_2$(New)	:	$\frac{1}{4}$	0	$\frac{-1}{6}$	$\frac{1}{3}$	$\frac{1}{12}$	$\frac{-1}{4}$
(Add)		+	+	+	+	+	+
$\therefore R_1$(New)	:	$\frac{5}{4}$	1	$-\frac{1}{2}$	0	$\frac{-1}{4}$	$\frac{-1}{4}$

Phase II

Now we consider the original LPP after introducing only surplus variables (s_1 and s_2)

Thus $\qquad \text{Max } Z = \frac{-15}{2} x_1 + 3x_2 + 0.x_3 + 0.s_1 + 0.s_2$

Subject to

$$3x_1 - x_2 - x_3 - s_2 = 3$$
$$x_1 - x_2 + x_3 - s_2 = 2$$
$$x_1, x_2, x_3, s_1, s_2 \geq 0$$

Using the solution of Iteration–2 of phase I, we use the usual simplex method to maximize the above problem.

Iteration–3

			$\frac{-15}{2}$	3	0	0	0
C_B	Y_B	X_B	x_1	x_2	x_3	s_1	s_2
$\frac{15}{2}$	x_1	$\frac{5}{4}$	1	$\frac{-1}{2}$	0	$\frac{-1}{4}$	$\frac{-1}{4}$
0	x_3	$\frac{3}{4}$	0	$\frac{-1}{2}$	1	$\frac{1}{4}$	$\frac{-3}{4}$
	$Z_j - C_j$	$\frac{75}{8}$	0	$\frac{3}{4}$	0	$\frac{15}{8}$	$\frac{15}{8}$

Since all $Z_j - C_j \geq 0$. Hence an optimum solution is same as found in Iteration–3 (or in Iteration–2).

$$\therefore \qquad Z_{max} = \frac{75}{8};\ x_1 = \frac{5}{4},\ x_2 = 0 \text{ and } x_3 = \frac{3}{4}$$

Remark: In phase II, the last table of phase I is considered with the only change in cost coefficients of the decision variables.

Example 24. *Use two phase simplex method to solve the following LPP.*

$$\text{Maximize } F = x_1 + 2x_2 - 3x_3$$
$$\text{Subject to } \quad -2x_1 + x_2 - 3x_3 = 2$$
$$2x_1 + 3x_2 + 4x_3 = 1$$
$$x_1, x_2 \geq 0.$$

Solution. Converting the given LPP into maximization form (*i.e.*, in standard form).

$$\text{Maximize } Z = -x_1 + 2x_2 + 3x_3 \text{ (as } Z = -F)$$

Now introducing only the artificial variables $A_1 \geq 0, A_2 \geq 0$

$\therefore$ The LPP can be rewritten as

$$\text{Maximize } Z = -x_1 + 2x_2 + 3x_3 - A_1 - A_2$$
$$\text{Subject to } \quad -2x_1 + x_2 + 3x_3 + A_1 = 2$$
$$2x_1 + 3x_2 + 4x_3 + A_2 = 1$$
$$x_1, x_2, x_3, A_1 \text{ and } A_2 \geq 0.$$

The initial solution is $A_1 = 2$ and $A_2 = 1$.

Phase I

$$\text{Maximize } Z^* = -A_1 - A_2.$$
$$\text{Subject to } \quad -2x_1 + x_2 + 3x_3 + A_1 = 2$$
$$2x_1 + 3x_2 + 4x_3 + A_2 = 1$$
$$x_1, x_2, x_3, A_1, A_2 \geq 0$$

Iteration–0

	$C_j \rightarrow$		0	0	0	1	1	
C_B	Y_B	X_B	x_1	x_2	x_3	A_1	A_2	Min. Ratio
–1	A_1	2	–2	1	3	1	0	$\frac{2}{3}$
–1	A_2	1	2	3	4*	0	1	$\frac{1}{4}$ ←
	$Z_j - C_j$	–3	0	–4	–7	0	0	
					↑			

Calculations for $Z_j - C_j$

$$Z_1 - C_1 = -1.(-2) + (-1)2 - 0 = 0$$
$$Z_2 - C_2 = -1.1 - 1.3 - 0 = -4$$
$$Z_3 - C_3 = -1.3 + -1.4 - 0 = -7$$

Similarly $\quad Z_4 - C_4$ and $Z_5 - C_5$ can be computed.

Since $Z_3 - C_3$ is most negative, thus x_3 enters the basis

Minimum ratio is computed as

$$\min.\left[\frac{2}{3}, \frac{1}{4}\right] = \frac{1}{4}$$

So A_2 leaves the basis and is dropped out.

Thus 4 becomes the pivot element.

Iteration–1

			0	0	0	–1
C_B	Y_B	X_B	x_1	x_2	x_3	A_1
–1	A_1	$\frac{5}{4}$	$\frac{-7}{2}$	$\frac{-5}{4}$	0	1
0	x_3	$\frac{1}{4}$	$\frac{1}{2}$	$\frac{3}{4}$	1	0
	$Z_j - C_j$	$\frac{-5}{4}$	$\frac{7}{2}$	$\frac{5}{4}$	0	0

Calculations for Row Operations (Iteration–1)

$R_2(\text{New}) \longrightarrow \frac{R_2}{4}(\text{Old})$

$$i.e., \quad \left(\frac{1}{4} \quad \frac{2}{4} \quad \frac{3}{4} \quad \frac{4}{4} \quad \frac{0}{4} \quad \frac{1}{4}\right)$$

$$\therefore R_2(\text{New}) \quad : \quad \left(\frac{1}{4} \quad \frac{1}{2} \quad \frac{3}{4} \quad 1 \quad 0 \quad \frac{1}{4}\right)$$

$R_1(\text{New}) \longrightarrow R_1(\text{Old}) + 3R_2(\text{New})$

$\therefore$ Now $R_1(\text{Old})$	:	2	–2	1	3	1
and $3R_2(\text{New})$	:	$\frac{3}{4}$	$\frac{3}{2}$	$\frac{9}{4}$	3	0
(Subtract)		–	–	–	–	–
$\therefore R_1(\text{New})$	:	$\frac{5}{4}$	$\frac{-7}{2}$	$\frac{-5}{4}$	0	1

Calculations for $Z_j - C_j$

$$Z_1 - C_1 = -1\left(\frac{-7}{2}\right) + 0.\frac{1}{2} - 0 = \frac{7}{2}$$

$$Z_2 - C_2 = -1\left(\frac{-5}{2}\right) + 0.\frac{3}{4} - 0 = \frac{5}{4}$$

$$Z_3 - C_3 = -1.0 + 0.1 - 0 = 0$$

$$Z_4 - C_4 = -1.1 + 0.0 + 1 = 0$$

Since all $Z_j - C_j \geq 0$, an optimum solution has been attained. But artificial variable A_1 still remains in the basic solution at a positive level and Z_{max}^* is negative.

Hence the original problem does not possess any feasible solution.

Remark. If there is no feasible solution in phase I then need not to go to phase II.

Example 25. *A patient requires 10, 12 and 12 units of protiens, minerals and vitamins respectively. Food X contain 5, 2 and 1 units of proteins, minerals and vitamins respectively, while food Y contains 1, 2 and 4 units of proteins, minerals and vitamins. If the cost of food X is ₹ 3 per unit and that of food Y is ₹ 2 per unit, then how many units of each food should he purchase to minimize the cost.*

Solution. Formulation of LPP

Let x_1: Number of units of food X.

x_2: Number of units of food Y.

$5x_1 + x_2 \geq 10$ Protein constraint

$2x_1 + 2x_2 \geq 12$ Mineral constraint

$x_1 + 4x_2 \geq 12$ Vitamin constraint

Thus the above problem can be written in the form of LPP as:

$$\text{Minimize F} = 3x_1 + 2x_2$$

$$\begin{aligned} \text{Subject to} \quad & 5x_1 + x_2 \geq 10 \\ & 2x_1 + 2x_2 \geq 12 \\ & x_1 + 4x_2 \geq 12 \\ & x_1, x_2 \geq 0. \end{aligned}$$

Converting the given problem into maximization form.

$$\text{Maximize Z} = -3x_1 - 2x_2$$

$$\begin{aligned} \text{Subject to} \quad & 5x_1 + x_2 \geq 10 \\ & 2x_1 + 2x_2 \geq 12 \\ & x_1 + 4x_2 \geq 12 \\ & x_1, x_2 \geq 0. \end{aligned}$$

Introducing surplus variables (s_1, s_2, s_3) and artificial variables A_1, A_2 and A_3 to convert the inequality constraints into equality constraints.

$$\begin{aligned} & 5x_1 + x_2 - s_1 + A_1 = 10 \\ & 2x_1 + 2x_2 - s_2 + A_2 = 12 \\ & x_1 + 4x_2 - s_3 + A_3 = 12 \\ & x_1, x_2, s_1, s_2, s_3, A_1, A_2, A_3 \geq 0. \end{aligned}$$

Thus the problem can be rewritten as:

$$\text{Maximize Z} = -3x_1 - 2x_2 + 0 \cdot s_1 + 0 \cdot s_2 + 0 \cdot s_3 - A_1 - A_2 - A_3$$

$$\begin{aligned} \text{Subject to} \quad & 5x_1 + x_2 - s_1 + A_1 = 10 \\ & 2x_1 + 2x_2 - s_2 + A_2 = 12 \\ & x_1 + 4x_2 - s_3 + A_3 = 12 \\ & x_1, x_2, s_1, s_2, s_3, A_1, A_2, A_3 \geq 0. \end{aligned}$$

To solve the above LPP using two phase simplex method.

Phase I

$$\text{Maximize } Z = -A_1 - A_2 - A_3$$

$$\begin{aligned} \text{Subject to} \quad & 5x_1 + x_2 - s_1 + A_1 = 10 \\ & 2x_1 + 2x_2 - s_2 + A_2 = 12 \\ & x_1 + 4x_2 - s_3 + A_3 = 12 \\ & x_1, x_2, s_1, s_2, s_3, A_1, A_2, A_3 \geq 0. \end{aligned}$$

The initial solution is

$$\begin{aligned} A_1 &= 10 \\ A_2 &= 12 \\ \text{and } A_3 &= 12. \end{aligned}$$

Iteration–0

		C_j	0	0	0	0	0	–1	–1	–1	
C_B	Y_B	X_B	x_1	x_2	s_1	s_2	s_3	A_1	A_2	A_3	Min. Ratio
–1	A_1	10	5	1	–1	0	0	1	0	0	$\frac{10}{5}$
–1	A_2	12	2	2	0	–1	0	0	1	0	$\frac{12}{2}$
–1	A_3	12	1	4	0	0	–1	0	0	1	$\frac{12}{1}$
$Z_j - C_j$		–34	–8 ↑	–7	1	1	1	0	0	0	

Since $Z_j - C_j$ (= –8) is most negative. Thus x_1 enters the basis and min ratio is 2 for R_1. So A_1 leaves the basis and is dropped out. Thus 5 becomes the pivot element.

Iteration–1

		C_j	0	0	0	0	0	–1	–1	
C_B	Y_B	X_B	x_1	x_2	s_1	s_2	s_3	A_2	A_3	Min. Ratio
0	x_1	2	1	$\frac{1}{5}$	$\frac{-1}{5}$	0	0	0	0	$\frac{2}{1/5}$
–1	A_2	8	0	$\frac{8}{5}$	$\frac{2}{5}$	–1	0	1	0	$\frac{8}{8/5}$
–1	A_3	10	0	$\frac{19^*}{5}$	$\frac{1}{5}$	0	–1	0	1	$\frac{10}{19/5}$ ←
$Z_j - C_j$		–18	0	$\frac{-27}{5}$ ↑	$\frac{-3}{5}$	1	1	0	0	

Calculations for Row Operations (Iteration–1)

$R_1(\text{New}) \longrightarrow \frac{R_1}{5}(\text{Old})$

$$\left(\frac{10}{5} \quad \frac{5}{3} \quad \frac{1}{5} \quad \frac{-1}{5} \quad \frac{0}{5} \quad \frac{0}{5} \quad \frac{0}{5} \quad \frac{0}{5}\right)$$

i.e., $R_1(\text{New}) \quad (2 \quad 1 \quad \frac{1}{5} \quad \frac{-1}{5} \quad 0 \quad 0 \quad 0 \quad 0)$

$R_2(\text{New}) \longrightarrow R_2(\text{Old}) - 2R_1(\text{New})$

Now R_2(Old)	:	12	2	2	0	–1	0	1	0
and $2R_1$(New)	:	4	2	$\frac{2}{5}$	$\frac{-2}{5}$	0	0	0	0
(Subtract)		–	–	–	+	–	–	–	–
∴ R_2(New)	:	8	0	$\frac{8}{5}$	$\frac{2}{5}$	–1	0	1	0

$R_3(\text{New}) \longrightarrow R_3(\text{Old}) - R_1(\text{New})$

Now R_3(Old)	:	12	1	4	0	0	–1	0	1
and R_1(New)	:	2	1	$\frac{1}{5}$	$\frac{-1}{5}$	0	0	0	0
(Subtract)		–	–	–	+	–	–	–	–
∴ R_3(New)	:	10	0	$\frac{19}{5}$	$\frac{1}{5}$	0	–1	0	1

Calculations for $Z_j - C_j$

$$Z_1 - C_1 = 0$$

$$Z_2 - C_2 = 0 - \frac{8}{5} - \frac{19}{5} - 0 = \frac{27}{5}$$

$$Z_3 - C_3 = 0$$

Similarly other net evaluations can be evaluated. Since $Z_2 - C_2$ is most negative, so x_2 enters the basis.

$$\min\left[\frac{2}{1/5}, \frac{8}{8/5}, \frac{10}{19/5}\right] = \min\left[10, 5, \frac{50}{19}\right] = \frac{50}{19}$$

So A_3 leaves the basis and is dropped out.

Thus $\frac{19}{15}$, becomes the pivot element.

Iteration–2

			0	0	0	0	0	–1	
C_B	Y_B	X_B	x_1	x_2	s_1	s_2	s_3	A_2	Min. Ratio
0	x_1	$\frac{28}{19}$	1	0	$\frac{-4}{19}$	0	$\frac{1}{19}$	0	28
–1	A_2	$\frac{72}{19}$	0	0	$\frac{-6}{19}$	–1	$\frac{8}{19}$*	1	9 ←
0	x_3	$\frac{50}{19}$	0	1	$\frac{1}{19}$	0	$\frac{-5}{19}$	0	–
	$Z_j - C_j$	$\frac{-72}{19}$	0	0	$\frac{-6}{19}$	1	$\frac{-8}{19}$ ↑	0	

We can compute $Z_j - C_j$ (the net evaluations) after applying elementary row operations in Iteration–2.

It is found that $Z_s - C_5$ is most negative, so, s_3 enters the basis.

As the minimum ratio is 9, so A_2 leaves the basis and is dropped out.

Iteration–3

			0	0	0	0	0
C_B	Y_B	X_B	x_1	x_2	s_1	s_2	s_3
0	x_1	1	1	0	$\frac{-1}{4}$	$\frac{1}{8}$	0
0	s_3	9	0	0	$\frac{3}{4}$	$\frac{-19}{8}$	1
0	x_2	5	0	1	$\frac{1}{4}$	$\frac{-5}{8}$	0
	$Z_j - C_j$	0	0	0	0	0	0

Since all $Z_j - C_j \geq 0$.

So, replace the costs of all the variables by their actual costs in following phase II.

Phase II

			–3	–2	0	0	0
C_B	Y_B	X_B	x_1	x_2	s_1	s_2	s_3
–3	x_1	1	1	0	$\frac{-1}{4}$	$\frac{1}{8}$	0
0	s_3	9	0	0	$\frac{3}{4}$	$\frac{-19}{8}$	1
–2	x_2	5	0	1	$\frac{1}{4}$	$\frac{-5}{8}$	0
	$Z_j - C_j$	–13	0	0	$\frac{1}{4}$	$\frac{7}{8}$	0

Since all $Z_j - C_j \geq 0$, thus optimal solution has been attained. So

$$Z_{max} = -13$$
$$x_1 = 1$$
$$x_2 = 5$$
$$\text{So } F_{min} = 13$$
$$x_1 = 1$$
$$x_2 = 5$$

2.8 DEGENERACY

While simplyfing the LP Problem, first of all the net evaluation $Z_j - C_j$ are evaluated, so that the "variable to be entered" to the basis is determined.

Then by minimum ratio $\left(\frac{x_{Br}}{x_{rk}}, x_{rk} > 0\right)$ is determined to evaluate the "variable to leave" the basis is determined but sometimes, there appears a tie (minimum ratio is same) for leaving the basis. Then there occurs degeneracy. However, degeneracy may also occur at the very first iteration, when the values of one or more basic variables in the x_B column (Right hand side of constraints) becomes equal to zero.

Whenever, if the minimum ratio is zero for two or more basic variables then degeneracy may result into the cycling, *i.e.*, the same sequence of simplex iterations are repeated endlessly without improving the solution.

Thus the solution obtained at one iteration may be obtained again after few iterations and therefore no optimum solution may be obtained in such situations.

2.9 RESOLVING DEGENERACY

The number of iterations required to arrive at an optimal solution can be minimized by adopting the following:

1. Divide the coefficients of slack variables in the simplex table where degeneracy is detected by the corresponding positive numbers of the key column in the row, starting from left to right.
2. The row that contains smallest ratio comparing from left to right column-wise becomes the key row.

Note: Whenever there is tie between a slack and artificial variables to leave the basis, the preference shall be given to artificial variable to leave the basis and there is no need to apply the procedure for resolving degeneracy in such situations.

Example 26. *Maximize* $Z = 3x_1 + 9x_2$

Subject to

$$x_1 + 4x_2 \leq 8$$
$$x_1 + 2x_2 \leq 4$$
$$x_1, x_2 \geq 0.$$

Solution. Adding slack variables $s_1 \geq 0$ and $s_2 \geq 0$, to both the constraints to convert the inequalities into equalities.

Thus after introducing slack variables, the LPP can be rewritten as:

Maximize $Z = 3x_1 + 9x_2 + 0.s_1 + 0.s_2$

Subject to

$$x_1 + 4x_2 + s_1 = 8$$
$$x_1 + 2x_2 + s_2 = 4$$
$$x_1, x_2 \geq 0.$$

The initial solution will be

$$s_1 = 8 \text{ and } s_2 = 4.$$

Iteration–0

	$C_j \rightarrow$		3	9	0	0	
C_B	Y_B	X_B	x_1	x_2	s_1	s_2	Min. Ratio
0	s_1	8	1	4	1	0	$8/4 = 2$ } tie
0	s_2	4	1	2*	0	1	$4/2 = 2$ } tie
	$Z_j - C_j$	0	–3	–9	0	0	

Since $Z_2 - C_2$ is most negative, so x_2 enters the basis. Since there exists a tie (= 2) in minimum ratio. Thus, it is a case of degeneracy.

Calculations for outgoing variable

We now divide the coefficients of slack variables s_1 and s_2 by the pivot column element as follows:

	Pivot column		s_1	s_2
Row_1	s_1	4	1	0
Row_2	s_2	2	0	1

Thus		s_1	s_2	Min. in s_1 column
Row_1	s_1	1/4	0/4	1/4
Row_2	s_2	0/2	1/2	0*

Since the minimum ratio occurs in s_1 column and that too for second row $(0/2 = 0)$, *i.e.*, s_2, thus s_2 will leave the basis.

Since x_2 enters the basis and s_2 leaves the basis, so, 2 will be the pivot element.

Iteration–1

			3	9	0	0
C_B	Y_B	X_B	x_1	x_2	s_1	s_2
0	s_1	0	–1	0	1	–2
9	x_2	2	1/2	1	0	1/2
	$Z_j - C_j$	18	3/2	0	0	9/2

Calculations for $Z_j - C_j$ (Iterations–1)

$$Z_1 - C_1 = 0.(-1) + 9.(1/2) - 1 = 3/2$$
$$Z_2 - C_2 = 0.0 + 9.1 - 9 = 0$$
$$Z_3 - C_3 = 0.1 + 9.0 - 0 = 0$$
$$Z_4 - C_4 = 0.(-2) + 9.\left(\frac{1}{2}\right) - 0 = \frac{9}{2}$$

Objective function Z = 0.0 + 9.2 = 18

Since all $Z_j - C_j \geq 0$

Thus an optimal solution has been attained. Therefore, the optimal basic feasible solution is

$$Z_{max} = 18$$
$$x_1 = 0$$
$$x_2 = 2.$$

Example 27. *Maximize* $Z = \frac{3}{4}x_1 - 150x_2 + \frac{1}{50}x_3 - 6x_4$

Subject to
$$\frac{1}{4}x_1 - 60x_2 - \frac{1}{25}x_3 + 9x_4 \leq 0$$
$$\frac{1}{2}x_1 - 90x_2 - \frac{1}{50}x_3 + 3x_4 \leq 0$$
$$x_3 \leq 1$$
$$x_1, x_2, x_3, x_4 \geq 0$$

Solution. Introducing slack variables s_1, s_2, s_3 and then rewriting the LPP.

Maximize $Z = \frac{3}{4}x_1 - 150x_2 + \frac{1}{50}x_3 - 6x_4 + 0 \cdot s_1 + 0 \cdot s_2 + 0 \cdot s_3$

Subject to
$$\frac{1}{4}x_1 - 60x_2 - \frac{1}{25}x_3 + 9x_4 + s_1 = 0$$
$$\frac{1}{2}x_1 - 90x_2 - \frac{1}{50}x_3 + 3x_4 + s_2 = 0$$
$$x_3 + s_3 = 1$$
$$x_1, ..., x_4, s_1, ..., s_3 \geq 0$$

The initial solution is $s_1 = 0$, $s_2 = 0$ and $s_3 = 1$.

Iteration–1

	$C_j \rightarrow$		3/4	–150	1/50	–6	0	0	0	
C_B	Y_B	X_B	x_1	x_2	x_3	x_4	s_1	s_2	s_3	Min. Ratio
0	s_1	0	1/4	–60	–1/25	9	1	0	0	0 } tie
0	s_2	0	1/2*	–90	–1/50	3	0	1	0	0 } tie
0	s_3	1	0	0	1	0	0	0	1	–
	$Z_j - C_j$	0	–3/4 ↑	150	–1/50	6	0	0	0	

Since $Z_1 - C_1$ is most negative, thus x_1 becomes the entering variable.

Since there is a tie to leave the basis, we apply the following rule:

		Pivot column	s_1	s_2	s_3
R_1	s_1	1/4	1	0	0
R_2	s_2	1/2	0	1	0
R_3	s_3	0	0	0	1

Thus

		s_1	s_2	s_3	Minimum in s_1 column
R_1	s_1	$\frac{1}{1/4}$	$\frac{1}{1/4}$	$\frac{1}{1/4}$	4
R_2	s_2	$\frac{0}{1/2}$	$\frac{0}{1/2}$	$\frac{0}{1/2}$	0*
R_3	s_3	–	–	–	–

Since minimum occurs for s_1 column and s_2 row thus s_2 will leave the basis.

Iteration–2

	$C_j \rightarrow$		3/4	–150	$\frac{1}{50}$	–60	0	0	0	
C_B	Y_B	X_B	x_1	x_2	x_3	x_4	s_1	s_2	s_3	Min. Ratio
0	s_1	0	0	–15	$-\frac{3}{100}$	$\frac{15}{2}$	1	$-\frac{1}{2}$	0	
3/4	x_1	0	1	–180	$\frac{1}{25}$	6	0	2	0	
0	s_3	1	0	0	1*	0	0	0	1	1
	$Z_j - C_j$	0	0	15	$-\frac{1}{20}$ ↑	$\frac{21}{2}$	0	$\frac{3}{2}$	1	

Since $Z_3 - C_3$ is most negative, therefore x_3 enters the basis.

Here $\min\left[-, -, \frac{1}{1}\right]$. ($\because$ –3/100 and –1/50 violates the conditions of minimum ratio as $x_{kc} > 0$)$\cdot$ s_3 leaves the basis and 1 becomes the pivot element.

Iteration–3

			$\frac{3}{4}$	–150	1/50	–60	0	0	0
C_B	Y_B	X_B	x_1	x_2	x_3	x_4	s_1	s_2	s_3
0	s_1	$\frac{3}{100}$	0	–1	0	$\frac{15}{2}$	1	$-\frac{1}{2}$	$\frac{3}{100}$
$\frac{3}{4}$	x_1	$\frac{1}{25}$	1	–180	0	6	0	2	$\frac{1}{25}$
$\frac{1}{50}$	x_3	1	0	0	1	0	0	0	1
	$Z_j - C_j$	$\frac{5}{100}$	0	15	0	$\frac{21}{2}$	0	$\frac{3}{2}$	$\frac{1}{20}$

Since all $Z_j - C_j \geq 0$.

Thus the optimal solution has been attained.

$$\therefore \quad Z_{max} = \frac{1}{20}$$

$$x_1 = \frac{1}{25}$$

$$x_2 = 0$$

$$x_3 = 1.$$

Example 28. *Solve the following LPP*

Maximize $Z = 10x_1 + 5x_2$

Subject to
$$4x_1 + 3x_2 \leq 12$$
$$4x_1 + x_2 \leq 8$$
$$4x_1 - x_2 \leq 8$$
$$x_1, x_2 \geq 0$$

Solution. Introducing slack variables $s_1 \geq 0$, $s_2 \geq 0$ and $s_3 \geq 0$.

Thus LPP can be written as

Maximize $Z = 10x_1 + 5x_2 + 0.s_1 + 0.s_2 + 0.s_3$

Subject to
$$4x_1 + 3x_2 + s_1 = 12$$
$$4x_1 + x_2 + s_2 = 8$$
$$4x_1 - x_2 + s_3 = 8$$
$$x_1, x_2, s_1, s_2, s_3 \geq 0.$$

The initial solution is

$s_1 = 12$, $s_2 = 8$ and $s_3 = 8$.

Iteration–0

	$C_j \rightarrow$		10	5	0	0	0	
C_B	Y_B	X_B	x_1	x_2	s_1	s_2	s_3	Min. Ratio
0	s_1	12	4	3	1	0	0	$\frac{12}{4}$
0	s_2	8	4	1	0	1	0	$\frac{8}{4}$ } = 2 (tie)
0	s_3	8	4*	–1	0	0	1	$\frac{8}{4}$ } = 2 (tie)
	$Z_j - C_j$	0	–10 ↑	–5	0	0	0	

Since $Z_1 - C_1$ is most negative, so x_1 enters the basis. Since there is a tie for R_2 and R_3 so we consider the slack variable.

		Pivot column	s_1	s_2	s_3
R_1	s_1	4	1	0	0
R_2	s_2	4	0	1	0
R_3	s_3	4	0	0	1

Thus

		s_1	s_2	s_3	Min. Ratio	
R_1	s_1	$\frac{1}{4}$	0	0	$\frac{1}{4}$	
R_2	s_2	0	$\frac{1}{4}$	0	0* } tie	$\frac{1}{4}$
R_3	s_3	0	0	$\frac{1}{4}$	0* } tie	0*

Since for first column, there is again a tie for minimum ratio (= 0), so we check the minimum ratio for next column (s_2) and found that minimum ratio occurs for row R_3 corresponding to s_3. So, s_3 leaves the basis.

Iteration–1

	$C_j \rightarrow$		10	5	0	0	0	
C_B	Y_B	X_B	x_1	x_2	s_1	s_2	s_3	Min. Ratio
0	s_1	4	0	4	1	0	–1	$\frac{4}{4}$
0	s_2	0	0	2*	0	1	–1	$\frac{0}{2}$ ←
10	x_1	2	1	$-\frac{1}{4}$	0	0	$\frac{1}{4}$	–
	$Z_j - C_j$	20	0	$-\frac{15}{2}$ ↑	0	0	$\frac{5}{2}$	

Since $Z_2 - C_2$ is most negative, so x_2 enters the basis. Minimum ratio corresponds to second row so, 2, becomes the pivot element and s_2 leaves the basis.

Iteration–2

			10	5	0	0	0
C_B	Y_B	X_B	x_1	x_2	s_1	s_2	s_3
0	s_1	4	0	0	1	–2	1
5	x_2	0	0	1	0	$\frac{1}{2}$	$-\frac{1}{2}$
10	x_1	2	1	0	0	$\frac{1}{8}$	$\frac{3}{8}$
	$Z_j - C_j$	20	0	0	0	$\frac{15}{4}$	$\frac{5}{4}$

Since all $Z_j - C_j \geq 0$, the optimal solution has been attained.

$\therefore \quad Z_{max} = 20$

$x_1 = 2$

$x_2 = 0.$

Example 29. *Maximize* $Z = 5x_1 - 2x_2 + 3x_2$

Subject to $2x_1 + 2x_2 - x_3 \geq 2$

$3x_1 - 4x_2 \leq 3$

$x_2 + 3x_3 \leq 5$

$x_1, x_2, x_3 \geq 0$

Solve the above LPP using simplex method.

Solution. Introducing slack, surplus and artificial variables, the above LP Problem can be rewritten as

Maximize $Z = 5x_1 - 2x_2 + 3x_3 + 0 \cdot s_1 + 0 \cdot s_2 + 0 \cdot s_3 - MA_1$

Subject to $2x_1 + 2x_2 - x_3 - s_1 + A_1 = 2$

$3x_1 - 4x_2 + s_2 = 3$

$x_2 + 3x_3 + s_3 = 5$

$x_1, x_2, x_3, s_1, s_2, s_3 = 0.$

Thus the initial solution is

$A_1 = 2$

$s_2 = 3$

and $s_3 = 5$

Iteration–0

$C_j \rightarrow$			5	–2	3	0	0	0	–M	
C_B	Y_B	X_B	x_1	x_2	x_3	s_1	s_2	s_3	A_1	Min. Ratio
–M	A_1	2	2*	2	–1	–1	0	0	1	$\frac{2}{2}$ tie
0	s_2	3	3	–4	0	0	1	1	0	$\frac{3}{3}$
0	s_3	5	0	1	3	0	0	1	0	–
$Z_j - C_j$		–2M	–2M – 5 ↑	–2M + 2	M – 3	M	0	0	0	

Since $Z_1 - C_1$ is most negative, so, x_1 enters the basis. Since there exists a tie in leaving variable (A_1 and s_2), thus there exists degeneracy.

Since there is a tie between a slack variable (s_2) and an artificial variable (A_1), preference is always given to the artificial variable.

Thus A_1 leaves the basis and is dropped out.

Iteration–1

			5	–2	3	0	0	0		
C_B	Y_B	X_B	x_1	x_2	x_3	s_1	s_2	s_3	Min. Ratio	
5	x_1	1	1	1	$-\frac{1}{2}$	$-\frac{1}{2}$	0	0	–	
0	s_2	0	0	–7	$\frac{3}{2}$*	$\frac{3}{2}$	1	0	0	←
0	s_3	5	0	1	3	0	0	1	$\frac{5}{3}$	
$Z_j - C_j$		5	0	7	$-\frac{11}{2}$ ↑	$-\frac{5}{2}$				

Since $Z_3 - C_3 = \dfrac{-11}{2}(<0)$ is most negative, thus, x_3 enters the basis. s_2 leaves the basis as it corresponds to minimum ratio (0). Here 3/2 is the pivot element.

Iteration–2

			5	–2	3	0	0	0	
C_B	Y_B	X_B	x_1	x_2	x_3	s_1	s_2	s_3	Min. Ratio
5	x_1	1	1	$-\frac{4}{3}$	0	0	$\frac{1}{3}$	0	–
3	x_3	0	0	$-\frac{14}{3}$	1	1	$\frac{2}{3}$	0	–
0	s_3	5	0	15*	0	–3	–2	1	$\frac{1}{3}$ ←
$Z_j - C_j$		5	0	$-\frac{56}{3}$ ↑	0	3	$\frac{11}{3}$	0	

Since $Z_2 - C_2$ is most negative, therefore x_2 enters the basis.

Iteration–3

C_B	Y_B	X_B	x_1	x_2	x_3	s_1	s_2	s_3	Min. Ratio
5	x_1	$\frac{13}{9}$	1	0	0	$-\frac{4}{15}$	$\frac{7}{45}$	$\frac{4}{45}$	
3	x_3	$\frac{14}{9}$	0	0	1	$\frac{1}{15}$*	$\frac{2}{45}$	$\frac{14}{45}$	$\frac{14/9}{1/15}$ ←
– 2	x_2	$\frac{1}{3}$	0	1	0	$-\frac{1}{5}$	$-\frac{2}{15}$	$\frac{1}{15}$	
$Z_j - C_j$		$\frac{101}{9}$	0	0	0	$-\frac{11}{15}$ ↑	$\frac{53}{45}$	$\frac{56}{45}$	

Since $Z_4 - C_4$ is most negative. So, s_1 enters the basis and by computing minimum ratio x_3 leaves the basis.

Iteration–4

C_B	Y_B	X_B	x_1	x_2	x_3	s_1	s_2	s_3
5	x_1	$\frac{23}{3}$	1	0	4	0	$\frac{1}{3}$	$\frac{4}{3}$
0	s_1	$\frac{70}{3}$	0	0	15	1	$\frac{2}{3}$	$\frac{14}{3}$
–2	x_2	5	0	1	3	0	0	1
$Z_j - C_j$		$\frac{85}{3}$	0	0	11	0	$\frac{5}{3}$	$\frac{14}{3}$

Since all $Z_j - C_j \geq 0$, therefore optimal solution has been attained.

Thus $Z_{max} = \frac{85}{3}$

$$x_1 = \frac{23}{3}$$

$$x_2 = 5$$

$$x_3 = 0.$$

Example 30. *Solve the following LPP using Big-M simplex method.*

$$\textit{Minimize } Z = -x_1 - \frac{3}{2}x_2 - 2x_3 - 5x_4$$

$$\begin{aligned} \textit{Subject to} \quad 3x_1 + 2x_2 + 4x_3 + x_4 &\le 6 \\ 2x_1 + x_2 + x_3 + 5x_4 &\le 4 \\ 2x_1 + 6x_2 - 8x_3 + 4x_4 &= 0 \\ x_1 + 3x_2 - 4x_3 + 3x_4 &= 0 \\ x_1, x_2, x_3, x_4 &\ge 0. \end{aligned}$$

Solution. Converting the minimization problem into maximization problem.

$$\text{Maximize } Z' = x_1 + \frac{3}{2}x_2 + 2x_3 + 5x_4$$

Then introducing slack variables $s_1 \ge 0$ and $s_2 \ge 0$, in the first two constraints to convert the inequality sign into equality sign.

Again, introducing artificial variables, $A_1 \ge 0$ and $A_2 \ge 0$ for the last two constraints.

Thus the above LPP can be written as:

$$\text{Maximize } Z' = x_1 + \frac{3}{2}x_2 + 2x_3 + 5x_4 + 0.s_1 + 0.s_2 - MA_1 - MA_2$$

$$\begin{aligned} \text{Subject to} \quad 3x_1 + 2x_2 + 4x_3 + x_1 + s_1 &= 6 \\ 2x_1 + x_2 + x_3 + 5x_4 + s_2 &= 4 \\ 2x_1 + 6x_2 - 8x_3 - 4x_4 + A_1 &= 0 \\ x_1 + 3x_2 - 4x_3 + 3x_4 + A_2 &= 0 \\ x_1, x_2, x_3, x_4 &\ge 0 \\ s_1, s_2, A_1, A_2 &\ge 0. \end{aligned}$$

The initial solution is obtained as:

$$s_1 = 6$$

$$s_2 = 4$$

$$A_1 = 0$$

$$A_2 = 0.$$

Iteration–0

			1	$\frac{3}{2}$	2	5	0	0	$-M$	$-M$	
C_B	Y_B	X_B	x_1	x_2	x_3	x_4	s_1	s_2	A_1	A_2	Min. Ratio
0	s_1	6	3	2	4	1	1	0	0	0	$\frac{6}{2}$
0	s_2	4	2	1	1	5	0	1	0	0	$\frac{4}{1}$
$-M$	A_1	0	2	6	-8	4	0	0	1	0	$\frac{0}{6}$ } tie
$-M$	A_2	0	1	3*	-4	3	0	0	0	1	$\frac{0}{6}$
	$Z_j - C_j$	0	$-3M$	$-9M$	$12M$	$-7M$	0	0	0	0	
			-1	$-\frac{3}{2}$	-2	-5					
				↑							

Since $Z_2 - C_2$ is most negative, therefore, x_2 enters the basis. Since there is tie among R_3 and R_4 for the variable to leave the basis, thus resulting in the occurence of degeneracy.

Thus we consider the slack and artificial variables for entering, the basis, since there are already two artificial variables (tie between artificial variables A_1 and A_2) to enter the basis.

So, considering only artificial variables as follows:

		Pivot column	A_1	A_2	Min. Ratio for A_1
R_3	A_1	6	1	0	$\frac{1}{6} = \frac{1}{6}$
R_4	A_2	3	0	1	$\frac{0}{6} = 0$*

Since minimum ratio]occurs for the first artificial variable, that is no need to calculate the minimum ratio for the second column A_2 (or artificial variable).

This minimum (zero), corresponds to R_4 (*i.e.*, to A_2), thus the leaving variable becomes A_4.

So, A_2 leaves the basis and is dropped out from the simplex tableau.

So, 3 becomes the pivot element.

Iteration–1

			1	$\frac{3}{2}$	2	5	0	0	$-M$	
C_B	Y_B	X_B	x_1	x_2	x_3	x_4	s_1	s_2	A_1	Min. Ratio
0	s_1	6	$\frac{7}{3}$	0	$\frac{20}{3}$*	-1	1	0	0	$\frac{9}{10}$ ←
0	s_2	4	$\frac{5}{3}$	0	$\frac{7}{3}$	4	0	1	0	$\frac{12}{7}$
$-M$	A_1	0	0	0	0	-2	0	0	+1	0
$\frac{3}{2}$	x_2	0	$\frac{1}{3}$	1	$-\frac{4}{3}$	1	0	0	0	–
$Z_j - C_j$		0	$-\frac{1}{2}$	0	-4 ↑	$2M-\frac{7}{2}$	0	0	0	

Calculations for Row Operations (Iteration–1)

R_4(New): $\frac{R_4}{3}$(Old)

i.e., $\left(\frac{0}{3}\ \frac{1}{3}\ \frac{3}{3}\ \frac{-4}{3}\ \frac{3}{3}\ \frac{0}{3}\ \frac{0}{3}\ \frac{0}{3}\right)$

$\therefore$ R_4(New): $\left(0\ \ \frac{1}{3}\ \ 1\ \ -\frac{4}{3}\ \ 1\ \ 0\ \ 0\ \ 0\right)$

R_1(New) $\longrightarrow$ R_1(Old) $-$ $2R_4$(New)

Now R_1(Old) :	6	3	2	4	1	1	0
and $2R_4$(New) :	0	$\frac{2}{3}$	2	$-\frac{8}{3}$	2	0	0
(Subtract) :	–	–	–	+	–	–	–
$\therefore$ R_1(New) :	6	$\frac{7}{3}$	0	$\frac{20}{3}$	-1	1	0

R_1(New) $\longrightarrow$ R_2(Old) $-$ R_1(New)

Now R_2(Old) :	4	2	1	1	5	0	1	0
and R_1(New) :	0	$\frac{1}{3}$	1	$-\frac{4}{3}$	1	0	0	0
(Subtract) :	–	–	–	+	–	–	–	–
$\therefore$ R_2(New) :	4	$\frac{5}{3}$	0	$\frac{7}{3}$	4	0	1	0

$R_3(\text{New}) \longrightarrow R_3(\text{Old}) - 6R_1(\text{New})$

Now R_3(Old) :	0	2	6	− 8	4	0	0	1
and $6R_1$(New) :	0	2	6	− 8	6	0	0	0
(Subtract) :	−	−	−	+	−	−	−	−
∴ R_3(New) :	0	0	0	0	− 2	0	0	1

Calculations for $Z_j - C_j$

$$Z_1 - C_1 = 0 + 0 + 0 + \frac{1}{2} - 1 = -\frac{1}{2}$$

$$Z_2 - C_2 = 0 + 0 + 0 + \frac{3}{2} - \frac{3}{2} = 0$$

$$Z_3 - C_3 = 0 + 0 + 0 - 2 - 2 = -4$$

$$Z_4 - C_4 = 0 + 0 + 2M + \frac{3}{2} - 5 = 2M - \frac{7}{2}$$

$$Z_5 - C_5 = 0 + 0 + 0 + 0 - 0 = 0$$

$$Z_6 - C_6 = 0 + 0 + 0 + 0 - 0 = 0$$

$$Z_7 - C_7 = 0 + 0 + M + 0 - M = 0$$

Since $Z_3 - C_3$ is most negative, therefore x_3 variable enters the basis and by minimum ratio s_1 leaves the basis.

So 20/3 becomes the pivot element.

Iteration–2

			1	$\frac{3}{2}$	2	5	0	0	$-M$
C_B	Y_B	X_B	x_1	x_2	x_3	x_4	s_1	s_2	A_1
2	x_3	$\frac{9}{10}$	$\frac{7}{20}$	0	1	$-\frac{3}{20}$	$\frac{3}{20}$	0	0
0	s_2	$\frac{19}{10}$	$\frac{51}{60}$	0	0	$\frac{87}{20}$	$-\frac{7}{20}$	1	0
$-M$	A_1	0	0	0	0	− 2	0	0	1
$\frac{3}{2}$	x_2	$\frac{6}{5}$	$\frac{4}{5}$	1	0	$\frac{4}{5}$	$\frac{1}{5}$	0	0
	$Z_j - C_j$	$\frac{18}{5}$	$\frac{7}{10}$	0	0	$2M - \frac{1}{10}$	$\frac{3}{5}$	0	0

Calculations of Row Operations (Iteration–2)

$$R_1(\text{New}) \longrightarrow \frac{R_1}{20/3}(\text{Old})$$

i.e., $\left(6\times\frac{3}{20}\quad \frac{7}{3}.\frac{3}{20}\quad 0.\frac{3}{20}\quad \frac{20}{3}.\frac{3}{20}\quad -1.\frac{3}{20}\quad 1.\frac{3}{20}\quad 0.\frac{3}{20}\quad 0.\frac{3}{20}\right)$

$\therefore\ R_1(\text{New}): \left(\frac{18}{20}\quad \frac{7}{20}\quad 0\quad 1\quad \frac{-3}{20}\quad \frac{3}{20}\quad 0\quad 0\right)$

$R_2(\text{New}) \longrightarrow R_2(\text{Old}) - \frac{7}{3}R_1(\text{New})$

Now R_2(Old) :	4	$\frac{5}{3}$	0	$\frac{7}{3}$	4	0	1	0
and $\frac{7}{3}R_1$(New) :	$\frac{21}{10}$	$\frac{49}{60}$	0	$\frac{7}{3}$	$\frac{-7}{20}$	$\frac{7}{20}$	0	0
(Subtract) :	–	–	–	–	+	–	–	–
$\therefore$ R_2(New) :	$\frac{19}{10}$	$\frac{51}{60}$	0	0	$\frac{87}{20}$	$\frac{-7}{20}$	1	0

$R_3(\text{New}) \longrightarrow R_3(\text{Old}) - 0.R_1(\text{New})$

$R_4(\text{New}) \longrightarrow R_4(\text{Old}) + \frac{4}{3}R_1(\text{New})$

Now R_4(Old) :	0	$\frac{1}{3}$	1	$\frac{-4}{3}$	1	0	0	0
and $\frac{4}{3}R_1$(New) :	$\frac{6}{5}$	$\frac{7}{15}$	0	$\frac{4}{3}$	$\frac{-1}{5}$	$\frac{1}{5}$	0	0
(Add) :	+	+	+	+	+	+	+	+
$\therefore$ R_4(New) :	$\frac{6}{5}$	$\frac{4}{5}$	1	0	$\frac{4}{5}$	$\frac{1}{5}$	0	0

Since all the net evaluations, $Z_j - C_j \geq 0$, therefore optimum solution has been attained as one artificial variable is in the basis at zero level.

Thus $Z_{\max} = \frac{18}{5}$

$x_1 = 0$

$x_2 = \frac{6}{5}$

$x_3 = \frac{9}{10}$

$x_4 = 0$

Since, the problem is of minimization.

Thus $Z_{\min} = -\frac{18}{5}$

$x_1 = 0,\quad x_3 = \frac{9}{10}$

$x_2 = \frac{6}{5},\ x_4 = 0.$

OBJECTIVE TYPE QUESTIONS

1. Which of the statement about degeneracy is correct?

(*a*) Degeneracy may be a temporary phenomenon

(*b*) Degeneracy may arise at the initial state

(*c*) Degeneracy may occur at any subsequent stage

(*d*) All of the above.

2. If there is at least one basic variable in the basis at zero level and all the index numbers are non-negative, then which of the following is true?

(*a*) The current solution is optimum

(*b*) The current solution is unbounded

(*c*) The current solution is degenerate

(*d*) The current solution has feasible solution.

3. Which of the following statement is correct regarding an LPP?

(*a*) A minimization LPP with non-negative variables cannot have unbounded solution.

(*b*) An unbounded solution can exist for any LPP

(*c*) A LPP can have multiple optimum solutions

(*d*) All of the above.

4. A necessary and sufficient condition for a basic feasible solution to a LPP to be an optimum (minimum) is:

(*a*) all $Z_j - C_j \geq 0$ (*b*) all $Z_j - C_j \leq 0$

(*c*) all $Z_j - C_j = 0$ (*d*) None of the above.

5. If there is no non-negative minimum ratio in the simplex tableaus, which is sought to be improved, then the solution is:

(*a*) unbounded (*b*) optimum

(*c*) feasible (*d*) degenerate.

6. In a maximization LPP, if at least one-artificial variable is in basis, but not at zero level and the coefficient of *M* in each of the net evaluations $Z_j - C_j$ is non-negative, then the solution is:

(*a*) feasible solution (*b*) optimum solution

(*c*) no feasible solution (*d*) degenerate solution.

7. In which of the following methods, a very high penalty (–*M*) is assigned to the artificial variables in the objective function.

(*a*) Simplex method (*b*) Big *M* method

(*c*) Two phase method (*d*) All of the above.

8. The method of penalty can be carried out in the simplex method.

(*a*) if there are constraints of ≥ type (*b*) if the constraints are of = sign

(*c*) if ≤ sign is used in the constraints (*d*) both (*a*) and (*b*).

9. Slack variables and artificial variables can be used when
   (*a*) the constraints are of ≤ type
   (*b*) the constraints are of ≥ type
   (*c*) the constraints are of = type
   (*d*) None of the above.

10. In two phase method, which of the following is true?
   (*a*) Assign a cost $-M$ or $+M$ accordingly to artificial variables.
   (*b*) Assign a cost –1 to each artificial variable.
   (*c*) Assign a cost 0 (zero) to all the variables other than artificial variables.
   (*d*) Assign a cost 0 (zero) to all the surplus variables.
   (*e*) Both (*b*) and (*c*).

11. The role of artificial variable in the simplex method is
   (*a*) to start phases of simplex method
   (*b*) to aid in finding an initial solution
   (*c*) to obtain the dual prices (optimal) in the final simplex tableau
   (*d*) All of the above.

12. If for a given solution, a slack variable is equal to zero, then the solution is
   (*a*) optimal (*b*) infeasible
   (*c*) degenerate (*d*) None of the above.

13. When even these is a tie between a slack and an artificial variable to leave the basis, then the preference shall be given to .... to leave the basis.
   (*a*) Slack variable (*b*) Artificial variable
   (*c*) Both of them (*d*) None of the above.

14. If an optimal solution is degenerate, then
   (*a*) there is a possibility of alternate optimal solution
   (*b*) the solution is infeasible
   (*c*) the solution cannot be obtained
   (*d*) None of the above.

15. A variable that does not appear in the basic variable column of simplex table is:
   (*a*) always equal to zero (*b*) never equal to zero
   (*c*) a basic variable (*e*) None of the above.

16. If the optimal simplex tableau contains $Z_j - C_j = 0$, then the solution is
   (*a*) unbounded (*b*) infeasible
   (*c*) degenerate (*e*) None of the above.

17. For a maximization problem, the objective function coefficient for an artificial variable is
   (*a*) $+M$ (*b*) $-M$
   (*c*) 0 (*d*) –1

18. For a minimization problem, the objective function coefficient for an artificial variable is:

(*a*) $+M$ (*b*) $-M$

(*c*) 0 (*d*) -1

19. If a non-basic variable corresponding to which $Z_j - C_j = 0$, is entered into the basis, then a new solution will be arrived at but the value of the objective function will

(*a*) increase (*b*) decrease

(*c*) not change (*d*) anything can happen.

20. The use of the simplex method requires that all the decision variables must have non-negative value at

(*a*) initial iteration (*b*) each iteration

(*c*) final iteration (*d*) None of the above.

UNSOLVED EXAMPLES

Solve the following using Penalty method or Big *M* Simplex method.

1. Maximize $Z = 4x_1 + 3x_2$

Subject to
$$x_1 + x_2 \le 50$$
$$x_1 + 2x_2 \ge 80$$
$$3x_1 + 2x_2 \ge 140$$
$$x_1, x_2 \ge 0$$

[**Ans:** No feasible solution]

2. Minimize $Z = 3x_1 + 2x_2$

Subject to
$$5x_1 + x_2 \ge 10$$
$$2x_1 + 2x_2 \ge 12$$
$$x_1 + 4x_2 \ge 12$$
$$x_1, x_2 \ge 0$$

[**Ans:** $x_1 = 1, x_2 = 5, Z_{min} = 13$]

3. Maximize $Z = 2x_1 + 3x_2$

Subject to
$$x_1 + x_2 \le 30$$
$$x_1 - x_2 \ge 0$$
$$x_2 \ge 3$$
$$x_1 \le 20$$
$$x_2 \le 12$$
$$x_1, x_2 \ge 0$$

[**Ans:** $x_1 = 18, x_2 = 12, Z_{max} = 72$]

4. Maximize $Z = 12x_1 + 20x_2$

Subject to
$$6x_1 + 8x_2 \ge 100$$
$$7x_1 + 12x_2 \ge 120$$
$$x_1, x_2 \ge 0$$

$\left[\textbf{Ans: } x_1 = 15, x_2 = \frac{5}{4}, Z_{min} = 205\right]$

5. Maximize $Z = 3x_1 + 2x_2 + x_3$

Subject to
$$-3x_1 + 2x_2 + 2x_3 = 8$$
$$-3x_1 + 4x_2 + x_3 = 7$$
$$x_1, x_2, x_3 \geq 0.$$

[**Ans:** Unbounded solution]

6. Minimize $Z = 3x_1 + 5x_2$

Subject to
$$x_1 + x_2 = 200$$
$$x_1 \leq 80$$
$$x_2 \geq 60$$
$$x_1, x_2 \geq 0.$$

[**Ans:** $x_1 = 80, x_2 = 120, Z_{min} = 840$]

7. Maximize $Z = -2x_1 - x_2$

Subject to
$$3x_1 + x_2 = 3$$
$$4x_1 + 3x_2 \geq 6$$
$$x_1 + 2x_2 \leq 3$$
$$x_1, x_2 \geq 0.$$

$\left[\textbf{Ans: } x_1 = \frac{3}{5}, x_2 = \frac{6}{5}, Z_{max} = -\frac{12}{5}\right]$

8. Minimize $Z = -6x_1 + 3x_2 - 2x_3$

Subject to
$$2x_1 + x_2 + x_3 \leq 16$$
$$3x_1 + 2x_2 + x_3 \leq 18$$
$$x_1 - 2x_3 \geq 8$$
$$x_1, x_2, x_3 \geq 0.$$

$\left[\textbf{Ans. } x_1 = \frac{2}{3}, x_2 = 8, x_3 = 0, Z_{min} = 20\right]$

9. Maximize $Z = -x_1 - x_2$

Subject to
$$3x_1 + 2x_2 \geq 30$$
$$2x_1 + 3x_2 \geq 30$$
$$x_1 + x_2 \leq 5$$
$$x_1, x_2 \geq 0.$$

[**Ans.** No feasible solution]

10. Maximize $Z = 3x_1 + 2x_2 + x_3$

Subject to
$$2x_1 + 5x_2 + x_3 = 12$$
$$3x_1 + 4x_2 = 11$$
$x_2, x_3 \geq 0$ and x_1 is unrestricted.

$\left[\textbf{Ans. } x_1 = \frac{11}{3}, x_2 = 0, x_3 = \frac{14}{3}, Z_{max} = \frac{47}{3}\right]$

11. Minimize $Z = -8x_1 - 15x_2 - 25x_3 + x_4$

Subject to
$$x_1 + 2x_2 + 3x_3 = 15$$
$$2x_1 + x_2 + 5x_3 = 20$$
$$x_1 + 2x_2 + x_3 + x_4 = 10$$
$$x_1, x_2, x_3, x_4 \geq 0.$$

$\left[\textbf{Ans. } x_1 = \frac{5}{2} = x_2 = x_3, x_4 = 0, Z_{max} = -120\right]$

12. Minimize $Z = -x_1 - x_2 - x_4$

Subject to
$$x_1 + x_2 + x_3 + x_4 = 4$$
$$x_1 + 2x_2 + x_3 + x_5 = 4$$
$$x_1 + 2x_2 + x_3 = 4$$
$$x_1, x_2, x_3, x_4, x_5 \geq 0$$

[**Ans.** $x_1 = 0 = x_3 = x_5, x_2 = 2, x_4 = 2, Z_{min} = -4$]

13. Maximize $Z = 2x_1 + x_2 + 3x_3$

Subject to
$$x_1 + x_2 + 2x_3 \leq 5$$
$$2x_1 + 3x_2 + 4x_3 = 12$$
$$x_1, x_2, x_3 \geq 0.$$

[**Ans.** $x_1 = 3, x_2 = 2, x_3 = 0, Z_{max} = 8$]

14. Maximize $Z = 2x_1 + 3x_2$

Subject to
$$-x_1 + 2x_2 \leq 4$$
$$-x_1 - x_2 \geq -6$$
$$x_1 + 3x_2 \leq 9$$

x_1, x_2 are unrestricted.

$\left[\textbf{Ans. } x_1 = \frac{9}{2}, x_2 = \frac{3}{2}, Z_{max} = \frac{27}{2}\right]$

Solve the following LPP using two phase method.

15. Maximize $Z = 107x_1 + x_2 + 2x_3$

Subject to
$$14x_1 + x_2 - 6x_3 + 3x_4 = 7$$
$$16x_1 + 0.5x_2 - 6x_3 \leq 5$$
$$3x_1 - x_2 - x_3 \leq 0$$
$$x_1, x_2, x_3, x_4 \geq 0.$$

[**Ans.** Unbounded solution]

16. Maximize $Z = 3x_1 + 2x_2$

Subject to
$$2x_1 + x_2 \leq 40$$
$$x_1 + x_2 \leq 24$$
$$2x_1 + 3x_2 \leq 60$$
$$x_1, x_2 \geq 0.$$

[**Ans.** $x_1 = 15, x_2 = 10, Z_{max} = 65$]

17. Maximize $Z = 5x_1 - 2x_2 - x_3$

Subject to
$$2x_1 + 2x_2 - x_3 \geq 2$$
$$3x_1 - 4x_2 \geq 3$$
$$x_1, x_2, x_3 \geq 0.$$

$\left[\textbf{Ans. } x_1 = \frac{13}{9}, x_2 = \frac{1}{3}, Z = \frac{14}{9}\right]$

18. Maximize $Z = -4x_1 - 3x_2$

Subject to
$$2x_1 + x_2 \geq 10$$
$$-3x_1 + 2x_2 \leq 6$$
$$x_1 + x_2 \geq 6$$
$$x_1, x_2 \geq 0.$$

[**Ans.** $x_1 = 4, x_2 = 2, Z_{max} = -22$]

19. Minimize $Z = -5x_1 - 8x_2$

Subject to
$$3x_1 + 2x_2 \geq 3$$
$$x_1 + 4x_2 \geq 4$$
$$x_1 + x_2 \leq 5$$
$$x_1, x_2 \geq 0.$$

[**Ans.** $x_1 = 0, x_2 = 5, Z_{min} = -40$]

20. Maximize $Z = 5x_1 - 4x_2 + 3x_3$

Subject to
$$2x_1 + x_2 - 6x_3 = 20$$
$$6x_1 + 5x_2 + 10x_3 \leq 76$$
$$8x_1 - 3x_2 + 6x_3 \leq 50$$
$$x_1, x_2, x_3 \geq 0.$$

$\left[\textbf{Ans. } x_1 = \frac{55}{7}, x_2 = \frac{30}{7}, Z_{max} = \frac{155}{7}\right]$

21. Maximize $Z = -0.75x_1 + 20x_2 - 0.5x_3 - 6x_4$

Subject to
$$0.25x_1 - 8x_2 - x_3 + 9x_4 \leq 0$$
$$0.5x_1 - 12x_2 - 0.5x_3 + 3x_4 \leq 0$$
$$x_3 \leq 1$$
$$x_1, x_2, x_3, x_4 \geq 0.$$

$\left[\textbf{Ans. } x_1 = 1 = x_3, x_2 = x_4 = 0, Z_{max} = \frac{5}{4}\right]$

22. Maximize $Z = \frac{1}{2}x_1 + 6x_2 + 5x_3$

Subject to
$$4x_1 + 6x_2 + 3x_3 \leq 24$$
$$x_1 + \frac{3}{2}x_2 + 3x_3 \leq 12$$
$$3x_1 + x_2 \leq 12$$
$$x_1, x_2, x_3 \geq 0.$$

[**Ans.** $x_1 = x_3 = 0, x_2 = 4, Z_{max} = 24$]

23. Maximize $Z = 3x_1 + 9x_2$

Subject to
$$x_1 + 4x_2 \leq 8$$
$$x_1 + 2x_2 \leq 4$$
$$x_1, x_2 \geq 0.$$

[**Ans.** $x_1 = 0, x_2 = 2, Z_{max} = 18$]

24. A company produces two types of products x_1 and x_2, where profit on both the products are ₹ 40 and ₹ 30 per unit respectively. Each product x_1 requires twice as much time as required by product x_2. The company can produce 1000 products per day, if the product to be produced is x_2. But the supply of raw material is only sufficient for producing 800 products per day. For finishing the product x_1, the packaging material required is 400, units/day, and for product x_2, the packaging material required is 700 units per day. How should the company manufacture these two products in order to maximize overall profit?

[**Ans.** Max $Z = 40x_1 + 30x_2$

Subject to
$$x_1 + x_2 \leq 800$$
$$2x_1 + x_2 \leq 1000$$
$$x_1 \leq 400 \text{ and } x_2 \leq 700$$
$$x_1, x_2 \geq 0]$$

25. A company manufactures two kinds of machines A and B, each requiring different techniques for their manufacture. Machine A requires 18 hours for labour and 8 hours for finishing the products. Machine A requires 3 hours of labour and 4 hours for finishing the products. The profit obtained by these machines are ₹ 400 and ₹ 200 respectively for A and B. The demand for machine B is more than 150. How much monthly the company should manufacture those machines so as to maximize overall profit?

26. A finished product must weigh exactly 150 grams. The two raw materials used in manufacturing the product are A, with a cost of ₹ 2 per unit and B with a cost of ₹ 8 per unit. At least 14 units of B and not more than 20 units of A must be used. Each unit of A and B weighs 5 grams and 10 grams respectively. How much of each type of raw material should be used for each unit of final product in order to minimize the cost?

27. A company produces three types of product X, Y and Z, that are to be processed on three different machines A, B and C. Product X requires 2 hours on machine A, 3 hours on machine B and 2 hours on machine C, while product Y requires 3 hours on machine A, 2 hours on machine B and 2 hours on machines C. But product Z requires 5 hours on machine B and 4 hours on machine C. There are 8 hours of time per day available on machine A, 10 hours on machine B and 15 hours on machine C. The profit gained from product A, B and C are respectively ₹ 3, ₹ 5 and ₹ 4. What should be the daily production of the company so as to maximize the profit?

[**Ans.** Max $Z = 3x_1 + 5x_2 + 4x_3$

Subject to
$$2x_1 + 3x_2 \le 8$$
$$2x_2 + 5x_3 \le 10$$
$$3x_1 + 2x_2 + 4x_3 \le 15, \quad x_1, x_2, x_3 \ge 0$$
$$x_1 = \frac{89}{41}, \; x_2 = \frac{50}{41}, \; x_3 = \frac{64}{41}, \; Z_{max} = \frac{775}{41}$$].

28. An animal feed company must produce 200 kg of a mixture consisting of ingredients x_1 and x_2 daily. The costs of x_1 is ₹ 3 kg while that of x_2 is ₹ 8 kg. Not more than 80 kg of x_1 can be used and at least 60 kg of x_2 must be used. Find how much of each ingredient should be used if the company wants to minimize costs.

[**Ans.** Max $C = 3x_1 + 8x_2$

Subject to
$$x_1 + x_2 = 200$$
$$x_1 \le 80$$
$$x_2 \ge 60, \quad x_1, x_2 \ge 0$$
$$x_1 = 80, \; x_2 = 120, \; Z_{max} = 1200].$$

29. A manufacturing company produces two products A and B. The company has a permanent contract of supplying atleast two tonnes of A and atleast 3 tonnes of B per day to the market. Each tonne of A requires 20 machine-hours production time and each tonne of B requires 50 machine-hours production time, while the daily maximum possible number of machine-hours is 360. The profit gained on product A is ₹ 80/tonne and ₹ 120/tonne for B. If the total production capacity of the firm is 9 tonnes/day, then determine that how much tonnes of each product A and B be produced in order to maximize the profit?

[**Ans.** A = 3 tonnes, B = 6 tonnes, $Z_{max} = 960$]

30. A manufacture company produces 3 products X, Y and Z. The profits are ₹ 30, ₹ 20 and ₹ 40 respectively. The firm has two different machines and the required processing time in hour for each machine on each product is given below:

Machine ↓ \ Product →	X	Y	Y
M_1	15	10	12
M_2	12	13	8

Machine M_1 and M_2 have 200 and 350 machine-hours respectively. The company must manufacture 130 X's, 270 Y's and 80 Z's, but not more than 250 X's. Solve the above LPP to maximize the profit.

[**Ans.** Max $P = 30x_1 + 20x_2 + 40x_3$

Subject to
$$15x_1 + 10x_2 + 12x_3 \leq 200$$
$$12x_1 + 13x_2 + 8x_3 \leq 350$$
$$130 \leq x_1 \leq 250,\ 0 \leq x_2 \leq 270$$
$$80 \leq x_3$$
$$x_3 \geq 0]$$

Answers for Objective Type Questions

1. (*d*)	2. (*c*)	3. (*d*)	4. (*b*)	5. (*a*)
6. (*c*)	7. (*b*)	8. (*d*)	9. (*d*)	10. (*e*)
11. (*d*)	12. (*d*)	13. (*b*)	14. (*a*)	15. (*a*)
16. (*d*)	17. (*b*)	18. (*a*)	19. (*c*)	20. (*b*)

❑❑❑

CHAPTER 3

Duality and Sensitivity Analysis in Linear Programming

3.1 DUALITY: ITS CONCEPT

Every linear programming problem is associated with another linear programming problem. The original (or the given) LPP is called the primal problem, where as the associated problem is called the dual problem. In general, either problem can be considered the primal, while the other remaining problem as dual.

If the optimal solution to one of the problem (either primal or dual), then the optimal solution of the remaining problem (*i.e.*, dual or primal) is readily available.

Sometimes, a situation arises, when the dual problem is more easier to solve than the original primal problem. One important thing is that the "dual of the dual" is the primal.

3.2 FORMULATION OF DUAL LINEAR PROGRAMMING PROBLEM

The forms of primal and dual problems are:

Let the primal LPP be given in the following form:

PP: Maximize $Z = c_1x_1 + c_2x_2 + \dots + c_nx_n$

Subject to the constraints

$$a_{11}x_1 + a_{12}x_2 + \dots + a_{1n}x_n \le b_1$$

$$a_{21}x_1 + a_{22}x_2 + \dots + a_{2n}x_n \le b_2$$

$$\vdots \quad \vdots \quad \vdots \quad \vdots$$

$$a_{m1}x_1 + a_{m2}x_2 + \dots + a_{mn}x_n \le b_m$$

and $x_1, x_2, \dots, x_n \ge 0$

or

Maximize $Z = \sum_{j=1}^{n} C_j x_j$

subject to $\sum_{j=1}^{n} a_{ij} x_j \le b_i$

$x_j \ge 0, \forall j$

Then the corresponding dual LPP will be written as follows:

DP: Minimize $W = b_1w_1 + b_2w_2 + \ldots + b_mw_m$

Subject to $a_{11}w_1 + a_{21}w_2 + \ldots + a_{m2}w_m \leq c_1$

$a_{12}w_1 + a_{22}w_2 + \ldots + a_{m2}w_m \leq c_2$

$\vdots \qquad \vdots$

$a_{1n}w_1 + a_{22}w_2 + \ldots + a_{mn}w_m \leq c_n$

$w_1, w_2, \ldots, w_m \geq 0$

or

Minimize $w = \sum_{i=1}^{m} b_i w_i$

Subject to $\sum_{i=1}^{m} a_{ji} w_i \geq c_j$

$w_i \geq 0, \ \forall i$

Whenever the linear programming problem is given in primal form as:

(*a*) objective function is to maximize

(*b*) $\leq$ type constraints

(*c*) variable x_j

(*d*) constraint i

(*e*) x_j is unrestricted in sign

(*f*) Constraint i is of = type sign

Then the dual should correspondingly contain the following:

(*a*) objective function must be of minimize

(*b*) $\geq$ type constraints

(*c*) constraint j

(*d*) variable w_i

(*e*) jth constraint is an equation

(*f*) variable w_i is unrestricted in sign.

3.3 CONSTRUCTION OF DUAL PROBLEM FROM PRIMAL PROBLEM

Various steps involved in the formulation of the dual problem from the primal problem are summarized as follows:

Step 1: Convert the given LPP in its standard form, and consider this problem as the primal problem (PP)

Step 2: If the primal problem has the objective function as maximization, then the dual problem must have the objective function as minimization; and vice versa.

Step 3: The inequality sign ($\leq$ or $\geq$) are reversed in the all the given constraints except the non-negativity conditions. *i.e.*, for a maximization primal problem containing $\leq$ sign, then the dual problem will be *a* of minimization type and $\geq$ sign in all the constraints.

Step 4: If there are m constraints and n variables in any given primal problem, then the dual will contain m variables and n constraints.

Step 5: The right hand side b_i $(i = 1, 2, ..., m)$ of the primal becomes the coefficients of the dual variables w_i $(i = 1, 2, ..., m)$ in the dual objective function w.

Step 6: The coefficients c_j $(j = 1, ..., n)$ of the primal variables x_j $(j = 1, 2, ..., n)$ in the objective function becomes the right hand side constants in the dual problem.

Step 7: The coefficients of the dual variables in the constraints are the same as the coefficients of the primal variables except that they are transposed, *i.e.*, columns in primal coefficients matrix becomes the rows in the dual coefficient matrix.

Dual Variables	*Primal Variables*				*Maximum Z*
	x_1	x_2	....	x_n	
w_1	a_{11}	a_{12}	....	a_{1n}	$\leq b_1$
w_2	a_{21}	a_{22}	....	a_{2n}	$\leq b_2$
$\vdots$	$\vdots$	$\vdots$		$\vdots$	$\vdots$
w_m	a_{m1}	a_{m2}	....	a_{mn}	$\leq b_m$
Minimum w	$\geq c_1 \geq c_2 ... \geqslant c_n$				

Example 1. *Maximize* $Z = 15x_1 + 13x_2$

Subject to
$$13x_1 + 15x_2 \leq 25$$
$$15x_1 + 12x_2 \leq 20$$
$$x_1, x_2 \geq 0$$

Write the dual of the above problem.

Solution.

PP: Maximize $Z = 15x_1 + 13x_2$

Subject to
$$13x_1 + 15x_2 \leq 25$$
$$15x_2 + 12x_2 \leq 20$$
$$x_1, x_2 \geq 0$$

DP: Minimize $W = 25w_1 + 20w_2$

Subject to
$$13w_1 + 15w_2 \geq 15$$
$$15w_1 + 12w_2 \geq 13$$
$$w_1, w_2 \geq 0$$

Example 2. *Formulate the dual of the following problem.*

Maximize $Z = 2x_1 - 3x_2 + 4x_3$

Subject to
$$2x_1 + 3x_2 + 5x_3 \leq 20$$
$$2x_1 - 2x_3 \leq 12$$
$$3x_1 - 3x_2 - 4x_3 \leq 16$$
$$x_1, x_2, x_3 \geq 0$$

Solution.

PP: Maximize $Z = 2x_1 - 3x_2 + 4x_3$

Subject to
$$2x_1 + 3x_2 + 5x_3 \leq 20$$
$$2x_1 - 2x_3 \leq 12$$
$$3x_1 - 3x_2 - 4x_3 \leq 16$$
$$x_1, x_2, x_3 \geq 0$$

DP: Minimize $W = 20w_1 + 12w_2 + 16w_3$

Subject to
$$2w_1 + 2w_2 + 3w_3 \geq 2$$
$$3w_1 - 3w_2 \geq -3$$
$$5w_1 - 2w_2 - 4w_3 \geq 4$$
$$w_1, w_2, w_3 \geq 0$$

Example 3. *Formulate the dual of the following LPP.*

Minimize $Z = x_1 - 2x_2 + 3x_3$

Subject to
$$x_1 + 2x_2 + 4x_3 \geq 7$$
$$4x_1 + x_2 + 3x_3 \geq 2$$
$$5x_1 - 2x_2 - x_3 \leq 8$$
$$x_1 - 2x_2 + 5x_3 \geq 1$$
$$2x_1 + 7x_2 - 2x_3 \geq 0$$
$$x_1, x_2, x_3 \geq 0$$

Solution. Since the primal problem is of minimization type, so change all the inequalities of ≤ type into ≥ type by multiplying by –1 to both the sides. Thus the standard form of LPP is:

PP: Minimize $Z = x_1 - 2x_2 + 3x_3$

Subject to
$$x_1 + 2x_2 + 4x_3 \geq 7$$
$$4x_1 + x_2 + 3x_3 \geq 2$$
$$-5x_1 + 2x_2 + x_3 \geq -8$$
$$x_1 - 2x_2 + 5x_3 \geq 1$$
$$2x_1 + 7x_2 - 2x_3 \geq 0$$
$$x_1, x_2, x_3 \geq 0$$

DP: Maximize $W = 7w_1 + 2w_2 - 8w_3 + w_4$

Subject to
$$w_1 + 4w_2 - 5w_3 + w_4 + 2w_5 \leq 1$$
$$2w_1 + w_2 + 2w_3 - 2w_4 + 7w_5 \leq -2$$
$$4w_1 + 3w_2 + w_3 + 5w_4 - 2w_5 \leq 3$$
$$w_1, w_2, w_3, w_4, w_5 \geq 0$$

Example 4. *Obtain the dual of the following problem.*

Minimize $Z = 2x_1 + 3x_2$

Subject to
$$3x_1 + 5x_2 \leq 16$$
$$2x_1 - 2x_2 = 15$$
$$x_1 \geq 5$$
$$x_1, x_2 \geq 0$$

Solution. Since the primal is of minimization type, so change all the ≤ and type inequalities into ≥ type inequalities by multiplying by –1 to both the sides of the constraint. Express the – type constraint equivalent to two constraints of ≥ and ≤ type. Thus

PP(1): Minimize $Z_1 = 2x_1 + 3x_2$

Subject to
$$3x_1 + 5x_2 \leq 16$$
$$2x_1 - 2x_2 = 15$$
$$x_1 \geq 45$$
$$x_1, x_2 \geq 0$$

PP(2): Minimize $Z_2 = 2x_1 + 3x_2$

Subject to
$$-3x_1 - 5x_2 \geq -16$$
$$\left.\begin{array}{l} 2x_1 - 2x_2 \geq 15 \\ 2x_1 - 2x_2 \leq +15 \end{array}\right\} \text{(Changing equality sign into } \geq \text{ and } \leq \text{ sign)}$$
$$x_1 \geq 15$$
$$x_1, x_2 \geq 0$$

PP(3): Minimize $Z_2 = 2x_1 + 3x_2$

Subject to
$$-3x_1 - 5x_2 \geq -16$$
$$2x_1 - 2x_2 \geq 15$$

DP(1): Maximize $W = -16w_1 + 15w_2 - 15w_3 + 45w_4$

Subject to
$$-3w_1 + 2w_2 - 2w_3 + w_4 \leq 2$$
$$-5w_1 - 2w_2 + 2w_3 \leq 3$$

$$-2x_1 + 2x_2 \geq -15 \qquad w_1, w_4 \geq 0$$
$$x_1 \geq 45$$
$$x_1, x_2 \geq 0$$

The above dual problem reduces to the following form if $w = w_2 - w_3$ (suppose)

DP(2):

Maximize $W = -16w_1 + 15w + 45w_4$

Subject to $\quad -3w_1 + 2w + w_4 \leq 2$
$$-5w_1 - 2w \leq 3$$
$$w_1, w_4 \geq 0$$

and w being unrestricted in sign.

Example 5. *Formulate the dual for the following primal LPP.*

Minimize $Z = x_1 - 2x_2 - 3x_3$

Subject to $\quad 4x_1 - 2x_2 + 3x_3 \leq 8$
$$3x_1 - 5x_2 \geq 13$$
$$-5x_1 + 4x_2 + 9x_3 = 11$$
$$x_1, x_2 \geq 0$$

and x_3 *unrestricted in sign.*

Solution. Since x_3 is unrestricted in sign, therefore x_3 can be expressed as the difference of two non-negative variables.

i.e., $x_3 = x_3' - x_3''$, where $x_3', x_3'' \geq 0$

So, the given LPP can be written as PP(1).

PP(1): Minimize $Z_1 = x_1 - 2x_2 - 3(x_3' - x_3'')$

Subject to $\quad 4x_1 - 2x_2 + 3(x_3' - x_3'') \leq 8$
$$3x_1 - 5x_2 \geq 13$$
$$-5x_1 + 4x_2 + 9(x_3' - x_3'') = 11$$
$$x_1, x_2, x_3', x_3'' \geq 0$$

PP(2): Minimize $Z_2 = x_1 - 2x_2 - 3(x_3' - x_3'')$

Subject to $\quad -4x_1 + 2x_2 - 3(x_3' - x_3'') \geq -8$
$$3x_1 - 5x_2 \geq 13$$
$$-5x_1 + 4x_2 + 9(x_3' - x_3'') = 11$$
$$x_1, x_2, x_3', x_3'' \geq 0$$

Let w_1, w_2 and w_3 be the dual variables corresponding to the constraints of the primal LPP. Multiplying by (–1) on both the sides to convert ≤ type sign into ≥ type sign, as the objective function is of minimization case.

Again, as the third constraint of the primal LPP is of = type sign, so, the third dual variable w_3 will be unrestricted in sign.

Therefore, the dual of the above primal LPP can be written as:

DP: Maximize $W = -8w_1 + 13w_2 + 11w_3$

Subject to $\quad -4w_1 + 3w_2 - 5w_3 \leq 1$

$$2w_1 - 5w_2 + 4w_3 \le -2$$
$$-3w_1 + 9w_3 \le -3$$
$$w_1, w_2 \ge 0$$

and w_3 unrestricted in sign.

Example 6. *Obtain the dual of the following primal LPP*

Maximize $Z = 4x_1 + 2x_2 + 3x_3 - 2x_4$

Subject to $3x_1 - 2x_2 + 4x_3 + 2x_4 = 10$

$$2x_1 + 2x_2 - 2x_3 + 2x_4 = 13$$
$$x_1, x_2 \ge 0$$

and x_3, x_4 *unrestricted in sign.*

Solution.

PP: Maximize $Z = 4x_1 + 2x_2 + 3x_3 - 2x_4$

Subject to $3x_1 - 2x_2 + 4x_3 + 2x_4 = 10$

$$2x_1 + 2x_2 - 2x_3 + 2x_4 = 13$$
$$x_1, x_2 \ge 0$$

and x_3, x_4 unrestricted

$\ge$ -2

DP: Minimize $W = 10w_1 + 13w_2$

Subject to $3w_1 + 2w_2 \ge 3$

$$-2w_1 + 2w_2 \ge -2$$
$$4w_1 - 2w_2 \ge 3$$
$$2w_1 + 2w_4$$

w_1, w_2 unrestricted in sign.

Example 7. *Write the dual of the following LPP*

Minimize $Z = x_1 + 2x_2 - 2x_3$

Subject to $2x_1 - 3x_2 + 4x_3 \ge 15$

$$2x_1 - 2x_2 \ge 16$$
$$3x_1 - x_3 \le 14$$
$$x_1, x_2, x_3 \ge 0$$

Solution.

PP(1): Minimize $Z = x_1 + 2x_2 - 2x_3$

Subject to $2x_1 - 3x_2 + 4x_3 \ge 15$

$$2x_1 - 2x_2 \ge 16$$
$$3x_1 - x_3 \le 14$$
$$x_1, x_2, x_3 \ge 0$$

The above problem is written as:

PP(2): Minimize $Z = x_1 + 2x_2 - 2x_3$

Subject to $2x_1 - 3x_2 + 4x_3 \ge 5$

$$2x_1 - 2x_2 \ge 6$$
$$-3x_1 + x_3 \ge -14$$
$$x_1, x_2, x_3 \ge 0$$

DP: Maximize $W = 15w_1 + 16w_2 - 14w_3$

Subject to $2w_1 + 2w_2 - 3w_3 \le 1$

$$-3w_1 - 2w_2 \le 2$$
$$4w_1 + w_3 \le -1$$
$$w_1, w_2, w_3 \ge 0$$

Example 8. *Obtain the dual of the following system*

Minimize $Z = 5x_1 + 6x_2 + 7x_3$

Subject to $2x_1 - 4x_2 + 5x_3 = 25$

$2x_1 - 3x_2 \leq 23$

$2x_2 - 3x_3 \geq 25$

$x_1, x_2 \geq 0$, x_3 *unrestricted in sign.*

Solution. Let us suppose $x_3 = x_3' - x_3''$

PP(1): Minimize $Z = 5x_1 + 6x_2 + 7(x_3' - x_3'')$

Subject to $2x_1 - 4x_2 + 5(x_3' - x_3'') \geq 25$

$2x_1 - 4x_2 + 5(x_3' - x_3'') \leq 25$

$2x_1 - 2x_2 \leq 23$

$2x_2 - 3(x_3' - x_3'') \geq 25$

$x_2, x_2, x_3', x_3'' \geq 0$

PP(2): Minimize $Z = 5x_1 + 6x_2 + 7(x_3' - x_3'')$

Subject to $2x_1 - 4x_2 + 5(x_3' - x_3'') \geq 25$

$-2x_1 + 4x_2 - 5(x_3' - x_3'') \geq -25$

$-2x_1 + 2x_2 \geq -23$

$2x_2 - 3(x_3' - x_3'') \geq 25$

$x_1, x_2, x_3', x_3'' \geq 0$

DP(1): Maximize $W = 25w_1' - 25w_1'' - 23w_2 + 25w_3$

Subject to $2w_1' - 2w_1'' - 2w_2 \leq 5$

$-4w_1' + 4w_1'' + 2w_2 + 2w_3 \leq 6$

$5w_1' - 5w_1'' - w_3 \leq 7$

$-5w_1' + 5w_1'' + w_3 \leq -7$

$w_1', w_1'', w_2, w_3 \geq 0$

Let $w_1' - w_1'' = w_1$, then

DP(2): Maximize $W = 25w_1 - 23w_2 + 25w_3$

Subject to $2w_1 - 2w_2 \leq 5$

$-4w_1 + 2w_2 + 2w_3 \leq 6$

$5w_1 - w_3 \leq 7$

$w_2, w_3 \geq 0$, w_1 is unrestricted in sign.

3.4 MAIN POINTS ON DUALITY

1. The dual of the dual linear programming problem is the primal problem.
2. If either the primal or the dual problem has an unbounded solution, then the other problem has no feasible solutions.
3. If either the primal or the dual problem has a finite optimal solution, then the other problem also has a finite optimal solution, and in this case, the optimal value for both the problem is same,

   i.e., Max Z = Min W

4. If the primal problem has no solution, then the dual has an unbounded solution is not always true, but instead, if the primal problem has no solution, then the dual will also has no solution.
5. The value of the objective function for any feasible solution of the primal problem is less than the value of the objective function for feasible solution of the dual problem.

3.5 ADVANTAGES OF DUALITY

1. It is advantageous to solve the dual of a primal problem, as the calculations are reduced even if the primal problem contains large number of rows and smaller number of variables.
2. It avoids the necessity of adding surplus variables and/or artificial variables (lengthy process, as artificial technique is used) and solves the problem quickly by the well known technique primal-dual method.
3. The dual variables can provide the economic interpretation of the final solution of a LPP.
4. The economic interpretation of dual helps the management to make future decisions.
5. It is also helpful in investigating the changes in parameters to an LPP and this technique is called as sensitivity analysis.
6. It is also helpful in solving the LPP by the simplex method, in which the initial solution is infeasible, and this technique is called as the dual simplex method.

3.6 COMPARISON OF SOLUTIONS TO THE PRIMAL AND ITS DUAL

In this section, the solution of primal problem and its dual problem has the same value of objective function, is shown.

PP(1): Maximize $Z = 4x_1 + 5x_2$

Subject to
$$x_1 + 2x_2 \leq 2$$
$$7x_1 + 3x_2 \leq 4$$
$$x_1, x_2 \geq 0$$

DP(1): Minimize $W = 2w_1 + 4w_2$

Subject to
$$w_1 + 7w_2 \geq 4$$
$$2w_1 + 3w_2 \geq 5$$
$$w_1, w_2 \geq 0$$

Now writing both the problems (Primal and Dual) in standard form.

Standard form

PP(2): Maximize $Z = 4x_1 + 5x_2$ Subject to $x_1 + 2x_2 + s_1 = 2$ $7x_1 + 3x_2 + s_2 = 4$ $x_1, x_2, s_1, s_2 \geq 0$ (where s_1 and s_2 are slack variables)	**DP(2):** Maximize $W' = -2w_1 - 4w_2$ Subject to $w_1 + 7w_2 - s_1 + A_1 = 4$ $2w_1 + 3w_2 - s_2 + A_2 = 5$ $w_1, w_2 \geq 0$ $s_1, s_2, A_1, A_2 \geq 0$ (where s_1, s_2 are surplus variables and A_1, A_2 are artificial variables)

Iteration–0 (Primal)

C_B	Y_B	X_B	x_1 (4)	x_2 (5)	s_1 (0)	s_2 (0)	Ratio
0	s_1	2	1	2*	1	0	1 ←
0	s_2	4	7	3	0	1	4/3
$Z_j - C_j$		0	–4	–5 ↑	0	0	

Iteration–0 (Dual)

C_B	Y_B	W_B	w_1 (–2)	w_2 (–4)	s_1 (0)	s_2 (0)	A_1 (–M)	A_2 (–M)	Ratio
–M	A_1	4	1	7*	–1	0	1	0	4/7
–M	A_2	5	2	3	0	–1	0	1	5/3
$Z_j - C_j$		–9M	–3M + 2	– 10M + 4 ↑	M	M	0	0	

Iteration–1 (Primal)

C_B	Y_B	X_B	x_1 (4)	x_2 (5)	s_1 (0)	s_2 (0)	Ratio
5	x_2	1	1/2	1	1/2	0	2
0	s_2	1	11/2*	0	–3/2	1	2/11 ←
$Z_j - C_j$		5	–3/2 ↑	0	5/2		

Iteration–1 (Dual)

C_B	Y_B	W_B	w_1 (–2)	w_2 (–4)	s_1 (0)	s_2 (0)	A_2 (–M)	Ratio
–4	w_2	4/7	1/7	1	–1/7	0	0	4
–M	A_2	23/7	11/7*	0	3/7	–1	1	23/11 ←
$Z_j - C_j$		$\frac{-23}{7}M - \frac{16}{7}$	$\frac{-11}{7}M + \frac{10}{7}$ ↑	0	$\frac{-3}{7}M + \frac{4}{7}$	M	0	

Iteration–2 (Primal)

C_B	V_B	X_B	x_1 (4)	x_2 (5)	s_1 (0)	s_2 (0)
5	x_2	10/11	0	1	7/11	–1/11
4	x_1	2/11	1	0	–3/11	2/11
$Z_j - C_j$		58/11	0	0	23/11	3/11

Iteration–2 (Dual)

C_B	V_B	W_B	w_1 (–2)	w_2 (–4)	s_1 (0)	s_2 (0)
–4	w_2	3/11	0	1	–2/11	+1/11
–2	w_1	23/11	1	0	3/11	–7/11
$Z_j - C_j$		–58/11	0	0	2/11	10/11

Since $Z_j - C_j \geq 0$
Optimal solution has been attained.
Here maximize Z = 58/11

Since $Z_j - C_j \geq 0$
Optimal solution has been attained.
Here Maximize Z = –(–58/11) = 58/11

Thus, from the above comparison between the two final tables of the problem (Primal and Dual problems), it is always concluded that the solution to a primal problem can always provide a solution to its dual problem.

In the above table

PP: Maximize $Z = 58/11$
$x_1 = 2/11$
$x_2 = 10/11$

DP: Maximize $Z = -(-58/11) = 58/11$
$w_1 = 23/11$
$w_2 = 3/11$

But $Z_3 - C_3 = \frac{23}{11} = w_1$

and $Z_4 - C_4 = \frac{3}{11} = w_2$

But $Z_3 - C_3 = \frac{2}{11} = x_1$

and $Z_4 - C_4 = \frac{10}{11} = x_2$

Example 9. *A company makes three products A, B, C out of three raw materials X, Y and Z. The number of raw materials required to produce one unit of product is given as follows:*

	A	B	C
X	2	3	0
Y	3	2	4
Z	0	2	5

The unit profit contribution of the products A, B and C are ₹ 3.00, ₹ 5.00 and ₹ 4.00 respectively. The number of raw materials available are 8, 15 and 10 units respectively.

(i) Determine the product mix that maximizes to total profit.

(ii) Through the final simplex tableau, write down the solution to the dual problem also.

Solution. Formulation of LPP

Maximize $Z = 3x_1 + 5x_2 + 4x_3$

Subject to
$$2x_1 + 3x_2 \leq 8$$
$$3x_1 + 2x_2 + 4x_3 \leq 15$$
$$2x_2 + 5x_3 \leq 10$$
$$x_1, x_2, x_3 \geq 0$$

By adding slack variables, the above LPP can be written as:

Maximize $Z = 3x_1 + 5x_2 + 4x_3 + 0 \cdot s_1 + 0 \cdot s_2 + 0 \cdot s_3$

Subject to
$$2x_1 + 3x_2 + 0x_3 + s_1 = 8$$
$$3x_1 + 2x_2 + 4x_3 + s_2 = 15$$
$$0x_1 + 2x_2 + 5x_3 + s_3 = 10$$
$$x_1, x_2, x_3 \geq 0$$
$$s_1, s_2, s_3 \geq 0$$

(where s_1, s_2 and s_3 are slack variables).

(*i*) **Iteration–0**

	$C_j \rightarrow$		3	5	4	0	0	0	
C_B	Y_B	X_B	x_1	x_2	x_3	s_1	s_2	s_3	Min. Ratio
0	s_1	8	2	3*	0	1	0	0	8/3 ←
0	s_2	15	3	2	4	0	1	0	15/2
0	s_3	10	0	2	5	0	0	1	10/2
	$Z_j - C_j$	0	–3	–5 ↑	–4	0	0	0	

Iteration–1

			3	5	4	0	0	0	
C_B	Y_B	X_B	x_1	x_2	x_3	s_1	s_2	s_3	Ratio
5	x_2	8/3	2/3	1	0	1/3	0	0	–
0	s_2	29/3	5/3	0	4	–2/3	1	0	29/3/4
0	s_3	14/3	–4/3	0	5*	–2/3	0	1	14/3/5 ←
$Z_j - C_j$		40/3	1/3	0	–4 ↑	5/3	0	0	

Iteration–2

			3	5	4	0	0	0	
C_B	Y_B	X_B	x_1	x_2	x_3	s_1	s_2	s_3	
5	x_2	8/3	2/3	1	0	1/3	0	0	
0	s_2	89/15	41/15 *	0	0	–2/15	1	–4/5	←
4	x_3	14/15	–4/15	0	1	–2/15	0	1/5	
			–11/15 ↑	0	0	17/15	0	4/5	

Iteration–3

C_B	Y_B	X_B	x_1	x_2	x_3	s_1	s_2	s_3
5	x_2	50/41	0	1	0	15/41	–10/41	8/41
3	x_1	89/41	1	0	0	–2/41	15/41	–12/41
4	x_3	62/41	0	0	1	–6/41	4/41	5/41
$Z_j - C_j$		765/41	0	0	0	45/41	11/41	24/41

Since all $Z_j - C_j \geq 0$, thus the optimal solution has been attained.

Thus $Z_{max} = 765/41$

$x_1 = 89/41$

$x_2 = 50/41$

$x_3 = 62/41$

(*ii*) Thus the dual problem of the above problem (primal) can be written as:

DP: Minimize $W = 8w_1 + 15w_2 + 10w_3$

Subject to
$$2w_1 + 3w_2 \geq 3$$
$$3w_1 + 2w_2 + 2w_3 \geq 5$$
$$4w_2 + 5w_3 \geq 4$$
$$w_1, w_2, w_3 \geq 0$$

Thus, from the final tableaus (simplex table) of primal problem, the solution of the dual (above) problem can be obtained from the net evaluations ($Z_j - C_j$) in slack columns (s_1, s_2 and s_3) as follows:

Since
$$\left.\begin{aligned} Z_4 - C_4 &= 45/41 \\ Z_5 - C_5 &= 11/41 \\ Z_6 - C_6 &= 24/41 \end{aligned}\right\} \text{From primal problem}$$

Thus
$$\left.\begin{aligned} w_1 &= 45/41 \\ w_2 &= 11/41 \\ w_3 &= 24/41 \end{aligned}\right\} \text{For dual problem}$$

Example 10. *Solve the following LPP*

Maximize $Z = 3x_1 + 2x_2 + 5x_3$

Subject to
$$x_1 + 2x_2 + x_3 \le 430$$
$$3x_1 + 2x_3 \le 460$$
$$x_1 + 4x_2 \le 420$$
$$x_1, x_2, x_3 \ge 0$$

Also, from the final table of the simlplex method, write the solution to the dual problem.

Solution. After adding slack variables s_1, s_2, s_3 the initial table is constructed as:

Iteration–0

	C_j		3	2	5	0	0	0	
C_B	Y_B	X_B	x_1	x_2	x_3	s_1	s_2	s_3	Min. Ratio
0	s_1	430	1	2	1	1	0	0	430/1
0	s_2	460	3	0	2*	0	1	0	460/2 ←
0	s_3	420	1	4	0	0	0	1	
	$Z_j - C_j$	0	–3	–2	–5 ↑	0	0	0	

Iteration-1

			3	2	5	0	0	0	
C_B	Y_B	X_B	x_1	x_2	x_3	s_1	s_2	s_3	
0	s_1	200	–1/2	2*	0	1	1/2	0	100 ←
5	x_3	230	3/2	0	1	0	–1/2	0	–
0	s_3	420	1	4	0	0	0	1	105
	$Z_j - C_j$	1150	9/2	–2 ↑	0	0	5/2	0	

Iteration–2

			3	2	5	0	0	0
C_B	Y_B	X_B	x_1	x_2	x_3	s_1	s_2	s_3
2	x_2	100	–1/4	1	0	1/2	–1/4	0
5	x_3	230	3/2	0	1	0	1/2	0
0	s_3	20	2	0	0	–2	1	1
	$Z_j - C_j$	1350	4	0	0	1	2	0

Since all $Z_j - C_j \ge 0$, therefore optimal solution has been obtained.

PP: $Z_{max} = 1350$, $x_1 = 0$, $x_2 = 100$, $x_3 = 230$

DP: $Z_{max} = 1350$, $w_1 = 1$, $w_2 = 2$, $w_3 = 0$

Example 11. *Solve the following primal LPP and its dual by simplex method*

$$\text{Maximize } Z = 4x_1 + 3x_2$$
$$\text{Subject to} \quad x_1 + x_2 \leq 50$$
$$x_1 + 2x_2 \geq 80$$
$$3x_1 + 2x_2 \geq 140$$
$$x_1, x_2 \geq 0.$$

Solution. After introducing slack, surplus and artificial variables. The above LPP can be written as:

$$\text{Maximize } Z = 4x_1 + 3x_2 + 0 \cdot s_1 + 0 \cdot s_2 + 0 \cdot s_3 - MA_1 - MA_2$$
$$\text{Subject to} \quad x_1 + x_2 + s_1 = 50$$
$$x_1 + 2x_2 - s_2 + A_1 = 80$$
$$3x_1 + 2x_2 - s_3 + A_2 = 140$$
$$x_1, x_2 \geq 0$$
$$s_1, s_2, s_3, A_1, A_2 \geq 0$$

(where s_1: slack variable; s_2, s_3: surplus variable; A_1, A_2: Artificial variable)

Iteration–0

$C_j \rightarrow$			4	3	0	0	0	$-M$	$-M$	
C_B	Y_B	X_B	x_1	x_2	s_1	s_2	s_3	A_1	A_2	Min. Ratio
0	s_1	50	1	1	1	0	0	0	0	50
$-M$	A_1	80	1	2 *	0	-1	0	1	0	40
$-M$	A_2	140	3	2	0	0	-1	0	1	70
$Z_j - C_j$		$-220M$	$4M-4$	$-4M-3$ ↑	0	M	M	0	0	

After 2 more iterations, the final table is obtained as follows:

Iteration–2

			4	3	0	0	0	$-M$
C_B	Y_B	X_B	x_1	x_2	s_1	s_2	s_3	A_2
4	x_1	20	1	0	2	1	0	0
3	x_2	30	0	1	-1	-1	0	0
$-M$	A_2	20	0	0	-4	-1	-1	1
$Z_j - C_j$		$-20M + 170$	0	0	$4M+5$	$M+1$	M	0

Since an artificial variable (A_2) remain in the basis at positive level and $Z_j - C_j \geq 0$. The above problem has no feasible solution.

Thus the dual problem does not possess any optimal basic feasible solution.

Example 12. *Solve the following primal LPP and its dual by simplex method*

$$\text{Maximize } Z = 2x_1 + x_2$$

$$\text{Subject to} \quad x_1 + 2x_2 \leq 10$$
$$x_1 + x_2 \leq 6$$
$$x_1 - x_2 \leq 2$$
$$x_1 - 2x_2 \leq 1$$
$$x_1, x_2 \geq 0$$

Solution. Adding slack variables s_1, s_2, s_3 and s_4

$$\text{Maximize } Z = 2x_1 + x_2 + 0s_1 + 0s_2 + 0s_3 + 0s_4$$

$$\text{Subject to} \quad x_1 + 2x_2 + s_1 = 10$$
$$x_1 + x_2 + s_2 = 6$$
$$x_1 - x_2 + s_3 = 2$$
$$x_1 - 2x_2 + s_4 = 1$$
$$x_1, x_2 \geq 0$$
$$s_1, s_2, s_3, s_4 \geq 0$$

Iteration–0

	C_j		2	1	0	0	0	0	
C_B	Y_B	X_B	x_1	x_2	s_1	s_2	s_3	s_4	
0	s_1	10	1	2	1	0	0	0	10
0	s_2	6	1	1	0	1	0	0	6
0	s_3	2	1	–1	0	0	1	0	2
0	s_4	1	1*	–2	0	0	0	1	1 →
	$Z_j - C_j$	0	–2 ↑	–1	0	0	0	0	

Iteration–1

			2	1	0	0	0	0	
C_B	Y_B	X_B	x_1	x_2	s_1	s_2	s_3	s_4	
0	s_1	9	0	4	1	0	0	–1	$\frac{9}{4}$
0	s_2	7	0	3	0	0	0	–1	$\frac{7}{3}$
0	s_3	1	0	1*	0	0	1	–1	1
2	x_1	1	1	–2	0	0	0	1	–
	$Z_j - C_j$	2	0	–5	0	0	0	0	

Iteration–2

			2	1	0	0	0	0	
C_B	Y_B	X_B	x_1	x_2	s_1	s_2	s_3	s_4	
0	s_1	5	0	0	1	0	–4	3*	$\frac{5}{3}$ ←
0	s_2	4	0	0	0	1	–3	2	$\frac{4}{2}$
1	x_2	1	0	1	0	0	1	–1	–
2	x_1	3	1	0	0	0	2	–1	–
$Z_j - C_j$			0	0	0	0	3	–3	

Iteration–3

			2	1	0	0	0	0
C_B	Y_B	X_B	x_1	x_2	s_1	s_2	s_3	s_4
0	s_4	$\frac{5}{3}$	0	0	$\frac{1}{3}$	0	$-\frac{4}{3}$	1
0	s_2	$\frac{2}{3}$	0	0	$-\frac{2}{3}$	1	$-\frac{1}{3}$	0
1	x_2	$\frac{8}{3}$	0	1	$\frac{1}{3}$	0	$-\frac{1}{3}$	0
2	x_1	$\frac{14}{3}$	1	0	$\frac{1}{3}$	0	$\frac{2}{3}$	0
$Z_j - C_j$		12	0	0	1	0	1	0

Since all $Z_j - C_j \geq 0$, thus optimal solution has been attained.

Now,

The dual problem of the above given problem is:

DP:

$$\text{Minimize } W = 10w_1 + 6w_2 + 2w_3 + w_4$$
$$\text{Subject to} \quad w_1 + w_2 + w_3 + w_4 \geq 2$$
$$2w_1 + w_2 - w_3 - 2w_4 \geq 1$$
$$w_1, w_2, w_3, w_4 \geq 0$$

Introducing surplus (s_1 and s_2) and the artificial variables (A_1 and A_2), the above problem (DP) can be written as:

$$\text{Minimize } W = 10w_1 + 6w_2 + 2w_3 + w_4$$
$$\text{Subject to} \quad w_1 + w_2 + w_3 + w_4 - s_1 + A_1 = 2$$

$$2w_1 + w_2 - w_3 - 2w_4 - s_2 + A_2 = 1$$
$$w_1, w_2, w_3, w_4 \geq 0$$
$$s_1, s_2, A_1, A_2 \geq 0$$

and the objective function can be written as follow:

$$\text{Maximize } W' = -10w_1 - 6w_2 - 2w_3 - w_4 + 0 \cdot s_1 + 0 \cdot s_2 - MA_1 - MA_2$$

Iteration–0

	C_j		-10	-6	-2	-1	0	0	$-M$	$-M$	
C_B	Y_B	X_B	w_1	w_2	w_3	w_4	s_1	s_2	A_1	A_2	Min. Ratio
$-M$	A_1	2	1	1	1	1	-1	0	1	0	$\frac{21}{1}$
$-M$	A_2	1	2^*	1	-1	-2	0	-1	0	1	$\frac{1}{2}$ ←
$Z_j - C_j$		$-3M$	$-3M + 10$ ↑	$-2M + 6$	2	$M + 1$	M	M	0	0	

Iteration–1

			-10	-6	-2	-1	0	0	$-M$	
C_B	Y_B	X_B	w_1	w_2	w_3	w_4	s_1	s_2	A_1	Min. Ratio
$-M$	A_1	$\frac{3}{2}$	0	$\frac{1}{2}$	$\frac{3}{2}^*$	2	-1	$\frac{1}{2}$	1	1 ←
-10	w_1	$\frac{1}{2}$	1	$\frac{1}{2}$	$\frac{-1}{2}$	-1	0	$\frac{-1}{2}$	0	–
$Z_j - C_j$		$\frac{-3}{2}M - 5$	0	$\frac{-M}{2} + 1$	$\frac{-3M}{2} + 7$ ↑	$-2M + 1$	M	$\frac{M}{2} + 5$	0	

Iteration–2

			-10	-6	-2	-1	0	0	
C_B	Y_B	X_B	w_1	w_2	w_3	w_4	s_1	s_2	
-2	w_3	1	0	$\frac{1}{3}$	1	$\frac{4}{3}$	$\frac{-2}{3}$	$\frac{1}{3}$	3
-10	w_1	1	1	$\frac{2}{3}^*$	0	$\frac{-1}{3}$	$\frac{-1}{3}$	$\frac{-1}{3}$	$\frac{3}{2}$ ←
$Z_j - C_j$		-12	0	$\frac{-4}{3}$ ↑	0	$\frac{5}{3}$	$\frac{14}{3}$	$\frac{8}{3}$	

Iteration–3

			–10	–6	–2	–1	0	0
C_B	Y_B	X_B	w_1	w_2	w_3	w_4	s_1	s_2
–2	w_3	$\frac{1}{2}$	$\frac{-1}{2}$	0	1	$\frac{3}{2}$	$\frac{1}{2}$	$\frac{1}{2}$
–6	w_2	$\frac{3}{2}$	$\frac{3}{2}$	1	0	$\frac{-1}{2}$	$\frac{-1}{2}$	$\frac{-1}{2}$
$Z_j - C_j$		–10	2	0	0	1	4 ↑ x_1	2 ↑ x_2

Since all $Z_j - C_j \geq 0$

The optional solution has been attained.

Thus

$$Z_{min} = -10$$

$$w_1 = 0 \quad \text{and} \quad x_1 = 4$$

$$w_2 = \frac{3}{2} \quad x_2 = 2$$

$$w_3 = \frac{1}{2}$$

$$w_4 = 0$$

$$\therefore \quad Z_{max} = 10 \quad Z_{max} = 10$$

$$w_1 = w_4 = 0 \quad \text{and} \quad x_1 = 4$$

$$w_2 = \frac{3}{2} \quad x_2 = 2$$

$$w_3 = \frac{1}{2}$$

3.7 DUAL SIMPLEX METHOD

In the previous section, it was observed that the optimality conditions ($Z_j - C_j \geq 0$) were independent of the right hand side of the constraint (b_i), in case of simplex method, which implies that one or more of the values of X_B column may be negative. In such cases, we can find a starting basic, but not feasible solution. This is called dual feasible. Thus a method (simplex method) by which we can obtain an optimum basic feasible solution maintaining the dual feasibility in a finite number of steps is known as dual simplex method. The computational procedure is summarized in the following steps:

Step 1: Express the given LP problem in its standard form and obtain an initial basic solution X_B and hence display it in the initial dual simplex table.

Step 2: (*a*) If all $x_{Bi} \geq 0$, then obtain the optimum solution using simplex method.

(*b*) If at least one $x_{Bi} < 0$, then go to next step.

Step 3: (*a*) If all $Z_j - C_j \geq 0$, then go to next step. However, if at this stage (with all $Z_j - C_j \geq 0$, and all the basic variables are non-negative also), then this solution becomes optimum.

(*b*) If at least one $Z_j - C_j < 0$, the method fails.

Step 4: (*a*) Select x_{Br} to be removed for pivot row such that

$$X_{Br} = \min_i \{x_{Bi}; x_{Bi} < 0\}$$

(*b*) Select x_r to enter the basis for pivot column such that

$$\frac{Z_r - C_r}{x_{kr}} = \max_j \left\{\frac{Z_j - C_j}{x_{kj}}, x_{kj} < 0\right\}$$

Then x_{kr} becomes the pivot element.

Step 5: After pivot element is found, apply simplex method procedure to find the optimal solution or till no feasible solution exists.

Example 13. *Solve the following problem using dual simplex method.*

$$\text{Minimize } F = 3x_1 + 2x_2 + x_3 + 4x_4$$

$$\text{Subject to} \quad 2x_1 + 4x_2 + 5x_3 + x_4 \geq 10$$

$$3x_1 - x_2 + 7x_3 - 2x_4 \geq 2$$

$$5x_1 + 2x_2 + x_3 + 6x_4 \geq 15$$

$$x_1, x_2, x_3, x_4 \geq 0$$

Solution. Converting the given minimization objective function into maximization

$$\text{Maximize } Z = -3x_1 - 2x_2 - x_3 - 4x_4$$

Again converting the inequality constraints $\geq$ type into $\leq$ type.

$$-2x_1 - 4x_2 - 5x_3 - x_4 \leq -10$$

$$-3x_1 + x_2 - 7x_3 + 2x_4 \leq -2$$

$$-5x_1 - 2x_2 - x_3 - 6x_4 \leq -15$$

Thus, the above LPP can now be written as follows after introducing slack variables $s_1 \geq 0$, $s_2 \geq 0$ and $s_3 \geq 0$.

$$\text{Maximize } Z = -3x_1 - 2x_2 - x_3 - 4x_4$$

$$\text{Subject to} \quad -2x_1 - 4x_2 - 5x_3 - x_4 + s_1 = -10$$

$$-3x_1 + x_2 - 7x_3 + 2x_4 + s_2 = -2$$

$$-5x_1 - 2x_2 - x_3 - 6x_4 + s_3 = -15$$

$$x_1, x_2, x_3, x_4, s_1, s_2, s_3 \geq 0$$

The initial solution is

$$s_1 = -10$$

$$s_2 = -2$$

$$s_3 = -15$$

Iteration–0

C_j			–3	–2	–1	–4	0	0	0	
C_B	Y_B	X_B	x_1	x_2	x_3	x_4	s_1	s_2	s_3	
0	s_1	–10	–2	–4	–5	–1	1	0	0	
0	s_2	–2	–3	1	–7	2	0	1	0	
0	s_3	–15	–5*	–2	–1	–6	0	0	1	←
$Z_j - C_j$			3	2	1	4	0	0	0	

Since all $Z_j - C_j \geq 0$, the optimal solution has been attained, but still this solution is in feasible as b_i's are negative.

Now $$X_{Br} = \text{Min } \{x_{Bi}, x_{Bi} < 0\} = \text{Min } \{-10, -2, -15\} = -15$$

Since –15 corresponds to R_3 (third row), thus R_3 becomes the pivot row. So, s_3 leaves the basis.

Again $$\underset{j}{\text{Max}} \left\{ \frac{Z_j - C_j}{x_{kj}}, x_{kj} < 0 \right\} = \frac{Z_r - C_r}{x_{kr}}$$

$$\therefore \quad \underset{j}{\text{Max}} \left\{ \frac{Z_j - C_j}{x_{3j}} \right\} = \text{Max} \left\{ -\frac{3}{5}, \frac{-2}{2}, \frac{-1}{1}, \frac{-4}{6} \right\} = \frac{-3}{5}$$

$$\therefore \quad \left\{ \frac{Z_1 - C_1}{x_{31}} \right\} = \frac{-3}{5}$$

Therefore, column one, *i.e.*, x_1 enters the basis, so the pivot element becomes –5.

To make the pivot element 1, divide the row third (R_3) by –5 and make appropriate row operation as usual to find the values of the remaining elements.

Iteration–1

$C_j \rightarrow$			–3	–2	–1	–4	0	0	0	
C_B	Y_B	X_B	x_1	x_2	x_3	x_4	s_1	s_2	s_3	
0	s_1	–4	0	$\frac{-16}{5}$	$\frac{-23}{5}$*	$\frac{7}{5}$	1	0	$\frac{-2}{5}$	←
0	s_2	7	0	$\frac{11}{5}$	$\frac{-32}{5}$	$\frac{28}{5}$	0	1	$\frac{-3}{5}$	
–3	s_3	3	1	$\frac{2}{5}$	$\frac{1}{5}$	$\frac{6}{5}$	0	0	$\frac{-1}{5}$	
$Z_j - C_j$		–9	0	$\frac{4}{5}$	$\frac{2}{5}$	$\frac{2}{5}$	0	0	$\frac{3}{5}$	
					↑					

Obviously, the above solution is infeasible but optimal as all $Z_j - C_j \geq 0$.

Remark: The elementary row operations are obtained as usual, as explained during simplex method.

Now $\quad X_{Br} = \text{Min}\{-4, -, -\}$ as $X_{Br} = \{X_{Bi}, X_{Bi} < 0\}$

$$= -4$$

which corresponds to first row (R_1). So, R_1 becomes the pivot row.

Again
$$\frac{Z_r - C_r}{x_{kr}} = \text{Max}\left\{\frac{Z_j - C_j}{x_{kj}}, x_{kj} < 0\right\}$$

$$= \text{Max}\left\{-, \frac{4/5}{-16/5}, \frac{2/5}{-23/5}, -, -, -, \frac{3/5}{(-2/5)}\right\}$$

$$= \text{Max}\left\{-, \frac{-1}{4}, \frac{-2}{23}, -, -, -, \frac{-3}{2}\right\}$$

$$= \text{Max}\{-, -0.25, -0.086, -, -, -, -1.5\}$$

$$\therefore \quad \frac{Z_3 - C_3}{x_{13}} = -0.086 = \frac{-2}{23}$$

Thus, column third becomes the pivot column and so x_3 enters the basis, there by making $\frac{-23}{5}$ as pivot element.

Divide R_1 by $\frac{-23}{5}$, to make the pivot element unity (1), and find the values of the remaining elements by elementary row transformations.

Iteration–2

	$C_j \rightarrow$		−3	−2	−1	−4	0	0	0
C_B	Y_B	X_B	x_1	x_2	x_3	x_4	s_1	s_2	s_3
−1	x_3	$\frac{20}{23}$	0	$\frac{16}{23}$	1	$\frac{-7}{23}$	$\frac{-5}{23}$	0	$\frac{2}{23}$
0	s_2	$\frac{289}{23}$	0	$\frac{153}{23}$	0	$\frac{84}{23}$	$\frac{-32}{23}$	1	$\frac{-1}{23}$
−3	x_1	$\frac{65}{23}$	1	$\frac{6}{23}$	0	$\frac{29}{23}$	$\frac{1}{23}$	0	$\frac{-13}{23}$
	$Z_j - C_j$	$\frac{-215}{23}$	0	$\frac{-12}{23}$	0	$\frac{-12}{23}$	$\frac{-2}{23}$	0	$\frac{-13}{23}$

Since all $X_{Bi} \geq 0$.

Therefore the optimal solution has been attained.

So
$$x_1 = \frac{65}{23}$$

$$x_2 = 0$$

$$x_3 = \frac{20}{23}$$

and $$Z_{max} = \frac{-215}{23}$$

∴ the optimal solution for the given problem is

$$F_{min} = \frac{215}{23}$$

$$x_1 = \frac{65}{23},\ x_2 = 0 \text{ and } x_3 = \frac{20}{23}$$

Example 14. *Solve the following LPP using dual simplex method.*

$$\text{Maximize } Z = -2x_1 - x_2$$
$$\text{Subject to} \quad 3x_1 + x_2 \geq 3$$
$$4x_1 + 3x_2 \geq 6$$
$$x_1 + 2x_2 \geq 3$$
$$x_1, x_2 \geq 0.$$

Solution. Converting the ≥ inequality into ≤ inequality, the above problem can be written as:

$$\text{Maximize } Z = -2x_1 - x_2 + 0{\cdot}s_1 + 0{\cdot}s_2 + 0{\cdot}s_3$$
$$\text{Subject to} \quad -3x_1 - x_2 \leq -3$$
$$-4x_1 - 3x_2 \leq -6$$
$$-x_1 - 2x_2 \leq -3$$
$$x_1, x_2 \geq 0$$

After adding slack variables s_1, s_2 and x_3 the initial solution can be written as $s_1 = -3$, $s_2 = -6$, $s_3 = -3$.

Iteration–0

$C_j \rightarrow$			−2	−1	0	0	0	
C_B	Y_B	X_B	x_1	x_2	s_1	s_2	s_3	
0	s_1	−3	−3	−1	1	0	0	
0	s_2	−6	−4	−3*	0	1	0	←
0	s_3	−3	−1	−2	0	0	1	
$Z_j - C_j$		0	2	1	0	0	0	
				↑				

Since $X_{Br} = \min\,[x_{Bi}, x_{Bi} < 0] = \min\,[-3, -6, -3] = -6 = x_{B2}$ and so s_2 leaves the basis

$$\frac{Z_k - C_k}{x_{kr}} = \max\left[\frac{Z_j - C_j}{x_{kr}}, x_{kr} < 0\right] = \max\left[\frac{2}{-4}, \frac{1}{-3}, -, -, -, 0\right] = \frac{-1}{3}$$

Thus x_2 enters the basis and −3 becomes pivot element.

Iteration–1

			–2	–1	0	0	0	
C_B	Y_B	X_B	x_1	x_2	s_1	s_2	s_3	
0	s_1	–1	$\frac{-5}{3}$*	0	1	$\frac{-1}{3}$	0	←
–1	x_2	2	$\frac{4}{3}$	1	0	$\frac{-1}{3}$	0	
0	x_3	1	$\frac{5}{3}$	0	0	$\frac{-2}{3}$	1	
$Z_j - C_j$		–2	$\frac{2}{3}$	0	0	$\frac{1}{3}$	0	
			↑					

$X_{Br} = \min\,[-1, -, -, x_{Bi}, < 0] = -1 = x_{B1}$

So s_1 leaves the basis.

$$\frac{Z_k - C_k}{x_{kr}} = \max\left[\frac{Z_j - C_j}{x_{kr}}, x_{ki} < 0\right]$$

$$= \max\left[\frac{2/3}{-5/3}, \frac{1/3}{-1/3}\right]$$

$$= \max\left[-\frac{2}{5}, -1\right]$$

$$= \frac{-2}{5}$$

So x_1 enters the basis and $\frac{-5}{3}$ becomes the pivot element.

Iteration–2

$C_j \rightarrow$			–2	–1	0	0	0
C_B	Y_B	X_B	x_1	x_2	s_1	s_2	s_3
–2	x_1	$\frac{3}{5}$	1	0	$\frac{-3}{5}$	$\frac{1}{5}$	0
–1	x_2	$\frac{6}{5}$	0	1	$\frac{4}{5}$	$\frac{-3}{5}$	0
0	s_3	0	0	0	1	–1	1
$Z_j - C_j$		$\frac{-12}{5}$	0	0	$\frac{2}{5}$	$\frac{1}{5}$	0

Since all $Z_j - C_j \geq 0$, optimal solution has been attained. As $b_i \geq 0$, therefore infeasibility is removed.

Thus the feasible optimal solution is

$$Z_{max} = \frac{-12}{5}$$

$$x_1 = \frac{3}{5}$$

$$x_2 = \frac{6}{5}$$

$$s_1 = 0$$
$$s_2 = 0$$
$$s_3 = 0$$

Example 15. *Solve the following problem using dual simplex method.*

$$\text{Minimize } Z = 20x_1 + 16x_2 + 12x_3$$
$$\text{Subject to } -x_1 + x_2 + x_3 \geq 2$$
$$3x_1 + x_2 - x_3 \geq 4$$
$$x_1, x_2, x_3 \geq 0.$$

Solution. Expressing the given LPP in maximization form and converting the constraint in equations (≥) type into (≤) type

$$x_1 - x_2 - x_3 \leq -2$$
$$-3x_1 - x_2 + x_3 \leq -4$$

Now introducing the slack variables $s_1 \geq 0$ and $s_2 \geq 0$ and rewriting the LPP as follows.

$$\text{Maximize F} = -20x_1 - 16x_2 - 12x_3 + 0 \cdot s_1 + 0 \cdot s_2$$
$$\text{Subject to } x_1 - x_2 - x_3 + s_1 = -2$$
$$-3x_1 - x_2 + x_3 + s_2 = -4$$
$$x_1, x_2, x_3, s_1, s_2 \geq 0$$

Thus the initial solution is $s_1 = -2$ and $s_2 = -4$.

Iteration–0

C_j			–20	–16	–12	0	0	
C_B	Y_B	X_B	x_1	x_2	x_3	s_1	s_2	
0	s_1	–2	1	–1	–1	1	0	
0	s_2	–4	–3*	–1	1	0	1	←
$Z_j - C_j$			20	16	12	0	0	
			↑					

Iteration–1

			–20	–16	–12	0	0	
C_B	Y_B	X_B	x_1	x_2	x_3	s_1	s_2	
0	s_1	$\frac{-10}{3}$	0	$\frac{-4}{3}$	$\frac{-2}{3}$*	0	$\frac{1}{3}$	←
–20	x_1	$\frac{4}{3}$	1	$\frac{1}{3}$	$\frac{-1}{3}$	0	$\frac{-1}{3}$	
	$Z_j - C_j$	$\frac{-80}{3}$	0	$\frac{28}{3}$	$\frac{56}{3}$	0	$\frac{20}{3}$	
					↑			

Iteration–2

			–20	–16	–12	0	0
C_B	Y_B	X_B	x_1	x_2	x_3	s_1	s_2
–12	x_3	5	0	2	1	0	$\frac{-1}{2}$
–20	x_1	3	1	$\frac{-1}{6}$	0	0	$\frac{-5}{6}$
$Z_j - C_j$		–120	0	$\frac{34}{3}$	0	0	$\frac{86}{6}$

Since all $Z_j - Z_j \geq 0$ and also all $x_{Bi} \geq 0$, optimum solution has been attained.

$\therefore\ x_1 = 3,\ x_2 = 0,\ x_3 = 5$ and $Z_{\min} = 120$.

3.8 SENSITIVITY ANALYSIS

In linear programming problems studied so far, it was assumed that all the coefficients (C_j, b_i and a_{ij}), are assumed to be constant and are not known with certainty, but are the estimates or they vary overtime. The optimal solution obtained in LPP depends upon the above parameters (C_j, b_i and a_{ij}).

But because of time factor, the parameters may change independently. For example, in any given problem, the cost of any product, raw material used or profit or return will change, that depends upon time. Thus, such changes in any of the above parameters may put forward the validity of the optimal solution in dark. This is because the parameters involved may change, depending upon the time period. So, the management has to take the decisions that how sensitive the optimal solution is to the changes in the parameters?

Thus, the changes in the optimal solution due to changes in the parameters (C_j, b_i and a_{ij}) is called the sensitivity analysis or post-optimality analysis. Sensitivity analysis is the study of sensitivity of the optimal solution of an LPP due to variations or changes in its parameters. The process of studying in the sensitivity of the optimal solution of an LPP is also called as post-optimality analysis as it is done after an optimal solution has been obtained for the model, under some assumption.

The objective of sensitivity analysis is to reduce the additional computational effort considerably which arise in solving the problem in new form. The changes usually occur in the linear programming problem are as:

(*i*) Coefficients (C_j) of the Objective Function

The coefficient C_j in the objective function of an LPP represents either profit, return or cost per unit of a variable (decision) x_j. Changes in the profit or cost coefficients in the objective function can occur for a basic variable (the variable in the solution mix) or a non-basic variable (the variable not in the solution mix). The sensitivity ranges for these variables are determined differently.

Such a change will only affect the optimality condition but not the values of the basic variables. Then after such changes, the revised optimum solution can be obtained from the optimal table of the original problem by using usual simplex method.

(*ii*) Changes in Right Hand Side (b_i)

The right hand side constant (resource availability) of one or more constraints of a linear programming model may be changed over a given period of time. This may affect the feasibility of the current optimal solution but not the optimality. Then after such changes, the revised optimum solution can be obtained by incorporating the new changes in right hand side constants.

(*iii*) Adding a New Constraint

Sometimes the programmer or the analysts, under certain situations, can consider few more constraints, and can add these new constraints to an existing linear programming model. Then, each of the basic variables in the new constraint is substituted with the corresponding expression based on the current optimal table, that yields a modified version of the new constraint in terms of only the current non-basic variables. The new constraint may or may not be satisfied by the values of the current basic variables. If affected; the modified version of the new constraint is to be augmented to the optimal table of the original problem and simplex method is used to obtain the optimal solution. If not, then the optimality of the original problem will not be affected after the addition of new constraint to the LP model.

(*iv*) Adding a New Variable

If a new decision variable is defined and is added to the existing LP model, then the new revised optimal solution can be obtained by the final tableau of the optimal solution.

Thus post optimal analysis enables us to assess the effect of changes in linear programming without solving the entire LP again. It is also possible to find the changes in the values of each C_j, each b_i in terms of range, within which the current optimal solution's optimality is maintained.

Example 16. *Solve the following LPP*

Maximize $Z = 20x_1 + 30x_2 + 40x_3$

Subject to $4x_1 + 8x_2 + 12x_3 \leq 48$

$$9x_1 + 18x_2 + 12x_3 \leq 60$$

$$x_1, x_2, x_3 \geq 0$$

Also compute the following:

(a) *Find the range of the objective function coefficients C_1 of variable x_1 and C_2 of variable x_2 such that the optimality is not affected.*

(b) *If the profit coefficients are changed from (20, 30 and 40) to (14, 28 and 30), then check whether the optimality is affected or not. If so, find the revised optimum solution.*

Solution.

$$\text{Maximize } Z = 20x_1 + 30x_2 + 40x_3 + 0 \cdot s_1 + 0 \cdot s_2$$
$$\text{Subject to} \quad 4x_1 + 8x_2 + 12x_3 + s_1 = 48$$
$$9x_1 + 18x_2 + 12x_3 + s_2 = 60$$
$$x_1, x_2, x_3, s_1, s_2 \geq 0$$

where s_1 and s_2 are slack variable.

Iteration–0

	C_j		20	30	40	0	0	
C_B	Y_B	X_B	x_1	x_2	x_3	s_1	s_2	Min. Ratio
0	s_1	48	4	8	12*	1	0	4 ←
0	s_2	60	9	18	12	0	1	5
	$Z_j - C_j$	0	–20	–30	–40 ↑	0	0	

Iteration–1

			20	30	40	0	0	
C_B	Y_B	X_B	x_1	x_2	x_3	s_1	s_2	
40	x_3	4	1/3	2/3	1	1/12	0	12
0	s_2	12	5*	10	0	–1	1	12/5
$Z_j - C_j$		160	–20/3 ↑	–10/3	0	10/3	0	

Now the above constraint is also included in the final optimal tableau as shown below.

			20	30	40	0	0	0	
C_B	Y_B	X_B	x_1	x_2	x_3	s_1	s_2	s_3	
40	x_3	16/5	0	0	1	3/10	0	0	
20	x_1	12/5	1	2	0	–1/5	1/5	0	
0	s_3	–14/5	0	0	0	–1/10	–7/5*	1	– ←
	$Z_j - C_j$	176	0	10	0	8	4 ↑	0	

In the above table since row R_3 contains negative value (–14/5), so the solution is infeasible which can be removed by using dual simplex method.

$x_{Br} = \min [x_{Bi}, x_{Bi} < 0]$

$x_{B3} = -14/5$

and $$\max_{x_{3j}} \frac{Z_j - c_j}{x_{3f}} = \max\left[\frac{8}{-1/10}, \frac{4}{7/5}\right] = \max\left\{-80, -\frac{20}{7}\right\} = \frac{-20}{7} = \frac{Z_5 - C_5}{x_{35}}$$

So s_2 enters the basis, while s_3 leaves the basis

			20	30	40	0	0	0
C_B	Y_B	X_B	x_1	x_2	x_3	s_1	s_2	s_3
40	x_3	16/5	0	0	1	3/10	0	0
20	x_1	2	1	2	0	–3/10	0	1/7
0	s_2	2	0	0	0	–1/10	1	–5/7
$Z_j - C_j$		168	0	10	0	6	0	20/7

Since all $x_{Bi} \geq 0$ and $Z_j - C_j \geq 0$

Optimal solution has been attained

$\therefore\ x_1 = 2, x_2 = 0, x_3 = 16/5$ and $Z_{max} = 168$

$\therefore$ The optimal solution after adding new constraint is

$$x_1 = 2, x_2 = 0, x_3 = \frac{16}{5}$$

$s_1 = 0, s_2 = 2, s_3 = 0$

and $Z_{max} = 168$

Iteration–2

			20	30	40	0	0
C_B	Y_B	X_B	x_1	x_2	x_3	s_1	s_2
40	x_3	16/5	0	0	1	3/20	0
20	x_1	12/5	1	2	0	–1/5	1/5
$Z_j - C_j$		176	0	10	0	2	0

Since all $Z_j - C_j \geq 0$, the optimal solution has been attained.

$\therefore\ Z_{max} = 176$

$$x_1 = \frac{12}{5}, x_2 = 0, x_3 = \frac{16}{5}$$

(*a*) **Determination of the range of the objective function.** If the optimality is not affected, by making few changes in the objective function coefficients, then the present set of basic variables will continue, and in that case $Z_j - C_j$ values of basic variables will be zero, but the $Z_j - C_j$ values of non-basic variables will change.

Now for C_1 of the variable x_1:

Since the variable x_1 with respect to the objective function coefficient C_1 is a basic variable in the optimal solution table. Then the values of $Z_j - C_j$ will change for non-basic variables x_2, s_1 and s_2 and their values can be computed in terms of C_1.

The expression of $Z_2 - C_2$ for x_2, $Z_4 - C_4$ for s_1 and $Z_5 - C_5$ for s_2, are respectively calculated as:

$$Z_2 - C_2 = [40\ C_1]\begin{bmatrix}0\\2\end{bmatrix} - 30$$

$$= [40 \times 0 + C_1 \times 2] - 30$$

$$= 2C_1 - 30$$

$$Z_4 - C_4 = [40\ C_1]\begin{bmatrix}3/20\\-1/5\end{bmatrix} - 0$$

$$= \left[40.\frac{3}{20} + C_1\left(\frac{-1}{5}\right)\right] - 0$$

$$= 6 - \frac{C_1}{5}$$

$$Z_5 - C_5 = [40\ C_1]\begin{bmatrix}0\\1/5\end{bmatrix} - 0$$

$$= \left[0 + \frac{1}{5}C_1\right] - C$$

$$= \frac{1}{5}C_1$$

The above relative contributions are restricted to at most zero (0) to maintain the optimality as:

$$2C_1 - 30 \geq 0 \quad \Rightarrow \quad 2C_1 \geq 30 \quad \Rightarrow \quad C_1 \geq 15$$

$$6 - \frac{C_1}{5} \geq 0 \quad \Rightarrow \quad 6 \geq \frac{C_1}{5} \quad \Rightarrow \quad C_1 \leq 30$$

$$\frac{1}{5}C_1 \geq 0 \quad \Rightarrow \quad C_1 \geq 0 \quad \Rightarrow \quad C_1 \geq 0$$

By combining the above inequalities

$\therefore\ 0 \leq C_1 \leq 30$

Thus in the above interval, the optimality is unaffected.

Now for C_2 of the variable x_2

Here C_2 corresponds to one of the non-basic variables x_2, the range of C_2 can be obtained by just restricting $C_2 - Z_2$ to 0.

$$\text{Thus } Z_2 - C_2 = [40\ 20]\begin{bmatrix}0\\2\end{bmatrix} - C_2 = 40.0 + 20.2 - C_2$$

$$= 0 + 40 - C_2$$

$$= 40 - C_2$$

Thus the relative contribution is restricted to atmost 0 for maintaining the optimality as:

$40 - C_2 \geq 0 \quad \Rightarrow \quad 40 \geq C_2 \quad \Rightarrow \quad C_2 \leq 40$

∴ From the above inequality, the optimality will be unchanged as long as the value of C_2 is less than or equal to 40.

(*b*) The new values of C_1, C_2 and C_3 are now considered as 14, 28 and 30. The corresponding modified relative contributions of all the variables are computed as follows:

			14	28	30	0	0
C_B	V_B	X_B	x_1	x_2	x_3	s_1	s_2
30	x_3	16/5	0	0	1	3/20	0
14	x_1	12/5	1	2	0	–1/5	1/5
$Z_j - C_j$		648/5	0	0	0	17/10	14/5

Calculations of $Z_j - C_j$

$Z_1 - C_1 = 30.0 + 14.1 - 14 = 0$

$Z_2 - C_2 = 30.0 + 14.2 - 28 = 0$

$Z_3 - C_3 = 30.1 + 14.0 - 30 = 0$

$$Z_4 - C_4 = 30.\frac{3}{20} - 14.\frac{1}{5} - 0 = \frac{17}{10}$$

$$Z_5 - C_5 = 30.0 + 14.\frac{1}{5} - 0 = \frac{14}{5}$$

Since all $Z_j - C_j \geq 0$, the optimal solution has been attained and the optimality is little bit affected as

$Z_{max} = 648/5$

$x_1 = 12/5$, $x_2 = 0$ and $x_3 = 16/5$

Example 17. *Solve the following LPP*

$$\text{Maximize } Z = 10x_1 + 20x_2$$
$$\text{Subject to } \quad 10x_1 + 20x_2 \leq 120$$
$$8x_1 + 8x_2 \leq 80$$
$$x_1, x_2 \geq 0$$

Then, again solve the above problem if

(a) the right hand side constraints I is changed from 120 to 60.

(b) the right hand side constraint I is changed from 120 to 130.

(c) the right hand side constraint II is changed from 80 to 100.

Solution. The standard LPP after adding slack variables s_1 and s_2 can be written as

$$\text{Maximize } Z = 10x_1 + 20x_2 + 0s_1 + 0s_2$$
$$\text{Subject to } \quad 10x_1 + 20x_2 + s_1 = 120$$
$$8x_1 + 8x_2 + s_2 = 80$$
$$x_1, x_2, s_1, s_2 \geq 0$$

Iteration–0

	C_j		10	20	0	0	
C_B	Y_B	X_B	x_1	x_2	s_1	s_2	
0	s_1	120	10	20 *	1	0	6 ←
0	s_2	80	8	8	0	1	10
$Z_j - C_j$		0	–10	–20 ↑	0	0	

Here, x_2 enters the basis while s_1 leaves the basis.

Iteration–1

	C_j		10	20	0	0
C_B	Y_B	X_B	x_1	x_2	s_1	s_2
20	x_2	6	1/2	1	1/20	0
0	s_1	32	4	0	–2/5	1
$Z_j - C_j$		120	0	0	1	0

Since $Z_j - C_j \geq 0$, optimal solution has been attained.

$$Z_{\max} = 120,\ x_1 = 0,\ x_2 = 6$$

(*a*) The revised right hand side constants after incorporating the changes in the constraints are obtained by the use of following formula

$$\begin{bmatrix}\text{Basic variables in}\\ \text{optimal table}\end{bmatrix} = \begin{bmatrix}\text{Technological coefficient columns}\\ \text{in optimal table w.r.t. basic}\\ \text{variables in initial table}\end{bmatrix} \cdot \begin{bmatrix}\text{New R.H.S. constants}\end{bmatrix}$$

i.e., $$\begin{bmatrix} x_2 \\ s_1 \end{bmatrix} = \begin{bmatrix} \frac{1}{20} & 0 \\ \frac{-2}{5} & 1 \end{bmatrix} \begin{bmatrix} 60 \\ 80 \end{bmatrix} \Rightarrow \qquad x_2 = \frac{1}{20} \times 60 + 0 \times 80 = 3$$

$$\text{and } s_1 = \frac{-2}{5} \times 60 + 1 \times 80 = 56$$

$\Rightarrow \qquad x_2 = 3$ and $s_1 = 56$

$\Rightarrow \qquad Z = 3 \times 20 + 56 \times 0 = 60$

Since these values are non-negative, the revised solution is feasible and optimal and the objective function values is decreased as 6.

(*b*) $$\begin{bmatrix} x_2 \\ s_1 \end{bmatrix} = \begin{bmatrix} 1/20 & 0 \\ -2/5 & 1 \end{bmatrix} \begin{bmatrix} 130 \\ 80 \end{bmatrix} \Rightarrow \qquad x_2 = \frac{1}{20} \times 130 = 13/2$$

$$\text{and } s_2 = \frac{-2}{5} \times 130 + 1 \times 80 = 28$$

$$\Rightarrow \quad Z_{max} = 20 \times \frac{13}{2} + 0 \times 28 = 130$$

(c) $$\begin{bmatrix} x_2 \\ s_1 \end{bmatrix} = \begin{bmatrix} 1/20 & 0 \\ -2/5 & 1 \end{bmatrix} \begin{bmatrix} 120 \\ 100 \end{bmatrix}$$

$$\Rightarrow \quad x_2 = 6 \text{ and } s_2 = 32$$

∴ There is no change.

Example 18. *Consider example 16. Maximize* $Z = 20x_1 + 30x_2 + 40x_3$

Subject to

$$4x_1 + 8x_2 + 12x_3 \leq 48$$
$$9x_1 + 18x_2 + 12x_3 \leq 60$$
$$x_1, x_2, x_3 \geq 0$$

(a) *If new constraint* $6x_1 + 2x_2 + 4x_3 \leq 70$, *is added, then check whether this new constraint affects the optimality or not. If yes, find the new optimum solution.*

(b) *If new constraint* $7x_1 + 2x_2 + 5x_3 \leq 30$, *is added, then find the new optimum solution, if it affects the optimality.*

Solution. $6x_1 + 2x_2 + 4x_3 \leq 70$. From the solved example 16, we have optimal solution as: $Z_{max} = 176$, $x_1 = 12/5$, $x_2 = 0$, $x_3 = 16/5$. The new constraint is satisfied by the values of the current basic variables ($x_1 = 12/5$ and $x_3 = 16/5$, $x_2 = 0$).

Hence, this new constraint is said to be redundant constraint and the optimality will not be affected even after including the new constraint into the existing linear programming model.

(b) $7x_1 + 2x_2 + 5x_3 \leq 30$.

Since the above new constraint is not satisfied by the values of the current basic variables ($x_1 = 12/5$, $x_2 = 0$ and $x_3 = 16/5$). So, the modified form of the new constraint in terms of only non-basic variables is obtained.

The standard form of the new constraint after adding slack variable $s_3 \geq 0$, is as:

$$7x_1 + 2x_2 + 5x_3 + s_3 = 30$$

Now the optimal tableau is written directly as

$C_j \rightarrow$			20	30	40	0	0
C_B	Y_B	X_B	x_1	x_2	x_3	s_1	s_2
40	x_3	16/5	0	0	1	3/10	0
20	x_1	12/5	1	2	0	–1/5	1/5
$Z_j - C_j$		176	0	10	0	2	0

From the above table

$$x_3 = \frac{3}{10}s_1 + 0s_2 = \frac{16}{5} \quad \text{and} \quad x_1 = \frac{-1}{5}s_1 + \frac{1}{5}s_2 = \frac{12}{5}$$

i.e., $$x_3 = \frac{16}{5} - \frac{3}{10}s_1 \text{ and } x_1 = \frac{12}{5} + \frac{1}{5}s_1 - \frac{1}{5}s_2$$

Then putting the values of x_1, x_2 and x_3 from above in the new constraint included.

$$7\left(\frac{12}{5} + \frac{1}{5}s_1 - \frac{1}{5}s_2\right) + 2(0) + 5\left(\frac{16}{5} - \frac{3}{10}s_1\right) + s_3 = 30$$

$$\therefore \frac{7}{5}s_1 - \frac{3}{2}s_1 - \frac{7}{5}s_2 + s_3 = 30 - \frac{84}{5} - \frac{80}{5}$$

$$-\frac{1}{10}s_1 - \frac{7}{5}s_2 + s_3 = -\frac{14}{5}$$

OBJECTIVE TYPE QUESTIONS

1. Which of the following is true regarding duality?
   (a) The dual of a dual is a primal
   (b) If the primal is minimization problem, then its dual will be a maximization problem.
   (c) If the primal is maximization problem, then its dual will be a minimization problem.
   (d) All of the above.
2. Which of the following is/are the advantage(s) of duality?
   (a) It avoids the necessity for adding surplus or artificial variables.
   (b) It solves the problem quickly.
   (c) It is used to solve an LPP by the simplex method in which the initial solution is infeasible.
   (d) All of the above.
3. Which of the following is incorrect?
   (a) The shadow price of non-binding constraint is always equal to zero.
   (b) The shadow price indicates the change in the value of the objective function, per unit increase in the value of the right hand side.
   (c) The shadow price is called as imputed value of resource.
   (d) None of the above.
4. The dual of the primal maximization problem having m constraints and n non-negative variables should have
   (a) m constraints and n non-negative variables.
   (b) n constraints and m non-negative variables.
   (c) m constraints and m non-negative variables.
   (d) n constraints and n non-negative variables.
5. Choose the correct statement
   (a) The dual of a dual is always a primal problem.
   (b) If dual has unbounded solution, then primal problem does not have feasible solution.
   (c) If either the primal or dual has a finite solution, then the other problem, dual or primal also have a finite optimum solution.
   (d) All of the above.

6. The shadow price is the:
   (*a*) price which is paid for purchase of resource.
   (*b*) increase in the objective function value by providing an additional unit of resource.
   (*c*) price which is paid for ordering the products.
   (*d*) increase in the constraints of its production.
7. Which of the following statement(s) is/are wrong?
   (*a*) All scarce resources have marginal profitability equal to zero.
   (*b*) If a constraint in the primal problem has negative value on the right-hand side, its dual cannot be constructed.
   (*c*) If the standard LPP is of maximization, then its dual is of minimization with $\geq$ constraints.
   (*d*) All of the above.
8. For the primal and its dual problem,
   (*a*) the primal problem will have an optimal solution iff its dual too has an optimal solution.
   (*b*) both primal and its corresponding dual problem cannot be infeasible.
   (*c*) both the problems have same value of the objective function.
   (*d*) None of the above.
9. Which of the following is correct?
   (*a*) For an unrestricted primal variable, the corresponding dual constraint is an equation.
   (*b*) The optimum solution of the primal problem can be obtained by inspecting the optimum table of the dual problem as well.
   (*c*) An equation in a constraint of a primal problem implies the associated variable in the dual problem to be unrestricted.
   (*d*) All of the above.
10. The right hand side (b_i) of a constraint in a primal LPP appears in the
   (*a*) right hand side of a constraint in the corresponding dual problem.
   (*b*) coefficient in the objective function in the corresponding dual problem.
   (*c*) non-negative restrictions of the corresponding dual problem.
   (*d*) None of the above.
11. The value of the dual variable represent
   (*a*) marginal profit of each additional unit of resource.
   (*b*) marginal cost of each additional unit of resource.
   (*c*) value of the additional unit of resource.
   (*d*) None of the above.

EXERCISES

1. Explain the term duality and dual.
2. Show that if any of the constraints in the primal is a strict equality, the corresponding dual variable is unrestricted in sign.

   (**Hint:** PP: Let Min Z = cx sb $\sum_{j=1}^{n} a_i x_j \geq b_i$ and $\sum_{j=1}^{n} a_{ij} x_j = b_i, x_j \geq 0$

   DP: Max $W = \sum_{j=1}^{n} b_i w_i + b_i(w_i' - w_i''), w_i \geq 0, w_i', w_i'' \geq 0$

   if $w_i = w_i' - w_i''$

   then DP: Max $Z = \sum_{j=1}^{n} b_i w_i$ st. $\sum_{j=1}^{n} a_{ji} w_i \leq C_j \ \forall_j = 1, 2, ..., n, w_i \geq 0; 1, 2 ...., m)$
3. Explain the properties of duality.
4. Describe an algorithm for primal-dual constructions of an LPP.
5. Discuss the relationship between primal and its dual.
6. What do you mean by primal and dual problems. Is the number of constraints in the primal and dual the same?
7. Prove that the necessary and sufficient condition for any linear programming problem and its dual to have optimal solutions is that both have feasible solutions.
8. Prove that if any variable of the primal problem is unrestricted in sign, then the corresponding constraint in the dual will be a strict equality.
9. Write a short note on "reading the solution to the dual problem from the final tableau of simplex method of the primal".
10. Given an optimal basic solution to LPP. Can one obtain an unbounded solution by changing only requirement vector?
11. What is the use of dual programming problem. Explain with the help of an example.
12. Define the dual of a LPP and prove that if the primal has an unbounded solution, the dual has no solution and vice-versa.
13. Prove that the dual of the dual of a given primal is the primal itself.
14. Prove that the variables in the dual of the LPP.

    $$\text{Max } Z = Cx$$
    $$\text{Subject to } Ax = b$$
    $$x \geq 0$$

    are unrestricted.
15. Write the advantages and the properties of duality.

UNSOLVED PROBLEMS

Write the dual of the following problem:

1. Minimize $Z = 6x_1 + 4x_2$

Subject to
$$5x_1 + x_2 \geq 13$$
$$x_1 + 5x_2 \geq 15$$
$$5x_1 + 6x_2 \geq 25$$
$$x_1, x_2 \geq 0$$

2. Maximize $Z = 4x_1 + 3x_2$

Subject to
$$2x_1 + 5x_2 \leq 20$$
$$3x_1 + 8x_2 \geq 40$$
$$x_1, x_2 \geq 0$$

3. Minimize $Z = 4x_1 + 11x_2$

Subject to
$$x_1 - x_2 \leq 5$$
$$3x_1 + 2x_2 = 9$$
$$4x_1 + 11x_2 \leq 6$$
$$x_1, x_2 \geq 0$$

4. Maximize $Z = 12x_1 + 15x_2 + 16x_3$

Subject to
$$4x_1 + 5x_2 - x_3 \leq 2$$
$$-2x_1 + x_2 + 3x_3 \leq 3$$
$$x_1 - 4x_2 + 2x_3 \leq 0$$
$$-2x_1 - 2x_2 + 6x_3 \leq 5$$
$$x_1, x_2, x_3 \geq 0$$

[**Ans.** Minimize $F = 2w_1 + 3w_2 + 5w_4$

Subject to
$$4w_1 - 2w_2 + w_3 - 2w_4 \geq 12$$
$$5w_1 + w_2 - 4w_3 - 2w_4 \geq 15$$
$$-w_1 + 3w_2 + 2w_3 + 6w_4 \geq 16$$
$$w_1, w_2, w_3 \geq 0]$$

5. Minimize $Z = 8x_1 + 5x_2 + 9x_3$

Subject to
$$5x_1 + 7x_2 + 6x_3 \geq 30$$
$$10x_1 + 5x_2 + 4x_3 \geq 10$$
$$4x_1 + 10x_2 + 8x_3 \leq 15$$
$$x_3 \geq 60$$
$$x_1 - x_2 \leq 0$$
$$x_1, x_2, x_3 \geq 0$$

6. Minimize $Z = 4x_1 - 3x_2 + 5x_3$

Subject to
$$2x_1 + 4x_2 + 3x_3 \geq 17$$
$$5x_1 + x_2 + 2x_3 \geq 3$$
$$6x_1 - x_2 - x_3 \leq 9$$
$$x_1 - x_2 + 4x_3 \geq 3$$
$$3x_1 + 6x_2 - x_3 \geq 1$$
$$x_1, x_2, x_3 \geq 0$$

[**Ans.** Maximize $W = 17w_1 + 3w_2 - 9w_3 + 3w_4 + w_5$

Subject to
$$2w_1 + 5w_2 - 6w_3 + w_4 + 3w_5 \leq 4$$
$$4w_1 + w_2 + w_3 - w_4 + 6w_5 \leq -3$$
$$3w_1 + 2w_2 + w_3 + 4w_4 - w_5 \leq 5$$
$$w_1, w_2, w_3, w_4, w_5 \geq 0]$$

7. Minimize $Z = 12x_1 + 14x_2 + 4x_3 - 13x_4$

Subject to
$$x_1 + x_2 + x_3 = 14$$
$$x_1 + 4x_2 + x_4 = 18$$
$$x_1, x_2, x_3, x_4 \geq 0$$

[**Ans.** Maximize $W = 14w_1 + 18w_2$

Subject to
$$w_1 + w_2 \geq 12$$
$$w_1 + 4w_2 \geq 14$$
$$w_1 \geq 4$$
$$w_2 \geq -13$$
w_1 and w_2 unrestricted in sign.]

8. Minimize $Z = 2x_3 + 3x_4 + 4x_5$

Subject to
$$2x_1 - 3x_3 + 4x_4 - 5x_5 = -12$$
$$x_2 - 2x_3 - x_4 + x_5 = 11$$
$$x_1, x_2, x_3, x_4, x_5 \geq 0$$

[**Ans.** Maximize $Z' = -12w_1 + 11w_2$

Subject to
$$2w_1 \leq 0$$
$$w_2 \leq 0$$
$$-3w_1 - 2w_2 \leq 2$$
$$4w_1 - w_2 \leq 3$$
$$-5w_1 + w_2 \leq 4$$
w_1, w_2 unrestricted in sign, $w_3, w_4, w_5 \geq 0$]

9. Minimize $Z = 5x_1 + 13x_2 + 7x_3$

Subject to
$$10x_1 + 4x_2 + 2x_3 \geq 18$$
$$6x_1 + 12x_2 + 8x_3 \geq 24$$
$$8x_1 + 2x_2 + 10x_3 \geq 11$$
$$2x_1 + 10x_2 + 6x_3 \geq 27$$
$$x_1, x_2, x_3 \geq 0$$

[**Ans.** Maximize $W = 18w_1 + 24w_2 + 11w_3 + 27w_4$

Subject to
$$10w_1 + 6w_2 + 8w_3 + 2w_4 \leq 5$$
$$4w_1 + 12w_2 + 2w_3 + 10w_4 \leq 13$$
$$2w_1 + 8w_2 + 10w_3 + 6w_4 \leq 7$$
$$w_1, w_2, w_3, w_4 \geq 0]$$

10. Maximize $Z = 2x_1 - 2x_2 + 6x_3$

Subject to
$$2x_1 + 3x_2 + 4x_3 \leq 12$$
$$2x_1 + 0x_2 - 3x_3 \leq 22$$
$$6x_1 - 6x_2 + 6x_3 \leq 16$$
$$x_1, x_2, x_3 \geq 0$$

[**Ans.** Minimize $W = 12w_1 + 22w_2 + 16w_3$

Subject to
$$2w_1 + 2w_2 + 6w_3 \geq 2$$
$$3w_1 - 6w_3 \geq -2$$
$$4w_1 - 3w_2 + 6w_3 \geq 6$$
$$w_1, w_2, w_3 \geq 0]$$

11. Minimize $Z = 2x_1 - 6x_2 - 4x_3$

Subject to
$$8x_1 - 2x_2 + 4x_3 \leq 27$$
$$3x_1 - 4x_2 \geq 24$$
$$-5x_1 + 13x_2 + 7x_3 = 36$$
$x_1, x_2 \geq 0$, and x_3 is unrestricted

[**Ans.** Maximize $W = -27w_1 + 24w_2 + 36w_3$

Subject to
$$-8w_1 + 3w_2 - 5w_3 \leq 2$$
$$2w_1 - 4w_2 + 13w_3 \leq -6$$
$$-4w_1 + 7w_3 \geq -4$$
$$w_1 \geq 0,\ w_2 \geq 0$$
w_3 unrestricted]

12. Minimize $Z = 2x_1 + 3x_2 + 6x_3$

Subject to
$$2x_1 - 13x_2 + 4x_3 = 25$$
$$12x_1 - 24x_2 \leq 23$$
$$22x_2 - 3x_3 \geq 25$$
$x_1, x_2 \geq 0$ and x_3 is unrestricted in sign

[**Ans.** Maximize $W = 25w_1 - 23w_2 + 25w_3$

Subject to
$$2w_1 - 12w_2 \leq 2$$
$$-13w_1 + 24w_2 \leq 3$$
$$4w_1 - 3w_2 = 6$$
$$w_2 \geq 0$$
w_1 unrestricted]

13. Maximize $Z = 3x_1 + 5x_2$

Subject to
$$2x_1 + 12x_2 \leq 20$$
$$3x_1 + 3x_2 = 16$$
$$2x_1 - 5x_2 \leq 12$$
$$x_1 - 2x_2 \leq 11$$
$$x_1, x_2, x_3 \geq 0$$

[**Ans.** Minimize $Z' = 20w_1 + 16w_2 + 12w_3 + 11w_4$

Subject to
$$2w_1 + 3w_2 + 2w_3 + w_4 \geq 3$$
$$12w_1 + 3w_2 - 5w_3 - 2w_4 \geq 5$$
$$w_1, w_2, w_3, w_4 \geq 0]$$

14. Minimize $Z = 8x_1 + 2x_2 + 4x_3$

Subject to
$$x_1 - 4x_2 - 2x_3 \geq 17$$
$$x_1 + x_2 - 3x_3 \geq -11$$
$$-3x_1 - x_2 + x_3 \geq 1$$
$$x_1, x_2, x_3 \geq 0$$

[**Ans.** Maximize $W = 17w_1 - 11w_2 + w_3$

Subject to
$$w_1 + w_2 + 3w_3 \leq 8$$
$$-4w_1 + w_2 - w_3 \leq 2$$
$$-2w_1 - 3w_2 + w_3 \leq 4$$
$$w_1, w_2, w_3 \geq 0]$$

15. Give the dual of the following problem in a form such that the dual variables are non-negative and no strict equations appear in the dual constraints.

Maximize $Z = x_1 + 2x_2$

Subject to
$$2x_1 + 3x_2 \geq 4$$
$$3x_1 + 4x_2 = 5$$
$x_1 \geq 0$ and x_2 is unrestricted.

[**Ans.** Minimize $W = -4w_1 + 5w_2 - 5w_3$

Subject to
$$-2w_1 + 3w_2 - 3w_3 \geq 1$$
$$-3w_1 + 4w_2 - 4w_3 \geq 2$$
$$3w_1 - 4w_2 + 4w_3 \geq -2$$
$$w_1, w_2, w_3 \geq 0]$$

16. Obtain the dual of the following LPP:

Maximize $Z = 12x_1 + 13x_2 + 14x_3$

Subject to
$$13x_1 - 12x_3 \leq 14$$
$$12x_1 + 10x_2 + 10x_3 \leq 53$$
$$12x_2 + 13x_3 \leq 36$$
$$x_1, x_2, x_3 \geq 0$$

[**Ans.** Minimize $W = 14w_1 + 53w_2 + 36w_3$

Subject to
$$13w_1 + 12w_2 \geq 12$$
$$10w_1 + 12w_2 \geq 13$$
$$-12w_1 + 10w_2 + 13w_3 \geq 14$$
$$w_1, w_2, w_3 \geq 0]$$

Solve the dual problem by simplex method and deduce from it the solution to the primal problem.

17. Obtain the dual of the following LPP:

Maximize $Z = 13x_1 + 10x_2 + 13x_3 - 10x_4$

Subject to
$$2x_1 - x_2 + 3x_3 + x_4 = 10$$
$$x_1 + x_2 - x_3 + x_4 = 13$$
$$x_1, x_2, x_3, x_4 \geq 0$$

[**Ans.** Minimize $W = 10w_1 + 13w_2$

Subject to
$$2w_1 + w_2 \geq 13$$
$$-w_1 + w_2 \geq 10$$
$$3w_1 - w_2 \geq 13$$
$$w_1 + w_2 \geq -10$$
w_1, w_2 unrestricted in sign]

18. Apply the simplex method to solve the following primal problem:

Maximize $Z = 30x_1 + 23x_2 + 29x_3$

Subject to
$$6x_1 + 5x_2 + 3x_3 \leq 26$$
$$4x_1 + 2x_2 + 6x_3 \leq 7$$
$$x_1, x_2, x_3 \geq 0$$

Also read the solution to the dual of the above problem from the final table.

[**Ans.** $Z = 161/2 \quad w_2 = w_5 = 23/2$]

19. Find the dual of the following problem:

Maximize $Z = 20x_1 - 10x_2$

Subject to
$$11x_1 + 12x_2 \leq 20$$
$$-3x_1 + x_2 = 26$$
$$15x_1 + 16x_2 \geq 12$$
$$x_1, x_2 \geq 0$$

Also, solve the primal problem by simplex method and deduce from it the solution to the dual.

20. Solve the following by the dual simplex algorithm:

Minimize $Z = x_1 + 2x_2$

Subject to
$$x_1 + 7x_2 \geq 7$$
$$2x_1 + x_2 \geq 4$$
$$x_1, x_2 \geq 0$$

[**Ans.** $Z_{min} = 41/13$, $x_1 = 21/13$, $x_2 = 10/13$]

21. Solve the following using dual simplex algorithm:

Maximize $Z = -3x_1 - x_2$

Subject to
$$x_1 + x_2 \geq 1$$
$$2x_1 + 3x_2 \geq 2$$
$$x_1, x_2 \geq 0$$

[**Ans.** $Z_{max} = -1.0$, $x_1 = 0$, $x_2 = 1$]

22. Using dual simplex method, solve the following LPP.

Minimize $Z = 6x_1 + 7x_2 + 3x_3 + 5x_4$

Subject to
$$5x_1 + 6x_2 - 3x_3 + 4x_4 \geq 12$$
$$2x_1 + 5x_2 + x_3 + x_4 \geq 8$$
$$x_2 + 5x_3 - 6x_4 \geq 10$$
$$x_1, x_2, x_3, x_4 \geq 0$$

[**Ans.** $Z_{min} = 258/11$, $x_1 = 0$, $x_2 = 30/11$, $x_3 = 16/11$, $x_4 = 0$]

23. Solve the following LPP using dual simplex method:

Minimize $Z = 2x_1 + 4x_2$

Subject to
$$2x_1 + x_2 \geq 4$$
$$2x_1 + 2x_2 \leq 12$$
$$x_1 + 2x_2 \geq 3$$
$$x_1, x_2 \geq 0$$

[**Ans.** $Z_{min} = 6$, $x_1 = 3$, $x_2 = 0$]

24. Use duality to obtain the optimal solution for the following:

Maximize $Z = 8x_1 + 6x_2$

Subject to
$$x_1 - x_2 \leq 3/5$$
$$x_1 - x_2 \geq 2$$
$$x_1, x_2 \geq 0$$

[**Ans.** DP has infeasible solution]

25. A firm makes three product A, B and C. Each product requires production on each of the two machines:

Machines	*Product A*	*Product B*	*Product C*	*Total Time Available (in hours)*
X	16	12	10	160
Y	11	5	8	130

Total time for the machines are given in the above table. The profit gained in selling the product A, B and C is ₹ 30, ₹ 35 and ₹ 55 respectively. Determine the optimum product mix and write the dual of this problem and give its economic interpretation.

26. Write the dual of the following LPP and solve it.

Maximize $Z = 4x_1 + 2x_2$

Subject to
$$-x_1 - x_2 \leq -3$$
$$-x_1 + x_2 \leq -2$$
$$x_1, x_2 \geq 0$$

Hence, otherwise write down the solution of the primal.

[**Ans.** DP has no optimum *bfs*. PP has no finite optimum solution]

27. Solve the following LPP (*i.e.*, primal problem) and its dual by simplex method.

Maximize $Z = 15x_1 + 2x_2 + 4x_3$

Subject to
$$2x_1 + 3x_2 + 5x_3 \leq 15$$
$$x_1 - 2x_2 + 3x_3 = 2$$
$$x_1, x_2, x_3 \geq 0$$

Verify that the solution of primal can be read from the optimal table of the dual and vice-versa.

28. Consider the following LPP and solve it:

Maximize $Z = 3x_1 + 4x_2 + x_3 + 7x_4$

Subject to
$$8x_1 + 3x_2 + 4x_3 + x_4 \leq 7$$
$$2x_1 + 6x_2 + x_3 + 5x_4 \leq 3$$
$$x_1 + 4x_2 + 5x_3 + 2x_4 \leq 8$$
$$x_1, x_2, x_3, x_4 \geq 0$$

If a new constraint $2x_1 + 3x_2 + x_3 + 5x_4 \leq 4$ is added to the constraints of the problem, then check whether there is any change in the optimum solution of the original problem.

[**Ans.** $x_1 = \frac{16}{19}, x_4 = \frac{5}{19}, x_2 = x_3 = 0$ the new constraint has decreased the optimum value and $Z_{max} = 113/38$]

29. Discuss the effect of adding a new non-negative variable x_3 to following LPP:

Maximize $Z = 3x_1 + 5x_2$

Subject to
$$x_1 + x_2 \leq 1$$
$$2x_1 + 3x_2 \leq 1$$
$$x_1, x_2 \geq 0$$

as Maximize $Z = 3x_1 + 5x_2 + 2x_3$

Subject to $x_1 + x_2 + x_3 \leq 1$

$2x_1 + 3x_2 - x_3 \leq 1$

$x_1, x_2, x_3 \geq 0$

On the optimality of the solution.

[**Ans.** $x_1 = 0$, $x_2 = 1/3$ and $Z_{max} = 5/3$ for New LPP $x_1 = 0$, $x_2 = 5/9$,

$x_3 = 1/2$, $Z_{max} = \frac{34}{9}$]

30. For the following LPP:

Maximize $Z = -x_1 + 2x_2 - x_3$

Subject to $3x_1 + x_2 - x_3 \leq 10$

$-x_1 + 4x_2 + x_3 \geq 6$

$x_2 + x_3 \leq 4$

$x_1, x_2, x_3 \geq 10$

(*a*) Determine an optimum solution.

(*b*) Determine the range of discrete changes in RHS b_2 and b_3 so as to maintain the optimality of the current optimum solution.

[**Ans.** (*a*) $Z_{max} = 8$, $x_1 = x_3 = 0$, $x_2 = 4$, (*b*) $\frac{-5}{2} \leq b_2 \leq 6$, $b_3 \geq 10$]

31. Write down the dual of the following LPP and solve it.

Maximize $Z = 4x_1 + 5x_2 - 3x_3 + 50$

Subject to $x_1 + x_2 + x_3 = 10$

$x_1 - x_2 \geq 1$

$2x_1 + 3x_2 + x_3 \leq 40$

$x_1, x_2, x_3 \geq 0$

Hence, otherwise write down the solution of the primal

[**Ans.** PP: $Z_{max} = 189/2$, $x_1 = 11/2$, $x_2 = 9/2$]

32. Food *X* contains 6 units of vitamin A per gram and 7 units of vitamin B per gram and costs 12 ₹ per gram. Food *Y* contains 8 units of vitamin A per gram and 12 units of vitamin B and costs ₹ 20 per gram. The daily minimum requirements of vitamin A and vitamin B are 100 units and 120 units respectively. Find the minimum cost of product minimization by simplex method.

Solve the above LPP and its dual by simplex method and verify the solution.

[**Ans.** Minimize $Z = 12x_1 + 20x_2$

Subject to $6x_1 + 8x_2 \geq 100$

$7x_1 + 12x_2 \geq 120$

$x_1, x_2 \geq 0$

PP: $Z_{min} = 205$, $x_1 = 15$, $x_2 = 5/4$]

33. A manufacturing company produces three product x, y and z. The profit obtained by these products per unit is ₹ 5, ₹ 10, ₹ 8 respectively. Each unit of product x requires 3 kg of material, 4 machine hours and 2 labour hours; each unit of product y requires 5 kg of material, 4 machine hours and 4 labour hours and each unit of product z requires 2 kg of material, 4 machine hours and 5 labour hours.

Only 60 kg of material, 72 machine hours and 100 labour hours are available. Find the best production strategy. Also investigate the effect on the solution of the following.

(*i*) an increase of 12 machine hours.

(*ii*) a decrease of 6 kg of material.

[**Ans.** $Z_{max} = 160$, $x_1 = 0$, $x_2 = 8$, $x_3 = 10$
(*i*) 5/3; $Z_{max} = 180$ (*ii*) –2/3; $Z_{max} = 156$]

34. Consider the LPP Maximize: $Z = 3x_1 + 5x_2$

Subject to
$$3x_1 + 2x_2 \le 18$$
$$x_1 \le 4$$
$$x_2 \le 6$$
$$x_1, x_2 \ge 0$$

Discuss the effect of optimality of solution when objective function is changed to $(3x_1 + x_2)$ from $(3x_1 + 5x_2)$ [**Ans.** $Z_{max} = 12$, $x_1 = 3$, $x_2 = 1$]

Answers for Objective Type Questions

1. (*d*)	**2.** (*d*)	**3.** (*d*)	**4.** (*b*)	**5.** (*d*)
6. (*b*)	**7.** (*d*)	**8.** (*a*)	**9.** (*d*)	**10.** (*b*)
11. (*a*)				

❑❑❑

CHAPTER 4

Transportation Problem

4.1 TRANSPORTATION PROBLEM

Transportation problems are one of the first types of problems analyzed in the early history of linear programming. This is also one of the sub classes of linear programming problems. The transportation problem can be solved by the regular simplex method. However, its special structure allows the development of a solution procedure, called the transportation technique, that is computationally more efficient.

The transportation technique can be, and often is, presented in an elementary manner that appears completely detached from the simplex method. The transportation problem can be extended to cover a number of important applications, including the assignment problem and the transshipment problem. However, the transportation problem and its extensions are also special cases of network models.

Transportation problem extend its scope of applications to a wider class of real-life problems. The general problem arises when goods available at several sources must be shipped to various destinations. With fixed amounts available at the sources and fixed demands to be met at the destination, the problem is to determine a shipping schedule that minimizes the transportation or shipping costs, involved in shipping the goods from one place to another. It is assumed that the costs of goods from a source to a destination are directly proportional to the amount of goods shipped. The standard form of the problem was originally formulated by Hitchcock, F.L. in 1941. Later, the problem was considered independently by T.C. Koopmans in 1949. Because of these early investigations, the problem sometimes is also called as the Hitchcock–Koopmans transportation problem, which have direct practical applications in many real life situations.

In the direct sense, the transportation problem seeks the determination of a transportation plan of a single commodity from a number of sources to a number of destinations. A transportation model contributes itself to modifications in such a way as to represent a variety of similar problems with only little change from the standard form.

4.2 MATHEMATICAL MODEL OF TRANSPORTATION PROBLEM

In general, let us consider that there be 'm' sources of supply $S_1, S_2, ..., S_m$ having a_i (i = 1, 2, ..., m) units of supply (or availability or capacity) respectively, to be transported among 'n' destinations $D_1, D_2, ..., D_n$ with b_j (j = 1, 2, ..., n) units of demand (or requirement) respectively. Let C_{ij} be the cost of shipping one unit of the commodity from source i to destination j for each route. If x_{ij} represents the number of units shipped per route from source i to destination j, then the problem is to determine the transportation schedule that minimizes the transportation cost satisfying supply and demand condition s. So, the problem may be mathematically stated as follows:

$$\text{Minimize } Z = \sum_{i=1}^{m}\sum_{j=1}^{n} C_{ij}\, x_{ij} \qquad ...(1)$$

Subject to the constraints

$$\sum_{j=1}^{n} x_{ij} = a_i, \quad i = 1, 2, ..., m \qquad \text{(Supply constraints) ...(2)}$$

$$\sum_{l=1}^{m} x_{ij} = b_j, \quad j = 1, 2, ..., n \qquad \text{(Demand constraints) ...(3)}$$

and $\quad x_{ij} \geq 0$ for all i and j ...(4)

The transportation problem is generally presented as shown in the Table (1).

Table 1

To / From	D_1	D_2	D_3	....	D_n a_i	*Supply*
S_1	C_{11} x_{11}	C_{12} x_{12}	C_{13} x_{13}	....	C_{1n} x_{1n}	a_1
S_2	C_{21} x_{21}	C_{22} x_{22}	C_{23} x_{23}	....	C_{2n} x_{2n}	a_2
S_3	C_{31} x_{31}	C_{32} x_{32}	C_{33} x_{33}	....	C_{3n} x_{3n}	a_3
⋮	⋮	⋮	⋮	....	....	⋮
S_m	C_{m1} x_{m1}	C_{m2} x_{m2}	C_{m3} x_{m3}	....	C_{mn} x_{mn}	a_m
Demand b_j	b_1	b_2	b_3	....	b_n	$\sum_{i=1}^{m} a_i = \sum_{j=1}^{n} b_j$

Remarks.

1. When the total supply equals total demand, then the problem is called a balanced transportation problem

i.e,
$$\sum_{i=1}^{m} a_i = \sum_{j=1}^{n} b_j$$

2. When the total supply exceeds the total demand or total demand exceeds total supply, then it is called an unbalanced transportation problem.

i.e,
$$\sum_{i=1}^{m} a_i > \sum_{j=1}^{n} b_j$$

or
$$\sum_{i=1}^{m} a_i < \sum_{j=1}^{n} b_j$$

Then the unbalanced transportation problem can be made balanced by adding a dummy supply (row) or a dummy demand (column) as per requirement.

3. Cells in the transportation table (Table 1) having positive allocation will be called occupied cells, otherwise empty or non-occupied cells.

4.3 SOME BASIC DEFINITIONS

Feasible solution. A set of non-negative individual allocation ($x_{ij} \geq 0$) which simultaneously removes deficiencies is called a feasible solution.

Basic feasible solution. An initial feasible solution with an allocation of $(m + n - 1)$ number of variables x_{ij} is called a basic feasible solution.

Optimum solution. A feasible solution (not necessarily basic) is said to be optimal if it minimizes the total transportation cost.

Degenerate basic feasible solution. Since the basic feasible solution has exactly $(m + n - 1)$ positive x_{ij}'s (or allocation or occupied cells) and if the number of occupied cells are less than $(m + n - 1)$ occupied cells, then it is called as degenerate basic feasible solution or simply degenerate solution.

4.4 LOOPS IN TRANSPORTATION TABLE AND THEIR PROPERTIES

Any basic feasible solution must contain $(m + n - 1)$ independent non-zero allocations. The independent non-zero allocations imply that one cannot form a closed loop (or circuit) by joining positive allocations by using horizontal and vertical lines. So, mathematically, a loop used in transportation can be defined as an ordered set of at least four cells in a table of transportation always forms a loop if

(*a*) any two adjacent cells of the ordered set lie either in the same row or in the same column, and

(*b*) no three or more adjacent cells in the ordered set lie in the same row or column.

(*c*) the first cell of the loop must also be the last cell of the loop.

(*d*) Every loop has an even number of cells and at least four.

Consider the following different cases in which we join the positive allocations by using horizontal and vertical lines and after joining these lines, a closed loop is obtained.

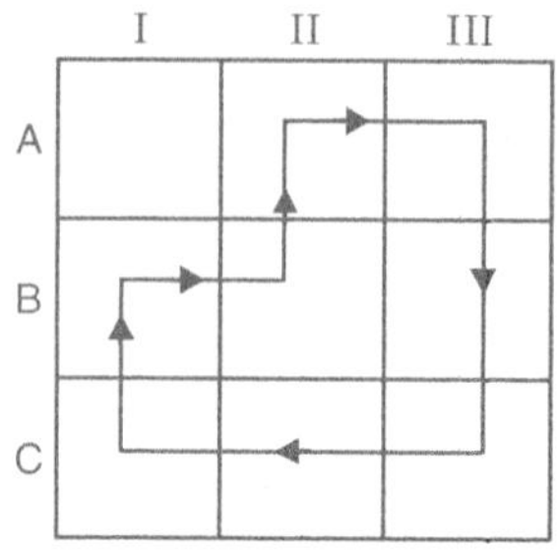

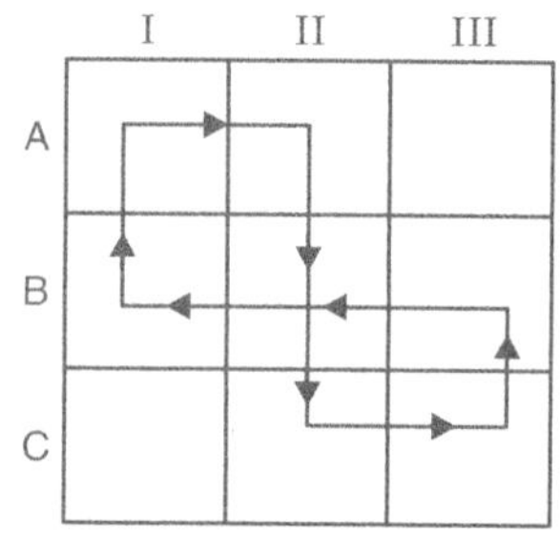

In the above tables, the loop in the first table is allowed where the loop in the second table is not allowed as one of the cell (B, II) is repeated twice.

Remarks.

(*a*) Closed loops may or may not be square or rectangular in shape.

(*b*) Each row and column in the transportation table should have only one plus and minus sign.

(*c*) All cells that have plus or a minus sign, except the starting unoccupied cell, must be occupied cells.

4.5 THE TRANSPORTATION METHOD

The algorithm for the solution of a transportation problem are summarized into the following steps.

Step 1: Formulate the objective function to be minimized, which is the total transportation cost and impose the constraints that are the supply and demand available at each source and destination, respectively.

Step 2: To obtain an initial basic feasible solution. There are several different methods to obtain an initial basic feasible solution of a transportation problem but this initial solution so obtained must satisfy the following conditions.

(*a*) The solution must be feasible, *i.e.*, it must satisfy all the supply and demand constraints.

(*b*) The number positive allocation must be equal to $(m + n - 1)$.

The initial basic solution can be obtained by the following methods which are discussed in detail later on, are:

(*a*) North-West Corner Method

(*b*) Least Cost Method or Matrix Minima Method

(*c*) The Row-Minima Method

(*d*) The Column-Minima Method

(*e*) Vogel's Approximation Method (or Penalty Method).

Step 3: Testing the initial solutions for optimality. After finding the initial basic feasible solution, in step 2, the next step is to check whether this initial solution is optimal or not.

If the current solution is optimal, then stop, otherwise, determine a new improved solution.

Step 4: Updating the solution. Repeat step 3 until we reach to obtain an optimal solution.

4.6 NORTH-WEST CORNER METHOD

This method is used to determine the initial basic feasible solution which is the simplest one. But this method does take into account the transportation cost on any route of transportation. North-West Corner Method can be summarized as follows:

Step 1: Start with the cell at the upper left (north-west) corner of the transportation matrix and allocate the maximum possible amount.

i.e., $x_{11} = \min(a_1, b_1)$, this is the value to be entered in the cell (1, 1) of the transportation problem.

Step 2: (*a*) If $b_1 > a_1$, then we move downward vertically to the second row and make the second allocation x_{21}.

i.e., $x_{21} = \min(a_2, b_1 - x_{11})$ in the cell (2, 1).

(*b*) If $b_1 < a_1$, then we move right in the horizontal direction to the second column and make the second allocation x_{12}.

i.e., $x_{12} = \min(a_1 - x_{11}, b_2)$ in the cell (1, 2).

(*c*) If $b_1 = a_1$, then we have a tie for the second allocation. One can make the second allocation as

$x_{12} = min(a_1 - a_1, b_1) = 0$ in the cell (1, 2).

or $x_{21} = min(a_2, b_1 - b_1) = 0$ in the cell (2, 1).

Step 3: Repeat step 1 and step 2 moving down towards the lower right corner of the transportation table until all the requirements are satisfied.

Remark. The initial basic feasible solution so obtained may be far from optimum, because in this costs are completely ignored.

Example 1. *Using North-West Corner Method, obtain the initial basic feasible solution for the following transportation problem.*

Requirement ↓	*I*	*II*	*III*	*IV*	*Available*
A	*10*	*12*	*14*	*17*	*100*
B	*19*	*6*	*8*	*4*	*200*
C	*12*	*7*	*16*	*18*	*200*
Requirement	*75*	*125*	*100*	*200*	

Solution. Since $\sum a_j = \sum b_j = 500$

This is a balanced transportation problem for which a feasible solution exists. The initial basic feasible solution can be obtained as follows:

By using the North-West Corner Method, the first allocation is made in the cell (1, 1).

i.e., x_{11} = min (100, 75) = 75

[75] 10	12	14	17	25
19	6	8	4	200
12	7	16	18	200
	125	100	200	

Then the second allocation is made in the cell (1, 2).

i.e., x_{12} = min (100 – 75, 200) = 25

[75] 10	[25] 12	14	17	
19	6	8	4	200
12	7	16	18	200
	100	100	200	

Then the third allocation is made in the cell (2, 2).

i.e., x_{22} = min (125 – 25, 200) = 100

[75] 10	[25] 12	14	17	
19	[100] 6	[100] 8	[100] 4	100
12	7	16	18	200
		100	200	

Then the fourth allocation is made in the cell (2, 3).

i.e. x_{23} = min (100, 200 – 100) = 100

[75] 10	[25] 12	14	17	
19	[100] 6	[100] 8	4	
12	7	16	18	200
			200	

There is a tie.

Then the fifth allocation is made in the cell (3, 4).

i.e., x_{34} = min (200, 200) = 200

[75] 10	[25] 12	14	17	100
19	[100] 6	[100] 8	4	200
12	7	16	18	300
75	125	100	200	

Again there is a tie.

Thus the initial basic feasible solution to the given transportation problem has been obtained and is displayed in the last table.

Thus the transportation cost according to the above route is

$$\begin{aligned} Z &= 75 \times 10 + 25 \times 12 + 100 \times 6 + 100 \times 8 + 200 \times 18 \\ &= 750 + 300 + 600 + 800 + 3600 \\ &= 6050 \end{aligned}$$

4.7 LEAST COST METHOD

Least cost method takes into account the minimum cost of transportation for obtaining the initial basic feasible solution and can be summarized as follows:

Step 1: Select the smallest cost in the given transportation table and allocate the maximum possible amount.
i.e., if C_{ij} is the lowest (smallest) cost, then
$x_{ij} = \min (a_i, b_j)$ in the cell (i, j).

Step 2: (*a*) If $x_{ij} = a_i$, then cross off the ith row of the transportation table and also decrease b_j by a_i.
(*b*) If $x_{ij} = b_j$, then cross off the jth column of the transportation table and also decrease a_i by b_j.
(*c*) If $x_{ij} = a_i = b_j$, then cross off either the ith row or jth column, but not both.

Step 3: Repeat step 1 and step 2 until the entire supply at various sources and demand at various destinations is satisfied

Remark. Whenever, there is a tie in minimum cost, then make an arbitrary choice and select the cell where maximum allocation can be made.

Example 2. *Using Least Cost Method, obtain the initial basic feasible solution for the following transportation problem.*

	I	*II*	*III*	*IV*	*Capacity*
A	*11*	*12*	*14*	*12*	*5*
B	*14*	*15*	*13*	*10*	*9*
C	*10*	*15*	*16*	*13*	*11*
Demand	*5*	*6*	*7*	*7*	

Solution. By using the Least-Cost Method, the first allocation is made in the cell (3, 1), as there is a tie.

i.e., $x_{31} = 5$ ($\because x_{31} = \min(5, 11)$)

This satisfies the demand at I and thus we cross of the first column from the given table.

	I	II	III	IV	
A					5
B					9
C	5 10				6
	5	6	7	7	

Then the second allocation is made in the cell (2, 4)

i.e., x_{24} = min (7, 9) = 7

	II	III	IV	
A				5
B			7 / 10	2
C				6
	6	7		

This satisfies the demand at IV and thus we cross of the fourth column from the given table as shown in the second table.

Then the third allocation is made in the cell (1, 2)

i.e., x_{12} = min (5, 6) = 5

This satisfies the capacity at first row and thus cross the first row from the given table.

	II	III	
A	5 / 12		5
B			2
C			6
	1	7	

Then the fourth allocation is made in the cell (2, 3).

i.e., x_{23} = min (2, 7) = 2

	II	III	
B		2 / 13	2
C			6
	1	7	

This satisfies the capacity at second row and thus we cross the second row from the given table.

Then the fifth allocation is made in the cell (3, 2).

i.e., x_{32} = min (1, 6) = 1

	II	III	
C	1 / 15		6
	1	5	

This satisfies the third demand, so we cross the second column from the table and finally the sixth allocation is made in the cell C(3, 3).

i.e., x_{33} = min (5, 5) = 5

This cell is crossed off.

	III	
C	5	5
	5	

The final tableau is given as in the last table for which the basic feasible solution is

$Z = 12 \times 5 + 2 \times 13 + 7 \times 10 + 5 \times 10 + 1 \times 15 + 5 \times 16 = 301$

	I	II	III	IV
A	11	5 / 12	14	12
B	14	15	2 / 13	7 / 10
C	5 / 10	1 / 15	5 / 16	13

4.8 THE ROW-MINIMA METHOD

Row Minima method takes into account the minimum cost of transportation for obtaining the initial basic feasible solution and can be summarized as follows:

Step 1: In the transportation table, determine the smallest cost (let it be C_{ij}) in the first row and allocate the maximum amount

i.e., $x_{1j} = \min (a_i, b_j)$ in the cell $(1, j)$, so that either the capacity at first origin or the requirement at jth destination or both of them are satisfied.

Step 2: (*a*) If $x_{1j} = a_1$, then the capacity at first origin is completely exhausted and cross out the first row of the table and move to the second row.

(*b*) If $x_{1j} = b_j$, then the requirement at jth destination is satisfied and cross out the jth column.

But in this case, the first row is again considered with the remaining availability at first origin.

(*c*) If $x_{1j} = a_1 = b_j$, then the capacity at first origin as well as the requirement at jth destination is completely satisfied. Then choose arbitrarily as a tie appears there.

Step 3: Repeat step 1 and step 2 until all the requirements are satisfied.

4.9 THE COLUMN-MINIMA METHOD

The column minima method takes into account the minimum cost of transportation for obtaining the initial basic feasible solution and can be summarized as follows:

Step 1: In the transportation table, determine the smallest cost (C_{1j}) in the first column and allocate the maximum amount.

i.e., $x_{i1} = \min (a_i, b_1)$

Step 2: (*a*) If $x_{i1} = b_1$, then the requirement at first destination is satisfied and move towards right to the second column of the transportation table after crossing the first column.

(*b*) If $x_{i1} = a_i$, then cross the ith row of the transportation table as the first row capacity is completely filled.

But in this case, the first column is again considered with the remaining demand.

(*c*) If $b_1 = a_i$, then the capacity of the first origin as well as the requirement at jth destination is completely satisfied. Cross the ith row and make the second allocation $x_{k1} = 0$ in the cell $(k, 1)$ as C_{k1} will become the new minimum cost in the first column. Cross the column and move towards right to the second column.

Step 3: Repeat step 1 and step 2 until all the requirements are satisfied.

Remark. The row-minima and the column-minima method are not generally preferred.

4.10 VOGEL'S APPROXIMATION METHOD (VAM)

Vogel's approximation method (penalty method) is preferred to the other methods described above because in this method, each allocation is made on the basis of the penalty cost that would have been incurred if allocations are made so that the penalty cost is minimized. The initial basic feasible solution obtained by using VAM is very near to the optimal solution. The VAM can be summarized as follows:

Step 1: Calculate the penalties for each row or column by taking the difference between the smallest and next smallest cost in the same row or column. The difference is the penalty or the extra cost that has to be paid if one fails to allocate to the cell with minimum cost. All these differences are written alongside the transportation table in extra rows and columns.

Step 2: Choose the row or column that has the largest difference among all the rows and columns and allocate the maximum possible amount to lowest cost cell in that row or column.

If a tie occurs, use any arbitrary tie-breaking choice.

If the minimum cost in C_{ij} in the ith row, that has the maximum difference then allocate

$x_{ij} = \min (a_i, b_j)$ in the (i, j) cell

and cross the ith row or jth column.

Step 3: Again calculate the row and column differences for the reduced transportation table and go to step 2.

Step 4: Repeat the procedure until an initial feasible solution is obtained.

Example 3. *Find the initial basic feasible solution for the following transportation table using Vogel's Approximation method.*

	I	*II*	*III*	*IV*	*Available*
A	*20*	*22*	*26*	*23*	*200*
B	*25*	*27*	*23*	*19*	*250*
C	*30*	*33*	*22*	*19*	*300*
Demand	*150*	*175*	*225*	*200*	

Solution. Using the Vogel's Approximation method, compute the differences between the smallest and next-to-smallest costs in each row and column.

	I	II	III	IV		Difference
A	[150] 20	22	26	23	200	2
B	25	27	23	19	250	4
C	30	33	22	19	300	3
	150	175	225	200		
Difference	5	5	1	0		

Since the largest difference is 5 (in columns I and II), we can choose arbitrarily the minimum cost in column I, *i.e.*, C_{11} (= 20) and allocate min (200, 150) = 150 in the cell (1, 1), so that the demand in first column is exhausted and so cross the first column.

Then again compute the row and column differences for the reduced transportation table.

	II	III	IV		Difference
A	[50] 22	26	23	50	1
B	27	23	19	250	4
C	33	22	19	300	3
	175	225	200		
Difference	5	1	0		

Again point out the largest difference *i.e.*, 5 which corresponds to column II and since C_{13} (= 22) is the minimum cost, so we allocate

$$x_{12} = \min (50, 175) = 50$$

and so row I capacity is fully satisfied and we cross the first row now and again compute the row and the column differences as we have done before.

	II	III	IV		Difference
B	[125] 27	23	19	250	4
C	33	22	19	300	3
	125	225	200		
Difference	5	1	0		

The largest difference is 5 (in second column) and the minimum cost in this column is C_{21} (= 27), so we allocate

$$x_{21} = \min (250, 125) = 125$$

and so the demand in the second column is satisfied and we cross this column.

Repeat this process and consequently the reduced tables so obtained are:

	III	IV		Difference
B	23	[125] 19	125	4
C	22	19	300	3
	225	200		
Difference	1	0		

	III	IV		Difference
C	[225] 22	[75] 19	300	3
Demand	225	75		

Thus the initial basic feasible solution (*i.e.*, the allocations) for the original transportation is shown as:

	I	II	III	IV	Capacity
A	[150] 20	[20] 22	26	23	200
B	25	[125] 27	23	[125] 19	250
C	30	33	[225] 22	[75] 19	300
Demand	150	175	225	200	

Thus the initial basic feasible solution is

$$Z = 150 \times 20 + 20 \times 22 + 125 \times 27 + 125 \times 19 + 225 \times 22 + 75 \times 19$$
$$= 3000 + 440 + 3375 + 2375 + 4950 + 1425$$
$$= 15565.$$

4.11 TEST FOR OPTIMALITY

Once an initial basic feasible solution is obtained, the next step is to check whether, the initial solution so obtained is an optimal solution or not, if not, we then try to calculate a new improved solution. This new solution will be the optimal solution if the total transportation cost is reduced and the solution cannot be further improved. An efficient technique called the modified–distribution (MODI) method (also called *u–v* method) that helps in relative advantage of alternative allocations for all the unoccupied cells simultaneously and is discussed below.

4.12 THE TRANSPORTATION SIMPLEX METHOD OR TRANSPORTATION ALGORITHM (MODI METHOD)

The following steps involved in solving the transportation problem, defines the transportation simplex method.

Step 1: If the problem under consideration is an unbalanced, then by using the dummy rows and dummy columns, make it a balanced transportation problem.

Step 2: Find the initial basic feasible solution by using any of the methods discussed so far.

Step 3: Check the number of occupied cells. If there are less than $(m + n - 1)$ cells, then there exists degeneracy and for this we have to introduce a very-very small positive assignment of $\in$ (= o) in suitable independent positions, so that the number of occuppied cells increases and becomes exactly equal to $(m + n - 1)$ cells.

Step 4: Use the fact that $u_i = 0$ and $u_i + v_j = C_{ij}$ for all basic variables to find the values of $(u_1, u_2, ..., u_m$ and $v_1, v_2, ..., v_n)$ for the current basic feasible solution.

Step 5: (*a*) (For a minimization problem)

If $u_i + v_j - C_{ij} \leq 0$, for all nonbasic variables, then the current basic feasible solution is optimal. Otherwise, we enter the variable with the most positive

$u_i + v_j - C_{ij}$ into the basis. This is usually denoted by d_{ij} and is entered in down right corner of the corresponding cell.

(*b*) (For a maximization problem)

If $u_i + v_j - C_{ij} \geq 0$, for all non-basic variables, the current basic feasible solution is optimal. Otherwise, we enter the variable with most negative $u_i + v_j - C_{ij}$ into the basis. Here too, it is denoted by d_{ij} and we enter them in down right corner of the corresponding cell.

Step 6: Using the new basic feasible solution, return to steps 3 and 4.

Step 7: Repeat the process until an optimum basic feasible solution is obtained.

4.13 STEPPING STONE SOLUTION

The alternative method for finding the optimal solution for a transportation problem is done by using stepping stone solution method, which can be summarized as follows:

Step 1: First of all obtain the initial basic feasible solution of the given transportation problem using any of the methods discussed above.

Step 2: Then check the number of basic cells, and if degeneracy occurs, then remove the degeneracy by introducing a very small quantity $\in$ ($\to 0$), so that the number of basic cells becomes $m + n - 1$.

Step 3: Then check various net costs for each of the unoccupied cells. This is usually done by calculating the net costs as follows. Consider the first unoccupied cell in the first column or first row. We want to convert this non-basic cell into the basic cell by assigning 1 unit, after tracing a closed path using the most direct route through at least three occupied cells used in the solution and then back to the original selected unoccupied cell. The cells in the path that lies at the turning points are considered only, and these cells at the turning points are called "stepping stones" on the path.

After tracing the closed path assign + and – signs alternatively on each corner of the closed path, that was just traced. It should be taken care that a plus (+) sign should be allotted to the selected unoccupied cell.

Then the net costs are evaluated by considering the + and – signs at each turning points. After calculating the net costs for each unoccupied cells with suitable closed path, check the sign (+ or –) of the net costs. If all net costs are greater than or equal to zero, then an optimal solution has been attained. If not, then improve the current solution and decrease the total shipping costs.

Step 4: Select that unoccupied cell having the most negative net cost and determine the maximum number of units that can be assigned to a cell marked with a minus (–) sign on the closed path corresponding to this cell. Then this amount is added to the unoccupied cell and act according to + (plus) and – (minus) sign of the closed path.

Step 5: This procedure is repeated until all net costs are positive *i.e.*, an optimal solution has been attained.

The above algorithm is illustrated by the following example.

Example 4.

	I	*II*	*III*	a_i
A	*21*	*25*	*17*	*20*
B	*19*	*13*	*23*	*16*
C	*31*	*29*	*21*	*9*
b_j	*18*	*12*	*15*	

Determine the optimum distribution for the above problem to minimize the costs by using the stepping stone method.

Solution. The initial basic feasible solution is obtained using the Vogel's approximation method.

	I	II	III	a_i
A	[14] 21	25	[6] 17	20
B	[4] 19	[12] 13	23	16
C	31	29	[9] 21	9
b_j	18	12	15	

Then we start selecting the unoccupied cells so that stepping stone method may be applied.

Since the unoccupied cells are

(A, II), (B, III), (C, I), (C, II).

Now we will consider these unoccupied cells to examine that whether this inclusion of cells would improve the initial solution or not. So let us choose the cell (A, II) of the initial basic feasible solution table and assign θ units to be shipped from source A to destination II.

				a_i
	[14] $-\theta$ 21	$+\theta$ 25	[6] 17	20
	[4] $+\theta$ 19	[12] $-\theta$ 13	23	16
	31	29	[9] 21	9
b_j	18	12	15	

Net change in cost 25 – 21 + 19 – 13 = 44 – 33 = +ve.

(We take 1 unit arbitrarily and add and subtract 1 unit from the turning points of the traced closed path).

Now we choose the cell (B, III) and trace to locate the close path as:

14 +θ 21	25	6 −θ 17
4 −θ 19	12 13	+θ 23
31	29	9 21

Net change in cost = 23 – 17 + 21 – 19 = 44 – 36 = +ve.

Next we choose the cell (C, I)

14 −θ 21	25	6 +θ 17
4 19	12 13	23
+θ 31	29	9 −θ 21

Net change in cost = 31– 21 + 17 – 21 = 48 – 42 = +ve.

Next we choose the cell (C, II)

14 −θ 21	25	6 +θ 17
4 +θ 19	12 −θ 13	23
31	+θ 29	9 −θ 21

∴ Net change in cost = 29 – 13 + 19 – 21 + 17 – 21 = 65 – 55 = +ve.

Since all the net changes in costs are obtained as positive, so the initial basic feasible solution obtained above will be the optimum solution of the transportation problem.

$$\begin{aligned}\text{Transportation cost} &= 14 \times 21 + 6 \times 17 + 4 \times 19 + 12 \times 13 + 9 \times 21 \\ &= 294 + 102 + 76 + 156 + 189 \\ &= ₹\ 817\end{aligned}$$

Example 5. *Determine the initial basic feasible solution by the following methods*

(a) North-West Corner Method

(b) Row Minimum Method

(c) Lowest Cost Method

(d) Vogel's Approximation Method

and then find the optimal basic feasible solution for the following transportation problem.

	I	II	III	Availability
A	50	30	220	1
B	90	45	170	3
C	250	200	50	4
Requirement	4	2	2	

Solution. (*a*) The initial basic feasible solution obtained by North-West Corner Method is as follows:

[1] 50	30	220	1
[3] 90	45	170	3
250	[2] 200	[2] 50	4
4	2	2	

$$\begin{aligned} \text{Cost } Z &= 1 \times 50 + 3 \times 90 + 2 \times 200 + 2 \times 50 \\ &= 50 + 270 + 400 + 100 \\ &= 820 \end{aligned}$$

(*b*) By using the Row Minima Method, the initial basic feasible solution can be obtained as follows:

Since in the first row

$$\min (50, 30, 220) = 30$$

Thus the first allocation is made in the cell (1, 2) as $C_{12} = 30$

i.e., $x_{12} = \min (1, 2) = 1$

Here the availability is completely satisfied for first origin A and this first row is then crossed out from the original transportation table.

50	[1] 30	220	1
90	45	170	3
250	200	50	4
4	2	2	

Now the reduced transportation table is

	[1]		
90	45	170	3
250	200	50	4
4	2	2	

Now in the second row: min (90, 45, 170) = 45

Thus the second allocation is made in the cell (2, 2) as $C_{22} = 45$.

i.e., $x_{22} = \min (3, 2 - 1) = 1$

So that the requirement at second destination is satisfied now and this second column II is now crossed off.

				Availability
		[1]		1
	90	[1] 45	170	3
	250	200	50	4
Requirement	4	2	2	

In the reduced transportation problem

Since in second row: min (90, 170) = 90

the third allocation is made in the cell (2, 1) is $C_{21} = 90$.

i.e., $x_{21} = \min (3 - 1, 4) = 2$

So that the availability at second origin is satisfied completely. This II row is now crossed out,

	[1]		
[2] 90	[1]	170	
250		50	4
4		2	

Similarly the next allocation is made in the cell (3, 3) as min (250, 50) = 50

i.e., $x_{33} = \min (4, 2) = 2$

so that the requirement at destination III is completely satisfied and this third column is crossed. The reduced transportation table is

	1	
2	1	
250		2 50
4		

Now the last allocation is made in the cell (3, 1)

i.e., $x_{31} = 2$

	1	
2	1	
2 250		2

The final tableau for the initial basic feasible solution is as:

50	1 30	220	1
2 90	1 45	170	3
2 250	200	2 50	4
4	2	2	

Since the basic cells do not form a loop, an initial basic feasible solution has been determined. Thus the transportation cost is:

$$
\begin{aligned}
Z &= 1 \times 30 + 2 \times 90 + 1 \times 45 + 2 \times 250 + 2 \times 50 \\
&= 30 + 180 + 45 + 500 + 100 \\
&= 855.
\end{aligned}
$$

(*c*) By using the Lowest Cost Method the initial basic feasible solution is obtained as follows.

50	1 30	220	1
2 90	1 45	170	3
2 250	200	2 50	4
4	2	2	

$$
\begin{aligned}
\therefore\ Z &= 1 \times 30 + 2 \times 90 + 1 \times 45 + 2 \times 250 + 2 \times 50 \\
&= 855
\end{aligned}
$$

(*d*) By using the Vogel's Approximation method, the initial basic feasible solution is obtained directly as follows:

[1] 30	30	220	1
[3] 90	45	170	3
250	[2] 200	[2] 50	4
4	2	2	

The transportation cost is formed to be:

$Z = 1 \times 50 + 3 \times 90 + 2 \times 200 + 2 \times 50$

$= 820$

Note: Readers should apply Least Cost Method as discussed before to obtain the initial basic feasible solution.

To find the optimal solution of the given transportation problem (original problem), we can consider any of the initial solution (obtained by different methods).

But here, we are considering the initial basic solution as obtained by Row-Minima Method and Lowest Cost Method (as both are 855) and not by North-West-Corner Method and Vogel's Approximation Method (as both are 820).

The following steps are involved towards the optimality after considering the initial solution is obtained by

	I	II	III	Availability
A		[1] 30		1
B	[2] 90	[1] 45		3
C	[2] 250		[2] 50	4
Requirement	4	2	2	

By applying $C_{ij} = u_i + v_j$ for all those i and j for which (i, j) cell is a basic cell.

Letting arbitrarily $u_2 = 0$ and solving sequentially, we have.

				a_i	u_i
		[1] 30		1	–15
	[2] 90	[1] 45		3	0
	[2] 250		[2] 50	4	160
b_j	4	2	2		
v_j	90	45	–110		

$u_2 + v_2 = C_{22} \Rightarrow u_2 + v_2 = 45 \Rightarrow 0 + v_2 = 45 \Rightarrow v_2 = 45$

$u_1 + v_2 = C_{12} \Rightarrow u_1 + v_1 = 30 \Rightarrow u_1 + 45 = 30 \Rightarrow u_1 = -15$

$u_2 + v_1 = C_{21} \Rightarrow 0 + u_2 = 90 \Rightarrow v_1 = 90$

$u_3 + v_1 = C_{31} \Rightarrow u_3 + 90 = 250 \Rightarrow u_3 = 160$

$u_3 + v_3 = C_{33} \Rightarrow 160 + v_3 = 50 \Rightarrow v_3 = -110$

Now making use of the above value of u_i and v_j in computing the net evaluations for each non-basic cell by using the relation $d_{ij} = u_i + v_j - C_{ij}$

For non-basic cells, we calculate

$d_{11} = u_1 + v_1 - C_{11} = -15 + 90 - 50 = 90 - 65 = +25^*$

$d_{13} = u_1 + v_3 - C_{13} = -15 + (-110) - 220 = -15 - 330 = -345$

$d_{23} = u_2 + v_3 - C_{23} = 0 + (-110) - 170 = -110 - 170 = -280$

$d_{32} = u_3 + v_2 - C_{32} = 160 + 45 - 200 = 205 - 200 = 5$

Since all the cell evaluations for the non-basic cells are not all positive, the solution under test is not an optimal one. Here d_{11} and d_{32}, both are positive.

Since $d_{11} = 25$ is positive (most positive d_{ij}), so allocate as much as possible to the cell (1, 1)

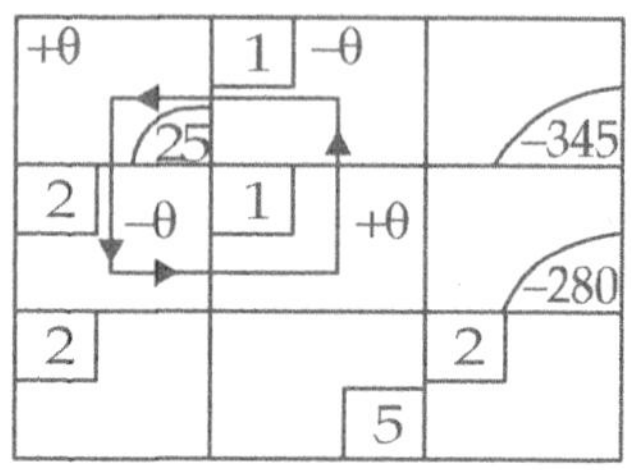

Now we choose the cell with min (–θ) [∵ min (1 – θ, 2 – θ) = 0 or 1 – θ = 0 or θ = 1]

i.e., min (1, 2) = 1

Now use $\theta^* = 1$, according to the signs (positive and negative) already displayed in the transportation table.

Thus for the new transportation table, the cell (1, 1) enters the basis, while the cell (1, 2) leave the basis and becomes empty.

<table>
<tr><td>1
50</td><td></td><td></td></tr>
<tr><td>1
90</td><td>2
45</td><td></td></tr>
<tr><td>2
250</td><td></td><td>2
50</td></tr>
</table>

$Z = 1 \times 50 + 1 \times 90 + 2 \times 45 + 2 \times 250 + 2 \times 50$

$= 50 + 90 + 90 + 500 + 100$

$= 830.$

Again to test the improved solution to be optimal, we proceed as previously.

			u_i
[1] 50	-25	-370	50
[1] 90	[2] 45	-280	90
[2] 250	+5	[2] 50	250
v_j: 0	-45	-200	

Using $C_{ij} = u_i + v_j$ for all those i and j for which (i, j) is a basic cell. Letting arbitrarily $v_1 = 0$ (as this column has maximum) number of basic cells, and solving sequentially, we have.

$u_1 + v_1 = C_{11} \Rightarrow u_1 + 0 = 50 \Rightarrow u_1 = 50$

$u_2 + v_1 = C_{21} \Rightarrow u_2 + 0 = 90 \Rightarrow u_2 = 90$

$u_2 + v_2 = C_{22} \Rightarrow 90 + v_2 = 45 \Rightarrow v_2 = -45$

$u_3 + v_1 = C_{31} \Rightarrow u_3 + 0 = 250 \Rightarrow u_3 = 250$

$u_3 + v_3 = C_{33} \Rightarrow 250 + v_3 = 50 \Rightarrow v_3 = -200$

Now making the use of above values of u_i and v_j in computing the net evaluation for non-basic cell as $d_{ij} = u_i + v_j - C_{ij}$.

$d_{12} = u_1 + v_2 - C_{12} = 50 - 45 - 30 = 50 - 75 = = -25$

$d_{13} = u_1 + v_3 - C_{13} = 50 - 200 - 220 = - 370$

$d_{23} = u_2 + v_3 - C_{23} = 90 - 200 - 170 = - 280$

$d_{32} = u_3 + v_2 - C_{32} = 250 - 45 - 200 = + 5^*$

Again here $d_{32} = 5$ is most positive, so cell (3, 2) enters the basis.

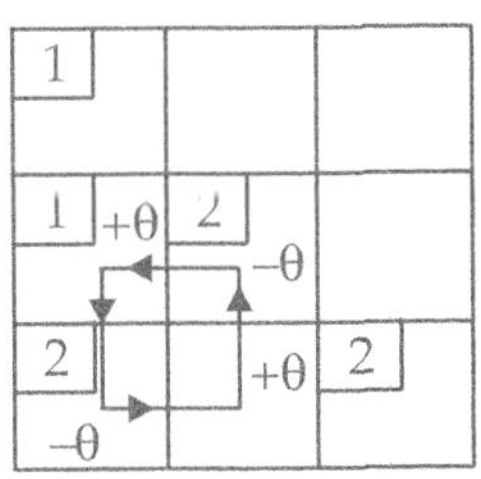

Here min $(2 - \theta, 2 - \theta) = 0$

or $2 - \theta = 0$ or $\theta = 2$

$\Rightarrow \theta^* = 2$

Thus we have new improved transportation table as the cell (3, 1) now leaves the basis. Here instead of cell (3, 1), cell (2, 2) can also be used to leave the basis.

[1] 50		
[3] 90	[0] 45	
	[2] 200	[2] 50

$$Z = 1 \times 50 + 3 \times 90 + 0 \times 45 + 2 \times 200 + 2 \times 50$$
$$= 50 + 270 + 0 + 400 + 100 = 820.$$

Again using $C_{ij} = u_i + v_j$ for all those i and j for which (i, j) is a basic cell. Letting arbitrarily $u_3 = 0$ and solving sequentially we have

				u_i
	1			–195
	3	0		–155
		2	2	0
v_j	245	200	50	

$$u_3 + v_3 = C_{33} \Rightarrow 0 + v_3 = 50 \Rightarrow v_3 = 50$$
$$u_3 + v_2 = C_{22} \Rightarrow 0 + v_2 = 200 \Rightarrow v_2 = 200$$
$$u_2 + v_2 = C_{22} \Rightarrow u_2 + 200 = 45 \Rightarrow u_2 = -155$$
$$u_2 + v_1 = C_{21} \Rightarrow -155 + v_1 = 90 \Rightarrow v_1 = 245$$
$$u_1 + v_1 = C_{11} \Rightarrow u_1 + 245 = 50 \Rightarrow u_1 = -195$$

Now making the use of above values of u_i and v_j in computing the net evaluation $d_{ij} = u_i + v_j - C_{ij}$ for non-basic cells.

$$d_{12} = u_2 + v_2 - C_{12} = -195 + 200 - 30 = -25$$
$$d_{13} = u_1 + v_3 - C_{13} = -195 + 50 - 220 = -365$$
$$d_{23} = u_2 + v_3 - C_{23} = -155 + 50 - 170 = -275$$
$$d_{31} = u_3 + v_1 - C_{31} = 0 + 245 - 250 = -5$$

Since all $d_{ij} \le 0$, we have attained the optimal solution.

At this stage $Z = 1 \times 50 + 3 \times 90 + 0 \times 45 + 2 \times 200 + 2 \times 50$
$= 820.$

This is the solution that was initially obtained by Vogel's Approximation Method as initial basic feasible solution. It is clear that VAM method is more appropriate as compared to other methods.

Example 6. *Solve the following transportation problem that involves four origins and three destinations. The cell entries in the transportation problem represents the unit costs.*

Destination ⟶

Origins↑	*I*	*II*	*III*	*Availability %*
A	2	7	4	5
B	3	3	1	8
C	5	4	7	7
D	1	6	2	14
Requirement	7	9	18	

Solution. The initial basic feasible solution is obtained using the Vogel's Approximation Method as follows:

[5] 2		
		[8] 1
	[7] 4	
[2] 1	[2] 6	[10] 2

The basic cells are shown in the above table.

$\therefore$ Z = 5 × 2 + 8 × 1 + 7 × 4 + 2 × 1 + 2 × 6 + 10 × 2

= 10 + 8 + 28 + 2 + 12 + 20

= ₹ 80.

After finding the initial basic feasible solution, we proceed to obtain the optimal solution using MODI method

				a_i	u_i
	[5] 2	7	4	5	1
	3	+θ 3	[8] −θ 1	8	−1
	5	[7] 4	7	7	−2
	[2] 1	[2] −θ 6	[10] +θ 2	14	0
b_j	7	9	18		
v_j	1	6	2		

We have $C_{ij} = u_i + v_j$ for all those i and j for which (i, j) is a basic cell. Letting $u_4 = 0$, and solving sequentially,

$u_4 + v_3 = C_{43} \Rightarrow 0 + v_3 = 2 \Rightarrow v_3 = 2$

$u_2 + v_3 = C_{23} \Rightarrow u_2 + 2 = 1 \Rightarrow u_2 = -1$

$u_4 + v_1 = C_{41} \Rightarrow 0 + v_1 = 1 \Rightarrow v_1 = 1$

$u_1 + v_1 = C_{11} \Rightarrow u_1 + 1 = 2 \Rightarrow u_1 = 1$

$u_4 + v_2 = C_{42} \Rightarrow 0 + v_2 = 6 \Rightarrow v_2 = 6$

$u_3 + v_2 = C_{32} \Rightarrow u_3 + 6 = 4 \Rightarrow u_3 = -2$

Now we make the use of the above values of u_i and v_j in computing the net evaluation, $d_{ij} = u_i + v_j - c_{ij}$ for the non-basic cells.

$d_{12} = u_1 + v_2 - C_{12} = 1 + 6 - 7 = 0$

$d_{13} = u_1 + v_3 - C_{13} = 1 + 2 - 4 = -1$

$d_{21} = u_2 + v_1 - C_{21} = -1 + 1 - 3 = -3$

$d_{22} = u_2 + v_2 - C_{22} = -1 + 6 - 3 = 2^*$

$d_{31} = u_3 + v_1 - C_{31} = -2 + 1 - 5 = -6$

$d_{33} = u_3 + v_3 - C_{33} = -2 + 2 - 7 = -7$

Since d_{22} is most positive ($d_{22} = 2$), so cell (2, 2) will enter the basis.

Here min $(8 - \theta, 2 - \theta) = 0$

or $2 - \theta = 0$

or $\theta = 2$

$\Rightarrow \theta^* = 2$

Thus we have new improved transprotation problem as the cell (4, 2) leaves the basis.

[5] 2		
	[2] 3	[6] 1
	[7] 4	
[2] 1		[12] 2

$$\begin{aligned} Z &= 5 \times 2 + 2 \times 3 + 6 \times 1 + 7 \times 4 + 2 \times 1 + 12 \times 2 \\ &= 10 + 6 + 6 + 28 + 2 + 24 \\ &= 76 \end{aligned}$$

The solution can be improved as follows:

			u_i
[5] 2			1
	[2] 3	[6] 1	–1
	[7] 4		0
[2] 1		[12] 2	0
v_j: 1	4	2	

$u_4 + v_1 = C_{41}$	$\Rightarrow$	$0 + v_1 = 1$	$\Rightarrow$	$v_1 = 1$
$u_4 + v_3 = C_{43}$	$\Rightarrow$	$0 + v_3 = 2$	$\Rightarrow$	$v_3 = 2$
$u_1 + v_1 = C_{11}$	$\Rightarrow$	$u_1 + 1 = 2$	$\Rightarrow$	$u_1 = 1$
$u_2 + v_3 = C_{23}$	$\Rightarrow$	$u_2 + 2 = 1$	$\Rightarrow$	$u_2 = -1$
$u_2 + v_2 = C_{22}$	$\Rightarrow$	$-1 + v_2 = 3$	$\Rightarrow$	$v_2 = 4$
$u_3 + v_2 = C_{32}$	$\Rightarrow$	$u_3 + 4 = 4$	$\Rightarrow$	$u_3 = 0$

Now, net evaluations d_{ij} are culculated as

$d_{12} = u_1 + v_2 - C_{12} = 1 + 4 - 7 = -2$

$d_{13} = u_1 + v_3 - C_{13} = 1 + 2 - 4 = -1$

$d_{21} = u_2 + v_1 - C_{21} = -1 + 1 - 3 = -3$

$d_{31} = u_3 + v_1 - C_{31} = 0 + 1 - 5 = -4$

$d_{42} = u_4 + v_2 - C_{42} = 0 + 4 - 6 = -2$

Since all $d_{ij} \le 0$, (negative). The optimal solution has been attained.

<table>
<tr><td>5
2</td><td></td><td></td></tr>
<tr><td></td><td>2
3</td><td>6
1</td></tr>
<tr><td></td><td>7
4</td><td></td></tr>
<tr><td>2
1</td><td></td><td>12
2</td></tr>
</table>

$Z = 5 \times 2 + 2 \times 3 + 6 \times 1 + 7 \times 4 + 2 \times 1 + 12 \times 2$

$= 10 + 6 + 6 + 28 + 2 + 24$

$= 76.$

The minimum cost for the transportation problem is ₹ 76.

4.14 DEGENERACY AND ITS RESOLUTION

A basic feasible solution for the general transportation must consists of exactly $(m + n - 1)$ positive allocations in independent positions in the transportation table.

If the number of occupied cells is less than $(m + n - 1)$, then degeneracy occurs. In such situations, the current solution cannot be further improved as it will not be possible to draw *a* closed path for every occupied cell. Further, the values of u_i and v_j cannot be computed.

Thus, to improve the given solution, the fundamental thing is that, the degeneracy in the transportation problem should be resolved any how. The degeneracy can be developed in the following two ways.

Case (1): *The degeneracy may occur while obtaining an initial basic feasible solution with number of occupied cells less than $(m + n - 1)$ allocations.*

Resolution. When the degeneracy occurs at the initial stage, then it can be resolved by proceeding as follows:

We allocate a very small quantity $\in$ (epsilon) nearly equal to zero, to one or more (if needed) to unoccupied cells so as to get a total of $(m + n - 1)$ number of occupied (basic) cells, which in turn does not affect at all the cost as well as the demand and the supply values. These small quantities are treated like any other basic cells and $\in$'s remain in the transportation table until temporary degeneracy is removed or until the optimum solution is obtained. After that $\in$ is set as $\in = 0$.

Case (2): *The degeneracy may occur at any iteration stage, while moving towards the optimal solution.*

Resolution. When the degeneracy occurs at any iteration stage, then it can be resolved by proceeding as follows:

When two or more occupied or basic cells are vacated (emptied) simultaneously, then allocate $\in$ to one or more of recently vacated cells so that the total number of basic cells become $(m + n - 1)$.

Example 7. *Solve the following transportation problem.*

				a_i
	12	8	9	20
	7	6	8	30
	8	9	11	50
b_j	40	10	50	

Solution. Using the North-West Corner Method, an initial basic feasible solution can be obtained as follows:

				a_i	u_i
	20			20	5
	20	10	$\in$	30	0
			50	50	3
b_j	40	10	50		
v_j	7	6	8		

Since the basic cells do not form a loop, the solution is basic. However, number of basic cells is 4, which is less than $(m + n - 1)$ $(= 3 + 3 - 1 = 5)$, the basic situation is degenerate. Thus in this example, case (1) of degeneracy occurs. So, in order to resolve the degeneracy proceed as follows. Since only one $(5 - 4 = 1)$ positive basic variable is needed, we select the cell (2, 3) and allocate $\in$ (negligible quantity) for x_{23}.

After the inclusion of the cell (2, 3), a loop cannot be formed. If we compute the net evaluation d_{ij} after calculating u_i & v_j, we find that all d_{ij} are positive.

$d_{12} = 3 + 6 - 8 = 1$

$d_{31} = 7 + 3 - 8 = 2$

$d_{13} = 5 + 8 - 9 = 4^*$

$d_{32} = 3 + 6 - 9 = 0$

The initial basic solution is not optimum as d_{13} is most positive (= 4).

The non-basic cell (1, 3) must enter the basis, and the basic cell (2, 3) leaves the basis as shown below.

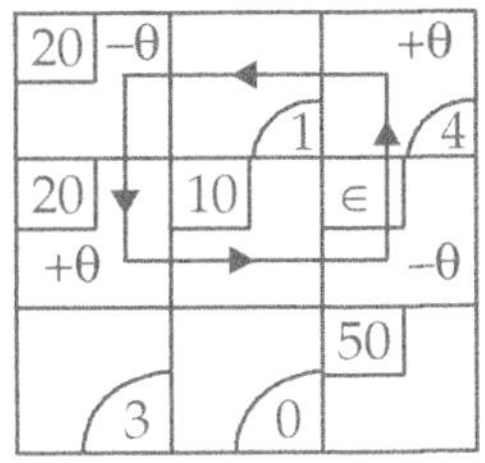

Here min $(2\theta - \theta, \in - \theta) = 0$

or $\in - \theta = 0$

$\Rightarrow \theta^* = \in$

Thus new transportation table looks like as:

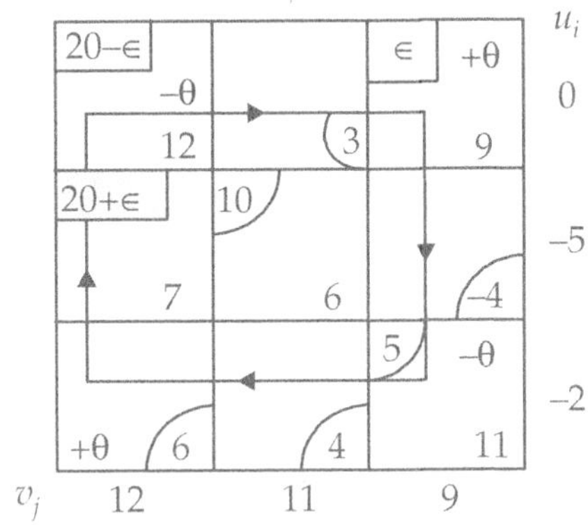

We calculate u_i and v_j and also the net evaluations d_{ij} as follows:

$d_{12} = 0 + 11 - 8 = 2;$ $\quad d_{23} = 9 - 5 - 8 = -4$

$d_{31} = 2 + 12 - 8 = 6^*;$ $\quad d_{32} = 2 + 11 - 9 = 4$

Since d_{31} is most positive (= 6), it enters the basis, *i.e.*, cell (3, 1) enters the basis.

Here min $(20 - \in - \theta, 50 - \theta)$

$\theta^* = -\in + 20 \Rightarrow \theta^* = 20 - \in$

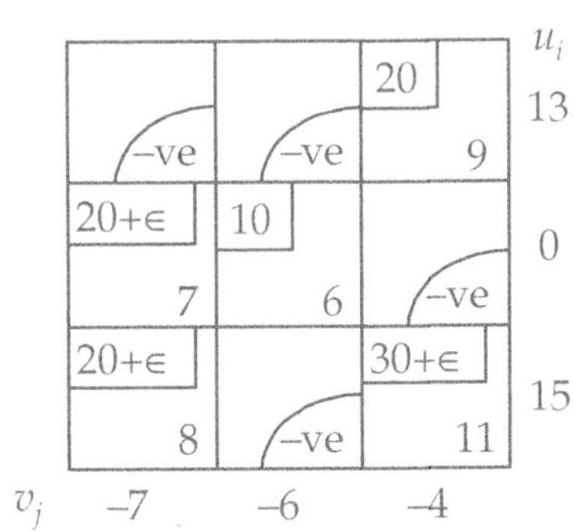

We again calculate u_i and v_j and also the net evaluations d_{ij} as follows.

$d_{11} = 13 - 7 - 12 = -6$

$d_{12} = 13 - 6 - 8 = -1$

$d_{23} = 0 - 4 - 8 = -12$

$d_{32} = 15 - 6 - 9 = 0$

Since all $d_{ij} \leq 0$, thus an optimal solution has been attained. Thus the transportation cost according to the given route is:

$$Z = 20 \times 9 + 20 + \in \times 7 + 10 \times 6 + 20 - \in \times 8 + 30 + \in \times 11$$
$$= 180 + 140 + 60 + 160 + 330 \qquad \& \in \to 0$$
$$= ₹\ 870$$

Thus the optimum cost is ₹ 870.

Example 8. *Determine the transportation schedule for the above transportation problem so that the cost is minimized.*

	I	II	III	a_i
A	10	7	8	100
B	17	12	14	60
C	5	11	12	60
b_j	130	60	30	

Solution. Using North-West Corner Method, the initial basic feasible solution is given as:

[100] 10	7	8	100
[30] 17	12	14	60
5	[30] 11	[30] 12	60
130	60	30	

To test the optimality of the solution, we calculate u_i, v_j and d_{ij} as shown below.

			u_i
[100] 10	(−2)	(−2)	−7
[30] −θ 17	[30] +θ 12	(−1)	0
+θ (11)	[30] −θ 11	[30] 12	−1
17	12	13	

Since d_{31} is most positive (= 11), therefore the cell (3, 1) enters the basis.

Here, min $(30 - \theta, 30 - \theta) = 0$

$30 - \theta = 0$

$\Rightarrow \theta^* = 30$

Now since $\theta^* = 30$, if allocated to the basic cells., then two cells ((2, 1) and (3, 2)) becomes unoccupied because these two have same allocations. Thus it leads to the required number of cells to 4, which is less than 5 (= $m + n - 1$). Hence this is a degenerate solution. To resolve degeneracy, a very small quantity $\in$ is assigned to any one of the cells that has just become unoccupied so that there are 5 (= $m + n + 1$) occupied cells.

	I	II	III	a_i
A	[100] 10	7	8	100
B	17	[60] 12	14	60
C	[30] 5	[∈] 11	[30] 12	60
b_j	130	60	30	

To test the optimality of the solution, we calculate u_i, v_j an.d d_{ij} as shown in the table given below.

				u_i
	[100] −θ 10	+θ 9	9	5
	−11	[60] 12	−1	1
	[30] +θ 5	[∈] −θ 11	[30] 12	0
v_j	5	11	12	

Since d_{12} and d_{13} are most positive (both equal to 9) so any of the cell either cell (1, 2) or cell (1, 3) can enter the basis. Let's choose cell (1, 2)

Here, min (100 – θ, ∈ – θ) = 0

$\Rightarrow \in - \theta = 0$

$\Rightarrow \theta' = \in$

Thus cell (3, 2) leaves the basis and so new transportation table is as:

				u_i
	[100] −θ 10	[∈] 7	+θ 9	5
	−2	[60] 12	8	10
	[30] +θ 5	−9	[30] −θ 12	0
v_j	5	2	12	

To test the optimality, u_i, v_j and d_{ij} are calculated again and are shown in above table.

So cell (1, 3) enters the basis and cell (3, 3) leaves the basis.

Here min (100 – θ, 30 – θ)

$\Rightarrow \theta^* = 30$

				a_i
	[70] 10	[∈] 7	[30] 8	100
	17	[60] 12	14	60
	[60] 5	11	12	60
b_j	130	60	30	

Now, again to test the optionality criteria, u_i, v_j and d_{ij} are calculated and are represented below:

				u_i
	[70] 10	[∈] 7	[30] 8	0
	(–2)	[60] 12	(–1)	5
	[60] 5	(–9)	(–9)	–5
v_j	10	7	8	

Since all d_{ij} are negative. Hence an optimal solution has been attained.

Then the transportation cost according to the given route is

$$Z = 70 \times 10 + \in \times 7 + 30 \times 8 + 60 \times 12 + 60 \times 5$$
$$= 700 + 240 + 720 + 300; \in \to 0$$
$$= ₹\ 1960.$$

4.15 PROHIBITED TRANSPORTATION ROUTES

So far all the routes from any source to sink have been treated as open and usable but in reality some routes may be prohibited (blocked) due to traffic regulations or other practical consideration such as snowfall, flood, security reasons, road construction, weight limits on bridges, etc.

The prohibited routes may sometimes lead to infeasibility even if the total supply exceeds or equals the maximum total demand. If so, one has no option but to adjust the supplies or the demands in order to obtain a feasible solution.

It is not possible to transport goods from certain sources to certain destination. Such type of problems can be handled by assigning a very large cost, say either M (or ∞) to that route (or cell). A numerical example is given below.

Example 9. *How many units of goods should be transported from sources to the destinations so that the total transportation cost is minimum? Here one route from origin C to destination III is prohibited because of road construction.*

	I	*II*	*III*	*Availability*
A	*7*	*7*	*8*	*10*
B	*9*	*6*	*7*	*15*
C	*6*	*8*	*X*	*40*
Requirement	*20*	*15*	*30*	

Solution. Since in the above transportation table one of the route, origin C to destination III is prohibited. Thus a large cost M is assigned to the cost C_{33} *i.e.*, in the cell (3, 3).

Destinations

Origin ↓	I	II	III	a_i
A	7	7	8	10
B	9	6	7	15
C	6	8	M	40
b_j	20	15	30	

Using Vogel's Approximation Method, the initial basic feasible solution is obtained as follows:

				a_i	Difference
	7	7	8	10	1
	9	6	7	15	1
	[20] 6	8	M	40	2
b_j	20	15	30		
Difference	1	1	1		

So we allocate 20 in the cell (3, 1) as C_{31} is minimum and cross out the column I.

Similarly we can allocate the remaining allocations after calculating the differences and finally the following tables are produced.

			10
		[15]	15
[20]			20
	15	30	

		[10] 8	10
		[15]	15
[20]			20
		15	

		[10] 8	
		[15]	
[20]	[15]	[5]	20
		5	

The initial basic feasible solution is shown in the following table.

	I	II	III	a_i
A	7	7	[10] 8	10
B	9	6	[15] 7	15
C	[20] 6	[15] 8	[5] M	20
b_j	20	15	30	

To test the optimality of the solution, we compute u_i, v_j and the net evaluations d_{ij}.

	I	II	III	u_i
A	(7–M)	(–7–M)	[10] 8	8–M
B	(4–M)	(–7–M)	[15] 7	7–M
C	[20] 6	[15] 8	[5] M	0
v_j	6	8	M	

$d_{11} = u_1 + v_1 - C_{11} = 8 - M + 6 - 7 = 7 - M$ (–ve quantity as M is very large and negative.)

$d_{12} = u_1 + v_2 - C_{12} = 8 - M + 8 - 7 = -7 - M$ (–ve)

$d_{21} = u_2 + v_1 - C_{21} = 7 - M + 6 - 9 = 4 - M$ (–ve)

$d_{22} = u_2 + v_2 - C_{22} = 7 - M - 8 - 6 = -7 - M$ (–ve)

Since here all $d_{ij} \leq 0$, thus the current solution is optimum.

Since the prohibited route cell (3, 3) also appears in the basis, so this solution is called as pseudo optimum feasible solution.

4.16 MAXIMIZATION TRANSPORTATION PROBLEM

Till now we have studied that, a total transportation cost is to be computed using the transportation table, for minimization of the costs. So, in, general, transportation problems are used for the cost minimization problem. However, instead of cost, C_{ij}, profit or payoff, P_{ij} are associated, with the given routes, then the problem becomes of maximization as profit is always to be maximized while cost is to be minimized. The objective function of the transportation problem, when it involves the profit or the payoffs, can be stated as follows:

$$\text{Maximize } Z = \sum_{i=1}^{m}\sum_{j=1}^{n} p_{ij} \cdot x_{ij}$$

The solution procedure can be summarized as follows:

Step 1: Convert the given problem into that of minimization by replacing each element of the transportation table by its difference from the maximum element of the table.

Step 2: Then the initial basic feasible solution is found using any of the methods described earlier.

Step 3: Then the optimum solution is obtained using MODI method.

Example 10. *The following table that involves profit is given below, otain the optimal solution for it.*

Profit Matrix

	I	II	III	IV	V	a_i
A	12	14	9	8	8	250
B	2	5	4	12	4	200
C	11	12	13	17	7	225
b_j	180	100	75	145	125	

Solution. The following matrix is obtained by subtracting each element from the largest (*i.e.*, 17)

					a_i
5	3	8	9	9	250
15	11	13	5	13	200
6	5	4	0	10	225
b_j 180	100	75	145	125	

Since $\sum_{i=1}^{m} a_i \neq \sum_{j=1}^{n} b_j$

Thus, it is an unbalanced transportation problem. To balance the problem, we introduce a dummy destination with demand $\left(\sum a_i - \sum b_j = 675 - 625 = 50\right)$ of 50 units.

So the problem now becomes.

						a_i
	5	3	8	9	9	0	250
	15	11	13	5	13	0	200
	6	5	4	0	10	0	225
b_j	180	100	75	145	125	50	

Using North-West Corner Rule, the initial basic feasible solution for the balanced transportation problem is as follows:

							u_i
	[180] 5	[70] 3	8	9	9	0	250
	15	[30] 11	[75] 13	[95] 5	13	0	200
	6	5	4	[50] 0	[125] 10	[50] 0	225
v_j	180	100	75	145	125	50	

Now, the initial solution so obtained by the North-West Corner Rule have 8 occupied cells (by $m + n - 1$). So, proceed further to obtain the optimal solution by using the MODI method.

							u_i
	[180] 5	[70] 3	−3	−12	−2	−3	−3
	−2	[30] 11	[75] 13	[95] −θ 5	2	+θ 5	5
	2	1	4	[50] +θ 0	[125] 10	[50] −θ 0	0
v_j	8	6	8	0	10	0	

Since $d_{26} = 5$ is most positive, so it enters the basis and the loop is formed.

Here min $(90 - \theta, 50 - \theta) = 0$

$50 - \theta = 0$

$\Rightarrow \theta^* = 50$

So the cell (3, 6) leaves the basis.

						u_i
180 / 5	70 / 3	−3	−12	−2	−8	−8
−2	30 / 11	75 −θ / 13	45 +θ / 5	2	50 / 0	0
2	1	+θ 4	100 −θ / 0	125 / 10	−5	−5
v_j 13	11	13	5	15	0	

Again computing the values of u_i, v_j and d_{ij} and they are noted down in the above table. Since d_{34} = 4 is most positive and the loop is formed.

Here min (75 – θ, 100 – θ) = 0

75 – θ = 0

⇒ θ* = 75

So the cell (2, 3) now leaves the basis.

						u_i
180 −θ / 5	70 +θ / 3	−7	−12	−2	−8	−3
	30 −θ / 11	−4	120 +θ / 5	2	50 / 0	5
2 / 2	1	75 / 4	25 −θ / 0	125 / 10	−5	0
v_j 8	6	4	0	10	0	

Again computing the values of u_i, v_j and d_{ij}. These values are noted in the above table.

Since $d_{31} = d_{25}$ = 2 (most positive), lets take arbitrarily the cell (3, 1) to enter the basis and the loop is formed.

Here min (180 – θ, 30 – θ, 25 – θ)

or 25 – θ = 0

⇒ θ* = 25.

So cell, (3, 4) leaves the basis.

						u_i
155 −θ / 5	95 +θ / 3	−5	−6	0	−8	−1
−2	5 −θ / 11	−2	145 / 5	+θ 4	50 / 0	7
25 +θ / 6	−1	75 / 4	−2	125 −θ / 10		0
v_j 6	4	4	−2	10	−7	

Again computing the values of u_i, v_j and d_{ij} and recording them in the above table. Since d_{25} = 4 is most positive, thus cell (2, 5) enters the basis and the loop is formed. Here min (155 – θ, 5 – θ, 125 – θ) = 0

5 – θ = 0

⇒ θ* = 5.

Now the cell (2, 2) leaves the basis

						u_i
150 5	100 3	–5	–8	0		–4
–6	–4	–6	145 –θ 5	5 +θ 13	50 0	0
30 6	–1	75 4	+θ 2	120 –θ 10		–3
v_j: 9	7	7	5	13	0	

Since d_{34} = 2, is most +ve it enters the basis.

Here θ* = 120

Now the cell (3, 5) leaves the basis.

						u_i
150 5	100 3	–5	–10	–2	–6	–1
–4	–2	–4	25 5	125 13	50 0	5
30 6	–1	75 4	120 0	–2	–5	0
v_j: 6	4	4	0	8	–5	

Since all $d_{ij} \le 0$ (*i.e.*, negative), an optimum solution has been attained.

The optimum allocations are

x_{11} = 150 x_{26} = 50

x_{12} = 100 x_{31} = 30

x_{24} = 25 x_{33} = 75

x_{25} = 125 x_{34} = 120

Total Profit = 150 × 5 + 100 × 3 + 25 × 5 + 125 × 13 + 50 × 0 + 30 × 6 + 75 × 4 + 120 × 0

= ₹ 3280.

Remark. The above problem is now solved by using Stepping Stone Solution Method as follows. Consider the problem when the initial basic feasible solution is obtained using North-West Rule.

						a_i
[180] 5	[70] 3	8	9	9	0	250
15	[30] 11	[75] 13	[95] 5	13	0	200
6	5	4	[50] 0	[125] 10	[50] 0	225
b_j: 180	100	75	145	125	50	

						a_i
[180] 5	[70] 3	8	9	9	0	250
15	[30] 11	[25] + 13	[145] 5	13	+ 0	200
6	5	[50] − 4	0	[125] 10	[50] − 0	225
b_j: 180	100	75	145	125	50	

By stepping stone method, the first table has been formed as follows. We select an unoccupied cell, where allocations can be made and with this cell, we trace a closed path, and calculate the net change in the cost along the closed path by adding and subtracting unit costs.

8 – 13 + 11 – 3 = 3 (+ve)

9 – 5 + 11 – 3 = 5 (+ve)

9 – 10 + 0 – 5 + 11 – 3 = 1 (+ve)

0 – 0 + 0 – 5 + 11 – 3 = 3 (+ve)

15 – 5 + 5 + 3 – 11 = –2 (–ve)

13 – 10 + 0 – 5 = –2 (–ve)

0 – 0 + 0 – 5 = –5 (–ve)

6 – 5 + 3 – 11 + 5 – 0 = –2 (–ve)

5 – 11 + 5 – 0 = –1 (–ve)

4 – 13 + 5 – 0 = –4* (–ve).

Since –4 is most negative for cell (2, 6).

(If all the net changes are +ve, an optimal solution has been attained. If not, the current solution can be improved). Thus cell (2, 6) enters the basis and $\theta^* = 25$.

Now cell (2, 3) leaves the basis and the same above procedure (stepping stone) is applied to improve the solution.

						a_i
180 −θ (5)	+θ 70 (3)	(8)	(9)	(9)	(0)	250
(15)	30 −θ (11)	(13)	145 (5)	(13)	25 +θ (0)	200
+θ (6)	(5)	75 (4)	(0)	125 (10)	25 −θ (0)	225
b_j 180	100	75	145	125	50	

In the above transportation table, cell (3, 1) enters the basis.

Here θ* = 25

Cell (3, 6) leaves the basis.

Thus the new transportation table is constructed as follows:

						a_i
155 −θ (5)	95 +θ (3)	(8)	(9)	(9)	(0)	250
(15)	5 θ (11)	(13)	145 (5)	+θ (13)	50 (0)	200
25 +θ (6)	(5)	75 (4)	(0)	125 −θ (10)	(0)	225
b_j 180	100	75	145	125	50	

Again the net changes are not all positive, so the solution can once again be improved.

Here θ* = 5

So, cell (2, 5) enters the basis and cell (2, 2) leaves the basis.

						a_i
150 (5)	100 (3)	(8)	(9)	(9)	(0)	250
(15)	(11)	(13)	145 −θ (5)	5 +θ (13)	50 (0)	200
30 (6)	(5)	75 (4)	+θ (0)	120 −θ (10)	(0)	225
b_j 180	100	75	145	125	50	

Again the net changes are not all positive, so the solution can once again be improved.

Here θ* = 120

So cell (3, 5) leaves the basis and cell (3, 4) enters the basis.

						a_i
	(150) 5	3	8	9	9	0	250
	15	11	13	(25) 5	(125) 13	(50) 0	200
	(30) 6	5	(75) 4	(120) 0	10	0	225
b_j	180	100	75	145	125	50	

After checking the sign of each net changes we have found that all the net changes are positive, so an optimal solution has been attained.

So the profit = 150 × 5 + 100 × 3 + 25 × 5 + 125 × 13 + 50 × 0 + 30 × 6 + 75 × 4 + 120 × 0

= 750 + 300 + 125 + 1625 + 0 + 180 + 300 + 0

= ₹ 3280.

So the optimum profit is ₹ 3280.

4.17 TRANSSHIPMENT PROBLEM

Till now, we have studied that in any transportation problem, the shipment of a commodity takes place only among sources and destinations. But instead of direct shipments to from a source to destinations, the commodity can also be transported to through one or more intermediate or transshipment points. Each of these intermediate or transshipment points in turn supply to other points.

Thus whenever, the shipment passes through a source to a source or from destination to destination, then we have a transshipment problem.

Transshipment problem

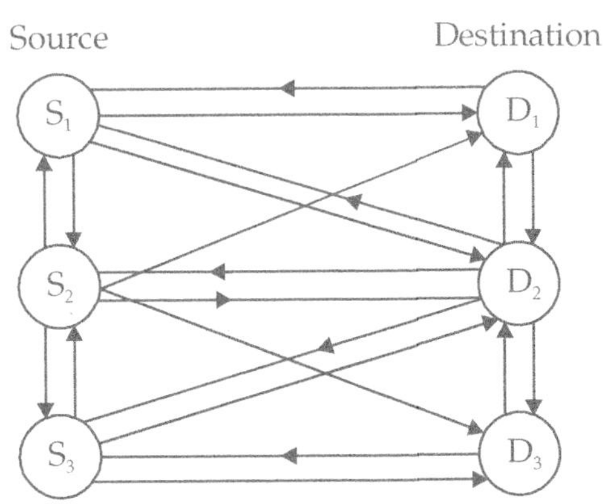

In the above ray diagram each source and each destination transport the goods to other sources and destinations. The symbol ⇄ is used to represent that shipment can be done in both ways.

The transshipment problem in first of all converted into a transportation problem, and then an optimal solution for the converted transportation problem is obtained after obtaining the initial basic feasible solution, for it. Consider a transshipment problem as:

If there are m sources and n sinks or destinations then the transportation problem can be constructed by using the above transshipment problem as follows. In the converted transportation problem, number of sources becomes $(m + n)$ and the number of destinations too becomes $(m + n)$.

Thus in the transportation problem with transshipment, instead of shipping direct from source to sink, it may be possible to tranship, *i.e.*, goods produced at some sourced and destined for some sink reach their ultimate destination *via* other sources and sinks and are transshipped at these points. If a point is a source, the net of what leaves that point must be a_i, and if a point is a sink, then the net of what arrives at that point must be b_j.

In the case of transshipment, one thing is that, each sink must be treated as two distinct sinks as it makes a difference whether the products are send from i to j or from j to i (even If $C_{ij} = C_{ji}$).

The cost of transportation from any source to source and destination to destination is always equal to zero.

Example 11. *Consider a transportation problem with transshipment as follows:*

		Source		*Sink*		
		A	*B*	*C*	*D*	*E*
Source	*A*	*0*	*13*	*12*	*13*	*14*
	B	*11*	*0*	*10*	*9*	*8*
Sink	*C*	*12*	*17*	*0*	*10*	*6*
	D	*6*	*10*	*6*	*0*	*5*
	E	*13*	*14*	*12*	*13*	*0*

Find the optimal shipping schedule and optimum transportation cost for the following transshipment problem, if the number of units available at A and B are 20 and 30 and the demands at C, D, and E are respectively 10, 15 and 25.

Solution. The maximum amount that can be transported through a source or sink is the total supply and demand.

i.e., supply + demand = Total Units

20 + 30 = 50

If all these 50 units are not transported through a source or a sink, then the remaining units will play the role of dummy. Thus the transshipment problem is now constructed as follows.

	A	B	C	D	E	a_i (supply)
A	0	13	12	13	14	20 + 50 = 70
B	11	0	10	9	8	30 + 50 = 80
C	12	17	0	10	6	50
D	6	10	6	0	5	50
E	13	14	12	13	0	50
(Demand) b_j	50	50	10 + 50 = 60	15 + 50 = 65	25 + 50 = 75	

The initial basic feasible solution for the above transportation problem is obtained by the method of Vogel's Approximation Method.

	C	D	E	a_i
A	[10] 12	[10] 13	14	20
B	10	[5] 9	[25] 8	30
b_j	10	15	25	

Now the initial basic feasible solution for the transshipment problem can be obtained by the initial basic feasible solution of transportation problem in addition with putting 50 units to each route on the diagonal of the transshipment problem. Thus the initial solution of the transshipment problem is shown as follows:

	A	B	C	D	E	a_i
A	[50] 0	13	[10] 12	[10] 13	14	70
B	11	[50] 0	10	[5] 9	[25] 8	80
C	12	17	[50] 0	10	6	50
D	6	10	6	[50] 0	5	50
E	13	14	12	13	[50] 0	50
b_j	50	50	60	65	75	

To find the optimum solution of the transshipment problem, we apply the UV–method (MODI method) and for this we have to first determine u_i and v_j and then d_{ij} for each unoccupied cells, as done before.

The values of u_i, v_j and d_{ij} are shown in next table.

	A	B	C	D	E	a_i	u_i
A	[50] 0	−9	[10] 12	[10] 13	−2	70	$u_1 = 4$
B	−15	[50] 0	−2	[5] 9	[25] 8	80	$u_2 = 0$
C	−24	−25	[50] 0	−9	−6	50	$u_3 = -8$
D	−19	−19	−7	[50] 0	−6	50	$u_4 = -9$
E	−25	−22	−12	−12	[50] 0	50	$u_5 = -8$
b_j	50	50	60	65	75	300	
v_j	$v_1 = -4$	$v_2 = 0$	$v_3 = 8$	$v_4 = 9$	$v_5 = 8$		

Since $u_i + v_j = C_{ij}$, we calculate all the values of u_i and v_j using this relation.

for cell (2, 5) $u_2 + v_5 = 8 \Rightarrow 0 + v_5 = 8 \Rightarrow v_5 = 0$

for cell (2, 4) $u_2 + v_4 = 9 \Rightarrow 0 + v_4 = 9 \Rightarrow v_4 = 9$

for cell (2, 2) $u_2 + v_2 = 0 \Rightarrow 0 + v_2 = 0 \Rightarrow v_2 = 0$

for cell (1, 4) $u_1 + v_4 = 13 \Rightarrow u_1 + 9 = 13 \Rightarrow u_1 = 4$

for cell (1, 1) $u_1 + v_1 = 0 \Rightarrow 4 + v_1 = 0 \Rightarrow v_1 = -4$

Similarly, we can find all the values of u_i and v_j.

Now we will calculate d_{ij} by the relation

$d_{ij} = u_i + v_j - C_{ij}$

$d_{12} = u_1 + v_2 - C_{12} = 4 + 0 - 13 = -9$

$d_{15} = u_1 + v_5 - C_{15} = 4 + 8 - 14 = -2$

$d_{21} = u_2 + v_1 - C_{21} = 0 + (-4) - 11 = -15$

$d_{23} = u_2 + v_3 - C_{23} = 0 + 8 - 10 = -2$

$d_{31} = u_3 + v_1 - C_{31} = -8 - 4 - 12 = -24$

$d_{32} = u_3 + v_2 - C_{32} = -8 + 0 - 17 = -25$

$d_{34} = u_3 + v_4 - C_{34} = -8 + 9 - 10 = -9$

$d_{35} = u_3 + v_5 - C_{35} = -8 + 8 - 6 = -6$

$d_{41} = u_4 + v_1 - C_{41} = -9 - 4 - 6 = -19$

$d_{42} = u_4 + v_2 - C_{42} = -9 + 0 - 10 = -19$

$d_{43} = u_4 + v_3 - C_{43} = -9 + 8 - 6 = -7$

$d_{45} = u_4 + v_5 - C_{45} = -9 + 8 - 5 = -6$
$d_{51} = u_5 + v_1 - C_{51} = -8 - 4 - 13 = -25$
$d_{52} = u_5 + v_2 - C_{52} = -8 + 0 - 14 = -22$
$d_{53} = u_5 + v_3 - C_{53} = -8 + 8 - 12 = -12$
$d_{54} = u_5 + v_4 - C_{54} = -8 + 9 - 13 = -12$

Since all d_{ij}'s are negative ($d_{ij} \leqslant 0$).

Thus the initial solution already calculated above will be the optimal solution.

Now, in order to interpret the optimal solution, allocations in the diagonal cells are ignored as these values show the extra dummies which have been added to allow as much as flow possible.

Thus the optimum transshipment cost is

$$\begin{aligned} TC &= 50 \times 0 + 10 \times 12 + 10 \times 13 + 50 \times 0 + 5 \times 9 + 25 \times 8 + 50 \times 0 + 50 \times 0 + 50 \times 0 \\ &= 0 + 120 + 130 + 0 + 45 + 200 + 0 + 0 + 0 \\ &= ₹\ 495. \end{aligned}$$

Thus the optimal solution is

$x_{11} = 50$ $\quad x_{22} = 0$ $\quad x_{33} = 50$
$x_{13} = 10$ $\quad x_{24} = 5$ $\quad x_{44} = 50$
$x_{14} = 10$ $\quad x_{25} = 25$ $\quad x_{55} = 50$

and the optimal at cost is ₹ 495.

Example 12. *In a flooded area, food packets have to be carried by three aircrafts from an airport and are dropped to five different places. The quantities (suitable units) that can be carried in one trip by these air crafts to the places are given below. The total number of trips per day that an aircraft can make to different places is given as below.*

		places →					
		P_1	P_2	P_3	P_4	P_5	*Trip per day by aircraft*
Air craft ↑	*AF1*	20	18	16	19	22	50
	AF2	15	13	18	14	20	90
	AF3	17	19	16	20	14	60
	Trips per day to places	100	80	70	40	20	

Then

(a) Formulate the problem as an LPP.

(b) Find the number of trips each craft should make to each place so that the total quantity of food transported is maximum.

Solution. Let x_{ij} be the amount of food packets transformed by ith aircraft to jth place.

As it is an unbalanced maximization problem.

Then Maximize Z $= 20x_{11} + 18x_{12} + 16x_{13} + 19x_{14} + 22x_{15} +$
$15x_{21} + 13x_{22} + 18x_{23} + 14x_{24} + 20x_{25} +$
$17x_{31} + 19x_{32} + 16x_{33} + 20x_{34} + 14x_{35} +$
$0.x_{41} + 0.x_{42} + 0.x_{43} + 0.x_{44} + 0.x_{45}$

Subject to

$$x_{11} + x_{12} + x_{13} + x_{14} + x_{15} = 50$$
$$x_{21} + x_{22} + x_{23} + x_{24} + x_{25} = 90$$
$$x_{31} + x_{32} + x_{33} + x_{34} + x_{35} = 60$$
$$x_{41} + x_{42} + x_{43} + x_{44} + x_{45} = 110$$
$$x_{11} + x_{21} + x_{31} + x_{41} = 100$$
$$x_{12} + x_{22} + x_{32} + x_{42} = 80$$
$$x_{13} + x_{23} + x_{33} + x_{43} = 70$$
$$x_{14} + x_{24} + x_{34} + x_{44} = 40$$
$$x_{15} + x_{25} + x_{35} + x_{45} = 20$$

$x_{ij} \geq 0; i = 1, 2, 3, 4$
and $j = 1, 2, 3, 4, 5$

Adding dummy row to balance the TP

	P_1	P_2	P_3	P_4	P_5	a_i
AF1	20	18	16	19	22	50
AF2	15	13	18	14	20	90
AF3	17	19	16	20	14	60
AF4	0	0	0	0	0	110
b_j	100	80	70	40	20	

	P_1	P_2	P_3	P_4	P_5	
AF1	2	4	6	3	0	50
AF2	7	9	4	8	2	90
AF3	5	3	6	2	8	60
AF4	22	22	22	22	22	110
	100	80	70	40	20	

By using Vogel's Approximation Method

						Penalties				
[50] 2	4	6	3	0	50	2	–			
7	9	[70] 4	8	[20] 2	90	2	2	2	3	3
5	[20] 3	6	[40] 2	8	60	1	1	3	2	–
[50] 22	[60] 22	[0] 22	22	22	110	0	0	0	0	0
100	80	70	40	20						
3	1	2	1	2						
2	6	2	6	6						
2	6	2	–	6						
2	6	2	–	–						
15	13	16								

Since for basic cells $C_{ij} = u_i + v_j = 0$ and for non-basic cells $d_{ij} = c_{ij} - (u_i + v_j)$

					u_i
50 / 2	2 / 4	4 / 6	2 / 3	0 / 0	$u_1 = -20$
3 / 7	5 / 9	70 / 4	5 / 8	20 / 2	$u_2 = -18$
2 / 5	20 / 3	3 / 6	40 / 2	7 / 8	$u_3 = -19$
50 / 22	60 / 22	0 / 22	1 / 22	2 / 22	$u_4 = 0$
$v_1 = 22$	$v_2 = 22$	$v_3 = 22$	$v_4 = 21$	$v_5 = 20$	v_j

Since all $d_{ij} \geq 0$, the solution obtained is optimal,

$\therefore$ Maximum quantity of food transported

$= 50 \times 20 + 70 \times 18 + 20 \times 20 + 19 \times 20 + 20 \times 40$

$= 1000 + 1260 + 400 + 380 + 800$

$= 3840$

Example 13. *A company ABC has four factories and it supplies warehouses to different districts. Monthly factory capacities are 350, 250, 400 and 320 units respectively. Monthly warehouse requirements are 150, 120, 220, 300 and 200 units respectively. The unit shipping costs from factories to warehouses are given as follows (in ₹):*

Warehouse →

Factory ↑	W_1	W_2	W_3	W_4	W_5
F1	13	14	16	12	23
F2	11	13	18	14	26
F3	25	12	15	16	13
F4	17	12	19	20	27

Solve the above transportation problem by MODI method and formulate it.

Solution. The given problem is an unbalanced one, so first of all balance it.

	W_1	W_2	W_3	W_4	W_5	W_6	a_i
F1	13	14	16	12	23	0	350
F2	11	13	18	14	26	0	250
F3	25	12	15	16	13	0	400
F4	17	12	19	20	27	0	320
b_j	150	120	220	300	200	330	

	W_1	W_2	W_3	W_4	W_5	W_6								
F1	13	14	16	[20] 12	23	[330] 0	350	12	12	1	1	4		
F2	[150] 11	13	18	[100] 14	26	0	250	11	11	2	3	4	4	
F3	25	12	[200] 15	16	[200] 13	0	400	12	12	3	1	1	1	1
F4	17	[120] 12	[20] 19	[180] 20	27	0	320	12	12	5	2	1	1	1
	150	120	220	300	200	330								
	2	0	1	2	13	0								
	2	0	1	2	–	0								
	2	0	1	2	–	–								
	2	–	1	2	–	–								
	–	–	1	2	–	–								
			3	2										
			4	4										

By Vogel's Approximation Method, we get an initial basic solution.

(4) 13	(10) 14	(5) 16	[20] +θ 12	(14) 23	[330] –θ 0	$u_1 = -8$
[150] 11	(7) 13	(5) 18	[100] 14	(15) 26	(–2) 0	$u_2 = -6$
(12) 25	(4) 12	[200] 15	(0) 16	[200] 13	(–4) 0	$u_3 = -4$
(0) 17	[120] 12	[20] 19	[180] –θ 20	(0) 27	(–8) 0	$u_4 = 0$
$v_1 = 17$	$v_2 = 12$	$v_3 = 19$	$v_4 = 120$	$v_5 = 17$	$v_6 = 8$	

Here $\theta^* = 200$

(4) 13	(2) 14	(−3) 16 + θ	[200] 12	(6) 23	[150] −θ 0	$u_1 = 0$
[150] 11	(−1) 13	(−3) 18	[100] 14	(7) 26	(−2) 0	$u_2 = 2$
(20) 25	(4) 12	[200] 15	(8) 16	[200] 13	(4) 0	$u_3 = -4$
(8) 17	[120] 12	[20] −θ 19	(8) 20	(10) 27	[180] +θ 0	$u_4 = 0$
$v_1 = 9$	$v_2 = 12$	$v_3 = 19$	$v_4 = 12$	$v_5 = 17$	$v_6 = 0$	

Here $\theta^* = 20$

(4) 13	(2) 14	[20] 16	[200] +θ 12	(9) 23	[130] −θ 0	$u_1 = 0$
[150] 11	(−1) 13	(0) 18	[100] −θ 14	(10) 26	+θ (−2) 0	$u_2 = 2$
(17) 25	(1) 12	[200] 15	(5) 16	[200] 13	(1) 0	$u_3 = -1$
(8) 17	[120] 12	(3) 19	(8) 20	(13) 27	[200] 0	$u_4 = 0$
$v_1 = 9$	$v_2 = 12$	$v_3 = 16$	$v_4 = 12$	$v_5 = 14$	$v_6 = 0$	

Here $\theta^* = 100$

(2) 13	(2) 14	[20] 16	[300] 12	(7) 23	[30] 0	$u_1 = 0$
[150] 11	(1) 13	(2) 18	(2) 14	(12) 26	[100] 0	$u_2 = 0$
(15) 25	(1) 12	[200] 15	(5) 16	[200] 13	(1) 0	$u_3 = -1$
(6) 17	[120] 12	(3) 19	(8) 20	(13) 27	[200] 0	$u_4 = 0$
$v_1 = 11$	$v_2 = 12$	$v_3 = 16$	$v_4 = 12$	$v_5 = 14$	$v_6 = 0$	

Since all $d_{ij} \geq 0$, the solution is optimal.

Total cost $= 20 \times 16 + 12 \times 300 + 11 \times 150 + 15 \times 200 + 13 \times 200 + 12 \times 120$

$= ₹\ 12{,}610$

Formulation. Let x_{ij} be the amount transported from *i*th factory to *j*th warehouse.

$$\begin{aligned}
\text{Minimize } Z = {} & 13x_{11} + 14x_{12} + 16x_{13} + 12x_{14} + 23x_{15} + 0.x_{16} + \\
& 11x_{21} + 13x_{22} + 18x_{23} + 14x_{24} + 26x_{25} + 0.x_{26} + \\
& 25x_{31} + 12x_{32} + 15x_{33} + 16x_{34} + 13x_{35} + 0.x_{36} + \\
& 17x_{41} + 12x_{42} + 19x_{43} + 20x_{44} + 27x_{45} + 0.x_{46}
\end{aligned}$$

Subject to

$$\begin{aligned}
x_{11} + x_{12} + x_{13} + x_{14} + x_{15} + x_{16} &= 350 \\
x_{21} + x_{22} + x_{23} + x_{24} + x_{25} + x_{26} &= 250 \\
x_{31} + x_{32} + x_{33} + x_{34} + x_{35} + x_{36} &= 400 \\
x_{41} + x_{42} + x_{43} + x_{44} + x_{45} + x_{46} &= 320 \\
x_{11} + x_{21} + x_{31} + x_{41} &= 150 \\
x_{12} + x_{22} + x_{32} + x_{42} &= 120 \\
x_{13} + x_{23} + x_{33} + x_{43} &= 220 \\
x_{14} + x_{24} + x_{34} + x_{44} &= 300 \\
x_{15} + x_{25} + x_{35} + x_{45} &= 200 \\
x_{16} + x_{26} + x_{36} + x_{46} &= 330
\end{aligned}$$

$x_{ij} \geq 0;\ i = 1, 2, 3, 4$

and $j = 1, 2, 3, 4, 5, 6$

OBJECTIVE TYPE QUESTIONS

1. The necessary and sufficient condition for the existence of a feasible solution to the transportation problem is:

   (*a*) $\sum_{i=1}^{m} a_i = \sum_{j=1}^{n} b_j$ (*b*) $\sum_{i=1}^{m} a_i + \sum_{j=1}^{n} b_j = N$

   (*c*) $\sum_{i=1}^{m} a_i \neq \sum_{j=1}^{n} b_j$ (*d*) None of the above.

2. The cells in the transportation table having positive allocations are called as:

   (*a*) non-occupied cells (*b*) occupied cells

   (*c*) entered cells (*d*) degenerate cells.

3. The method to find an initial basic feasible solution is

   (*a*) North-West Corner Method (*b*) Least Cost Method

   (*c*) Vogel's Approximation Method (*d*) All of the above.

4. In North-West Corner rule,

   (*a*) cost of transportation on any route is given priority

   (*b*) cost of transportation on any route is neglected

   (*c*) cost of transportation on any route is used to be minimized

   (*d*) cost of transportation on any route is used to be maximized.

5. The initial solution obtained by any method must satisfy the condition (*s*):
   (*a*) The solution must be feasible.
   (*b*) The number of basic cells should be equal to $(m + n - 1)$
   (*c*) $\sum a_i = \sum b_j$ should be satisfied
   (*d*) All of the above.
6. Whenever the cell evaluation matrix corresponding to the optimal solution a transportation problem has zero entry in an empty cell, then there exits a/an
   (*a*) optimal solution (*b*) alternate optimal solution
   (*c*) no solution (*d*) unbounded solution.
7. In Vogel's Approximation Method, the opportunity cost associated with a row is determined by the difference between the
   (*a*) smallest cost and the next smallest cost in that row
   (*b*) smallest unused cost and the next smallest unused cost in that row
   (*c*) smallest cost and the next smallest unused cost in that row
   (*d*) None of the above.
8. Degeneracy in transportation occurs when
   (*a*) there are less than $(m + n - 1)$ cells used
   (*b*) demand exceeds supply
   (*c*) supply exceeds demand
   (*d*) None
9. A transportation problem where shipment is possible from an origin to an origin or a destination as well as from destination to an origin or a destination is better known as
   (*a*) capacitated transportation problem
   (*b*) transshipment problem
   (*c*) unbalanced transportation problem
   (*d*) None of the above.

EXERCISES

1. State a transportation problem. When does the transportation problem attains a unique solution?
2. What is a transportation problem? Write its mathematical model.
3. What do you understand by balanced transportation problem?
4. Explain in brief about transportation problem and show that it can be treated as a linear programming problem.
5. What are the various methods to compute an initial basic feasible solution for a transportation problem.

6. Briefly explain the following method for obtaining an initial basic feasible solution for the transportation problem.
   (*a*) North-West Corner Method
   (*b*) Minimum Matrix Method
   (*c*) Vogel's Approximation Method
   (*d*) The Row Minima Method.
7. Give examples to explain the following methods for solving any given transportation problem.
   (*a*) Stepping Stone Method
   (*b*) MODI Method
   (*c*) Vogel's Approximation Method.
8. What is degeneracy in transportation problem and how can it be removed?
9. What is an unbalanced transportation problem? Write a procedure to solve it with suitable example.
10. Differentiate between the transportation and transshipment problem.
11. Explain various steps involved in getting an optimal solution to a transportation problem.

UNSOLVED EXERCISES

1. Find the initial basic feasible solution using North-West Corner Method

	I	II	III	IV	a_i
A	42	36	12	18	30
B	21	40	15	11	40
C	10	26	29	43	10
b_j	15	10	15	40	

(**Hint:** $x_{11} = 15$, $x_{12} = 10$, $x_{13} = 5$, $x_{23} = 10$, $x_{24} = 30$, $x_{34} = 10$)

2. Find the initial basic feasible solution for the following transportation problem using Row-Minima Method.

	I	II	III	IV	a_i
A	2	3	11	7	6
B	1	0	6	1	1
C	5	8	15	2	10
b_j	7	5	3	2	

(**Hint:** $x_{11} = 6$, $x_{22} = 1$, $x_{31} = 1$, $x_{32} = 4$, $x_{33} = 3$, $x_{34} = 2$, TC = ₹ 11,200)

3. Find the initial basic feasible solution for the following transportation problem using Least Cost Method.

					a_i
	1	2	5	8	10
	6	4	3	2	12
	1	0	5	6	16
b_j	10	9	9	10	

4. Find the initial basic feasible solution for the following transportation problem using Vogel's Approximation Method.

	I	II	III	IV	a_i
A	2	3	11	7	6
B	1	0	6	1	1
C	5	8	15	9	10
b_j	7	5	3	1	

(**Hint:** $x_{11} = 1$, $x_{12} = 5$, $x_{12} = 1$, $x_{23} = 1$, $x_{31} = 6$, $x_{33} = 3$, $x_{34} = 1$, TC = ₹ 10,200)

5. A company has 4 factories and 5 warehouses, then find the optimum solution (cost) for the company if

	W_1	W_2	W_3	W_4	W_5	Availability
F1	70	60	40	50	90	400
F2	80	50	60	70	80	300
F3	60	80	90	60	50	200
F4	50	70	70	80	60	100
Requirement	300	300	150	200	50	

(**Hint:** $x_{11} = 50$, $x_{13} = 150$, $x_{14} = 200$, $x_{22} = 300$, $x_{31} = 150$, $x_{35} = 50$, $x_{41} = 100$)

6. A product is produced in four factories F_1, F_2, F_3 and F_4. These four factories supply the product to 4 different demand centres D_1, D_2, D_3, and D_4. The production capacity for the factories are 500, 700, 300 and 500 units, while the demands at different destinations are 250, 350, 1050 and 200 units respectively. The unit transportation costs in rupees from each factory to each destination is given as

	D_1	D_2	D_3	D_4
F1	40	60	80	130
F2	130	110	100	80
F3	140	40	100	130
F4	90	110	130	80

Determine the optimum minimum cost.

7. Solve the following transportations problem:

	A	B	C	D	E	F	a_i
I	11	12	21	14	15	12	300
II	13	13	12	11	14	13	500
III	14	12	15	19	16	12	750
IV	13	11	17	13	14	16	200
b_j	200	400	300	100	500	250	

8. Consider the following transportation problem.

	A	B	C	a_i
I	10	6	12	10
II	11	9	11	80
III	8	7	10	15
IV	10	8	7	–
b_j	75	20	50	145

Find the optimum solution for the above problem.

9. A company has four different factories F_1, F_2, F_3, and F_4 and five warehouses W_1, W_2, W_3 W_4, and W_5. The product is produced at these factories and are then supplied to these warehouses. The total availability at each factory is 100, 200, 150, 150 units respectively, whereas the requirement at each warehouse is 50 units, 100 units, 150 units, 200 units and 100 units. The transportation cost from factory to destination is given in the following table as:

	W_1	W_2	W_3	W_4	W_5
F1	12	6	7	1	5
F2	2	1	5	2	1
F3	7	6	1	3	5
F4	8	7	5	6	1

Find the optimum scheduling cost.

10. A company XYZ has three factories and five demand centres. The transportation cost for shipping the product from factories to demand centres are shown in the following table:

Demand centres

		D_1	D_2	D_3	D_4	D_5	Capacities
	F1	9	7	8	7	11	80
Factories	F2	10	9	10	7	6	120
	F3	11	10	9	12	8	140
Requirement		40	40	60	80	80	

What is an optimal scheduling schedule?

11. A company has 3 factories located at different places but all these factories produce the same identical product. The cost of production, distribution cost for each factory to the three different demand centres, the sale price at each demand centre and the individual capacities for both the factories and the demand centres are given as:

Distribution to Demand Centres	Factories			Sale Price	Demand Centres Capacity
	F_1	F_2	F_3		
D_1	8	14	10	39	100
D_2	6	12	9	37	90
D_3	10	13	8	36	160
Raw material	20	23	19		
Other expenses	15	14	17		
Capacity of factory	100	120	160		

Find the distribution pattern so as to maximize profit after introducing suitable dummy demand centre/factory.

[**Hint:** The profit table can be obtained by the following equation

Profit = sale price – production cost – raw material cost – transportation cost.

i.e., for I cell profit = 39 – 15 – 20 – 8 = 39 – 43 = –4

Thus the profit matrix is obtained as

Demand centres

		D_1	D_2	D_3	Available
Factories	F1	6	–4	–9	100
	F2	–12	–12	–1	120
	F3	–7	–8	–8	160
Requirement		100	90	160	

This is an unbalanced transportation problem and can be solved using usual method.]

12. A company ABC Ltd. has three different factories F1, F2 and F3 which supply to warehouses located at W_1, W_2, W_3, W_4 and W_5. The monthly capacities are 80, 50 and 90 units respectively and the monthly warehouses requirement are 40, 40, 50, 40 and 80 units respectively. The unit transportation costs in rupees are given as.

Warehouse →

Factory ↑	W_1	W_2	W_3	W_4	W_5
F_1	8	11	9	9	6
F_2	7	10	10	9	8
F_3	11	7	9	9	7

Determine an optimum distribution for the company so as to minimize the total transportation cost.

[**Hint:** Since in the above problem $\sum a_i \neq \sum b_j$. It is an example of an unbalanced transportation problem.

i.e., $\sum a_i = 80 + 50 + 90 = 220$ units

and $\sum b_j = 40 + 40 + 50 + 40 + 80 = 250$ units

So a dummy factory is introduced having all the transportation costs as zero and the availability as (250 – 220) = 30 units.

Thus the following transportation problem can be solved by usual methods.

	W_1	W_2	W_3	W_4	W_5	a_i
F_1	8	11	9	9	6	80
F_2	7	10	10	9	8	50
F_3	11	7	9	9	7	90
	0	0	0	0	0	30
b_j	40	40	50	40	80	

The optimum transportation cost is ₹ 920.]

13. Determine the optimal solution to the following degenerate transportation problem.

	I	II	III	IV	V	a_i
A	6	9	5	10	4	4
B	3	6	9	5	10	7
C	9	4	6	9	9	9
D	6	10	4	6	9	2
b_j	8	3	7	2	2	

14. Consider the following transportation problem.

	I	II	III	IV	a_i
A	6	8	10	15	50
B	15	13	12	10	70
C	16	6	12	15	30
D	11	13	15	10	50
b_j	25	35	105	20	

Test the above problem for optimality.

15. ABC company has three factories which manufactures some scientific instruments. The company markets its product through four different outlets. The quantities to be supplied to each outlet (in hundreds), the production capacity (in hundreds) at each of the factories and the cost of transporting one instrument from each of the factories to each of the outlets is given in the following table.

Out let →

Factory ↓	1	2	3	4	a_i ↓
I	11	9	12	10	14
II	10	13	11	13	27
III	15	12	14	12	14
b_j →	15	19	11	10	

Determine an optimal distribution schedule for the company.

16. Consider a company having two factories. The company is to transport its product from factories to two retail stores. The number of units available at factories A and B are 5 and 25 respectively. Rather than shipping directly from sources to destinations, the firm decides to investigate the possibility of transshipment. The unit transportation costs (in ₹) are given as follows:

		Factories A	Factories B	Retail Stores R_1	Retail Stores R_2
Factories	A	0	2	3	4
	B	2	0	2	4
Retail Stores	R_1	3	2	0	1
	R_2	4	4	1	0

Find the optimal solution of the above problem.

17. Solve the following transportation problem where all the entries are unit costs of a product shipped from 5 origin to 5 different destinations.

	I	II	III	IV	V	a_i
A	74	41	10	80	21	8
B	63	94	97	9	14	7
C	97	66	81	51	66	9
D	58	59	30	13	88	3
E	57	24	88	19	13	5
b_j	6	8	10	4	4	

18. Solve the following transportation problem with prohibited routes.

	A	B	C	D	a_i
I	15	16	17	18	400
II	–	17	18	19	500
III	–	–	16	17	300
IV	–	–	–	18	500
b_j	200	300	500	400	

[**Hint:** Since it is an unbalanced problem, we introduce a dummy requirements as 300 (1700 – 1400) units having all the transportation costs as zero. We then apply the initial basic solution procedure by VAM and find the optimal solution.]

19. Solve the following TP:

	I	II	III	IV	a_i
A	12	13	14	16	6
B	10	16	13	12	1
C	9	28	8	17	2
b_j	7	5	3	2	

20. Solve the following TP:

	1	2	3	4	5	a_i
I	8	6	7	6	10	8
II	9	8	9	6	5	12
III	10	9	8	11	7	14
b_j	4	4	6	8	8	

Answers for Objective Type Questions

1. (*a*) **2.** (*b*) **3.** (*d*) **4.** (*a*) **5.** (*d*)

6. (*b*) **7.** (*a*) **8.** (*a*) **9.** (*b*)

❑❑❑

CHAPTER 5

Assignment Problems

5.1 ASSIGNMENT PROBLEMS

Assignment problem applies to the problems where the objective is to assign a number of jobs (origins) to the equal number of persons (destination) at a minimum cost (or maximum profit).

The assignment problem is a special type of transportation problem. In this assignment problem, the assignment is made on a one-to-one basis, *i.e.*, no two jobs will be assigned to same one person or machine.

If there are n jobs for a factory and the factory has n different machines. So that these jobs may be processed on these machines. A job (i = 1, 2, ..., n) when processed by the machine j (j = 1, 2, ..., n) is assumed that a cost incurred is c_{ij}. The assignment is to be made in such a way that each job can associate with one and only one machine. Then the main aim or the objective is to assign the jobs to the machines so as to minimize the over all cost.

5.2 MATHEMATICAL MODEL OF ASSIGNMENT PROBLEM

Let us define

$$x_{ij} = \begin{cases} 0, \text{ if the } i\text{th job is not assigned to the } j\text{th machine} \\ 1, \text{ if the } i\text{th job is assigned to the } j\text{th machine} \end{cases}$$

Now $\sum_{i=1}^{n} x_{ij} = 1$ and $\sum_{j=1}^{n} x_{ij} = 1$

Since only one job is to be assigned to each machine.

The total assignment cost involved is given by

$$Z = \sum_{j=1}^{n} \sum_{i=1}^{n} C_{ij} \, x_{ij}$$

Thus the mathematical model of assignment problem is as:

$$\text{Minimize } Z = \sum_{j=1}^{n} \sum_{i=1}^{n} C_{ij}\, x_{ij}$$

Subject to constraints

$$\sum_{i=1}^{n} x_{ij} = 1 \qquad j = 1, \ldots, n$$

$$\sum_{j=1}^{n} x_{ij} = 1 \qquad i = 1, \ldots, n$$

with $x_{ij} = 0$ or 1

5.3 SOLUTION OF ASSIGNMENT PROBLEM

We shall apply the Hungarian Method (or Reduced Matrix Method) to solve the assignment problem which involves the following steps:

Step 1: Subtract the minimum element of each row of the given matrix from all the elements of the row. Examine if there is at least one zero in each row and in each column.

If this happens, then stop.

Otherwise subtract the minimum element of each column from all the elements of the column.

Step 2: Examine the rows of the current matrix successively until a row with exactly one unmarked zero is found. Then mark this zero, (*i.e.*, encircle the zero) which indicates that an assignment will be done here later on. Then mark all other zeros (*i.e.*, × cross out) lying in the column of above zero (encircled).

Then the cross out zeros (×) will not be considered for future assignment.

The process is continued until all the rows have been taken into consideration.

Step 3: Examine each column successively until a column with exactly one unmarked zero is found. Then encircle the zero, which indicates that an assignment will be done here later on. Then all other zeros in the column of the above encircled zero is crossed out (×).

The process continues until all the columns have been taken into consideration.

Step 4: The assignment problem is then checked for its optimality. Steps 2 and 3 are done successively till one of the following occurs.

(*a*) There is no row and no column without assignment. It means that an optimal solution has been attained.

(*b*) There may be few rows or columns without an assignment. It means that the current solution is not optimal and proceed to next step.

Step 5: Draw the minimum number of lines crossing all zeros as follows:

(*a*) Mark the notation (✓) to the rows in which assignment has not been made.

(*b*) Mark the notation (✓) to the columns (not already marked) which have zeros in the marked rows.

(*c*) Mark the notation (✓) to the rows (not already marked) which have assignments in marked columns.

(*d*) Repeat the steps 5(*b*) and 5(*c*) until no more marking is possible.

(*e*) Draw horizontal and vertical lines so that it passes through all unmarked rows and unmarked columns. Let the total number of these lines be N and let the order of the matrix be n. Then

(*i*) If $N = n$, then current assignment is optimal.

(*ii*) If $N < n$, then current assignment is not optimal.

Step 6: Examine the elements that do not have a line through them and select the smallest of these elements and subtract the same from all the elements that do not have a line passing through them. Add this smallest element to every element that lies on the intersection of a horizontal and a vertical line.

Then this new matrix so formed will be considered.

Step 7: Go to step 2 and repeat the whole process until an optimal solution is obtained.

Example 1. *Consider the problem of assigning five jobs to five persons. The assignment costs are as follows.*

Jobs ⟶

Persons ↓	1	2	3	4	5
A	9	5	3	7	2
B	1	10	6	6	5
C	4	9	10	3	7
D	5	4	2	1	4
E	10	6	9	10	6

Determine the optimum assignment schedule.

Solution. In the given matrix, from each row, we select the minimum and subtract this cost from all the elements of the respective row.

	1	2	3	4	5	Minimum
A	9	5	3	7	2	2
B	1	10	6	6	5	1
C	4	9	10	3	7	3
D	5	4	2	1	4	1
E	10	6	9	10	6	6

	1	2	3	4	5
A	7	3	1	5	0
B	0	9	5	5	4
C	1	6	7	0	4
D	4	3	1	0	3
E	4	0	3	4	0
Minimum	0	0	1	0	0

Similarly we select the minimum cost from each column and subtract from respective columns.

	1	2	3	4	5
A	7	3	0	5	0
B	0	9	4	5	4
C	1	6	6	0	4
D	4	3	0	0	3
E	4	0	2	4	0

Then we try to draw the minimum possible number of horizontal and vertical lines so as to corner all the zero show in the matrix.

	1	2	3	4	5
A	7	3	0	5	0
B	0	9	4	5	4
C	1	6	6	0	4
D	4	3	0	0	3
E	4	0	2	4	0

Since the number of lines is 5 and is equal to the order of the cost matrix, *i.e.*, 5, an optimum assignment (solution) has been obtained. For determining the optimum assignment, we now consider only the zero elements of the matrix as follows.

	1	2	3	4	5
A			0		0
B	0				
C				0	
D			0	0	
E		0			0

In the above matrix of zeros, Row B and Row C has a single unmarked zero. So we encircle these zeros and cross out (×) all the remaining zeros in the respective columns.

		1	2	3	4	5
	A			0		0
Person	B	(0)				
	C				(0)	
	D			0	~~0~~	
	E		0			0

The crossed out zeros are not considered for future assignment. Then again we examine the rows successively and find that in Row D, a single unmarked zero is there in the third column. Encircle this zero and cross out all zeros in the third column.

	1	2	3	4	5
A			~~0~~		0
B	(0)				
C				(0)	
D			(0)	~~0~~	
E		0			0

Again in Row A, a single unmarked zero is found, this zero is encircled and the remaining zeros in that column (column 5) are crossed out. Then similarly in Row E we can make an assignment.

		1	2	3	4	5
Thus	A			~~0~~		(0)
	B	(0)				
	C				(0)	
	D			(0)	~~0~~	
	E		(0)			~~0~~

Since in the above matrix each row and each column has exactly one encircle zero, an optimal solution has been attained. Thus the optimum assignment schedule will be:

$$A \longrightarrow 5$$
$$B \longrightarrow 1$$
$$C \longrightarrow 4$$
$$D \longrightarrow 3$$
$$E \longrightarrow 2$$

The minimum assignment cost is

$Z = 2 + 1 + 3 + 2 + 6$

$= 14$

5.4 MAXIMIZATION PROBLEM

Sometimes the assignment problem deals with maximization of an objective function. The maximization problem has to be reduced to minimization problem before Hungarian method may be applied. It is done by subtracting from the highest element, all the elements of the matrix.

Example 2. *A drug company XYZ has 5 Medical representative and 5 sales districts. The company estimates that sales of drugs per month (in hundred rupees) for each Medical representative for each salesman in each district is as follows:*

Districts →

Medical Representative ↓	*1*	*2*	*3*	*4*	*5*
A	*52*	*58*	*60*	*48*	*60*
B	*60*	*44*	*48*	*41*	*56*
C	*61*	*47*	*53*	*50*	*57*
D	*42*	*58*	*61*	*56*	*56*
E	*49*	*53*	*60*	*55*	*59*

Find the assignment of medical representative to each districts so as to maximize the sales.

Solution. Since the aim is to maximize the sales, so we have to convert the given maximization problem into a minimization problem by making all the cell values negative in the above given matrix,

because Max Z = –Min (–Z)

Now subtract the minimum element of each column from the elements of that column and also subtract the minimum element of each row from the elements of that row.

	1	2	3	4	5	Minimum
A	52	58	60	48	60	48
B	60	44	48	41	56	41
C	61	47	53	50	57	47
D	42	58	61	56	56	42
E	49	53	60	55	59	49

	1	2	3	4	5
A	4	10	12	0	12
B	19	3	7	0	15
C	14	0	6	3	10
D	0	16	19	14	14
E	0	4	11	6	10
Minimum	0	0	6	0	10

	1	2	3	4	5
A	4	10	6	0	2
B	19	3	1	0	5
C	14	0	0	3	0
D	0	16	13	14	4
E	0	4	5	6	0

	1	2	3	4	5
A	4	10	6	0	2
B	19	3	1	0	5
C	14	0	0	3	0
D	0	16	13	14	4
E	0	4	5	6	0

Now we have draw minimum number of lines (horizontal and vertical) that covers all the zeros of the matrix.

Since the number of lines is less than the order of the matrix

i.e., 4 < 5

So, we select the smallest element in the above matrix, which is not covered by any line.

The element is 1. So subtract 1 from all the elements of the matrix and add to the element that lies in intersection of the lines.

	1	2	3	4	5
A	4	9	5	0	2
B	19	2	0	0	5
C	15	0	0	4	1
D	0	15	12	14	4
E	0	3	4	6	0

Again we draw the minimum number of lines to cover maximum zeros. This time the total number of lives is 5, Which is equal to the order of matrix (*i.e.*, 5 = 5).

So an optimal solution has been attained. To determine the optimum assignment, we consider only the zero elements of the above matrix.

	1	2	3	4	5
A				0	
B			0	0	
C		0	0		
D	0				
E	0				0

Now we choose the rows, that have exactly one zeros in it.

i.e., Row A and Row D

Then we encircle these zeros and cross out other zeros in respective columns *i.e.,* in column 4 and column 1 as follows.

	1	2	3	4	5
A				⓪	
B			0	~~0~~	
C		0	0		
D	⓪				
E	~~0~~				0

Now we proceed with treating single zeros in row and cross out the remaining zeros in that column.

	1	2	3	4	5
A				⓪	
B			⓪	~~0~~	
C		⓪	~~0~~		
D	⓪				
E	~~0~~				⓪

Since each row and each column now contains exactly one zero (encircled one), so the following optimum schedule for assignment is as follows:

$$A \longrightarrow 4$$
$$B \longrightarrow 3$$
$$C \longrightarrow 2$$
$$D \longrightarrow 1$$
$$E \longrightarrow 5$$

Thus the maximum assignment profit is

$Z = 48 + 48 + 47 + 42 + 59$

$= 244$

Example 3. *Solve the following assignment problem.*

	1	2	3	4
A	12	13	14	15
B	14	15	16	17
C	17	18	19	18
D	13	15	18	14

Solution.

	1	2	3	4	Minimum
A	12	13	14	15	12
B	14	15	16	17	14
C	17	18	19	18	17
D	13	15	18	14	13

Subtract the minimum values from their respective rows.

	1	2	3	4
A	0	1	2	3
B	0	1	2	3
C	0	1	2	1
D	0	2	5	1
Minimum	0	1	2	1

Subtract the minimum values from their respective columns.

	1	2	3	4
A	0	0	0	2
B	0	0	0	2
C	0	0	0	0
D	0	1	3	0

Since number of lines is equal to the number of order of matrix, an optimum solution has been attained. So we will now consider only the zeros of the matrix for further calculation of optimum solution.

	1	2	3	4
A	0	0	0	2
B	0	0	0	2
C	0	0	0	0
D	0	1	3	0

In Row D, there are two zeros, so we may choose any arbitrarily zero to select (lets consider cell (D, 1)). Encircle this zero in cell (D,1) and cross out all the remaining zeros in the column 1 and row 4 of the matrix.

	1	2	3	4
A	⊗	0	0	
B	⊗	0	0	
C	⊗	0	0	0
D	⓪			⊗

Now in column 4, only one unmarked zero is there, so we encircle that zero in cell (C, 4) and cross out all the remaining zeros in that row, and similarly we can proceed to reach the optimal solution.

	1	2	3	4
A	⊗	⓪	⊗	
B	⊗	⊗	⓪	
C	⊗	⊗	⊗	⓪
D	⊗			⊗

Thus the optimal solution is

$A \longrightarrow 2$
$B \longrightarrow 3$
$C \longrightarrow 4$
$D \longrightarrow 1$

and the total minimum cost

$$Z = 13 + 16 + 18 + 13$$
$$= ₹\ 60$$

5.5 ALTERNATE OPTIMAL SOLUTIONS

Sometimes while solving the assignment problems, it is possible to have two or more ways to strike off all zero elements in the final reduced matrix for a given problem thus resulting in a tie. In such cases there will be alternate optimal solution, but with the same cost. Alternate optimal solutions offer a great flexibility to the management since it can select the one which is most suitable to its requirement. This can be understood by the following example.

Example 4. *A company wishes to depute its four repairman to 4 different districts A, B, C and D for repairing the machines. The repairman according to their skills provided the following estimated result based on man hours spent while repairing the machines in their particular districts. The man hour for all the repairman are given in the table below.*

Districts →

Repairman ↓	*A*	*B*	*C*	*D*
1	*50*	*30*	*20*	*80*
2	*70*	*90*	*20*	*60*
3	*60*	*40*	*50*	*70*
4	*50*	*70*	*70*	*80*

Find the optimum assignment that will minimize the total man hour needed while repairing the machine.

Solution.

	A	B	C	D
1	50	30	20	80
2	70	90	20	60
3	60	40	50	70
4	50	70	70	80

We select the smallest element from each row and then subtract it from their respective rows.

	A	B	C	D	Minimum
1	30	10	0	60	20
2	50	70	0	40	20
3	20	0	10	30	40
4	0	20	20	30	50

Again we select the minimum element from each column and then subtract it from their respective columns.

	A	B	C	D
1	30	10	0	30
2	50	70	0	10
3	20	0	10	0
4	0	20	20	0
Minimum	0	0	0	30

Now we consider only the zeros for obtaining the optimal assignment.

	A	B	C	D
1			⓪	
2			~~0~~	
3		⓪		0
4	⓪			0

The optimal solution has not been attained, since no zero has been encircled in second and fourth row.

So we draw the minimum number of horizontal and vertical lines.

	A	B	C	D
1	30	10	(0)	30
2	50	70	X	10
3	20	(0)	10	0
4	(0)	20	20	0

No we select the smallest element not covered with the lines. Then we subtract this element from all the elements not covered by the lines and add it to the elements lying at the intersection of the lines. Thus we choose 10, as the smallest element.

	A	B	C	D
1	20	0	0	20
2	40	60	0	0
3	20	0	20	0
4	0	20	30	0

Thus again, we select the zeros for assignment as

	A	B	C	D
1		(0)	X	
2			(0)	X
3		X		(0)
4	(0)			X

Optional Assignment

1 ⟶ B
2 ⟶ C
3 ⟶ D
4 ⟶ 1

Man hours
= 30 + 20 + 70 + 50
= 170 hours

We select first row and encircle the first zero in cell (1, B) and cross out the remaining zeros in that column B.

Proceeding in the similar way we attain the optimal solution as above.

There can be one more alternative optimum assignment as follows.

	A	B	C	D
1		✗	⓪	
2			✗	⓪
3		⓪		✗
4	⓪			✗

Optional Assignment

1 ⟶ C
2 ⟶ D
3 ⟶ B
4 ⟶ A

Man hours

= 20 + 60 + 40 + 50

= 170 hours

If we select the zero in III row or IV row, we can proceed in the usual manner but with different assignments as given above.

In both the cases, the optimal assignment, has the man hours as 170 hours.

5.6 UNBALANCED ASSIGNMENT PROBLEM

The assignment problem solved by Hungarian Method, so far, involved a square matrix (*i.e.*, the number of columns were same as number of rows).

But whenever the matrix of an assignment problem is not a square matrix (*i.e.*, number of rows ≠ number of columns), or in other words, the number of sources is not equal to the number of destinations, then this type of assignment problem is called as unbalanced assignment problem. To solve such types of problems, we add dummy rows and (or) dummy columns in the matrix so that it becomes a square matrix. Then this balanced (square matrix) is solved by Hungarian method as usual.

Example 5. *Solve the following assignment problem.*

	A	*B*	*C*	*D*
1	*11*	*16*	*21*	*17*
2	*9*	*19*	*22*	*21*
3	*11*	*20*	*23*	*20*
4	*12*	*14*	*20*	*21*
5	*12*	*17*	*23*	*18*

Solution. Since in the above problem, the matrix is not a square matrix, so we introduce one dummy column (E) with zero costs as follows:

	A	B	C	D	E
1	11	16	21	17	0
2	9	19	22	21	0
3	11	20	23	20	0
4	12	14	20	21	0
5	12	17	23	18	0

Now applying the Hungarian method, we choose the smallest element in rows and columns and subtract them from their respective rows and columns. Since in all the rows, the minimum is zero, so we search in columns only.

	A	B	C	D	E
1	2	2	1	0	0
2	0	5	2	4	0
3	2	6	3	3	0
4	3	0	0	4	0
5	3	3	3	1	0
Minimum	9	14	20	17	0

Then we draw minimum number of lines to cover all zeros in the above matrix

	A	B	C	D	E
1	2	2	1	0	0
2	0	5	2	4	0
3	2	6	3	3	0
4	3	0	0	4	0
5	3	3	3	1	0

Since number of lines is less than the order of the matrix, we proceed as.

Then we subtract the smallest uncovered element from the matrix and add to the element that lies at the intersection of two lines. Here smallest uncovered element is 1.

	A	B	C	D	E
1	1	1	0	0	0
2	0	5	2	5	1
3	1	5	2	3	0
4	3	0	0	5	0
5	2	2	2	1	0

Again we draw lines to cover the zeros.

Since number of lines < order of matrix. Now smallest uncovered element is 1 and we again subtract it from uncovered element and add to the intersection of the lines.

	A	B	C	D	E
1	1	1	0	0	1
2	0	5	2	5	2
3	0	4	1	2	0
4	3	0	0	5	1
5	1	1	1	0	0

Now we consider only the zeros for optimal assignments as.

	A	B	C	D	E
1			⓪	⊠	
2	⓪				
3	⊠				⓪
4		⓪	⊠		
5				⓪	⊠

Then the optimal assignment is as follows:

$$1 \longrightarrow C$$
$$2 \longrightarrow A$$
$$3 \longrightarrow E$$
$$4 \longrightarrow B$$
$$5 \longrightarrow D$$

The minimum assignment cost is

i.e., Z = 21 + 9 + 0 + 14 + 18

Example 6. *A company XYZ has one deficit truck and one surplus truck in each of the cities 1, 2, 3, 4, 5 and 6 and A, B, C, D and E. The distance between the cities are shown in the following matrix.*

	1	2	3	4	5	6
A	10	8	13	20	16	6
B	8	16	23	13	14	10
C	9	8	1	6	3	7
D	4	12	8	11	11	10
E	6	10	9	5	11	8

Solution. Since in the above matrix number of rows is not equal to number of columns; it is an unbalanced assignment problem and to solve it, we introduced a dummy row.

	1	2	3	4	5	6
A	10	8	13	20	16	6
B	8	16	23	13	14	10
C	9	8	1	6	3	7
D	4	12	8	11	11	10
E	6	10	9	5	11	8
F	0	0	0	0	0	0

Now we select the smallest element in each row and each column and subtract them from their respective rows.

	1	2	3	4	5	6	Minimum
A	4	2	7	14	10	0	6
B	0	8	15	5	6	2	8
C	8	7	0	5	2	6	1
D	0	8	4	7	7	6	4
E	1	5	4	0	6	3	5
F	0	0	0	0	0	0	0

Since after drawing horizontal and vertical lines, we find that the number of lines is less than the order of matrix.

$$i.e., 5 < 6$$

Now choose the smallest element from the uncovered matrix, and subtract the same from the uncovered elements and add it to the elements that lie on the intersections of two lines.

Here minimum element is 2.

	1	2	3	4	5	6
A	4	0	7	14	8	0
B	0	6	15	5	4	2
C	8	5	0	5	0	6
D	0	6	4	7	5	6
E	1	3	4	0	4	3
F	1	0	1	1	0	1

Again number of lines (5) < order of matrix (6).

So again we choose the smallest element from the uncovered elements *i.e.*, 4 and proceed in the same manner as before.

	1	2	3	4	5	6
A	4	0	3	14	4	0
B	0	6	11	5	0	2
C	12	9	0	9	0	10
D	0	6	0	7	1	6
E	1	3	0	0	0	3
F	5	4	1	5	0	5

Smallest element is 2

	1	2	3	4	5	6
A	6	0	5	14	6	0
B	0	4	11	3	0	0
C	12	7	0	7	0	8
D	0	4	0	5	1	4
E	3	3	2	0	2	3
F	5	2	1	3	0	3

Since number of lines is equal to order of matrix, an optimal solution has been attained. Now we consider only zeros for opitmal assignment.

	1	2	3	4	5	6
A		⓪				⊠
B	⊠				⊠	⓪
C			⓪		⊠	
D	⓪		⊠			
E				⓪		
F					⓪	

The optimal patterns is

Then

A ⟶ 2
B ⟶ 6
C ⟶ 3
D ⟶ 1
E ⟶ 4
F ⟶ 5

The minimum distance travelled is

= 8 + 10 + 1 + 4 + 5 + 0

= 28 km.

Example 7. *Five lathes are to be allotted to five operators (one for each). The following table gives weekly output figures (in pieces):*

Weekly output in lathe

		A	*B*	*C*	*D*	*E*
	M	*31*	*33*	*38*	*43*	*47*
	N	*30*	*34*	*40*	*45*	*51*
Operators	*O*	*34*	*39*	*46*	*50*	*45*
	P	*32*	*39*	*42*	*48*	*53*
	Q	*35*	*39*	*42*	*47*	*52*

If the profit per piece is ₹ 40, then find the maximum profit.

Solution. Since the given problem is of maximization. So before solving it convert the above problem into minimization and the largest cost is ₹ 53.

Now we have to minimize

	A	B	C	D	E
M	22	20	15	10	6
N	23	19	13	8	2
O	19	14	7	3	8
P	21	14	11	5	0
Q	18	14	11	6	1

Applying Row operations, we have

16	14	9	4	0
21	17	11	6	0
16	11	4	0	5
21	14	11	5	0
17	13	10	5	0

Now applying column operation, we have

⓪	3	5	4	✗
5	6	7	6	⓪
✗	⓪	✗	✗	5
5	3	7	5	0
1	2	6	5	0

⓪	3	5	4	1
4	5	6	5	⓪
✗	⓪	✗	✗	6
4	2	6	4	✗
✗	1	5	4	✗

⓪	2	4	3	1
4	4	5	4	⓪
1	✗	⓪	✗	7
4	1	5	3	✗
✗	⓪	4	3	✗

⓪	2	4	3	2
3	3	4	3	⓪
1	✗	⓪	✗	8
3	⓪	4	2	✗
✗	✗	4	3	1

⓪	2	2	1	2
3	3	2	1	⓪
3	2	⓪	✗	10
3	⓪	2	⓪	✗
✗	⓪	2	1	1

So, the assignments are

$$M \longrightarrow A$$
$$N \longrightarrow E$$
$$O \longrightarrow C$$
$$P \longrightarrow D$$
$$Q \longrightarrow B$$

with maximum output = 31 + 51 + 46 + 48 + 39
= 215

∴ Maximum Profit = ₹ 215 × 40
= ₹ 8600

5.7 RESTRICTIONS ON ASSIGNMENTS IN ASSIGNMENT PROBLEM

Sometimes there is a restriction imposed that a particular resource (say a man or a machine) cannot be assigned to perform a particular job (say activitiy). The restrictions usually arises due to inefficiency of a worker, or a particular machine should be kept ideal for sometime while processing etc.

To overcome this difficulty, a very high cost (say M or ∞) is considered so as to that this entry (M or ∞) does not appears in the final solution (optimal).

Example 8. *A factory XYZ is to be setup with new machines* M_1, M_2, M_3 *and* M_4. *But because of some space problem, there is a condition that in the available spaces at points A, B, C, D and E,* M_2 *machine and* M_3 *machine cannot be placed at palces C and A respectively. The cost of placing the machines at any of the places among A, B, C, D and E are as follows:*

		Places				
		A	*B*	*C*	*D*	*E*
	M_1	12	14	18	13	14
Machines	M_2	15	12	—	13	12
	M_3	—	14	17	14	10
	M_4	17	11	15	10	11

Find the optimal assignment of the machines.

Solution. Since the problem is an unbalanced assignment problem, we have to introduce one dummy machine M_5 (or row) with a zero cost element. Again there are two restrictions imposed on machine M_2 and Machine M_3, we introduce a very high cost M in the cell (M_2, C) and (M_3, A).

Thus the above problem can now be written along with restrictions and dummy rows as follows.

	A	B	C	D	E
M_1	12	14	18	13	14
M_2	15	12	M	13	12
M_3	M	14	17	14	10
M_4	17	11	15	10	11
M_5	0	0	0	0	0

Now we use Hungarian method to solve the above problem.

	A	B	C	D	E	Minimum	Remark
M_1	0	2	6	1	2	12	M − 12 = M
M_2	3	0	M	1	0	12	and M − 10 = M
M_3	M	4	7	4	0	10	
M_4	7	1	5	0	1	10	
M_5	0	0	0	0	0	0	
Minimum	0	0	0	0	0		

Since number of lines is equal to the order of matrix

i.e., 5 = 5

Now we consider only zeros for optimal assignments.

	A	B	C	D	E
M_1	⓪				
M_2		⓪			✗
M_3					⓪
M_4				⓪	
M_5	✗	✗	⓪	✗	✗

Thus the optimal assignment is

$M_1 \longrightarrow A$
$M_2 \longrightarrow B$
$M_3 \longrightarrow E$
$M_4 \longrightarrow D$
$M_5 \longrightarrow C$

and the total minimum cost in

$z = 12 + 12 + 10 + 10 + 0$

$= ₹\ 44$

Example 9. *A company's salesman travels from city to city to maintain accounts. This week he has to leave his home base and visit each other city and return home. The table shows the distances (in kms)* *between the various cities. The home city is city A. Use the assignment method to determine the tour that will minimize the total distances of visitings all cities and returning home.*

To city ⟶

		I	*II*	*III*	*IV*	*V*
	I	—	255	480	30	70
	II	255	—	180	230	55
From city ↑	*III*	480	180	—	230	380
	IV	30	230	230	—	180
	V	70	55	380	180	—

Solution.

	I	II	III	IV	V
I	∞	245	450	0	40
II	200	∞	125	175	0
III	300	0	∞	50	200
IV	0	200	200	∞	150
V	15	0	325	125	∞

I	II	III	IV	V
∞	245	325	(0)	40
200	∞	(0)	175	~~0~~
300	(0)	∞	50	200
(0)	200	75	∞	150
15	~~0~~	200	125	∞

I	II	III	IV	V
∞	260	325	(0)	40
200	∞	(0)	175	0
285	(0)	∞	35	185
(0)	215	75	∞	135
~~0~~	~~0~~	185	110	∞

I	II	III	IV	V
∞	295	325	(0)	40
235	∞	(0)	175	~~0~~
285	(0)	∞	~~0~~	150
(0)	215	40	∞	100
~~0~~	~~0~~	150	75	∞

I	II	III	IV	V
∞	295	285	(0)	0
275	∞	~~0~~	215	(0)
285	(0)	∞	~~0~~	110
~~0~~	215	~~0~~	∞	60
(0)	~~0~~	110	75	∞

Thus route is : I ⟶ IV ⟶ III ⟶ II ⟶ V ⟶ I

with minimum distance = 30 + 230 + 180 + 55 + 70 = 565 km.

Example 10. *A marketing manager has 5 salesman in 5 cities. Considering the capabilities of the salesman and the nature of, cities, the marketing manager estimates that sales per month (in' 00 ₹) for each salesman in each city would be as follows:*

Sales City ⟶

		I	*II*	*III*	*IV*	*V*
	A	37	43	45	33	45
	B	45	—	33	26	41
Salesman ↓	*C*	46	32	38	—	42
	D	27	43	46	41	41
	E	—	37	45	40	44

What is the maximum sale that may be expected if an optimum assignment is made? In the above question a '—' indicates that the particular salesman is not interested in travelling a particular city.

Solution. Since the given problem is of maximization as well as prohibited. So, convert the given problem into minimization problem. Here the largest element is 46.

	I	II	III	IV	V
A	9	3	1	13	1
B	1	M	13	20	5
C	0	14	8	M	4
D	19	3	0	5	5
E	M	19	1	6	2

Applying row operation, we get

8	2	0	12	0
0	M	12	19	4
0	14	8	M	4
19	3	0	5	5
M	18	0	5	1

Applying column operation, we have

8	(0)	×	7	0
(0)	M	12	14	4
0	12	8	M	4
19	1	(0)	×	5
M	16	×	(0)	1

	I	II	III	IV	V
A	12	(0)	×	7	×
B	(0)	M	8	10	×
C	×	8	4	M	(0)
D	23	1	×	(0)	5
E	M	16	(0)	0	1

Assignments are

A ⟶ II, B ⟶ I, C ⟶ V, D ⟶ IV, E ⟶ III,

(Here an alternative solution exist)

Maximum sale = 43 + 45 + 42 + 41 + 45 = 216

5.8 TRAVELLING SALESMAN PROBLEM

Suppose a salesman has to visit 'm' different cities and wishes to start from any particular city, after visiting each city he returns back to the starting city. In this type of problem, the main objective is to select that sequence in which the cities are visited so that the total travelling time is minimized. If the salesman starts from city 1 (say), then he may have a total of (m – 1)! different sequences (possible trips). Since he has to visit all the 'm' cities, the optimal solution remains independent of selection of the starting city.

This travelling salesman problem is very similar to the assignment problem except that the travelling salesman problem has an additional restrictions. Thus the problem can be solved by satisfying the additional restrictions too. If the solution of the problem does not satisfies the additional restrictions, then after solving the problem by Hungarian method, the enumeration method is used. The following example illustrates the method.

Example 11. *The salesman of a company has to visit five different cities to collect the order of the product. The distance between the cities are given below in the form of the matrix as:*

From↓ \ *To*→	*1*	*2*	*3*	*4*	*5*
1	—	*14*	*26*	*27*	*17*
2	*8*	—	*18*	*20*	*9*
3	*12*	*13*	—	*20*	*14*
4	*16*	*19*	*24*	—	*18*
5	*14*	*15*	*25*	*27*	—

If the salesman starts from city 1 and has to come back to city 1, then which route would you advise him to follow so that the total distance travelled by him is minimized?

Solution. We apply the Hungarian method to solve the above travelling salesman problem (or assignment problem) by applying restriction procedure (*i.e.*, allocating M), on the restricted route.

	1	2	3	4	5	Minimum
1	M	14	26	27	17	14
2	8	M	18	20	9	8
3	12	13	M	20	14	12
4	16	19	24	M	18	16
5	14	15	25	27	M	14

	1	2	3	4	5
1	M	0	12	13	3
2	0	M	10	12	1
3	0	1	M	8	2
4	0	3	8	M	2
5	0	1	11	13	M
Minimum	0	0	8	8	1

	1	2	3	4	5
1	M	0	4	5	2
2	0	M	2	4	0
3	0	1	M	0	1
4	0	3	0	M	1
5	0	1	3	5	M

Now we will draw horizontal and vertical lines to cover the maximum number of zeros.

	1	2	3	4	5
1	M	0	4	5	2
2	0	M	2	4	0
3	0	1	M	0	1
4	0	3	0	M	1
5	0	1	3	5	M

Since number of lines is equal to the order of matrix

i.e., 5 = 5

We have attained the optimal solution.

Now consider only zero for optimal assignment

	1	2	3	4	5
1		⓪			
2	~~0~~				⓪
3	~~0~~			⓪	
4	~~0~~		⓪		
5	⓪				

Thus the optimal assignments are

$$1 \longrightarrow 2$$
$$2 \longrightarrow 5$$
$$3 \longrightarrow 4$$
$$4 \longrightarrow 3$$
$$5 \longrightarrow 1$$

The total minimum distance is Z = 14 + 9 + 20 + 24 + 14 = 81 km.

Since in the above optimal solution so obtained, the route does not provide the best route as the salesman travels from city 1 to city 2, then city 2 to city 5 and from city 5 back to city 1, and without attending the cities 3 and 4.

Thus, we try the next best solution, that satisfies the above condition imposed as well as all the cities are attended. So we choose the next minimum (non zero) element in the matrix is 1. So we now try to solve the problem.

	1	2	3	4	5
1	M	⓪	4	5	2
2	~~0~~	M	②	4	~~0~~
3	~~0~~	1	M	⓪	1
4	~~0~~	3	~~0~~	M	①
5	⓪	1	3	5	M

Now, the next minimum element in the above matrix is 1 (after zero). So we consider 1 and proceed towards the solution. So for this, we start with encircling the element in the cell (4, 5). Thus the optimal solution is

$$1 \longrightarrow 2$$
$$2 \longrightarrow 3$$
$$3 \longrightarrow 4$$
$$4 \longrightarrow 5$$
$$5 \longrightarrow 1$$

The total minimum distance is = 14 + 18 + 20 + 18 + 14 = 84 km.

The alternate solution can also be obtained as

$$1 \longrightarrow 2$$
$$2 \longrightarrow 5$$
$$5 \longrightarrow 3$$
$$3 \longrightarrow 4$$
$$4 \longrightarrow 1$$

and Total minimum distance

= 14 + 9 + 25 + 20 + 16

= 84 km.

Since 81 km is the shortest route but it does not satisfies the given restriction of travelling salesman.

OBJECTIVE TYPE QUESTIONS

1. The assignment problem

(*a*) special case of the transportation problem.

(*b*) can also be solved using simplex method.

(*c*) when treated as a linear programming, always has an optimal integer solution.

(*d*) all of the above.

2. The main drawback in using the methods of transportation problem in solving an assignment problem is that

(*a*) the assignment problem is an unbalanced transportation problem.

(*b*) the assignment problem can never be formulated as a transportation problem.

(*c*) a degeneracy occurs from every improvement in the total cost.
(*d*) none of the above.

3. Which of the following is true about the assignment problem?
(*a*) AP is a set of costs associated with jobs and facility
(*b*) AP contains number of supplies and demands
(*c*) AP may or may not be balanced
(*d*) All of the above.

4. The method used in solving an assignment problem is
(*a*) Hungarian method
(*b*) Reduced Matrix Method
(*c*) Flood's Technique
(*d*) All of the above.

5. The assignment problem can consists of
(*a*) multiple optimal problems
(*b*) maximization type problems
(*c*) restriction type problems
(*d*) All of the above.

6. If the cost matrix of an assignment problem is not a square matrix, then the assignment problem is called as
(*a*) transportation problem
(*b*) degenerate problem
(*c*) unbounded problem
(*d*) unbalanced assignment problem

7. Which of the following are used while moving towards optimality in solving assignment problem?
(*a*) Drawing horizontal lines to cover maximum number of zeros.
(*b*) Drawing vertical lines to cover maximum number of zeros.
(*c*) Encircle the single zero and crossing out the remaining zeros in that row and column.
(*d*) All of the above.

8. The maximal subset of P (set of zero elements in given matrix) provides an optimal assignment when the
(*a*) minimum number of lines to cover all the elements of P is equal to the order of C (cost matrix).
(*b*) maximum number of lines to cover all are elements of P is equal to the order of C (cost matrix).
(*c*) the number of horizontal lines must be equal to the number of vertical lines.
(*d*) None of the above.

9. The main aim of an assignment problem is to find an assignment so that the total cost for performing all jobs is
(*a*) maximized
(*b*) minimized
(*c*) cost is not considered for optimal solution
(*d*) the number of lines should be minimum covering all zeros.

EXERCISES

1. Describe the assignment problem and write its mathematical formulation.
2. Write the mathematical formulation of an assignment problem.
3. Describe using a suitable example, the assignment problem.
4. What is the difference between transportation and assignment problem.
5. Write the Hungarian algorithm used in solving the assignment problem.
6. Explain the concept of assignment, and then assignment problem using suitable example. Also give any two areas of its applications.
7. How can you use linear programming to model an assignment problem?
8. How is an assignment problem with restrictions (or prohibited assignment) be solved.
9. Briefly explain an assignment problem and compare it with transportation problem.
10. Explain the modifications needed in an assignment problem, what the objective is of maximization type.
11. Explain how an assignment problem can be treated as a linear programming problem.
12. Describe any method of solving an assignment problem.
13. Show that the lines drawn in the assignment method pass through all the zeros and have the property that every line passes through one and only one assignment.
14. Show that in any assignment problem, if we multiply each element of the given cost matrix by some fixed constant, then the optimal solution remain unchanged.

UNSOLVED PROBLEMS

1. Solve the following assignment problem.

	1	2	3
A	80	60	40
B	40	50	70
C	70	100	80

[**Ans.** 160 minutes.]

2. Solve the following assignment problem.

	I	II	III	IV
A	6	4	3	9
B	8	10	3	7
C	7	5	6	8
D	6	8	8	9

[**Ans.** 17]

3. Five repairman can repair 5 different machines, and from the past records, the time consumed by each man to repair the machines in hours is known and is given in the following matrix.

Machines

	M_1	M_2	M_3	M_4	M_5
1	12	19	12	17	11
2	16	18	17	16	11
3	14	16	15	13	11
4	14	12	17	13	11
5	15	13	19	15	11

[**Ans.** 63 hours]

4. A truck company who rents each of its truck at five depots A, B, C, D and E. The customer in each of the five towns T_1, T_2, T_3, T_4 and T_5 requires a truck. The distances between the towns and the depots are given in the following matrix.

Depot ⟶

Town ↓	A	B	C	D	E
T_1	150	120	166	180	190
T_2	125	110	120	150	165
T_3	130	100	145	160	175
T_4	40	40	70	70	100
T_5	45	25	60	70	95

Find the optimal assignment of trucks to various customers to find the total distance travelled by 5 trucks. [**Ans.** T_1 – E, T_2 – C, T_3 – B, T_4 – A, T_5 – D.]

5. Solve the following assignment problem.

	A	B	C	D
I	9	17	16	14
II	22	11	21	15
III	20	21	23	18
IV	11	22	20	16

[**Ans.** I ⟶ C, II ⟶ B, III ⟶ D, IV ⟶ A]

6. A companyABC has four salesman and 4 products to sale. The salesman differ in efficiency and products differ with each other. The estimates of the profit (in rupees) each salesman would earn is given in the following matrix. How should the products be sold, by each salesman so as to maximize the total earnings?

	P_1	P_2	P_3	P_4
S_1	15	50	30	15
S_2	35	45	40	35
S_3	25	35	30	30
S_4	25	15	40	25

[**Ans.** ₹ 150]

7. Find the optimal assignment for the given assignment problem with the following cost matrix.

	1	2	3	4
A	9	7	5	12
B	11	13	6	10
C	10	8	9	11
D	9	11	11	10

[**Ans.** A $\longrightarrow$ 3, B $\longrightarrow$ 4, C $\longrightarrow$ 2, D $\longrightarrow$ 1, Min value 8
and A $\longrightarrow$ 2, B $\longrightarrow$ 3, C $\longrightarrow$ 4, D $\longrightarrow$ 1, Min value 8]

8. A company assigns 4 trucks T_2, T_2, T_3 and T_4 to vacant spaces S_1, S_2, S_3, S_4 and S_5 so that the distance travelled is minimized.

	P_1	P_2	P_3	P_4
S_1	65	55	75	35
S_2	45	45	55	45
S_3	75	35	45	35
S_4	45	45	35	45
S_5	25	35	25	45

[**Ans.** Total Minimum distance 130 km]

9. A compnay ABC has to install its machines M_1, M_2, M_3, M_4, M_5 and M_6 at different places *A, B, C, D, E* and *F*. The cost of installing the machines at different places are given in the following matrix.

	A	B	C	D	E	F
M_1	21	24	19	11	17	21
M_2	51	21	18	17	16	12
M_3	61	31	41	56	9	8
M_4	7	8	11	21	26	10
M_5	19	20	29	18	61	71
M_6	10	11	21	31	41	56

Find the optimum assignment and the minimum total cost

[**Ans.** $M_1 \to$ A, $M_2 \to$ F, $M_3 \to$ E, $M_4 \to$ C, $M_5 \to$ A, $M_6 \to$ B, TC = ₹ 71]

10. Find the minimum cost solution for the following assignment problem whose cost coefficents are given in the following matrix

	A	B	C	D	E
I	–2	–4	–8	–6	–1
II	0	–9	–5	–5	–4
III	–3	–8	–9	–2	–6
IV	–4	–3	–1	0	–3
V	–9	–5	–8	–9	–5

[**Ans.** I → C, II → B, III → E, IV → A, V → D, Min TC = –36]

11. A company has five jobs to be done. The following matrix shows the return of assigning *i*th machine (i = 1, 2, ..., 5) to *j*th job (j = 1, 2, ..., 5). Assign the five jobs to the five machines so as to maximize the total expected profit.

	A	B	C	D	E
1	12	18	17	19	11
2	9	11	13	10	12
3	10	19	12	21	13
4	13	21	11	18	14
5	14	16	15	19	12

[**Ans.** TC Min = 78]

Answers for Objective Type Questions

1. (*d*) 2. (*c*) 3. (*d*) 4. (*d*) 5. (*d*)

6. (*d*) 7. (*d*) 8. (*a*) 9. (*b*)

❑❑❑

CHAPTER 6

Dynamic Programming

6.1 INTRODUCTION

Dynamic programming is a mathematical technique dealing with the optimization of multistage decision problems. Dynamic programming was developed by Richard Bellman and G.B. Dantzig in 1950s. In the beginning this technique was termed as stochastic linear programming or linear programming dealing with uncertainty. Dynamic programming can be given a more significant name as recursive optimization. In dynamic programming the term 'dynamic' stands for its usefulness in problems where decisions have to be taken at several distinct stages and 'programming' is used in a mathematical sense of selecting an optimum allocation of resources. In dynamic programming a large problem having n variables is divided into n subproblems (stages), each of which involves one variable. The optimum solution is obtained in an orderly manner starting from one stage to the next and continued till the final stage is reached.

There are two terms stage and state in dynamic programming. Each point in the problem where a decision must be made is known as stage. Each stage has a number of states associated with it. The states are various possible conditions in which the system might find itself at that stage of the problem.

Dynamic programming technique is applicable in solving a wide variety of problems including inventory control, allocations, long-term corporate planning, replacement, etc.

Dynamic programming works on the Bellman's principle of optimality.

6.2 BELLMAN'S PRINCIPLE OF OPTIMALITY

It states that "An optimal policy (set of decisions) has the property that whatever be the initial state and decisions are, the remaining decisions must constitute an optimal policy regardless of the policy adopted in previous stages."

6.3 CHARACTERISTICS OF DYNAMIC PROGRAMMING

The basic features which characterize dynamic programming problem are as follows:

1. The problem can be sub divided into stages with a policy decision required at each stage.
2. Each stage has a number of states associated with it.
3. The effect of the policy decision at each stage is to transform the current state into a state associated with the next stage.
4. The state of the system at a stage is described by a set of variables, called state variables.
5. Remaining decisions constitutes an optimal policy regardless of the policy adopted in previous stage, *i.e.*, given the current stage, an optimal policy for the remaining stages is independent of the policy adopted in previous stage.
6. A recursive equation is formed that connect the optimal solution of the previous stage and the contribution of the current stage, to identify the optimal policy for each state with $(n - 1)$ stages.
7. Using this recursive equation, the solution procedure moves backward stage by stage to get the optimal policy for each state of that stage until the optimal policy for the initial stage.

6.4 FORWARD AND BACKWARD RECURSION

If the computational procedure proceed from stage-1 to stage-n then it is called forward recursion. If the computational procedure proceed from stage-n to stage-1 then it is called backward recursion.

Both the forward and backward recursions gives the same solution. Generally, backward recursion is used, as it is more convenient.

6.5 BASIC STEPS OF DYNAMIC PROGRAMMING

The basic steps for the solution of problem by dynamic programming are as follows:

1. Identify the decision variables and specify the objective function to be optimized.
2. Divide the given problem into a number of sub-problems (stages) and identify the state variables at each stage.
3. Deveolp the recursive equation for computing the optimal policy. Decide whether forward or backward recursion approach is to be used for the solution of the problem.
4. Construct appropriate stages to show the required values of the return function at each stage.
5. Move backward stage by stage to find the overall optimal solution and its value. There may be more than one optimal solution of the problem.

6.6 APPLICATIONS OF DYNAMIC PROGRAMMING

Dynamic programming can be used to solve many real-life problems. Some of the important applications of dynamic programming are as follows:

1. Linear programming problem
2. Inventory control problem
3. Replacement problem
4. Capital budgeting problem
5. Shortest route problem
6. Cargo loading problem
7. Production planning and scheduling
8. Investment analysis
9. Reliability problem

6.7 MODEL–I: SINGLE ADDITIVE CONSTRAINT, MULTIPLICATIVE SEPARABLE RETURN

The general form of the recursive equation to solve this type of problem by dynamic programming can be illustrated by considering following problem.

Suppose we have separable return functions $f_j(x_j)$; $j = 1, 2, ..., n$ and we want to

$$\text{Maximize } Z = f_1(x_1) \cdot f_2(x_2) \ ..., f_n(x_n)$$

$$\text{Subject to} \quad a_1x_1 + a_2x_2 + ... + a_nx_n = b$$

$$x_j, a_j, b \geq 0 \text{ for all } j = 1, 2, ..., n.$$

where j = jth number of stage ($j = 1, 2, ..., n$).

x_j = decision variable at jth stage

Now define state variables $s_1, s_2, ..., s_n$ such that

$$s_n = a_1x_1 + a_2x_2 + ... + a_nx_n = b$$

$$s_{n-1} = a_1x_1 + a_2x_2 + ... + a_{n-1}x_{n-1} = s_n - a_nx_n$$

$$\vdots$$

$$s_{j-1} = s_j - a_jx_j$$

$$\vdots$$

$$s_1 = s_2 - a_2x_2$$

At the nth stage, s_n is expressed as the function of decision variables. Thus the maximum value of Z denoted by $f_n^*(s_n)$ for any feasible value of s_n is given by

$$f_n^*(s_n) = \underset{x_j>0}{\text{Maximum}} \{f_1(x_1) \,.\, f_2(x_2) \ ..., \,.\, f_n(x_n)\}$$

$$\text{Subject to} \quad s_n = b$$

Now keeping a particular value of x_n fixed, the maximum value of Z will be given by

$$f_n(x_n) \cdot \underset{x_j>0}{\text{Max}} \{f_1(x_1) \cdot f_2(x_2) \ ..., f_{n-1}(x_{n-1})\};\ j = 1, 2, ..., n-1$$

$$= f_n(x_n) \cdot f_{n-1}^*(s_{n-1})$$

The maximum value $f_{n-1}{}^*(x_{n-1})$ of Z due to decision variables x_j ($j = 1, 2, ..., n - 1$) depends upon the state variables s_{n-1}. The maximum of Z for any feasible value of all decision variables will be given by

$$f_j^*(s_j) = \underset{x_j>0}{\text{Max}} \{f_j(x_j) \cdot f_{j-1}{}^*(s_{j-1})\};\ j = n, n-1, ..., 2$$

$$f_1^*(s_1) = f_1(x_1)$$

where $$s_{j-1} = f_j(s_j, x_j)$$

The value of $f_j^*(s_j)$ represents the general recursive equation.

Example 1. *Use dynamic programming to solve the following problem.*

$$\textit{Maximize } Z = x_1 \cdot x_2 \cdot x_3$$

$$\textit{Subject to} \quad x_1 + x_2 + x_3 = 20$$

$$x_1, x_2, x_3 \geq 0$$

Solution. Let the state variable s_j ($j = 1, 2, 3$) such that

$$s_3 = x_1 + x_2 + x_3 = 20 \qquad \text{(stage 3)}$$

$$s_2 = s_3 - x_3 = x_1 + x_2 \qquad \text{(stage 2)}$$

$$s_1 = s_2 - x_2 = x_1 \qquad \text{(stage 1)}$$

The maximum value of Z for any feasible value of state variable is given by

$$f_3(s_3) = \underset{x_3}{\text{Max}} \{x_3 \cdot f_2(s_2)\}$$

$$f_2(s_2) = \underset{x_2}{\text{Max}} \{x_2 \cdot f_1(s_1)\}$$

$$f_1(s_1) = x_1 = s_2 - x_2$$

Thus $$f_2(s_2) = \underset{x_2}{\text{Max}} \{x_2 \cdot (s_2 - x_2)\}$$

$$= \text{Max} \{x_2 s_2 - x_2^2\}$$

Now differentiating $f_2(s_2)$ with respect to x_2 and then equating to zero (using the condition for maxima or minimia of a function), we have

$$s_2 - 2x_2 = 0 \text{ or } x_2 = \frac{s_2}{2}$$

Now, $$f_2(s_2) = \left(\frac{s_2}{2}\right) \cdot s_2 - \left(\frac{s_2}{2}\right)^2 = \frac{s_2^2}{4}$$

and $$f_3(s_3) = \underset{x_3}{\text{Max}} \{x_3 \cdot f_2(s_2)\}$$

$$= \underset{x_3}{\text{Max}} \left\{x_3 \cdot \left(\frac{s_2^2}{4}\right)\right\}$$

$$= \text{Max} \left\{x_3 \cdot \frac{(s_3 - x_3)^2}{4}\right\}$$

Now differentiating $f_3(s_3)$ with respect to x_3 and equating to zero, we have

$$\frac{1}{4}\left\{x_3 \cdot 2(s_3 - x_3)(-1) + (s_3 - x_3)^2 \cdot 1\right\} = 0$$

$$(s_3 - x_3)(-2x_3 + s_3 - x_3) = 0$$

$$(s_3 - x_3)(s_3 - 3x_3) = 0$$

Now either $x_3 = s_3$ which is trivial as $x_1 + x_2 + x_3 = s_3$

or $s_3 - 3x_3 = 0$ or $x_3 = \frac{s_3}{3} = \frac{20}{3}$.

Therefore, $x_2 = \frac{s_2}{2} = \frac{s_3 - x_3}{2} = \frac{1}{2}\left(20 - \frac{20}{3}\right) = \frac{20}{3}$

$$x_1 = s_2 - x_2 = \frac{40}{3} - \frac{20}{3} = \frac{20}{3}$$

So, $x_1 = x_2 = x_3 = \frac{20}{3}$ and Max. $Z = \left(\frac{20}{3}\right)^3 = \frac{8000}{27}$ **Ans.**

6.8 MODEL–II: SINGLE ADDITIVE CONSTRAINT, ADDITIVE SEPARABLE RETURN

The general form of the recursive equation to solve this type of problem by dynamic programming can be illustrated by considering following problem:

Suppose we want to

$$\text{Minimize } Z = f_1(x_1) + f_2(x_2) + \ldots + f_n(x_n)$$

$$\text{Subject to } a_1x_1 + a_2x_2 + \ldots + a_nx_n \geq b$$

$$x_j, a, b \geq 0 \text{ for all } j = 1, 2, \ldots, n$$

Where j = jth number of stage ($j = 1, 2, \ldots, n$).

x_j = decision variable at jth stage.

Now define state variables $s_1, s_2, \ldots, s_n$ such that

$$s_n = a_1x_1 + a_2x_2 + \ldots + a_nx_n \geq b$$

$$s_{n-1} = a_1x_1 + a_2x_2 + \ldots + a_{n-1}x_{n-1} = s_n - a_nx_n$$

$$\vdots$$

$$s_{j-1} = s_j - a_jx_j$$

$$\vdots$$

$$s_1 = s_2 - a_2x_2$$

At the nth stage, s_n is expressed as the function of decision variables. Thus the minimum value of Z denoted by $f_n^*(s_n)$ for any feasible value of s_n is given by

$$f_n^*(s_n) = \underset{x_j > 0}{\text{Minimize}} \sum_{j=1}^{n} f_j(x_j)$$

subject to $s_n \geq b$

Now keeping a particular value of x_n fixed, the minimum value of Z will be given by

$$f_n(x_n) + \underset{x_j>1}{\text{Min}} \sum_{j=1}^{n-1} f_j(x_j) = f_n(x_n) + f_{n-1}^*(s_{n-1})$$

The minimum value $f_{n-1}^*(x_{n-1})$ of Z due to decision variables x_j ($j = 1, 2, ..., n - 1$) depends upon the state variables s_{n-1}. The minimum value of Z for any feasible value of all decision variables will be given by

$$f_j^*(s_j) = \underset{x_j>0}{\text{Min}} \{f_j(x_j) + f_{j-1}^*(s_{j-1})\};\ j = n, n-1, ..., 2$$

$$f_1^*(s_1) = f_1(x_1)$$

where $\quad s_{j-1} = t_j(s_j, x_j)$

The value of $f_j^*(s_j)$ represents the general recursive equation.

Example 2. *Use dynamic programming to solve the following problem:*

$$\textit{Minimize } Z = x_1^2 + x_2^2 + x_3^2$$

$$\textit{Subject to} \quad x_1 + x_2 + x_3 = 20$$

$$x_1, x_2, x_j \geq 0$$

Solution. Let the state variables s_j ($j = 1, 2, 3$) such that

$$s_3 = x_1 + x_2 + x_3 = 20 \qquad \text{(stage 3)}$$

$$s_2 = s_3 - x_3 = x_1 + x_2 \qquad \text{(stage 2)}$$

$$s_1 = s_2 - x_2 = x_1 \qquad \text{(stage 1)}$$

The minimum value of Z for any feasible value of state variable is given by

$$f_3(s_3) = \underset{x_3}{\text{Min}} \{x_3^2 + f_2(s_2)\}$$

$$f_2(s_2) = \underset{x_2}{\text{Min}} \{x_2^2 + f_1(s_1)\}$$

$$f_1(s_1) = \underset{x_1}{\text{Min}} \{x_1^2\} = x_1^2 = (s_2 - x_2)^2$$

Thus, $\quad f_2(s_2) = \underset{x_2}{\text{Min}} \{x_2^2 + (s_2 - x_2^2)\}$

Now differentiating $f_2(s_2)$ with respect to x_2 and then equating to zero (using the condition for maxima or minima of a function), we have

$$2x_2 + 2(s_2 - x_2)(-1) = 0 \text{ or } x_2 = \frac{s_2}{2}$$

Now, $\quad f_2(s_2) = \left(\frac{s_2}{2}\right)^2 + \left(s_2 - \frac{s_2}{2}\right)^2 = \frac{s_2^2}{2}$

and $\quad f_3(s_3) = \underset{x_3}{\text{Min}} \{x_3^2 + f_2(s_2)\}$

$$= \underset{x_3}{\text{Min}} \left\{x_3^2 + \frac{s_2^2}{2}\right\}$$

$$= \underset{x_3}{\text{Min}} \left\{x_3^2 + \frac{(s_3 - x_3)^2}{2}\right\}$$

Now differentiating $f_3(s_3)$ with respect to x_3 and equating to zero, we have

$$2x_3 + \frac{2(s_3 - x_3)}{2}(-1) = 0 \text{ or } x_3 = \frac{s_3}{3}$$

Thus,
$$f_3(s_3) = \left(\frac{s_3}{3}\right)^2 + \frac{1}{2}\left(s_3 - \frac{s_3}{3}\right)^2 = \frac{s_3^{\,2}}{3}$$

$$f_3(s_3) = \frac{(20)^3}{3} = \frac{400}{3} \qquad (\because s_3 = 20)$$

$$x_3 = \frac{s_3}{3} = \frac{20}{3}$$

$$x_2 = \frac{s_2}{2} = \frac{(s_3 - x_3)}{2} = \frac{\left(20 - \frac{20}{3}\right)}{2} = \frac{20}{3}$$

$$x_1 = s_2 - x_2 = \frac{40}{3} - \frac{20}{3} = \frac{20}{3}$$

So $x_1 = x_2 = x_3 = \dfrac{20}{3}$ and Minimize $Z = \dfrac{(20)^2}{3} = \dfrac{400}{3}$ **Ans.**

6.9 MODEL–III: SINGLE MULTIPLICATIVE CONSTRAINT, ADDITIVELY SEPARABLE RETURN

The general form of the recursive equation to solve this type of problem by dynamic programming can be illustrated by considering following problem:

Suppose we want to

$$\text{Minimize } Z = f_1(x_1) + f_2(x_2) + \ldots + f_n(x_n)$$

$$\text{Subject to, } \quad x_1 \cdot x_2 \ldots . x_n \geq b$$

$$x_j, b \geq 0 \text{ for all } j = 1, 2, \ldots, n$$

where j = jth number of stage ($j = 1, 2, \ldots, n$)

x_j = decision variable at jth stage

Now define state variables $s_1, s_2, \ldots, s_n$ such that

$$s_n = x_n \cdot x_{n-1} \ldots x_2 \cdot x_1 \geq b$$

$$s_{n-1} = x_{n-1} \cdot x_{n-2} \ldots x_2 \cdot x_1 = \frac{s_n}{x_n}$$

$$\vdots$$

$$s_{j-1} = \frac{s_j}{x_j}; j = 2, 3, \ldots, n$$

The minimum value of Z denoted by $f_n^*(s_n)$ for any feasible value of s_n is given by

$$f_n^*(s_n) = \min_{x_j > 0} \sum_{j=1}^{n} f_j(x_j)$$

Subject to $\quad s_n \geq b$

The minimum value $f_{n-1}^*(x_{n-1})$ of Z due to decision variables x_j ($j = 1, 2, ..., n - 1$) depends upon the state variables s_{n-1}. The minimum of Z for any feasible value of all decision variables will be given by

$$f_j^*(s_j) = \underset{x_j > 0}{\text{Min}} \{f_j(x_j) + f_{j-1}^*(s_{j-1})\}; \quad (j = 2, 3, ..., n)$$

$$f_1^*(s_1) = f_1(x_1)$$

where $\quad s_{j-1} = t_j(s_j, x_j)$

The value of $f_j^*(s_j)$ represents the general recursive equation.

Example 3. *Use dynamic programming to solve the following problem:*

$$\textit{Minimize } Z = x_1^2 + x_2^2 + ... + x_n^2$$

$$\textit{Subject to} \quad x_1 \cdot x_2 \dots x_n = C$$

$$x_j \geq 0;\ j = 1, 2, ..., n$$

Solution. Let $f_n(c)$ be the minimum attainable sum of $x_1^2 + x_2^2 + ... + x_n^2$ when c is divided into n factors.

For $n = 1$, we have $x_1 = c$

So $\quad f_1(c) = \underset{x_1 = c}{\text{Min}} \{x_1^2\} = c^2.$

For $n = 2$, Let $x_1 = y$ and $x_2 = \dfrac{c}{x_1} = \dfrac{c}{y}$, then

$$f_2(c) = \underset{0 \leq y \leq c}{\text{Min}} \{x_1^2 + x_2^2\}$$

$$= \underset{0 \leq y \leq c}{\text{Min}} \left\{y^2 + \left(\frac{c}{y}\right)^2\right\}$$

$$= \underset{0 \leq y \leq c}{\text{Min}} \left\{y^2 + f_1\left(\frac{c}{y}\right)\right\} \qquad \left(\because f_1(c) = c^2, \text{ so } f_1\left(\frac{c}{y}\right) = \left(\frac{c}{y}\right)^2\right)$$

For $n = 3$, Let $x_1 = y$ and $x_2 \cdot x_3 = \dfrac{c}{y}$, then

$$f_3(c) = \underset{0 \leq y \leq c}{\text{Min}} \{x_1^2 + x_2^2 + x_3^2\}$$

$$= \underset{0 \leq y \leq c}{\text{Min}} \left\{y^2 + f_2\left(\frac{c}{y}\right)\right\}$$

Proceeding in the same way, we have

$$f_n(c) = \underset{0 \leq y \leq c}{\text{Min}} \left\{y^2 + f_{n-1}\left(\frac{c}{y}\right)\right\}$$

Now, the solution to the recursive equation to get the optimal policy can be obtained by using the principle of maxima and minima of function.

Let $$f(y) = y^2 + \left(\frac{c}{y}\right)^2$$

$$\frac{df}{dy} = 2y - \frac{2c^2}{y^2} = 0 \qquad y = (c)^{1/2}$$

Therefore, $$x_1 = (c)^{1/2} \text{ and } x_2 = \frac{c}{y} = \frac{c}{c^{1/2}} = (c)^{1/2}$$

Since the second derivative of $f(y)$ with respect to y is positive, so $f(y)$ minimum. Also

$$f_2(c) = \underset{0 \le y \le c}{\text{Min}} \left\{ y^2 + \left(\frac{c}{y}\right)^2 \right\}$$

$$= \left(c^{1/2}\right)^2 + \left(\frac{c}{c^{1/2}}\right)^2 = 2c$$

Thus, $$f_2(c/y) = 2(c/y)$$

Hence, the optimal policy is $(c^{1/2}, c^{1/2})$ and $f_2(c) = 2c$.

Again,

$$f_3(c) = \underset{0 \le y \le c}{\text{Min}} \left\{ y^2 + f_2\left(\frac{c}{y}\right) \right\}$$

$$= \underset{0 \le y \le c}{\text{Min}} \left\{ y^2 + 2\left(\frac{c}{y}\right) \right\}$$

$$= \left(c^{1/3}\right)^2 + 2\left(\frac{c}{c^{1/3}}\right)^2 = 3c^{2/3}$$

Since minimum of $f(y) = y^2 + \dfrac{c}{y}$ is attained at $y = c^{1/3}$.

Hence the optimal policy is $(c^{1/3}, c^{1/3}, c^{1/3})$ and $f_3(c) = 3c^{2/3}$

Now, on continuing in the same manner, we can get the optimal policy for an n stage problem as

$(c^{1/n}, c^{1/n}, ..., c^{1/n})$ and $f_n(c) = nc^{2/n}$.

6.10 MODEL–IV SHORTEST ROUTE PROBLEM

Example 4. *Consider the following diagram where circles denote cities, and lines between two such circles represent highways connecting the cities. The numbers inside the circles represents city numbers and those given beside the lines denote the distance between the cities connected by the lines. Suppose a salesman start from city 1 and would like to go to city 10. What is the shortest route from city 1 to city 10 and what is the minimum distance?*

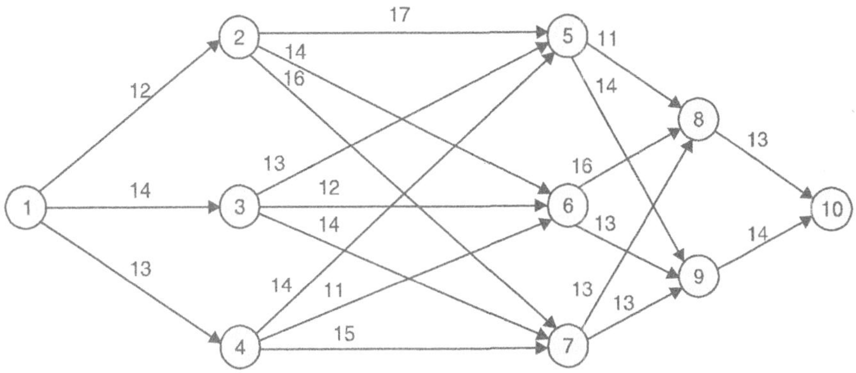

Solution. The given problem is 5 stage problem as:

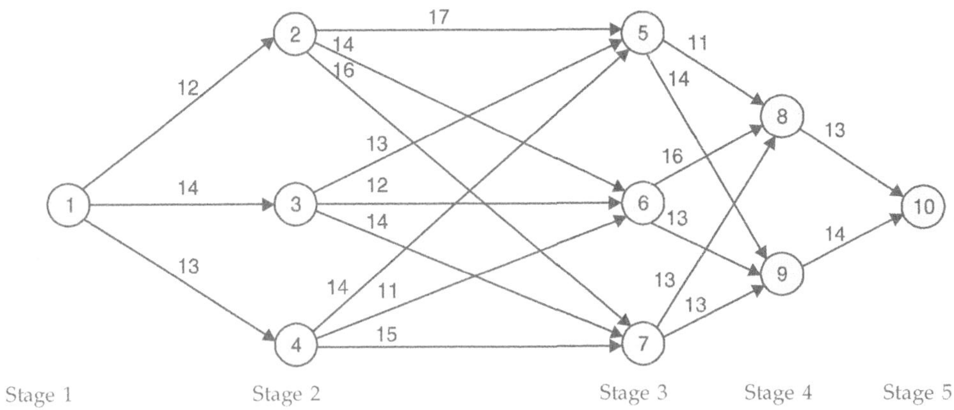

The backward recursive equation for the problem is:

$$f_i(x_i) = \underset{\substack{\text{all feasible} \\ \text{routes } (x_i, x_{i+1})}}{\text{Min}} \{d(x_i, x_{i+1}) + f_{i+1}(x_{i+1})\}; \quad i = 1, 2, 3, 4$$

where x_i = the state of the system at stage i

$f_i(x_i)$ = the shortest distance to node x_i at stage i

Here, $f_5(x_5) = 0$ for $x_5 = 10$. The associated order of computations is $f_4 \longrightarrow f_3 \longrightarrow f_2 \longrightarrow f_1$.

Stage 4. Because node 10 ($x_5 = 10$) is connected to nodes 8 and 9 ($x_4 = 8$ and 9) with exactly one route each, there are no alternatives to choose from and stage 4 results can be represented as

	$d(x_4, x_5)$	*Optimum solution*	
x_4	$x_5 = 10$	$f_4(x_4)$	x_5^*
8	13	13	10
9	14	14	10

Stage 3. Here, we have two alternatives each from nodes 5, 6 and 7 respectively. Given $f_4(x_4)$ from stage 4. Now stage 3 result can be represented as

	$d(x_3, x_4) + f_4(x_4)$		Optimum solution	
x_3	$x_4 = 8$	$x_4 = 9$	$f_3(x_3)$	x_4^*
5	11 + 13 = 24	14 + 14 = 28	24	8
6	16 + 13 = 29	13 + 14 = 27	27	9
7	13 + 13 = 26	13 + 14 = 27	26	8

Stage 2. Here, we have three alternatives each from nodes 2, 3 and 4 respectively. Given $f_3(x_3)$ from stage 3. Now stage 2 result can be represented as

	$d(x_2, x_3) + f_3(x_3)$			Optimum solution	
x_2	$x_3 = 5$	$x_3 = 6$	$x_3 = 7$	$f_2(x_2)$	x_3^*
2	17 + 24 = 41	14 + 27 = 41	16 + 26 = 42	41	5 or 6
3	13 + 24 = 37	12 + 27 = 39	14 + 26 = 40	37	5
4	14 + 24 = 38	11 + 27 = 38	15 + 26 = 41	38	5 or 6

Stage 1. Here, we have three alternatives from node 1. Given $f_2(x_2)$ from stage 2. Now stage 1 result can be represented as

	$d(x_1, x_2) + f_2(x_2)$			Optimum solution	
x_1	$x_2 = 2$	$x_2 = 3$	$x_2 = 4$	$f_1(x_1)$	x_2^*
1	12 + 41 = 53	14 + 37 = 51	13 + 38 = 51	51	3 or 4

The optimum solution of the problem, using optimum solutions of stage 1, stage 2, stage 3 and stage 4 is

$1 \to 3 \to 5 \to 8 \to 10$ or $1 \to 4 \to 5 \to 8 \to 10$ or $1 \to 4 \to 6 \to 9 \to 10$ and the minimum distance = 51 units

6.11 SOLUTION OF SOME OTHER PROBLEMS BY USING DYNAMIC PROGRAMMING

Example 5. (Cargo Loading Problem) *A 40 ton vessel is to be loaded with one or more of three items. The following table gives the unit weight w_i (in tonnes) and the unit revenue r_i (in thousands of ₹) for items i.*

Item (*i*)	w_i	r_i
1	20	31
2	30	47
3	10	14

How should the vessel be loaded to maximize the total return?

Solution. First, we formulate the problem as:

$$\text{Maximize } Z = 31y_1 + 47y_2 + 14y_3$$
$$\text{Subject to } 20y_1 + 30y_2 + 10y_3 \le 40$$
$$y_1, y_2, y_3 \ge 0 \text{ and integer}$$

Now, the backward recursive equation for the optimization is

$$f_i(x_i) = \underset{\substack{y_i = 0, 10, \ldots, \left[\frac{W}{w_i}\right] \\ x_i = 0, 10, \ldots, W}}{Max} \{r_i y_i + f_{i+1}(x_i + 1)\};\ i = 1, 2, 3$$

where $f_{n+1} \cdot (x_{n+1}) = 0$, $x_{i+1} = x_i - w_i y_i$ and W = capacity of the vessel

There are 3 stages in the given problem.

Stage 3. The weight to be allocated in stage 3 must take one of the values 0, 10, ..., 40 ($\because$ W = 40 tonnes).

The maximum number of units of item 3 that can be loaded is $\left[\frac{40}{10}\right] = 4$, which means the possible values of y_3 are 0, 1, 2, 3 and 4. An alternative y_3 is feasible only if $w_3 y_3 \le x_3$. Thus, all the infeasible alternatives (those for which $w_3 y_3 > x_3$) are excluded. So,

$$f_3(x_3) = \underset{y_3}{\text{Max}} \{14 y_3\};\ \text{maximum } y_3 = \left[\frac{40}{10}\right] = 4$$

The stage 3 result can be represented as

x_3	$14y_3$					*Optimum solution*	
	$y_3 = 0$	$y_3 = 1$	$y_3 = 2$	$y_3 = 3$	$y_3 = 4$	$f_3(x_3)$	y_3^*
0	0	—	—	—	—	0	0
10	0	14	—	—	—	14	1
20	0	14	28	—	—	28	2
30	0	14	28	42	—	42	3
40	0	14	28	42	56	56	4

Stage 2. Here,

$$f_2(x_2) = \underset{y_2}{\text{Max}} \left\{47y_2 + f_3(x_2 - 30y_2)\right\};\ \text{maximum } y_2 = \left[\frac{40}{30}\right] = 1$$

The stage 2 result can be represented as

x_2	$47y_2 + f_3(x_2 - 30y_2)$		*Optimum solution*	
	$y_2 = 0$	$y_2 = 1$	$f_2(x_2)$	y_2^*
0	0 + 0 = 0	—	0	0
10	0 + 14 = 14	—	14	0
20	0 + 28 = 28	—	28	0
30	0 + 42 = 42	47 + 0 = 47	47	1
40	0 + 56 = 56	47 + 14 = 61	61	1

Stage 1. Here,

$$f_1(x_1) = \underset{y_1}{\text{Max}} \{31y_1 + f_2(x_1 - 20y_1)\}; \text{ maximum } y_1 = \left[\frac{40}{20}\right] = 2$$

The stage 1 result can be represented as

	$31y_1 + f_2(x_1 - 20y_1)$			Optimum solution	
x_1	$y_1 = 0$	$y_1 = 1$	$y_1 = 2$	$f_1(x_1)$	y_1^*
0	0 + 0 = 0	—	—	0	0
10	0 + 14 = 14	—	—	14	0
20	0 + 28 = 28	31 + 0 = 31	—	31	1
30	0 + 47 = 47	31 + 14 = 45	—	47	0
40	0 + 61 = 61	31 + 28 = 59	62 + 0 = 62	62	2

The optimum solution is now determined as follows:

Given $W = 40$ tonnes, from stage 1 table $x_1 = 40$ gives the optimum alternative $y_1^* = 2$, which means that 2 units of item 1 will be loaded on the vessel. This allocation leaves $x_2 = x_1 - 20y_1^* = 40 - 20 \times 2 = 0$, from stage 2 table $x_2 = 0$ gives the optimum alternative $y_2^* = 0$. This allocation leaves $x_3 = x_2 - 30y_2 = 0 - 30 \times 0 = 0$, from stage 3 table $x_3 = 0$ gives the optimum alternative $y_3^* = 0$.

Thus, the optimum solution of the problem is

$y_1 = 2$, $y_2 = 0$, $y_3 = 0$ and maximum return is ₹ 62,000.

Example 6. (Inventory control) *A man is engaged in buying and selling identical items. He operates from a warehouse that can hold 500 items. Each month he can sell any quantity that he chooses upto the stock at the beginning of the month. Each month he can buy as much as he wishes for delivery at the end of the month so as his stock does not exceed 500 items. For the next four months, he has the following error free forecasts of cost, sales prices:*

Month	*(i)*	1	2	3	4
Cost	(c_i)	27	24	26	28
Sales price	(p_i)	28	25	25	27

If he currently has a stock of 200 units, what quantities should he sell and buy in the next four months? Find the solution using dynamic programming.

Solution. Let x_i = amount of sell during the month i

y_i = amount of ordered during the month i

b_i = stock level at the beginning of the month i

Let $f_n(b)$ be the maximum possible return when there are n months left with the initial stock level b at the beginning of this month.

Here, we use the backward recursive approach. The problem can be solved in four stages as follows:

Stage 4. Let us be in the 4th month starting with the stock level $b = b_4$ at the beginning of this month.

So, $$f_1(b_4) = \underset{x_4,\, y_4}{\text{Max}} \{p_4x_4 - c_4y_2\}$$

where $0 \le x_4 \le b_4$, $y_4 \ge 0$ and $b_4 - x_4 + y_4 \le 0$

or $$f_1(b_4) = \underset{\substack{0 \le x_4 \le b_4 \\ 0 \le y_4 \le x_4 - b_4}}{\text{Max}} \{27x_4 - 28y_4\}$$

It is obvious that Max $(27x_2 - 28y_4)$ occurs at $x_4 = b_4$, $y_4 = 0$

$\therefore$ $$f_1(b_4) = 27b_4 - 28 \times 0 = 27b_4$$

$\therefore$ Optimal decisions are $x_4 = b_4$, $y_4 = 0$ and $f_1(b_4) = 27b_4$ ...(1)

Stage 3. Let us be in the 3rd month, *i.e.*, two months are left with the initial stock b_3 at the beginning of this month. Since stock $b_4 = b_3 - x_3 + y_3$ will remain available at the beginning of next month.

So $$f_2(b_3) = \underset{x_3,\, y_3}{\text{Max}} \{p_3x_3 - c_3y_3 + f_1(b_3 - y_3 + y_3)\}$$

where $0 \le x_3 \le b_3$, $y_3 \ge 0$ and $b_3 - x_3 + y_3 \le 500$

or $$f_2(b_3) = \underset{\substack{0 \le x_3 \le b_3 \\ 0 \le y_3 \le 500 - b_3 - x_3}}{\text{Max}} \{25x_3 - 26y_3 + 27(b_3 - x_3 + y_3)\} \quad \text{[from (}i\text{)]}$$

$$= \underset{\substack{0 \le x_3 \le b_3 \\ 0 \le y_3 \le 500 - b_3 + x_3}}{\text{Max}} \{27b_3 - 2x_3 + y_3\}$$

$$f_2(b_3) = \underset{0 \le x_3 \le b_3}{\text{Max}} \{27b_3 - 2x_3 + (500 - b_3 + x_3)\}$$

$$= \underset{0 \le x_3 \le b_3}{\text{Max}} \{26b_3 - x_3 + 500\}$$

which occurs at $x_3 = 0$.

$\therefore$ Optimal decisions are $x_3 = 0$, $y_3 = 500 - b_3 + x_3 = 500 - b_3$ and $f_2(b_3) = 26b_3 + 500$ ...(2)

Stage 2. Let us be in the 2nd month, *i.e.*, 3 months are left with the initial stock level b_2 at the beginning of this month. Since stock $b_3 = b_2 - x_2 + y_2$ will remain available at the beginning of the next month.

So, $$f_3(b_2) = \underset{x_2,\, y_2}{\text{Max}} \{p_2x_2 - c_2y_2 + f_2(b_2 - x_2 + y_2)\}$$

where $0 \le x_2 \le b_2$, $y_2 \ge 0$ and $b_2 - x_2 + y_2 \le 500$

or $$f_3(b_2) = \underset{\substack{0 \le x_2 \le b_2 \\ 0 \le y_2 \le 500 - b_2 + x_2}}{\text{Max}} \{25x_2 - 24y_2 + 26(b_2 - x_3 + y_2) + 500\} \text{ [from (2)]}$$

$$= \underset{\substack{0 \le x_2 \le b_2 \\ 0 \le y_2 \le 500 - b_2 + x_2}}{\text{Max}} \{-x_2 + 2y_2 + 26b_2 + 500\}$$

$$= \underset{0 \le x_2 \le b_2}{\text{Max}} \{-x_2 + 2(500 - b_2 + x_2) + 26b_2 + 500\}$$

$$= \underset{0 \le x_2 \le b_2}{\text{Max}} \{24b_2 + x_2 + 1500\}$$

which occurs at $x_2 = b_2$.

$\therefore$ Optimal decisions are $x_2 = b_2, y_2 = 500 - b_2 + x_2 = 500$

and $f_3(b_2) = 24b_2 + b_2 + 1500 = 25b_2 + 1500$ ...(3)

Stage 1. Let us be in the 1st month, *i.e.*, 4 months are left with the initial stock level b_1 at the beginning of this month. Since stock $b_2 = b_1 - x_1 + y_1$ will remain available at the beginning of the next month.

So. $$f_4(b_1) = \max_{x_1, y_1} \{p_1 x_1 - c_1 y_1 + f_3(b_1 - x_1 + y_1)\}$$

where $0 \le x_1 \le b_1, y_1 \ge 0$ and $b_1 - x_1 + y_1 \le 500$

or $$f_4(b_1) = \max_{\substack{0 \le x_1 \le b_1 \\ 0 \le y_1 \le 500 - b_1 + x_1}} \{28x_1 - 27y_1 + 25(b_1 - x_1 + y_1) + 1500\}$$

$$= \max_{0 \le x_1 \le b_1} \{3x_1 - 2y_1 + 25b_1 + 1500\}$$

which occurs at $x_1 = b_1, y_1 = 0$.

$\therefore$ Optimal decisions are $x_1 = b_1, y_1 = 0$ and $f_4(b_1) = 28b_1 + 1500$ ...(4)

But the stock at the beginning of 1st month is 200 units.

$\therefore$ $b_1 = 200$, so that $x_1 = 200$ $y_1 = 0$

$b_2 = b_1 - x_1 + y_1 = 200 - 200 + 0 = 0, x_2 = b_2 = 0, y_2 = 500$

$b_3 = b_2 - x_2 + y_2 = 0 - 0 + 500 = 500, x_3 = 0, y_3 = 500 - b_3 = 0$

$b_4 = b_3 - x_3 + y_3 = 500 - 0 + 0 = 500, x_4 = b_4 = 500, y_4 = 0$

Hence, the optimal solution for 4 years is

Month	(i)	1	2	3	4
Purchase	(y_i)	0	500	0	0
Sale	(x_i)	200	0	0	500

and maximum profit $= f_4(b_1) = 28 \times 200 + 1500 =$ ₹ 7100.

Example 7. (Reliability Problem) *Consider the problem of designing an electronic device consisting of three main components. The three components are arranged in series so that the failure of one of the components will result in the failure of the whole device. Therefore, it is decided that reliability of the device can be increased by installing parallel units on each component. Each component may be installed at most three parallel units. The total capital (in thousand ₹) available for the device is 10. Following data is available.*

Solution.

	$i = 1$		$i = 2$		$i = 3$	
m_i	r_1	c_1	r_2	c_2	r_3	c_3
1	0.5	2	0.7	3	0.6	1
2	0.7	4	0.8	5	0.8	2
3	0.9	5	0.9	6	0.9	3

Here, m_i is the number of parallel units placed with the ith component, r_i is the reliability of the component and c_i is the cost for the ith component. Determine m_i which will maximize the total reliability of the system without exceeding the given capital.

Solution. Let R be the total reliability of a system of n components arranged in series and m parallel units per component i (i = 1, 2, 3). Thus, the problem is

$$\text{Maximize } R = r_1 r_2 r_3$$

$$\text{Subject to } c_1 + c_2 + c_3 \le c$$

where c = total capital available

Let x_i = the capital allocated to states i (i = 1, 2, 3)

$x_i(c_i)$ = reliability r_i is a function of c_i

$f_i(x_i)$ = reliability of components (stages), 1 through i inclusive given that $0 \le x_i \le c$.

Since x_i are the states of the system, the forward recursive equations are given by

$$f_1(x_1) = \max_{0 \le c_1 \le x_1} \{r_1(c_1)\} \text{ for } m_1 = 1, 2, 3$$

and
$$f_i(x_i) = \max_{0 \le c_i \le x_i} \{r_i(c_i) \cdot f_{i-1}(x_i - c_i)\};\ i = 1, 2, 3, \ldots;\ m_i = 1, 2, 3.$$

There are 3 stages in the given problem

Stage 1. The stage 1 result can be represented as

	$f_1(x_1) = r_1(c_1)$			*Max. Reliability*	
	$m_1 = 1$	$m_1 = 2$	$m_1 = 3$		
x_1	$r_1 = 0.5,\ c_1 = 2$	$r_1 = 0.7,\ c_1 = 4$	$r_1 = 0.9,\ c_1 = 5$	$f_1(x_1)$	m_1^*
2	0.5	—	—	0.5	1
3	0.5	—	—	0.5	1
4	0.5	0.7	—	0.7	2
5	0.5	0.7	0.9	0.9	3
6	0.5	0.7	0.9	0.9	3

Stage 2. The stage 2 result can be represented as

	$f_2(x_2) = r_2(c_2) \cdot f_1(x_2 - c_2)$			*Max. Reliability*	
	$m_2 = 1$	$m_2 = 2$	$m_2 = 3$		
x_2	$r_2 = 0.7,\ c_2 = 3$	$r_2 = 0.8,\ c_2 = 5$	$r_2 = 0.9,\ c_2 = 6$	$f_2(x_2)$	m_2^*
3	0.7 × (–) = —	—	—	—	—
4	0.7 × (–) = —	—	—	—	—
5	0.7 × (0.5) = 0.35	0.8 × (–) = —	—	0.35	1
6	0.7 × (0.5) = 0.35	0.8 × (–) = —	0.9 × (–) = —	0.35	1
7	0.7 × (0.7) = 0.49	0.8 × (0.5) = 0.40	0.9 × (–) = —	0.49	1
8	0.7 × (0.9) = 0.63	0.8 × (0.5) = 0.40	0.9 × (0.5) = 0.45	0.63	1
9	0.7 × (0.9) = 0.63	0.8 × (0.7) = 0.56	0.9 × (0.5) = 0.45	0.63	1

Stage 3. The stage 3 result can be represented as

	$f_3(x_3) = r_3(c_3) \cdot f_2(x_3 - c_3)$			*Max. Reliability*	
	$m_3 = 1$	$m_3 = 2$	$m_3 = 3$		
x_3	$r_3 = 0.6,\ c_3 = 1$	$r_3 = 0.8,\ c_3 = 2$	$r_3 = 0.9,\ c_3 = 3$	$f_3(x_3)$	m_3^*
10	0.6 × 0.63 = 0.378	0.8 × 0.63 = 0.504	0.9 × 0.49 = 0.441	0.504	2

The optimal solution is $m_1^* = 3$, $m_2^* = 1$, $m_3^* = 2$ with maximum reliability = 0.504.

6.12 SOLUTION OF LINEAR PROGRAMMING PROBLEM BY DYNAMIC PROGRAMMING

Consider the general linear programming problem

$$\text{Maximize } Z = \sum_{j=1}^{n} c_j x_j$$

$$\text{Subject to} \quad \sum_{j=1}^{n} a_{ij} x_j \le b_i\ ;\ i = 1, 2, \ldots, m$$

$$x_j \ge 0;\ i = 1, 2, \ldots, n$$

We consider determination of variable x_j (activity j), ($j = 1, 2, \ldots, n$) as a stage. So it is a n stage problem. The value of x_j at several stages can be obtained by the forward computational procedure or the backward computational procedure. The state variables at each stage are the amount of resources available for allocation to the current stage and subsequent stages. The constants $b_1, b_2, \ldots, b_m$ are the amounts of the available resources.

Let $f_n(b_1, b_2, \ldots, b_m)$ be the optimal value of the objective function defined above for stages $x_1, x_2, \ldots, x_n$ for states $b_1, b_2, \ldots, b_m$. We shall use backward computational procedure here.

The recursive equation for optimization is

$$f_j(b_1, b_2, \ldots, b_m) = \underset{0 \le a_{ij} x_j \le b_i}{\text{Max}} \{c_j x_j + f_{j+1}(b_1 - a_{1j} x_j, b_2 - a_{2j} x_j, \ldots, b_m - a_{mj} x_j)\}$$

Example 8. *Solve the following linear programming problem by dynamic programming:*

$$\text{Maximize } Z = 5x_1 + 7x_2$$

$$\text{Subject to} \quad x_1 + x_2 \le 4$$

$$3x_1 + 8x_2 \le 24$$

$$10x_1 + 7x_2 \le 35$$

$$x_1, x_2 \ge 0$$

Solution.

1. Stage i corresponds to $i = 1, 2$
2. Alternative x_i for $i = 1, 2$
3. State (u_2, v_2, w_2) represents the amounts of resoures 1, 2 and 3 used in stage 2.
4. State (u_1, v_1, w_1) represents the amounts of resourecs 1, 2 and 3 used in stages 1 and 2.

Stage 2. Define $f_2(u_2, v_2, w_2)$ as the maximum profit for stage 2 given the state (u_2, v_2, w_2). Then

$$f_2(u_2, v_2, w_2) = \underset{\substack{0 \le x_2 \le u_2 \\ 0 \le 8x_2 \le v_2 \\ 0 \le 7x_2 \le w_2}}{\text{Max}} \{7x_2\}$$

Thus max $\{7x_2\}$ occurs at $x_2 = \min\{u_2, v_2, w_2\}$ and the solution for stage 2 is

State	*Optimum solution*	
	$f_2(u_2, v_2, w_2)$	x_2
(u_2, v_2, w_2)	$7\min(u_2, v_2\ w_2)$	$\min(u_2, v_2\ w_2)$

Stage 1.

$$f_1(u_1, v_1, w_1) = \underset{\substack{0 \le x_1 \le u_1 \\ 0 \le 3x_1 \le v_1 \\ 0 \le 10x_1 \le w_1}}{\text{Max}} \left\{5x_1 + f_2\left(u_1 - x_1, \frac{v_1 - 3x_1}{8}, \frac{w_1 - 10x_1}{7}\right)\right\}$$

$$= \underset{\substack{0 \le x_1 \le u_1 \\ 0 \le 3x_1 \le v_1 \\ 0 \le 10x_1 \le w_1}}{\text{Max}} \left\{5x_1 + 7\min\left(u_1 - x_1, \frac{v_1 - 3x_1}{8}, \frac{w_1 - 10x_1}{7}\right)\right\}$$

The optimization of stage 1 requires the solution of a minimax problem. For this problem, we get $u_1 = 4$, $v_1 = 24$ and $w_1 = 35$ which gives $0 \le x_1 \le 4$, $0 \le 3x_1 \le 24$ and $0 \le 10x_1 \le 35$. Because $\min\left(4 - x_1, \frac{24 - 3x_1}{8}, \frac{35 - 10x_1}{7}\right)$ is the lower envelope of the two intersecting lines it follows that

$$\min\left(4 - x_1, \frac{24 - 3x_1}{8}, \frac{35 - 10x_1}{7}\right) = \begin{cases} \frac{24 - 3x_1}{8}; & 0 \le x_1 \le 8/5 \\ 4 - x_1; & 8/5 \le x_1 \le 7/3 \\ \frac{35 - 10x_1}{7}; & 7/3 \le x_1 \le 7/2 \end{cases}$$

$$\left[\begin{array}{c}\text{To check minimum put } x_1 = 0 \text{ and select minimum one so it will be lower limit} \\ \text{of minimum (I) one and for upper limit of I and lower limit of II solve} \\ \text{I and II for } x_1\text{. Now for upper limit of II and lower limit of III solve} \\ \text{II and III for } x_1 \text{ and for upper limit of III one take} \\ x_1 = \min(u_1, v_1, w_1) = \min\left(4, \frac{24}{3}, \frac{35}{10}\right) = 3.5 = \frac{7}{2}\end{array}\right]$$

$$\text{Now } f_1(4, 24, 35) = \max_{x_1} \begin{cases} 5x_1 + \frac{7}{8}(24 - 3x_1); & 0 \le x_1 \le 8/5 \\ 5x_1 + 7(4 - x_1); & 8/5 \le x_1 \le 7/3 \\ 5x_1 + (35 - 10x_1); & 7/3 \le x_1 \le 7/2 \end{cases}$$

$$= \max_{x_1} \begin{cases} \dfrac{19}{8}x_1 + 21; & 0 \le x_1 \le 8/5 \\ -2x_1 + 28; & 8/5 \le x_1 \le 7/3 \\ -5x_1 + 35; & 7/3 \le x_1 \le 7/2 \end{cases}$$

$$= \max \begin{cases} 21 & \text{for} \quad x_1 = 0 \\ \dfrac{124}{5} & \text{for} \quad x_1 = 8/5 \\ \dfrac{70}{3} & \text{for} \quad x_1 = 7/3 \\ \dfrac{35}{2} & \text{for} \quad x_1 = 7/2 \end{cases}$$

$$= \frac{124}{5} \text{ at } x_1 = \frac{8}{5}$$

State	*Optimum solution*	
	$f_1(u_1, v_1, w_1)$	x_1
(4, 24, 35)	$\frac{124}{5}$	$\frac{8}{5}$

To determine the optimum value of x_2, we note that

$$u_2 = u_1 - x_1 = 4 - \frac{8}{5} = \frac{12}{5}; \; v_2 = \frac{v_1 - 3x_1}{8} = \frac{24 - 24/5}{8} = \frac{12}{5};$$

$$w_2 = \frac{w_1 - 10x_1}{7} = \frac{35 - \frac{80}{5}}{7} = \frac{19}{7}$$

So $\quad x_2 = \min(u_2, v_2, w_2) = \min\left(\frac{12}{5}, \frac{12}{5}, \frac{19}{7}\right) = \frac{12}{5}$

Hence, the optimum solution is

$$x_1 = \frac{8}{5}, \; x_2 = \frac{12}{5} \text{ and Maximize } Z = \frac{124}{5}$$

Example 9. *Solve the following linear programming problem by dynamic programming.*

$$\text{Maximize } Z = 2x_1 + 5x_2$$
$$\text{Subject to } \quad 2x_1 + x_2 \le 430$$
$$x_2 \le 230$$
$$x_1, x_2 \ge 0$$

Solution.

1. Stage i corresponds to $i = 1, 2$
2. Alternative x_i for $i = 1, 2$
3. State (v_2, w_2) represents the amounts of resources 1 and 2 used in stage 2.
4. State (v_2, w_1) represents the amounts of resources 1 and 2 used in stages 1 and 2.

Stage 2. Define $f_2(v_2, w_2)$ as the maximum profit for stage 2 given the state (v_2, w_2). Then

$$f_2(v_2, w_2) = \max_{\substack{0 \le x_2 \le v_2 \\ 0 \le x_2 \le w_2}} \{5x_2\}$$

Thus, max $\{5x_2\}$ occurs at $x_2 = \min\{v_2, w_2\}$ and the solution for stage 2 is

State	Optimum solution	
	$f_2(v_2, w_2)$	x_2
(v_2, w_2)	$5 \min(v_2, w_2)$	$\min(v_2, w_2)$

Stage 1.

$$f_1(v_1, w_1) = \max_{0 \le 2x_1 \le v_1} \{2x_1 + f_2(v_1 - 2x_1, w_1)\}$$

$$= \max_{0 \le 2x_1 \le v_1} \{2x_1 + 5 \min(v_1 - 2x_1, w_1)\}$$

The optimization of stage 1 requires the solution of a minimax problem. For this problem, we get $v_1 = 430$ and $w_1 = 230$ which gives $0 \le 2x_1 \le 430$. Because $\min(430 - 2x_1, 230)$ is the lower envelope of two intersecting lines, it follows that

$$\min(430 - 2x_1, 230) = \begin{cases} 230; & 0 \le x_1 \le 100 \\ 430 - 2x_1; & 100 \le x_1 \le 215 \end{cases}$$

[To check minimum put $x_1 = 10$ and select minimum one so it will be lower limit of minimum (I) one and for upper limit of I and lower limit of II solve I and II for x_1 and for upper limit of II one take

$$x_1 = \min(v_1, w_1) = \min\left(\frac{430}{2}, 230\right) = 215$$]

Now $$f_1(430, 230) = \max_{x_1} \begin{cases} 2x_1 + 5 \times 230; & 0 \le x_1 \le 100 \\ 2x_1 + 5 \times (430 - 2x_1); & 100 \le x_1 \le 215 \end{cases}$$

$$= \max_{x_1} \begin{cases} 2x_1 + 1150; & 0 \le x_1 \le 100 \\ 2150 - 8x_1; & 100 \le x_1 \le 215 \end{cases}$$

$$= \max \begin{cases} 1150 & \text{for} \quad x_1 = 0 \\ 1350 & \text{for} \quad x_1 = 100 \\ 430 & \text{for} \quad x_1 = 215 \end{cases}$$

$$= 1350 \text{ at } x_1 = 100$$

State	Optimum solution	
	$f_1(v_1, w_1)$	x_1
(430, 230)	1350	100

To determine the optimum value of x_2 we note that

$$v_2 = v_1 - 2x_1 = 430 - 200 = 230; \; w_2 = w_1 - 0 = 230$$

So, $$x_2 = \min(v_2, w_2) = \min(230, 230) = 230$$

Hence, the solution is

$$x_1 = 100, \; x_2 = 230 \text{ and Maximize } Z = 1350$$

EXERCISES

1. Explain dynamic programming. What are applications of dynamic programming?
2. State the 'Bellman's Principle of optimality' in dynamic programming and give a mathematical formulation of dynamic programming.
3. Define dynamic programming problem. List and explain the terminologies of dynamic programming problem, also applications of this technique. *(UPTU, 2004–05)*
4. What do you understand from multistage decision process? Give example. State the 'Principle of optimality' and explain it giving examples. What do you understand from the 'concept of sub-optimization'?
5. State the essential characteristics of dynamic programming problems.
6. State the various steps involved for solving the multistage problem by dynamic programming.
7. Use dynamic programming to solve the following problem:

   Maximize $Z = x_1 \cdot x_2 \cdot x_3$

   Subject to $x_1 + x_2 + x_3 = 5$

   $x_1, x_2, x_3 \geq 0$ $\left[\textbf{Ans. } x_1 = x_2 = x_3 = \frac{5}{3}, \max Z = \frac{125}{27}\right]$

8. Use dynamic programming to solve the following problem:

   Minimize $Z = x_1^2 + x_2^2 + x_3^2$

   Subject to $x_1 + x_2 + x_3 = 5$

   $x_1, x_2, x_3 \geq 0$ $\left[\textbf{Ans. } x_1 = x_2 = x_3 = \frac{5}{3}, \max Z = \frac{25}{3}\right]$

9. Use dynamic programming to solve the following problem:

   Minimize $Z = x_1^2 + x_2^2 + x_3^2$

   Subject to $x_1 + x_2 + x_3 = 27$

   $x_1, x_2, x_3 \geq 0$ [**Ans.** $x_1 = x_2 = x_3 = 3$, max $Z = 27$]

10. Consider the following diagram where circles denote cities, and lines between two such circles represent highways connecting the cities. The numbers inside the circles represents city numbers and those given beside the lines denote the distance between the cities connected by the lines. Suppose a salesman start from city 1 and would like to go to city 15. What is the shortest route from city 1 to city 15 and what is the minimum distance?

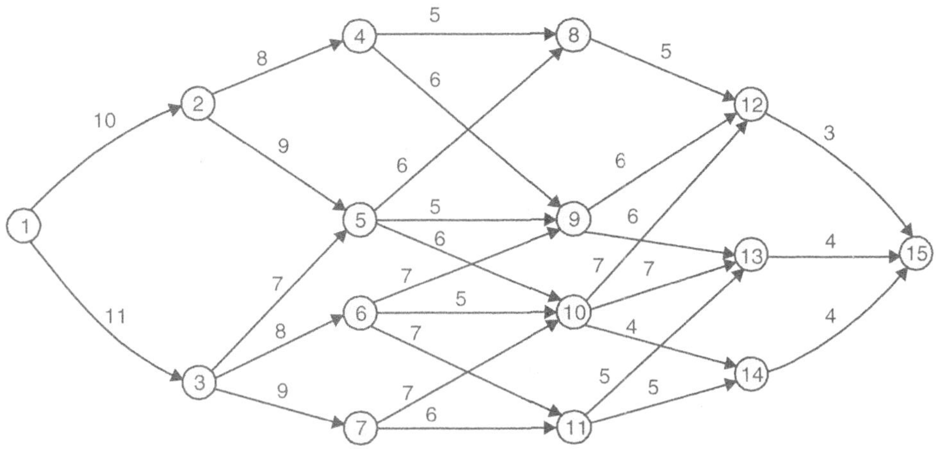

[**Ans.** 1 → 2 → 4 → 8 → 12 → 15; 31 units]

11. XYZ roadways has four types of packages A,B,C and D to be carried in their parcel van. The bulk density of each package is different. As per the company's rule, the packages fall under different categories of freight classification and therefore, the revenue per unit of each package also varies. Data regarding the weights and the expected revenue for each package are available:

Type of package (*i*)	*Weight per unit* (*kg*) w_i	*Expected unit revenue* (₹) r_i
1	2000	200
2	4000	425
3	5000	550
4	3000	350

Determine the number of units of each package that would maximize the revenue, given that the capacity of the van is limited to 10,000 kg.

[**Ans.** 1 – 0 unit, 2 – 1 unit, 3 – 0 unit, 4 – 2 units; mas revenue = ₹ 1125]

12. An electronic device consists of three components, each of which must function for the system to function. The system reliability can be improved by installing parallel units in one or more of the components. The reliability (*r*) of a component with one, two or three parallel units and the corresponding cost (*c*) are given in the table below. The maximum amount available for this device is 10. The problem is to determine the number of parallel units in each component.

No. of units (m_i)	$i = 1$		$i = 2$		$i = 3$	
	r_1	c_1	r_2	c_2	r_3	c_3
1	0.6	2	0.8	3	0.7	1
2	0.7	4	0.8	5	0.8	2
3	0.9	5	0.9	6	0.9	3

[**Ans.** $m_1^* = 3$, $m_2^* = 1$, $m_3^* = 2$.]

13. A company has five salesmen, who have to be allocated to four marketing zones. The return (or profit) from each zone depends upon the number of salesman working in that zone. The expected returns for different number of salesman in different zones, as estimated from the past records are given below. Determine the optimal allocation policy.

Number of Salesmen	*Marketing zones*		
	1	*2*	*3*
0	45	30	35
1	58	45	45
2	70	60	52
3	82	70	64
4	93	79	72
5	101	90	82

[**Ans.** Zone 1 – 3, Zone 2 – 2, Zone 1 – 0; optimal return = 177 units]

14. Use dynamic programming to solve the following linear programming problem.

Maximize $Z = 8x_1 + 7x_2$

Subject to $2x_1 + x_2 \le 8$

$5x_1 + 2x_2 \le 15$

$x_1, x_2 \ge 0$ [**Ans.** $x_1 = 3, x_2 = 0$; Max Z = 24]

15. Use dynamic programming to solve the following linear programming problem:

Maximize $Z = 50x_1 + 100x_2$

Subject to $2x_1 + 3x_2 \le 48$

$x_1 + 3x_2 \le 42$

$x_1 + x_2 \le 21$

$x_1, x_2 \ge 0$ [**Ans.** $x_1 = 6, x_2 = 12$; Max Z = 1500]

16. Use dynamic programming to solve the following linear programming problem:

Maximize $Z = 3x_1 + 4x_2$

Subject to $2x_1 + x_2 \le 40$

$2x_1 + 5x_2 \le 180$

$x_1, x_2 \ge 0$ [**Ans.** $x_1 = \frac{5}{2}, x_2 = 35$; Max Z = 147.50.]

CHAPTER 7

Decision Theory

7.1 INTRODUCTION

Decision analysis involves the use of a rational process for selecting the best of several alternatives. The goodness of a selected alternative depends on the quality of the data used in describing the decision situation. A decision-making process falls into one of the three categories; decision-making under certainty, decision-making under uncertainty and decision-making under risk.

Nowadays, management students, businessman, engineers, persons from industries and government, etc., are giving much emphasis over decision-making under conditions of uncertainty as mostly situations involves making choices under uncertainty. The study of making decisions to choose the best among a number of alternative courses of action is known as **decision theory** or **statistical decision theory**.

7.2 ELEMENTS OF A DECISION PROBLEM

There are certain essential elements which are common to all decision-making categories:

1. **The decision-maker.** The decision-maker is charged with the responsibility for making the decisions. The decision-maker can be an individual, a group of individuals, any company, an industrial body, etc.
2. **Acts.** The acts are the alternative courses of action or strategies that are available to decision-maker.
3. **Events.** The events also known as states of nature. The events identify the occurrences which are not under the control of decision-maker and which determines the level of success for a given act.
4. **Pay-off.** Each combination of a course of action and an event is associated with a pay-off. It is a quantitative measure of the value to the decision-maker of the outcomes. It measures the net benefit to the decision-maker from a given combination of course of action and an event. The pay-off usually represents the net monetary gain (profit), but some other measures can also be used, as cost is negative profit.

5. **Pay-off table.** Suppose the problem under consideration has m possible events (state of nature denoted by $E_1, E_2, ..., E_m$ and n alternative acts (strategies) denoted by $A_1, A_2, ..., A_n$. Then the pay-off corresponding to strategy A_j of the decision-maker under the state of nature E_i will be denoted by p_{ij} $(i = 1, 2, ..., m; j = 1, 2, ..., n)$.

   The totality of mn pay-offs-arranged in a tabular form is known as **pay-off table.**

Events (States of nature)	*Pay-off (₹) Courses of actions/acts/strategies*			
	A_1	A_2	...	A_n
E_1	p_{11}	p_{12}	...	p_{1n}
E_2	p_{21}	p_{22}	...	p_{2n}
.	.	.	.	
.	.	.	.	
.	.	.	.	
E_m	p_{m1}	p_{m2}	...	p_{mn}

6. **Regret or opportunity loss table.** An opportunity loss has been defined to be the difference between the highest possible profit for a state of nature and the actual profit obtained for a particular action taken, *i.e.*, an opportunity loss is the loss incurred due to failure of not adopting the best possible action. For a given state of nature, the opportunity loss of a course of action is the difference between the pay-off of that course of action and the pay-off for the best course of action that could have been selected.

Events (States of nature)	*Opportunity loss (₹) Courses of actions/acts/strategies*			
	A_1	A_2	...	A_n
E_1	$M_1 - p_{11}$	$M_1 - p_{12}$	...	$M_1 - p_{1n}$
E_2	$M_2 - p_{21}$	$M_2 - p_{22}$	...	$M_2 - p_{2n}$
.	.	.	.	
.	.	.	.	
.	.	.	.	
E_m	$M_m - p_{m1}$	$M_m - p_{m2}$	...	$M_m - p_{mn}$

where $M_1, M_2, ..., M_m$ are the maximum of these quantities respectively.

7.3 TYPES OF DECISION-MAKING ENVIRONMENT

There are three categories of decision-making environment:

1. **Decision-making under certainty.** In this environment the decision-maker knows with certainty the consequence of every alternative or decision choice. There will be only one outcome for each alternative. Examples of such decision problems are linear programming, dynamic programming, transportation, assignment, integer programming, etc.
2. **Decision-making under uncertainty.** In this environment, the decision-maker cannot assess the outcome probability with confidence. In other words, if the information about

the outcomes is incomplete and the available information cannot be described in terms of probability density. Decisions under uncertainty refer to situations where more than one outcome can result from any single decision.

3. **Decision-making under risk.** In this environment the pay-offs associated with each decision alternative are usually described by probability distributions. For this reason, decision-making under risk is usually based on the expected monetary value criterion or expected opportunity loss of the expected pay-off.

7.4 DECISION-MAKING UNDER UNCERTAINTY

Different rules for making a decision under such environment are as follows:

1. **Maximax or Minimin Criterion (Criterion of Optimism).** This criterion is based upon 'extreme optimism'. The basic steps of this criterion are as follows:
   (*i*) Determine the maximum possible pay-off for each alternative.
   (*ii*) Choose that alternative which corresponds to the maximum of the above maximum pay-offs.

   In decision problems dealing with costs, the minimum for each alternative is determined and then the alternative which minimizes the above minimum cost is selected.

2. **Maximin or Minimax Criterion (Criterion of Pessimism).** This criterion is based upon the 'conservative approach' to assume that the worst possible is going to happen. The basic steps of this criterion are as follows:
   (*i*) Determine the minimum possible pay-off for each alternative.
   (*ii*) Choose that alternative which corresponds to the maximum of the above minimum pay-offs.

   In decision problems dealing with costs, the maximum for each alternative is determined and then the alternative which minimizes the above maximum cost is selected.

3. **Laplace Criterion (Equally Likely Decisions).** The Laplace criterion uses all the information by assigning equal probabilities to all events of each alternative, as there is no information about probabilities of occurrence. The basic steps of this criterion are as follows:
   (*i*) Assign equal probabilities $\frac{1}{n}$ to each pay-off of a strategy (having n pay-offs).
   (*ii*) Determine the expected pay-off value for each alternative by multiplying each pay-off by its probability and then adding.
   (*iii*) Choose that alternative which corresponds to the maximum of the expected pay-offs. In decision problems dealing with costs, select that alternative which corresponds to the minimum of the expected pay-offs.

4. **Savage Criterion (Criterion of Regret).** The savage criterion is based on the concept of regret (or opportunity loss). This criterion also known as **minimax regret criterion**. The basic steps of this criterion are as follows:
   (*i*) Construct the regret table.

$$\text{Regret (opportunity loss)} = \begin{cases} \text{pay-off} - \text{max. pay-off; if the pay-offs represent profits} \\ \text{pay-off} - \text{min. pay-off; if the pay-offs represent costs} \end{cases}$$

(*ii*) Determine the maximum regret for each alternative.

(*iii*) Choose the alternative with minimum regret out of these maximum regrets.

5. **Hurwicz Criterion.** The Hurwicz criterion is based on the concept that the decision-makers are neither completely pessimistic nor completely optimistic, but are a combination of the two extremes. Therefore, we should give attention to both. The basic steps of this criterion are as follows:

(*i*) Choose an appropriate degree of optimism (or pessimism) of the decision-maker. Let α $(0 \le \alpha \le 1)$ be his degree of optimism (so $1 - \alpha$ is his degree of pessimism).

(*ii*) Determine the maximum as well as minimum pay-off for each alternative and obtain the quantities D (decision index) as

$$D = \alpha \cdot \text{maximum pay-off} + (1 - \alpha) \cdot \text{minimum pay-off}$$

for each alternative.

(*iii*) Choose the maximum value of D when profits are given (Choose the minimum value of D when costs are given).

ILLUSTRATIVE EXAMPLES

Example 1. *Given the following profit pay-off table:*

Strategy	*States of nature*			
	S1	*S2*	*S3*	*S4*
A1	*16*	*10*	*12*	*7*
A2	*13*	*12*	*9*	*9*
A3	*11*	*14*	*15*	*14*

Which strategy should the decision-maker choose on the basis of

(*i*) *Maximin criterion* (*ii*) *Maximax criterion*

(*iii*) *Minimax regret criterion* (*iv*) *Laplace criterion?*

Solution.

(*i*) Maximin criterion:

Strategy	*States of nature*				*Minimum of each Strategy*
	S1	S2	S3	S4	
A1	16	10	12	7	7
A2	13	12	9	9	9
A3	11	14	15	14	**11**

Using maximin criterion, maximum of these minimum is 11 corresponding to strategy A3. So A3 should be selected.

(*ii*) Maximax criterion:

Strategy	*States of nature*				*Maximum of each Strategy*
	S1	*S2*	*S3*	*S4*	
A1	16	10	12	7	**16**
A2	13	12	9	9	13
A3	11	14	15	14	15

Using maximax criterion, maximum of these maximum is 16 corresponding to strategy A1. So A1 should be selected.

(*iii*) **Minimax regret criterion:**

Regret table

Strategy	*States of nature*				*Maximum Regret*
	S1	*S2*	*S3*	*S4*	
A1	16 – 16 = 0	14 – 10 = 4	15 – 12 = 3	14 – 7 = 7	**7**
A2	16 – 13 = 3	14 – 12 = 2	15 – 9 = 6	14 – 9 = 5	6
A3	16 – 11 = 5	14 – 14 = 0	15 – 15 = 0	14 – 14 = 0	**5**

Using minimax regret criterion, minimum of these maximum regrets is 5 corresponding to strategy A3. So A3 should be selected.

(*iv*) **Laplace criterion:**

Here, $p = \frac{1}{4}$

$$\text{EMV (Strategy A1)} = \frac{1}{4} \times 16 + \frac{1}{4} \times 10 + \frac{1}{4} \times 12 + \frac{1}{4} \times 7$$

$$= \frac{1}{4}(16 + 10 + 12 + 7) = \frac{45}{4} = 11.25$$

$$\text{EMV (Strategy A2)} = \frac{1}{4}(13 + 12 + 9 + 9) = \frac{43}{4} = 10.75$$

$$\text{EMV (Strategy A3)} = \frac{1}{4}(11 + 14 + 15 + 14) = \frac{54}{4} = 13.50$$

Since the EMV is maximum for strategy A3, so A3 should be selected.

Example 2. *The research department of Hindustan Lever has recommended to the marketing department to launch a shampoo of three different types. The marketing manager has to decide one of the types of shampoo to be launched under the following estimated pay-offs various levels of sales:*

Types of shampoo	*Estimate levels of sales (units)*		
	15,000	*10,000*	*5,000*
Egg shampoo	30	10	10
Clinic shampoo	40	15	5
Delux shampoo	55	20	3

What should be the marketing manager decision using:

(*i*) *Maximin criterion*

(*ii*) *Minimax criterion*

(*iii*) *Maxnimax criterion*

(*iv*) *Laplace criterion*

(*v*) *Minimax regret criterion?*

Solution. (*i*) Maximin criterion:

Types of shampoo	*Estimated levels of sales (units)*			*Minimum of each decision*
	15,000	*10,000*	*5,000*	
Egg shampoo	30	10	10	**10**
Clinic shampoo	40	15	5	5
Delux shampoo	55	20	3	3

Using maximin criterion, maximum of these minimum is 10 corresponding to Egg shampoo. So Egg shampoo should be launched.

(*ii*) Minimax criterion:

Types of shampoo	*Estimated levels of sales (units)*			*Maximum of each decision*
	15,000	*10,000*	*5,000*	
Egg shampoo	30	10	10	**30**
Clinic shampoo	40	15	5	40
Delux shampoo	55	20	3	55

Using minimax criterion, minimum of these maximum is 30 corresponding to Egg shampoo. So Egg shampoo should be launched.

(*iii*) Maximax criterion:

Types of shampoo	*Estimated levels of sales (units)*			*Maximum of each decision*
	15,000	*10,000*	*5,000*	
Egg shampoo	30	10	10	**30**
Clinic shampoo	40	15	5	**40**
Delux shampoo	55	20	3	**55**

Using maximax criterion, maximum of these maximum is 55 corresponding to Delux shampoo. So Delux shampoo should be launched.

(*iv*) Laplace criterion:

Here, $p = \frac{1}{3}$

$$\text{EMV (Egg shampoo)} = \frac{1}{3} \times 30 + \frac{1}{3} \times 10 + \frac{1}{3} \times 10$$

$$= \frac{1}{3}(30 + 10 + 10)\ \frac{50}{3} = 16.67$$

$$\text{EMV (Clinic shampoo)} = \frac{1}{3}(40 + 15 + 5) = \frac{60}{3} = 20$$

$$\text{EMV (Delux shampoo)} = \frac{1}{3}(55 + 20 + 3)\ \frac{78}{3} = 26$$

Since the EMV is maximum for Delux shampoo. So Delux shampoo should be launched.

(*v*) Minimax regret criterion:

Regret table

Types of shampoo	*Estimated levels of sales (units)*			*Maximum Regret*
	15,000	*10,000*	*5,000*	
Egg shampoo	55 – 30 = 25	20 – 10 = 10	10 – 10 = 0	**25**
Clinic shampoo	55 – 40 = 15	20 – 10 = 10	10 – 5 = 5	15
Delux shampoo	55 – 55 = 0	20 – 10 = 10	10 – 3 = 7	7

Using minimax regret criterion, minimum of these maximum regrets is 7 corresponding to Delux shampoo. So Delux shampoo should be launched.

Example 3. *A farmer wants to plan which of the three crops he should plant on his 100 acre farm. The profit of each crop depends upon the rainfall during the growing season. The rainfall could be high, medium and low. The estimated profit of the farmer for each of the crops is shown in the table:*

Rain fall	*Estimated conditional profit*		
	Crop A	*Crop B*	*Crop C*
High	*6000*	*3000*	*7000*
Medium	*4000*	*4500*	*4000*
Low	*2000*	*5000*	*5000*

The farmer decides to plant only one crop, which would be his best crop using the following:

(i) Maximax criterion *(ii) Maximin criterion*

(iii) Laplace criterion *(iv) Minimax regret criterion.*

Solution.

(*i*) Maximax criterion:

Type of crop	*Estimated conditional profit rainfall*			*Maximum of each crop*
	High	*Medium*	*Low*	
Crop A	6000	3000	2000	**6000**
Crop B	3000	4500	5000	5000
Crop C	7000	4000	5000	**7000**

Using maximax criterion, maximum of these maximum is 7000 corresponding to crop C. So crop C is the best crop.

(*ii*) Maximin criterion:

Type of crop	*Estimated conditional profit rainfall*			*Minimum of Each crop*
	High	*Medium*	*Low*	
Crop A	6000	3000	2000	**2000**
Crop B	3000	4500	5000	3000
Crop C	7000	4000	5000	**4000**

Using maximin criterion, maximum of these minimum is 4000 corresponding to crop C. So crop C is the best crop.

(*iii*) Laplace criterion:

Here, $p = \frac{1}{3}$

$$\text{EMV (Crop A)} = \frac{1}{3} \times 6000 + \frac{1}{3} \times 4000 + \frac{1}{3} \times 2000$$

$$= \frac{1}{3}(6000 + 4000 + 2000) = \frac{12000}{3} = 4000$$

$$\text{EMV (Crop B)} = \frac{1}{3}(3000 + 4500 + 5000) = \frac{12500}{3} = 4166.67$$

$$\text{EMV (Crop C)} = \frac{1}{3}(7000 + 4000 + 5000) = \frac{16000}{3} = 5333.33$$

Since the EMV is maximum for crop C. So crop C is the best crop.

(*iv*) Minimax regret criterion:

Regret table

Type of crop	*Rainfall*			*Maximum Regret*
	High	*Medium*	*Low*	
Crop A	7000 – 6000 = 1000	4500 – 4000 = 500	5000 – 2000 = 3000	3000
Crop B	7000 – 3000 = 4000	4500 – 4500 = 0	5000 – 5000 = 0	4000
Crop C	7000 – 7000 = 0	4500 – 4000 = 500	5000 – 5000 = 0	500

Using minimax regret criterion, minimum of these maximum regrets is 500 corresponding to crop C. So crop C is best crop.

Example 4. *Consider the following pay-off (profit) matrix:*

Alternative	*Events*			
	E1	*E2*	*E3*	*E4*
A1	*5*	*10*	*18*	*25*
A2	*8*	*7*	*8*	*23*
A3	*21*	*18*	*12*	*21*
A4	*30*	*22*	*19*	*15*

Find optimum alternative using Hurwicz criterion with $\alpha = 0.75$.

Solution. Here $\alpha = 0.75$ so $1 - \alpha = 1 - 0.75 = 0.25$

Alternative	*Maximum pay-off (i)*	*Minimum pay-off (ii)*	$D = \alpha \times (i) + (1 - \alpha) \times (ii)$
A1	25	5	25 × 0.75 + 5 × 0.25 = 20
A2	23	7	23 × 0.75 + 7 × 0.25 = 19
A3	21	12	21 × 0.75 + 12 × 0.25 = 18.75
A4	30	15	30 × 0.75 + 15 × 0.25 = **26.25**

According to Hurwicz criterion, maximum value of D is 26.25 corresponding to A4. So A4 is optimum alternative.

7.5 DECISION-MAKING UNDER RISK

Different criterion for making a decision under such environment are as follows:

1. **Expected Monetary Value (EMV) Criterion.** The expected monetary value criterion seeks the maximization of expected profit or the minimization of expected cost. The basic steps of this criterion are as follows:
   (*i*) Construct the pay-off table listing all possible courses of actions and events (states of nature), along with the corresponding event probabilities.

(*ii*) Determine the expected conditional profit values for each course of action.

(*iii*) Determine EMV for each course of action (strategy) by

$$\text{EMV } A_i = p_{i1}\, P(E_1) + p_{i2}\, P(E_2) + \ldots + p_{im}\, P(E_m)$$

(*iv*) Choose that course of action (strategy) having highest EMV.

2. **Expected Opportunity Loss (EOL) Criterion.** An alternative approach to maximizing expected monetary value (EMV) is to minimize expected opportunity loss (EOL). The basic steps of this criterion are as follows:

(*i*) Construct the opportunity loss table listing all possible courses of actions and events (states of nature), along with the corresponding event probabilities.

(*ii*) Determine the conditional opportunity loss values for each event.

(*iii*) Determine the expected conditional opportunity loss values and sum these values to get the expected opportunity loss (EOL) for each course of action by

$$\text{EOL}(A) = (M_1 - P_1)\, P(E_1) + (M_2 - P_2)\, P(E_2) + \ldots + (M_m - P_m)\, P(E_m)$$

(*iv*) Choose that course of action (strategy) having lowest EOL.

3. **Expected Value of Perfect Information (EVPI).** The expected value with perfect information is the expected or average return, in the long run, if we have perfect information before a decision is made. The EVPI may be defined as the maximum amounts spend by the decision-maker to get perfect (additional) information. Expected pay-off under perfect information (EPPI) can be calculated by finding the sum of product of pay-off of best outcome of each state of nature and its probability of occurrence.

The expected value of perfect information (EVPI) is the expected outcome with perfect information minus the expected outcome without perfect information (maximum EMV).

$$\text{EVPI} = \text{EPPI} - \text{max. EMV}$$

ILLUSTRATIVE EXAMPLES

Example 5. *A management is faced with the problem of choosing one of three products for manufacturing. The potential demand for each product may turn out to be good, moderate or poor. The probabilities for each of the states of nature were estimated as follows:*

Product	*Nature of demand*		
	Good	*Moderate*	*Poor*
X	0.70	0.20	0.10
Y	0.50	0.30	0.20
Z	0.40	0.50	0.10

The estimated profit or loss (in ₹) under the three states may be taken as:

Product	*Nature of demand*		
	Good	*Moderate*	*Poor*
X	300,000	200,000	100,000
Y	600,000	300,000	200,000
Z	400,000	100,000	–150,000

Prepare the expected value table and advice the management about the choice of the product.

Solution.

Nature of demand	*Expected pay-off (in ₹ Lacs) for various acts*								
	X			Y			Z		
	x_{1j}	p_{1j}	$x_{1j}p_{1j}$	x_{2j}	p_{2j}	$x_{2j}p_{2j}$	x_{3j}	p_{3j}	$x_{3j}p_{3j}$
Good	3	0.7	2.1	6	0.5	3.0	4	0.4	1.6
Moderate	2	0.2	0.4	3	0.3	0.9	1	0.5	0.5
Poor	1	0.1	0.1	2	0.2	0.4	–1.5	0.1	–0.15
EMV			2.6			**4.3**			1.95

Since the EMV is maximum for product Y, so Y should be selected as the best product.

Example 6. *Pay-offs of three acts X, Y, Z and the states of nature P, Q, R are as follows:*

State of nature	*Pay-off (₹)*		
	Y	*Y*	*Z*
P	*–120*	*–80*	*100*
Q	*200*	*400*	*–300*
R	*260*	*–260*	*600*

The probabilities of the states of nature are 0.3, 0.5 and 0.2 respectively. Tabulate the expected monetary values (EMVs) for the above data and state which can be selected as the best act.

Solution.

States of nature	*Pay-offs (Acts)*								
	X			Y			Z		
	x_{1j}	p_{1j}	$x_{1j}p_{1j}$	x_{2j}	p_{2j}	$x_{2j}p_{2j}$	x_{3j}	p_{3j}	$x_{3j}p_{3j}$
P	–120	0.3	–36	–80	0.3	–24	100	0.3	30
Q	200	0.5	100	400	0.5	200	–300	0.5	–150
R	260	0.2	52	–260	0.2	–52	600	0.2	120
EMV			116			**124**			0

Since the EMV is maximum for act Y, so Y should be selected as the best act.

Example 7. *A newspaper distributor assigns probabilities to the demand for a magazine as follows:*

Copies demanded	*1*	*2*	*3*	*4*
Probability	*0.4*	*0.3*	*0.2*	*0*

A copy of magazine sells for ₹ 7 and costs ₹ 6. What can be the maximum possible expected monetary value (EMV) if the distributor can return unsold copies for ₹ 5 each?

Solution. Cost of magazine = ₹ 6

Selling price of magazine = ₹ 7

Profit per magazine = ₹ (7 – 6) = ₹ 1

Loss on each unsold magazine = ₹ (6 – 5) = ₹ 1.

$$\text{Conditional profit} = \begin{cases} 1\times S = S & \text{if } D \geq S \\ 1\times D - 1\times(S-D) = 2D - S & \text{if } D < S \end{cases}$$

Where D = number of magazines demanded

S = number of magazines in stock

The resulting pay-off and corresponding expected pay-offs are as follows:

Event (Demand)	*Probability*	*Conditional pay-off (₹) Acts (Stock)*				*Expected pay-off (₹) Acts (Stock)*			
D	*(i)*	*1 (ii)*	*2 (iii)*	*3 (iv)*	*4 (v)*	*1 (i) × (ii)*	*2 (i) × (iii)*	*3 (i) × (iv)*	*4 (i) × (v)*
1	0.4	1	0	–1	–2	0.4	0.0	–0.4	–0.8
2	0.3	1	2	1	0	0.3	0.6	0.3	0.0
3	0.2	1	2	3	2	0.2	0.4	0.6	0.4
4	0.1	1	2	3	4	0.1	0.2	0.3	0.4
					EMV	1.0	1.2	0.8	0.0

Since the EMV is maximum for act (stock) 2, so the optimum act for the distributor would be to stock 2 copies of magazine.

Example 8. *The following pay-off table is given:*

Acts	*Events*			
	E1	*E2*	*E3*	*E4*
A1	*40*	*200*	*–200*	*100*
A2	*200*	*0*	*200*	*0*
A3	*0*	*100*	*0*	*150*
A4	*–50*	*400*	*100*	*0*

Suppose that the probabilities of the events are: p(E1) = 0.20, p(E2) = 0.15, p(E3) = 0.40 and p(E4) = 0.25. Calculate the expected pay-off and the expected loss of each action. Find the optimum act using EMV and EOL criterion.

Solution. Computation of expected pay-offs:

Event (Demand)	*Probability*	*Conditional pay-off (₹) Acts (Stock)*				*Expected pay-off (₹) Acts (Stock)*			
D	*(i)*	*A1 (ii)*	*A2 (iii)*	*A3 (iv)*	*A4 (v)*	*A1 (i) × (ii)*	*A2 (i) × (iii)*	*A3 (i) × (iv)*	*A4 (i) × (v)*
E1	0.20	40	200	0	–50	8	40	0	–10
E2	0.15	200	0	100	400	30	0	15	60
E3	0.40	–200	200	0	100	–80	80	0	40
E4	0.25	100	0	150	0	25	0	37.5	0
					EMV	–17	**120**	52.5	90

Since the EMV is maximum for act A2, so A2 is the optimum act.

Computation of expected loss

Event (Demand)	*Prob-ability*	*Opportunity loss Acts*				*Expected loss Acts (Stock)*			
D	*(i)*	*A1 (ii)*	*A2 (iii)*	*A3 (iv)*	*A4 (v)*	*A1 (i) × (ii)*	*A2 (i) × (iii)*	*A3 (i) × (iv)*	*A4 (i) × (v)*
E1	0.20	200 – 40 = 160	200 – 200 = 0	200 – 0 = 200	200 + 50 = 250	32	0	40	50
E2	0.15	400 – 200 = 200	400 – 0 = 400	400 – 100 = 300	400 – 400 = 0	30	60	45	0
E3	0.40	200 + 200 = 400	200 – 200 = 0	200 – 0 = 200	200 – 100 = 100	160	0	80	40
E4	0.25	150 – 100 = 50	150 – 0 = 150	150 – 150 = 0	150 – 0 = 150	12.5	37.5	0	37.5
						234.5	**97.5**	**165**	**127.5**

Since the EOL is minimum for act A2, so A2 is the optimum act.

Example 9. *A grocery with a bakery department is faced with the problem of how many cakes to buy in order to meet the day's demand. The grocer prefers not to day-old goods in competition with fresh products; leftover cakes are, therefore, a complete loss. On the other hand, if a customer desires a cake and all of them have been sold, the disappointed customer will buy elsewhere and the sales will be lost. The grocer has, therefore, collected information on the past sale on a selected 100 day period as follows:*

Sales per day	*No of days*	*Probability*
25	10	0.10
26	30	0.30
27	50	0.50
28	10	0.10

A cake costs ₹ 80 and sells for ₹ 100. Construct the pay-off table and opportunity loss table. What is the optimum number of cakes that should be bought each day?

Solution. Let A_i = alternative strategy (act) of stocking i cakes

E_j = a daily demand of j cakes states of nature (event)

Cost of a cake = ₹ 80

Selling price of a cake = ₹ 100

Profit per cake sold = ₹ (100 – 80) = ₹ 20

Loss on each unsold cake = ₹ 80

$$\text{Conditional profit} = \begin{cases} 20S & \text{if } D \geq S \\ 20D - 80(S-D) = 100D - 80S & \text{if } D < S \end{cases}$$

Where D = number of cakes demanded

S = number of cakes in stock

The resulting pay-off (conditional profit) are as follows:

Even (demand) D	*Probability*	*Conditional pay-offs (₹) Acts (Stock)*			
		A1 : 25	*A2 : 26*	*A3 : 27*	*A4 : 28*
E1 : 25	0.10	500	420	340	260
E2 : 26	0.30	500	520	440	360
E3 : 27	0.50	500	520	540	460
E4 : 28	0.10	500	520	540	560

The expected conditional pay-off are computed as follows:

Even (demand) D	*Probability*	*Expected conditional pay-offs (₹) Acts (Stock)*			
		A1 : 25	*A2 : 26*	*A3 : 27*	*A4 : 28*
E1 : 25	0.10	50	42	34	26
E2 : 26	0.30	150	156	132	108
E3 : 27	0.50	250	160	270	230
E4 : 28	0.10	50	52	54	56
	EMV	500	**510**	490	420

Since the EMV is maximum for act A2, so 26 cakes should be bought (stocked) each day. The conditional opportunity loss are computed as follows:

Event (Demand) D	*Probability*	*Conditional opportunity loss (₹) Acts (Stock)*			
		A1 : 25	*A2 : 26*	*A3 : 27*	*A4 : 28*
E1 : 25	0.10	0	80	160	240
E2 : 26	0.30	20	0	80	160
E3 : 27	0.50	40	20	0	80
E4 : 28	0.10	60	40	20	0

The expected conditional opportunity losses are computed as follows:

Event (Demand) D	*Probability*	*Conditional opportunity loss (₹) Acts (Stock)*			
		A1 : 25	*A2 : 26*	*A3 : 27*	*A4 : 28*
E1 : 25	0.10	0	8	16	24
E2 : 26	0.30	6	0	24	48
E3 : 27	0.50	20	10	0	40
E4 : 28	0.10	6	4	2	0
	EOL	32	**22**	42	112

Since the EOL is minimum for act A2, so 26 cakes should be bought (stocked) each day.

Example 10. *A wholesaler of sports goods has an opportunity to buy 5000 pairs of gloves that have been declared surplus by the government. The wholesaler will pay ₹ 50 per pair and can obtain ₹ 100 a pair by selling gloves to retailers. The price is well established, but the wholesaler is in doubt as to just how many pairs he will able to sell. Any gloves leftover, he can sell to discount outlets at ₹ 20 a pair. After careful consideration of the past data, the wholesaler assigns probabilities to the demand as follows.*

Retailer's demand	*Probability*
1000 pairs	*0.6*
3000 pairs	*0.3*
5000 pairs	*0.1*

(i) Compute the conditional monetary and expected monetary values.

(ii) Compute the expected profit with a perfect predicting device.

(iii) Compute the EVPI.

Solution.

Cost of a pair = ₹ 50

Selling price per pair = ₹ 100

Profit per pair = ₹ (100 – 50) = ₹ 50 (on sold pair)

Loss on each unsold pair = ₹ (50 – 20) = ₹ 30

$$\text{Conditional pay-off (profit)} = \begin{cases} 50S & \text{if } D \geq S \\ 50D - 30(S - D) = 80D - 30S & \text{if } D < S \end{cases}$$

Where D = number of pairs demanded

S = number of pairs in stock

(*i*) The resulting conditional pay-offs and corresponding expected pay-offs are computed as follows:

Retailer's Demand D	*Probability*	*Conditional pay-offs (₹'000) Stock per week*			*Expected pay-offs (₹'000) Stock per week*		
		1000 pairs	***3000 pairs***	***5000 pairs***	***1000 pairs***	***3000 pairs***	***5000 pairs***
1000 pairs	0.6	50	–10	–70	30	–6	–42
3000 pairs	0.3	50	150	90	15	45	27
5000 pairs	0.1	50	150	250	5	15	25
				EMV	50	54	10

(*ii*) The expected profit under perfect information (EPPI) is computed as follows:

Retailer's Demand	*Probability*	*Conditional pay-offs (₹ '000) Stock per week*			*Under perfect information (₹ '000)*	
D		*1000 Pairs*	*3000 Pairs*	*5000 Pairs*	*Maximum pay-off (v)*	*Expected pay-off*
	(i)	*(ii)*	*(iii)*	*(iv)*	*[from (ii), (iii), (iv)]*	*(i) × (ii)*
1000 pairs	0.6	50	–10	–70	50	30
3000 pairs	0.3	50	150	90	150	45
5000 pairs	0.1	50	150	250	250	25
						EPPI = 100

(*iii*) EVPI = EPPI = max EMV = 100 – 54 = 46

Thus, EVPI = ₹ 46,000.

Example 11. *Pay-off of three acts, A1, A2 and A3 and state of nature X, Y, Z are as follows:*

States of nature	*Pay-off (₹) Acts*		
	A1	*A2*	*A3*
X	*–20*	*–50*	*200*
Y	*200*	*–100*	*–50*
Z	*400*	*600*	*300*

The probabilities of the state of nature are 0.3, 0.4 and 0.3 respectively. Calculate the EMV for the given data and select the best act. Also find the expected value of perfect information (EVPI).

Solution. Computation of expected pay-off

States of nature	*Probability*	*Pay-off (₹) Acts*			*Expected pay-off (₹) Acts*		
		A1	*A2*	*A3*	*A1*	*A2*	*A3*
	(i)	*(ii)*	*(iii)*	*(iv)*	*(i) × (ii)*	*(i) × (iii)*	*(i) × (iv)*
X	0.3	–20	–50	200	–6	–15	60
Y	0.4	200	–100	–50	80	–40	–20
Z	0.3	400	600	300	120	180	90
				EMV	**194**	125	130

Since the EMV is maximum for act A1, so A1 is the best act.

The expected profit under perfect information (EPPI) is computed as follows:

States of nature	*Probability*	*Pay-off* (₹)			*Under perfect information* (₹)	
			Acts		*Maximum*	*Expected*
	(i)	*A1* *(ii)*	*A2* *(iii)*	*A3* *(iv)*	*pay-off (v)* *[from (ii), (iii), (iv)]*	*pay-off* *(i) × (v)*
X	0.3	–20	–50	200	200	60
Y	0.4	200	–100	–50	200	80
Z	0.3	400	600	300	600	180
						EPPI = 320

EVPI = EPPI – max EMV = 320 – 194 = 126

Thus, EVPI = ₹ 126.

7.6 DECISION TREE

A decision tree is a graphical representation of the various alternatives and sequence of events in a decision problem. Decision tree is a simple method for making a decision, where all the options are clearly open to the decision-maker in concise form. Decision tree is beneficial for simple as well as complex decision-making situations. Basically decision tree is drawn for those problems where more than one decisions are to be taken and the decision taken to one stage affects the subsequent decision.

There are some basic rules for drawing a decision tree.

(*i*) Identify all decisions to be made and the order in which they must be made.

(*iii*) Identify the chance events that can occur after each decision.

(*iii*) Develop a tree diagram showing the sequence of decisions and chance events. The tree is constructed starting from left and moving towards right. The 'square box' denotes a decision point at which the available strategies are considered. The 'circle' represents the chance node or event, the various state of nature or outcomes emanate from this.

(*iv*) Obtain probability estimate of the chances of each outcome's occurrence.

(*v*) Obtain estimates of the consequences of all possible outcomes or actions.

(*vi*) Calculate the expected value of all possible actions.

(*vii*) Select the action offering the most attractive expected value.

ILLUSTRATIVE EXAMPLES

Example 12. *XYZ Ltd. has invented a picture cell phone. It is faced with selecting one alternative out of the following strategies:*

(*i*) *Manufacture the cell phone*

(*ii*) *Take royalty from another manufacturer*

(*iii*) *Sell the rights for the invention and take a lumpsum amount.*

Profit in thousands of rupees which can be incurred and the probability associated with such alternative are shown in the following table.

Event	*Probability*	*Manufacture*	*Royalty*	*Sell rights*
High	*0.25*	*200*	*60*	*50*
Medium	*0.40*	*50*	*40*	*50*
Low	*0.35*	*–10*	*20*	*50*

Represent the company's problem in the form of the decision tree and suggest what decision the company should take to maximize profit.

Solution.

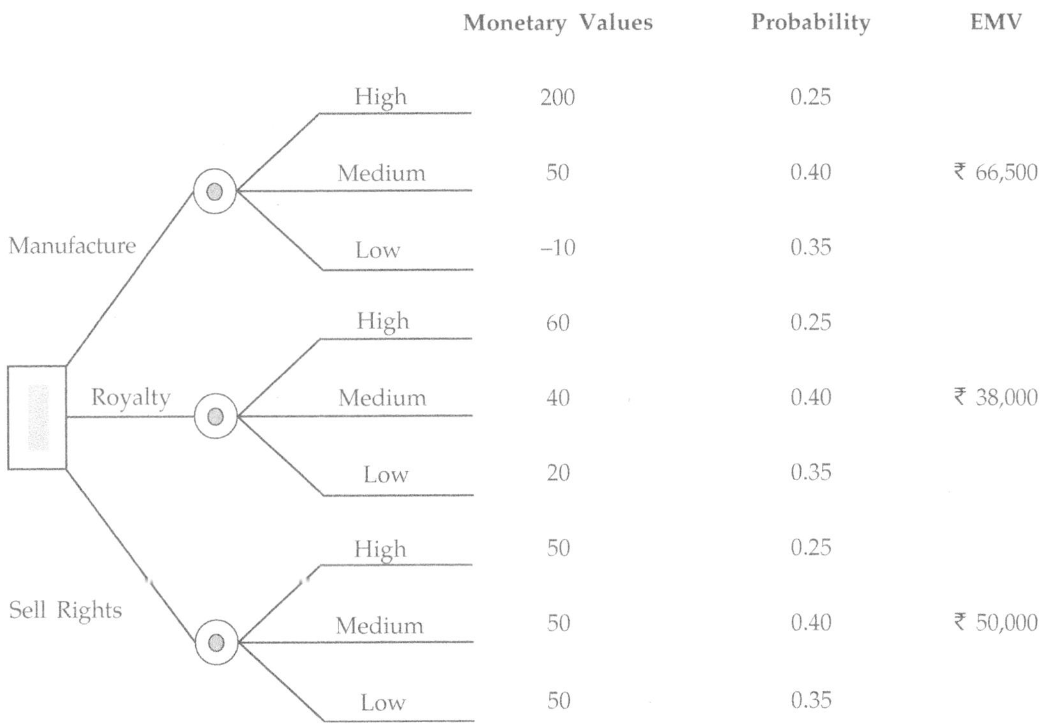

The EMV for strategy (*i*) manufacture the cell phone is maximum. So the best decision by XYZ Ltd. is to manufacture the picture cell phone itself to get profit of ₹ 66,500.

Example 13. *A company is evaluating four alternative single period investment opportunities whose returns are based on the state of the economy. The possible states of the economy and the associated probability distribution are as follows:*

State	*Fair*	*Good*	*Great*
Probability	*0.2*	*0.5*	*0.3*

The returns for each investment opportunity and each state of the economy are as follows:

Alternative	*State of Economy*		
	Fair (₹)	*Good (₹)*	*Great (₹)*
A	*1000*	*3000*	*6000*
B	*500*	*4500*	*6800*
C	*0*	*5000*	*8000*
D	*–4000*	*6000*	*8500*

Using the decision tree approach, determine the expected return for each alternative. Which alternative investment proposal would you recommend if the expected monetary value criterion is to be employed?

Solution.

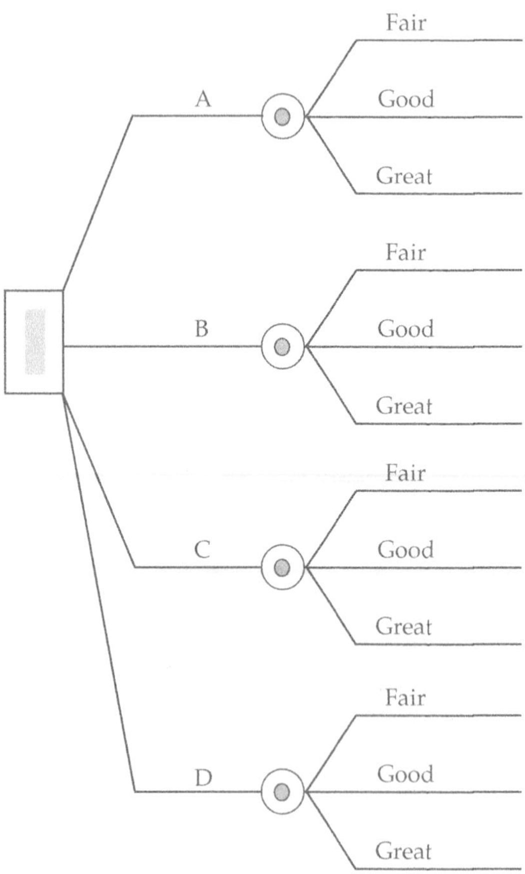

Monetary Values (₹)	Probability	EMV
1,000	0.2	
3,000	0.5	₹ 3,500
6,000	0.3	
500	0.2	
4,500	0.5	₹ 4,390
6,800	0.3	
0	0.2	
5,000	0.5	₹ 4,900
8,000	0.3	
–4,000	0.2	
6,000	0.5	₹ 4,750
8,500	0.3	

Thus, EMV for C is maximum, so alternative C is the best with maximum return of ₹ 4,900.

Example 14. *A manager has a choice between (i) a risky contract promising ₹ 7 lakhs with probability 0.6 and ₹ 4 lakhs with probability 0.4, (ii) a diversified portfolio consisting of two contracts with independent outcomes promising ₹ 3.5 lakhs with probability of 0.6 and ₹ 2 lakhs with probability of 0.4. Construct a decision tree and suggest which choice the manager should opt using EMV criterion.*

Solution.

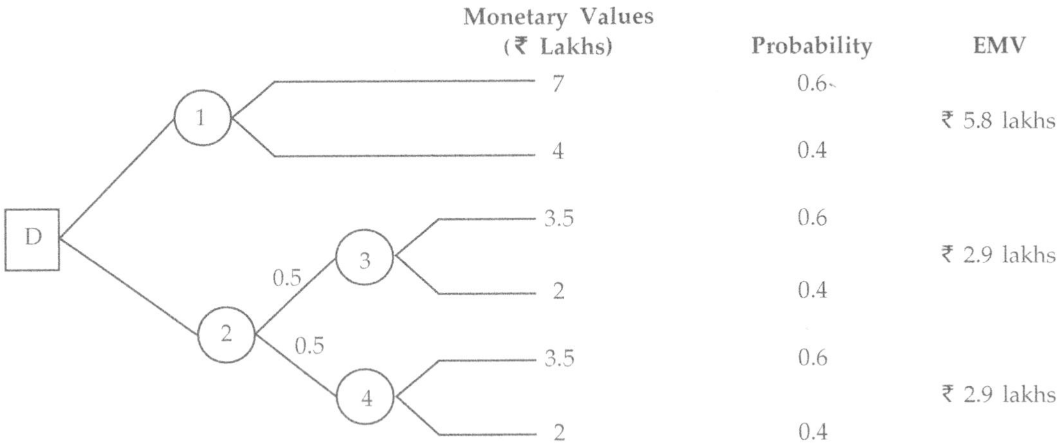

EMV at node 2 = (2.9 x 0.5) + (2.9 x 0.5) = ₹ 2.9 lakhs.

Thus, EMV for strategy (*i*) risky contract is maximum. So manager should opt choice (*i*).

Example 15. *A shopkeeper has the facility to store a large number of perishable items. He buys them at a rate of ₹ 3 per item and sells at the rate of ₹ 5 per item. If an item is not sold at the end of the day, then there is a loss of ₹ 3 per item. The daily demand of the item has the following probability distribution.*

No. of items sold	4	5	6
Probability	0.2	0.5	0.3

How many items should he store so that his daily expected profit is maximum? Use decision tree approach.

Solution. Profit per item = ₹ (5 – 3) = ₹ 2

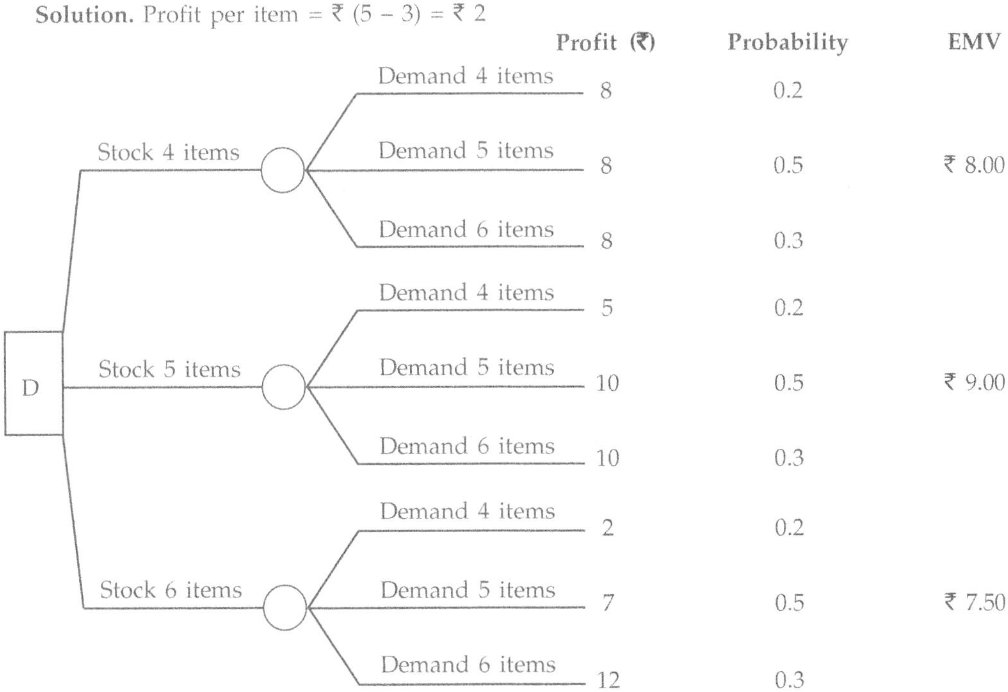

Thus, EMV for strategy second is maximum. So shopkeeper should stock 5 items.

Example 16. *Matrix company is planning to launch a new product, which can be introduced initially in Western India or in the entire country. If the product is introduced only in Western India, the investment outlay will be ₹ 12 million. After two years, Matrix can evaluate the project to determine whether it should cover the entire country. For such expansion it will have to incur an additional investment of ₹ 10 million. To introduce the product in the entire country right in the beginning would involve an outlay of ₹ 20 million. The product, in any case, will have a life of 5 years after which the plant will have zero net value. If the product is introduced only in Western India, demand would be high or low with the probabilities of 0.8 and 0.2 respectively and annual cash-flow of ₹ 4 million and ₹ 2.5 million respectively. If the product is introduced in the entire country right in the beginning the demand would be high or low with probabilities of 0.6 and 0.4 respectively and annual cash inflows of ₹ 8 million and ₹ 5 million respectively.*

Based on the observed demand in Western India, if the product is introduced in the entire country the following probabilities would exist for high and low demand on an all India basis.

Western India	*Entire Country*	
	High demand	*Low demand*
High demand	0.9	0.1
Low demand	0.4	0.6

The hurdle rate applicable to this project is 12 percent.

(i) *Set up a decision tree for the investment situation.*

(ii) *Advice Matrix company on the investment policy it should follow. Support your advice with appropriate reasoning.*

Solution.

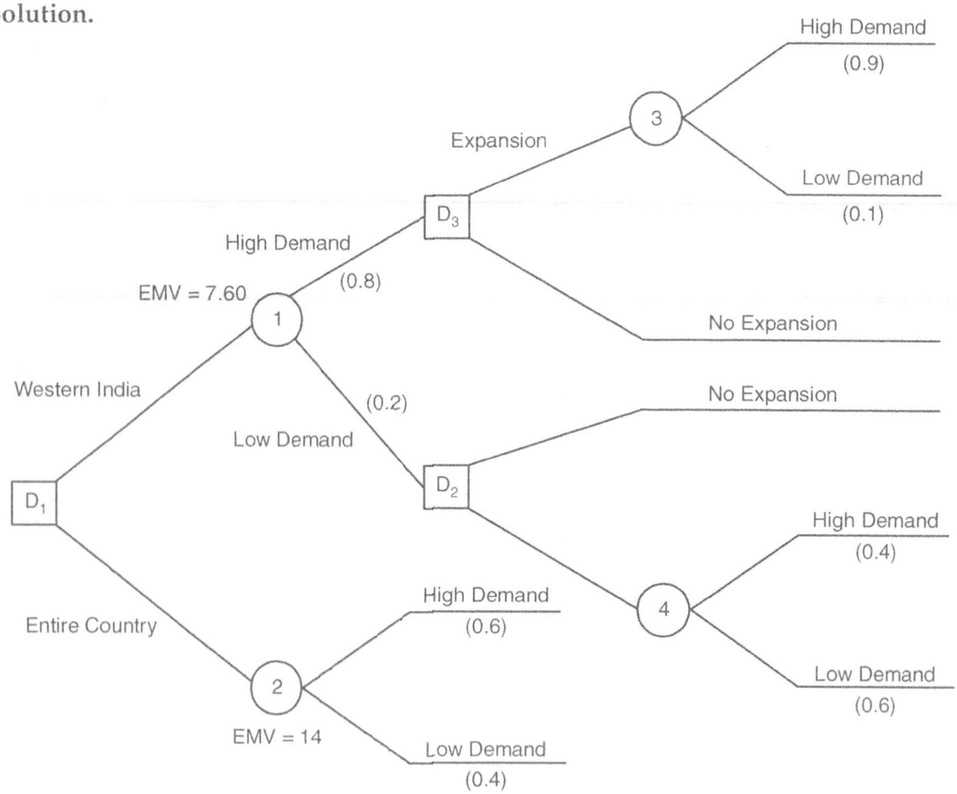

	Decision point	*Outcome*	*Probability*	*Conditional value (₹)*	*Expected value*
D3	(Demand high in Western India				
	(*i*) Expansion	High demand	0.9	8	7.2
		Low demand	0.1	5	0.5
					7.7
					7.7 × 3 years = 23.1
					Less cost = 10.0
					Total = 13.1
	(*ii*) No expansion				0.0
					Total expected profit = 13.1
D2	(Demand low in Western India)				
	(*i*) Expansion	High demand	0.4	8	3.2
		Low demand	0.6	5	3.0
					6.2
					6.2 × 3 years = 18.6
					Less cost = 10.0
					Total = 8.6
					0.0
	(*i*) No expansion				Total expected profit = 8.6
D1	(*i*) Introduction Entire country	High demand	0.6	8	4.8
		Low demand	0.4	5	2.0
					6.8
					6.5 × 5 years = 34.0
					Less cost = 20.0
					Total expected profit = 14.0
	(*ii*) Introduction Western India	High demand	0.8	4	0.8 (4 × 2 + 13.1) = 16.88
		Low demand	0.2	2.5	0.2 (2.5 × 2 + 8.6) = 2.72
					19.60
					Less cost = 12.00
					Total expected profit = 7.6

Thus, the EMV at node 2 is maximum, make a decision to launch the product in entire country.

EXERCISES

1. The ABC company is faced with four decision alternatives relating to investments in a capital expansion programme. Since these investments are made in future, the company foresees different market conditions as expressed in the form of states of nature. The following table summarizes the decision alternatives, the various states of nature and the rate of return associated with each state of nature.

Decision	*States of Nature*		
	Q1	*Q2*	*Q3*
D1	17%	15%	8%
D2	18%	16%	9%
D3	21%	14%	9%
D4	19%	12%	10%

If the company has no information regarding the probability of occurrence of the three states of nature, give the recommended decision for the decision criterion as follows:

(*i*) Maximax criterion (*ii*) Maximin criterion

(*iii*) Minimax regret criterion (*iv*) Laplace criterion

[**Ans.** (*i*) D3 (*ii*) D4 (*iii*) D3 (*iv*) D3]

2. A food products company is contemplating the introduction of a revolutionary new product with new packaging to replace the existing product at much higher price (A1) or a moderate change in the composition of the existing product with a new packaging at a small increase in price (A2) or a small change in the composition of the existing except the word 'New' with a negligible increase in price (A3). The three possible states of nature or events are (*i*) high increase in sales (S1), (*ii*) no change in sales (S2) and decrease in sales (S3). The marketing department of the company worked out the pay-offs in terms of yearly net profits for each of the strtegies of three events (expected sales). This is represented in the following table.

Strategy	*States of Nature* *Pay-offs (in ₹)*		
	S1	*S2*	*S3*
A1	7,00,000	3,00,000	1,50,000
A2	5,00,000	4,50,000	0
A3	3,00,000	3,00,000	3,00,000

Which strategy should the concerned executive choose on the basis of

(*i*) Maximin criterion (*ii*) Maximax criterion

(*iii*) Minimax regret criterion (*iv*) Laplace criterion?

[**Ans.** (*i*) A3 (*ii*) A1, (*iii*) A1, (*iv*) A1 (*iv*) Bonds]

3. A person wants to invest in one of three alternative investment plans: stock, bonds or a savings account. It is assumed that the person wishes to invest all of the funds in one plan. The conditional pay-offs of the investments are based on three potential economic conditions: accelerated, normal or slow growth. The pay-off matrix is given as:

Alternative Investment	*Economic conditions Pay-offs (in ₹)*		
	Accelerated growth	*Normal growth*	*Slow growth*
Stocks	10,000	6,500	–4,000
Bonds	8,000	6,000	1000
Savings	5,000	5,000	5,000

Determine the best investment plan using each of the following:

(*i*) Maximin criterion (*ii*) Maximax criterion

(*iii*) Laplace criterion (*iv*) Hurwicz criterion with $\alpha = 0.6$

[**Ans.** (*i*) Savings (*ii*) Stock (*iii*) Bonds or Savings]

4. Consider the following cost matrix.

Alternatives	*States of Nature*			
	S1	*S2*	*S3*	*S4*
A1	1	3	8	5
A2	2	5	4	7
A3	4	6	6	3
A4	6	8	3	5

Determine the best alternative using:

(*i*) Minimax criterion

(*ii*) Minimin criterion

(*iii*) Minimax regret criterion. [**Ans.** (*i*) A3 (*ii*) A1 (*iii*) A3]

5. Pay-offs (in ₹) of three acts A1, A2 and A3 and the possible states of nature S1, S2 and S3 are as follows:

States of nature	*Acts*		
	A1	*A2*	*A3*
S1	–20	–50	200
S2	200	–100	–50
S3	400	600	300

The probabilities of the states of nature are 0.3, 0.4 and 0.3 respectively. Tabulate the expected monetary values (EMVs) for the above data and state which can be selected as the best act. [**Ans.** A1]

6. An investor is given the following investment alternatives and percentage rates of return:

Strategy	*States of Nature (Market conditions)*		
	Low	*Medium*	*High*
Regular shares	7%	10%	15%
Risky shares	–10%	12%	25%
Property	–12%	18%	30%

Over the past 300 days, 150 days have been medium market conditions and 60 days have been high market conditions. [**Ans.** Property]

On the basis of these data, state the optimum investment strategy for the investment.

7. Pay-offs (₹) of three acts A1, A2 and A3 and the states of nature S1, S2, and S3 are as follows:

States of nature	*Pay-offs (₹) Acts*		
	A1	*A2*	*A3*
S1	25	–10	–125
S2	400	440	400
S3	650	740	750

The probabilities of the states of nature are 0.1, 0.7 and 0.2 respectively. Tabulate the expected monetary values (EMVs) and state which can be selected as the best act.

[**Ans.** A2]

8. XYZ flower shop promises its customers delivery within four hours on all flower orders. All flowers are purchased on the prior day and delivered to XYZ by 8:00 the next morning. XYZ's daily demand for roses is as follows:

Roses (in dozens)	7	8	9	10
Probability	0.1	0.2	0.4	0.3

XYZ purchases roses for ₹ 10.00 per dozen and sells them for ₹ 30.00. All unsold roses are donated to a local hospital. How many dozens of roses should XYZ order each evening to maximize its profit? What is the optimum expected profit?

[**Ans.** 9 dozen, ₹ 168]

9. A producer of boats has estimated the following distribution of demand for a particular kind of boat:

No. demanded	0	1	2	3	4	5	6
Probability	0.14	0.27	0.27	0.18	0.09	0.04	0.01

Each boat cost him ₹ 7,000 and he sells them for ₹ 10,000 each. Any boat that are left unsold at the end of the season must be disposed off for ₹ 6,000 each. How many boats should be in stock so as to maximize his expected profit?

[**Ans.** 3 boats]

10. Consider the following pay-off table.

Act	Events			
	E1	*E2*	*E3*	*E4*
A1	18	10	12	8
A2	16	12	10	10
A3	12	13	11	12

The probabilities of events E1, E2, E3, and E4 are 0.25, 0.40, 0.15 and 0.20 respectively. Find the optimum act using expected opportunity loss (EOL) criterion. [**Ans.** A2]

11. A man has the choice of running either a hot-snack stall or an ice-cream stall at a seaside resort during the summer season. If it is a fairly cool summer, he should make ₹ 5,000 by running the hot-snack stall, but if the summer is quite hot he can only expect to make ₹ 1000. On the other hand, if he operates the ice-cream stall, his profit is estimated at ₹ 6500 if the summer is hot, but only ₹ 1000 if it is cool. There is a 40% chance of the summer being hot. Should he opt for running the hot-snack stall or the ice-cream stall? Give mathematical argument. [**Ans.** Hot-snack stall]

12. The cost of making an item is ₹ 25, the selling price of the item is ₹ 30, if it is sold within a week, and it could be disposed off at ₹ 20 per piece at the end of week if unsold. Frequency of weekly sales is given as:

Weekly sales	(≤ 3)	4	5	6	7	(≥ 8)
No. of weeks	0	10	20	40	30	0

Find the optimum number of items per week the industry should make using EMV and EOL criterion. Also find, the EVPI. [**Ans.** 6 items, ₹ 3.50]

13. A company wants to know whether or not a new shaving cream should be marketed. The present value of all future profits for the success of the cream is ₹ 1,000,000 and its failure would results in a net loss of ₹ 5,00,000. Not marketing it would not change the profits. The chances of the success of the new cream are 50%. Determine the optimum act and find the EVPI. [**Ans.** Market the cream, ₹ 2,50,000]

14. A modern home appliances dealer finds that the cost of holding a mini-cooking range in stock for a month is ₹ 200 (insurance, minor deterioration, interest on borrowed capital, etc.). Customer who cannot obtain a cooking range immediately tends to go to other dealers and he estimates that for every customer who cannot get immediate delivery, he loses an average of ₹ 500. The probabilities of a demand of 0, 1, 2, 3, 4 and 5 cooking ranges in a month are 0.05, 0.10, 0.20, 0.30, 0.20 and 0.15 respectively. Determine the optimum stock level of cooking range. Also find the EVPI.

[**Ans.** 4 cooking ranges, ₹ 315]

15. A manufacturer of leather goods must decide whether to expand his plant capacity now or wait at least another year. His advisors tell him that if he expands now and economic conditions remained good, there will be a profit of ₹ 164,000 during the next year. If he expands now and there is recession, there will be a loss of ₹ 40,000. If he waits at least another year and economic conditions remain good, there will be a profit of ₹ 80,000 and if he waits at least another year and there is a recession, there will be a small profit of ₹ 8,000. What should the manufacturer decide to do if he wants to minimize the expected loss during next year and he feels that the odds are 2 : 1 that there will be recession. Use decision tree approach. [**Ans.** Wait for one year]

16. XYZ Ltd. wants to update/change its existing manufacturing prices for product A. It wants to strengthen its research and development cell and conduct research for finding a better product of manufacturing, which can get them higher profits. At present the company is earning a profit of ₹ 20,000 after paying for material, labour and overheads. XYZ Ltd. has the following four alternatives:

(*i*) The company continues with the existing process.

(*ii*) The company conducts research P, which costs ₹ 20,000, has 75% probability of success and can get the profit of ₹ 5,000.

(*iii*) The company conducts research Q, which costs ₹ 10,000, has 50% probability of success and can get the profit of ₹ 25,000.

(*iv*) The company pays ₹ 10,000 as royalty for a new product and can get profit of ₹ 20,000.

The company can carry out only one out of the two types of research P and Q because of certain limitations. Draw a decision tree diagram and find the best strategy for XYZ Ltd. [**Ans.** Conduct research P to find a new product]

17. The investment staff of a bank is considering four investment proposals for clients, shares, bonds, real estate and saving certificates, these investments will be held for one year. The past data regarding the four proposals is given as follows:

Shares. There is 25% chance that shares will decline by 10%, 30% chance that they will remain stable and 45% chance that will increase in value by 15%. Also the shares under consideration do not pay any dividends.

Bonds. These bonds stand a 40% chance of increase in value by 5% and 60% chance of remaining stable and they yield 12%.

Real Estate. This proposal has a 20% chance of increasing 30% in value, a 25% chance of increasing 20% in value, a 40% chance of increasing 10% in value, 10% chance of remaining stable and a 5% chance of loosing 5% of its value.

Saving Certificates. These certificates will yields 8.5% with certainty.

Use a decision tree to structure the alternatives available to the investment staff and using the expected monetary value criteria choose the alternative with the highest expected value. [**Ans.** Invest in real estate]

18. A manufacturing company has to select one of the two products A or B for manufacturing product A requires investment of ₹ 20,000 and product B ₹ 40,000. Market research survey shows high, medium and low demands with corresponding probabilities and return from sales, in ₹ thousand, for the two products in the following table.

Market	*Probability*		*Return for sales*	
	A	*B*	*A*	*B*
High	0.4	0.3	50	80
Medium	0.3	0.5	30	60
Low	0.3	0.2	10	50

Construct an appropriate decision tree. What decision the company should take?

[**Ans.** Product B]

❑❑❑

CHAPTER 8

Theory of Games

8.1 INTRODUCTION

In all the various types of optimization problems there is a single decision maker whose interest lies in selecting the variables in such a way as to optimize objective function, there being no conflict in deciding what the objective is. But in many practical problems, it is required to take decision in a situation, where there are two or more decision makers with conflicting interests and the action of one depends upon the action taken by the other. This situation is known as competitive situation (game). Game theory is a distinct and interdisciplinary approach to the study of human behaviour. The disciplines in the game theory are mathematics, economics and the other social and behavioural sciences.

Some game theoretic ideas can be traced to the 18th century, but a decisive event in the development of the theory was the publication in 1944 of the book "Theory of Games and Economic Behaviour" by John Von Neumann and Oscar Morgentern which established the foundations of the game theory. The theory of games is based on the minimax principle derived by John Von Neumann, which states that each player will try to minimize his maximum loss (or maximize his minimum gain).

8.2 ASSUMPTIONS OF THE GAME

1. There are finite number of participants called players.
2. Each players has a finite number of possible strategies (alternatives). The possible strategies may not be same for each player.
3. Each player knows all the possible alternatives available to others but does not know which of them is going to be chosen by them.
4. Every combination of strategies determines an outcome which results in gains to the players.
5. The gain of a player depends not only on his own actions but also those of others.
6. Each player knows the full information contained in the pay-off matrix.
7. The players make individual decisions without direct communication.

8.3 BASIC TERMINOLOGY

- **A Competitive Game:** A competitive situation with a finite number of competitions with conflicting interests and where the action of one depends upon the action taken by the other.
- **Strategy:** The number of competitive actions (alternatives) that are available for a player are called strategies to that player.
- **Pay-off:** It is the outcome of playing the game.
- **Pay-off-Matrix:** It is a tabular representation of the outcomes or pay-off of different strategies of the game. Generally, pay-off matrix is generated in favour of first player.
- **Optimal Strategy:** The particular strategy by which a player optimize his gains or losses without knowing the competitor's strategies is called optimal strategy.
- **Pure Strategy:** It is a decision which is taken by the player to select the particular strategy (alternative).
- **Mixed Strategy:** If a player in a game chooses among two or more strategies at random according to specific probabilities, this choice is called a mixed strategy.
- **Zero-Sum Game:** If we add up the gains and losses in a game, treating losses as negatives, and we find that the sum is zero for each set of strategies chosen, then the game is a zero-sum game.
- **Saddle Point:** A saddle point of a pay-off matrix is that position in the matrix where the maximum of the row minima coincides with the minimum of the column maxima. The pay-off at the saddle point is called the value of the game and is obviously equal to the maximin and minimax values of the game. In general, the value of the game satisfies the inequations.

$$\text{maximin value} \leq v \leq \text{minimax value}$$

$$\underline{v} \leq v \leq \overline{v}$$

A game is said to be a fair game, if the value of the game is zero, *i.e.*, $v = 0$.

A game is said to be strictly determinable, if maximin value = minimax value $= v$.

8.4 TWO PERSON ZERO-SUM GAMES

Zero-sum games with two players are called two person zero-sum games or rectangular games. In two person zero-sum games the gain of one player is exactly equal to the loss of the other. The assumptions of such games are:

1. There are two players only.
2. The number of strategies available to each player is finite.
3. There is a pay-off for each specific strategy.
4. The amount won by one player is exactly equal to the amount lost by the other.
5. First player tries to maximize gains and second players tries to minimize losses.

8.5 MINIMAX THEOREM

The minimax theorem is given by John Von Neumann which states that "For every two-person zero-sum game with finite strategies, there exists a value v and a mixed strategy for each player," *i.e.*,

1. Given second player's strategy, the best pay-off possible for player first is v, and
2. Given first player's strategy, the best pay-off possible for player second is $-v$.

8.6 SOLUTION OF GAMES WITH SADDLE POINT (*Pure Strategy Games*)

The following rules are used to determine the saddle point:

1. Select the minimum element of each row of the pay-off matrix and encircle them.
2. Select the maximum element of each column of the pay-off matrix and enclose them in a square.
3. If there appears an element in the pay-off matrix which is enclosed by circle and square both, the position of that element is called the saddle point.

Note: If a pay-off matrix involve more than one saddle point then there exists more than one solution of the game.

Example 1. *Solve the game whose pay-off matrix is:*

			B	
		I	*II*	*III*
	I	–3	–2	6
A	*II*	2	0	2
	III	5	–2	–4

(UPTU, 2004–05)

Solution. First we try to find a saddle point of the game. To find the saddle point, circle the minimum of each row and square the maximum of each column.

			B		
		I	II	III	Row minimum
	I	(–3)	–2	[6]	–3
A	II	2	[(0)]	2	0 ← Maximin
	III	[5]	–2	(–4)	–4
Column maximum		5	0	6	
			↑ Minimax		

Clearly, there is a saddle point, *i.e.*, cell (II, II). Thus, the solution of the game is:

Optimal strategy for player A is II.

Optimal strategy for player B is II.

Value of the game = value of the saddle point

= 0

Example 2. *For the following two-person zero-sum game, find the optimal strategies for the two players and value of the game.*

		Player B		
		B1	B2	B3
Player A	A1	5	9	3
	A2	6	–12	–11
	A3	8	16	10

(IU 2007–08)

Solution. First we try to find a saddle point of the game. To find the saddle point, circle the minimum of each row and square the maximum of each column.

		Player B			
		B1	B2	B3	Row minimum
Player A	A1	5	9	(3)	3
	A2	6	(–12)	–11	–12
	A3	[(8)]	[16]	[10]	8 ← Maximin
Column maximum		8 ↑ Minimax	16	10	

Clearly, there is a saddle point, *i.e.*, cell (A3, B1). Thus, the solution of the game is:

Optimal strategy for player A is A3.

Optimal strategy for player B is B1.

Value of the game = Value of the saddle point

= 8

Example 3. *For the game with pay-off matrix:*

		Player B				
		B1	B2	B3	B4	B5
Player A	A1	9	3	1	8	0
	A2	6	5	4	6	7
	A3	2	4	3	3	8
	A4	5	6	2	2	1

Determine the best strategies for players A and B. Also determine the value of the game. Is this game (a) strictly determinable? (b) fair?

Solution. First we try to find a saddle point of the game. To find the saddle point, circle the minimum of each row and square the maximum of each column.

Player B

		B1	B2	B3	B4	B5	Row minimum
Player A	A1	9	3	1	8	0	0
	A2	6	5	4	6	7	4 ← Maximin
	A3	2	4	3	3	8	2
	A4	5	6	2	2	1	1
Column maximum		9	6	4	8	8	
				↑ Minimax			

Clearly, there is a saddle point, *i.e.*, cell (A2, B3). Thus, the solution of the game is:

Optimal strategy for player A is A2.

Optimal strategy for player B is B3.

Value of the game = Value of the saddle point

= 4

The game is strictly determinable, because value of the game $\neq 0$. The game is not a fair game.

Example 4. *For what value of λ, the following game is strictly determinable?*

Player B

		B1	*B2*	*B3*
Player A	*A1*	λ	*6*	*3*
	A2	*–1*	λ	*–6*
	A3	*–3*	*5*	λ

Solution. Ignoring the value of λ, we determine maximin and minimax value of the given pay-off matrix.

Player B

		B1	B2	B3	Row minimum
	A1	λ	6	3	3 ← Maximin
Player A	A2	–1	λ	–6	–6
	A3	–3	5	λ	–3
Column maximum		–1	6	3	
		↑ Minimax			

Here, maximin = 3 and minimax = –1

So the value of the game lies between –1 and 3

$$-1 \leq v \leq 3.$$

We know that a game is strictly determinable if

maximin = minimax = v

Therefore, λ must be between –1 and 3, *i.e.*,

$$-1 \leq \lambda \leq 3.$$

Example 5. *Find the ranges of p and q which will render the entry (2, 2) a saddle point for the game,*

		Player B		
		B1	*B2*	*B3*
	A1	2	4	5
Player A	*A2*	10	7	*q*
	A3	4	*p*	6

Solution. Ignoring the values of p and q, we determine the maximin and minimax value of pay-off matrix

		Player B			
		B1	B2	B3	Row minimum
	A1	2	4	5	2
Player A	A2	10	7	q	7 ← Maximin
	A3	4	p	6	4
Column maximum		10	7 ↑ Minimax	6	

Here, maximin = minimax = 7

For the entry (2, 2) a saddle point, $p \le 7$ and $q \ge 7$. Hence, the range of p and q will be $p \le 7$, $q \ge 7$.

8.7 SOLUTION OF GAMES WITHOUT SADDLE POINT (MIXED STRATEGIES GAMES)

There may be situations when no saddle point exists, *i.e.*, there is no pure strategy solution for games. In such cases the concept of mixed strategies is used. A mixed strategy game can be solved by the following methods:

1. Arithmetic method
2. Graphical method
3. Linear programming method

1. Arithmetic Method

For any 2 × 2 two person zero sum game in which each of the players, say A and B, has strategies A1 and A2 and B1 and B2 respectively. If p_1 is the probability with which A plays strategy A1 and if q_1 is the probability that B plays strategy B1, the pay-off matrix for player A is given by:

		Player B	
		B1	B2
Player A	A1	a_{11}	a_{12}
	A2	a_{21}	a_{22}

The optimum mixed strategies for players A and B are given by

$$S_A = \begin{bmatrix} A1 & A2 \\ p_1 & p_2 \end{bmatrix} \quad \text{and} \quad S_B = \begin{bmatrix} B1 & B2 \\ q_1 & q_2 \end{bmatrix}$$

where p_1, p_2, q_1 and q_2 are the probabilities to be determined by

$$\frac{p_1}{p_2} = \frac{a_{22} - a_{21}}{a_{11} - a_{12}}, \quad \frac{q_1}{q_2} = \frac{a_{22} - a_{12}}{a_{11} - a_{21}}$$

where $p_1 + p_2 = 1$ and $q_1 + q_2 = 1$.

The value of the game v for player A is given by

$$v = \frac{a_{11}a_{22} - a_{12}a_{21}}{(a_{11} + a_{22}) - (a_{12} + a_{21})}$$

The value of p_1 and q_1 can also be find by using

$$p_1 = \frac{a_{22} - a_{21}}{(a_{11} + a_{22}) - (a_{12} + a_{21})}; \quad q_1 = \frac{a_{22} - a_{12}}{(a_{11} + a_{22}) - (a_{12} + a_{21})}$$

$$p_2 = 1 - p_1; \quad q_2 = 1 - q_1$$

Dominance in Games

The concept of dominance can be applied to any two person zero sum game with any number of strategies for each player. For a pay-off matrix of large size, the rule of dominance can be used to reduce its size, by eliminating certain strategies whose removal will not affect the final solution.

In general, the following rules of dominance are used to reduce the size of the pay-off matrix:

Rule 1: If all the elements of ith row are less than or equal to the corresponding elements of the jth row, then ith row is dominated by the jth row of the pay-off matrix. Hence, ith row can be deleted from the pay-off matrix.

Rule 2: If all the elements of rth column are greater than or equal to the corresponding elements of the sth column, then rth column is dominated by the sth column of the pay-off matrix. Hence, rth column can be deleted from the pay-off matrix.

Rule 3: A strategy can also be dominated if it is inferior to an average of two or more other pure strategies. If a strategy dominates the convex linear combination of some other pure strategies, then one of the pure strategies in the combination may be deleted. The decision for dominance is taken by using rule 1 and rule 2.

Example 6. *Players A and B play a game in which each has three coins, a 5p, 10p and a 20p. Each selects a coin without the knowledge of the other's choice. If the sum of the coins is an odd amount, then A wins B's coin. But, if the sum is even, then B wins A's coin. Find the best strategy for each player and the value of the game.*

Solution. The pay-off matrix for player A is as follows:

		Player B		
		B1 : 5p	B2 : 10p	B3 : 20p
	A1 : 5p	–5	10	20
Player A	A2 : 10p	5	–10	–10
	A3 : 20p	5	–20	–20

There is no saddle point of this game. Therefore, we try to reduce the size of the pay-off matrix by use of dominance rules. Since every element of third column is greater than or equal to the corresponding element of the second column, therefore, the third column is dominated by the second column, *i.e.*, delete the third column from the pay-off matrix. So we get the following reduced matrix.

		Player B	
		B1 : 5*p*	B2 : 10*p*
Player A	A1 : 5*p*	–5	10
	A2 : 10*p*	5	–10
	A3 : 20*p*	5	–20

Since every element of the third row is less than or equal to the corresponding element of the second row, therefore, the third row is dominated by second row, *i.e.*, delete the third row from the pay-off matrix. So we get the following reduced 2 × 2 matrix.

		Player B	
		B1 : 5*p*	B2 : 10*p*
Player A	A1 : 5*p*	–5	10
	A2 : 10*p*	5	–10

Now we solve the 2 × 2 problem by using the formulas as follows:

Here, $a_{11} = -5$, $a_{12} = 10$, $a_{21} = 5$, $a_{22} = -10$

$$p_1 = \frac{a_{22} - a_{21}}{(a_{11} + a_{22}) - (a_{12} + a_{21})} = \frac{-10-5}{(-5-10)-(10+5)} = \frac{-15}{-30} = \frac{1}{2}$$

$$p_2 = 1 - p_1 = 1 - \frac{1}{2} = \frac{1}{2}$$

$$q_1 = \frac{a_{22} - a_{12}}{(a_{11} + a_{22}) - (a_{12} + a_{21})} = \frac{-10-10}{(-5-10)-(10+5)} = \frac{-20}{-30} = \frac{2}{3}$$

$$q_2 = 1 - q_1 = 1 - \frac{2}{3} = \frac{1}{3}$$

$$v = \frac{a_{11}a_{22} - a_{12}a_{21}}{(a_{11} + a_{22}) - (a_{12} + a_{21})} = \frac{(-5\times-10)-(10\times5))}{(-5-10)-(10+5)} = \frac{0}{-30} = 0$$

Hence, an optimal solution of the given game is:

Optimal strategy for player A

$$S_A = \begin{bmatrix} A1 & A2 & A3 \\ \frac{1}{2} & \frac{1}{2} & 0 \end{bmatrix}$$

Optimal strategy for player B

$$S_B = \begin{bmatrix} B1 & B2 & B3 \\ \frac{2}{3} & \frac{1}{3} & 0 \end{bmatrix}$$

and the value of the game $v = 0$.

Example 7. *Solve the game whose pay-off matrix is as follows:*

		B1	B2	B3
	A1	1	0	10
A	A2	9	7	1
	A3	8	2	14

Solution. The given problem does not have a saddle point. Therefore, we try to reduce the size of the pay-off matrix by use of dominance rules. Since every element of the first row is less than or equal to the corresponding element of the third row, therefore, the first row is dominated by the third row, *i.e.*, delete the first row from the pay-off matrix. So we get the following reduced matrix.

		B1	B2	B3
A	A2	9	7	1
	A3	8	2	14

Since every element of the first column is greater than or equal to the corresponding element of the second column, therefore, the first column is dominated by the second column, *i.e.*, delete the first column from the pay-off matrix. So we get the following reduced 2 × 2 matrix.

		B2	B3
A	A2	7	1
	A3	2	14

Now we solve the 2 × 2 problem by using the formulas as follows:

Here, $a_{11} = 7$, $a_{12} = 1$, $a_{21} = 2$, $a_{22} = 14$

$$p_1 = \frac{a_{22} - a_{21}}{(a_{11} + a_{22}) - (a_{12} + a_{21})} = \frac{14-2}{(7+14)-(1+2)} = \frac{12}{18} = \frac{2}{3}$$

$$p_2 = 1 - p_1 = 1 - \frac{2}{3} = \frac{1}{3}$$

$$q_1 = \frac{a_{22} - a_{12}}{(a_{11} + a_{22}) - (a_{12} + a_{21})} = \frac{14-1}{(7+14)-(1+2)} = \frac{13}{18}$$

$$q_2 = 1 - q_1 = 1 - \frac{13}{18} = \frac{5}{18}$$

$$v = \frac{a_{11}a_{22} - a_{12}a_{21}}{(a_{11} + a_{22}) - (a_{12} + a_{21})} = \frac{7 \times 14 - 1 \times 2}{(7+14)-(1+2)} = \frac{96}{18} = \frac{16}{3}$$

Hence, an optimal solution of the given game is:

Optimal strategy for player A

$$S_A = \begin{bmatrix} A1 & A2 & A3 \\ 0 & \frac{2}{3} & \frac{1}{3} \end{bmatrix}$$

Optimal strategy for player B

$$S_B = \begin{bmatrix} B1 & B2 & B3 \\ 0 & \frac{13}{18} & \frac{5}{18} \end{bmatrix}$$

and the value of the game $v = \frac{16}{3}$

Example 8. *Solve the game whose pay-off matrix is as follows:*

		B I	B II	B III
A	I	1	7	2
	II	6	2	7
	III	5	1	6

Solution. The given problem does not have a saddle point. Therefore, we try to reduce the size of the pay-off matrix by use of dominance rules. Since every element of the third column is greater than or equal to the corresponding element of the first column, therefore, the third column is dominated by the first column, *i.e.*, delete the third column from the pay-off matrix. So we get the following reduced matrix.

		B I	B II
A	I	1	7
	II	6	2
	III	5	1

Since every element of the third row is less than or equal to the corresponding element of the second row, therefore, the third row is dominated by the second row, *i.e.*, delete the third row from the pay-off matrix. So we get the following reduced 2 × 2 matrix.

		B I	B II
A	I	1	7
	II	6	2

Now we solve the 2 × 2 game by using the formulas as follows:

Here, $a_{11} = 1$, $a_{12} = 7$, $a_{21} = 6$, $a_{22} = 2$

$$p_1 = \frac{a_{22} - a_{21}}{(a_{11} + a_{22}) - (a_{12} + a_{21})} = \frac{2-6}{(1+2)-(7+6)} = \frac{-4}{-10} = \frac{2}{5}$$

$$p_2 = 1 - p_1 = 1 - \frac{2}{5} = \frac{3}{5}$$

$$q_1 = \frac{a_{22} - a_{12}}{(a_{11} + a_{22}) - (a_{12} + a_{21})} = \frac{2-7}{(1+2)-(7+6)} = \frac{-5}{-10} = \frac{1}{2}$$

$$q_2 = 1 - q_1 = 1 - \frac{1}{2} = \frac{1}{2}$$

$$v = \frac{a_{11}a_{22} - a_{12}a_{21}}{(a_{11}+a_{22})-(a_{12}+a_{21})} = \frac{1\times2-7\times6}{(1+2)-(7+6)} = \frac{2-42}{-10} = 4$$

Hence, an optimal solution of the given game is:

Optimal strategy for player A

$$S_A = \begin{bmatrix} \text{I} & \text{II} & \text{III} \\ \frac{2}{5} & \frac{3}{5} & 0 \end{bmatrix}$$

Optimal strategy for player B

$$S_B = \begin{bmatrix} \text{I} & \text{II} & \text{III} \\ \frac{1}{2} & \frac{1}{2} & 0 \end{bmatrix}$$

and the value of the game $v = 4$.

Example 9. *Solve the game whose pay-off matrix is as follows:*

		B			
		B1	*B2*	*B3*	*B4*
A	*A1*	2	1	3	–1
	A2	2	3	1	3
	A3	3	1	3	–1
	A4	–1	3	–1	7

Solution. The given problem does not have a saddle point. Therefore, we try to reduce the size of the pay-off matrix by use of dominance rules. Since every element of the first row is less than or equal to the corresponding element of the third row, therefore, the first row is dominated by the third row, *i.e.*, delete the first row from the pay-off matrix. So we get the following reduced matrix.

		B			
		B1	B2	B3	B4
A	A2	2	3	1	3
	A3	3	1	3	–1
	A4	–1	3	–1	7

Now, the first column is dominated by the third column, *i.e.*, delete the first column from the pay-off matrix. So we get the following reduced matrix.

		B		
		B2	B3	B4
A	A2	3	1	3
	A3	1	3	–1
	A4	3	–1	7

In order to check the further reduction of this matrix, the average of the player B's B3 and B4 pure strategies give $\left\{\frac{1+3}{2}, \frac{3-1}{2}, \frac{-1+7}{2}\right\}$ or {2, 1, 3} which is less than or equal to the corresponding elements of the second column, *i.e.*, B2, therefore the second column is deleted from the matrix. So we get the following reduced matrix.

		B3	B4
	A2	1	3
A	A3	3	–1
	A4	–1	7

(B above columns B3, B4)

Now the average of the player A's A3 and A4 pure strategies give $\left\{\frac{3-1}{2}, \frac{-1+7}{2}\right\}$ or {1, 3} which is same as the player A's A2 strategy. Hence deleting the player A's A2 strategy we get the following reduced 2 × 2 matrix

		B3	B4
A	A3	3	–1
	A4	–1	–7

(B above columns B3, B4)

Now, we solve the 2 × 2 game by using the formulas as follows:

Here, $a_{11} = 3, a_{12} = -1, a_{21} = -1, a_{22} = 7$

$$p_1 = \frac{a_{22}-a_{21}}{(a_{11}+a_{22})-(a_{12}+a_{21})} = \frac{7-(-1)}{(3+7)-(-1-1)} = \frac{8}{12} = \frac{2}{3}$$

$$p_2 = 1 - p_1 = 1-\frac{2}{3} = \frac{1}{3}$$

$$q_1 = \frac{a_{22}-a_{12}}{(a_{11}+a_{22})-(a_{12}+a_{21})} = \frac{7-(-1)}{(3+7)-(-1-1)} = \frac{8}{12} = \frac{2}{3}$$

$$q_2 = 1 - q_1 = 1-\frac{2}{3} = \frac{1}{3}$$

$$v = \frac{a_{11}a_{22}-a_{12}a_{21}}{(a_{11}+a_{22})-(a_{12}+a_{21})} = \frac{3\times7-(-1\times-1)}{(3+7)-(-1-1)} = \frac{20}{12} = \frac{5}{3}$$

Hence, an optimal solution of the given game is:

Optimal strategy for player A

$$S_A = \begin{bmatrix} A1 & A2 & A3 & A4 \\ 0 & 0 & \frac{2}{3} & \frac{1}{3} \end{bmatrix}$$

Optimal strategy for player B

$$S_A = \begin{bmatrix} B1 & B2 & B3 & B4 \\ 0 & 0 & \frac{2}{3} & \frac{1}{3} \end{bmatrix}$$

and the value of the game $v = \frac{5}{3}$.

Example 10. *Solve the game whose pay-off matrix is as follows:*

Player B

		I	*II*	*III*	*IV*	*V*	*VI*
	1	*4*	*2*	*0*	*2*	*1*	*1*
	2	*4*	*3*	*1*	*3*	*2*	*2*
Player A	*3*	*4*	*3*	*7*	*–5*	*1*	*2*
	4	*4*	*3*	*4*	*–1*	*2*	*2*
	5	*4*	*3*	*3*	*–2*	*2*	*2*

Solution. The given problem does not have a saddle point. Therefore, we try to reduce the size of the pay-off matrix by use of dominance rules. Since every element of the first row is less than or equal to the corresponding element of the second row, therefore, the first row is dominated by the second row, *i.e.,* delete the first row from the pay-off matrix. Similarly fifth row is dominated by fourth row, *i.e.,* delete the fifth row from the pay-off matrix. So we get the following reduced matrix.

Player B

		I	II	III	IV	V	VI
	2	4	3	1	3	2	2
Player A	3	4	3	7	–5	1	2
	4	4	3	4	–1	2	2

Now, columns I and II are dominated by columns IV, V and VI and column VI is dominated by column V. Therefore, columns I, II and VI are deleted from the pay-off matrix. So we get the following reduced matrix.

Player B

		III	VI	V
	2	1	3	2
Player A	3	7	–5	1
	4	4	–1	2

Here, column V is dominated by the average of the column. III and IV, which is $\left\{\frac{1+3}{2}, \frac{7-5}{2}, \frac{4-1}{2}\right\}$ or $\left\{2, 1, \frac{3}{2}\right\}$. Therefore column V is deleted and we get the following reduced matrix.

Player B

		III	IV
	2	1	3
Player A	3	7	–5
	4	4	–1

Here, fourth row is dominated by the average of second and third row, which is $\left\{\frac{1+7}{2}, \frac{3-5}{2}\right\}$ or {4, –1}. Therefore, fourth row is deleted and we get the following reduced matrix

		Player B	
		III	IV
Player A	2	1	3
	3	7	–5

Now, we solve the 2 × 2 game by using the formulas as follows:

Here, $a_{11} = 1$, $a_{12} = 3$, $a_{21} = 7$, $a_{22} = -5$

$$p_1 = \frac{a_{22}-a_{21}}{(a_{11}+a_{22})-(a_{12}+a_{21})} = \frac{-5-7}{(1-5)-(3+7)} = \frac{-12}{-14} = \frac{6}{7}$$

$$p_2 = 1 - p_1 = 1-\frac{6}{7} = \frac{1}{7}$$

$$q_1 = \frac{a_{22}-a_{12}}{(a_{11}+a_{22})-(a_{12}+a_{21})} = \frac{-5-3}{(1-5)-(3+7)} = \frac{-8}{-14} = \frac{4}{7}$$

$$q_2 = 1 - q_1 = 1-\frac{4}{7} = \frac{3}{7}$$

$$v = \frac{a_{11}a_{22}-a_{12}a_{21}}{(a_{11}+a_{22})-(a_{12}+a_{21})} = \frac{(1\times -5)-(3\times 7)}{(1-5)-(3+7)} = \frac{-26}{-14} = \frac{13}{7}$$

Hence, an optimal solution of the given game is: Optimal strategy for player A

$$S_A = \begin{bmatrix} 1 & 2 & 3 & 4 & 5 \\ 0 & \frac{6}{7} & \frac{1}{7} & 0 & 0 \end{bmatrix}$$

Optimal strategy for player B

$$S_B = \begin{bmatrix} \text{I} & \text{II} & \text{III} & \text{IV} & \text{V} & \text{VI} \\ 0 & 0 & \frac{4}{7} & \frac{3}{7} & 0 & 0 \end{bmatrix}$$

and the value of the game $v = \frac{13}{7}$.

2. Graphical Method

The graphical method is applicable for the game where the pay-off matrix is of the size $2 \times n$ or $m \times 2$, *i.e.*, the game with mixed strategies that has only two undominated pure strategies for one of the players in the two-person zero-sum game. It reduces the $2 \times n$ or $m \times 2$ game to 2×2 game by identifying and deleting the dominated strategies and then solve by the method discussed earlier. The resulting solution is also the solution to the original problem. The method is interesting as it explains the idea of the saddle point graphically. Consider the following $2 \times n$ game without saddle point whose pay-off matrix is given by

		Player B				
		B1	B2	...	Bn	Probability
Player A	A1	a_{11}	a_{12}	...	a_{1n}	p_1
	A2	a_{21}	a_{22}	...	a_{2n}	p_2
Probability		q_1	q_2	...	q_n	

Player A has two strategies A1 and A2 with he mixes with probabilities p_1 and p_2 respectively, such that $p_1 + p_2 = 1$ and $0 \le p_1 \le 1$. Player B has n strategies B1, B2, ..., B_n which he mixes with probabilities $q_1, q_2, ..., q_n$ where $q_1, q_2, ..., q_n \ge 0$ and $q_1 + q_2 + ... + q_n = 1$.

Expected pay-off for player A corresponding to the pure strategies of player B are as follows:

B's pure strategies	*A's expected pay-off*
B1	$a_{11}p_1 + a_{21}p_2$
B2	$a_{12}p_1 + a_{22}p_2$
.	.
.	.
.	.
Bn	$a_{1n}p_1 + a_{2n}p_2$

According to the maximin criterion for mixed strategy games, player A should select that value of p_1 and p_2 which maximizes his minimum expected pay-offs. This may be done by plotting the straight lines representing player A's expected pay-off values.

The highest point on the lower boundary (lower envelope) of these lines will give maximum expected pay-off among the minimum expected pay-off and the optimum value of p_1 and p_2.

Now the two strategies of player B are given by the two lines which pass through this maximin point. By doing this, we have 2 × 2 game which can be solved by the method discussed earlier.

The $m \times 2$ games are also treated in the same way except that the upper boundary (upper envelope) of the straight lines corresponding to player B's expected pay-off will give the maximum expected pay-off to player B and the lowest point on this boundary will then give the minimum expected pay-off (minimax value) and the optimum value of q_1 and q_2.

Example 11. *Solve the following game using graphical method:*

		Player B		
		B1	*B2*	*B3*
Player A	*A1*	*1*	*3*	*10*
	A2	*7*	*4*	*2*

Solution. The given game does not have a saddle point. A's expected pay-offs corresponding to B's pure strategies are given by

B's pure strategies	*A's expected pay-off*
B1	$p_1 + 7p_2 \;=\; -6p_1 + 7$
B2	$3p_1 + 4p_2 \;=\; -p_1 + 4$
B3	$10p_1 + 2p_1 = 8p_1 + 2$

These three expected pay-off lines can be plotted as functions of p_1 on the graph to solve the game. The following figure shows the pay-offs of each column represented as points on two vertical axes 1 and 2, unit distance apart.

As the player A wishes to maximize his minimum expected pay-off, we take the highest point of intersection on the lower envelope (maximin point). Maximin point is the point of intersection of lines B2 and B3 (relevant moves). So, we delete B1. The original 2 × 3 game reduces to that of 2 × 2 game as follows:

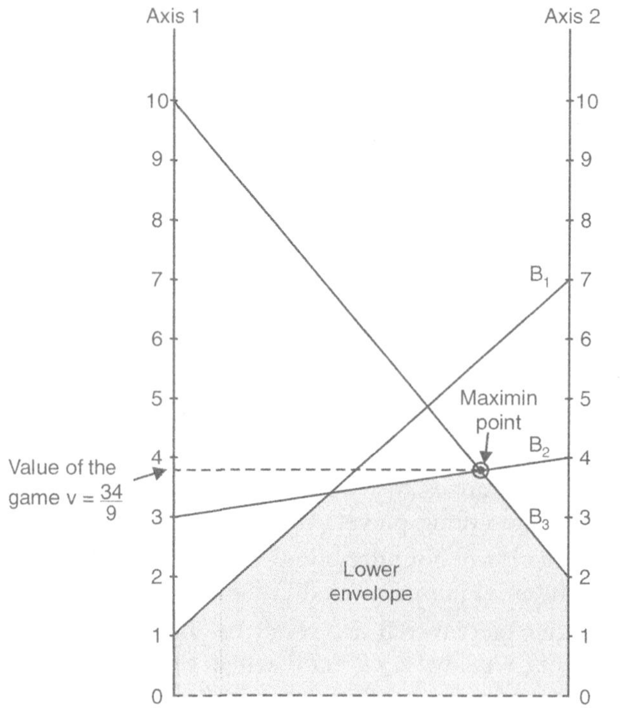

		Player B	
		B2	B3
Player A	A1	3	10
	A2	4	2

Now, we solve the 2 × 2 game by using the formulas as follows:

Here, $a_{11} = 3$, $a_{12} = 10$, $a_{21} = 4$, $a_{22} = 2$

$$p_1 = \frac{a_{22} - a_{21}}{(a_{11} + a_{22}) - (a_{12} + a_{21})} = \frac{2-4}{(3+2)-(10+4)} = \frac{-2}{-9} = \frac{2}{9}$$

$$p_2 = 1 - p_1 = 1 - \frac{2}{9} = \frac{7}{9}$$

$$q_1 = \frac{a_{22} - a_{12}}{(a_{11} + a_{22}) - (a_{12} + a_{21})} = \frac{2-10}{(3+2)-(10+4)} = \frac{-8}{-9} = \frac{8}{9}$$

$$q_2 = 1 - q_1 = 1 - \frac{8}{9} = \frac{1}{9}$$

$$v = \frac{a_{11}a_{22} - a_{12}a_{21}}{(a_{11} + a_{22}) - (a_{12} + a_{21})} = \frac{(3 \times 2) - (10 \times 4)}{(3+2) - (10+4)} = \frac{-34}{-9} = \frac{34}{9}$$

Hence, an optimal solution of the given game is:

Optimal strategy for player A

$$S_A = \begin{bmatrix} A2 & A2 \\ \frac{2}{9} & \frac{7}{9} \end{bmatrix}$$

Optimal strategy for player B

$$S_B = \begin{bmatrix} B1 & B2 & B3 \\ 0 & \frac{8}{9} & \frac{1}{9} \end{bmatrix}$$

and the value of the game $v = \frac{34}{9}$.

Example 12. *Solve the following game using graphical method:*

		Player B			
		B1	*B2*	*B3*	*B4*
Player A	*A1*	–5	5	0	8
	A2	8	–4	–1	–5

Solution. The given game does not have a saddle point. A's expected pay-offs corresponding to B's pure strategies are given by

B's pure strategies	*A's expected pay-off*
B1	$-5p_1 + 8p_2 = -13p_1 + 8$
B2	$5p_1 - 4p_2 = 9p_1 - 4$
B3	$0.p_1 - p_2 = p_1 - 1$
B4	$8p_1 - 5p_2 = 13p_1 - 5$

These four expected pay-off lines can be plotted as functions of p_1 on the graph to solve the game. The following figure shows the pay-offs of each column represented as points on two vertical axes 1 and 2, unit distance apart.

As the player A wishes to maximize his minimum expected pay-off, we take highest point of intersection on the lower envelope (maximin point). Maximin point is the point intersection of lines B1 and B3 (relevant moves). So we delete B2 and B4. The original 2 × 4 game reduces to that of 2 × 2 game as follows:

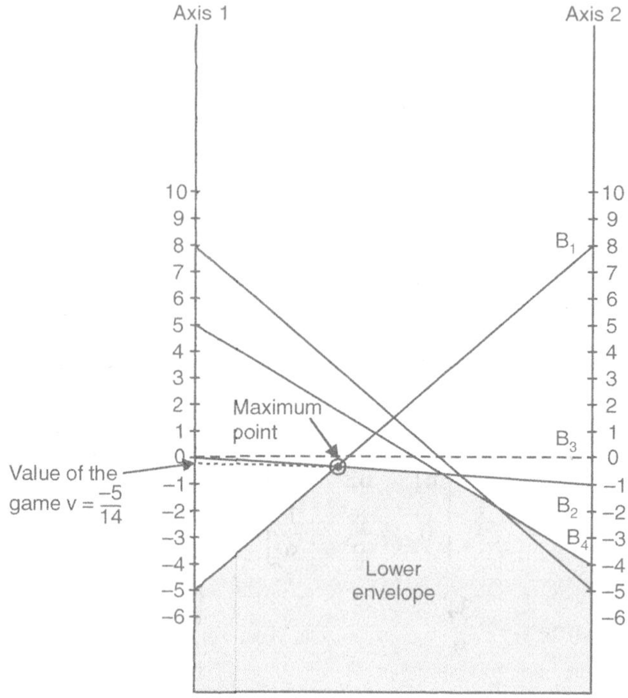

Player B

		B1	B3
Player A	A1	–5	0
	A2	8	–1

Now, we solve the 2 × 2 game by using the formulas as follows:

Here, $a_{11} = -5$, $a_{12} = 0$, $a_{21} = 8$, $a_{22} = -1$

$$p_1 = \frac{a_{22}-a_{21}}{(a_{11}+a_{22})-(a_{12}+a_{21})} = \frac{-1-8}{(-5-1)-(0+8)} = \frac{-9}{-14} = \frac{9}{14}$$

$$p_2 = 1 - p_1 = 1-\frac{9}{14} = \frac{5}{14}$$

$$q_1 = \frac{a_{22}-a_{12}}{(a_{11}+a_{22})-(a_{12}+a_{21})} = \frac{-1-0}{(-5-1)-(0+8)} = \frac{-1}{-14} = \frac{1}{14}$$

$$q_2 = 1 - q_1 = 1-\frac{1}{14} = \frac{13}{14}$$

$$v = \frac{a_{11}a_{22}-a_{12}a_{21}}{(a_{11}+a_{22})-(a_{12}+a_{21})} = \frac{(-5\times-1)-(0\times8)}{(-5-1)-(0+8)} = \frac{5}{-14} = -\frac{5}{14}$$

Hence, an optimal solution of the given game is:

Optimal strategy for player A

$$S_A = \begin{bmatrix} A1 & A2 \\ \frac{9}{14} & \frac{5}{14} \end{bmatrix}$$

Optimal strategy for player B

$$S_B = \begin{bmatrix} B1 & B2 & B3 & B4 \\ \frac{1}{14} & 0 & \frac{13}{14} & 0 \end{bmatrix}$$

and the value of the game $v = -\frac{5}{14}$.

Example 13. *Solve the following game using graphical method:*

		Player B	
		B2	*B3*
Player A	*A1*	4	2
	A2	3	8
	A3	2	12

Solution. The given game does not have a saddle point. B's expected pay-offs corresponding to A's pure strategies are given by

A's pure strategies	*B's expected pay-off*
A1	$4q_1 + 2q_2 = 2q_1 + 2$
A2	$3q_1 + 8q_2 = -5q_1 + 8$
A3	$2q_1 + 12q_2 = -10q_1 + 12$

These three expected pay-off lines can be plotted as functions of q_1 on the graph to solve the game. The following figure shows the pay-off of each row represented as points on two vertical axes 1 and 2, unit distance apart.

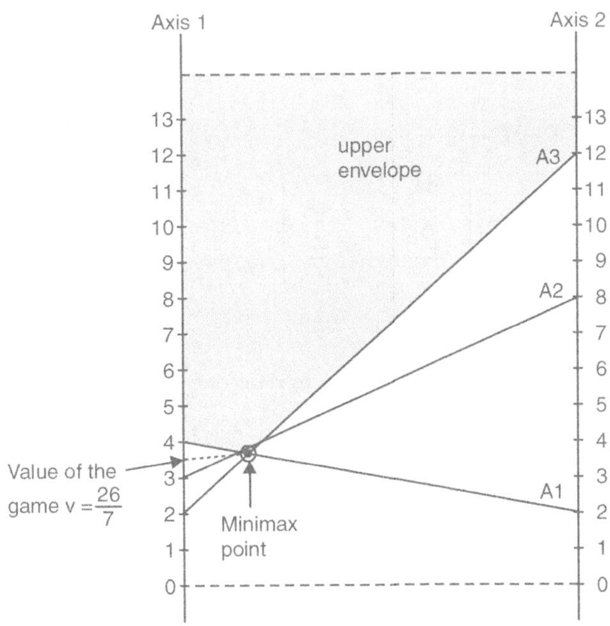

As the player B wishes to minimize his maximum expected pay-off, we take lowest point of intersection on the upper envelope (minimax point). Minimax point is the point of intersection of lines A1 and A2 (relevant moves). So we delete A3. The original 3 × 2 game reduces to that of 2 × 2 game as follows:

Player B

Player A		B1	B2
	A1	4	2
	A2	3	8

Now, we solve the 2 × 2 game by using the formulas as follows:

Here, $a_{11} = 4$, $a_{12} = 2$, $a_{21} = 3$, $a_{22} = 8$

$$p_1 = \frac{a_{22} - a_{21}}{(a_{11} + a_{22}) - (a_{12} + a_{21})} = \frac{8-3}{(4+8)-(2+3)} = \frac{5}{7}$$

$$p_2 = 1 - p_1 = 1 - \frac{5}{7} = \frac{2}{7}$$

$$q_1 = \frac{a_{22} - a_{12}}{(a_{11} + a_{22}) - (a_{12} + a_{21})} = \frac{8-2}{(4+8)-(2+3)} = \frac{6}{7}$$

$$q_2 = 1 - q_1 = 1 - \frac{6}{7} = \frac{1}{7}$$

$$v = \frac{a_{11}a_{22} - a_{12}a_{21}}{(a_{11} + a_{22}) - (a_{12} + a_{21})} = \frac{(4 \times 8)-(2 \times 3)}{(4+8)-(2+3)} = \frac{26}{7}$$

Hence, an optimal solution of the given game is:

Optimal strategy for player A

$$S_A = \begin{bmatrix} A1 & A2 & A3 \\ \frac{5}{7} & \frac{2}{7} & 0 \end{bmatrix}$$

Optimal strategy for player B

$$S_B = \begin{bmatrix} B1 & B2 \\ \frac{6}{7} & \frac{1}{7} \end{bmatrix}$$

and the value of the game $v = \frac{26}{7}$.

3. Linear Programming Method

The two-person zero-sum games can also be solved by linear programming. For problems of higher order pay-off matrices (*i.e.*, 3 × 3 or higher) having neither a saddle point nor any dominance, linear programming approach offers the best solution. For solving a game by linear programming, we consider a game whose pay-off matrix is $[a_{ij}]_{m \times n}$. Let $(x_1, x_2, ..., x_m)$ and $(y_1, y_2, ..., y_n)$ are the probabilities with which players A and B adopt their mixed strategies

$(A_1, A_2, ..., A_m)$ and $(B_1, B_2, ..., B_n)$ respectively. If v is the value of the game, then expected gain to player A for this game when player B select strategies $B_1, B_2, ..., B_n$ one by one is given by left-hand side of simultaneous linear equations respectively. The aim of player A is to select a set of strategies with probability x_i $(i = 1, 2, ..., m)$ on any play of game such that he can maximize his minimum expected gains. Thus to maximize the minimum expected gains, it is necessary that

$$\left.\begin{array}{rl} a_{11}x_1 + a_{21}x_2 + ... + a_{m1}x_m & \geq v \\ a_{12}x_1 + a_{22}x_2 + ... + a_{m2}x_m & \geq v \\ ... \quad ... \quad ... & ... \\ ... \quad ... \quad ... & ... \\ a_{1n}x_1 + a_{2n}x_2 + ... + a_{mn}x_m & \geq v \\ x_1 + x_2 + ... + x_m & = 1 \\ \text{and} \qquad x_1, x_2, ..., x_m & \geq 0 \end{array}\right\} \quad ...(1)$$

Similarly, the aim of player B is to select a set of strategies with probability y_j $(j = 1, 2, ..., n)$ on any play of game such that he can minimize his maximum expected loss. Thus to minimize the maximum expected loss, it is necessary that

$$\left.\begin{array}{rl} a_{11}y_1 + a_{12}y_2 + ... + a_{1n}y_n & \leq v \\ a_{21}y_1 + a_{22}y_2 + ... + a_{2n}y_n & \leq v \\ ... \quad ... \quad ... \quad ... & ... \\ ... \quad ... \quad ... \quad ... & ... \\ a_{m1}y_1 + a_{m2}y_2 + ... + a_{mn}y_n & \leq v \\ y_1 + y_2 + ... + y_n & = 1 \\ \text{and} \qquad y_1, y_2, ..., y_n & \geq 0 \end{array}\right\} \quad ...(2)$$

Let us divide each of the relationships in (1) and (2) by v and let

$$X_i = \frac{x_i}{v} \text{ and } Y_j = \frac{y_j}{v}$$

We see that $\quad \Sigma X_i = \frac{1}{v}\Sigma x_i = \frac{1}{v}$

and $\quad \Sigma Y_j = \frac{1}{v}\Sigma y_j = \frac{1}{v}$

Hence, by minimize ΣX_i, player A will maximize the value of the game and by maximize ΣY_j, player B will minimize the value of the game. Thus, (1) and (2) can be written as a linear programming problem as follows:

The Primal Problem:

$$\text{Minimize } Z_x = X_1 + X_2 + ... + X_m$$

$$\begin{array}{lrl} \text{Subject to} & a_{11}X_1 + a_{21}X_2 + ... + a_{m1}X_m & \geq 1 \\ & a_{12}X_1 + a_{22}X_2 + ... + a_{m2}X_m & \geq 1 \\ & ... \quad ... \quad ... \quad ... & ... \\ & ... \quad ... \quad ... \quad ... & ... \\ & a_{1n}X_1 + a_{2n}X_2 + ... + a_{mn}X_m & \geq 1 \\ \text{and} & X_i \geq 0;\ i = 1, 2, ..., m & \end{array}$$

The Dual Problem:

Minimize $Z_y = Y_1 + Y_2 + \ldots + Y_n$

Subject to

$$a_{11}Y_1 + a_{12}Y_2 + \ldots + a_{1n}Y_n \leq 1$$
$$a_{12}Y_1 + a_{22}Y_2 + \ldots + a_{2n}Y_n \leq 1$$
$$\ldots \quad \ldots \quad \ldots \quad \ldots$$
$$\ldots \quad \ldots \quad \ldots \quad \ldots$$
$$a_{m1}Y_1 + a_{m2}Y_2 + \ldots + a_{mn}Y_n \leq 1$$

and $Y_j \geq 0 \,;\, j = 1, 2, \ldots, n$

Note:

1. Since every game has a solution, optimum solution to the above problems exists and

Minimize ΣX_i = Maximize $\Sigma Y_j = \dfrac{1}{v}$

2. The linear programming problem for player B is the dual of linear programming problem for player A. Thus the solution of the dual problem can be obtained from the primal simplex table and vice-versa.

Example 14. *Solve the following game by linear programming method:*

		Player B		
		B1	B2	B3
	A1	4	1	–3
Player A	A2	3	1	6
	A3	–3	4	–2

Solution. Let the value of the game (to A) be v. Consider the game from B's point of view. B is trying to minimize v, then against A's strategies, we have

$$4y_1 + y_2 - 3y_3 \leq v$$
$$3y_1 + y_2 + 6y_3 \leq v$$
$$-3y_1 + 4y_2 - 2y_3 \leq v$$
$$y_1 + y_2 + y_3 = 1$$
$$y_1, y_2, y_3 \geq 0$$

on dividing by v, we have

$$\frac{4y_1}{v} + \frac{y_2}{v} - \frac{3y_3}{v} \leq 1$$

$$\frac{3y_1}{v} + \frac{y_2}{v} + \frac{6y_3}{v} \leq 1$$

$$-\frac{3y_1}{v} + \frac{y_2}{v} - \frac{2y_3}{v} \leq 1$$

$$\frac{y_1}{v} + \frac{y_2}{v} + \frac{y_3}{v} = \frac{1}{v}$$

$$\frac{y_1}{v}, \frac{y_2}{v}, \frac{y_3}{v} \geq 0$$

Let $Y_1 = \frac{y_1}{v}$, $Y_2 = \frac{y_2}{v}$, $Y_3 = \frac{y_3}{v}$

then
$$4Y_1 + Y_2 - 3Y_3 \leq 1$$
$$3Y_1 + Y_2 + 6Y_3 \leq 1$$
$$-3Y_1 + 4Y_2 - 2Y_3 \leq 1$$
$$Y_1 + Y_2 + Y_3 = \frac{1}{v}$$
$$Y_1, Y_2, Y_3 \geq 0$$

Since B is trying to minimize v, he must maximize $\frac{1}{v}$. Thus the problem as a linear programming problem becomes as

Maximize $Z_y \left(\text{or} \frac{1}{v}\right) = Y_1 + Y_2 + Y_3$

Subject to
$$4Y_1 + Y_2 - 3Y_3 \leq 1$$
$$3Y_1 + Y_2 + 6Y_3 \leq 1$$
$$-3Y_1 + 4Y_2 - 2Y_3 \leq 1$$
$$Y_1, Y_2, Y_3 = 0$$

Since the problem is of maximization and the right hand side of the inequality (b_i) are already positive. Thus introducing slack variables s_1, s_2 and $s_3 \geq 0$.

Thus the above problem can be re-written as

Maximize $Z_y = Y_1 + Y_2 + Y_3 + 0.s_1 + 0.s_2 + 0.s_3$

Subject to
$$4Y_1 + Y_2 - 3Y_3 + s_1 = 1$$
$$3Y_1 + Y_2 + 6Y_3 + s_2 = 1$$
$$-3Y_1 + 4Y_2 - 2Y_3 + s_3 = 1$$
$$Y_1, Y_2, Y_3, s_1, s_2, s_3 \geq 0$$

Iteration–0

	$C_j \rightarrow$		1	1	1	0	0	0	
C_B	Y_B	X_B	Y_1	Y_2	Y_3	s_1	s_2	s_3	Min Ratio
0	s_1	1	4*	1	–3	1	0	0	1/4 ←
0	s_2	1	3	1	6	0	1	0	1/3
0	s_3	1	–3	4	–2	0	0	1	—
	$Z_j - C_j$	0	–1	–1	–1	0	0	0	

Iteration–1

	$C_j \rightarrow$		1	1	1	0	0	0	
C_B	Y_B	X_B	Y_1	Y_2	Y_3	s_1	s_2	s_3	Min. Ratio
1	Y_1	1/4	1	1/4	–3/4	1/4	0	0	—
0	s_2	1/4	0	1/4	33/4	–3/4	1	0	1/33 ←
0	s_3	7/4	0	19/4	–17/4	3/4	0	1	—
	$Z_j - C_j$	1/4	0	–3/4	–7/4	1/4	0	0	

Iteration–2

	$C_j \rightarrow$		1	1	1	0	0	0	
C_B	Y_B	X_B	Y_1	Y_2	Y_3	s_1	s_2	s_3	Min. Ratio
1	Y_1	3/11	1	3/11	0	2/11	1/11	0	1
1	Y_3	1/33	0	1/33	1	–1/11	4/33	0	1
0	s_3	7/4	0	161/33	0	4/11	17/33	1	62/161 ←
	$Z_j - C_j$	10/33	0	–23/33	0	1/11	7/33	0	

Iteration–3

	$C_j \rightarrow$		1	1	1	0	0	0
C_B	Y_B	X_B	Y_1	Y_2	Y_3	s_1	s_2	s_3
1	Y_1	27/161	1	0	0	26/161	10/161	–9/161
1	Y_3	3/161	0	0	1	–15/161	19/161	–1/161
1	Y_2	62/161	0	1	0	12/161	17/161	33/161
	$Z_j - C_j$	92/161	0	0	0	23/161	46/161	23/161

Since all $Z_j - C_j$ in iteration –3 are positive *i.e.*, all $Z_j - C_j \geq 0$.

Thus an optimal solution has been attained.

$$\therefore \quad \text{Maximize}\left(\frac{1}{v}\right) = \frac{4}{7}$$

$$Y_1 = \frac{27}{161}, \; Y_2 = \frac{62}{161}, \quad Y_3 = \frac{3}{161}.$$

The value of the game $v = \dfrac{7}{4}$

Now, $y_1 = Y_1.v = \dfrac{27}{161} \times \dfrac{7}{4} = \dfrac{27}{92}$

$$y_2 = Y_2.v = \frac{62}{161} \times \frac{7}{4} = \frac{62}{92}$$

$$y_3 = Y_3.v = \frac{3}{161} \times \frac{7}{4} = \frac{3}{92}$$

A's best strategies appear in $Z_j - C_j$ row of the optimal table (iteration–3) under s_1, s_2 and s_3 columns.

$$X_1 = \frac{23}{161}, X_2 = \frac{46}{161}, X_3 = \frac{23}{161}$$

Now, $$x_1 = X_1.v = \frac{23}{161} \times \frac{7}{4} = \frac{1}{4}$$

$$x_2 = X_2.v = \frac{46}{161} \times \frac{7}{4} = \frac{1}{2}$$

$$x_3 = X_3.v = \frac{23}{161} \times \frac{7}{4} = \frac{1}{4}$$

Hence, an optimal solution of the given game is:

Optimal strategy for player A

$$S_A = \begin{bmatrix} A1 & A2 & A3 \\ \frac{1}{4} & \frac{1}{2} & \frac{1}{4} \end{bmatrix}$$

Optimal strategy for player B

$$S_B = \begin{bmatrix} B1 & B2 & B3 \\ \frac{27}{92} & \frac{62}{92} & \frac{3}{92} \end{bmatrix}$$

and the value of the game $v = \frac{7}{4}$.

Example 15. *Solve the following game by linear programming method:*

		Player B		
		B1	*B2*	*B3*
Player A	*A1*	3	–2	4
	A2	–1	4	2
	A3	2	2	6

Solution. Let the value of the game (to A) be v. Consider the game from B's point of view. B is trying to minimize v, then against A's strategies, we have

$$3y_1 - 2y_2 + 4y_3 \le v$$

$$-y_1 + 4y_2 + 2y_3 \le v$$

$$2y_1 + 2y_2 + 6y_3 \le v$$

$$y_1 + y_2 + y_3 = 1$$

$$y_1, y_2, y_3 \ge 0$$

on dividing by v, we have

$$\frac{3y_1}{v} - \frac{2y_2}{v} + \frac{4y_3}{v} \le 1$$

$$-\frac{y_1}{v} + \frac{4y_2}{v} + \frac{2y_3}{v} \le 1$$

$$\frac{2y_1}{v} + \frac{2y_2}{v} + \frac{6y_3}{v} \le 1$$

$$\frac{y_1}{v} + \frac{y_2}{v} + \frac{y_3}{v} = \frac{1}{v}$$

$$\frac{y_1}{v}, \frac{y_2}{v}, \frac{y_3}{v} \ge 0$$

Let $Y_1 = \frac{y_1}{v}$, $Y_2 = \frac{y_2}{v}$, $Y_3 = \frac{y_3}{v}$

then

$$3Y_1 - 2Y_2 + 4Y_3 \le 1$$
$$-Y_1 + 4Y_2 + 2Y_3 \le 1$$
$$2Y_1 + 2Y_2 + 6Y_3 \le 1$$
$$Y_1 + Y_2 + Y_3 = \frac{1}{v}$$
$$Y_1, Y_2, Y_3 \ge 0$$

Since B is trying to minimize v, he must maximize $\frac{1}{v}$. Thus the problem as a linear programming problem becomes as

Maximize $Z_y \left(\text{or } \frac{1}{v}\right) = Y_1 + Y_2 + Y_3$

Subject to

$$3Y_1 - 2Y_2 + 4Y_3 \le 1$$
$$-Y_1 + 4Y_2 + 2Y_3 \le 1$$
$$2Y_1 + 2Y_2 + 6Y_3 \le 1$$
$$Y_1, Y_2, Y_3 \ge 0$$

Since the problem is of maximization and the right hand side of the inequality (b_i) are already positive. Thus introducing slack variables s_1, s_2 and $s_3 \ge 0$.

Thus the above problem can be written as

Maximize $Z_y = Y_1 + Y_2 + Y_3 + 0.s_1 + 0.s_2 + 0.s_3$

Subject to

$$3Y_1 - 2Y_2 + 4Y_3 + s_1 = 1$$
$$-Y_1 + 4Y_2 + 2Y_3 + s_2 = 1$$
$$2Y_1 + 2Y_2 + 6Y_3 + s_3 = 1$$
$$Y_1, Y_2, Y_3, s_1, s_2, s_3 \ge 0$$

Iteration–0

	$C_j \rightarrow$		1	1	1	0	0	0	
C_B	Y_B	X_B	Y_1	Y_2	Y_3	s_1	s_2	s_3	Min. Ratio
0	s_1	1	3*	–2	4	1	0	0	1/3 ←
0	s_2	1	–1	4	2	0	1	0	—
0	s_3	1	2	2	6	0	0	1	1/2
	$Z_j - C_j$	0	–1	–1	–1	0	0	0	

Iteration–1

	$C_j \rightarrow$		1	1	1	0	0	0	
C_B	Y_B	X_B	Y_1	Y_2	Y_3	s_1	s_2	s_3	Min. Ratio
1	Y_1	1/3	1	–2/3	4/3	1/3	0	0	—
0	s_2	4/3	0	10/3	10/3	1/3	1	0	2/5
0	s_3	1/3	0	10/3*	10/3	–2/3	0	1	1/10 ←
	$Z_j - C_j$	1/3	0	–5/3	1/3	1/3	0	0	

Iteration–2

	$C_j \rightarrow$		1	1	1	0	0	0
C_B	Y_B	X_B	Y_1	Y_2	Y_3	s_1	s_2	s_3
1	Y_1	2/5	1	0	2	1/5	0	1/5
0	s_2	1	0	0	0	1	1	–1
1	Y_2	1/10	0	1	1	–1/5	0	3/10
	$Z_j - C_j$	1/2	0	0	2	0	0	1/2

Since all $Z_j - C_j$ in iteration-2 are positive *i.e.*, all $Z_j - C_j \geq 0$.

Thus an optimal solution has been attained.

$$\therefore \text{ Maximize } \left(\frac{1}{v}\right) = \frac{1}{2}$$

$$Y_1 = \frac{2}{5},\ Y_2 = \frac{1}{10},\ Y_3 = 0$$

The value of the game $v = 2$.

Now $y_1 = Y_1.v = \frac{2}{5} \times 2 = \frac{4}{5}$

$$y_2 = Y_2.v = \frac{1}{10} \times 2 = \frac{1}{5}$$

$$y_3 = Y_3.v = 0 \times 2 = 0$$

A's best strategies appear in $Z_j - C_j$ row of the optimal table (iteration-2) under s_1, s_2 and s_3 columns.

$X_1 = 0, X_2 = 0, X_3 = \frac{1}{2}$

Now, $x_1 = X_1.v = 0 \times 2 = 0$

$x_2 = X_2.v = 0 \times 2 = 0$

$x_3 = X_3.v = \frac{1}{2} \times 2 = 1$

Hence, an optimal solution of the given game is:

Optimal strategy for player A

$$S_A = \begin{bmatrix} A1 & A2 & A3 \\ 0 & 0 & 1 \end{bmatrix}$$

Optimal strategy for player B

$$S_B = \begin{bmatrix} B1 & B2 & B3 \\ \frac{4}{5} & \frac{1}{5} & 0 \end{bmatrix}$$

and the value of the game $v = 2$.

Limitations of Game Theory

1. A fixed number of players. In real life situation, there can be more than expected number of players. Analysis of a game becomes complex and difficult as the number of players increases.
2. Assumption that players have complete knowledge of the strategies (alternatives) is not practical.
3. The information about the available strategies and pay-offs may be incomplete and uncertain. Risk and uncertainty are not taken into account.
4. Sum of the gains and losses of the players may not be zero (non-zero sum games). Zero-sum game is not realistic.
5. All the situations cannot be tackled by the rules of games.

EXERCISES

1. Explain the assumptions underlying game theory.
2. Define: pay-off matrix, pure strategy, mixed strategies, saddle point and two person zero-sum games.
3. What is a strictly determinable game?
4. Explain the method to formulate a game as a linear programming problem.
5. How is the concept of dominance used in simplifying the solution of a rectangular game?

6. Determine optimum strategies and value of the following game:

		Player B			
		B1	B2	B3	B4
Player A	A1	–3	4	2	9
	A2	7	8	6	10
	A3	6	2	4	–1

[**Ans.** A2, B3; v = 6]

7. Determine the optimum strategies and value of the following game:

		Player B				
		B1	B2	B3	B4	B5
Player A	A1	11	5	3	10	2
	A2	8	7	6	8	9
	A3	4	6	5	5	10
	A4	7	8	4	4	3

[**Ans.** A2, B3; v = 6]

8. Verify that the following game is a fair game.

		Player B			
		B1	B2	B3	B4
Player A	A1	1	9	6	0
	A2	3	4	7	–1
	A3	–5	–2	11	–3
	A4	8	5	–3	–6

9. Verify that the following game is strictly determinable.

		Player B		
		B1	B2	B3
Player A	A1	5	–3	–4
	A2	0	–3	–8
	A3	7	8	–7
	A4	8	4	–8

10. Find the range of values of p and q so that the entry (2, 2) is a saddle point of the following game:

		Player B		
		B1	B2	B3
Player A	A1	2	q	4
	A2	p	8	12
	A3	9	2	5

[**Ans.** $p \le 8$, $q \ge 8$]

11. Two players A and B match coins. If the coins match, then A wins one unit of value; if the coins do not match, then B wins one unit of value. Determine the optimum strategies for each player and the value of the game. [**Ans.** $S_A = \left[\frac{1}{2}, \frac{1}{2}\right]$, $S_B = \left[\frac{1}{2}, \frac{1}{2}\right]$; $v = 0$]

12. In a game of matching coins with two players A and B, A wins one unit of value when there are two heads, wins nothing when there are two tails and loses $\frac{1}{2}$ unit of value when there is one head and one tail. Determine the optimum strategies for each player and the value of the game. [**Ans.** $S_A = \left[\frac{1}{4}, \frac{3}{4}\right]$, $S_B = \left[\frac{1}{4}, \frac{3}{4}\right]$; $v = -\frac{1}{8}$]

13. Two companies are competing for the same product. Their different strategies are given in the following pay-off matrix:

Company B

		B1	B2	B3
Company A	A1	–1	–2	8
	A2	7	5	–1
	A3	6	0	12

[**Ans.** $S_A = \left[0, \frac{2}{3}, \frac{1}{3}\right]$, $S_B = \left[0, \frac{13}{18}, \frac{5}{18}\right]$; $v = \frac{10}{3}$]

14. Solve the game whose pay-off matrix is as follows:

Player B

		B1	B2	B3	B4
Player A	A1	3	2	4	0
	A2	2	4	2	4
	A3	4	2	4	0
	A4	0	4	0	8

[**Ans.** $S_A = \left[0, 0, \frac{2}{3}, \frac{1}{3}\right]$, $S_B = \left[0, 0, \frac{2}{3}, \frac{1}{3}\right]$; $v = \frac{8}{3}$]

15. Solve the game whose pay-off matrix is as follows:

Player B

		B1	B2	B3	B4
Player A	A1	6	2	4	8
	A2	2	–1	1	12
	A3	2	3	3	9
	A4	5	2	6	10

[**Ans.** $S_A = \left[\frac{1}{5}, 0, \frac{4}{5}, 0\right]$, $S_B = \left[\frac{1}{5}, \frac{4}{5}, 0, 0\right]$; $v = \frac{14}{5}$]

16. Solve the following game using graphical method:

		Player B		
		B1	B2	B3
Player A	A1	1	3	11
	A2	8	5	2

[**Ans.** $S_A = \left[\frac{3}{11}, \frac{8}{11}\right], S_B = \left[0, \frac{9}{11}, \frac{2}{11}\right]; v = \frac{49}{11}$]

17. Solve the following game using graphical method:

		Company B		
		B1	B2	B3
Company A	A1	20	30	60
	A2	45	45	30

[**Ans.** $S_A = \left[\frac{3}{11}, \frac{8}{11}\right], S_B = \left[\frac{6}{11}, 0, \frac{5}{11}\right]; v = \frac{420}{11}$]

18. Solve the following game using graphical method:

		Player B	
		B1	B2
Player A	A1	3	–4
	A2	2	5
	A3	–2	8

[**Ans.** $S_A = \left[\frac{3}{10}, \frac{7}{10}, 0\right], S_B = \left[\frac{9}{10}, \frac{1}{10}\right]; v = \frac{23}{10}$]

19. Solve the following game using graphical method:

		Player B	
		B1	B2
Player A	A1	–4	3
	A2	–7	–1
	A3	–2	–4
	A4	–5	–2
	A5	–1	–6

[**Ans.** $S_A = \left[\frac{5}{12}, 0, 0, 0, \frac{7}{12}\right], S_B = \left[\frac{9}{12}, \frac{3}{12}\right]; v = -\frac{9}{4}$]

20. Solve the following game by linear programming method:

		Player B		
		B1	B2	B3
Company A	A1	1	–1	3
	A2	3	5	–3
	A3	6	2	–2

$$\left[\textbf{Ans. } S_A = \left[\frac{2}{3}, \frac{1}{3}, 0\right], \; S_B = \left[0, \frac{1}{2}, \frac{1}{2}\right]; \; v = 1\right]$$

21. Solve the following game by linear programming method:

		Player B		
		B1	B2	B3
Player A	A1	0	2	2
	A2	3	–1	3
	A3	4	4	–2

$$\left[\textbf{Ans. } S_A = \left[\frac{6}{11}, \frac{3}{11}, \frac{2}{11}\right], \; S_B = \left[\frac{5}{22}, \frac{8}{22}, \frac{9}{22}\right]; \; v = \frac{17}{11}\right]$$

❑❑❑

CHAPTER 9

Stochastic Inventory Models

9.1 INTRODUCTION

Inventory is defined as a stock of goods which is kept for the purpose of future use. The stock of goods can be in the form of raw materials, parts, finished or semi-finished goods, machinery etc.

Inventory can also be defined as the stock of goods, items other economic resources that are stored or kept to ensure smooth and efficient running of business operations.

9.2 INVENTORY CONTROL

Inventory control is defined as the scientific method of finding how much stock of goods should be maintained in order to meet the production demands and be able to provide right type of materials at right time in the right quantities and at competitive prices.

9.3 NEED OF INVENTORY

No business activity can be performed without inventories. Maintaining an inventory is necessary because of the following reasons:

1. It helps in smooth and efficient running of business.
2. It provides service to the customer in a short time.
3. It takes advantage of price discounts by purchasing larger quantities.
4. It takes the advantage of price fluctuations.
5. It ensure against scarcity of materials in the market.
6. It keeps better relations with customers.
7. It ensure against delays in deliveries.
8. It has a better utilization of men and machinery.

9. It reduces the possibility of duplication of orders.
10. It helps in minimizing the loss due to deterioration, damage etc.
11. It acts as buffer stock when raw materials are received late and many items are rejected.
12. To protect against future price and delivery uncertainties, such as price increases, inflation and strikes.

9.4 INVENTORY CLASSIFICATION

Inventory may be classified into the following types:

1. **Direct Inventories.** The items which play a direct role in the manufacture of a product and become an integral part of the finished product are called direct inventories. These are as below:
   (*a*) **Raw material inventory.** Raw materials which are kept in stock for using in the production of goods such as copper, tin, wood, plastic, rubber, steel, leather, cotton, cement etc.
   (*b*) **In process inventory.** In process inventories are the semifinished goods at various stages of manufacturing.
   (*c*) **Finished goods.** Finished goods inventories contain the output of the production process. These are the finished products ready for dispatching to the customers.
2. **Indirect Inventories.** These are the items which are necessarily required for manufacturing but do not become the components of finished products, *e.g.*, office material, tools, oil, grease, welding electrodes punches, petrol, diesel etc.

9.5 TYPES OF INVENTORIES

The following types of inventory generally an enterprise use for a variety of purposes.

1. **Transportation Inventory.** This inventory is also called as transit or pipe line inventory. These are the inventory items which are transported from different locations to different manufacturing centres.
2. **Buffer Inventories.** These inventories are used to meet the uncertainty of demand and supply. Buffer inventories are necessary, because, when an order is placed for a raw material, it cannot be possible to receive the material at the same time. There is a 'lead time' between the order placed and the availability of the material.
3. **Decoupling Inventories.** The stocks used to reduce the interdependence of various stages of production system are known as decoupling inventories.
4. **Lot Size Inventories.** These are held to take advantage of discounts which are usually available for purchase of large quantities.
5. **Anticipation Inventories.** These inventories are kept in anticipation of a big selling season, a promotion programme or for satisfying the customer demand for the plant shut down period.

9.6 INVENTORY COSTS

The various costs involved in inventory problems are as follows:

1. **Carrying Cost or Holding Cost or Storage Cost.** The costs associated with the holding or storage of the inventory are known as carrying costs or holding costs or storage costs. These costs are directly proportional to size of the inventory and the time for which the items are held in stock. Various components of the carrying costs are as follows:
   (*i*) Rent for the space or the cost of depreciation of the space, in case the own space, required to store the goods.
   (*ii*) Insurance and taxes.
   (*iii*) **Handling cost.** These include all the costs associated with the movement of goods, such as cost of labour, transportation cost etc.
   (*iv*) Administrative and record keeping costs.
   (*v*) Deterioration costs, which arise due to deterioration of items during the inventory *e.g.*, fashion items, fragile items, perishable goods, items that changes chemically etc.
   (*vi*) Obsolescence cost, which arise due to the technical advancement, *e.g.*, electronic items, computer components etc.

   The carrying cost is generally denoted by C_1 per unit of quantity per unit of time.
2. **Shortage Cost or Stock Out Cost or Penalty Cost.** The costs associated with a delay in meeting demands in the stock out period is known as shortage cost or stock out cost or penalty cost. This cost is usually of two types. In case the unfilled demand can be filled at a later stage known as backlog cases, these costs are proportional to the quantity short and the delay in delivery time. In case the unfilled demand is lost known as no backlog case, these costs are proportional to the quantity short only.

   The shortages may result in the cancellation of orders, loss of sales, loss of profit, loss of goodwill etc. The shortage cost is generally denoted by C_2.
3. **Setup Cost or Ordering Cost or Replenishment Cost.** The cost associated with the setting a machine before it starts production or placing of an order or replenishing the inventory is known as setup cost or ordering cost or replenishment cost. It is independent of the quantity ordered or produced but directly proportional to the number of orders placed. The setup cost is generally denoted by C_s.

9.7 OTHER ELEMENTS OF INVENTORY PROBLEM

There are different important elements of inventory problem, which are as follows:

1. **Demand.** The number of items required per period is called demand. The demand may be deterministic *i.e.*, exactly known or probabilistic (stochastic) *i.e.*, not known with certainty.
2. **Lead Time.** The time gap between placing of an order and its arrival in the inventory is called as lead time.
3. **Order Cycle.** The time period between placements of two successive orders is called as an order cycle.

4. **Re-order Level.** The level between the maximum and minimum level of stock at which purchasing activities must start or manufacturing process must start for replenishment is called re-order level.
5. **Time Horizon.** The time period over which the inventory is controlled is called time horizon.
6. **Buffer Stock or Safety Stock.** The extra stock which is kept for the situations of uncertainties in demand and lead time is known as buffer stock or safety stock. It is maintained to avoid the stock out situation.

9.8 ECONOMIC ORDER QUANTITY (EOQ)

The inventory problems in which demand is assumed to be fixed and completely predetermined are known as the economic order quantity problems.

Economic order quantity is that size of order which minimizes the total cost of inventory *i.e.*, carrying costs, shortage costs and ordering costs. Economic order quantity is that quantity for which the ordering costs are equal to the carrying costs. This situation is shown in the following figure:

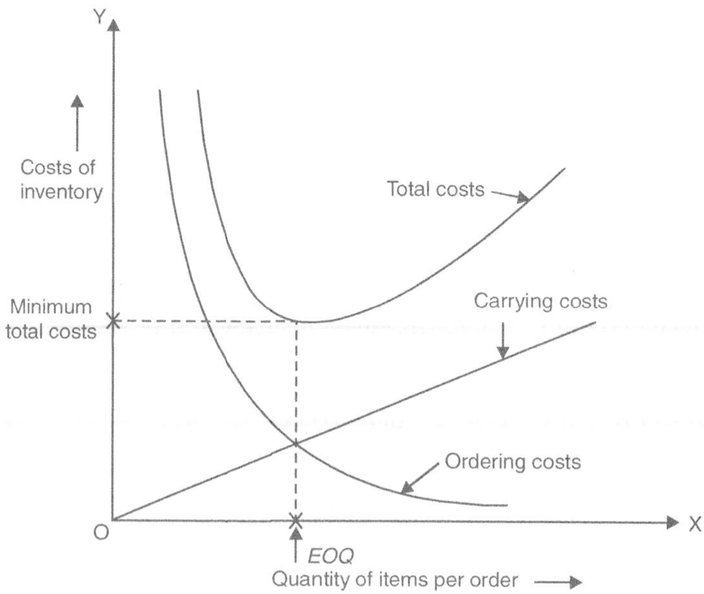

The economic order quantity can be obtained by the following formula,

$$EOQ(Q^*) = \sqrt{\frac{2DC_S}{C_1}}\ ;\ C_1 = KI$$

for which the total inventory cost is given by

$$TC(Q^*) = DK + \frac{D}{Q^*}C_S + \frac{1}{2}Q^*C_1$$

Where Q^* = Optimal number of units per order (EOQ)

D = Annual demand of the inventory item

C_1 = Carrying cost per unit per year

C_S = Ordering cost or set up cost per order

K = Cost of purchasing or manufacturing per unit

I = Inventory carrying cost per year.

9.9 INVENTORY MODELS

The inventory models may be classified as follows:

1. Deterministic Models
2. Probabilistic or Stochastic Models.

(*a*) **Deterministic Models.** Deterministic inventory models are the models in which demand is fixed and known with certainty.

(*b*) **Probabilistic or Stochastic Models.** Probabilistic or stochastic inventory models are the models in which probability distribution of future demand is known. The probability distribution of future demand is determined from the past experience collected data. In probabilistic or stochastic inventory models we minimize the expected costs rather than the actual costs. There are two types of inventory models; single period inventory model and multi-period inventory model.

The single period inventory models are as follows:

9.10 MODEL (1)

Uniform Demand, No Set-up Cost and Lead Time Zero

In this model, the demand is uniform over a period. Let it be q units per time period. The set-up cost is not included, lead time is zero. Let C_1 be the carrying cost per item per unit time, C_2 be the shortage cost per item per unit time and Q be the inventory level at any time t.

The problem is to determine the optimal order level Q where $q \le Q$ or $q > Q$ at the beginning of each time period. The inventory situation in both the cases is shown as follows:

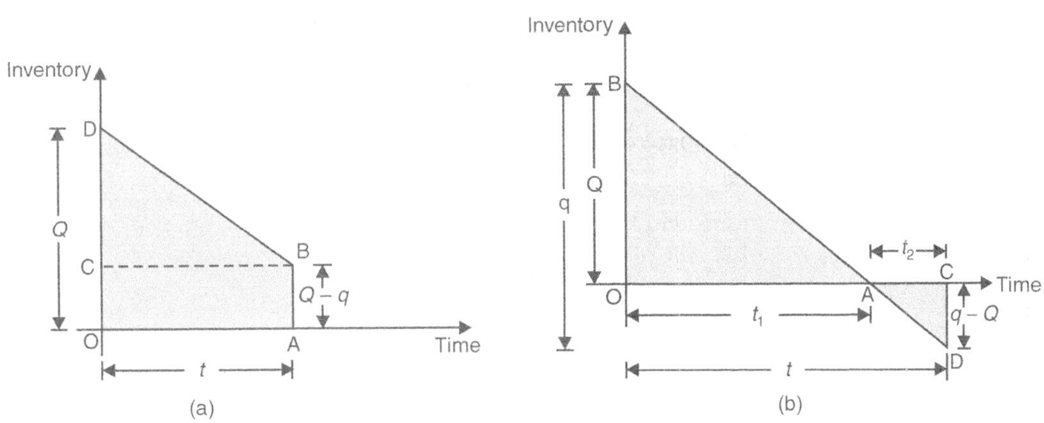

When $q \le Q$ as shown in Fig. (*a*), there are no shortages,

When $q > Q$ as shown in Fig. (*b*), shortages occur.

Case 1. Discrete Units

When $q \le Q$, there is no shortage cost, only carrying cost is there.

$$\text{Carrying cost} = C_1 \times \text{Area of trapezium}$$

$$= C_1 \times \frac{1}{2} OA(AB + OD)$$

$$= C_1 \times \frac{1}{2}(2Q - q)t = \frac{1}{2} C_1 t(2Q - q)$$

$$\text{Expected carrying cost} = \frac{1}{2} C_1 t \sum_{d=0}^{Q} (2Q - q)p(q)$$

When $q > Q$, both the costs are there.

$$\text{Carrying cost} = C_1 \times \text{Area of } \Delta OAB$$

$$= C_1 \times \frac{1}{2} Qt_1 = \frac{1}{2} C_1 Q t_1$$

$$\text{Shortage cost} = C_2 \times \text{Area of } \Delta ACD$$

$$= C_2 \times \frac{1}{2}(q - Q)t_2 = \frac{1}{2} C_2 (q - Q)t_2$$

Now using the property of similar triangles in Fig. (*b*), we have

$$\frac{t_1}{t} = \frac{Q}{q} \quad \text{and} \quad \frac{t_2}{t} = \frac{q-Q}{q}$$

$$\Rightarrow \quad t_1 = \frac{Q}{q} t \quad \text{and} \quad t_2 = \frac{q-Q}{q} t$$

$$\text{Expected cost (carrying + shortage)} = \sum_{q=Q+1}^{\infty} \left[\frac{1}{2} QC_1 \frac{Q}{q} t + \frac{1}{2}(q-Q)C_2 \frac{q-Q}{q} t \right] p(q)$$

Thus, the total expected cost (TC) is given by

$$TC = C_1 t \sum_{q=0}^{Q} \left(Q - \frac{q}{2} \right) p(q) + \sum_{q=Q+1}^{\infty} t \left[C_1 Q^2 + C_2 (q-Q)^2 \right] \frac{p(q)}{2q}$$

The total average cost is given by

$$TC(Q) = C_1 \sum_{q=0}^{Q} \left(Q - \frac{q}{2} \right) p(q) + \sum_{q=Q+1}^{\infty} \left[C_1 Q^2 + C_2 (q-Q)^2 \right] \frac{p(q)}{2q}$$

Now to obtain the optimum value of Q for which $TC(Q)$ is minimum, we use the following conditions of difference calculus $\Delta TC(Q - 1) < 0 < \Delta TC(Q)$

$$\Delta TC(Q) = TC(Q + 1) - TC(Q) > 0 \quad \text{and} \quad \Delta TC(Q - 1) = TC(Q) - TC(Q - 1) < 0$$

Now, putting $Q + 1$ in place of Q in the expression of $TC(Q)$, we have

$$TC(Q+1) = C_1 \sum_{q=0}^{Q+1}\left(Q+1-\frac{q}{2}\right)p(q) + \sum_{q=Q+2}^{\infty}\left[C_1(Q+1)^2 + C_2(q-Q-1)^2\right]\frac{p(q)}{2q}$$

$$\Delta TC(Q) = TC(Q+1) - TC(Q)$$

$$= C_1 \sum_{q=0}^{Q+1}\left(Q+1-\frac{q}{2}\right)p(q) + \sum_{q=Q+2}^{\infty}\left[C_1(Q+1)^2 + C_2(q-Q-1)^2\right]\frac{p(q)}{2q}$$

$$- C_1 \sum_{q=0}^{Q}\left(Q-\frac{q}{2}\right)p(q) - \sum_{q=Q+1}^{\infty}\left[C_1Q^2 + C_2(q-Q)^2\right]\frac{p(q)}{2q}$$

$$= C_1 \sum_{q=0}^{Q}\left[\left(Q+1-\frac{q}{2}\right)-\left(Q-\frac{q}{2}\right)\right]p(q) + C_1(Q+1-\frac{Q+1}{2}\,p(Q+1)$$

$$+ C_1 \sum_{q=Q+1}^{\infty}\left[(Q+1)^2 - Q^2\right]\frac{p(q)}{2q} - C_1(Q+1)^2\frac{p(Q+1)}{2(Q+1)}$$

$$+ C_2 \sum_{q=Q+1}^{\infty}\left[(q-Q-1)^2 - (q-Q)^2\right]\frac{p(q)}{2q} - C_2(Q+1-Q-1)\frac{p(Q+1)}{2(Q+1)}$$

$$= C_1 \sum_{q=0}^{Q}p(q) + \frac{C_1}{2}(2Q+1)\sum_{q=Q+1}^{\infty}\frac{p(q)}{q} + C_2\sum_{q=Q+1}^{\infty}(1-2q+2Q)\frac{p(q)}{2q}$$

$$= C_1 \sum_{q=0}^{Q}p(q) + C_1\left(Q+\frac{1}{2}\right)\sum_{q=Q+1}^{\infty}\frac{p(q)}{q} + C_2\left(Q+\frac{1}{2}\right)\sum_{q=Q+1}^{\infty}\frac{p(q)}{q} - C_2\sum_{q=Q+1}^{\infty}p(q)$$

$$= C_1 \sum_{q=0}^{Q}p(q) + (C_1+C_2)\left(Q+\frac{1}{2}\right)\sum_{q=Q+1}^{\infty}\frac{p(q)}{q} - C_2\left[\sum_{q=0}^{\infty}p(q) - \sum_{q=0}^{Q}p(q)\right]$$

$$= (C_1+C_2)\left[\sum_{q=0}^{Q}p(q) + \left(Q+\frac{1}{2}\right)\sum_{q=Q+1}^{\infty}\frac{p(q)}{q}\right] - C_2 \qquad \left(\because \sum_{q=0}^{\infty}p(q) = 1\right)$$

$$= (C_1+C_2)\,F(Q) - C_2 \qquad \text{where } F(Q) = \sum_{q=0}^{Q}p(q) + \left(Q+\frac{1}{2}\right)\sum_{q=Q+1}^{\infty}\frac{p(q)}{q}$$

Now, $\Delta TC(Q) > 0 \Rightarrow (C_1 + C_2)\,F(Q) - C_2 > 0$

or $$F(Q) > \frac{C_2}{(C_1+C_2)} \qquad \text{...(1)}$$

Similarly,

$$\Delta TC(Q-1) = TC(Q) - TC(Q-1)$$

$$= (C_1+C_2)\,F(Q-1) - C_2 \qquad \text{where } F(Q-1) = \sum_{q=0}^{Q-1}p(q) + \left(Q-\frac{1}{2}\right)\sum_{q=Q}^{\infty}\frac{p(q)}{q}$$

Now $\Delta TC(Q-1) < 0 \Rightarrow (C_1 + C_2)\,F(Q-1) - C_2 < 0$

or
$$F(Q-1) < \frac{C_2}{(C_1 + C_2)} \qquad ...(2)$$

From equations (1) and (2), we have

$$F(Q-1) < \frac{C_2}{(C_1 + C_2)} < F(Q)$$

Case 2. Continuous Units

Here, all the conditions are same as in case 1 but demand is continuous. So the cost equation of inventory involves integral in place of summation and $p(q)$ are replaced by $f(q)\,dq$.

Now proceeding in the same manner as in case 1, the total average cost is given by

$$TC(Q) = C_1\int_0^Q \left(Q - \frac{q}{2}\right) f(q)\,dq + \int_Q^\infty \left[C_1Q^2 + C_2(q-Q)^2\right]\frac{f(q)}{2q}\,dq$$

$$TC(Q) = C_1\int_0^Q \left(Q - \frac{q}{2}\right) f(q)\,dq + C_1\int_Q^\infty Q^2\frac{f(q)}{2q}\,dq + C_2\int_Q^\infty (q-Q)^2\frac{f(q)}{2q}\,dq$$

For optimum value of Q,

$$\frac{d}{dQ}[TC(Q)] = 0 \Rightarrow C_1\int_0^Q f(q)dq + C_1\int_Q^\infty \frac{Q}{q} f(q)dq - C_2\int_Q^\infty\left(\frac{q-Q}{q}\right) f(q)dq = 0$$

or
$$C_1\int_0^Q f(q)dq + C_1\int_Q^\infty \frac{Q}{q} f(q)dq - C_2\left[\int_0^\infty f(q)dq - \int_0^Q f(q)dq\right] + C_2\int_Q^\infty \frac{Q}{q} f(q)dq = 0$$

$$(C_1 + C_2)\left[\int_0^Q f(q)dq + \int_Q^\infty \frac{Q}{q} f(q)dq\right]^Q - C_2 = 0 \qquad \left(\because \int_0^\infty f(q)dq = 1\right)$$

or
$$F(Q) = \frac{C_2}{(C_1 + C_2)}, \quad \text{where } F(Q) = \int_0^Q f(q)dq + \int_Q^\infty \frac{Q}{q} f(q)dq$$

Now
$$\frac{d^2[TC(Q)]}{dQ^2}\Big/Q = (C_1 + C_2)\int_Q^\infty \frac{f(q)}{q}\,dq > 0$$

which shows that $TC(Q)$ is minimum for the value of Q given by $F(Q) = \dfrac{C_2}{(C_1 + C_2)}$.

Example 1. *The probability distribution of monthly sales of a certain item is as follows:*

Monthly Sales :	0	1	2	3	4	5	6
Probability :	0.02	0.05	0.30	0.27	0.20	0.10	0.06

The cost of carrying inventory is ₹ 10.00 per unit per month. The current policy is to maintain a stock of four items at the beginning of each month. Assuming that the cost of shortage is proportional to both time and quantity short, obtain the imputed cost of a shortage of one item for one time unit.

Solution. Here, $C_1 = 10$, $Q = 4$

The monthly sales q is given from 0 to 6 times in discrete units, we have

$$F(Q-1) < \frac{C_2}{(C_1+C_2)} < F(Q)$$

where $$F(Q) = \sum_{q=0}^{Q} p(q) + \left(Q+\frac{1}{2}\right)\sum_{q=Q+1}^{\infty} \frac{p(q)}{q}$$

Now least value of C_2 is determined by

$$\frac{C_2}{C_1+C_2} = F(Q-1) \Rightarrow \frac{C_2}{10+C_2} = \sum_{q=0}^{3} p(q) + \frac{7}{2}\sum_{q=4}^{6} \frac{p(q)}{q}$$

or $$\frac{C_2}{10+C_2} = [p(0)+p(1)+p(2)+p(3)] + \frac{7}{2}\left[\frac{p(4)}{4}+\frac{p(5)}{5}+\frac{p(6)}{6}\right]$$

$$= [0.02+0.05+0.30+0.27] + \frac{7}{2}\left[\frac{0.20}{4}+\frac{0.10}{5}+\frac{0.06}{6}\right]$$

$$= 0.92$$

or $C_2 = ₹\ 115$

Similarly, the greatest value of C_2 is determined by

$$\frac{C_2}{C_1+C_2} = F(Q) \Rightarrow \frac{C_2}{10+C_2} = \sum_{q=0}^{4} p(q) + \frac{9}{2}\sum_{q=5}^{6} \frac{p(q)}{q}$$

or $$\frac{C_2}{10+C_2} = [p(0)+p(1)+p(2)+p(3)+p(4)] + \frac{9}{2}\left[\frac{p(5)}{5}+\frac{p(6)}{6}\right]$$

$$= [0.02+0.05+0.30+0.27+0.20] + \frac{9}{2}\left[\frac{0.10}{5}+\frac{0.06}{6}\right]$$

$$= 0.975$$

or $C_2 = ₹\ 390$

Hence, the range of values of the imputed cost of a shortage is given by

$$₹\ 115 < C_2 < ₹\ 390$$ **Ans.**

Example 2. *The demand for a particular product is continuous and shows the following probability distribution:*

Demand	:	*0*	*1*	*2*	*3*	*4*	*5*	*6 or more*
Probability	:	*0.40*	*0.24*	*0.20*	*0.10*	*0.05*	*0.01*	*0.00*

Find out the optimum stock level, if the cost of shortage is ₹ 1000 per unit and cost of holding is ₹ 100 per unit. The shortage cost is proportional to both time and quantity short.

Solution. Here, $C_1 = 100$, $C_2 = 1000$

$$\frac{C_2}{C_1+C_2} = \frac{1000}{100+1000} = 0.909$$

The optimum stock level is given by

$$F(Q-1) < \frac{C_2}{(C_1+C_2)} < F(Q)$$

or $$F(Q-1) < 0.909 < F(Q) \qquad ...(1)$$

For finding the value of Q, we use the following table:

Q	q	$p(q)$	$Q+\frac{1}{2}$	$\sum_{q=0}^{Q} p(q)$	$\sum_{q=Q+1}^{\infty} \frac{p(q)}{q}$	$\left(Q+\frac{1}{2}\right)\sum_{q=Q+1}^{\infty} \frac{p(q)}{q}$	$F(Q)$
0	0	0.40	0.5	0.40	0.3875	0.19375	0.59375
1	1	0.24	1.5	0.64	0.1475	0.22125	0.86125
2	2	0.20	2.5	0.84	0.0475	0.11875	0.95874

It is clear from the table for $Q = 2$ the condition $F(1) < 0.909 < F(2)$.

Hence, optimum stock level $Q = 2$ **Ans.**

9.11 MODEL (2)

Instantaneous Demand, No Set-up Cost and Lead Time Zero

In this model, the demand is instantaneous. The set-up cost is not included, lead time is zero. Let demand be q units per time period, C_1 be the carrying cost per item per unit time, C_2 be the shortage cost per item per unit time and Q be the inventory level at any time t.

The problem is to determine the optimal order level Q where $q \le Q$ or $q > Q$ at the beginning of each time period. The inventory situation in both the cases is shown as follows:

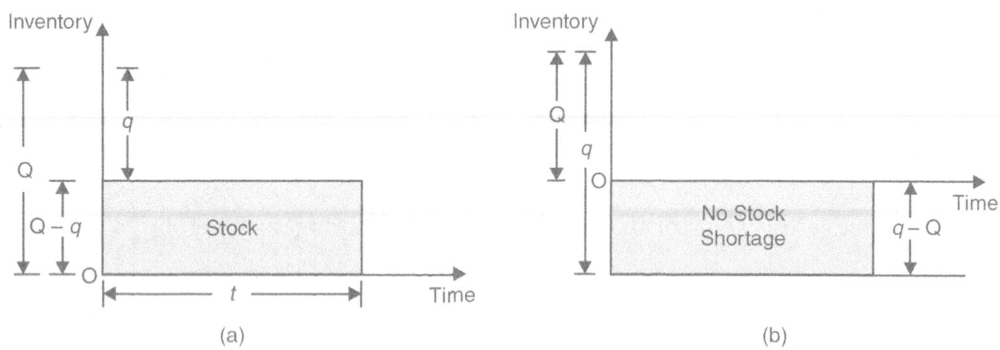

When $q \le Q$ as shown in Fig. (*a*), there are no shortages,

When $q > Q$ as shown in Fig. (*b*), shortages occur.

Case 1. Discrete Units

When $q \le Q$, there is no shortage, only carrying cost is there.

Carrying cost per unit time $= C_1(Q - q)$

$$\text{Expected carrying cost} = C_1 \sum_{q=0}^{Q}(Q-q)p(q)$$

When $q > Q$, only shortage cost is there.

Shortage cost per unit time $= C_2(q - Q)$

Expected shortage cost $= C_2 \sum_{q=Q}^{\infty}(q-Q)\, p(q).$

Thus, the total expected cost (TC) is given by

$$TC(Q) = C_1 \sum_{q=0}^{Q}(Q-q)\, p(q) + C_2 \sum_{q=Q+1}^{\infty}(q-Q)p(q)$$

Now to obtain the optimum value of Q for which $TC(Q)$ is minimum, we use the following conditions of difference calculus

$\Delta TC(Q-1) < 0 < \Delta TC(Q)$

$\Delta TC(Q) = TC(Q+1) - TC(Q) > 0$ and $\Delta TC(Q-1) = TC(Q) - TC(Q-1) < 0$

Now, putting $Q + 1$ in place of Q in the expression of $TC(Q)$, we have

$$TC(Q+1) = C_1 \sum_{q=0}^{Q+1}(Q+1-q)\, p(q) + C_2 \sum_{q=Q+2}^{\infty}(q-Q-1)p(q)$$

$$\begin{aligned}
\Delta TC(Q) &= TC(Q+1) - TC(Q) \\
&= C_1 \sum_{q=0}^{Q+1}(Q+1-q)p(q) + C_2 \sum_{q=Q+2}^{\infty}(q-Q-1)\, p(q) \\
&\quad - C_1 \sum_{q=0}^{Q}(Q-q)p(q) - C_2 \sum_{q=Q+1}^{\infty}(q-Q)p(q) \\
&= C_1 \sum_{q=0}^{Q}(Q+1-q)p(q) + C_1(Q+1-Q-1)p(Q+1) \\
&\quad + C_2 \sum_{q=Q+1}^{\infty}(q-Q-1)\, p(q) - C_2(Q+1-Q-1)\, p\,(Q+1) \\
&\quad - C_1 \sum_{q=0}^{Q}(Q-q)p(q) - C_2 \sum_{q=Q+1}^{\infty}(q-Q)p(q) \\
&= C_1 \sum_{q=0}^{Q} p(q) - C_2 \sum_{q=Q+1}^{\infty} p(q) \\
&= C_1 \sum_{q=0}^{Q} p(q) - C_2 \left[\sum_{q=0}^{\infty} p(q) - \sum_{q=0}^{Q} p(q)\right]
\end{aligned}$$

$$= (C_1 + C_2)\sum_{q=0}^{Q} p(q) - C_2 \qquad \left(\because \sum_{q=0}^{\infty} p(q) = 1\right)$$

$$= (C_1 + C_2)\, F(Q) - C_2 \qquad \text{where } F(Q) = \sum_{q=0}^{Q} p(q)$$

Now $\Delta TC(Q) > 0 \Rightarrow (C_1 + C_2)\, F(Q) - C_2 > 0$

or $$F(Q) > \frac{C_2}{(C_1 + C_2)} \qquad ...(1)$$

Similarly,

$$\Delta TC(Q-1) = TC(Q) - TC(Q-1)$$

$$= (C_1 + C_2)\, F(Q-1) - C_2 \qquad \text{where } F(Q-1) = \sum_{q=0}^{Q-1} p(q)$$

Now $\Delta TC(Q-1) < 0 \Rightarrow (C_1 + C_2)\, F(Q-1) - C_2 < 0$

or $$F(Q-1) < \frac{C_2}{(C_1 + C_2)} \qquad ...(2)$$

From equations (1) and (2), we have

$$F(Q-1) < \frac{C_2}{(C_1 + C_2)} < F(Q)$$

Case 2. Continuous Units

Here, all the conditions are same as in case 1 but demand is continuous. So the cost equation of inventory involves integral in place of summation and $p(q)$ are replaced by $f(q)dq$.

Now proceeding in the same manner as in case 1, the total expected cost is given by

$$TC(Q) = C_1 \int_0^Q (Q-q) f(q)dq + C_2 \int_Q^{\infty} (q-Q) f(q)dq$$

For optimum value of Q,

$$\frac{d[TC(Q)]}{dQ} = 0 \Rightarrow C_1 \int_0^Q f(q)dq - C_2 \int_Q^{\infty} f(q)\,dq = 0$$

or $$C_1 \int_0^Q f(q)dq - C_2\left[\int_0^{\infty} f(q)dq - \int_{\infty}^{Q} f(q)dq\right] = 0$$

$$(C_1 + C_2) \int_0^Q f(q)dq - C_2 = 0 \qquad \left(\because \int_0^{\infty} f(q)dq = 1\right)$$

or $$\int_0^Q f(q)dq = \frac{C_2}{(C_1 + C_2)}$$

or $$F(Q) = \frac{C_2}{(C_1 + C_2)} \qquad \text{where } F(Q) = \int_0^Q f(q)dq$$

Now $$\frac{d^2[TC(Q)]}{dQ^2}\Big/Q = (C_1 + C_2)\, F(Q) > 0$$

Which shows that $TC(Q)$ is minimum for the value of Q given by $F(Q) = \frac{C_2}{(C_1 + C_2)}$.

Example 3. *A newspaper boy buys papers for ₹1.50 each and sells them for ₹2.0 each. He cannot return unsold newspapers. Daily demand has the following distribution.*

No of customers :	23	24	25	26	27	28	29	30	31	32
Probability :	0.01	0.03	0.06	0.10	0.20	0.25	0.15	0.10	0.05	0.05

If each day's demand is independent of the previous day's, how many newspapers should be ordered each day?

Solution. Here, $C_1 = 1.50$, $C_2 = 2.0 - 1.5 = 0.50$

$$\frac{C_2}{C_1 + C_2} = \frac{0.50}{1.50 + 0.50} = 0.25$$

q	23	24	25	26	27	28	29	30	31	32
$p(q)$	0.01	0.03	0.06	0.10	0.20	0.25	0.15	0.10	0.05	0.05
$\Sigma\, p(q)$	0.01	0.04	0.10	0.20	0.40	0.65	0.80	0.90	0.95	1.00

The optimum value of Q is obtained by

$$F(Q - 1) < \frac{C_2}{C_1 + C_2} < F(Q)$$

i.e., $$0.20 < 0.25 < 0.40$$

Number of newspapers ordered $(Q) = 27$. **Ans.**

Example 4. *A baking company sells one of its types of cakes by weight. It makes a profit of ₹19 on every kg of cake sold on the day it is baked. It disposes of all cakes not sold on the date these are baked at a loss of ₹3.00 per kg. If demand is known to be rectangular between 400 and 500 kg, determine the optimum amount baked.*

Solution. Here, $C_1 = 3.00$, $C_2 = 19$

$$f(q) = \frac{1}{q_2 - q_1} = \frac{1}{500 - 400} = \frac{1}{100}$$

(For rectangular distribution $f(x) = \frac{1}{b - a};\ a < x < b$)

Optimum value of Q is obtained by

$$\int_0^Q f(q)\,dq = \frac{C_2}{C_1 + C_2}$$

$$\int_{400}^{Q} \frac{1}{100}\,dq = \frac{19}{3 + 19}$$

$$\frac{1}{100}(Q - 400) = 0.8636$$

$$Q = 400 + 86.36 = 486.36 \text{ kg}$$ **Ans.**

Example 5. *An ice-cream company sells one of its types of ice-cream by weight. If the product is not sold on the day it is prepared, it can be sold at a loss of 50 paise per pound. But there is an unlimited market for one-day old ice-cream. On the other hand the company makes a profit of ₹ 3.20 on every pound of ice-cream sold on the day it is prepared. Past daily orders form as distribution with*

$f(q) = 0.02 - 0.0002q,\ 0 \le q \le 100.$

How many pounds of ice-cream, should the company prepare every day?

Solution. Here, $C_1 = 0.50$, $C_2 = 3.20$, $f(q) = 0.02 - 0.0002q$

Optimum value of Q is obtained by

$$\int_0^Q f(q)dq = \frac{C_2}{C_1 + C_2}$$

$$\int_0^Q (0.02 - 0.0002q)dq = \frac{3.20}{0.50 + 3.20}$$

$$\left(0.02q - 0.0002\frac{q^2}{2}\right)_0^Q = 0.865$$

$$0.02Q - 0.0002\frac{Q^2}{2} = 0.865$$

$$0.0001Q^2 - 0.02Q + 0.865 = 0$$

or $$Q = 63.3 \text{ pounds}$$

9.12 MODEL (3)

Continuous Demand, No Set-up Cost and Constant Lead Time

In this model demand is continuous. The set up cost is not included. Let C_1 be the carrying cost per item per unit time, C_2 be the shortage cost per item per unit time and Q be the inventory level at any time t. t is the constant interval between order. Let x is the demand during the time t with probability $F(x)$, y is the demand during the lead time L with probability $G(y)$.

The problem is to determine the optimum order level Q.

Case 1. Discrete Units

There are three situations depending upon the values of x, y and Q.

(*a*) When $0 \le y \le Q$, $0 < x \le Q - y$

Here, the demand during the lead time L is $y \le Q$. The period t starts with a stock $(Q - y)$ and ends with the stock $(Q - y - x)$. This situation can be represented in the figure on next page.

Only carrying cost is involved and no shortage cost.

$$\text{Total cost} = C_1 \times \text{Area of trapezium}$$

$$= C_1 \times \frac{1}{2} AB(BC + AD) = C_1 \times \frac{1}{2} t(Q - y - x + Q - y)$$

$$\text{Total cost} = C_1(Q - y - \frac{x}{2})t$$

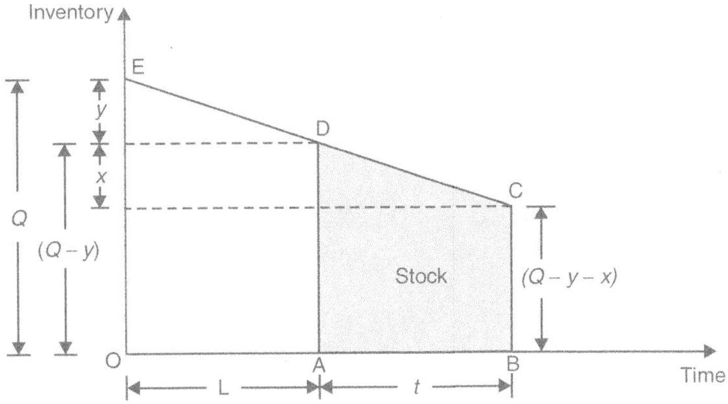

(*b*) When $0 \le y \le Q$, $x > Q - y$

Here, the demand during the lead time L is $y \le Q$. The period t starts with a stock $(Q - y)$ and ends with shortage $(x + y - Q)$. This situation can be represented in the following figure:

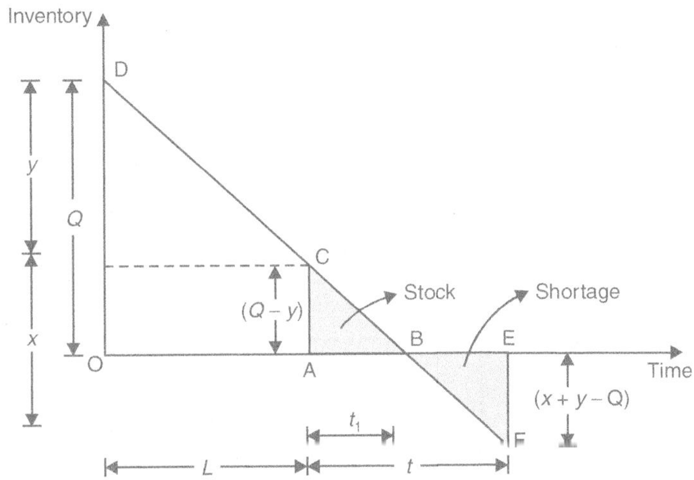

Both the costs are involved here.

$$\text{Carrying cost} = C_1 \times \text{Area of } \Delta ABC$$

$$= C_1 \times \frac{1}{2} t_1 (Q - y)$$

$$= C_1 \times \frac{1}{2}\left(\frac{Q-y}{x}\right) t\,(Q - y) \qquad \left[\because t_1 = \frac{(Q-y)}{x} t\right]$$

$$= C_1 \frac{(Q-y)^2}{2x} t$$

$$\text{Shortage cost} = C_2 \times \text{Area of } \Delta BEF$$

$$= C_2 \times \frac{1}{2}(t - t_1)\,(x + y - Q)$$

$$= C_2 \times \frac{1}{2}\left[t - \frac{(Q-y)}{x}t\right](x + y - Q)$$

$$= C_2 \frac{(x+y-Q)^2}{2x}t$$

$$\text{Total cost} = C_1 \frac{(Q-y)^2}{2x}t + C_2 \frac{(x+y-Q)^2}{2x}t$$

(*c*) When $y > Q$, $x > 0$

Here, the demand during the lead time L is $y > Q$. The period t starts with a shortage $(y - Q)$ and ends with shortage $(x + y - Q)$. This situation can be represented in the following figure.

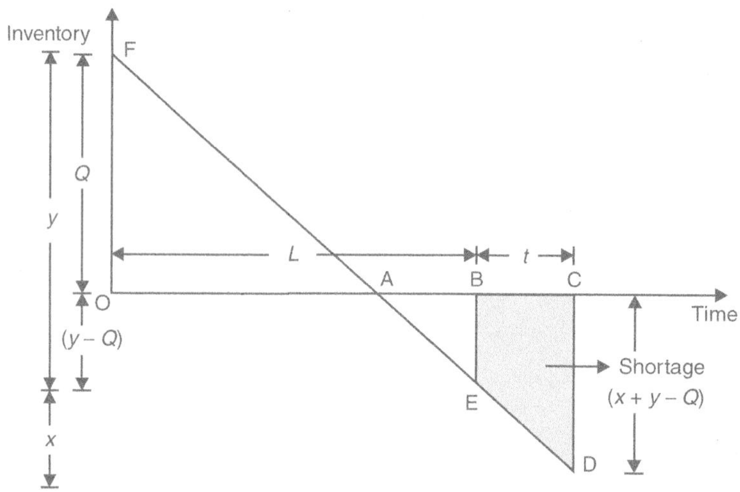

Only shortage cost is involved here.

$$\text{Shortage cost} = C_2 \times \text{Area of trapezium}$$

$$= C_2 \times \frac{1}{2} BC(BE + CD)$$

$$= C_2 \times \frac{1}{2} t\,[(y - Q) + (x + y - Q)]$$

$$= C_2 \times \left[\frac{x}{2} + y - Q\right]t$$

Now, the total expected cost (TC) is given by

$$TC = \sum_{y=0}^{Q}\sum_{x=0}^{Q-y} C_1\left(Q - y - \frac{x}{2}\right) t\,F(x)\,G(y)$$

$$+ \sum_{y=0}^{Q}\sum_{x=Q-y+1}^{\infty} \frac{1}{2x}\left[C_1(Q-y)^2 + C_2(x+y-Q)^2\right] t\,F(x)\,G(y) + \sum_{y=Q+1}^{\infty}\sum_{x=0}^{\infty} C_2\left(\frac{x}{2} + y - Q\right) t\,F(x)\,G(y)$$

The total average cost is given by

$$TC(Q) = \sum_{y=0}^{Q}\sum_{x=0}^{Q-y} C_1\left(Q-y-\frac{x}{2}\right)F(x)\,G(y) + \sum_{y=0}^{Q}\sum_{x=Q-y+1}^{\infty}\frac{1}{2x}\left[C_1(Q-y)^2+C_2(x+y-Q)^2\right]F(x)G(y)$$

$$+ \sum_{y=Q+1}^{\infty}\sum_{x=0}^{\infty} C_1\left(\frac{x}{2}+y-Q\right)F(x)G(y)$$

Now to obtain the optimum value of Q for which $TC(Q)$ is minimum, we use the following conditions of difference calculus

$\Delta TC(Q-1) < 0 < \Delta TC(Q)$

After simplifications, we have

$$\sum_{y=0}^{Q-1} G(y)\left[\sum_{x=0}^{Q-y-1}F(x)+\left(Q-y-\frac{1}{2}\right)\sum_{x=Q-y}^{\infty}\frac{F(x)}{x}\right] < \frac{C_2}{C_1+C_2}$$

$$< \sum_{y=0}^{Q} G(y)\left[\sum_{x=0}^{Q-y}F(x)+\left(Q-y+\frac{1}{2}\right)\sum_{x=Q-y+1}^{\infty}\frac{F(x)}{x}\right]$$

Case 2. Continuous Units

Here, all the conditions are same as in case 1 but demand is continuous. So the cost equation of inventory involves integral in place of summation and $F(x)$ and $G(y)$ are replaced by $f(x)\,dx$ and $g(y)\,dy$ respectively.

Now proceeding in the same manner as in case 1, the total average cost is given by

$$TC(Q) = C_1\int_0^Q g(y)dy\int_0^{Q-y}\left(Q-y-\frac{x}{2}\right)f(x)dx$$

$$+ \int_0^Q g(y)dy\int_{Q-y}^{\infty}\frac{1}{2x}[C_1(Q-y)^2+C_2(x+y-Q)^2]f(x)dx$$

$$+ C_2\int_Q^{\infty} g(y)dy\int_0^{\infty}\left(\frac{x}{2}+y-Q\right)f(x)dx$$

For optimum value of Q,

$$\frac{d[TC(Q)]}{dQ} = 0 \Rightarrow (C_1+C_2)\int_0^Q g(y)dy\left[\int_0^{Q-y}f(x)dx+(Q-y)\int_{Q-y}^{\infty}\frac{f(x)}{x}dx\right] - C_2 = 0$$

The optimum value of Q can be obtained by following relationship.

$$\int_0^Q g(y)dy\left[\int_0^{Q-y}f(x)dx+(Q-y)\int_{Q-y}^{\infty}\frac{f(x)}{x}dx\right] = \frac{C_2}{(C_1+C_2)}$$

The multiperiod inventory model is as follows:

9.13 MODEL (4)

Multiperiod Model with Constant Lead Time, Fixed Reorder Quantity

In this model, the demand for a single product and the lead time both are discrete random variables with known probability distribution functions. Here, the demand represents the number of units of product demanded by customers per unit of time, whereas the lead time represents the number of units of time from the time a replenishment order is placed until it is received. It is imperative that the same unit of time be used for both demand and lead time. Although demand and lead time are random variables, we assume their distributions remains the same from cycle to cycle, where a cycle is defined to be the number of units of time between the receipt of two consecutive replenishment orders. Since cycle time is a function of demand and lead time, it will also be a random variable.

In this model, there are following assumptions:

1. A fixed reorder point, fixed reorder quantity.
2. The demand and lead time are discrete random variables with known probability distribution functions.
3. The demand and lead time distributions remains the same from cycle to cycle.
4. Backordering is allowed.
5. The three costs are involved *i.e.,* ordering costs, carrying costs and shortage costs.
6. The planning period is one year.

Units of the product that are requested after the inventory level reaches zero are called stockouts. These units are backordered in the sense that they will supply the unfilled demands when the next replenishment order is received.

The notations used are as follows:

D = Expected annual demand
Q = Reorder quantity
C_1 = Carrying cost per unit per year
C_2 = Shortage cost per unit
C_S = Ordering cost or setup cost per order
LT = Lead time
d_{LT} = Demand during lead time
$p(d_{LT})$ = Distribution of demand during lead time
r = Reorder point quantity

The fixed reorder quantity, fixed reorder point model with random demand and lead time is illustrated in the following figure:

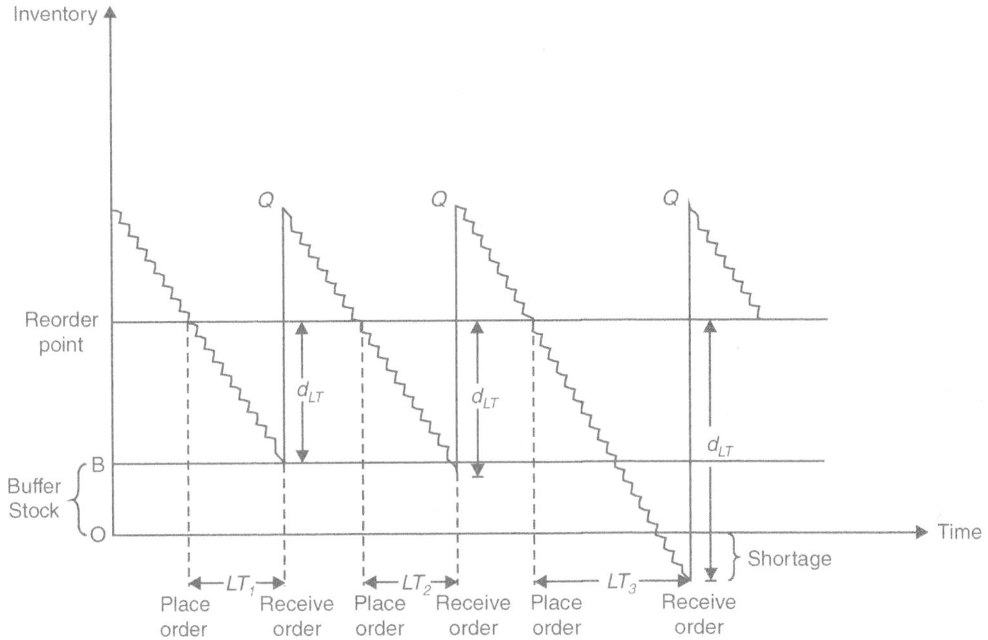

In the above figure, three cycles are shown. In first cycle, replenishment is received at the moment inventory level reaches to buffer stock level. In second cycle, lead time is longer as compared to lead time of first cycle and demand cuts into the buffer stock before replenishment is received. In third cycle, lead time is longer as compared to previous lead times and demand not only cuts the buffer stock but also a shortage is there before replenishment is received.

Since demand is uncertain there may be surpluses or shortages depending upon the demand during lead time (d_{LT}). If d_{LT} is less than the reorder point quantity (r), then there is a surplus of ($r - d_{LT}$) units, remains in the inventory. Otherwise, there is a shortage of ($d_{LT} - r$) units. Therefore, three costs are involved *i.e.*, ordering cost, carrying cost and shortage cost in the model.

Now, Ordering cost $= \frac{D}{Q}C_S$

Carrying cost $= \frac{Q}{2}C_1$

Shortage cost $= (d_{LT} - r)\ C_2$

We have to maintain a buffer stock against shortages,

so increased carrying cost $= (r - d_{LT})C_1$

Expected ordering cost $= \frac{D}{Q}C_S$

Expected carrying cost $= \frac{Q}{2}C_1 + (r - d_{LT})\ C_1$

$$= \left(\frac{Q}{2} + r - d_{LT}\right)C_1$$

Expected shortage cost per cycle = $C_2 \sum (d_{LT} - r)\, p(d_{LT})$

Expected annual shortage cost = $C_2\left(\frac{D}{Q}\right)\sum (d_{LT} - r)\, p(d_{LT})$

Now, the total annual expected cost is given by

$$TC = \frac{D}{Q}C_S + C_1\left(\frac{Q}{2} + r - d_{LT}\right) + C_2\left(\frac{D}{Q}\right)\sum (d_{LT} - r)p(d_{LT})$$

Now, the objective is to find the values of Q and r that simultaneously minimize the total annual expected cost TC.

The following formula provides an approximated optimal order quantity (Q^*)

$$EOQ(Q^*) = \sqrt{\frac{2DC_S}{C_1}}$$

Now, the value of Q^* can be used to find the value of r to minimize buffer stock costs. The optimal value of r can be obtained by using the following cost equation:

$$\text{Cost} = C_1(r - d_{LT}) + C_2\left(\frac{D}{Q^*}\right)\sum (d_{LT} - r)p(d_{LT})$$

Example 6. *The annual demand for a particular product is 1600 units. The carrying cost is ₹ 20 per unit, the stockout cost is ₹ 20 and the cost of placing an order is ₹ 640. The demand during the lead time is randomly distributed throughout the year and has the following distribution.*

Demand during lead time (d_{LT})	:	10	15	20	25	30	35
Probability $p(d_{LT})$	:	0.04	0.08	0.26	0.24	0.22	0.16

Determine the optimal order quantity and reorder point quantity.

Solution. Here, $D = 1600$ units/year.

$C_1 = ₹\ 20;\ C_2 = ₹\ 20,\ C_S = ₹\ 640$

$$\text{Optimal order quantity } (Q^*) = \sqrt{\frac{2DC_S}{C_1}}$$

$$= \sqrt{\frac{2 \times 1600 \times 640}{20}} = 320 \text{ units}$$

Expected demand during the lead time is given by

$$ED_{LT} = d_{LT_1} \cdot p(d_{LT_1}) + d_{LT_2} \cdot p(d_{LT_2}) + \ldots + d_{LT_6} \cdot p(d_{LT_6})$$
$$= (10 \times 0.04) + (15 \times 0.08) + (20 \times 0.26) + (25 \times 0.24) + (30 \times 0.22) + (35 \times 0.16)$$
$$= 25 \text{ units}$$

It buffer stock is not there, then shortage will occur when the demand during lead time is greater than 25 units. The expected number of shortage units per reorder cycle are calculated as follows:

Reorder point quantity (r)	Buffer stock (B)	Demand during lead time (d_{LT})	Shortages during lead time $(d_{LT} - r)$	Probability of demand during lead time $p(d_{LT})$	Expected shortage $(d_{LT} - r)$ $p(d_{LT})$	Expected units short per reorder cycle $\Sigma(d_{LT} - r)$ $p(d_{LT})$
25	0	25	0	0.24	0	
		30	5	0.22	1.10	
		35	10	0.16	1.60	2.70
30	5	30	0	0.22	0	
		35	5	0.16	0.80	0.80
35	10	35	0	0.16	0	0

From the above table, it is clear that the expected number of units short per reorder cycle are 2.70, when there is no buffer stock. But expected number of units short per reorder cycle are 0.80 and 0 when buffer stock of 5 and 10 units is there respectively.

Now, the expected annual shortage cost is calculated as follows:

Buffer Stock (B)	Expected units Short per reorder cycle $\Sigma(d_{LT} - r)$ $p(d_{LT})$	Expected annual shortage cost $C_2 \left(\frac{D}{Q^*}\right) \Sigma(d_{LT} - r)$ $p(d_{LT})$
0	2.70	$20 \times \frac{1600}{320} \times 2.70 = 270$
5	0.80	$20 \times \frac{1600}{320} \times 0.80 = 80$
10	0	$20 \times \frac{1600}{320} \times 0 = 0$

Now, the total annual expected cost is calculated as follows:

Buffer Stock (B)	Buffer stock carrying cost $(C_1 \times B)$	Expected annual shortage cost	Totat annual expected cost
0	$20 \times 0 = 0$	270	$0 + 270 = 270$
5	$20 \times 5 = 100$	80	$100 + 80 = 180$
10	$20 \times 10 = 200$	0	$200 + 0 = 200$

It is clear from the above table that the total annual expected cost is minimum when the buffer stock level is of 5 units.

So, the optimal reorder point quantity is

$$
\begin{aligned}
r &= B + ED_{LT} \\
&= 5 + 25 = 30 \text{ units.}
\end{aligned}
$$

Example 7. *The annual demand for an item is 1800 units. The carrying cost is ₹10 per unit, the stockout cost is ₹10 and the cost of placing an order is ₹40. The demand during the lead time is randomly distributed throughout the year and has the following distribution.*

Demand during lead time (d_{LT}) :	12	13	14	15	16	17	18
Probability $p(d_{LT})$:	0.05	0.15	0.20	0.25	0.12	0.16	0.07

Determine the optimal order quantity and reorder point quantity.

Solution. Here, $D = 1800$ units/year

$C_1 = ₹\ 10,\quad C_2 = ₹\ 10,\quad C_S = ₹\ 40$

$$\text{Optimal order quantity } (Q^*) = \sqrt{\frac{2DC_S}{C_1}}$$

$$= \sqrt{\frac{2 \times 1800 \times 40}{10}} = 120 \text{ units}$$

Expected demand during the lead time is given by

$$ED_{LT} = d_{LT_1} \cdot p(d_{LT_1}) + d_{LT_2} \cdot p(d_{LT_2}) + ... + d_{LT_7} \cdot p(d_{LT_7})$$

$$= (12 \times 0.05) + (13 \times 0.15) + (14 \times 0.20) + (15 \times 0.25)$$

$$+ (16 \times 0.12) + (17 \times 0.16) + (18 \times 0.07)$$

$$= 15 \text{ units}$$

If buffer stock is not there, then shortage will occur when the demand during lead time is greater than 15 units. The expected number of shortage units per reorder cycle are calculated as follows:

Reorder point quantity (r)	*Buffer stock (B)*	*Demand during lead time (d_{LT})*	*Shortages during lead time ($d_{LT} - r$)*	*Probability of demand during lead time $p(d_{LT})$*	*Expected shortage ($d_{LT} - r$) $p(d_{LT})$*	*Expected units short per reorder cycle* $\Sigma(d_{LT} - r)\, p(d_{LT})$
15	0	15	0	0.25	0	
		16	1	0.12	0.12	
		17	2	0.16	0.32	
		18	3	0.07	0.21	0.65
16	1	16	0	0.12	0	
		17	1	0.16	0.16	
		18	2	0.07	0.14	0.30
17	2	17	0	0.16	0	
		18	1	0.07	0.07	0.07
18	3	18	0	0.07	0	0

From the above table, it is clear that the expected number of units short per reorder cycle are 0.65, when there is no buffer stock. But expected number of units short per reorder cycle are 0.30, 0.07 and 0 when buffer stock of 1, 2 and 3 units is there respectively.

Now, the expected annual shortage cost is calculated as follows:

Buffer stock (*B*)	*Expected units short per reorder cycle* $\Sigma(d_{LT} - r)\ p(d_{LT})$	*Expected annual shortage cost* $C_2 \left(\frac{D}{Q^*}\right) \Sigma(d_{LT} - r)\ p(d_{LT})$
0	0.65	$10 \times \frac{1800}{120} \times 0.65 = 97.5$
1	0.30	$10 \times \frac{1800}{120} \times 0.30 = 45.0$
2	0.07	$10 \times \frac{1800}{120} \times 0.07 = 10.5$
3	0	$10 \times \frac{1800}{120} \times 0 = 0.0$

Now, the total annual expected cost is calculated as follows:

Buffer stock (*B*)	*Buffer stock carrying cost* ($C_1 \times B$)	*Expected annual shortage cost*	*Totat annual expected cost*
0	$10 \times 0 = 0$	97.5	$0 + 97.5 = 97.5$
1	$10 \times 1 = 10$	45.0	$10 + 45.0 = 55.0$
2	$10 \times 2 = 20$	10.5	$20 + 10.5 = 30.5$
3	$10 \times 3 = 30$	0.0	$30 + 0.0 = 30.0$

It is clear from the above table that the total annual expected cost is minimum when the buffer stock level is of 3 units.

So, the optimal reorder point quantity is

$$r = B + ED_{LT}$$
$$= 3 + 15 = 18 \text{ units.}$$

9.14 EOQ PROBLEMS WITH PRICE BREAKS

The *EOQ* formula under the basic *EOQ* model is based on the assumption that the price per unit is fixed irrespective of the order quantity. Sometimes suppliers offers discount if the quantities are purchased in bulk. Such discounts are referred to as quantity discounts or price breaks.

The *EOQ* formula is

$$Q^* = \sqrt{\frac{2DC_S}{C_1}}; \quad C_1 = KI$$

where
D = Consumption rate (demand in one year)
C_S = Set-up cost per order
C_1 = Carrying cost per unit per year
K = Cost of purchasing or manufacturing per unit
I = Inventory carrying cost per year

The total inventory cost of Q^* is given by

$$TC(Q^*) = DK + \frac{D}{Q^*} C_S + \frac{1}{2} Q^*KI$$

9.15 EOQ PROBLEM WITH ONE PRICE BREAK

One price break problem can be represented as follows:

Range of quantity	Purchase cost per unit
$0 \le Q_1 < b_1$	K_{11}
$b_1 \le Q_2$	K_{12}

where $K_{12} < K_{11}$.

The following procedure is used for obtaining *EOQ* in such case:

Step 1: Calculate Q_2^* and compare it with b_1.

Step 2: If $Q_2^* \ge b_1$, then *EOQ* or optimum order quantity will be Q_2^*, *i.e.*, $Q° = Q_2^*$. Otherwise go to next step.

Step 3: If $Q_2^* < b_1$, then in order to obtain the optimum order quantity, we have to compare the total inventory cost for Q_1^* with b_1.

Step 4: If $TC(Q_1^*) > TC(b_1)$, then optimum order quantity $Q° = b_1$ otherwise $Q° = Q_1^*$.

Example 8. *Find the optimum order quantity for a product for which the price breaks are as follows:*

Quantity	*Unit price (₹)*
$0 \le Q_1 < 300$	*10.00*
$300 \le Q_2$	*9.25*

The annual demand for the product is 2400 units, the cost of storage is 2% of the unit cost and the ordering cost is ₹ 350.

Solution. Here, $D = 2400, \quad C_S = 350$

$I = 2\% = 0.02, K_{11} = 10.00$ and $K_{12} = 9.25$

$$Q_2^* = \sqrt{\frac{2DC_S}{K_{12}I}} = \sqrt{\frac{2 \times 2400 \times 350}{9.25 \times 0.02}} = 3013.48 \simeq 3013 \text{ units}$$

Now Q_2^* (3013) > 300. Therefore, the optimum order quantity is given by $Q° = Q_2^* = 3013$ units.

Example 9. *Find the optimum order quantity for a product for which the price breaks are as follows:*

Quantity	*Unit price (₹)*
$0 \le Q_1 < 500$	10.00
$500 \le Q_2$	9.80

The annual demand for the product is 1600 units, the cost of storage is 10% of the unit cost and the ordering cost is ₹ 5.00.

Solution. Here, $D = 1600, \quad C_S = 5$

$$I = 10\% = 0.10, K_{11} = 10.00, \quad K_{12} = 9.80$$

$$Q_2^* = \sqrt{\frac{2DC_S}{K_{12}I}} = \sqrt{\frac{2\times 1600\times 5}{9.80\times 0.10}} = 127.77 \simeq 128 \text{ units}$$

Here Q_2^* (128) < b_1 (500)

So $$Q_1^* = \sqrt{\frac{2DC_S}{K_{11}I}} = \sqrt{\frac{2\times 1600\times 5}{10.00\times 0.10}} = 126.49 \simeq 126 \text{ units}$$

Now we will find $TC(Q_1^*)$ and $TC(b_1)$.

$$TC(Q_1^*) = DK_{11} + \frac{D}{Q_1^*}C_S + \frac{1}{2}Q_1^*K_{11}I$$

$$= 1600 \times 10 + \frac{1600}{126} \times 5 + \frac{1}{2} \times 126 \times 10 \times 0.10$$

$$= ₹\ 16126.49$$

$$TC(b_1) = DK_{12} + \frac{D}{b_1}C_S + \frac{1}{2}b_1K_{12}I$$

$$= 1600 \times 9.8 + \frac{1600}{500} \times 5 + \frac{1}{2} \times 500 \times 9.8 \times 0.10$$

$$= ₹\ 15941$$

Since $TC(b_1) < TC(Q_1^*)$.

So optimum order quantity is $Q^\circ = b_1 = 500$ units.

9.16 EOQ PROBLEM WITH TWO PRICE BREAKS

Two price break problem can be represented as follows:

Range of quantity	Purchase cost per unit
$0 \le Q_1 < b_1$	K_{11}
$b_1 \le Q_2 < b_2$	K_{12}
$b_2 \le Q_3$	K_{13}

where $K_{13} < K_{12} < K_{11}$.

The following procedure is used for obtaining *EOQ* in such case:

Step 1: Calculate Q_3^* and compare it with b_2.

Step 2: If $Q_3^* \geq b_2$, then EOQ or optimum order quantity will be Q_3^*, *i.e.*, $Q^\circ = Q_3^*$. Otherwise go to next step.

Step 3: If $Q_3^* < b_2$, then calculate Q_2^*. Since $Q_3^* < b_2$, $Q_2^* < b_2$ ($\because Q_1^* < Q_2^* < Q_3^*$).
Thus either $Q_2^* < b_1$ or $b_1 \leq Q_2^* < b_2$.

Step 4: If $Q_2^* < b_2$ and $b_1 \leq Q_2^* < b_2$ then follow the same procedure as in the case of one price break, *i.e.*, to find EOQ compare $TC(Q_2^*)$ with $TC(b_2)$.

Step 5: If $Q_2^* < b_2$ and $Q_2^* < b_1$, then calculate Q_1^*. Now to find EOQ compare $TC(Q_1^*)$, $TC(b_1)$ and $TC(b_2)$.

Example 10. *Derive the optimal order quantity from the following data:*

Quantity	*Unit price (₹)*
$0 \leq Q_1 < 500$	10.00
$500 \leq Q_2 < 750$	9.25
$750 \leq Q_3$	8.75

The annual demand for the product is 200 units, the cost of storage is 2% of the unit cost and the ordering cost is ₹ 350.

Solution. Here, $D = 200$,

$C_S = 350 \quad I = 2\% = 0.02,\ K_{11} = 10.00,\ \ K_{12} = 9.25$ and $K_{13} = 8.75$

$$Q_3^* = \sqrt{\frac{2DC_S}{K_{13}I}} = \sqrt{\frac{2\times 200\times 350}{8.75\times 0.02}} = 894.43 \simeq 894$$

Now $Q_3^*(894) > 750$. Therefore, the optimum order quantity is given by $Q^\circ = Q_3^* = 894$ units.

Example 11. *Find the optimum order quantity from the following data:*

Quantity	*Unit price (₹)*
$0 \leq Q_1 < 1000$	1.00
$1000 \leq Q_2 < 2000$	0.95
$2000 \leq Q_3$	0.93

The annual demand for the product is 2000 units, the cost of storage is 16% of the unit cost and the ordering cost is ₹ 10.

Solution. Here, $D = 2000, \qquad C_S = 10,$

$I = 16\% = 0.16,\ K_{11} = 1.00,\ \ K_{12} = 0.95$ and $K_{13} = 0.93$

$$Q_3^* = \sqrt{\frac{2DC_S}{K_{13}I}} = \sqrt{\frac{2\times 2000\times 10}{0.93\times 0.16}} = 518.47 \simeq 518 \text{ units}$$

$Q_3^*(518) < b_2(2000)$, we have to find

$$Q_2^* = \sqrt{\frac{2DC_S}{K_{12}I}} = \sqrt{\frac{2\times 2000\times 10}{0.95\times 0.16}} = 512.989 \simeq 513 \text{ units}$$

$Q_2^*(513) < b_1(1000)$, we have to find

$$Q_1^* = \sqrt{\frac{2DC_S}{K_{11}I}} = \sqrt{\frac{2\times 2000\times 10}{1.00\times 0.16}} = 500 \text{ units}$$

Now,

$$TC(Q_1^*) = DK_{11} + \frac{D}{Q_1^*}C_S + \frac{1}{2}Q_1^*K_{11}I$$

$$TC(500) = 2000 \times 1 + \frac{2000}{5000} \times 10 + \frac{1}{2} \times 500 \times 1 \times 0.16$$

$$= ₹\ 2080$$

$$TC(b_1) = DK_{12} + \frac{D}{b_1}C_S + \frac{1}{2}b_1K_{12}I$$

$$TC(1000) = 2000 \times 0.95 + \frac{2000}{1000} \times 10 + \frac{1}{2} \times 1000 \times 0.95 \times 0.16$$

$$= ₹\ 1996$$

$$TC(b_2) = DK_{13} + \frac{D}{b_2}C_S + \frac{1}{2}b_2K_{13}I$$

$$TC(2000) = 2000 \times 0.93 + \frac{2000}{2000} \times 10 + \frac{1}{2} \times 2000 \times 0.93 \times 0.16$$

$$= ₹\ 2018.80$$

Since $TC(b_1)$ is the lowest cost. So the optimum order quantity is $Q^\circ = b_1 = 1000$ units.

Example 12. *A manufacturing concern requires 64000 units of a material per year. The ordering cost is ₹10 per order, while carrying cost of one unit for a year is 20 percent. The purchase price is ₹10 per unit. If a discount of 2 percent is available on an order of at least 1000 units at a time, and a discount of 5 percent is available on an order of at least 5000 units at a time. What purchase quantity would you recommend?*

Solution. Here, $D = 64000$, $C_S = 10$, $I = 20\% = 0.20$.

The price breaks can be represented as

Quantity	Unit price (₹)
$0 \le Q_1 < 1000$	10.00
$1000 \le Q_2 < 5000$	9.80
$5000 \le Q_3$	9.50

$$Q_3^* = \sqrt{\frac{2DC_S}{K_{13}I}} = \sqrt{\frac{2 \times 64000 \times 10}{9.50 \times 0.20}} = 820.78 \simeq 821 \text{ units}$$

$Q_3^*(821) < b_2(5000)$, we have to find

$$Q_2^* = \sqrt{\frac{2DC_S}{K_{12}I}} = \sqrt{\frac{2 \times 64000 \times 10}{9.8 \times 0.20}} = 808.12 \simeq 808 \text{ units}$$

$Q_2^*(808) < b_1(1000)$, we have to find

$$Q_1^* = \sqrt{\frac{2DC_S}{K_{11}I}} = \sqrt{\frac{2 \times 64000 \times 10}{10 \times 0.20}} = 800 \text{ units}$$

Now,

$$TC(Q_1^*) = DK_{11} + \frac{D}{Q_1^*} C_S + \frac{1}{2} Q_1^* K_{11} I$$

$$TC(800) = 64000 \times 10 + \frac{64000}{800} \times 10 + \frac{1}{2} \times 800 \times 10 \times 0.20$$

$$= ₹\ 641600$$

$$TC(b_1) = DK_{12} + \frac{D}{b_1} C_S + \frac{1}{2} b_1 K_{12} I$$

$$TC(1000) = 64000 \times 9.8 + \frac{64000}{1000} \times 10 + \frac{1}{2} \times 1000 \times 9.8 \times 0.20$$

$$= ₹\ 628820$$

$$TC(b_2) = DK_{13} + \frac{D}{b_2} C_S + \frac{1}{2} b_2 K_{13} I$$

$$TC(5000) = 64000 \times 9.5 + \frac{64000}{5000} \times 10 + \frac{1}{2} \times 5000 \times 9.5 \times 0.20$$

$$= ₹\ 612878$$

Since $TC(b_2)$ is the lowest cost. So the optimum order quantity is $Q^\circ = b_2 = 5000$ units.

9.17 EOQ PROBLEM WITH *n* PRICE BREAKS

n price break problem can be represented as follows:

Range of quantity	Purchase cost per unit
$0 \le Q_1 < b_1$	K_{11}
$b_1 \le Q_2 < b_2$	K_{12}
$\vdots$	$\vdots$
$b_{n-1} \le Q_n$	K_{1n}

where $K_{1n} < \ldots < K_{12} < K_{11}$.

The following procedure is used for obtaining EOQ in such case:

Step 1: Calculate Q_n^* and compare it with b_{n-1}.

Step 2: If $Q_n^* \ge b_{n-1}$, then EOQ or optimum order quantity will be Q_n^*, *i.e.*, $Q^\circ = Q_n^*$. Otherwise go to next step.

Step 3: If $Q_n^* < b_{n-1}$, then calculate Q_{n-1}^*.

Step 4: If $Q_{n-1}^* \ge b_{n-2}$ then follow the same procedure as in the case of one price break, *i.e.*, to find EOQ compare $TC\left(Q_{n-1}^*\right)$ with $TC(b_{n-1})$.

Step 5: If $Q_{n-1}^* < b_{n-2}$, then calculate Q_{n-2}^*.

Step 6: If $Q^*_{n-2} \geq b_{n-3}$, then follows the same procedure as in the case of two price breaks, *i.e.*, to find *EOQ* compare $TC\left(Q^*_{n-2}\right)$ with $TC(b_{n-2})$ and $TC(b_{n-1})$.

Step 7: If $Q^*_{n-2} < b_{n-3}$. The proceed as in step 3 to step 6.

Step 8: We continue this procedure until we reach to an EOQ.

Example 13. *Find the optimum order quantity for a product for which the price breaks are as follows:*

Quantity	*Unit price (₹)*
$0 \leq Q_1 < 500$	15.00
$500 \leq Q_2 < 1500$	14.80
$1500 \leq Q_3 < 3000$	14.60
$3000 \leq Q_4$	14.40

The annual demand for the product is 500 units, the cost of storage is 10% of the unit cost per year and the ordering cost per order is ₹ 180.

Solution. Here, $D = 500, \quad C_S = 180,$

$I = 10\% = 0.10,\ K_{11} = 15.00,\ K_{12} = 14.80,\ K_{13} = 14.60$, and $K_{14} = 14.40$

$$Q_4^* = \sqrt{\frac{2DC_S}{K_{14}I}} = \sqrt{\frac{2\times 500\times 180}{14.40\times 0.10}} = 353.55 \simeq 354 \text{ units}$$

$Q_4^*(354) < b_3(3000)$, we have to find

$$Q_3^* = \sqrt{\frac{2DC_S}{K_{13}I}} = \sqrt{\frac{2\times 500\times 180}{14.60\times 0.10}} = 351.12 \simeq 351 \text{ units}$$

$Q_3^*(351) < b_2(1500)$, we have to find

$$Q_2^* = \sqrt{\frac{2DC_S}{K_{12}I}} = \sqrt{\frac{2\times 500\times 180}{14.80\times 0.10}} = 348.74 \simeq 349 \text{ units}$$

$Q_2^*(349) < b_1(500)$, we have to find

$$Q_1^* = \sqrt{\frac{2DC_S}{K_{11}I}} = \sqrt{\frac{2\times 500\times 180}{15.00\times 0.10}} = 346.41 \simeq 346 \text{ units}$$

Now,

$$TC(Q_1^*) = DK_{11} + \frac{D}{Q_1^*}C_S + \frac{1}{2}Q_1^*K_{11}I$$

$$TC(346) = 500\times 15 + \frac{500}{346}\times 180 + \frac{1}{2}\times 346\times 15\times 0.10$$

$$= ₹\ 8019.615$$

$$TC(b_1) = DK_{12} + \frac{D}{b_1} C_S + \frac{1}{2} b_1 K_{12} I$$

$$TC(500) = 500 \times 14.80 + \frac{500}{500} \times 180 + \frac{1}{2} \times 500 \times 14.80 \times 0.10$$

$$= ₹\ 7950$$

$$TC(b_2) = DK_{13} + \frac{D}{b_2} C_S + \frac{1}{2} b_2 K_{13} I$$

$$TC(1500) = 500 \times 14.60 + \frac{500}{1500} \times 180 + \frac{1}{2} \times 1500 \times 14.60 \times 0.10$$

$$= ₹\ 8455$$

$$TC(b_3) = DK_{14} + \frac{D}{b_3} C_S + \frac{1}{2} b_3 K_{14} I$$

$$TC(3000) = 500 \times 14.40 + \frac{500}{3000} \times 180 + \frac{1}{2} \times 3000 \times 14.40 \times 0.10$$

$$= ₹\ 9390$$

Since $TC(b_1)$ is the lowest cost. So the optimum order quantity is $Q^\circ = b_1 = 500$ units.

EXERCISES

1. The probability distribution of monthly sales of a certain item is as follows:

Monthly Sales :	0	1	2	3	4	5	6	7	8
Probability :	0.01	0.05	0.24	0.33	0.20	0.07	0.06	0.02	0.02

The cost of holding inventory is ₹ 10 per unit per month. A stock of 5 items is maintained at the start of each month. If the shortage cost is proportional to both time and quantity short, find the imputed cost of shortage of unit item for unit time.

[**Ans.** ₹ 253.85 < C_2 < ₹ 633.086]

2. The demand for a particular product is continuous and shows the following probability distribution:

Demand :	0	1	2	3	4	5	6
Probability :	0.02	0.05	0.30	0.27	0.20	0.10	0.06

Find out the optimum stock level, if the cost of shortage is ₹ 110 per unit and cost of holding is ₹ 5 per unit. The shortage is proportional to both time and quantity short.

[**Ans.** 4 units]

3. Let the probability density of demand of a certain item during a week be

$$f(q) = \begin{cases} 0.1, & 0 \leq q \leq 10 \\ 0, & \text{otherwise} \end{cases}$$

The demand is assumed to occur with a uniform pattern over the week. Let the unit carrying cost of the item in inventory be ₹ 2 per week and unit shortage cost be ₹ 8 per week. How would you determine the optimal order level of the inventory?

[**Ans.** 4.5 units]

4. A newspaper boy buys papers for ₹ 5 each and sells them for ₹ 6 each. He cannot return unsold newspapers. Daily demand has the following distribution:

No. of customers	:	10	11	12	13	14	15	16
Probability	:	0.05	0.15	0.40	0.20	0.10	0.05	0.05

If each day's demand is independent of the previous day's, how many papers should be ordered each day? [**Ans.** 11]

5. Some of the spare parts of a ship cost ₹ 50,000 each. These spare parts can only be ordered together with the ship. If not ordered at the time the ship is constructed, these parts cannot be available on need. Suppose that a loss of ₹ 4,500,000 is suffered for each spare that is needed when none is available in the stock. Further suppose that the probabilities that the spares will be needed as replacement during the life term of the class of ship discussed are

Spares required	:	0	1	2	3	4	5	6 or more
Probability	:	0.900	0.040	0.025	0.020	0.010	0.005	0.000

How many spare parts should be procured? [**Ans.** 4]

6. The cost of holding an item in stock is ₹ 2 per unit and the shortage cost is ₹ 8. If ₹ 2 is the purchasing cost per unit, determine the optimal order level of inventory, given the following probability distribution:

q	:	0	1	2	3	4	5
$p(q)$	:	0.05	0.25	0.20	0.15	0.20	0.15

[**Ans.** 3]

7. A baking company sells cake by kg weight. It makes a profit of ₹ 5 per kg sold on the day it is baked. It disposes off, all cakes not sold on the date it is baked at a loss of ₹ 1.20 a kg. If demand is known to be rectangular between 2000 and 3000 kg, determine the optimal daily amount baked. [**Ans.** 2806.45 kg]

8. A fish stall sells a variety of fish at the rate of ₹ 5 per kg on the day of the catch. If the stall fails to sell the catch on the same day, it pays for shortages at the rate of ₹ 0.30 per kg and the price fatched is ₹ 4.50 per kg on the next day. Past records show that there is an unlimited demand for the fish one day old. The problem is to ascertain how much fish should be procured every day, so that the total expected cost is the minimum. It has been found from the past records that daily demand follows an exponential distribution with

$$f(q) = 0.02\,\bar{e}^{0.02q}, \; 0 \leq q \leq \infty$$ [**Ans.** 99 kg]

9. An item has annual demand of 2000 units. The cost of placing an order is ₹ 400 and the annual carrying cost is ₹ 10 per unit. The costs of stock out are estimated to average ₹ 10. The demand during lead time tends to be randomly distributed throughout the year, so that a Poisson distribution can be assumed. There are 250 working days per year and lead time is 5 working days:

Demand during lead time	:	70	75	80	85	90	95	100
Probability	:	0.02	0.14	0.23	0.24	0.21	0.12	0.04

Determine the optimal order quantity and reorder level quantity.

[**Ans.** 400 units; 90 units]

10. Find the optimum order quantity for a product for which the price breaks are as follows:

Quantity	Unit price (₹)
$0 \le Q_1 < 500$	10.00
$500 \le Q_2$	9.25

The annual demand for the product is 2400 units, the cost of storage is 2% of the unit cost and the ordering cost is ₹ 100. [**Ans.** 500]

11. Find the optimum order quantity for a product for which the price breaks are as follows:

Quantity	Unit price (₹)
$0 \le Q_1 < 500$	10.00
$500 \le Q_2$	9.25

The annual demand for the product is 2400 units, the cost of storage is 2% of the unit cost and the ordering cost is ₹ 350. [**Ans.** 870]

12. Find the optimum order quantity for a product for which the price breaks are as follows:

Quantity	Unit price (₹)
$0 \le Q_1 < 300$	10.00
$300 \le Q_2$	9.25

The annual demand for the product is 2400 units, the cost of storage is 2% of the unit cost and the ordering cost is ₹ 100. [**Ans.** 465]

13. Find the optimum order quantity for a product for which the price breaks are as follows:

Quantity	Unit price (₹)
$0 \le Q_1 < 100$	20
$100 \le Q_2 < 200$	18
$200 \le Q_3$	16

The annual demand for the product is 400 units, the cost of storage is 20% of the unit cost and the ordering cost is ₹ 25 per order. [**Ans.** 200]

14. Find the optimum order quantity for a product for which the price breaks are as follows:

Quantity	Unit price (₹)
$0 \le Q_1 < 500$	0.39
$500 \le Q_2 < 1000$	0.29
$1000 \le Q_3$	0.28

The annual demand for the product is 600 units, the cost of storage is 20% of the unit cost and the ordering cost is ₹ 800. [**Ans.** 4140]

15. Find the optimum order quantity for a product for which the price breaks are as follows:

Quantity	Unit price (₹)
$0 \le Q_1 < 500$	10.00
$500 \le Q_2 < 750$	9.25
$750 \le Q_3$	8.75

The monthly demand for the product is 200 units, the cost of storage is 2% of the unit cost and the ordering cost is ₹ 100. [**Ans.** 750]

16. Find the optimum order quantity for a product for which the price breaks are as follows:

Quantity	Unit price (₹)
$0 \le Q_1 < 3000$	10.00
$3000 \le Q_2 < 5000$	9.25
$5000 \le Q_3$	8.75

The monthly demand for the product is 200 units, the cost of storage is 2% of the unit cost and the ordering cost is ₹ 100. [**Ans.** 447]

17. Find the optimum order quantity for a product for which the price breaks are as follows:

Quantity	Unit price (₹)
$0 \le Q_1 < 1000$	22.00
$1000 \le Q_2 < 1500$	20.00
$1500 \le Q_3 < 2000$	19.00
$2000 \le Q_4$	18.50

The annual demand for the product is 8000 units, the cost of storage is 10% of the unit cost and the ordering cost is ₹ 180 per order. [**Ans.** 2000]

18. Find the optimum order quantity for a products for which the price breaks are as follows:

Quantity	Unit price (₹)
$0 \le Q_1 < 500$	25.00
$500 \le Q_2 < 1500$	24.80
$1500 \le Q_3 < 3000$	24.60
$3000 \le Q_4$	24.40

The annual demand for the product is 500 units, the cost of storage is 10% of the unit cost and the ordering cost is ₹ 180 per order. [**Ans.** 268]

❑❑❑

CHAPTER 10

Simulation

10.1 INTRODUCTION

The mathematical models can help to describe and analyse a wide variety of problems. But, all real life problems cannot be converted into a mathematical form due to the complexity of the situations. In such cases, simulation is a very useful technique. Today, simulation is one of the most multifaceted topics that can face an industrial engineer in the workplace. It is also very important to a corporation, regardless of the industry. It can be used as a tool to increase the production capacity.

Simulation is a flexible methodology we can use to analyse the behaviour of a present or proposed business activity, new product, manufacturing line or plant expansion etc.

In simulation, we perform experiments on a model of the real system, rather than the real system itself, because it is faster, cheaper or safer to perform experiments on the model. Each experiment is called a trial and a simulation run includes many trials. Simulation is described by Shannon as:

"Simulation is the process of designing a model of the real system and conducting experiments with this model for the purpose of understanding the behaviour for the operation of the system."

By performing simulations and analyzing the results, we can gain an understanding of how a present system operates, and what would happen if we changed it, or we can estimate how a proposed new system would behave. Sometimes, a simulation deals with uncertainty in the system itself or in the world around it. When the simulation deals with uncertainty, the model will include uncertain variables, whose values are not under our control as well as decision variables that we can control.

10.2 THE BASIC STEPS OF SIMULATION PROCESS

The steps involved in simulation process are as follows:

1. **Problem Definition:** The initial step involves the goals of the study and determining the kind of problem that can be solved by the simulation technique.

2. **Project Planning:** The tasks for completing the project are broken down into work packages with a responsible group assigned to each package. Milestones are indicated for tracking the progress. This schedule is necessary to determine if sufficient time and resources are available for completion.

   The steps of simulation process are incorporated into a flowchart as follows:
3. **System Definition:** It involves the identification of the system components to be modeled and the performance measures to be analyzed.
4. **Construction of Model:** A model is constructed to be analyzed. The model so constructed should represent the real system as closely as possible but should not be so complex to understand.
5. **Validation of Model:** Validation of the model ensures that no significant difference exists between the model and the real system and that the model reflects reality.
6. **Experimentation:** Experimentation involves developing the alternative model(s), executing the simulation run and statistically comparing the alternative(s) system performance with that of the real system.
7. **Run the simulation model:** Use the computer to get the output in the form of operating characteristics by running the model.
8. **Examine the Results:** Examine the results of the problem to check whether we have achieved what we wanted to achieve by using simulation.
9. **Implementation:** The best course of action is identified, recommended and justified.

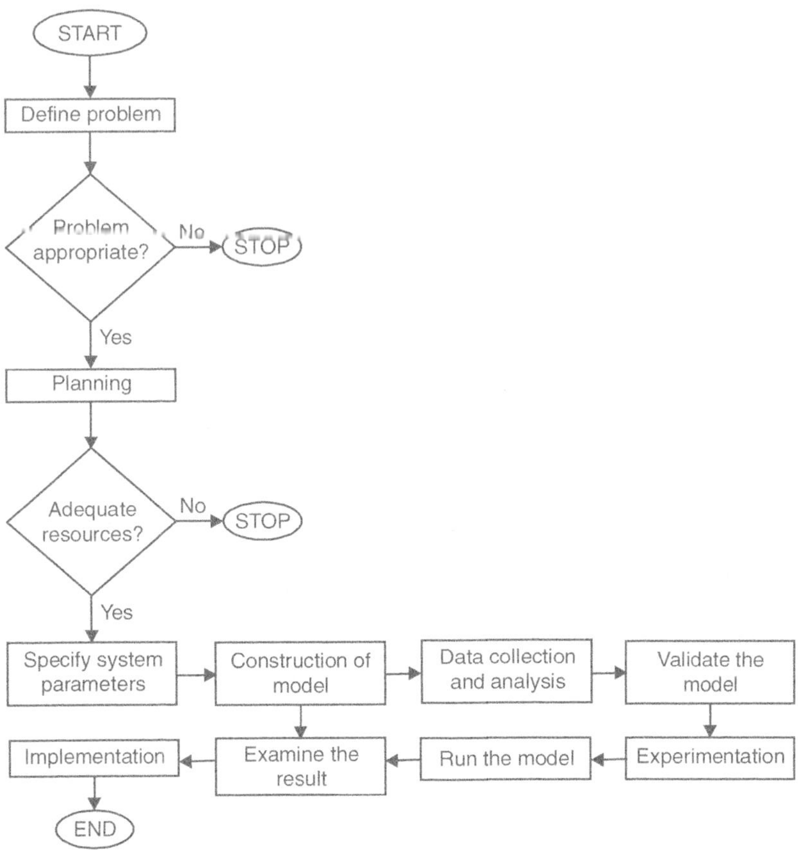

10.3 ADVANTAGES OF SIMULATION TECHNIQUE

The simulation technique, when compared with mathematical model analysis has so many advantages. Some of the important advantages are as below:

1. Simulation technique is suitable for the analysis of complex real life problems.
2. It is useful for sensitivity anaylsis of complex problems. In other words, it can be modified to suit the changing situation and to that extent are flexible.
3. It enables the decision maker to assess the possible risk involved in a new policy before implementing it.
4. Simulation technique is easier than mathematical models in many cases.
5. Simulation technique provides the solution when other techniques fail.
6. If well designed, learning how to operate a computer simulation program generally requires little effort.
7. Simulation technique can be used to verify analytic solutions.
8. Building a model can lead to system improvements and greater understandings.

10.4 DISADVANTAGES OF SIMULATION TECHNIQUE

There are not only advantages connected with the simulation technique. Some of the disadvantages (or limitations) are as below:

1. Simulation technique does not provide optimum solution. The solution may be differ with the use of different random numbers.
2. Simulation concerns the manipulation of a number of variables of a model representing a real system. However, manipulation of a single variable often means that the reality of the system as a whole can be lost.

   Certain system of a realistic situation are not transparent. Some factors have a lot of influence on the whole, but they have indistinct relations in the whole and can therefore not be represented in a model.
3. It provides only estimates of solution.
4. Simulation can take a large amount of development and (or) computer time. Do not use computer simulation if an analytical solution is available or if simulation costs outweigh benefits.
5. Each application of simulation is ad hoc to a great extent which indicates simulation does not require standard probability distribution.

10.5 APPLICATIONS OF SIMULATION

There are wide variety of problems or areas where simulation is used. Some of the applications where simulation is used are as below:

Manufacturing

Finance

Transportation

Inventory
Computer systems
Telecommunications
E-business
Forecasting
Planning etc.

10.6 MONTE CARLO SIMULATION

The Monte Carlo method is a technique that involves random numbers and probability to solve problems.

The term Monte Carlo method was given by Stainslaw Ulam and Nicholas Metropolis in reference to games of chance, a popular game in Monte Carlo, Monaco where the Casinos have games of chance. Monte Carlo simulation is a technique that converts uncertainties in input variables of a model into probability distributions. By combining the distributions and randomly selected values from them, it recalculates the simulated model many times and provides the probability of the output. This is a method for iteratively evaluating a deterministic model using the sequence of random numbers as inputs. Monte Carlo simulation is generally used when the model is complex.

The steps involved in Monte Carlo simulation are as below:

1. Identify the variables to be analysed and set up a probability distribution for these variables.
2. Generate a cumulative probability distribution for each variable.
3. Get a sequence of random numbers to represent value or interval of values for each variable.
4. Make a simulation experiment by means of random sampling.
5. Repeat step-4 until the required number of simulation runs has been generated.

10.7 BASIC CHARACTERISTICS

Monte Carlo simulation allows several inputs to be used at the same time to create the probability distribution of one or more than one outputs. For the inputs of the model different types of probability distributions can be assigned. The use of random numbers characterizes Monte Carlo simulation as a stochastic method. The random numbers have to be independent, no correlation should exist between them. Monte Carlo simulation generates the output as a range instead of a fixed value and shows how likely the output value is to occur in the range.

10.8 SIMULATION LANGUAGES

A computer simulation language describe the operation of a simulation on a computer. There are various computer languages to write the simulation programmes. FORTRAN is a general purpose language and can be used for any type of simulation. FORTRAN is more efficient in computer time and storage requirements so it is quite often used to write the simulation programmes. However, programming in FORTRAN is very difficult and time consuming in comparison the special simulation languages. There are two major types of simulation: continuous and discrete event type though more modern languages can handle both types of events.

GASP and SIMSCRIPT are two widely used general simulation languages. The most commonly used simulation language is GPSS (General purpose simulation system), which was developed in 1960s. SIMSCRIPT, SLAM and SIMAN allow the user to write (a portion of) the model in higher level language such as FORTRAN or C. In 80s, SIMANIV and CINEMAIV was developed. In 1984 the first simulation language specifically designed for modeling manufacturing system was developed. In the late 80s with the development of the discrete event simulation model, the management was able to assess the cost-benefits of alternatives, maintenance strategies and capital replacements etc. In the early 90s software EMS version of GPSS/PC, MIC-SIM version 3.0 was developed.

A new process oriented simulation language called SIMNET II is designed to allow modeling complex situations directly. Some of the simulation languages are: SIMULA, SOL, GASP2, ASCL, Dynamo, SIMULINK, SPICE, SIMIO.

Example 1. *The automobile company manufactures around 150 scooters. The daily production varies from 146 to 154 depending upon the availability of raw materials and other working conditions.*

Production per day	*Probability*
146	0.04
147	0.09
148	0.12
149	0.14
150	0.11
151	0.10
152	0.20
153	0.12
154	0.08

The finished scooters are transported in a specially arranged lorry accommodating 150 scooters. Using following random numbers:

80, 81, 76, 75, 64, 43, 18, 26, 10, 12, 65, 68, 69, 61, 57 simulate the process to find out:

(i) What will be the average number of scooters waiting in the factory?

(ii) What will be the average number of empty space on the lorry?

Solution. We determine the random numbers intervals as below:

Production per day	*Probability*	*Cumulative probability*	*Random number intervals*
146	0.04	0.04	00–03
147	0.09	0.13	04–12
148	0.12	0.25	13–24
149	0.14	0.39	25–38
150	0.11	0.50	39–49
151	0.10	0.60	50–59
152	0.20	0.80	60–79
153	0.12	0.92	80–91
154	0.08	1.00	92–99

Now using the given random numbers, we simulate the production per day as below:

S. No.	*Random Number*	*Production per day*	*Number of scooters waiting*	*Number of empty spaces in the lorry*
1	80	153	3	
2	81	153	3	
3	76	152	2	
4	75	152	2	
5	64	152	2	
6	43	150	0	0
7	18	148		2
8	26	149		1
9	10	147		3
10	12	147		3
11	65	152	2	
12	68	152	2	
13	69	152	2	
14	61	152	2	
15	57	151	1	
Total			21	9

(*i*) Average numbers of scooters waiting $= \dfrac{21}{15} = 1.4$ per day

(*ii*) Average number of empty space on the lorry $= \dfrac{9}{15} = 0.6$ per day

Example 2. *The occurrence of rain in a city on a day is dependent upon whether or not it rained on the previous day. It is rained on the previous day, the rain distribution is given by:*

Event	*No rain*	*1 cm rain*	*2 cm rain*	*3 cm rain*	*4 cm rain*	*5 cm rain*
Probability	*0.50*	*0.25*	*0.15*	*0.05*	*0.03*	*0.02*

If it did not rain the previous day, the rain distribution is given by:

Event	*No rain*	*1 cm rain*	*2 cm rain*	*3 cm rain*
Probability	*0.75*	*0.15*	*0.06*	*0.04*

Simulate the city's weather for 10 days and determine by simulation the total days without rain as well as the total rainfall during the period. Use the following random numbers for simulation.

67, 63, 39, 55, 29, 78, 70, 06, 78, 76

Assume that for the first day of the simulation it had not rained the day before.

Solution. If it rained on the previous day, the rain distribution and the random number intervals are as below:

Previous day rain distribution

Event	*Probability*	*Cumulative probability*	*Random number intervals*
No rain	0.50	0.50	00–49
1 cm rain	0.25	0.75	50–74
2 cm rain	0.15	0.90	75–89
3 cm rain	0.05	0.95	90–94
4 cm rain	0.03	0.98	95–97
5 cm rain	0.02	1.00	98–99

If it did not rain on the previous day, the rain distribution and the random number intervals are as below:

Previous day no rain distribution

Event	*Probability*	*Cumulative probability*	*Random number intervals*
No rain	0.75	0.75	00–74
1 cm rain	0.15	0.90	75–89
2 cm rain	0.06	0.96	90–95
3 cm rain	0.04	1.00	96–99

Now using the given random numbers, we simulate the rainfall for 10 days as below:

Day	*Random number*	*Event*	*Cumulative rain*
1	67	No rain	—
2	63	No rain	—
3	39	No rain	—
4	55	No rain	—
5	29	No rain	—
6	78	1 cm rain	1 cm
7	70	1 cm rain	2 cm
8	06	No rain	2 cm
9	78	1 cm rain	3 cm
10	76	2 cm rain	5 cm

Total number of days without rainfall = 6 days

Total rainfall during the period = 5 cm.

Example 3. *Customers arrive at a milk booth for taking delivery of the milk packets. Assume that inter arrival and service times are constant and given by 1.8 and 4 times units respectively. Simulate the system for 14 time units. What is the average waiting time per customer? What is the percentage idle time of the facility? (Assume the system starts at $t = 0$).*

Solution. According to the data, arrival occurs after every 1.8 time units, *i.e.*, first customer arrives at $t = 0$, second customer arrives at $t = 1.8$, third customer arrives at $t = 1.8 + 1.8 = 3.6$ and so on. Service time is 4 units, *i.e.*, first customer is getting service upto $t = 4$, second customer starts getting service at $t = 4$ and service is completed at $t = 8$ and so on. During service customers are arriving at the interval of $t = 1.8$. The whole situation can be represented as below:

Time (t)	*Event*	*Customer number*	*Waiting time*
0.0	Arrival	1	
1.8	Arrival	2	
3.6	Arrival	3	
4.0	Departure	1	4 – 1.8 = 2.2 (customer 2)
5.4	Arrival	4	
7.2	Arrival	5	
8.0	Departure	2	8 – 3.6 = 4.4 (customer 3)
9.0	Arrival	6	
10.8	Arrival	7	
12.0	Departure	3	12 – 5.4 = 6.6 (customer 4)
12.6	Arrival	8	14 – 7.2 = 6.8 (customer 5)
14.0	End		14 – 9.0 = 5.0 (customer 6)
			14 – 10.8 = 3.2 (customer 7)
			14 – 12.6 = 1.4 (customer 8)

Average waiting time per customer $= \dfrac{2.2+4.4+6.6+6.8+5.0+3.2+1.4}{8} = \dfrac{29.6}{8} = 3.7$ units.

Percentage idle time of the facility = 0%.

Example 4. *A bakery keeps stock of a popular brand of cake. Previous experience shows the daily demand pattern for the item with associated probabilities, as given below:*

Daily demand	0	10	20	30	40	50
Probability	0.01	0.20	0.15	0.50	0.12	0.02

Use the following sequence of random numbers to simulate the demand for next 10 days.

25 39 65 76 12 05 73 89 19 49

Also, estimate the daily average demand for the cakes on the basis of simulated data.

Solution. We determine the random number intervals as below:

Daily demand	*Probability*	*Cumulative probability*	*Random number interval*
0	0.01	0.01	0–00
10	0.20	0.21	01–20
20	0.15	0.36	21–35
30	0.50	0.86	36–85
40	0.12	0.98	86–97
50	0.02	1.00	98–99

Now using the given random numbers, we simulate the demand for next 10 days as below:

Days	*Random number*	*Demand*
1	25	20
2	39	30
3	65	30
4	76	30
5	12	10
6	05	10
7	73	30
8	89	40
9	19	10
10	49	30
Total		**240**

Daily average demand $= \dfrac{240}{10} = 24$ units per day

Example 5. *The management of ABC company is considering the question of marketing a new product. The fixed cost required in the project is ₹4,000. Three factors are uncertain, viz., the selling price, variable cost and the annual sales volume. The product has a life of only one year. The management has the data on these three factors as under.*

Selling price (₹)	*Probability*	*Variable cost (₹)*	*Probability*	*Sales volume (Units)*	*Probability*
3	0.2	1	0.3	2000	0.3
4	0.5	2	0.6	3000	0.3
5	0.3	3	0.1	4000	0.4

Consider the following sequence of random numbers.

81 32 60 04 46 31 67 25 24 10 40 02 39

68 08 59 66 90 12 64 79 31 86 68 82 89

25 11 98 16

Using the sequence (first three random numbers for the first trial, etc.), simulate the average profit for the above project on the basis of ten trials.

Solution. We determine the random number intervals for each of the three variables as follows:

Selling price (₹)	*Probability*	*Cumulative probability*	*Random number intervals*
3	0.2	0.2	0–19
4	0.5	0.7	20–69
5	0.3	1.0	70–99

Variable cost (₹)	*Probability*	*Cumulative probability*	*Random number intervals*
1	0.3	0.3	0–29
2	0.6	0.9	30–89
3	0.1	1.0	90–99

Sales volume (Units)	*Probability*	*Cumulative probability*	*Random number intervals*
2000	0.3	0.3	0–29
3000	0.3	0.6	30–59
4000	0.4	1.0	60–99

Now, using the given random numbers, we simulate for each of the three variables for ten trials as follows:

S. No.	Random number	Selling price (₹)	Random number	Variable cost (₹)	Random number	Sales volume (Units)
1	81	5	32	2	60	4000
2	04	3	46	2	31	3000
3	67	4	25	1	24	2000
4	10	3	40	2	02	2000
5	39	4	68	2	08	2000
6	59	4	66	2	90	4000
7	12	3	64	2	79	4000
8	31	4	86	2	68	4000
9	82	5	89	2	25	2000
10	11	3	98	3	16	2000

Now, the profit can be obtained by using

Profit = (Selling price – variable cost) × Sales volume – Fixed cost

Simulated profit in ten trials will be as below:

S. No.	Profit (₹) = (Selling price – variable cost) × Sales volume – Fixed cost
1	(5 – 2) × 4000 – 4000 = 8000
2	(3 – 2) × 3000 – 4000 = –1000
3	(4 – 1) × 2000 – 4000 = 2000
4	(3 – 2) × 2000 – 4000 = –2000
5	(4 – 2) × 2000 – 4000 = 0
6	(4 – 2) × 4000 – 4000 = 4000
7	(3 – 2) × 4000 – 4000 = 0
8	(4 – 2) × 4000 – 4000 = 4000
9	(5 – 2) × 2000 – 4000 = 2000
10	(3 – 3) × 2000 – 4000 = –4000
Total	13000

Average profit per trial = ₹ $\frac{13000}{10}$ = ₹ 1300.

Example 6. *A company manufactures 20 items per day. The sale of these items depends upon demand which has the following distribution:*

Sales (Units)	*17*	*18*	*19*	*20*	*21*	*22*
Probability	*0.10*	*0.15*	*0.20*	*0.35*	*0.15*	*0.05*

The production cost is ₹ 40 per unit and the selling price is ₹ 50 per unit. Any unsold item is to be disposed of at a loss of ₹ 15 per unit. There is a penalty of ₹ 5 per unit if the demand is not met.

Using the following random numbers estimate total profit/loss for the company of the next 10 days:

10 99 65 99 95 01 79 11 16 20

It the company decides to produce 19 items per day, what is the advantage or disadvantage to the company?

Solution. We determine the random number intervals as below:

Sale (Units)	*Probability*	*Cumulative probability*	*Random number intervals*
17	0.10	0.10	0–09
18	0.15	0.25	10–24
19	0.20	0.45	25–44
20	0.35	0.80	45–79
21	0.15	0.95	80–94
22	0.05	1.00	95–99

The profit can be obtained by using

$$\text{Profit} = \begin{cases} ES \times 10 - (20 - ES) \times 15 & \text{if } ES \le 20 \\ 20 \times 10 - (ES - 20) \times 5 & \text{if } ES > 20 \end{cases}$$

ES → estimated sale

Note: For profit, in case of production of 19 items per day, use 19 in place of 20 in the above formula.

Now, using the given random numbers, we simulate the estimated sale and profit in each case as below:

Days	*Random Number*	*Estimated Sale*	*Profit (₹) (Production 20 items per day)*	*Profit (₹) (Production 19 items per day)*
1	10	18	18 × 10 – 2 × 15 = 150	18 × 10 – 1 × 15 = 165
2	99	22	20 × 10 – 2 × 5 = 190	19 × 10 – 3 × 5 = 175
3	65	20	20 × 10 = 200	19 × 10 – 1 × 5 = 185
4	99	22	20 × 10 – 2 × 5 = 190	19 × 10 – 3 × 5 = 175
5	95	22	20 × 10 – 2 × 5 = 190	19 × 10 – 3 × 5 = 175
6	01	17	17 × 10 – 3 × 15 = 125	17 × 10 – 2 × 15 = 140
7	79	20	20 × 10 = 200	19 × 10 – 1 × 5 = 185
8	11	18	18 × 10 – 2 × 15 = 150	18 × 10 – 1 × 15 = 165
9	16	18	18 × 10 – 2 × 15 = 150	18 × 10 – 1 × 15 = 165
10	20	18	18 × 10 – 2 × 15 = 150	18 × 10 – 1 × 15 = 165
Total			₹ 1695	₹ 1695

There is no advantage or disadvantage to the company if the production is reduced to 19 items per day.

Example 7. *Observations of past data show the following patterns in respect of inter arrival duration in a single channel queueing system.*

Interarrival time	
Minutes	*Probability*
2	0.15
4	0.23
6	0.35
8	0.17
10	0.10

Service time	
Minutes	*Probability*
1	0.10
3	0.22
5	0.35
7	0.23
9	0.10

Using the following random numbers, simulate the queue behaviour for a period of 60 minutes.

9371 1463 7214 1053 2164 8142 8707 9054 3866 1053

Also estimate the average queue length, average waiting time of customer before service, average service idle time, average service time.

Solution. We determine the random number intervals as below:

Arrival time			
Minutes	*Probability*	*Cumulative probability*	*Random number intervals*
2	0.15	0.15	0–14
4	0.23	0.38	15–37
6	0.35	0.73	38–72
8	0.17	0.90	73–89
10	0.10	1.00	90–99

Service time			
Minutes	*Probability*	*Cumulative probability*	*Random number intervals*
1	0.10	0.10	0–09
3	0.22	0.32	10–31
5	0.35	0.67	32–66
7	0.23	0.90	67–89
9	0.10	1.00	90–99

Now, using the given random numbers, we simulate the queue behaviour as follows: (Assume that service is available at 10 : 00 A.M.)

Random number	Time till arrivals (minutes)	Arrival time (A.M.)	Service starts (A.M.)	Random number	Service time (minutes)	Service ends (A.M.)	Waiting		
							Attendents (minutes)	Customers (minutes)	Number of customers
93	10	10 : 10	10 : 10	71	7	10 : 17	10	—	—
14	2	10 : 12	10 : 17	63	5	10 : 22	—	5	1
72	6	10 : 18	10 : 22	14	3	10 : 25	—	4	1
10	2	10 : 20	10 : 25	53	5	10 : 30	—	5	1
21	4	10 : 24	10 : 30	64	5	10 : 35	—	6	1
81	8	10 : 32	10 : 35	42	5	10 : 40	—	3	1
87	8	10 : 40	10 : 40	07	1	10 : 41	—	—	—
90	10	10 : 50	10 : 50	54	5	10 : 55	9	—	—
38	6	10 : 56	10 : 56	66	5	11 : 01	1	—	—
Total	56				41		20	23	5

Average queue length $= \frac{5}{9} = 0.56$

Average waiting of customer before service $= \frac{23}{9} = 2.56$ minutes

Average service idle time $= \frac{20}{9} = 2.22$ minutes

Average service time $= \frac{41}{9} = 4.56$ minutes.

Example 8. *(i) A businessman is considering taking over a certain new business. Based on past information and his own knowledge of the business, he works out the probability distributions of the daily costs and sales revenues, as given here:*

Cost (₹)	*Probability*	*Sales (₹)*	*Probability*
8500	0.10	9500	0.10
9000	0.10	10000	0.10
9500	0.40	10500	0.20
10000	0.20	11000	0.40
10500	0.20	11500	0.15
		12000	0.05

Use the following sequence of random numbers to be used for estimating costs and revenues. Obtain the probability distribution of the daily net revenue.

Sequence 1 : 81, 83, 27, 81, 35, 91, 72, 90, 62, 28, 26, 25, 91, 62, 82, 02, 12, 38, 10, 18.

Sequence 2 : 38, 71, 37, 28, 70, 82, 18, 71, 91, 58, 48, 38, 71, 93, 02, 91, 73, 17, 09, 04.

(ii) Repeat the analysis in (i) by using the following random numbers:

Sequence 1 : 21, 64, 47, 17, 46, 42, 45, 67, 88, 27, 79, 41, 30, 93, 22, 37, 58, 04, 29, 09.

Sequence 2 : 24, 58, 99, 85, 52, 30, 42, 12, 67, 31, 42, 81, 63, 75, 65, 27, 42, 41, 98, 16.

Solution. We determine the random number intervals as below:

Cost	*Probability*	*Cumulative probability*	*Random number intervals*	*Revenue*	*Probability*	*Cumulative probability*	*Random number intervals*
8500	0.10	0.10	0–09	9500	0.10	0.10	0–09
9000	0.10	0.20	10–19	10000	0.10	0.20	10–19
9500	0.40	0.60	20–59	10500	0.20	0.40	20–39
10000	0.20	0.80	60–79	11000	0.40	0.80	40–79
10500	0.20	1.00	80–99	11500	0.15	0.95	80–94
				12000	0.05	1.00	95–99

(*i*) Now using the sequence 1 and sequence 2 of random numbers, we simulate the cost and revenue as below:

Random number	*Cost (₹)*	*Random number*	*Revenue (₹)*	*Net revenue*
81	10500	38	10500	0
83	10500	71	11000	500
27	9500	37	10500	1000
81	10500	28	10500	0
35	9500	70	11000	1500
91	10500	82	11500	1000
72	10000	18	10000	0
90	10500	71	11000	500
62	10000	91	11500	1500
28	9500	58	11000	1500
26	9500	48	11000	1500
25	9500	38	10500	1000
91	10500	71	11000	500
62	10000	93	11500	1500
82	10500	02	9500	-1000
02	8500	91	11500	3000
12	9000	73	11000	2000
38	9500	17	10000	500
10	9000	09	9500	500
18	9000	04	9500	500

(*ii*) Now, using the sequence 1 and sequence 2 of random numbers, we simulate the cost and revenue as below:

Random number	*Cost (₹)*	*Random number*	*Revenue (₹)*	*Net revenue*
21	9500	24	10500	1000
64	10000	58	11000	1000
47	9500	99	12000	2500
17	9000	85	11500	2500
46	9500	52	11000	1500
42	9500	30	10500	1000
45	9500	42	11000	1500
67	10000	12	10000	0
88	10500	67	11000	500
27	9500	31	10500	1000
79	10000	42	11000	1000
41	9500	81	11500	2000
30	9500	63	11000	1500
93	10500	75	11000	500
22	9500	65	11000	1500
37	9500	27	10500	1000
58	9500	42	11000	1500
04	8500	41	11000	2500
29	9500	98	12000	2500
09	8500	16	10000	1500

Now, the probability distribution of the daily net revenue can be obtained as below:

Net revenue	*Part (i)*		*Part (ii)*	
	Frequency	*Probability*	*Frequency*	*Probability*
–1000	1	0.05	0	0.00
0	3	0.15	1	0.05
500	6	0.30	2	0.10
1000	3	0.15	6	0.30
1500	5	0.25	6	0.30
2000	1	0.05	1	0.05
2500	0	0.00	4	0.20
3000	1	0.05	0	0.00

Example 9. *Consider an inventory control problem in which demand during lead time as well as lead time distribution is as below:*

Demand	*Probability*	*Lead time (Weeks)*	*Probability*
0	0.10	2	0.20
1	0.45	3	0.65
2	0.30	4	0.15
3	0.15		

The reorder point is 6 units and reorder quantity is 12 units. If the ordering cost is ₹200 per order, inventory carrying cost is ₹5 per unit per week and the shortage cost is ₹80 per unit per week. Using the following random numbers for the demand

49, 67, 06, 30, 95, 03, 10, 70, 80, 66, 69, 78, 85, 56, 84

and the following random numbers for the lead time

83, 78, 14, 02.

Find the total inventory cost for 15 weeks. Assume an initial inventory of 10 units.

Solution. We determine the random number intervals for demand and lead time as below:

Demand	*Probability*	*Cumulative probability*	*Random number intervals*
0	0.10	0.10	0–09
1	0.45	0.55	10–54
2	0.30	0.85	55–84
3	0.15	1.00	85–99

Lead time (Weeks)	*Probability*	*Cumulative probability*	*Random number intervals*
2	0.20	0.20	0–19
3	0.65	0.85	20–84
4	0.15	1.00	85–99

Now, assume that all orders all placed at the beginning of the week and deliveries against these orders are also received at the beginning of the week.

Now, using the sequence of random numbers, we simulate the demand and lead time for 15 weeks as follows:

Week number	Stock on the begining of week number	Demand		Quantity received	Stock at the end of week number	Shortage	Lead time	
		Random number	Quantity demanded				Random number	Period (weeks)
1	10	49	1	–	9	–	–	–
2	9	67	2	–	7	–	–	–
3	7	06	0	–	7	–	–	–
4	7	30	1	–	6	–	–	–
5	6	95	3	–	3	–	83	3
6	3	03	0	–	3	–	–	–
7	3	10	1	–	2	–	–	–
8	2	70	2	12	12	–	–	–
9	12	80	2	–	10	–	–	–
10	10	66	2	–	'8	–	–	–
11	8	69	2	–	6	–	–	–
12	6	78	2	–	4	–	78	3
13	4	85	2	–	1	–	–	–
14	1	56	2	–	0	1	–	–
15	0	84	2	–	10	–	–	–
Total	**88**				**88**	**1**		

$$\text{Total average inventory in 15 weeks} = \frac{88+88}{2} = 88 \text{ units.}$$

Inventory carring cost = ₹ 5 × 88 = ₹ 440

Ordering cost = ₹ 200 × 2 = ₹ 400

Shortage cost = ₹ 80 × 1 = ₹ 80

Total inventory cost in 15 weeks = ₹ (440 + 400 + 80)

= ₹ 920

EXERCISES

1. What is simulation? Explain why is it used?
2. What is Monte Carlo simulation? Why is it called so?
3. Explain the steps involved in Monte-Carlo simulation.
4. Explain the advantages and disadvantages of simulation technique.
5. What is simulation? Explain the theory of Monte-Carlo simulation. Write the names and applications of various simulation languages. *(I.U., 2007–08; UPTU, 2005–06)*

6. What do you understand by simulation? Explain different types of simulation models, in brief, with application. *(UPTU, 2004–05)*

7. A production line turns out about 50 cars per day with the following probability distribution:

Production per day :	45	47	49	51	53	55	46	48	50	52	54
Probability :	0.03	0.07	0.15	0.15	0.07	0.03	0.05	0.10	0.20	0.10	0.05

Finished cars are transported by train at the end of the day. If the train capacity is only 51, what will be the average number of cars waiting to be shipped and what will be the average number of empty spaces on the train? Simulate a 8 day operation with random number of 37, 35, 63, 25, 50, 71, 95, 16.

[**Ans.** No. of cars waiting to be shipped in a 8 day period = 3
Empty spaces in a 8 day period = 7]

8. A dentist schedules all her patients for 30 minutes appointments. Some of the patients take more or less than 30 minutes depending on the type of dental work to be done. The following summary shows the various categories of the work, their probabilities and the time needed to complete the work.

Category	*Time required (minutes)*	*Probability*
Filling	45	0.40
Crown	60	0.15
Cleaning	15	0.15
Extraction	45	0.10
Checkup	15	0.20

Simulate the dentist's clinic for four hours and determine the average waiting time for the patients as well as idleness of the doctor. Assume that all the patients show up at the clinic at exactly their scheduled arrival times, starting at 10 A.M. use the following random numbers for handling the above problem:

40, 82, 11, 34, 25, 66, 17 and 79.

[**Ans.** 35.625 minutes; Nil]

9. A bakery keeps stock of a popular brand of cake. Previous experience shows the daily demand pattern for the item with associated probabilities, as given below:

Daily demand :	0	15	25	35	45	50
Probability :	0.01	0.15	0.20	0.50	0.12	0.02

Use the following sequence of random numbers to simulate the demand for next 10 days:
48, 78, 09, 51, 56, 77, 15, 14, 68, 09.

Also, estimate the daily average demand for the cakes on the basis of simulated data.

[**Ans.** 27 cakes]

10. Popa Ltd. trade in a perishable commodity. Each day Popa Ltd. receives supplies of the goods from a wholesaler but the quantity supplied is a random variable, as is the subsequent retail customer demand for the commodity. Both supply and demand

are expressed in batches of 50 units and over the past working year (300 days), Popa Ltd. has kept records of supplies and demands. The results are as follows:

Wholesaler supplies	*No. of days occurring*	*Customer's demand*	*No. of days occurring*
50	60	50	60
100	90	100	60
150	90	150	150
200	60	200	30

Popa Ltd. buys the commodity at ₹ 6 per unit and sells at ₹ 10 per unit. At present unsold units at the end of the day are worthless and there are no storage facilities. Popa Ltd. estimates that each unit of unsatisfied demand on any day costs them ₹ 2. Using the following random numbers:

8, 4, 8, 0, 3, 3, 4, 7, 9, 6, 1 and 5.

(*a*) simulate six days trading and estimate the annual profit.

(*b*) repeat the exercise to estimate the value of storage facilities.

[**Ans.** (*a*) ₹ 80,000 (*b*) ₹ 600]

11. Consider an inventory control problem in which demand during lead time as well as lead time distribution are given as follows:

Demand	*Probability*	*Lead time (Week)*	*Probability*
0	0.10	2	0.20
1	0.45	3	0.65
2	0.30	4	0.15
3	0.15		

The reorder point is 6 units and reorder quantity is 12 units. If the ordering cost is ₹ 100 per order, inventory carrying cost is ₹ 4 per unit per week and the shortage cost is ₹ 60 per unit per week. Find the total inventory cost for 15 weeks. Assume an initial inventory of 10 units.

Assume the following random numbers for the demand.

49, 67, 06, 30, 95, 01, 10, 70, 80, 66, 69, 76, 85, 56, 84.

Also assume the following random numbers for the lead time:

84, 79, 15, 03.

[**Ans.** ₹ 612]

12. A book store wishes to carry a particular book in stock. Demand is probabilistic and replenishment of stocks takes 2 days (*i.e.*, if an order is placed on day 1, it will be delivered at the end of day 3). The probabilities of demand are given below:

Daily demand	0	1	2	3	4
Probability	0.05	0.10	0.30	0.45	0.10

Each time an order is placed, the incurs an ordering cost of ₹ 10 per order. The store also incurs a carrying cost of ₹ 0.05 per book per day. The inventory carrying cost is calculated on the basis of stock at the end of each day.

The manager of the book store wishes to compare two options for his inventory decision.

A. Order 5 books when the inventory at the beginning of the day plus orders outstanding is less than 8 books.

B. Order 8 books when the inventory at the begining of the day plus orders outstanding is less than 8 books.

Currently (beginning of 1st day) the store has a stock of 8 books plus 6 books ordered two days ago and expected to arrive next day.

Using Monte Carlo simulation for 10 cycles, recommend with option the manager should choose.

Use the following random numbers:

89, 34, 78, 63, 61, 81, 39, 16, 13, 73

[**Ans.** Option B (∵ Total cost for option B, ₹ 52.50 < Total cost for option A, ₹ 59.50)]

13. A bookshop has studied the weekly receipts and payments over the past 200 days and has developed the following set of information:

Daily receipts (₹)	*Probability*	*Weekly payments* (₹)	*Probability*
30,000	0.20	40,000	0.30
50,000	0.30	60,000	0.40
70,000	0.40	80,000	0.20
120,000	0.10	100,000	0.10

Using the following set of random numbers, simulate the weekly pattern of receipts and payments for the 15 days of the next fortnight, assuming further that the begining bank balance is ₹ 80,000. What is expected balance at the end of the 15 days period? What is the highest fortnightly balance during the fortnight? What is the average balance for the fortnight? Random number:

For receipts : 02, 93, 42, 58, 18, 49, 31, 45, 65, 71, 27, 20, 76, 07, 84

For payments : 64, 98, 32, 34, 07, 86, 48, 27, 83, 16, 74, 92, 04, 41, 81.

[**Ans.** ₹ 10,000; ₹ 70,000; ₹ 3307.69]

14. A plant has a large number of similar machines. The machine breakdowns or failures are random and independent. The shift incharge of the plant collected the data about the various machines breakdown times and the repair time required on hourly basis, and the record for the past 100 observations as follows:

Time between recorded machine breakdowns (hours)	*Probability*	*Repair time required (hours)*	*Probability*
0.5	0.05	1	0.28
1.0	0.06	2	0.52
1.5	0.16	3	0.20
2.0	0.33		
2.5	0.21		
3.0	0.19		

For each hour that one machine is down due to being or waiting to be repaired, the plant loses ₹ 70 by way of lost production. A repairman is paid at ₹ 20 per hour.

Use the following random numbers, to

(*i*) Simulate this maintenance system for 15 breakdowns.

(*ii*) How many repairman should the plant hire for repair work?

Random numbers:

For breakdowns : 61 85 16 46 88 08 82 56 22 49 44 33 77 87 54

For repair time : 87 39 28 97 69 87 52 52 15 85 41 82 98 99 23

[**Ans.** One additional repairman]

15. The director of finance for a firm co-operative is concerned about the yields per acre he can expect from this year's corn crop. The probability distribution of the yields for the current weather conditions is given below:

Yield in kg./acre	:	120	140	160	180
Probability	:	0.18	0.26	0.44	0.12

He should like to see a simulation of the yields he might expect over the next 10 years for weather conditions similar to those he is now experiencing.

(*i*) Simulate the average yield he might expect per acre using the following random numbers:

20 72 34 54 30 22 48 74 76 02

He is also interested in the effect of market-price fluctuations on the co-operative's farm revenue. He makes the estimate of per-kg prices for corn:

Price/kg (in ₹)	:	2.00	2.10	2.20	2.30	2.40	2.50
Probability	:	0.05	0.15	0.30	0.25	0.15	0.10

(*ii*) Simulate the price he might expect to observe over the next 10 years using the following random numbers:

82 95 18 96 20 84 56 11 52 03.

(*iii*) Assuming that prices are independent of yields, combine these two into the revenue per acre and also find out the average revenue per acre he might expect every year.

[**Ans.** Average yield = 148 kg./acre
Average revenue per acre = ₹ 338.60]

16. The output of a production line is checked by an inspector for one or more of three different types of defects, called defects *A*, *B* and *C*. If defects *A* occurs, the item is scrapped. If defect *B* or *C* occurs, the item must be reworked. The time required to rework a *B* defect is 15 minutes and the time required to rework a *C* defect is 30 minutes. The probabilities of an *A*, *B* and *C* defects are 0.15, 0.20, 0.10 respectively. For ten itmes coming off the assembly line, determine the number of times without any defects, the number scrapped and the total minutes rework time. Use the following random numbers:

Random numbers:

For defect A :	48	55	91	40	93	01	83	63	47	52
For defect B :	47	36	57	04	79	55	10	13	57	09
For defect C :	82	95	18	96	20	84	56	11	52	03

[**Ans.** Five items out of ten had no defects; one item was scrapped; 90 minutes of total rework time was required by three items.]

17. An investment corporation wants to study the investment projects based on three factors: market demand in units, price per unit minus cost per unit and the investment required. These factors are felt to the independent of each other. In analysing a new consumer product, the corporation estimates the following probability distributions:

Annual demand		*(Price-cost) Per unit*		*Investment required*	
Units	*Probability*	₹	*Probability*	₹	*Probability*
20,000	0.05	3.00	0.10	17,50,000	0.25
25,000	0.10	5.00	0.20	20,00,000	0.50
30,000	0.20	7.00	0.40	25,00,000	0.25
35,000	0.30	9.00	0.20		
40,000	0.20	10.00	0.10		
45,000	0.10				
50,000	0.05				

Using simulation process, repeat the trial 10 times, compute the return on investment for each trial taking these three factors into account approximately. What is the most likely return?

Use the following random numbers:

For demand :	28	57	60	17	64	20	27	58	61	30
For profit/unit :	19	07	90	02	57	28	29	83	58	41
For investment :	18	67	16	71	43	68	47	24	19	97

[**Ans.** Highest likely return is 20% corresponding to the annual demand of 35,000 units resulting in a profit of ₹ 10 per unit and the required investment will be 1,750,000.]

❑❑❑

CHAPTER 11

Queueing Models

11.1 INTRODUCTION

Queueing theory is the study of queues (sometimes are called waiting lines). Most people are familiar with the concept of queues, they exist all around us in daily lives. Queueing theory can be used to describe these real world queues. Queueing theory is the branch of operations research which explores the relationships between demand on a service system and the delays suffered by the users of that system. Queue occurs whenever arriving customers wait in a line to get service at one or more service point. It is formed when the number of customers arriving is greater than the number of customers being served during a period of time.

Its applications in different places are as follows:

1. Traffic flow
2. Scheduling
3. Airports
4. Railway reservation counters
5. Supermarkets
6. Manufacturing process
7. Hair dressers
8. Restaurants
9. Hospital appointment bookings
10. Banks
11. Petrol pumps, etc.

Since queueing theory is applied in different fields, also the terms job and task are often used instead customer. The service counter is often named processor or machine.

11.2 QUEUEING SYSTEM

The basic queueing system can be described as a system in which customers arrive at service station for service, wait for their turn in the queue if the server is busy in the service of the other customer and gets service when server is free. Finally the customer leave the system after the service.

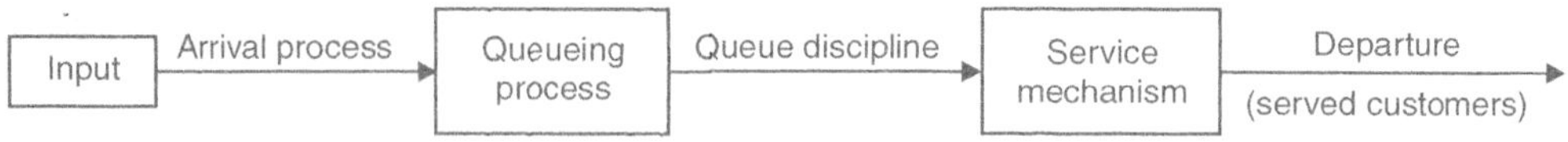

11.3 ELEMENTS OF THE QUEUEING SYSTEM

The various elements of the queueing system are as below:

1. **The Input (or Arrival Pattern):** The input describes the arrival pattern of customers for service. The arrival of customers may be either at a constant rate or at random. Generally customers arrive in a random fashion, therefore their arrival pattern is described in terms of probabilities. We assume that they arrive according to a Poisson process.
2. **Queue (or Waiting Line):** A flow of customers towards the service station form a queue. A queue is characterized by the maximum permissible number of customers that it contains.
3. **The Service Discipline (or Service Pattern):** The service discipline refers to the manner in which the customers in the queue are chosen for service. Some common service disciplines are as below:

   FIFO (First in First Out): According to FIFO, the customers are served in the order of their arrival. In other words, a customer that finds the server busy goes to the end of the queue.

   LIFO (Last in First Out): According to LIFO, the customer arriving last gets the service first. In other words, a customer that finds the server busy proceeds immediately to the head of the queue, and will be served next, given that no further customers arrive.

   SIRO (Service in Random Order): According to SIRO, the customers in the queue are served in random order.

   SIP (Service in Priority): According to SIP, certain customers are given priority over other customers. This scheme can use preemption or not.

   SIRR (Service in Round Robin): According to SIRR, every customer gets a time slice. If the service is not completed, customer will reenter the queue.
4. **Service Mechanism:** The uncertainties involved in the service mechanism are the number of servers, the number of customers getting served at anytime, and the duration and mode of service. Networks of queues consist of more than one servers arranged in series and/or parallel. Random variables are used to represent service times, and the number of servers, when appropriate.
5. **Customer's Behaviours:** The customers generally behave in the following ways:

   (*a*) **Balking:** Customers deciding not to join the queue if it is too long.

   (*b*) **Reneging:** Customers leave the queue if they have waited too long for service.

(c) **Collusion:** Some customers may collaborate and only one of them may join the queue. However, when their turn comes for service, the customers who were in collusion demand service.

(d) **Jockeying:** Customers switch between queues, if they think they will get served faster by so doing.

11.4 DISTRIBUTION OF ARRIVALS (*Pure Brith Model*)

The model in which only arrivals are counted and no departure takes place are called pure birth models. The number of arrivals in a time interval (0, t) is a random variable which follows a Poission distribution with parameter $\lambda(t)$ is,

$$P_n(t) = e^{-\lambda t}\frac{(\lambda t)^n}{n!}\ ;\ n \geq 0.$$

11.5 DISTRIBUTION OF INTER-ARRIVAL TIMES (*Exponential Process*)

Inter-arrival times are defined as the time intervals between two successive arrivals. If the arrival process follows the poisson distribution, an associated random variable defined as the time between successive arrivals follows the exponential distribution $f(t) = \lambda e^{-\lambda t}$ and vice versa.

Let the random variable T be the time between successive arrivals, then

$$P(T > t) = P\text{ (no arrival in time } t)$$
$$= P_0(t) = e^{-\lambda t}$$

The cumulative distribution function of T is

$$F(t) = P(T \leq t) = 1 - P(T > t) = 1 - e^{-\lambda t};\ 0 \leq t \leq \infty.$$

The density function $f(t)$ for inter-arrival times is

$$f(t) = \frac{d}{dt}F(t) = \begin{cases} \lambda e^{-\lambda t}; & 0 \leq t \leq \infty \\ 0\ ; & t < 0. \end{cases}$$

The expected time of inter-arrival is given by

$$E(t) = \int_0^{\infty} t\,f(t)dt = \int_0^{t} \lambda\,te^{-\lambda t}dt = \frac{1}{\lambda}.$$

Thus, T has the exponential distribution with mean $\frac{1}{\lambda}$.

11.6 DISTRIBUTION OF SERVICE TIMES

The time t to complete the service on a customer follows an exponential distribution is given by

$$g(t) = \begin{cases} \mu e^{-\mu t}; & 0 \leq t \leq \infty \\ 0\ ; & t < 0 \end{cases}$$

where μ is the mean service rate for a particular service station.

11.7 KENDAL'S NOTATION FOR REPRESENTING QUEUEING MODELS

The queueing models may be completely specified in the following symbolic form,

$$(a/b/c) : (d/e)$$

where

a = type of distribution of inter-arrival time

b = type of distribution of inter-service time

c = number of service stations

d = capacity of the system (maximum number of customers allowed in the system)

e = queue discipline.

11.8 TERMINOLOGY AND NOTATIONS FOR QUEUEING MODELS

The following notations are used in different queueing models:

n = number of customers in the system, both waiting and service

m = number of customers in the queue

λ = mean arrival rate (units/unit time)

μ = mean service rate (units/unit time)

ρ = $\frac{\lambda}{\mu}$ = traffic intensity

S = number of service stations

N = Capacity of the system

$P_n(t)$ = Probability of n customers in the system at any time t, both waiting and in service.

P_n = Probability (time independent) of n customers in the system, both waiting and in service.

$E(n)$ = expected number of customers in the system, both waiting and in service.

$E(m)$ = expected number of customers in the queue, waiting for service.

$E(T)$ = expected time spent by a customer in the system, both waiting and in service.

$E(w)$ = expected waiting time in the queue by a customer.

11.9 DEFINITION OF TRANSIENT AND STEADY STATE

A system is said to be in transient state when its operating characteristics (input, output etc.) are dependent on time. This state occurs at the beginning of the operation of the system.

A system is said to be in steady state when its operating characteristics become independent of time. This state occurs in the long run of the system.

If $P_n(t)$ denotes the probability that there are n customers in the system at any time t, then in the steady state case,

$$\lim_{t \to \infty} = P_n \text{ (independent of time } t)$$

11.10 MODEL 1

(M/M/1) : (∞/FIFO): This model deals with a queueing system with Poisson arrival, exponential service, single server, infinite capacity and the service on the basis 'first in first out'.

Let $P_n(t)$ be the probability that there are n customers in the system at time t.

Then the probability of n customers in the system at time $(t + \Delta t)$ can be expressed as

$$\begin{aligned} P_n(t + \Delta t) &= P_n(t).P(\text{no arrival in } \Delta t).P(\text{no service completed in } \Delta t) \\ &\quad + P_n(t).P(\text{one arrival in } \Delta t).P(\text{one service completed in } \Delta t) \\ &\quad + P_{n+1}(t).P(\text{no arrvial in } \Delta t).P(\text{one service completed in } \Delta t) \\ &\quad + P_{n-1}(t).P(\text{one arrival in } \Delta t).P(\text{no service completed in } \Delta t) \\ &= P_n(t)\,[1 - \lambda\Delta t]\,[1 - \mu\Delta t] + P_n(t)\,[\lambda\Delta t]\,[\mu\Delta t] \\ &\quad + P_{n+1}(t)\,[1 - \lambda\Delta t]\,[\mu\Delta t] + P_{n-1}(t)\,[\lambda\Delta t]\,[1 - \mu\Delta t] \end{aligned}$$

On neglecting the terms of $(\Delta t)^2$, we have

$$P_n(t + \Delta t) = P_n(t) - (\lambda + \mu)\,P_n(t)\Delta t + \mu P_{n+1}(t)\Delta t + \lambda P_{n-1}(t)\Delta t$$

$$\frac{P_n(t+\Delta t) - P_n(t)}{\Delta t} = -(\lambda + \mu)\,P_n(t) + \mu P_{n+1}(t) + \lambda P_{n-1}(t).$$

Now, taking the limit as $\Delta t \to 0$, we have

$$\lim_{\Delta t \to 0} \frac{P_n(t+\Delta t) - P_n(t)}{\Delta t} = -(\lambda + \mu)\,P_n(t) + \mu P_{n+1}(t) + \lambda P_{n-1}(t)$$

$$\frac{d}{dt} P_n(t) = -(\lambda + \mu)\,P_n(t) + \mu P_{n+1}(t) + \lambda P_{n-1}(t);\ n \ge 1. \quad \text{...(1)}$$

For $n = 0$, the probability of zero customers in the system at time $(t + \Delta t)$ can be expressed as,

$$\begin{aligned} P_0(t + \Delta t) &= P_0(t).P[\text{no arrival in } \Delta t] + P_1(t).P(\text{no arrival in } \Delta t).P(\text{one service completed in } \Delta t) \\ &= P_0(t)[1 - \lambda\Delta t] + P_1(t)\,[1 - \lambda\Delta t]\,[\mu\Delta t] \end{aligned}$$

On neglecting the terms of $(\Delta t)^2$, we have

$$P_0(t + \Delta t) = P_0(t)\,[1 - \lambda\Delta t] + P_1(t).\mu\Delta t$$

$$\frac{P_0(t+\Delta t) - P_0(t)}{\Delta t} = -\lambda P_0(t) + \mu P_1(t)$$

Now, taking the limit as $\Delta t \to 0$, we have

$$\lim_{\Delta t \to 0} \frac{P_0(t+\Delta t) - P_0(t)}{\Delta t} = -\lambda P_0(t) + \mu P_1(t)$$

$$\frac{d}{dt} P_0(t) \quad -\lambda P_0(t) + \mu P_1(t)\ ;\ n = 0. \quad \text{...(2)}$$

Now when the system reaches in steady state,

$$\lim_{t \to \infty} P_n(t) = P_n \text{ and } \frac{d}{dt} P_n(t) = 0 \text{ as } t \to \infty.$$

Under steady state of the system, the equations (1) and (2) reduces to

$$0 = -(\lambda + \mu)P_n + \mu P_{n+1} + \lambda P_{n-1}; \quad n \geq 1 \qquad ...(3)$$

$$0 = -\lambda P_0 + \mu P_1; \quad n = 0. \qquad ...(4)$$

Now, from (4), we have

$$P_1 = \left(\frac{\lambda}{\mu}\right) P_0$$

On putting $n = 1, 2, ...$ in the above equation (3), we have

$$P_2 = \frac{\lambda+\mu}{\mu} P_1 - \frac{\lambda}{\mu} P_0 = \left(\frac{\lambda}{\mu}\right)^2 P_0$$

$$P_3 = \left(\frac{\lambda}{\mu}\right)^3 P_0$$

$$\vdots$$

$$P_n = \left(\frac{\lambda}{\mu}\right)^n P_0; \quad n \geq 0$$

$$= \rho^n P_0.$$

To obtain the value of P_0, we use the boundary condition

$$\sum_{n=0}^{\infty} P_n = 1$$

$$\sum_{n=0}^{\infty} \rho^n P_0 = 1 \text{ or } P_0 [1 + \rho + \rho^2 + ...] = 1$$

$$P_0 \left[\frac{1}{1-\rho}\right] = 1 \text{ or } P_0 = (1 - \rho)$$

$$\therefore \quad P_n = \rho^n (1 - \rho).$$

Characteristics of (M/M/1) : (∞/FIFO)

1. Expected number of customers in the system,

$$E(n) = \sum_{n=0}^{\infty} nP_n = \sum_{n=0}^{\infty} n(1-\rho)\rho^n = (1-\rho)\sum_{n=0}^{\infty} n\rho^n$$

$$= (1 - \rho)[0 + 1.\rho + 2.\rho^2 + 3\rho^3 + ...]$$

$$= (1 - \rho)\rho[1 + 2\rho + 3\rho^2 + ...] = (1 - \rho)\rho(1 - \rho)^{-2}$$

$$= \frac{\rho}{(1-\rho)} = \frac{\lambda}{(\mu-\lambda)}.$$

2. Expected number of customers in the queue,

$$E(m) = E(n) - \rho$$

$$= \frac{\rho}{1-\rho} - \rho = \frac{\rho^2}{(1-\rho)} = \frac{\lambda^2}{\mu(\mu-\lambda)}.$$

3. Expected time a customer spends in the system,

$$E(T) = \frac{\text{Expected number of customers in the system}}{\text{Arrival rate}}$$

$$= \frac{E(n)}{\lambda} = \frac{\lambda/(\mu-\lambda)}{\lambda} = \frac{1}{\mu-\lambda}$$

4. Expected time a customer spends in the queue,

$$E(w) = \text{Expected time in the system–time in service}$$

$$= E(T)-\frac{1}{\mu} = \frac{1}{\mu-\lambda}-\frac{1}{\mu} = \frac{\lambda}{\mu(\mu-\lambda)}.$$

5. Expected length of a non-empty queue

$$E(m/m > 0) = \frac{\text{Expected length of queue}}{\text{Probability of non-empty queue}}$$

$$= \frac{E(m)}{P(m>0)} = \frac{E(m)}{P(n>1)} \qquad (\because\ m = n - 1)$$

$$= \frac{\rho^2/(1-\rho)}{\sum_{n=0}^{\infty} P_n - P_0 - P_1} = \frac{\rho^2/(1-\rho)}{1-(1-\rho)-\rho(1-\rho)}$$

$$= \frac{1}{(1-\rho)} = \frac{\mu}{(\mu-\lambda)}.$$

6. Probability of queue size being greater than or equal to n,

$$P(\geq n) = \sum_{k=n}^{\infty} P_k = \sum_{k=n}^{\infty}(1-\rho)\rho^k = (1-\rho)\rho^n \sum_{n=0}^{\infty} \rho^{k-n}$$

$$= (1-\rho)\,\rho^n[1+\rho+\rho^2+\ldots]$$

$$= (1-\rho)\,\rho^n.\frac{1}{1-\rho} = \rho^n = \left(\frac{\lambda}{\mu}\right)^n.$$

7. Idle rate, *i.e.*, the server is idle (no customer in the system),

$$P_0 = 1-\rho = 1-\left(\frac{\lambda}{\mu}\right).$$

Expected idle time (for service facility) $= \left(1-\frac{\lambda}{\mu}\right) \times$ Total service time.

8. Probability that a customer has to wait w units of time is $= e^{-(\mu-\lambda)w}$

Example 1. *A telephone exchange receives one call for every 4 minutes and connects one call for every 3 minutes. If the rate of arrivals follows Poisson distribution and service time follows exponential distribution, find:*

(a) *Expected number of customers in the system.*

(b) *Expected number of customers in the queue.*

(c) *Expected time spend in the system.*

(d) *Expected waiting time for a call.*

Solution. Here,

$$\lambda = \text{arrival rate} = \frac{1}{4} \text{ per minute}$$

$$\mu = \text{service rate} = \frac{1}{3} \text{ per minute.}$$

(a) Expected number of customers in the system,

$$E(n) = \frac{\lambda}{\mu-\lambda} = \frac{1/4}{1/3-1/4} = \text{calls.}$$

(b) Expected number of customers in the queue,

$$E(m) = \frac{\lambda^2}{\mu(\mu-\lambda)} = \frac{\left(\frac{1}{4}\right)^2}{\frac{1}{3}\left(\frac{1}{3}-\frac{1}{4}\right)} = \frac{9}{4} \text{ calls}$$

(c) Expected time spend in the system,

$$E(T) = \frac{1}{\mu-\lambda} = \frac{1}{\frac{1}{3}-\frac{1}{4}} = 12 \text{ minutes.}$$

(d) Expected waiting time for a call,

$$E(w) = \frac{\lambda}{\mu(\mu-\lambda)} = \frac{\frac{1}{4}}{\frac{1}{3}\left(\frac{1}{3}-\frac{1}{4}\right)} = 9 \text{ minutes.}$$

Ans.

Example 2. *A supermarket has a single cashier. During the peak hours, customers arrive at a rate of 20 customers per hour. The average number of customers that can be processed by the cashier is 24 per hour.*

Calculate:

(a) *The probability that the cashier is idle.*

(b) *The average number of customers in the queuing system.*

(c) *The average time a customer spends in the system.*

(d) *The average number of customers in the queue.*

(e) *The average time a customer spends in the queue waiting for service.*

Solution. Here

$$\lambda = 20 \text{ customers per hour}$$

$$\mu = 24 \text{ customers per hour.}$$

(a) Probability that the cashier is idle,

$$P_0 = 1-\frac{\lambda}{\mu} = 1-\frac{20}{24} = \frac{1}{6}$$

(*b*) Average number of customers in the system,

$$E(n) = \frac{\lambda}{\mu-\lambda} = \frac{20}{24-20} = 5.$$

(*c*) Average time a customer spends in the system,

$$E(T) = \frac{1}{\mu-\lambda} = \frac{1}{24-20} = \frac{1}{4} \text{ hour or 15 minutes.}$$

(*d*) Average number of customers in the queue,

$$E(m) = \frac{\lambda^2}{\mu(\mu-\lambda)} = \frac{(20)^2}{24(24-20)} = \frac{25}{6} \text{ or } 4.167.$$

(*e*) Average time a customer spends in the queue,

$$E(w) = \frac{\lambda}{\mu(\mu-\lambda)} = \frac{20}{24(24-20)} = \frac{5}{24} \text{ hour or 12.5 minutes.}$$ **Ans.**

Example 3. *At a one man barbershop, it takes on the average 30 minutes for a haircut, and customers arrive at an average rate of one per every 45 minutes. If the Poisson exponential model is assumed, at any point in time on the average,*

(*a*) *How many customers will be there in the shop?*

(*b*) *What time will a customer spend in the shop?*

(*c*) *Of this time, what part be spent waiting to be served?*

(*d*) *What portion of the day will barber be idle?*

(*e*) *What is the porbability that a customer has to wait for 30 minutes?*

Solution. Here, $\lambda = \frac{60}{45} = \frac{4}{3}$ per hour

$$\mu = \frac{60}{30} = 2 \text{ per hour.}$$

(*a*) Average number of customers in the shop,

$$E(n) = \frac{\lambda}{\mu-\lambda} = \frac{\frac{4}{3}}{2-\frac{4}{3}} = 2.$$

(*b*) Average time a customer spends in the shop

$$E(T) = \frac{1}{\mu-\lambda} = \frac{1}{2-\frac{4}{3}} = \frac{3}{2} = 1\frac{1}{2} \text{ hours.}$$

(*c*) Average time spent waiting in the shop to be served,

$$E(w) = \frac{\lambda}{\mu(\mu-\lambda)} = \frac{\frac{4}{3}}{2\left(2-\frac{4}{3}\right)} = 1 \text{ hour.}$$

(*d*) The barber remains idle $= 1-\dfrac{\lambda}{\mu}$

$$= 1-\frac{\frac{4}{3}}{2} = \frac{1}{3} \text{ of the day.}$$

(*e*) Probability that a customer has to wait for $\frac{1}{2}$ hour,

$$= e^{-(\mu - \lambda)w}$$

$$= e^{-\left(2-\frac{4}{3}\right)\frac{1}{2}} = e^{-\frac{1}{3}} = 0.71653$$

Ans.

Example 4. *The rate of arrival of customers at a public telephone booth follows Poisson distribution, with an average time of 10 minutes between one customer and the next. The duration of a phone call is assumed to follow exponential distribution, with mean time of 3 minutes.*

(*a*) *What is the probability that a person arriving at the booth will have to wait?*

(*b*) *What is the average length of non-empty queues that form from time to time?*

(*c*) *The Mahanagar Telephone Nigam Ltd. will install a second booth when it is convinced that the customers would expect waiting for at least 3 minutes for their turn to make a call. By how much time should the flow of customers increase in order to justify a second booth?*

Solution. Here,

$$\lambda = \frac{60}{10} = 6 \text{ per hour}$$

$$\mu = \frac{60}{3} = 20 \text{ per hour}$$

(*a*) Probability that a person arriving at the booth will have to wait

$$= 1 - P_0 = 1-\left(1-\frac{\lambda}{\mu}\right) = \frac{\lambda}{\mu} = \frac{6}{20} = 0.3.$$

(*b*) Average length of non-empty queues

$$= \frac{\mu}{\mu-\lambda} = \frac{20}{20-6} = 1.43 \text{ customers}$$

(*c*) The installation of second booth will be justified, if the arrival rate is greater than the waiting time. Now, if λ' denotes the increased arrival rate, average time spend waiting in the booth will be

$$E(w) = \frac{\lambda'}{\mu(\mu-\lambda')}$$

$$\frac{3}{60} = \frac{\lambda'}{20(20-\lambda')}$$

$$\Rightarrow \lambda' = 10.$$

Hence, increase in the arrival rate = 10 – 6 = 4 customers per hour to justify the second booth.

Ans.

Example 5. *In a supermarket, the average arrival rate of customers is 20 per hour following Poisson process. The average time taken by a cashier to list and calculate the customer's purchase is* $2\frac{1}{2}$ *minutes following exponential distribution. Find:*

(a) The porbability that the queue length exceeds 7.

(b) The expected time spent by a customer in the system.

Solution. Here,

$$\lambda = 20 \text{ per hour}$$

$$\mu = \frac{60}{2.5} = 24 \text{ per hour.}$$

(*a*) The probability that the queue length exceeds 7,

$$P(>7) = \left(\frac{\lambda}{\mu}\right)^7 = \left(\frac{20}{24}\right)^7 = 0.27908.$$

(*b*) The expected time spent by a customer in the system,

$$E(T) = \frac{1}{\mu-\lambda} = \frac{1}{24-20} = 0.25 \text{ hour or 15 minutes.}$$ **Ans.**

Example 6. *On an average 96 patients per 24-hour day require the service of an emergency clinic. Also on average, a patient requires 10 minutes of active attention. Assume that the facility can handle only one emergency at a time. Suppose that it costs the clinic ₹ 100 per patient treated to obtain an average servicing time of 10 minutes, and that each minute of decrease in this average time would cost ₹ 10 per patient treated. How much would have to be budgeted by the clinic to decrease the average size of the queue from* $1\frac{1}{3}$ *patients to* $\frac{1}{2}$ *patient.*

Solution. Here

$$\lambda = 96 \text{ patients per day}$$

$$\mu = \frac{24\times 60}{10} = 144 \text{ patients per day.}$$

Expected number of patients in the queue,

$$E(m) = \frac{\lambda^2}{\mu(\mu-\lambda)} = \frac{96\times 96}{144(144-96)} = \frac{4}{3} = 1.333.$$

This number is to be reduced from $1\frac{1}{3}$ to $\frac{1}{2}$. So, we require new value of μ, say μ'.

Now,

$$\frac{1}{2} = \frac{\lambda^2}{\mu'(\mu'-\lambda)}$$

or

$$\frac{1}{2} = \frac{96\times 96}{\mu'(\mu'-96)}$$

or

$$\mu' = 192 \text{ patients per day.}$$

Therefore, average time required for treatment of each patient $= \frac{60\times 24}{192} = 7\frac{1}{2}$ minutes.

So, decrease in time required to attend a patient = 10 – 7.5 = $2\frac{1}{2}$ minutes.

The budget required for each patient is = ₹ (100 + 2.5 × 10) = ₹ 125.

Hence, in order to decrease the size of the queue, budget requirement per patient should be increased from ₹ 100 to ₹ 125. **Ans.**

Example 7. *At a car service centre, cars arrive according to Poisson process with mean 3 per hour. The time for servicing each car is exponentially distributed with mean 15 minutes per car. The facility can handle one car at a time, compute:*

(*a*) *Average queue length*

(*b*) *Average number of cars in the queueing system*

(*c*) *Waiting time in the system, and*

(*d*) *Percentage utilization of service.* (IU, 2006–07; UPTU, 2003–04)

Solution. Here, $\lambda = 3$ per hour

$$\mu = \frac{60}{15} = 4 \text{ per hour.}$$

(*a*) Average queue length,

$$E(m) = \frac{\lambda^2}{\mu(\mu-\lambda)} = \frac{3\times 3}{4(4-3)} = \frac{9}{4} \text{ cars.}$$

(*b*) Average number of cars in the queueing system,

$$E(n) = \frac{\lambda}{\mu-\lambda} = \frac{3}{4-3} = 3.$$

(*c*) Waiting time in the system,

$$E(T) = \frac{1}{\mu-\lambda} = \frac{1}{4-3} = 1 \text{ hour or 60 minutes.}$$

(*d*) Percentage utilization of service,

$$\rho = \frac{\lambda}{\mu} = \frac{3}{4} = 0.75 \text{ or } 75\%.$$ **Ans.**

Example 8. *In a railway marshalling yard, goods train arrive at a rate of 30 trains per day. Assuming that the inter-arrival time follows an exponential distribution and the service time distribution is also exponential with an average of 36 minutes. Calculate the following:*

(*i*) *The mean queue size (line length), and*

(*ii*) *The probability that the queue size exceeds 10.*

If the input of trains increases to an average 33 per day, what will be the change in (i) and (ii)?

Solution. Here, λ = arrival rate = $\frac{30}{24} = \frac{5}{4}$ per hour or $\frac{1}{48}$ per minute

$$\mu = \text{service rate} = \frac{1}{36} \text{ per minute.}$$

(*i*) The mean queue size,

$$E(n) = \frac{\lambda}{\mu-\lambda} = \frac{\frac{1}{48}}{\frac{1}{36}-\frac{1}{48}} = 3 \text{ trains.}$$

(*ii*) The probability that the queue size exceeds 10,

$$P(>10) = \left(\frac{\lambda}{\mu}\right)^{10} = \left(\frac{\frac{1}{48}}{\frac{1}{36}}\right)^{10} = 0.0563.$$

Now, if the input increases to 33 trains per day, then we have $\lambda = \frac{33}{24}$ per hour or $\frac{33}{24\times 60} = \frac{11}{480}$ per minute and $\mu = \frac{1}{36}$ per minute, then charge in;

(*i*) The mean queue size,

$$E(n) = \frac{\lambda}{\mu-\lambda} = \frac{\frac{11}{480}}{\frac{1}{36}-\frac{11}{480}} = 4.7143 \approx 5 \text{ trains.}$$

(*ii*) The probability that the queue size exceeds 10,

$$P\,(>10) = \left(\frac{\lambda}{\mu}\right)^{10} = \left(\frac{\frac{11}{480}}{\frac{1}{36}}\right)^{10} = 0.1461.$$

11.11 MODEL 2

(M/M/1) : (N/FIFO): This model differs from that of Model-1 in the sense that the maximum number of customers in the system is limited to N. When waiting space is limited, a number of minor modifications must be made to the Model-1.

The steady state equations are identical to those used in Model-1 with additional difference equation for $n = N$.

The probability of N customers in the system at time $(t + \Delta t)$ can be expressed as,

$$\begin{aligned} P_N(t + \Delta t) &= P_N(t).P(\text{no service completed in } \Delta t) \\ &\quad + P_{N-1}(t).P(\text{no arrival in } \Delta t).P(\text{no service completed in } \Delta t) \\ &= P_N(t)\,[1 - \mu\Delta t] + P_{N-1}(t)\,[\lambda\Delta t]\,[1 - \mu\Delta t] \end{aligned}$$

On neglecting the term of $(\Delta t)^2$, we have

$$P_N(t + \Delta t) = P_N(t)[1 - \mu\Delta t] + P_{N-1}(t)\,\lambda\Delta t$$

$$\frac{P_N(t+\Delta t)-P_N(t)}{\Delta t} = -\mu P_N(t) + P_{N-1}(t).$$

Now, taking the limit as $\Delta t \to 0$, we have

$$\frac{d}{dt}P_N(t) = -\mu P_N(t) + \lambda P_{N-1}(t).$$

Under steady state of the system, the equation reduces to

$$0 = -\mu P_N + \lambda P_{N-1}$$

The complete set of steady state equations can be written as:

$$\begin{aligned} \mu P_1 &= \lambda P_0 &&; n = 0 \\ \mu P_{n+1} &= (\lambda + \mu)P_n - \lambda P_{n-1} &&; 1 \le n \le N-1 \\ \mu P_N &= \lambda P_{N-1} &&; n = N \end{aligned}$$

we have,

$$\begin{aligned} P_n &= \left(\frac{\lambda}{\mu}\right)^n P_0 &&; n \le N \\ &= e^n P_0. \end{aligned}$$

To obtain the value of P_0, we use the boundary condition

$$\sum_{n=0}^{N} P_N = 1$$

$$\sum_{n=0}^{N} P_0 \rho^n = 1 \text{ or } P_0[1 + \rho + \rho^2 + \ldots + \rho^N] = 1$$

$$P_0\left[\frac{1-\rho^{N+1}}{1-\rho}\right] = 1 \text{ or } P_0 = \frac{1-\rho}{1-\rho^{N+1}}; \text{ for } \rho \neq 1$$

Thus,

$$P_n = \begin{cases} \dfrac{(1-\rho)\rho^n}{1-\rho^{N+1}}; & \rho \neq 1 \\ \dfrac{1}{N+1} & ; \rho = 1. \end{cases}$$

Characteristics of (M/M/1) : (N/FIFO)

1. Expected number of customers in the system

$$\begin{aligned} E(n) &= \sum_{n=0}^{N} nP_n = P_0 \sum_{n=0}^{N} n\rho^n = P_0\rho \sum_{n=0}^{N} \frac{d}{d\rho}(\rho^n) \\ &= P_0\rho \frac{d}{d\rho}\sum_{n=0}^{N} \rho^n = P_0\rho \frac{d}{d\rho}\left[\frac{1-\rho^{N+1}}{1-\rho}\right] \\ &= P_0\rho\left[\frac{-(1-\rho)(N+1)\rho^N + \left(1-\rho^{N+1}\right)}{(1-\rho)^2}\right] \\ &= \rho\left[\frac{1 - (N+1)\rho^N + N\rho^{N+1}}{(1-\rho)\left(1-\rho^{N+1}\right)}\right]; \quad \rho \neq 1 \\ &= \frac{N}{2}; \quad \rho = 1. \end{aligned}$$

2. Expected number of customers in the queue

$$E(m) = \sum_{n=1}^{N}(n-1)P_n = \sum_{n=1}^{N} nP_n - \sum_{n=1}^{N} P_n$$

$$= E(n) - \left[\sum_{n=0}^{N} P_n - P_0\right] = E(n) - (1 - P_0)$$

$$= \rho\left[\frac{1-(N+1)\rho^N + N\rho^{N+1}}{(1-\rho)(1-\rho^{N+1})}\right] - \left[1-\left(\frac{1-\rho}{1-\rho^{N+1}}\right)\right]$$

$$= \frac{\rho^2 - N\rho^{N+1} + (N-1)\rho^{N+2}}{(1-\rho)(1-\rho^{N+1})}$$

$$= \rho^2\left[\frac{1-N\rho^{N-1}+(N-1)\rho^N}{(1-\rho)(1-\rho^{N+1})}\right] ;\ \rho \neq 1.$$

(No queue when $\lambda = \mu$ *i.e.*, $\frac{\lambda}{\mu} = \rho = 1$).

3. Expected time a customer spends in the system.

$$E(T) = \frac{E(n)}{\lambda'} \text{ where } \lambda' = \lambda(1 - P_N),\ P_N = \rho^N P_0$$

4. Expected time a customer spends in the queue,

$$E(w) = \frac{E(m)}{\lambda'} \text{ or } E(T) - \frac{1}{\mu}.$$

Example 9. *Trains arrive at the yard every 12 minutes and the service time is 35 minutes. If the capacity of the yard is limited to 4 trains find:*

(*a*) *Probability that the yard is empty.*

(*b*) *The average number of trains in the system.*

(*c*) *The average number of trains in the queue.*

Solution. Here, $\lambda = \frac{1}{12}$ per minutes or 5 per hour

$\mu = \frac{1}{35}$ per minute or $\frac{12}{7}$ per hour

and $N = 4.$

Now, $\rho = \frac{\lambda}{\mu} = \frac{5}{\frac{12}{7}} = 2.917\ (>1).$

(*a*) Probability that the yard is empty,

$$P_0 = \frac{\rho - 1}{\rho^{N+1} - 1} = \frac{2.917 - 1}{(2.917)^5 - 1} = \frac{1.917}{210.1943} = 0.00912.$$

(*b*) Average number of trains in the system,

$$E(n) = \sum_{n=0}^{N} n\,Pn \qquad \text{where } Pn = \rho^n P_0$$

$$= 0 \cdot P_0 + 1 \cdot P_1 + 2 \cdot P_2 + 3 \cdot P_3 + 4 \cdot P_4$$

$$= \rho^1 P_0 + 2\rho^2 P_0 + 3\rho^3 P_0 + 4\rho^4 P_0$$

$$= P_0 [\rho + 2\rho^2 + 3\rho^3 + 4\rho^4]$$

$$= 0.00912[2.917 + 2(2.917)^2 + 3(2.917)^3 + 4(2.917)^4]$$

$$= 3.502 \approx 3 \text{ trains.}$$

(*c*) Average number of trains in the queue,

$$E(m) = \sum_{n=1}^{N} (n-1) P_n = \sum_{n=1}^{4} (n-1) P_n$$

$$= 0 \cdot P_1 + 2 \cdot P_2 + 2 \cdot P_3 + 3 \cdot P_4$$

$$E(m) = P_0 [\rho^2 + 2\rho^3 + 3\rho^4]$$

$$= 0.00912\ [(2.917)^2 + 2(2.917)^3 + 3(2.917)^4]$$

$$= 2.511 \approx 2 \text{ trains.}$$

Ans.

Example 10. *Consider a single server queueing system with Poisson input, exponential service times. Suppose the mean arrival rate is 3 calling units per hour, the expected service time is 0.25 hour and the maximum permissible number calling units in the system is two. Derive the steady-state probability distribution of number of calling units in the system and then calculate the expected number in the system.*

Solution. Here, $\lambda = 3$ per hour

$$\mu = \frac{1}{0.25} = 4 \text{ per hour}$$

and $N = 2$

Now, $\rho = \dfrac{\lambda}{\mu} = \dfrac{3}{4} = 0.75.$

The steady state probability distribution of number of calling units (number of n customers) in the system is,

$$P_n = \rho^n P_0 \text{ and } P_0 = \frac{1-\rho}{1-\rho^{N+1}}$$

$$P_0 = \frac{1-\rho}{1-\rho^{N+1}} = \frac{1-0.75}{1-(0.75)^3} = \frac{0.25}{0.578125} = 0.4324$$

$$P_n = \rho^n P_0 = (0.75)^n \times 0.4324 = 0.4324(0.75)^n$$

Expected number of calling units in the system,

$$E(n) = \sum_{n=0}^{N} nP_n = \sum_{n=0}^{2} n(0.75)^n \times 0.4324$$

$$= 0.4324\,[(0.75) + 2\,(0.75)^2] = 0.81075 \approx 1 \text{ unit.}$$ **Ans.**

Example 11. *A one person barbershop has a space to accommodate 5 customers four waiting and one being attended at a time. If a customer comes to his shop and finds it full, he goes to the next shop. Customers arrive at an average rate of 4 per hour and service time is 10 minutesh, find:*

(a) Probability that a customer can get the service directly on arrival without waiting.

(b) Expected number of customers waiting in the shop.

(c) Expected number of customers in the shop.

(d) The time a customer expects to spend in the shop.

Solution: Here, $\lambda = 4$ per hour

$$\mu = \frac{60}{10} = 6 \text{ per hour}$$

and $N = 5.$

Now, $$\rho = \frac{\lambda}{\mu} = \frac{4}{6} = \frac{2}{3} = 0.67$$

(*a*) Probability that a customer can get the service directly on arrival without waiting,

$$P_0 = \frac{1-\rho}{1-\rho^{N+1}} = \frac{1-0.67}{1-(0.67)^6} = \frac{0.33}{0.9095} = 0.363.$$

(*b*) Expected number of customers waiting in the shop,

$$E(m) = \sum_{n=1}^{N}(n-1)P_n = \sum_{n=1}^{5}(n-1)P_n$$

$$= 0.P_1 + 1.P_2 + 2.P_3 + 3.P_4 + 4.P_5$$

$$= P_0[\rho^2 + 2\rho^3 + 3\rho^4 + 4\rho^5]$$

$$= 0.363[(0.67)^2 + 2(0.67)^3 + 3(0.67)^4 + 4(0.67)^5]$$

$$= 0.7968 \approx 1 \text{ customer.}$$

(*c*) Expected number of customers in the shop,

$$E(n) = \sum_{n=0}^{N} nP_n = \sum_{n=0}^{5} nP_n$$

$$= 0.P_0 + 1.P_1 + 2.P_2 + 3.P_3 + 4.P_4 + 5.P_5$$

$$= P_0[\rho + 2\rho^2 + 3\rho^3 + 4\rho^4 + 5\rho^5]$$

$$= 0.363[(0.67) + 2(0.67)^2 + 3(0.67)^3 + 4(0.67)^4 + 5(0.67)^5]$$

$$= 1.4343 \text{ customers.}$$

(*d*) The time a customer expects to spend in the shop,

$$E(T) = \frac{E(n)}{\lambda'} \text{ where } \qquad \lambda' = \lambda(1 - P_c),\ P_N = \rho^N P_0$$

$$= \frac{1.4343}{3.804} \qquad P_5 = (0.67)^5 \times 0.363 = 0.049$$

$$= 0.377 \text{ hour} \qquad \lambda' = 4\,(1 - 0.049)$$

$$\text{or } 22.632 \text{ minutes} \qquad = 3.804.$$

Ans.

Example 12. *A car park contains 4 cars. The arrival of cars is Poisson at a mean rate of 10 per hour. The length of time each car spends in the car park is negative exponential distribution with mean of 2 hours. How many cars in the car park on average?*

Solution. Here, $\lambda = 10$ per hour

$$\mu = \frac{1}{2} \text{ per hour}$$

and $N = 4$.

Now,

$$\rho = \frac{\lambda}{\mu} = \frac{10}{\frac{1}{2}} = 20 \qquad (\rho > 1)$$

$$P_0 = \frac{\rho - 1}{\rho^{N+1} - 1} = \frac{20 - 1}{20^5 - 1} = \frac{19}{3199999} = 0.00000594$$

Average number of cars in the park,

$$E(n) = \sum_{n=0}^{N} nP_n$$

$$= \sum_{n=0}^{4} nP_n = P_1 + 2P_2 + 3P_3 + 4P_4$$

$$= P_0\,[\rho + 2\rho^2 + 3\rho^3 + 4\rho^4]$$

$$= 0.00000594[20 + 2(20)^2 + 3(20)^3 + 4(20)^4]$$

$$= 3.9224 \approx 4 \text{ cars.}$$

Ans.

11.12 MULTICHANNEL QUEUEING MODELS

Multichannel queueing theory treats the condition in which there are several service stations S (say) in parallel and each customer in the waiting line can be served by any service station. Each service station has the same type of service and is equipped with the same type of facilities. The new arrival selects one service station without any external pressure.

11.13 MODEL 3

(M/M/S) : (∞/FIFO): This model deals with a queueing system having S parallel service stations. The arrival rate is λ and the service rate per service station is μ. The capacity of the system is infinite and the service on the basis 'first in first out'.

When number of customers $n < S$, there is no queue because all the arriving customers are being serviced, and the rate of servicing will be $n\mu$. When $n = S$, all service stations will be working and when $n > S$, there will be $(n - S)$ customers in the queue and the rate of service will be $S\mu$. Thus λ_n and μ_n are defined as,

$$\lambda_n = \lambda;\ n \geq 0$$

and
$$\mu_n = \begin{cases} n\mu;\ 0 \leq n < S \\ S\mu;\ n \geq S \end{cases}$$

The steady state solution is

$$P_n = \begin{cases} \dfrac{1}{n!}\left(\dfrac{\lambda}{\mu}\right)^n P_0;\ 0 \leq n < S \\ \dfrac{1}{S^{n-S}\,S!}\left(\dfrac{\lambda}{\mu}\right)^n P_0;\ n \geq S. \end{cases}$$

To obtain the value of P_0, we use the boundary condition

$$\sum_{n=0}^{\infty} P_n = 1$$

or
$$\sum_{n=0}^{S-1} P_n + \sum_{n=S}^{\infty} P_n = 1$$

or
$$\left[\sum_{n=0}^{S-1} \frac{1}{n!}\left(\frac{\lambda}{\mu}\right)^n + \sum_{n=S}^{\infty} \frac{1}{S^{n-s}\,S!}\left(\frac{\lambda}{\mu}\right)^n\right] P_0 = 1$$

or
$$P_0 = \left[\sum_{n=0}^{S-1} \frac{1}{n!}\left(\frac{\lambda}{\mu}\right)^n + \frac{1}{S!}\left(\frac{\lambda}{\mu}\right)^S \frac{S\mu}{S\mu - \lambda}\right]^{-1}.$$

Characteristics of (M/M/S) : (∞/FIFO)

1. Expected number of customers in the system,

$$E(n) = \frac{\lambda\mu\left(\dfrac{\lambda}{\mu}\right)^S P_0}{(S-1)!\,(S\mu - \lambda)^2} + \frac{\lambda}{\mu}.$$

2. Expected number of customers in the queue,

$$E(m) = \sum_{n=S}^{\infty} (n-S) P_n \text{ or } E(n) - S.\frac{\lambda}{S\mu}$$

$$= \frac{\lambda\mu\left(\dfrac{\lambda}{\mu}\right)^S P_0}{(S-1)!(S\mu - \lambda)^2}.$$

3. Expected time a customer spends in the system,

$$E(T) = \frac{E(n)}{\lambda} = \frac{\mu\left(\frac{\lambda}{\mu}\right)^S P_0}{(S-1)!\,(S\mu-\lambda)^2} + \frac{1}{\mu} \text{ or } E(w) + \frac{1}{\mu}.$$

4. Expected time a customer spends in the queue

$$E(w) = \frac{E(m)}{\lambda} = \frac{\mu\left(\frac{\lambda}{\mu}\right)^S P_0}{(S-1)!\,(S\mu-\lambda)^2}.$$

5. Probability that a customer has to wait,

$$P(n \geq S) = \sum_{n=S}^{\infty} P_n = \sum_{n=S}^{\infty} \frac{1}{S!\,S^{n-S}}\left(\frac{\lambda}{\mu}\right)^n P_0 = \frac{S\mu\left(\frac{\lambda}{\mu}\right)^S P_0}{S!\,(S\mu-\lambda)}.$$

6. Probability that a customer enters the service without wait,

$$= 1 - P(n \geq S) = 1 - \frac{S\mu\left(\frac{\lambda}{\mu}\right)^S P_0}{S!(S\mu-\lambda)}.$$

7. Utilization rate $(\rho) = \frac{\lambda}{S\mu}$.

8. Efficiency of the model $= \frac{\text{Average number of customers served}}{\text{Total number of customers served}}$.

9. Average number of idle servers = S – average numbers of customers served.

Example 13. *A petrol pump has two service stations. The service time follows the exponential distribution with mean 3 minutes and cars arrive in a Poisson process at the rate of 10 cars per hour. Find the probability that a car has to wait for service. What proportion of time the service station remains idle?*

Solution. Here, $\lambda = 10$ per hour

$$\mu = \frac{60}{3} = 20 \text{ per hour}$$

and $S = 2.$

Now,

$$P_0 = \left[\sum_{n=0}^{S-1} \frac{1}{n!}\left(\frac{\lambda}{\mu}\right)^n + \frac{1}{S!}\left(\frac{\lambda}{\mu}\right)^S \frac{S\mu}{S\mu-\lambda}\right]^{-1}$$

$$= \left[\sum_{n=0}^{1} \frac{1}{n!}\left(\frac{10}{20}\right)^n + \frac{1}{2!}\left(\frac{10}{20}\right)^2 \frac{40}{40-10}\right]^{-1}$$

$$= \left[1 + \frac{1}{2} + \frac{1}{6}\right]^{-1} = \frac{3}{5} = 0.6.$$

The probability of a car to wait for service,

$$P(n \geq 2) = \sum_{n=2}^{\infty} P_n = \sum_{n=2}^{\infty} \frac{1}{2!2^{n-2}}\left(\frac{10}{20}\right)^n P_0$$

$$= \frac{\left(\frac{10}{20}\right)^2 .40}{2!(40-10)} \times 0.6 = 0.1.$$

The proportion of time, petrol pump remains busy $= \frac{\lambda}{S\mu} = \frac{10}{40} = \frac{1}{4}$.

The proportion of time, petrol pump remains idle $= 1 - \frac{1}{4} = \frac{3}{4}$.

So, percentage of idle time is 75%. **Ans.**

Example 14. *A tax consulting firm has four service stations in its office to attend the problems of the peoples. Average 80 persons arrives in an 8-hour service day. Each tax advisor spends an irregular amount of time servicing the arrivals which have been found to have an exponential distribution. The average service time is 20 minutes. Find:*

(*a*) *The average number of customers waiting to be serviced.*

(*b*) *The average number of customers in the system.*

(*c*) *Average waiting time for a customer for service.*

(*d*) *Average time a customer spends in the system.*

(*e*) *The probability that a customer has to wait before service.*

Solution. Here, $\lambda = \frac{80}{8} = 10$ per hour

$\mu = \frac{60}{20} = 3$ per hour

and $S = 4$.

Now, $$P_0 = \left[\sum_{n=0}^{S-1} \frac{1}{n!}\left(\frac{\lambda}{\mu}\right)^n + \frac{1}{S!}\left(\frac{\lambda}{\mu}\right)^S \frac{S\mu}{S\mu - \lambda}\right]^{-1} = \left[\sum_{n=0}^{3} \frac{1}{n!}\left(\frac{10}{3}\right)^n + \frac{1}{4!}\left(\frac{10}{3}\right)^4 \frac{12}{12-10}\right]^{-1}$$

$$= \left[1 + \frac{10}{3} + \frac{1}{2}\left(\frac{10}{3}\right)^2 + \frac{1}{6}\left(\frac{10}{3}\right)^3 + \frac{1}{24}\left(\frac{10}{3}\right)^4 \times 6\right]^{-1} = 0.02131.$$

(*a*) The average number of customers waiting to be serviced,

$$E(m) = \sum_{n=4}^{\infty} (n-4)P_n = \frac{\lambda\mu\left(\frac{\lambda}{\mu}\right)^S P_0}{(S-1)!(S\mu - \lambda)^2} = \frac{10 \times 3 \times \left(\frac{10}{3}\right)^4 \times 0.02131}{3!(12-10)^2}$$

$$= 3.289.$$

(*b*) The average number of customers in the system,

$$E(n) = E(m)+\frac{\lambda}{\mu} = 3.289 + \frac{10}{3} = 6.6223.$$

(*c*) Average waiting time for a customer for service,

$$E(w) = \frac{E(m)}{\lambda} = \frac{\mu\left(\frac{\lambda}{\mu}\right)^S P_0}{(S-1)!\,(S\mu-\lambda)^2}. = \frac{3\times\left(\frac{10}{3}\right)^4 \times 0.02131}{3!\,(12-10)^2}$$

$$= 0.3289 \text{ hour or } 19.734 \text{ minutes.}$$

(*d*) Average time a customer spends in the system,

$$E(T) = E(w) + \frac{1}{\mu} = 0.3289 + \frac{1}{3}$$

$$= 0.66223 \text{ hour or } 39.734 \text{ minutes}$$

(*e*) The probability that a customer has to wait before service,

$$P(n \geq 4) = \sum_{n=4}^{\infty} P_n = \frac{\left(\frac{\lambda}{\mu}\right)^4 \times 4\mu}{4!(4\mu-\lambda)} \times P_0 = \frac{\left(\frac{10}{3}\right)^4 \times 4\times 3}{24\times(12-10)} \times 0.02131$$

$$= 0.0006577.$$ **Ans.**

Example 15. *A super market has three sales girls at the sales counters. If the service time for each customer is exponential with a mean of 4 minutes, and if the customers arrive in a Poisson fashion at the rate of 10 per hour. Find:*

(*a*) *Probability that there is no customer in the system.*

(*b*) *Average number of customers in the queue.*

(*c*) *Average number of customers in the system.*

(*d*) *Average waiting time in the queue.*

(*e*) *Utilization factor.*

Solution. Here, $\lambda = 10$ per hour

$$\mu = \frac{60}{4} = 15 \text{ per hour}$$

and $S = 3$.

(*a*) Probability that there is no customer in the system,

$$P_0 = \left[\sum_{n=0}^{S-1}\frac{1}{n!}\left(\frac{\lambda}{\mu}\right)^n + \frac{1}{S!}\left(\frac{\lambda}{\mu}\right)^S \frac{S\mu}{S\mu-\lambda}\right]^{-1} = \left[\sum_{n=0}^{2}\frac{1}{n!}\left(\frac{10}{15}\right)^n + \frac{1}{3!}\left(\frac{10}{15}\right)^3 \frac{45}{45-10}\right]^{-1}$$

$$= \left[1+\left(\frac{10}{15}\right)+\frac{1}{2}\left(\frac{10}{15}\right)^2+\frac{1}{6}\left(\frac{10}{15}\right)^3\frac{45}{35}\right]^{-1}$$

$$= 0.5122$$

(*b*) Average number of customers in the queue,

$$E(m) = \frac{\lambda\mu\left(\frac{\lambda}{\mu}\right)^S P_0}{(S-1)!\,(S\mu-\lambda)^2} = \frac{10\times 15\times\left(\frac{10}{15}\right)^3\times 0.5122}{2!(45-10)^2}$$

$$= 0.00929.$$

(*c*) Average number of customers in the system,

$$E(n) = E(m)+\frac{\lambda}{\mu} = 0.00929+\frac{10}{15}$$

$$= 0.676.$$

(*d*) Average waiting time in the queue,

$$E(w) = \frac{E(m)}{\lambda} = \frac{0.00929}{10}$$

$$= 0.000929 \text{ hour or } 0.056 \text{ minutes.}$$

(*e*) Utilization factor,

$$\rho = \frac{\lambda}{S\mu} = \frac{10}{45}$$

$$= 0.222$$

Ans.

Example 16. *A library wants to improve its service facilities in terms of the waiting time of its borrowers. The library has two counters at present and borrowers arrive according to Poisson distribution with arrival rate 1 every 6 minutes and service time follows exponential distribution with a mean of 10 minutes. The library has relaxed its membership rules and a substantial increase in the number of borrowers is expected. Find the number of additional counters to be provided if the arrival rate is expected to be twice the present value and the average waiting time of the borrower must be limited to half the present value.*

Solution. Here, $\lambda = \frac{1}{6}$ per minute or $\frac{60}{6} = 10$ per hour

$\mu = \frac{1}{10}$ per minute or $\frac{60}{10} = 6$ per hour

and $S = 2.$

Now,

$$P_0 = \left[\sum_{n=0}^{S-1}\frac{1}{n!}\left(\frac{\lambda}{\mu}\right)^n + \frac{1}{S!}\left(\frac{\lambda}{\mu}\right)^S \frac{S\mu}{S\mu-\lambda}\right]^{-1}$$

$$= \left[\sum_{n=0}^{1}\frac{1}{n!}\left(\frac{10}{6}\right)^n + \frac{1}{2!}\left(\frac{10}{6}\right)^2 \times\frac{12}{12-10}\right]^{-1}$$

$$= \left[1+\frac{5}{3}+\frac{25}{3}\right]^{-1} = \frac{1}{11} = 0.091$$

Average waiting time of a borrower for service,

$$E(w) = \frac{E(m)}{\lambda} = \frac{\mu\left(\frac{\lambda}{\mu}\right)^S P_0}{(S-1)!\,(S\mu-\lambda)^2}$$

$$= \frac{6\times\left(\frac{10}{6}\right)^2}{1!\,(12-10)^2}\times 0.091 = 0.379 \text{ hour or } 22.75 \text{ minutes.}$$

$$\text{New arrival rate } (\lambda) = 2\times\frac{1}{6} = 1/3 \text{ per minutes or } \frac{60}{3} = 20 \text{ per hour}$$

$$\mu = 6 \text{ per hour.}$$

The average waiting time of a borrower is to be calculated for different number of counters. If $S = 3$.

$$\text{Utilization factor} = \frac{\lambda}{S\mu} = \frac{20}{3\times 6} = \frac{10}{9} > 1$$

It shows that the arrival rate of the system is more than its service rate. The state of the system is in explosive state.

If $S = 4$

$$\text{Utilization factor} = \frac{\lambda}{S\mu} = \frac{20}{4\times 6} = \frac{5}{6} < 1$$

Now,
$$P_0 = \left[\sum_{n=0}^{3}\frac{1}{n!}\left(\frac{20}{6}\right)^n + \frac{1}{3!}\left(\frac{20}{6}\right)^3 \times \frac{24}{24-20}\right]^{-1}$$

$$= \left[1+\frac{10}{3}+\frac{50}{9}+\frac{500}{81}+\frac{1000}{27}\right]^{-1} = 0.0188.$$

Average waiting time of a borrower for service,

$$E(w) = \frac{E(m)}{\lambda} = \frac{\mu\left(\frac{\lambda}{\mu}\right)^S P_0}{(S-1)!\,(S\mu-\lambda)^2}$$

$$= \frac{6\times\left(\frac{20}{6}\right)^4}{3!\,(24-20)^2}\times 0.0188 = 0.145 \text{ hour or } 8.7 \text{ minutes}$$

which is less than half the present value of 22.75 minutes, *i.e.*, 8.7 < 11.375.

Hence two additional counters are to be provided. **Ans.**

11.14 MODEL 4

(M/M/S) : (N/FIFO): This model deals with a queueing system having s parallel service stations. The arrival rate is λ and the service rate per service station is μ. The capacity of the system is limited to N and the service on the basis 'first in first out'. Also $N > S$.

Here, the value of λ_n will be zero when the value of $n \geq N$. Thus λ_n and μ_n are defined as

$$\lambda_n = \begin{cases} \lambda; \ 0 \leq n < N \\ 0; \ n \geq N \end{cases}$$

and
$$\mu_n = \begin{cases} n\mu; \ 0 \leq n < S \\ S\mu; \ S \leq n \leq N. \end{cases}$$

The steady state solution is,

$$P_n = \begin{cases} \dfrac{1}{n!}\left(\dfrac{\lambda}{\mu}\right)^n P_0; \ 0 \leq n < S \\ \dfrac{1}{S!S^{n-s}}\left(\dfrac{\lambda}{\mu}\right)^n P_0; \ S \leq n \leq N. \end{cases}$$

To obtain the value of P_0, we use the boundary condition,

$$\sum_{n=0}^{N} P_n = 1$$

or
$$\sum_{n=0}^{S-1} P_n + \sum_{n=S}^{N} P_n = 1$$

or
$$\left[\sum_{n=0}^{S-1} \frac{1}{n!}\left(\frac{\lambda}{\mu}\right)^n + \sum_{n=S}^{N} \frac{1}{S!S^{n-S}}\left(\frac{\lambda}{\mu}\right)^n\right] P_0 = 1$$

or
$$P_0 = \left[\sum_{n=0}^{S-1} \frac{1}{n!}\left(\frac{\lambda}{\mu}\right)^n + \sum_{n=S}^{N} \frac{1}{S!S^{n-S}}\left(\frac{\lambda}{\mu}\right)^n\right]^{-1}.$$

Characteristics of (M/M/S): (N/FIFO)

1. Expected number of customers in the queue,

$$E(m) = \sum_{n=S}^{N} (n-S)P_n$$

$$= \frac{(S\rho)^S \rho P_0}{S!(1-\rho)^2}\left[1-\rho^{N-S+1}-(1-\rho)(N-S+1)\rho^{N-S}\right]$$

where
$$\rho = \frac{\lambda}{S\mu}.$$

2. Expected number of customers in the system,

$$E(n) = \sum_{n=0}^{N} nP_n = E(m) + S - P_0 \sum_{n=0}^{S-1} \frac{(S-n)(\rho S)^n}{n!}.$$

3. Expected time a customer spends in the system,

$$E(T) = \frac{E(n)}{\lambda'} \text{ where } \lambda' = \lambda(1 - P_N).$$

4. Expected time a customer spends in the queue,

$$E(w) = \frac{E(m)}{\lambda'} \quad \text{or} \quad E(T) - \frac{1}{\mu} \quad \text{where } \lambda' = \lambda(1 - P_N).$$

Example 17. *At a port, let there be six unloading berths and four unloading crews. When all the berths are full, arriving ships are diverted to an overflow capacity 25 kms. down the river. Tankers arrive according to a Poisson process with a mean of one every two hour. It takes an unloading crew on the average, ten hours to unload a tanker, the unloading time follows an exponential distribution. Find:*

(*a*) *The average number of tankers at the port.*

(*b*) *The average waiting time in the system.*

Solution. Here, $\lambda = \frac{1}{2}$ per hour, $\mu = \frac{1}{10}$ per hour

$S = 4$ and $N = 6$

$$P_0 = \left[\sum_{n=0}^{S-1} \frac{1}{n!}\left(\frac{\lambda}{\mu}\right)^n + \sum_{n=S}^{N} \frac{1}{S!S^{n-S}}\left(\frac{\lambda}{\mu}\right)^n\right]^{-1}$$

$$= \left[\sum_{n=0}^{3} \frac{1}{n!}(5)^n + \sum_{n=4}^{6} \frac{1}{4!(4)^{n-4}}(5)^n\right]^{-1}$$

$$= \left[1 + (5) + \frac{1}{2!}(5)^2 + \frac{1}{3!}(5)^3 + \frac{1}{4!(4)^0}(5)^4 + \frac{1}{4!(4)^1}(5)^5 + \frac{1}{4!(4)^2}(5)^6\right]^{-1}$$

$= 0.007214.$

(*a*) Average number of tankers at the port is given by,

$$E(n) = E(m) + S - P_0 \sum_{n=0}^{S-1} \frac{(S-n)(\rho S)^n}{n!}; \; \rho = \frac{\lambda}{S\mu}$$

$$= \sum_{n=S}^{N} (n-S)P_n + S - P_0 \sum_{n=0}^{S-1} \frac{(S-n)(\rho S)^n}{n!}$$

$$= \sum_{n=4}^{6} (n-4)P_n + 4 - P_0 \sum_{n=0}^{3} \frac{(4-n)(5)^n}{n!}$$

$$= P_5 + 2P_6 + 4 - P_0\left[4 + 15 + 25 + \frac{125}{6}\right]$$

$$= \frac{1}{4!\times 4}\times(5)^5\times 0.007214+\frac{1}{4!\times 4}\times(5)^6\times 0.007214+4-0.007214\times 64.833$$

$$= 4.354 \approx 4 \text{ tankers.}$$

(*b*) Average waiting time in the system is given by,

$$E(T) = \frac{E(n)}{\lambda'} \quad \text{where } \lambda' = \lambda(1-P_N)$$

$$P_6 = \frac{1}{4!\times(4)^2}\times(5)^6\times 0.007214 = 0.2935$$

$$\lambda' = \frac{1}{2}(1-0.2935) = 0.3532.$$

Now, $E(T) = \dfrac{4.354}{0.3532} = 12.327$ hour. **Ans.**

Example 18. *A Car servicing station has 3 stalls where service can be offered simultaneously. The Cars wait in such a way that when a stall becomes vacant, the car at the head of the line pulls upto it. The station can accommodate atmost 4 cars waiting (seven in the station) at one time. The arrival pattern is Poisson with a mean of one car per minute during the peak hours. The service time is exponential with mean six minutes. Find:*

(*a*) *Expected number of cars in the queue.*

(*b*) *Expected number of cars in the service station.*

(*c*) *Expected waiting time a car spends in the system.*

(*d*) *Expected number of cars per hour that can not enter the station.*

Solution. Here, $\lambda = 1$ per minute, $\mu = \dfrac{1}{6}$ per minute

$S = 3$ and $N = 7$

$$P_0 = \left[\sum_{n=0}^{S-1}\frac{1}{n!}\left(\frac{\lambda}{\mu}\right)^n+\sum_{n=S}^{N}\frac{1}{S!S^{n-S}}\left(\frac{\lambda}{\mu}\right)^n\right]^{-1} = \left[\sum_{n=0}^{2}\frac{1}{n!}(6)^n+\sum_{n=3}^{7}\frac{1}{3!3^{n-3}}(6)^n\right]^{-1}$$

$$= \left[1+(6)+\frac{1}{2!}(6)^2+\frac{1}{3!}(6)^3+\frac{1}{3!3}(6)^4\right.$$

$$\left.+\frac{1}{3!(3)^2}(6)^5+\frac{1}{3!(3)^3}(6)^6+\frac{1}{3!(3)^4}(6)^7\right]^{-1}$$

$$= 0.000876.$$

(*a*) Expected number of cars in the queue,

$$E(m) = \sum_{n=S}^{N}(n-S)P_n = \sum_{n=3}^{7}(n-3)P_n$$

$$= P_4 + 2P_5 + 3P_6 + 4P_7$$

$$= \left[\frac{1}{3!3}\times(6)^4+\frac{2}{3!(3)^2}\times(6)^5+\frac{3}{3!(3)^3}\times(6)^6+\frac{4}{3!(3)^4}\times(6)^7\right]\times 0.000876$$

$$= 3.09 \approx 3 \text{ cars.}$$

(*b*) Expected number of cars in the service station,

$$E(n) = E(m) + S - P_0 \sum_{n=0}^{S-1} \frac{(S-n)(\rho S)^n}{n!}$$

$$= 3.09 + 3 - 0.000876 \sum_{n=0}^{2} \frac{(3-n)(6)^n}{n!}$$

$$= 6.09 - 0.000876\,[3 + 12 + 18] = 6.061 \approx 6 \text{ cars.}$$

(*c*) Expected waiting time a car spends in the system,

$$E(T) = \frac{E(n)}{\lambda'} \quad \text{where } \lambda' = \lambda\,(1 - P_N)$$

$$= \frac{6.061}{0.495} \qquad P_7 = \frac{1}{3!3^4}(6)^7 \times 0.000876 = 0.505$$

$$= 12.244 \text{ minutes} \qquad \lambda' = 1(1 - 0.505) = 0.495.$$

(*d*) Expected number of cars per hour that cannot enter the station is,

$$60\lambda\, P_N = 60 \times 1 \times 0.505$$

$$= 30.3 \text{ car per hour.}$$

Ans.

EXERCISES

1. The machines in production shop breakdown at an average of 2 per hour. The non-productive time of any machine costs ₹ 30 per hour. If the cost of repairman is ₹ 50 per hour and the repair rate is 3 per hour.

   Calculate:

   (*a*) Number of machines not working at any point of time.

   (*b*) Average time that a machine is waiting for the repairman.

   (*c*) Cost of non-productive time of the machine operator.

   (*d*) Expected cost of system per hour. [**Ans.** (*a*) 2 (*b*) $\frac{2}{3}$ hours (*c*) ₹ 60 (*d*) ₹ 110]

2. Arrival rate of telephone calls at a telephone both is according to Poisson distribution, with an average time of 9 minutes between two consecutive arrivals. The lengths of telephone calls is assumed to be exponentially distributed with mean 3 minutes.

   (*a*) Determine the probability that a person arriving at the both will have to wait.

   (*b*) Find the average queue length.

   (*c*) Find the fraction of the day that the phone will be in use.

   (*d*) The telephone company will install a second booth when convinced that an arrival would expect to have to wait at least 4 minutes for phone. Find the increase in flow of arrivals which will justify a second booth.

   [**Ans.** (*a*) 0.33 (*b*) 3 (*c*) 0.33 (*d*) $\frac{100}{21}$ per hour]

3. A self-service store employs one cashier at its counter. Nine customers arrive on an average every 5 minutes while the cashier can serve ten customers in 5 minutes. Assuming Poisson distribution for arrival rate and exponential distribution for service rate, find

   (*a*) Average number of customers in the system.

   (*b*) Average number of customers in the queue.

   (*c*) Average time a customer spends in the system.

   (*d*) Average time a customer waits before being served.

   [**Ans.** (*a*) 9 (*b*) 8.1 (*c*) 5 minutes (*d*) 4.5 minutes]

4. A road transport company has one reservation clerk on duty at a time. He handles information of bus schedules and makes reservations. Customers arrive at a rate of 8 per hour and the clerk can service 12 customers on an average per hour. Compute:

   (*a*) Average number of customers waiting for the service of the clerk.

   (*b*) Average time a customer has to wait before getting service.

   (*c*) Average time spent by a customer in the system.

   [**Ans.** (*a*) 2 (*b*) 10 minutes (*c*) 15 minutes]

5. Customers arrive at a box office window, being manned by a single individual according to a Poisson input process with a mean rate of 30 per hour. The time required to serve a customer has an exponential distribution with a mean of 90 seconds. Find the average waiting time of a customer. Also determine the average number of customers in the system and average queue length. [**Ans.** 4.5 minutes; 3; 0.25]

6. In a bank, cheques are cashed at a single 'teller' counter. Customers arrive at the counter in a Poisson manner at an average rate of 30 customers per hour. The teller takes, on an average, a minute and a half to cash cheque. The service time has been shown to be exponentially distributed.

   (*a*) Calculate the percentage of time the teller is busy.

   (*b*) Calculate the average time a customer is expected to wait.

   [**Ans.** (*a*) 75% of its time (*b*) 6 minutes]

7. A repair shop attended by a single mechanic has an average of four customers an hour who bring small appliances for repair. The mechanic inspects them for defects render a diagnosis. This takes him six minutes, on an average. Arrivals are Poisson and service time has the exponential distribution. Compute:

   (*a*) The proportion of time during which the shop is empty.

   (*b*) The probability of finding at least one customer in the shop.

   (*c*) Average number of customers in the system.

   (*d*) Average time spent by the customer in the system.

   [**Ans.** (*a*) 0.6 (*b*) 0.4 (*c*) $\frac{2}{3}$ (*d*) 10 minutes]

(M/M/1 : N/FIFO)

8. Trains arrive at the yard every 15 minutes and the service time is 33 minutes. If the line capacity of the yard is limited to 5 trains, find the probability that the yard is empty and the average number of trains in the system. [**Ans.** 0.01068 ; 2.019]

9. A local one-person barber shop has a space to accommodate 4 customers three waiting and one being attended at a time. If a customer comes to his shop and finds it full, he goes to the next shop. Customers arrive at random at an average rate of 4 per hour and the barber's service time is negative exponential with an average rate of 10 minutes.

   (*a*) What is the probability that a customer can get the service directly on arrival without waiting?

   (*b*) What is the expected number of customers waiting in the barber's shop?

   (*c*) What is the expected number of customers in the barber shop?

   (*d*) How much time can a customer expect to spend in the barber shop?

[**Ans.** (*a*) 0.3838 (*b*) 0.6253 (*c*) 1.2411 (*d*) 18.61 minutes]

10. Consider a single server queueing system with Poisson input, exponential service times. Suppose the mean arrival rate is 6 calling units per hour, the expected service time is 0.125 hour and the maximum permissible calling units in the system is two. Derive the steady state probability distribution of the number of calling units in the system, and then calculate the expected number in the system. [**Ans.** $(0.431)\ (0.75)^n$; 0.81]

11. If for a period of 2 hours in the day (8–10 A.M.) trains arrive at the yard every 20 minutes but the service time continues to remain 36 minutes, calculate for this period,

   (*a*) The probability that the yard is empty.

   (*b*) Average queue length (units in the system).

   Assume that the line capacity of the yard is limited to 4 trains only.

[**Ans.** (*a*) 0.04 (*b*) 2.7]

12. Patients arrive at a clinic according to a Poisson distribution at the rate of 30 patients per hour. The waiting room does not accomodate more than 14 patients. Examination time per patient is exponential with mean rate 20 per hour.

   (*a*) Find the effective arrival rate at the clinic.

   (*b*) What is the probability that an arriving patient will not wait?

   (*c*) What is the expected waiting time until a patient is discharged from the clinic?

[**Ans.** (*a*) 19.98 (*b*) 0.67 (*c*) 0.65 hours]

(M/M/S : ∞ /FIFO)

13. A telephone exchange has two long distance operators. The telephone company finds that, during the peak load, long distance calls arrive in Poisson fashion at an average rate of 15 per hour. The length of service on these calls is approximately exponentially distributed with mean length 5 minutes.

   (*a*) What is the probability that a subscriber will have to wait for his long distance call during the peak hours of the day?

   (*b*) If the subscribers will wait and serviced in turn, what is the expected waiting time?

[**Ans.** (*a*) 0.48 (*b*) 3.2 minutes]

14. Four counters are being run on the frontier of a country to check the passports and necessary papers of the tourists. The tourists choose counter at random. If the arrivals at the frontier is Poisson at the rate of λ and the service time is exponential with parameter $\frac{\lambda}{2}$, what is the steady-state average queue at each counter? [**Ans.** $\frac{4}{23}$]

15. A super market has two sales girls at the sales counters. If the service time for each customer is exponential with mean 4 minutes, and if people arrive in a Poisson fashion at the counter at the rate of 10 an hour.

(*a*) What is the probability of having to wait for service?

(*b*) What is the expected percentage of idle time for each girl?

(*c*) If a customer has to wait, what is the expected length of his waiting time?

[**Ans.** (*a*) 0.167 (*b*) 67% (*c*) 3 minutes]

16. A store is manned by three salesmen. Any salesman can provide desired service to any customer. The customers arrive at the counter according to Poisson distribution at an average rate of 30 per hour. The service time is exponential with a mean rate of 3 minutes.

(*a*) What fraction of time are all three salesmen busy?

(*b*) What is the mean number of customers waiting to be attended?

(*c*) What average time does a customer spend at the shop?

(*d*) What is the probability that a customer has to wait?

[**Ans.** (*a*) 0.50 (*b*) 7.1053 (*c*) 0.1684 (*d*) 0.2368]

17. A barber shop has two barbers and three chairs for customers. Assume that the customers arrive in a Poisson fashion at rate of 5 per hour and that each barber service customers according to an exponential distribution with mean of 15 minutes. Furtherh if a customer arrives and there are no empty chairs in the shop, he will leave. What is the probability that the shop is empty? What is the expected number of customers in the shop?

[**Ans.** 0.2841; 1.226.]

❑❑❑

Index

V

W

❑❑❑